AN ARTHUR A. COHEN READER

AN ARTHUR A. COHEN READER

SELECTED FICTION AND WRITINGS ON JUDAISM, THEOLOGY, LITERATURE, AND CULTURE

Edited by
David Stern and Paul Mendes-Flohr

 WAYNE STATE UNIVERSITY PRESS   DETROIT

02 01 00 99 98   5 4 3 2 1

Library of Congress Cataloging-in-Publication Data

Cohen, Arthur Allen, 1928–
    [Selections.   1998]
    An Arthur A. Cohen reader : selected fiction and writings on
Judaism, theology, literature, and culture / edited by David Stern
and Paul Mendes-Flohr.
        p.   cm.
    Includes bibliographical references.
    ISBN 0-8143-2282-4 (pbk. : alk. paper)
    1. Judaism.   2. Judaism—Relations—Christianity.   3. Christianity
and other religions—Judaism.   4. Holocaust (Jewish theology)
5. Jews—Intellectual life.   6. Literature, Modern—History and
criticism.   I. Stern, David, 1949–   .   II. Mendes-Flohr, Paul R.
III. Title.
BM45.C5835   1998
296—dc21   97-23839

CONTENTS

ACKNOWLEDGMENTS

The editors wish to express their gratitude and appreciation to Professor Alan Udoff, who originally proposed the idea of this volume; to Lorraine Berry-Andrews, who helped with organizing the material and securing the rights to the published essays; to Arthur Evans and the editorial staff of Wayne State University Press; and most of all, to Elaine Lustig Cohen, whose encouragement, support, and intelligence was instrumental throughout the process of selecting and shaping this book.

THE NATURAL AND THE SUPERNATURAL ARTHUR A. COHEN: AN INTRODUCTION

David Stern

Throughout his life, Arthur Cohen was exceptional. Even now, some eight years after his untimely death at the age of fifty-eight, he remains an anomalous figure, difficult to categorize or assimilate to the usual patterns of American Jewish life. A theologian by vocation and training, he devoted his best energies during the last fifteen years of his life to writing novels. Though he was best known as a novelist and theologian, he also pursued successful careers as a highly regarded editor and publisher, as an expert collector and dealer in rare books and documents on twentieth-century art, and as a man of letters and cultural critic who wrote with equal authority on modern European literature, medieval Jewish mysticism, the history of Dada and surrealism, and modern typography and design. Most people who knew him in one or two of these guises were hardly aware of the others.

In his personal life, Cohen was no less difficult to categorize. While one would expect his natural home to have been a university, Cohen assiduously eschewed all formal professional affiliations with academic institutions and with the trappings of academic life (except for a brief stint or two as a visiting professor). A successful businessman, he maintained an at times almost flamboyant lifestyle that was at odds with the spartan and austere existence usually associated with the life of a theologian. So, too, despite his passionate preoccupation with the survival of

Judaism in the modern world, Cohen avoided for most of his life associating himself with the organized movements of American Judaism. Nor could he ever fit comfortably within their frameworks and ideologies. Although his theology was enormously respectful of halakhah, traditional Jewish law, he was personally (save for one brief period in his twenties) almost completely unobservant of its rules and regulations. Utterly self-disciplined, fastidious in appearance, meticulous in manner—his work desk was a picture of perfect order—there was nonetheless a deeply antinomian streak in his character. His closest friends were other writers and artists, not rabbis or professors.

Yet, for all these contradictions, Cohen remains one of the few truly preeminent figures in American Jewish intellectual life in the past several decades, an author and thinker who continues to command our attention. A man of contradictions, he embodied in his person many of the contradictions of American Jewish life in these last decades of the twentieth century—not to mention the incongruities and disparities of being an American Jewish intellectual in our time.

Arthur Cohen was born in New York City in 1928 and grew up in an affluent, assimilated Jewish home, the second of two children. His parents were second-generation Americans, his father a prosperous clothing manufacturer. Cohen's childhood, despite its material luxury, was not very happy. Bedridden as an infant with tuberculosis and nephrosis, shunted off to boarding school by his parents before he was seven, the young boy was unusually precocious, almost handicapped at times by his intellect, and emotionally isolated. He was, he wrote later, "a stunted child with a large imagination and a mind that guarded the secrets of loneliness and vulnerability with a frighteningly mature ferocity." Whether the source of those feelings was a difficult relationship with an overbearing father or a more pervasive feeling of powerlessness, that combination of emotional vulnerability and intellectual ferocity would be familiar to all who knew Cohen for the rest of his life. It bred in him both a great empathy for others whom he felt shared the same vulnerability and a great impatience toward those whom he felt to be imposters either emotionally or intellectually.

At the age of sixteen, Cohen entered the University of Chicago, which, under the leadership of Robert Maynard Hutchins, was probably the most intellectual, cerebral university in America at the time. In this heady atmosphere, Cohen first came into his own. In Chicago's famous humanities courses, he read the classics of Western literature and studied philosophy and religion. Out of these studies, however, he directly entered into a "crisis" that was to have the most decisive effect upon his life. The crisis began—as he explained in "Why I Choose to be a Jew," the 1959 essay in *Harper's Magazine* that first brought Cohen to public attention—with his recognition "that Western culture is a Christian culture." This recognition, abetted by his "unreligious background, a growing and intense concern with religious problems, and the ready access to compelling Christian literature," led him to consider converting to Christianity. Whether he actually confided this possibility to his parents, or whether it was simply his refusal to attend High Holy Day services in 1945 that tipped them off to the plan, it is not difficult to imagine his parents' horror when they found out. Sensing the danger of the moment, they rushed their son off for help—not to a psychiatrist, but to a rabbi.

To Cohen's great good fortune, the rabbi to whom his parents sent him was Milton Steinberg, arguably the most original and searching American Jewish religious thinker of his generation and a leading figure in the movement just then gaining force to revive interest in theology as a matter of serious Jewish intellectual concern. Under Steinberg's patient tutelage, Cohen embarked on an introductory course of study in Judaism. He began to learn Hebrew and thus was led on "the path backward through Christianity to Judaism, revealing the groundwork of Jewish thought and experience which supported . . . the scaffolding of Christian 'unreason.'"

Exactly how deep Cohen's religious crisis was is difficult to gauge. When Cohen himself referred to it later in his life, he nearly always did so with a great deal of irony. What is more important about the entire episode is the significance it came to hold in Cohen's own mind: Like his later hero and theological model, Franz Rosenzweig, Cohen would always see himself as having come to Judaism "through the medium of Christianity." As a result, Cohen's theology of Judaism would always, to some extent, be predicated upon the existence of Christianity as a promise and a reality to be denied by the Jew. That is to say, Cohen's Judaism was always shadowed by the otherness of Christianity, by the presence of a Christian "alternative" to the life of the Jew. To be sure, Cohen emerged from the crisis feeling himself to be a "self-chosen Jew." Indeed, the idea that Judaism was not an "unavoidable fate, but a destiny to be chosen freely" was an equally important result of his "conversion" experience. But this self-chosen destiny was inevitably a conversion *from* something, a refusal of another destiny, or fate, that he could have chosen had he wished.

In 1946, after two years at Chicago, Cohen received his B.A. and immediately entered Chicago's graduate school in the Department of Philosophy. In 1949, he received an M.A. for a thesis on "The Concept of Paradox in Kierkegaard and Nietzsche." Upon graduation, at the urging of Milton Steinberg, Cohen spent the second half of 1949 in Jerusalem, where he studied Hebrew, took courses at the Hebrew University, and made the acquaintance of the Jewish thinkers and philosophers then living in Jerusalem including Martin Buber, Ernst Simon, and Hugo Bergmann. Out of this experience came Cohen's first scholarly article, "Being and Existence: The Prospect of Israel Philosophy," which was published in 1951.

Upon returning from Israel, Cohen enrolled at the Jewish Theological Seminary in New York in order to study medieval Jewish philosophy. Unhappily, the intellectual life at the seminary, rich as it was, did not satisfy Cohen, who found it insulated and unexciting compared to Chicago. Even though he was told by one of the seminary's more distinguished faculty that he had the intellectual gifts to become his generation's Maimonides, Cohen was not persuaded to make the effort (nor, it appears, was his ego sufficiently enlarged by the possibility of remaking himself in someone else's image, even if it was Maimonides'). Shortly later, the Korean War broke out, and Cohen was told that in order to receive a deferment from the draft he would have to enroll in the seminary's Rabbinical School. This seemed to him a very poor reason to become a rabbi and—after receiving a medical deferment on account of his childhood tuberculosis—he left the seminary in 1951.

This move ended Cohen's formal education. It also initiated the next phase of his life, his remarkable career as a publisher and editor. With a friend, the poet Cecil Hemley, Cohen founded the Noonday Press. A small house, it quickly gathered a very distinguished list of authors including Louise Bogan, Ortega y Gasset, and Machado de Assis as well as such Yiddish authors as Sholom Aleichem and Isaac Bashevis Singer, whom Cohen was one of the first to introduce to an American audience in translation.

As it turned out, Noonday was sufficiently successful that in 1954 Cohen founded a subsidiary, Meridian Books, which was one of the first publishing houses to put out paperback books of quality, original works as well as books intended for adoption in schools. The idea to market inexpensive paperbacks as textbooks was revolutionary and prescient; it was also enormously successful. Meridian Books was distinguished as well by Cohen's use of avant-garde designers like Alvin Lustig, one of the major figures in introducing European modernism into America, and Lustig's wife Elaine, to design innovative layouts and covers for the house's books. From this professional association, Cohen and the two

Lustigs became closest friends, and after Alvin Lustig's death in 1955, Cohen and Elaine Lustig married.

In 1956, Cohen decided to sell his shares in Noonday to Hemley in order to devote himself full-time to Meridian. Four years later—on the same day in 1960 on which his daughter Tamar was born—he sold Meridian to the World Publishing House. Its new owner retained Cohen as Meridian's director, but the partnership was not a happy one. After a year, Cohen left to become head of religious books at Holt, Rinehart, and Winston, then one of America's largest publishing houses. Three years later, in 1964, Cohen became editor in chief and vice president of the trade book division of Holt, Rinehart, and Winston, a position in which he remained for the next five years.

During this entire eighteen-year period—from 1951 to 1969—publishing was, however, Cohen's "day job" only. At night, he devoted himself to theology. Over the same period, Cohen wrote and published two books, *Martin Buber* and *The Natural and Supernatural Jew;* he edited *A Handbook of Christian Theology* as well as an edition of Milton Steinberg's classic *The Anatomy of Faith;* and in addition, he wrote more than eighty essays and reviews, most of them on theology or on the place of religion in American culture. Taken together, these books and essays set forth the basic structure of Cohen's religious thinking.

The ground of that structure is the distinction between the natural and the supernatural Jew. The natural Jew, Cohen wrote, is "a creature situated in nature and activated by history"—that is, one whose fate is essentially defined by his or her cultural and social circumstances and who cannot alone transcend the determinations of nature and history. In contrast, the supernatural Jew is "a messianic being," the Jew aware of being called by God to a transhistorical vocation, to the work of redemption, who must nonetheless testify for all time that "there is *no* redemption until *all* history is redeemed." These two types, Cohen emphasized, are not to be understood as opposites or as exclusive: they "are joined in every Jew." For while "the supernatural Jew may occasionally forget that he is also flesh and blood"—that is, fated to live *in* history—such a Jew, Cohen wrote, "is as much in error as is the natural Jew who forgets what links him to eternity." The renewal of the Jewish vocation—the eschatological consummation ahead—lies in the reuniting in the Jew of his or her natural and supernatural selves, in the turning of Judaism toward history and culture in such a way that the forms and events of history will be made into "bearers of ultimate and consummate meaning."

Cohen was not the first American Jewish thinker to present a distinction of this kind between two sides of Jewish existence, one historical and culturally situated, the other transcendent and metahistorical. As Arnold Eisen points out in his illuminating study, *The Chosen People in America* (1983), the making of this distinction was itself a sign of the time. Cohen was part of a new generation of American Jewish thinkers who emerged after the war and in the early fifties, a group that included Will Herberg, Steven Schwartzchild, Eugene Borowitz, Emil Fackenheim, Joseph Soloveitchik, and still others. Like many American intellectuals in general during those early, bitter years of the cold war, Cohen and the other Jewish thinkers of his generation had grown disillusioned with cultural liberalism and the ideals of progressivism that had characterized earlier American religious and philosophical thought. Deeply influenced by the new existentialist philosophy coming out of Europe, Cohen and his generation rebelled against the ideological rationalism that had characterized earlier schools of Jewish thinkers in America, and their faith in the unproblematic possibility of Jews assimilating into American society. In Cohen's own work, the terms natural and supernatural were essentially polemical, reactions against and critiques of the "naturalism" and anti-"supernaturalism" espoused by Mordechai Kaplan, the most important Jewish thinker of the previous generation. Kaplan had argued vehemently against the persistence of "supernatural" elements in Judaism, like the belief in a transcendent God who had chosen Israel as His elect nation. In their place, he and his disciples had sought to find modern or functional equivalents to Israel's ancient ideals in values like those of American democracy.

Cohen and the new Jewish theologians of his generation repudiated Kaplan's naturalism and what they saw as Kaplan's inability to address the true theological issues underlying the crisis of faith afflicting contemporary Judaism in America. Arguing for a renewal of Jewish theology as a prerequisite for the renewing of Judaism itself, Cohen and his peers reasserted the centrality of such concepts as faith, revelation, chosenness, and messianism, all the supernatural elements that Kaplan had dismissed.

Within the context of this larger movement, Cohen's particular contribution lay in several areas, both substantive and methodological. First, profoundly influenced by Franz Rosenzweig's *The Star of Redemption* (the English translation of which Cohen commissioned when he was editor at Holt, Rinehart, and Winston), Cohen emphasized more than others the messianic, eschatological side of Judaism—the unredeemed state of the present world. Second, in *The Natural and the Supernatural Jew*, Cohen was the first to use the new theological perspective of his age to write a history of Jewish thought, from the early Middle Ages until his own time. To be sure, some of his contemporaries wrote books of Jewish theology, and others composed histories of Jewish thought. Yet Cohen was really the first to apply the exacting rigor of a historiographical study to the theological project itself.

Third, and finally, Cohen brought an eloquence and passion to the language of Jewish theology that it had hitherto lacked in its American setting. Cohen wrote theology as though it were poetry. This was because he regarded poetry as "the language of existence—the means by which the paradoxes of theology can be rendered into life," as he wrote about the dedication to language shared by his two models, Franz Rosenzweig and the great medieval Jewish poet and philosopher Judah Halevi. To be sure, Cohen's ornate writing at times verged upon the rhetorical and the opaque. Yet his language was never gratuitous or intentionally obscure. It was always moved by the desire to capture through the resonances and inflections of speech the mystery of existence beholden to a divine reality, and that often required stretching and pushing and reinventing his language in order to express thoughts that were truly difficult and far from obvious.

Cohen's elegant theological writing anticipates his later fiction; in fact, this is one of the subterranean continuities that links the diverse aspects of Cohen's life. Another such link is the natural-supernatural distinction, which, one might say, was not simply a theological concept for Cohen. In many respects, it actually describes the shape of Cohen's own life, his living a "natural" existence as a publisher and editor and a "supernatural" one as a theologian and writer. Unlike the other Jewish theologians of his generation, who virtually all pursued their theological study as the basis of their livelihood—as academics or professional rabbis—Cohen's publishing career bore only a tangential relationship to his life as a theologian. There was, however, nothing schizophrenic about this dual existence; indeed, to the contrary, the very disparity between Cohen's separate lives seems to have been for him a genuine resource, a fount of his remarkable productivity and a source of intellectual energy.

Publishing and theology were also not the only centers of his varied interests during the sixties. This was the decade in which Cohen received his education in modern art, and when he became an avid collector (after starting out, as he used to say, "a visual idiot"). Through his wife Elaine Lustig Cohen, the graphic designer and painter, Arthur met and became close friends with many painters and sculptors. Out of one of these friendships—with Robert Motherwell—there evolved a famous series, The Documents of 20th-Century Art, published by Viking, for which Motherwell served as general editor and Cohen as managing editor, and to which Cohen eventually contributed his own volume, *The New Art of Color: The Writings of Robert and Sonia Delaunay* (1978). The Cohens's closest friendship from this period, however, was with a young architect named Richard Meier whom they met one day at Wittenborn, the great art book store in New York City. Through their friendship with Meier, the Cohens's living room also became the regular meeting place for the New York Five, the now-legendary group of young architects including Meier, Michael Graves, and Charles Gwathmey who essentially remade postmodern architecture in America in the sixties and seventies.

Then, in 1967, Cohen's life took another turn. In the midst of a personal crisis, he decided to leave Holt, Rinehart, and Winston, and publishing in general, in order to devote himself full-time to writing. Not coincidentally, this was the year that he published his first novel, *The Carpenter Years,* an account of a "secret" Jew, Morris Edelman, who one day abandons his family and life to become Edgar Morrison, a Christian, only to be rediscovered years later by his son Danny. This was also the year in which Cohen began writing *In the Days of Simon Stern,* his best-known and most ambitious work of fiction, completed and published in 1973. Over the next thirteen years, he published three additional novels: *A Hero in His Time* (1976), *Acts of Theft* (1980), and *An Admirable Woman* (1983), and the posthumously published collection, *Artists and Enemies: Three Novellas* (1987).

Cohen's turning to fiction represents the pivotal moment in his career, and it requires some words of elaboration. Cohen was not a born novelist. His skills as a writer of fiction, however impressive they may have been, were acquired. Indeed, exactly why Cohen chose to begin writing novels remains something of a mystery. In part, he may have been unconsciously emulating his early mentor, Milton Steinberg, who published one novel, *Driven as a Leaf,* which has since become a kind of classic of Jewish belles lettres, and who left a second, unfinished novel at his death. Partly, too, Cohen doubtless turned to fiction in order to reach a larger audience than he could ever acquire through his theological writing, despite his growing reputation in the field. He certainly wanted greater exposure for his ideas and talents.

Yet there was more to his writing novels than either ambition or the desire to emulate a theological mentor. Cohen wrote fiction because there were subjects about which he could not otherwise write. Cohen is often described as a novelist of ideas—preeminently of a theological order— but even though this is a mainly accurate description of *In the Days of Simon Stern,* most of his novels are not novels of ideas. They are rather fictions about characters captivated by ideas—poets, artists, intellectuals, all obsessed by dreams of the intellect.

To the extent that these works share a theme, it is about the difference between the false and the failed or, as Cohen would have put it, "the excellence of failure" (as he titled a lecture he delivered upon receiving an honorary degree from Spertus College in 1985). For Cohen, the "true failure" was a real source of heroism, perhaps the only authentic heroism possible in our time and worth struggling for. This is the struggle of Yuri Maximovich, the Russian poet and protagonist of *A Hero in His Time,* of the sculptor and art thief Stefan Mauger in *Acts of Theft,* and of Erika Hertz, the German-Jewish emigré intellectual whose ruminations and memoirs are the subject of *An Admirable Woman.* These characters are all, in one way or another, struggling for an authenticity that does not depend upon a worldly success that is guaranteed only by visible or tangible measures. By ordinary, objective standards, all these characters fail. Yet failure, in Cohen's personal vocabulary, was not a negative term, a sign for defeat; rather, it was a mark that proved, time and again, only that the world remained unredeemed, unfulfilled. Cohen's characters, each in its own way, thus relive the drama of *unredemption,* the only drama that Cohen believed could authentically transpire as long as history persisted, and so long as the *eschaton* had not arrived.

From this perspective it is perhaps best to look upon Cohen's fiction writing as his own attempt to find authenticity, indeed as a strategy and medium through which he could reflect upon his search for an authentic voice. It is this presence of reflection as an activity that gives his novels their metaphysical aura. To this extent, the protagonists of all his novels may therefore be said to be surrogates for Cohen himself. There is no question, though, that in the character of Erika Hertz, Cohen discovered the intellectual persona closest to himself. This last fact is telling—that Cohen should have found his most compelling fictional persona in the character of a woman, a German-Jewish intellectual emigré. As a novelist and as an intellectual, Cohen did not fit into the mold of the great American tradition, the line of a Hemingway and a Fitzgerald and an Edmund Wilson. There was always something intensely European—German-Jewish especially—about his work. As a novelist, he more closely modeled himself upon Thomas Mann than Saul Bellow; as a man of letters he was more like Walter Benjamin than Irving Howe. Cohen did not even fit neatly into the New York Jewish intellectual world: he was too much the *flaneur,* too metaphysical and baroque in his style, too much the theologian, never sufficiently political or bent on controversy.

Cohen's success as a novelist was mixed. He never quite received the wide, unequivocally positive reception that he sought. The novels, though always consummately intelligent, often suffer from too obvious an effort of invention, from being too much creations of their author's head. Yet this evaluation of Cohen's fiction is misleading, not entirely fair. For Cohen's most important and single best work, In the Days of Simon Stern, may be his least successful novel qua novel, but it is nonetheless an epic work of theological imagining, and in this quite unlike anything else in modern Jewish writing. The story of Simon Stern, a millionaire real estate dealer on the Lower East Side who never in his lifetime steps beyond the island of Manhattan, as though it were the Holy Land, the novel recounts Stern's attempt in the aftermath of the Holocaust to save the remnants of Jewry (a select number of survivors chosen by Stern for their capacity to "endure" history) by building them a temple-like sanctuary in New York City. This narrative is, then, explicitly the story of a messiah but one of a "failed" (though not false) messiah. That is to say, Simon Stern is a genuine messiah but his messianic mission is to prove the impossibility of redemption so long as history lasts. In this novel, Cohen actually succeeded in recreating a Jewish myth, but it is precisely the book's uncategorizable shape—as it sprawls in every direction trying to encompass the boundless Jewish yearning for redemption and the equally boundless disappointment of failure—that makes it so unique. Cohen liked to quote Rosenzweig's statement that Judaism must be smuggled into life. In Simon Stern Cohen used fiction to smuggle Judaism into art.

Simon Stern, the real estate developer who becomes a messiah, is also another transmogrification of the natural and supernatural Jew. Furthermore, from the time Cohen began working full-time on Simon Stern, he too lived, one might say, still another version of the doubled identity, but now as theologian and novelist. For some people, this dual existence was even more difficult to comprehend than his previous life as a successful publisher and a serious theologian. For Cohen himself, though, his dual commitments to theology and fiction did not create visible conflict. In the course of this period, during the same time that he wrote four novels and the several novellas published posthumously, he also produced a steady stream of theological works—a collection of essays entitled The Myth of the Judaeo-Christian Tradition (1970); the remarkable anthology Arguments and Doctrines: A Reader of Jewish Thinking in the Aftermath of the Holocaust (1970); If Not Now, When? Toward a Reconstitution of the Jewish People: Conversations between Mordecai M. Kaplan and Arthur A. Cohen (1973); The Jew: Essays from Martin Buber's Journal Der Jude: 1916–1928 (1980); and The Tremendum: A Theological Interpretation *of the Holocaust* (1981). Over the same period, Cohen also underwent psychoanalysis, the influence of which can be seen in his essay-length psycho-biographical studies of Franz Rosenzweig and Sabbetai Zevi.

Nor was this all. In 1973, Cohen founded, with his wife Elaine, an antiquarian bookstore named Ex Libris that specialized in books and documents of twentieth-century art, particularly Dada, Surrealism, and early Russian Constructivism. In founding Ex Libris, the Cohens drew with great success upon their joint expertise in the history of modern art. For Cohen himself, this new immersion in art and Russian culture also produced, over the next decade, a host of related books and writings—*Osip Emilevich Mandelstam: An Essay in Antiphon* (1974); *Sonia Delaunay* (1975), *The Avant-Garde in Print* (1981); and *Herbert Bayer: The Collected Works* (1984). Cohen's "natural" existence at this time was clearly the background as well for the material in *A Hero in His Time, Acts of Theft,* and the three novellas that appeared posthumously in *Artists and Enemies.* One glimpses here a few more of the hidden threads in Cohen's work that joined the disparate parts of his life.

These years—from 1975 to 1985—were in many respects the most contented ones in Cohen's life. Extraordinarily productive, he began to study Hebrew again, even corresponding with colleagues and friends in Israel in Hebrew, and he became actively involved in two organizations, the YIVO Institute for Jewish Research and the American PEN Center, two institutions that served, as it were, as corrolaries for his two existences as novelist and Jewish intellectual. This happy period was, alas, brought to an abrupt halt by Cohen's untimely death from leukemia in 1986. True to his character, Cohen worked throughout the period of his illness. By the time of his death, he had finished coediting (with Paul Mendes-Flohr) a final book, the monumental *Contemporary Jewish Religious Thought: Original Essays on Critical Concepts, Movements, and Beliefs.* Fittingly, the more than a hundred contributions in this book captured the mode of speculative and constructive theological thinking that Cohen had sought throughout his life to encourage. Despite being an anthology of essays by many different authors, the book as a whole is powerful testimony to Cohen's passionate conviction that Judaism's survival and vitality can only be guaranteed by rigorous theological discourse.

On several occasions, Cohen expressed the wish that he be remembered and judged for the totality of his work, his entire corpus, not on the basis of one or two books or for his theology or his fiction alone. There exists a totality—that is, an abiding coherence—to the complete body of his work. In the course of this biographical sketch, I have pointed to a few of the links between the different areas of his life and thought. Its deeper unity lies, though, in its author's singular, distinctive voice, in the shifting dialectic of Cohen's thinking, which his writing uncannily replicated.

That dialectic was essentially theological, or better yet, metaphysical—that is, concerned with "ultimate and consummate meaning." The coherence behind his work lay in its sharing in this metaphysical insight, which is partly to say that it was Jewish—that is, concerned with the metaphysics of Judaism—even when it wasn't explicitly about Judaism. Cohen's theological writings stand in the same relation to his nontheological writings as does the Jew's supernatural vocation to his natural one. If, as Cohen once wrote, the function of the supernatural Jew is not to *make* history but "to make of culture a partial consummation of history," then one might say that Cohen sought, in his nontheological writings, to make of culture a partial reflection of Judaism—or, as he was wont to do in more covert moments, of its metaphysical or theological values. To do this—that is, to smuggle Judaism into culture, again to use Rosenzweig's phrase—it was necessary, Cohen believed, to treat culture, *all* culture, with utmost seriousness, and then to bring to it the supernatural critique that could turn facts of culture into "bearers of ultimate and consummate meaning."

Cohen's aim in all of this was not so much to create a Jewish critique of culture—he was generally suspicious of attempts to use Judaism as a monolithic standard or convenient yardstick by which to legislate behavior or ideas—as it was to uncover the Jewish or theological lode hidden within culture, to unveil the secret religious aura surrounding the cultural artifact. The shape of this project can be seen in many of Cohen's writings, but for a particularly unusual example, the reader is referred to Cohen's essay entitled "The Typographic Revolution: Antecedents and Legacy of Dada Graphic Design" (1979). On its surface, this dense and complex study traces the prehistory and influence of Dada typography—those wonderfully chaotic and inventive arrangements of letters and print familiar to all students of early twentieth-century art as being among the most defiant icons of modernism. Within the essay, though, Cohen juxtaposes arguments that complicate this history: the idea of Dada as inherent contradiction; the notion that all written languages—that is, letters—are essentially ideograms, abstractions of the living voice; the various attempts through the ancient and medieval periods to embellish the written word—so as to renew "the rhythm of the living voice"; and the correlative effort in Dada and its precursors "to oblige a reconception of the relation of spoken word, written speech, settled meaning, and the pictorial ideogram which was once the alphabet and is now twenty-six beautiful and exotic shapes which can slink or lurk, stand erect or be flattened by bar lines, hemmed within squares, wrinkled by italic or compelled to call forth, tiny letter surrounded by giant capitals, to drown beneath the weight of fat faces or lie down on their sides to rest or to hide," as Cohen wrote in his exposition of the subject. Fittingly, the intellectual epiphany of this remarkable essay comes only at its conclusion, when Cohen proposes that the Dadaist desire to make type come alive so as to be "reapprehended as living voice, speaking volumes, shouting and making love" be understood in conjunction with the inquiries of such contemporary philosophers and theologians as Ferdinand Ebner, Nicolai Berdyaev, Martin Buber, and Franz Rosenzweig, all of whom sought to reconceive the direct speech between man and God and thus to reclaim those "realms of intimacy" in which the living voice of the divine once spoke to man. The brilliance of this essay—a brilliance absolutely typical of Cohen's strongest writing—comes not only from the unexpected connection it makes between two distinct subjects—Dada typography and early modern theology—but from the startling illumination that this perspicacious connection sends forth, exposing to our view the theological kernel silently residing within even the outrageous clamor of Dadaist nonsense.

Cohen's gift for revealing transcendent meaning in such unlikely artifacts of culture was one sign of his special genius. Yet it also suggests some of the reasons for his isolated, relatively unappreciated status within American Jewish intellectual life. Part of the reason why Arthur Cohen was an anomaly in American Jewish life was that he made connections that were beyond the ken of most American Jews. He refused to popularize Judaism. He refused not to be difficult (when difficulty was required). He refused as well to cater to the conventional pieties of American Jews, to use the State of Israel or Zionism (for example) as staples of Jewish identity. Even his stance toward the Holocaust, with which Cohen became most closely identified (as "a Holocaust thinker") at the end of his life, was unpopular. As Cohen saw it, the primary implication of the Holocaust was not homiletical, political, or cautionary, but theological— the requirement it enforced to rethink the very bases of Jewish belief, particularly the Jewish conception of God, and thus to move beyond the frozen stances of faith and observance promulgated by "official" Judaism in any of its varieties.

Cohen's lack of academic or institutional affiliation, his refusal to pledge allegiance to or align himself with a major organized cause, partly explains, no doubt, his relatively minor influence upon the larger movements within American Judaism. He was, to a certain extent, inconsistent, or better yet, unpredictable; he could be very difficult to pin down, and if one knew him solely by reputation or from a distance, his life could seem a puzzle, a bewilderment, certainly not a model to be held up to the masses. It is therefore understandable that his greatest impact came upon individuals in social or private encounters, and particularly upon young writers and intellectuals, like the author of this introduction, all of whom can testify to his extraordinary generosity, and his loyalty as a friend and supporter.

One of Cohen's greatest talents was his sociability. He was genuinely interested in people, and he was able to recognize their worth and merit when they were as yet unrecognized. He liked bringing such people together, especially if they were dissimilar, in the same way that he liked making connections between unpredictable and seemingly unlike or unfashionable topics, like theology and literature. His living room was like a nineteenth-century European salon in which one was as likely to meet the most interesting writers—Donald Barthelme, Cynthia Ozick, Jerzy Kozinski—as the most influential intellectuals of the time, figures like Yosef Haim Yerushalmi or David Tracy, and artists and architects, like Mel Bochner or Richard Meier.

This anthology brings together a selection of Cohen's writings from as many areas and disciplines as has been possible in order to convey to the reader the shape of his life and work in their entirety. The selections have been chosen both for their intrinsic merit and for their relation to the whole of his oeuvre, however complex and differentiated it was. Yet what an anthology like this cannot represent or reproduce is Cohen's living presence—how he embodied a kind of juncture, a meeting point, for the most diverse and unrelated types, and how he personally served as a center that seemed able to hold it all together in the fragmented and scattered intellectual and Jewish worlds of New York City in the seventies and eighties, just as he was able to bring together the most contradictory aspects in his own personality.

More even than his writings, it was this living example that Cohen set, the example of his presence, the example of his life lived in all its contradictions, that had such an impact upon those who knew him. Cohen was not a saintly figure by any measure, but he was deeply charismatic in the way saints often can be—that is, capable of touching and provoking and shaping those with whom the saint comes into contact through the force of his or her sheer presence. Cohen's personality possessed that kind of presence. Ultimately, too, it is that presence to which his writings, his theology as much as the fiction and the cultural criticism, give expression. The remarkable character of all his writing lay in

Cohen's efforts to invent a discourse, a language, that could record and convey the charisma of his presence and the singular matters—religious and imaginative—that obsessed him. The writing that resulted was like nothing else in American Jewish culture in our time.

A Note on the Selection of Texts

As even a casual glance at his complete bibliography will reveal, Cohen's output was enormous in both its quantity and range. Accordingly, the task of deciding upon selections for this anthology was no less challenging. In the separate introductions to the sections of this book, we discuss the reasons for some of our choices; other factors included the length of the piece, its originality and accessibility, and, to some degree, the extent to which the text contributed to the larger shape of this volume and its picture of Cohen's oeuvre in its entirety. In a few cases—where we thought parts of essays were uneven either in quality or in their abiding interest—we took the liberty of abridging or selecting from a text. In all cases, full bibliography citations are supplied in the anthology, and the reader dissatisfied with our procedure is encouraged to look up the essay in its original publication.

The original manuscripts and page proofs of all Cohen's published works are deposited in the Beinicke Library at Yale University. Unpublished manuscripts from the Estate of Arthur A. Cohen are in the possession of Elaine Lustig Cohen.

I.

JEWISH
THEOLOGY

Introduction

Paul Mendes-Flohr

Arthur A. Cohen was a theological Jew. For him theology had an existential urgency borne of his need to be a Jew by faith and religious commitment. As an American Jew, relatively free of the anxiety of anti-Semitism and feeling sufficiently secure within the social and cultural fabric of his country, he was faced with the possibility of indifference to his ancestral identity and religion, and even the option of adopting another faith. Finding the imperatives of sentiment and primordial loyalty not sufficiently compelling, he understood his abiding attachment to Judaism—as a system of religious discourse and practice—to be one of choice. Yet as a conscious choice it required sustained intellectual clarification and justification. It required theology.

In his quest for a theological grounding for belief, Cohen soon realized that Judaism, certainly American Jewry, had a deeply ingrained "distrust of theology." This disdain for theology, he concluded, could only partially be explained by the oft-repeated suspicion that theology was inherently a Christian exercise. A deeper reason, he felt, was an unwillingness to face the questions raised by theology. For theology "often produces a recognition of the insufficiency" of one's categories, it perforce addresses doubts and despair, and acknowledges that "much in human life—evil, suffering, guilt, and love—is terrifyingly real without ever being rationally comprehensible." Indeed, as Cohen understood it, theology is "inherently deconstructive—an inevitable challenge to complacent, unthoughtful attitudes and lives."

It is not true, Cohen also argued, that theology is alien to Judaism. Jews have always asked theological questions—about God, the nature of His rule, the meaning of His dominion, and its bearing on the destiny of humanity and Israel. Indeed, as Cohen aphoristically put it, "theology in Judaism . . . [has] a continuous history, but a discontinuous tradition." Although Judaism, unlike Christianity, knows no established forms of theological discourse, its literature—from the Bible to the Midrash, from the writings of the medieval philosophers to those of modern Jewish thinkers, particularly in Central Europe, like Moses Mendelssohn, Hermann Cohen, Franz Rosenzweig, and Martin Buber—abounds in theological reflection.

Because it is not part of a standard curriculum of Jewish learning, theology in Judaism has a spontaneous quality, invariably emerging in response to a felt existential need; indeed, Cohen observed, in the course of Jewish thought, theological questions are most forcefully posed in those critical moments "in the life of the believer when the materials of faith . . . are no longer self-confirming." As an existentially urgent exercise in clarification, theology becomes relevant to Jews in precisely those situations when historical experience and intellectual developments converge, pressing the issues of faith and thus threatening to weaken one's bonds to the tradition and its principles of belief and practice.

It was Cohen's conviction that at the present juncture of Jewish history, when the presuppositions of Jewish faith are no longer self-evident, the "refusal to think about theological questions within Judaism is [not only] no longer possible, [it] is dangerously irresponsible." Moreover, he held, especially in his later years, in the wake of the Holocaust Jewish theology—a grounding of faith in honest, rational reflection—is that much more exigent. "There can be no Jewish theology in this most terrible of centuries unless it is prepared to ask: what do we know *now* about the creator God in whose universe such horror is permitted?" Hence, "the task of theology is no longer optional and secondary to Jewish tradition, but unavoidably primary."

The essays in this section span the entire course of Cohen's career. "Why I Choose to be a Jew" (1959), originally published in *Harper's Magazine,* first brought Cohen to wide attention; in this essay, Cohen spelled out what he believed to be the modern condition of Jewishness, that is, its volitional character—one may "choose *not* to remain a Jew"— and the theological and religious responsibilities that condition entailed. "Some Existential Dogmas" and "The Renewal of the Jewish Vocation," respectively the introduction and the epilogue to *The Natural and the Supernatural Jew* (1962), articulate the essential parameters of Cohen's early theology. The essay "Art and Theology" (1963) originally appeared as part of a catalog essay Cohen wrote for an art exhibit he curated at the Jewish Museum in New York City entitled "The Hebrew Bible in Christian, Jewish, and Muslim Art"; as its title indicates, this essay was one of Cohen's earliest attempts to spell out the complicated relationship between the visual and the religious imaginations. The fifth selection in the section, "The Negative Way" (1964), consists of ten "propositions," aphorisms on metaphysical topics, that Cohen composed and originally published in a private edition accompanied by lithographs by the artist Paul Brach; this work anticipates the often arcane aphorisms and metaphysical comments that dot much of Cohen's later writing as well as his private notebooks. "Reflections on Theological Method: The Task of Jewish Theology," never before published, was originally written for a conference on Jewish philosophy held at Columbia University in November 1967; the essay is one of Cohen's more ambitious attempts at delineating the need for Jewish theology at the present time, while also acknowledging the limits of the theological project. "Life amid the Paradigms or the Absence of a Jewish Critique of Culture," delivered as a plenary address at the 1985 Annual Meeting of the American Academy of Religion, is a characteristic work of Cohen's later theology. Arguing *against* a self-conscious Jewish critique of culture, Cohen postulated the notion of a "paradigmatic core of Jewish life," a series of events or "paradigms" like the Exodus that rule Jewish history and that stand indifferently beside— and thus dialectically critical of—general history and culture. Finally, the last three essays in the section, "Theology," "Resurrection of the Dead," and "Eschatology," were all written specially for the monumental anthology of theological essays, *Contemporary Jewish Religious Thought* (1987) that Cohen coedited with Paul Mendes-Flohr during the last years of his life; among the most powerful of all Cohen's writings, these essays eloquently and defiantly defend the veracity of some of the most embattled concepts in modern Jewish thought.

WHY I CHOOSE TO BE A JEW

Until the present day, the Jew could not *choose* to be a Jew—history forced him to accept what his birth had already defined.

During the Middle Ages he was expected to live as a Jew. He could escape by surrendering to Islam or Christianity, but he could *not* choose to remain anonymous. In the nineteenth century, with the growth of nationalism, Christianity became the ally of patriotism. The Jews of Europe were compelled to prove that their religion did not compromise their loyalty to king, emperor, kaiser, or tsar. But no matter how desperately they tried to allay suspicion by assimilation or conversion, the fact of their birth returned to plague them. Finally, in the Europe of Nazism and Communism, the Jew could not choose—on any terms—to exist at all.

In the United States today, it is at last possible to choose *not* to remain a Jew. The mass migrations of Jews from Europe have ended and the immigrant generation which was tied to the European pattern of poverty and voluntary segregation is dying off. Their children, the second generation, were as suspicious of the gentile American society in which they grew up as they were condescending toward the ghetto world of

Harper's Magazine 218, no. 1307 (April 1959): 63–66. Copyright © 1959 by *Harper's Magazine*. All rights reserved. Reprinted from the April issue by special permission.

their parents. The second generation, however, made the Jewish community economically secure and fought anti-Semitism so effectively that, though still present, it is no longer severe. *Their* children—the third generation of Jews now in its twenties and thirties—are able to choose.

For this generation the old arguments no longer hold. It was once possible to appeal to history to prove that Jewish birth was inescapable, but history is no proof to those who are—as many Jews are—indifferent to its evidence. Loyalty to the Jewish people and pride in the State of Israel are no longer enough to justify the choice to be a Jew. The postwar American Jew no longer needs the securities which European Jewry found in Jewish Socialism, Jewish nationalism, the revival of Hebrew, and the Zionist movement. *Fear*—the fear of anti-Semitism—and *hope*—the hope for the restoration of Israel—are no longer effective reasons for holding onto Jewish identity. The fear has waned and the hope has been fulfilled.

The irresistible forces of history no longer *compel* the Jew to choose Judaism. In many cases, moreover, he is choosing to repudiate Judaism or to embrace Christianity. I do not say the numbers are alarming. That they exist at all is, however, symptomatic. It is only the exceptional—those who are searching deeply or are moved profoundly, who ever reject or embrace. The majority tend more often to undramatic indifference—to slide into the routine of maturity without asking questions for which no meaningful answers have been offered.

Given the freedom to choose I have decided to embrace Judaism. I have not done so out of loyalty to the Jewish people or the Jewish state. My choice was religious. I chose to believe in the God of Abraham, Isaac, and Jacob; to acknowledge the law of Moses as the Word of God; to accept the people of Israel as the holy instrument of divine fulfillment; to await the coming of the Messiah and the redemption of history.

Many Jews will find my beliefs unfamiliar or unacceptable—perhaps outrageous. The manner in which I arrived at them is not very interesting in itself, but I think two aspects of my experience are worth noting because they are fairly common: I come from a fundamentally unobservant Jewish home and my first religious inclination was to become a Christian.

My parents are both second-generation American Jews whose own parents were moderately religious, but, newly come to America, lacked either the education or the opportunity, patience, and time to transmit to their children their own understanding of Judaism. My parents went to synagogue to observe the great Jewish holidays—Passover, the New Year, and the Day of Atonement—but worship at home, knowledge of the liturgy, familiarity with Hebrew, concern with religious thought and problems, did not occupy them. Their real concern—and they were not unique—was adjusting to American life, achieving security, and passing to their children and those less fortunate the rewards of their struggle.

It would be ungrateful to deny the accomplishments of my parents' generation. They managed to provide their children with secular education and security. But although the flesh was nourished, the spirit was left unattended. When I had finished high school and was ready to leave for college I took with me little sense of what my religion, or any religion, involved. I knew only that in these matters I would have to fend for myself.

When an American Jew studies at an American university, it is difficult for him not to be overwhelmed—as I was at the University of Chicago—by the recognition that Western culture is a Christian culture, that Western values are rooted in the Greek and Christian tradition. He may hear such phrases as "Judaeo-Christian tradition" or "the Hebraic element in Western culture," but he cannot be deluded into thinking that this is more than a casual compliment. The University of Chicago, moreover, insisted that its students study seriously the philosophic sources of Western culture, which, if not outspokenly Christian, were surely non-Jewish. I soon found myself reading the classics of Christian theology and devotion—from St. Augustine and St. Anselm through the sermons of Meister Eckhart.

It was not long before my unreligious background, a growing and intense concern with religious problems, and the ready access to compelling Christian literature all combined to produce a crisis—or at least my parents and I flattered ourselves that this normal intellectual experience was a religious crisis. The possibility of being a Christian was, however, altogether real. I was rushed, not to a psychoanalyst, but to a rabbi—the late Milton Steinberg, one of the most gifted and profound Jewish thinkers of recent years. Leading me gently, he retraced the path backward through Christianity to Judaism, revealing the groundwork of Jewish thought and experience which supported what I have come to regard as the scaffolding of Christian "unreason."

It was extremely important to me to return to Judaism through the medium of Christianity—to choose after having first received the impress of Western education and Christian thought. Since it would have been possible to become a Christian—to accept Christian history as my history, to accept the Christian version of Judaism as the grounds of my own repudiation of Judaism, to believe that a Messiah had redeemed *me*—I could only conclude that Judaism was not an unavoidable fate, but a destiny to be chosen freely.

My own conversion and, I suspect, the conversion of many other Jews to Judaism, was effected, therefore, through study, reflection, and thought. What first seized my attention was not the day-to-day religious life of the Jewish community around me, but rather principles, concepts, and values. I had first to examine the pressing theological claims of a seemingly triumphant Christianity, before I could accept the ancient claims of a dispersed, tormented, and suffering Jewry.

This may sound reasonable enough to a gentile, but I must point out that it is an extremely unconventional attitude for a Jew. Historically, Judaism has often looked with disfavor upon theology. And today, despite the fact that traditional emotional ties can no longer be relied upon to bind the third generation to Jewish life, American Jewish leadership has not seen fit to encourage the examination of the theological bases of Jewish faith. In fact, the leading rabbinical seminaries teach little Jewish theology as such, give scant attention to Jewish philosophical literature, and have allowed the apologetic comparison of religious beliefs to become a moribund discipline. Even practical problems involving some theological insight—the nature of marriage, the Jewish attitude toward converts, the life of prayer—are dispatched with stratospheric platitudes, or not discussed at all.

Why this distrust of theology? I suspect that some Jewish leaders fear—perhaps not unjustifiably—that theological scrutiny of what they mean by God, Israel, and Law might reveal that they have no theology at all. Others no doubt fear—again not unjustifiably—that their unbending interpretations of Jewish Law and life might have to be revised and rethought. Theology often produces a recognition of insufficiency, an awareness that valid doctrine is being held for the wrong reasons and that erroneous doctrine is being used to rationalize right action. But the major Jewish argument against Jewish theology is that it is a Christian pastime—that it may, by insinuation and subtle influence, Christianize Judaism. In this view, Christianity is a religion of faith, dogma, and theology and Judaism is a religion which emphasizes *observance* of God's Law, not speculation about it.

For me this argument is a vast oversimplification. Christianity is not without its own structure of discipline, requirements, and laws—the Roman sacraments and the Lutheran and Anglican liturgy, for example— and this structure does not move with the Holy Spirit as easily as St. Paul might have wished. Judaism, on the other hand, is not tied to the pure act. It has matured through the centuries a massive speculative and mystic tradition which attempts to explain the principles upon which right action is founded. Judaism need not, therefore, regret the renewal of theology. It already has one. It is merely a question of making what is now a minor chord in Jewish tradition sound a more commanding note.

As a "convert" who thinks that theology must come first, what do I believe?

The convert, I must point out, is unavoidably both a thinker and a believer—he thinks patiently and believes suddenly. Yet belief, by itself, cannot evict the demons of doubt and despair. As a believer I can communicate my beliefs, but as a thinker I cannot guarantee that they are certain or will never change. As all things that record the encounter of God and man, beliefs are subject to the conditions of time and history, and the pitiable limitation of our capacity to understand such enormous mysteries. As I shall try to show, however, the four beliefs which I have already set down lie at the center of my faith as a Jew. They depend upon one another; they form a whole; they differ profoundly from the substance of Christian belief.

First, I chose to believe in the God of Abraham, Isaac, and Jacob. This is to affirm the reality of a God who acts in history and addresses man. Although this God may well be the same as the abstract gods formulated by philosophers, he is still more than these—he is the God who commanded Abraham to quit the land of the Chaldeans and who wrestled with Jacob throughout the night.

The philosopher and the believer must differ in their method. The philosopher begins by examining that portion of reality to which reason allows him access. The believer, however, must at some point move beyond the limits which reason has defined. He may rightly contend that reason points beyond itself, that the rational is real, but that much in human life—evil, suffering, guilt, and love—is terrifyingly real without ever being rationally comprehensible.

Reason may thus push a man to belief, and it is inaccurate to speak of the believer as though he had deserted or betrayed reason. Informed belief demands philosophic criticism and refinement. The believer is bound to uphold his faith in things he cannot see or verify; but he is foolish if he does not try to define what that belief is and clarify the unique ways in which it makes reality meaningful for him.

For me then to believe in the Biblical God, the God of the Patriarchs, the smoking mountain, the burning bush, was not to surrender reason, but to go beyond it. More than accepting the literal words of the Bible, it meant believing in the Lord of History—the God who creates and unfolds history, and observes its tragic rifts and displacements—from the Tower of Babel to the cold war; who, in his disgust, once destroyed the world with flood and later repented his anger; who, forgoing anger, gave to the world counsels of revelation, commencing with the gift of Torah to Moses and continuing through the inspired writings of the ancient rabbis; and who finally—through his involvement with the work of creation—prepares it for redemption.

It may seem difficult—indeed for many years it was—to consider the Bible, which is the source of this belief, as more than the unreliable account of an obscure Semitic tribe. But gradually I came to discover in it an authentic statement of the grandeur and misery of man's daily existence—a statement which I could accept only if I believed in a God who could be addressed as "Lord, Lord."

My second belief is an acknowledgment that *the Law of Moses is the Word of God.* The Bible tells us that the Word of God broke out over the six hundred thousand Hebrews who assembled at the foot of Sinai. That Word was heard by Moses—he who had been appointed to approach and receive. The Word became human—in its humanity, it undoubtedly suffers from the limitation of our understanding—but it lost none of its divinity.

The Law is always a paradox: it is both the free Word of God and the frozen formality of human laws. But the Law of Moses was vastly different from what we usually understand law to be. It is true that in the days before the temple was destroyed by Titus in 70 A.D. divine law was the enforceable law of the judge and the court; but later the great rabbis who interpreted it conceived of the revelation of God to Israel, not as law in its common usage, but as *Torah*—teaching.

Torah is a fundamental concept for the Jew. Narrowly conceived, it refers to the Pentateuch—the first five books of the Bible which are the pristine source of all Jewish tradition. In them are the laws of the Sabbath and the festivals: the foundations of family and communal morality; and the essentials of Jewish faith—the unity of God, the election of Israel, and the definition of its special mission. But, broadly conceived, Torah refers to *any* teaching which brings man closer to the true God, who is the God of Israel and the Lord of History.

Torah has two aspects—the actual way of law and observance (the *halakhah* as it is called in Hebrew) and the theology of the rabbis which interprets that way (called the *aggadah*). By means of both, according to Jewish tradition, God proposes to lead *all* of his creation to fulfillment, to perfect its imperfections, to mend the brokenness of his creatures. The Jewish people—the guardian of the *halakhah* and the *aggadah*—has been elected to be pedagogue to all the nations of the world, to become on its behalf "a kingdom of priests and a holy people."

Jews can achieve holiness—the primary objective, I believe, of their religion—neither by prayer nor meditation alone. Judaism values prayer only in conjunction with the act; it praises study only in relation to life.

God does not propose or suggest ways to achieve holiness; he commands them. According to Torah, he lays upon each Jew "the yoke of the commandments." To observe the Sabbath is as much a commandment as is the obligation to daily prayer; the grace which accompanies eating as essential as the study of sacred literature. Although tradition distinguishes between practical and intellectual commandments, it considers both to be equally the expressed will of God. The arbitrary and the reasonable—the dietary laws and the prohibition of homosexuality for example—both proceed from God.

Judaism begins with an explicit fact: the revelation of Torah. Many of its commandments may seem trivial. But it should not be expected that God will leave the trivial to man and concern himself only with the broad, general, and universal. The corruption of man takes place not only in the province of principle, but in the small and petty routine of life. The Torah is therefore exalted and picayune, universal and particular, occupied equally with principle and the details of practice. It tolerates no separation between the holy and the profane—all that is secular must become sacred, all that is profane must be kept open to the transforming power of God.

The exact degree to which Jews should fulfill all the commandments of the Law is one of the most difficult and perplexing dilemmas for modern Jews. Orthodox Jews are in principle obligated to observe all of Jewish Law. Reformed Jews have cut observance to a minimum (though there is a movement to increase it). Conservative Jews stand somewhere in between. I will not attempt it in this space, but I believe it is possible to show that the fundamental question is not whether the Jew performs the required acts of observance, but whether he is truly aware of the sacred intention of these acts. One can, for example, recite the blessings over the food one eats and feel nothing of the sanctity of food; on the other hand one can silently acknowledge the holiness of eating, and fulfill the command of God. Both are needed—the blessing and the inner acknowledgment, but the former is surely incomplete without the latter.

The third of my beliefs is, as I have indicated, simply an element of God's revelation in Torah—that *the Jewish people has been chosen as a special instrument of God.*

The Jews did not request the attentions of God. There is significant truth—truth moreover which the rabbis of the Talmud endorse—in the popular couplet: "How odd of God, to choose the Jews." Odd, and unsolicited. The ancient rabbis disclaim particular merit. If anyone possessed merit, they repeat, it was not the generation that fled Egypt and braved the wilderness for forty years, but the generations of the Biblical patriarchs—Abraham, Isaac, and Jacob. They had no organizer such as Moses, nor strength of numbers, nor the miracles of the well, manna, and quail. They made a covenant with God on sheer trust. The generation of Sinai was *compelled* to become the people of God or perish. A God of History grows impatient with delay. The God of Israel was profoundly impatient on Sinai.

This tradition of election should not be confused with racial pride or an attitude of arrogant exclusion toward others. The Jew believes neither that the truth flows in his blood nor that the gentile cannot come to possess it. Judaism is exclusive only in the sense that we affirm we possess important truth which is available to all—everyone can join but only on our terms.

The election of Israel is not a conclusion drawn from history—the survival and endurance of the Jews through twenty centuries of destructive persecution could be no more than blind accident. At best it could be construed as a compliment to the resiliency and stubbornness of the Jewish people. Judaism has insisted however—not as a declaration after the fact, but as a principle of its very existence—that it is both a holy nation chosen by God to be his own and a suffering nation destined to ensure martyrdom for his sake. God announces not only that "Ye shall be holy unto me; for I the Lord am Holy, and have separated you from the peoples, that ye should be mine" (Leviticus 20:26) but that "You only have I known of all the families of the earth: therefore I will visit upon you all your iniquities" (Amos 3:2).

Israel is thus called not only to be the example to the nations, but, being the example, is tried all the more sorely for its transgressions. To be sure, this is not a doctrine for the uncouraged. No one even slightly familiar with the agonies of Jewish history could claim that the election of Israel has brought with it particular reward and security. It is however precisely the fact of Jewish suffering which makes its election and mission all the more pertinent to the modern world. To have believed and survived in spite of history is perhaps the only evidence which Judaism can offer to the accuracy of its conviction that it is called to be a holy community.

In the face of Christendom and the obvious success which its claims have enjoyed, it may seem foolish or presumptuous for Judaism—a small and insignificant community of believers—to assert my fourth belief: that *Jesus is not the Messiah of which the Bible speaks,* that Christianity has conceived but one more imperfect image of the end, and that *a Messiah is yet to come who will redeem history.*

But there are enduring reasons why Jews cannot accept Jesus as the Messiah. Both Christian and Jew begin with the conviction of the imperfection of man. The Christian argues, however, that creation has been so corrupted by man as to be saved only through the mediation of Jesus. The Jew considers creation imperfect but, rather than corrupt, he finds it rich with unfulfilled possibility. The role of man is to bring creation to that point at which the Messiah can come to glorify man by bringing him the praise of God—not to save him from self-destruction, as Christianity would have it. According to Jewish tradition, Moses died from the kiss of God. It would be fitting to conceive the advent of the Messiah and the Kingdom of God as the bestowal of a kiss.

This does not mean that God congratulates man for his good works but rather that he shares both in the agony of history and in its sanctification. Judaism does not imagine that every day we are getting better and better, and that finally we will reach a point where the Messiah will come. As likely as not, it seems to me, history is coming closer each day to suicide. The mission of Judaism is not to stave off disaster but to enlarge man's awareness of the Divine Presence.

Jews believe, if they are to remain Jews, that the Messiah has not come. They can accept Jesus of Nazareth as little more than a courageous witness to truths to which his own contemporaries in Pharisaic Judaism by and large subscribed. Jesus was, as Martin Buber has suggested, one in the line of "suffering servants" whom God sends forth to instruct the nations. It is to the dogmatizing work of St. Paul that one must ascribe the transformation of "prophet" into "Christ"—and it is therefore St. Paul who severs Jesus from the life of Israel. The rejection of Jesus must now stand to the end of time.

The role of Israel and Judaism, until the advent of the true Messiah, is to outlast the world and its solutions—to examine its complacencies, to deflate its securities, to put its principles to the test of prophetic judgment. This is an aristocratic and painful mission, for though Judaism may address the world and lay claim to it, it does not seek to convert it.

Judaism does not say "The world is not changed—therefore we do not believe in the Messiah." This is only partially true, for the coming of the Messiah will mean more than a reformed world in which the wolf and lamb shall share bread together and war shall cease. This social image of salvation is true as far as it goes, but it does not go far enough. The Messiah is not a handyman or a plumber—his task does not consist in "mending" a world that is temporarily faulty but is essentially perfect. The world is to be transformed—not reformed—by the Messiah.

This transformation will come to pass, Judaism believes, only when the world wishes it so deeply that it cannot abide itself more a single moment. At that moment the Messiah may come. This moment of expectancy has not yet arrived. The rabbis have taught us that I, and all of the House of Israel, prevent him from coming. Of this there is no question, but we cannot avoid concluding that he has not come.

For the Jew who comfortably repeats the rituals of his religion without confronting the principles of faith which they express, and for the Jew who was not aware that Judaism had any principles of faith at all, this personal statement may seem shocking. But I do not think my position or my background are by any means unique. If, as I have argued, the present generation of American Jews is indeed the first generation of Jews in centuries who are free to choose to believe as Jews, then, in my terms at least, my argument is important. Now as never before it will be possible for the Jewish people and the State of Israel to survive, but for Jewish *religion* to perish. For me, and for other believing Jews, it is crucial for mankind that Judaism survive. The mission of Judaism is not completed nor the task of the Jewish people fulfilled. If the Jewish people is an instrument sharpened by God for his own purposes, it must go on serving that purpose, sustaining its burden, and keeping that trust which alone can bring all men to redemption.

Some Existential Dogmas

The classic credos of Western religion conceal behind their verbal façade an edifice of argument which it has required centuries of disputation to construct. The passage of time, however, manages to spread over the seams and cracks of ancient controversy a tapestry of composure and equanimity. In this, history misrepresents the precarious situation of faith, for an illusion of wholeness and integrity, which conceals the knots and wormholes of disagreement and unbelief, is transmitted to the present and the future. Hopefully, the artificial peace is sometimes broken. At such moments believer and heretic, traditionalist and dissident—from whose disputation doctrine was originally fashioned—tangle once more.

The content of religious doctrine is founded on the presumption that God does not change. The endurance of religious doctrine, however, must presuppose that man changes, that his volatility is not mere caprice and inconstancy, but a response to the historical flux in which God and man met once and meet again and again. Doctrine emerges, therefore, as the reflection of the constancy of God and the temporality and historicity of man.

Doctrine may be eternally true, yet die in history. It may continue to

From *The Natural and Supernatural Jew.* New York: Pantheon, 1962, 3–9. Estate of Arthur A. Cohen.

enjoy some abstract and remote validity, preserved pure and undefiled in apocalyptic enclaves, but it ceases to a living force in history. History both authenticates and compromises the truth of doctrine. The process of authentication is truth become historical, liberated from its stony abstractness. The truth itself is not affected by the power of history: God continues to exist, hidden and secret. If he does not exist in history, however, he is as though he were dead. History is the medium through which God passes into human life.

To speak of religious doctrine is, therefore, to speak of history. We cannot even withdraw to the apodictic and compelling consolations of revelation to protect us from the ravages of history; since in revelation God's Word is as much in time and history as though he were present in all his immediacy. In no sense, therefore, can religious doctrine escape history.

Religious doctrine cannot escape history; Judaism cannot escape history. The day-to-day existence of Judaism is wholly historical. It may transmute the events of time, wrenching them out of the orbit of the routine and elevating them into a new time. By so doing it does not negate time. It only succeeds in giving to temporal events a symbolic and sacramental status. The commandments of Judaism, wherein time is sanctified, project the image of the end of time. The commandments are the constant symbols of Jewish redemption. They anticipate the end of time, for they are so consciously refusals to take normal time and natural history for what they are: the subverters of redemption. The performance of each commandment carries with it the injunction to think upon the meaning toward which time and history point. The hallowing of time and history consists in the prescient recognition that they are linked to the *beyond-time* and the *beyond-history*. Sanctification is symbolic, and holiness, wherever it exists, is little more than an anticipation amid creation of what it is that God prepares as the fulfillment of history.

The confession with which I begin is a statement of existential dogma—that is, what *I* say here *I* must believe, because without it there is nothing I consider *ultimately* relevant or meaningful to believe.

I feel obliged, however, to qualify immediately this assertion of dogma. Obviously the dogmas I shall define are not dogmas of tradition nor even formulas founded upon the reworking of inherited principles of Jewish faith. They are, rather, evocations of meaning implicit in the "dogmatics" set forth during earlier ages of Jewish faith; but even this historical foundation does not permit me to make claim for their being authentically Jewish.

The dogmatics I employ has primarily a *heuristic* value, for it enables me to define the ground from which my investigation will depart. My dogmas are conclusions drawn from my understanding of the actual situation of the Jew—in this sense they are *empirical;* they are also judgments upon the events of Jewish history which transmit meaning and instruction regarding the predicament of the Jew amid the nations—in this sense they are *historical;* and lastly they define a view of the Jew's involvement with ultimate reality, his connection with a destiny which commands him, with that which makes him, in fact, Jewish—in this sense they are *transhistorical,* possibly metaphysical, and certainly theological.

The thing to remember, however, is that I do not consider these dogmas to be necessarily valid for all time. They may be, but they need not be. What is crucial is that they serve me and assist in clarifying my understanding of the times in which we live. They are, I believe, properly termed existential dogmas.

The dogmas are these:

One: There is a distinction between the natural and the supernatural Jew. The natural Jew is a creature situated in nature and activated by history. His natural environment shapes his physical person and his contingent personality and disposition; the interaction of his natural environment and the events which come to form his personal history—his country of birth, the language he speaks, the wars in which he fights, the national culture he espouses, the work he does—define a nexus which is fatalistically limited. Only if he exercises his freedom to intend transcendence, to become conscious of the limitations to which environment and personal history compel him to submit, is he able to break out of fate into destiny. In a community such as that of the Jew, which believes itself not only open before God, but the one to whom God has opened himself, one can speak of a supernatural community. God has covenanted with the Jewish people that it shall transcend nature and history to him alone. He has confirmed in the Jewish people the possibility (which all men possess) of *intending* its transcendence. Moreover, God has converted the fatality of nature and history into the destiny of the Jew, that he transcend his natural situation to Him. Without the command to sustain one's supernatural vocation (that is, the belief that God has called the Jew to Himself) to call oneself a Jew is but a half-truth—a mere designation without ultimate meaning.

Two: The consciousness of supernatural vocation, as a condition of Jewish existence, is made doubly important by the continuing significance of the Exile. The Exile, as I understand it, is not an accident of history, remedied by security within the Diaspora or national fulfillment in the State of Israel. It is not only a historical predicament, but a theological category. The Exile is the historical coefficient of being unredeemed.

Three: Since the Exile is the coefficient of being unredeemed, the purpose of the supernatural vocation of the Jew is to make all history alive to its incompleteness. This is no more than to reaffirm that the Jew is a messianic being for whom there is *no* redemption until *all* history is redeemed.

Four: Although the Jew is a messianic being, he cannot be a messianist in isolation from the community of Jews and the whole of mankind. If he remains single, isolate, and alone he compromises the demanding assumption of his supernature, that not in solitude but in community was he joined in covenant to God. God elects, not the single Jew, but the Jewish people. The obligation to engage in concert in the work of redemption joins the people of Israel to the fortunes of all peoples. The Jewish people has not itself alone to redeem.

Five: Insofar as the Jewish people has both a natural and a supernatural dimension (and it is understood that neither can exist distillate and pure) it is obliged to acknowledge that its situation at any given moment is fashioned not only by God but by the events of time and history. It has law and tradition, teaching and belief, *halakhah* and *aggadah,* but these are involved—as is all else—in the dialectical contrariety of divine prescription and historical freedom. It does as much violence to our supernature to trivialize our lives in submission to the accommodations which time and history may recommend as it does violence to our human condition amid time and history to pronounce the Word of God, as once stated, to be final.

The preceding assertions, complex though they may be, are unqualified. They define something infinitely more precious than the triumph of thought and argument. They are what enables me to understand myself as a Jew. Such affirmations are not, however, without their correlative intellectual imperatives, for they do not enjoy a merely subjective status in my thought.

There is little question that my reflections on history have no resemblance to the formal discipline of the historian, but this does not mean that my reflections are therefore false. Every man who confronts his world with the question of meaning is raising a fundamentally historical question. He is not only asking whether an event occurred; he is asking why it occurred. The question of "why" is rarely a dispassionate question. It is asked not only because man has curiosity about his past, but because he has concern about his future. The search for meaning in history may be the modest effort to enrich self-understanding (which is, after all, what

R. G. Collingwood considered the sufficient purpose of historiography) or it may be the grander and more unscientific effort to fathom a unity and to define a purpose immanent within history, or to locate an end-point toward which history is directed and through which it is fulfilled. The variety of meanings which have been discerned in history, whatever their questionable status as scientific truth, may have the value of illuminating the life of reflective men, of strengthening character, of shaping conviction, of giving to each new moment a quality of excitement and expectation which otherwise it might lack. It is true that such metaphysicians of history might well be satisfied with meanings discerned *within* the flow of historical events. However, a partisan of existential dogmatics might add something more: no longer do we know the end for which we strive; but if, indeed, there is an end, each moment prefigures something of it. Each moment becomes a prism through which the murky light of history and the clear light of God become one. This is, perhaps, all that eschatology can say to history, for any doctrine of the last event seems captious and gratuitous while we stand amid the agonies of actual history.[1] We may be assured of the beginning of history and we may demand its end, but all we have is the present and it is in the present, *the time between creation and redemption,* that we must live. It is for these reasons that any dogmatics is unavoidably existential, because its truth and power arise out of a decision with respect to *our history* and *our eternal task.*

If the dogmas which I have affirmed are authentic Jewish dogmas they must have been latent in the past against which Jewish thought developed and matured. It is obviously of little interest to project a view of Jewish destiny so at variance with possibilities present in Jewish history as to be ludicrously implausible and tendentious. Undoubtedly my view is a harsh view. However, I am afraid less of harshness than of inauthenticity. I am afraid less of abnormalizing the Jew than of normalizing him. This is so because my concern is less with Jewish history as such, with the works of the Jewish mind, with the identification of its peculiar cast and accent, its spirit and force, than with a specific phenomenon: the Jewish mind as it has thought and continues to think about its supernatural vocation.

NOTES

1. Arthur A. Cohen, "The Past and Future of Eschatological Thinking," in Harold Stahmer, ed., *Religion and Contemporary Society* (New York: Collier Books, 1963).

The Renewal of the Jewish Vocation

A natural history of the Jewish mind is impossible. The Jewish mind, as a natural and empirical phenomenon, is an absurdity. It consists in but the pale images of theological models—prophetism and messianism transformed into social and political ideologies, Exile recast as social alienation, the loneliness and spiritual discomfort of biblical man translated into the self-estrangement of modern man. For the natural Jew all that remains of the supernatural community is a treasury of inspiriting maxims and heroic legends, divested not only of their mythological content but of their divinity as well. Judaism has been quietly and unconsciously demythologizing its tradition for centuries; but the purgation of myth has not been accompanied by a sharper, more compelling awareness of the personal truth and meaning of its history (much demythologizing, but little kerygma).

The Jewish mind is demythologized, but the natural Jew has lost, in the process, all contact with and approach to his supernatural life. For centuries the supernatural Jew struggled to survive, and though he perished in the flesh, he did survive. Faith in the promise of the past and trust in the consummating action of God enabled him to survive the

From *The Natural and Supernatural Jew*. New York: Pantheon, 1962, 311–14. Estate of Arthur A. Cohen.

assaults of Christendom and Islam. The loss in our time of that supernatural pride which is called the "stubbornness" of the Jew is partially responsible for the loss of contact with the legacy of tradition and the passion to give witness to the incomplete sanctity of the natural order; moreover, the immolation of European Jewry in this century has exploded the last vestige of Jewish mythology—an eschatological trust which was indifferent to the course of world history and culture.

The supernatural Jew, defined as he is by those concerns and preoccupations which form the historic consensus of the Jewish mind, is the last of the eschatologists, for the Jew, more than any other man, lives on the recollection of first things and the anticipation of the last. Each moment comes to the supernatural Jew full of unrealized meaning, for each moment is abundant with the unrealized possibility of God in history. Every moment is potentially an eschatological moment; every moment collects the history of the past and portends the unfulfilled future. There is no such thing for the supernatural Jew as the denial of history, the repudiation of its meaning, the despair of its justification. Where the natural Jew may know despair, the supernatural Jew knows only trust.

But the natural and the supernatural Jew are joined in every Jew. The supernatural Jew may occasionally forget that he is also flesh and blood; he may detach himself from the world and disengage himself from history that he may pursue a path of self-denial and private illumination. Such a Jew is as much in error as is the natural Jew who forgets what links him to eternity. The natural Jew, enmeshed in the historical, cannot help but despair; destiny disappears for him and only the hard and implacable fatality of his life remains. The despair of the historical is but the consequence of fate obliterating destiny; while the ecstasy of the mystic, no less an example of fate, is centered exclusively upon the actuality of God, indifferent to his involvement in the contingent and dangerous war of history.

The religious dilemma which makes the unity of the natural and the supernatural so imperative for the Jewish mind is that the representation of God in history is not pure actuality but actuality committed to the unfulfilled possibility of history. The eschatological consummation toward which Judaism turns its face is history with God, the actual God realizing new creation, and new concreteness. As such, each moment of the present may become a redemptive moment, a moment in which the new possibility of God and the renewed sensibility of the Jew may meet and sanctify.

The renewal of the historical, the reunion of the Jew with general culture, the reassertion of the catholic claim of Judaism depend upon the

rediscovery of the implicit polarity and dialectic of the Jewish nature—
that it is a natural, participating in all the forms and events of history
and culture, and supernatural, transforming those forms and events into
bearers of ultimate and consummate meaning. God is not an eschatolo-
gist nor is God a messianist. God does what can be done—this is indeed
part of the tragedy which we may sense when we speak of God, for God
cannot compel history to fulfillment, he can but enrich the moment with
those possibilities which become the bearers of meaning. It is man who
victimizes God. God maintains freedom and the free destiny; it is human
obduracy and folly which refuses such terrifying freedom and finds con-
solation in the refusal of destiny and the comforting delusion of fate.

The historic moment that bears ultimate meaning is always at hand.
But when the argument is done and the historic precedents of the Jewish
mind have been adduced and displayed and the consensus of Judaism
has been recapitulated, the same question recurs: Can the testimony of all
truth compel human decision? Is it possible that the sense of supernatural
vocation—lost as it is in the abyss of natural fate—may be renewed? This
question still remains, and only Jews can answer it.

ART AND THEOLOGY

The theologian perforce uses art, as he uses all life, as a means by which to think more clearly, to understand more profoundly, and to love more ardently the God in whom he believes. He cannot fail to be struck therefore by the incongruity, the almost antiquarian anomalousness that an exhibition of the influence of the Hebrew Bible upon the imagination must have when presented in this decade, in this city, and at this moment. Can one not fail to be struck by what appears to be the hopeless and irremediable alienation of religion and art in our time? That ancient conjunction of the religious sensibility and the creative imagination would appear sufficiently dead as to have no justification for recollection, other than for purposes of simple recall. The fact that the holy and the beautiful are radically polarized and incommunicate is not of itself sufficient to convict their ancient communication of falsity or the effort which this exhibition makes to reawaken the sense of their historical and continuing community of irrelevant intellectualizing. The fact is that for many theologians, not alone myself, it is the arts (taken here to embrace not only painting and sculpture, but dance, literature, architecture, and music) which have been and continue to be the most vivid, direct, and

From *The Hebrew Bible in Christian, Jewish, and Muslim Art*. New York: Jewish Museum, 1963.

profound means by which man expresses his understanding of the universe and the sources of power and order which give it meaning. The arts alone succeed in making concrete the forms of thought, of adumbrating in rhythm, movement, line, and material the myths and symbols of the historical consciousness. Each art has its specific talent, its unique angularity which enables it more perfectly than does another art to express the distance and nearness of man to his external environment, to suggest temporality or timelessness, to articulate what actually is or to project the inner vision which one discerns beneath the seeming. In a word, every art is, in some sense, a metaphysical gloss or exegesis of the world, for it expresses a view of man's position in the universe—what he can know, what he must do, what he can hope for. It is proper, therefore, for the theologian to concern himself with the presentation of art. He does so less in order to instruct the artist about his history and purpose than to communicate with him and his history as human beings together in search of significant meaning.

Both the collaboration of theologian and artist as well as the hostility between theologian and artist have elaborate and unbroken histories. The threat and opportunity which the image offered the expression of religious ideas are enormously ancient and enormously contemporary. In ancient and primitive art, in the art of Latin and Byzantine Christendom, to a lesser extent in the art of Judaism and Islam, there has been a continuing tension between iconoclasm and iconomachy, between the repudiation of the image and the intensification of the image.

Whether the image be employed that God might be approached more meaningfully or the ascetic renunciation of the image be insisted upon is not really the issue. The tension is not simply that between the image and the imageless so stated, but rather between the beautiful and the holy. It may be recalled that in ancient Greece the Xoanon, an image of God made of wood, "rough and scarcely human" (G. Van der Leeuw, *Sacred and Profane Beauty: The Holy in Art*) was preferred in public religious processions to the sculptures of a Phidias or a Praxiteles. Similarly it may be observed in Mexico, or Spain, or Southern Italy that some handsome, clean-cut, baroque religious sculpture of a saint is less evocative of popular devotion than would be a smoke-blackened, worn, wax-covered image. The one object has a history of veneration and responsiveness; the other is only beautiful. It may well be that the beautiful object could in time come to enjoy the same quality of fervor and affection, but it would have accomplished this not by the power of its beauty, but by its manifest concentration of holy power.

The focus of discussion must then be shifted from what it is that is produced (although surely we can never lose sight of this) to what it is that the artist believes he is producing. For example, the primitive artist, interested though he may be in the representation of feeling (whether we call this his sentimentalism or romanticism) or in the achievement of a satisfactory visual statement, is primarily interested in conveying with his entire personality the existence, power, and reality of that which he is representing. The effects of his art—the artifact, mask, shield—may be wholly unrealistic to our lights, but nevertheless be a faithful rehearsal of a mythology which concentrates a significant sector of the natural and supernatural power to which he is dedicated. The beauty of primitive art is a by-product of its efficacy; undoubtedly it often occurred that the beautiful object was considered more sacred because it was a more perfect realization and balancing of the elements for which sacred myth required expression, but such a coincidence was more likely accidental. What was primary was that the artist was dealing with the holy and that figuratively, and in some cultures literally, at least, his life was staked upon his achievement.

The supposed alienation of religion and the artist in contemporary culture—what convinces many of the contemporary painters and sculptors exhibited here to choose remote or abstract titles for their works in order to signal their independence from a given sacred tradition—is not, I believe, a simple consequence of the emancipation of the ego or auto-centric individualism or deference to scientific specialization or even to the secularization of Western culture. Such explanations are historicist versions of the truth; they depend upon a fatal employment of historical events to explain historical events. Such explanations do not work, although they are rhetorically useful, contributing frills and ruffles to what seems to me to be a more significant explanation.

The Hebrew tradition, and in turn the traditions of Christianity and Islam, and latterly the Hindu revival sparked by Sri Ramakrishna, depends upon the efficacy of Divine action. It mattered little whether God spoke and then lapsed into silence, whether he chose to work wonders on one occasion and at another equally providential moment elected to passivity. What counted was that having expressed power once—vividly, directly, overwhelmingly—he was credited with all power and accorded unceasing attentiveness and concern. The involvement of God in nature demanded response and the artists of the ancient world were eminently responsive. Their task, like the task of poets, musicians, architects, was to consecrate and preserve the Divine-human experience in such a form as to insure its endurance and efficacy long after the actual moment was over. The artist fashioned in order that divinity might be recollected through his work. The holy image became rather more dangerous and compromising when it passed into representation, when the object became the divinity, when the occasioning event was forgotten and the image of recollection substituted for the god itself. Such idolatry was always anathema, even to religions which preserve the sacred function of images. But, whatever the tension and dynamic which existed between the making and the denying of images, the embodying or spiritualizing of the sacred event, what counted was that God was felt to have performed and that man was struck with joy or terror by his performance.

Without belaboring the history of transformation through which the major religions have passed since their formative days, it may be said unhesitantly that the artist of this day (however much he may remain a religious man) is not making paintings or sculptures in a tradition which may be recognized as historically religious. He may make sentimental or romantic studies of the popular evocative symbols of institutional religion, but his best work is not institutionally religious. This is only to say that the institutions through which the religions founded upon the Hebrew Bible are conserved have not enabled the artist to create contemporary religious art. This is not to say that motifs and emphases which these institutions have peripherally sustained—preserving for them an iconographic and symbolic history—are not influential. That would be to debar the work of many painters and sculptors who are Christian or Jewish and who have used figures or events from their scriptural traditions to make certain kinds of statements. But there are precious few living artists of whom it might be said, as it once might have been said, that their whole work was the celebration of a specific sacred history. This does not, of course, rule out the possibility that many artists who have never employed a biblical theme might well be celebrating at all times and throughout all their work their own understanding of God. To say this—and it is said seriously—is to suggest that something has happened to the artist *and* to religious institutions which make the pictorial and plastic images of the artist disjunct and alien from the verbal and conceptual traditions which religious institutions conserve.

The artist is perforce always temporalizing his images. He is (particularly today) a creature, severed and cut off from institutions, divorced from historical traditions of any age or authority. He is, he believes, a freed man and since freed he sees himself empowered to embody, without restriction, his own views of what is valuable. Religion, on the other hand, eternalizes a past moment, believing as it does that that past moment is only past to the relative eye of historical judgment. If the artist is freed of all institutions (not only the institutions of religion, but other institutions as well) it might be thought, however, that his freedom is illusory. One wonders whether there can be autonomy without contrariety, without the pitting of oneself against something other which is genuinely and authentically forceful and commanding. If we may trust the seismographic symposia which record the volatile brainwaves of the present younger generation, there are really no institutions against which it feels itself pitted, no establishment worthy enough to be opposed, and no system of values sufficiently dogmatic and uncompromising to provoke its heretical dissent. If this is the true state of affairs, then the situation is genuinely bleak, for it may be doubted whether the artist—or any other creative person for that matter—is really free. The artist may be autarchic, but he is not autonomous; he may be obliged to live on his own straitened intellectual and emotional capital, but he lacks sovereignty or transcendence. Where there is no opponent against which the artist must struggle, no values worth denying, no gods to be slain, and none to resurrect, then the prospect for "holy beauty" becomes rather dim. Not then the eclipse of religion (about which too much has already been written), but the eclipse of man is the real predicament of our times.

The Negative Way

The One was itself,
unique and solitary.
Lest the One be overcome
by its own magnitude,
it chose to extrude the many
in order that it might
apprehend itself.

Every determination
is a negation.
The undifferentiated
is specified by negation:
being caused to become different
by ceasing to be alike;
negating multiplicity
in order to affirm itself,
itself to become unique,
unique to become like
the One.

Privately published, 1964. Estate of Arthur A. Cohen.

The finite
is a determination of the manifold;
it negates the indeterminate
in order that it shall
become itself.
The Infinite, without parts and place,
without number and motion,
assumes the forms of finitude
in order to exhibit its own
existence.

The One enables the world
in order to become God
and the world sustains God
out of negation.
The world negates the All
that is within the One
for the sake of some thing
and the manifold negates
its multiplicity
in order to become
one thing.

The One desires
to become the God
of the many.
Without the many
the plenitude of the One
is as though it was nothing;
with the many the One
overflows.

The many desires
that God become One.
Without the vision
of the One,
each specification of the manifold
would seek to become God.
It is not the Oneness of God
which is the terror
of the many,

but rather his
plenitude.

What does death end.
More than the beginning.
What does birth begin.
More than dying.
What is between.
More than the courage to
fill the abyss.

To desire all things
is to desire no thing,
for all things are the
portion of the One.
To desire no thing
is to desire to become
the One;
however the One can be only itself.
Wisdom is to desire all things,
and to expect none.

If God is that being
who has his center everywhere
and his circumference nowhere,
man is that being
who has his center and
his circumference somewhere.
God's nowhere is a portion
of man's somewhere and
man's somewhere would vanish
were God nowhere.
It is for this reason
that God's center is everywhere
in order that man's center
might be somewhere.

Reflections on Theological Method: The Task of Jewish Theology

I

I confess to being baffled by the assignment. There was a part of me, a not insubstantial part, that rejected the assignment as specious and dishonest. How could I give myself with any degree of conviction to the defense of a discipline that I believed *as a discipline* needed no defense? It might be necessary, I would agree, to defend the existence of God, the immutability of Torah, or the eternity of the Jewish people. Such doctrines, involving as they do the assertion of attitudes and convictions that appeal for substantiation to personal experience, to the subjective interpretation of a public history; which purport to be general propositions, while remaining credally narrow and specific, obligate their defenders to explication. Of course, any theological statement can be received without explication. Belief may exist without interpretation; the articulation of belief, however, requires interpretation. Speech obliges interpretation; communication demands defense.

If we were content to stand upon the reception of revealed sentences, we should have little need to speak—the individual believer hears, and hearing as individual, he need not speak. It is only when believer joins with believer to form community that the requirement for explication is

Unpublished manuscript, 1967. Estate of Arthur A. Cohen.

felt. Explication, clarification, elucidation—these objectives of discourse are felt by the community seeking to establish a normative language of faith. It is recognized nonetheless that one can achieve explication, clarification, and elucidation without stating truth, for the judgment of truth involves some collaboration between language and reality, between the intellect conceptualizing feeling and the accuracy with which feeling records and transmits the impact of the actual, the real event.

The defense of doctrines involves the defense of assertions that are held as true because they are received and believed, not the defense of a method of correlating such assertions. The assertions of a believer with respect to what he believes may have no public referent other than the grammar and order of his language, for if there is no consensus respecting the existence, reality, or meaning of the terms his language employs, it is hopeless to expect that his assertions will carry with them any claim upon general assent, any intrinsic persuasiveness.

The promulgation of discrete and independent propositions that derive their force from the suasion of faith can yield no public communication, no consensual discourse, and certainly no systematic teaching, except insofar as many believers, responding out of their own personal conviction, choose to accept particular doctrines as doctrines they collectively believe. There is a distinction between theological propositions and theology as such; statements of belief, faith, and expectation may be eccentrically held, may be minimal or maximal, may be formulated apodictically, without appeal to any source of confirmation other than the force of the assertion itself, may be absolute despite their privacy and subjectivity, or may be absolute in their reliance upon the sufficient warrant of a sacred source, but such assertions, however theological in character, need not reflect upon the nature of theology.

The defense of theology is independent, therefore, of any defense of Jewish theology. It may well be the case that Jewish life can endure without theology, that there is no need for the development of a discourse that interrelates the docta of Jewish faith in order to better illuminate its unique claims, its general coherence, its vision of God, man, and history, and its participation in the collective human pursuit of wisdom. I am willing to acknowledge that such is obviously the conviction of those who oppose Jewish theology, who regard it as a divisive, alien, Christianizing discipline; a discipline suspiciously redolent with the aromas of gnosticism; a pagan discipline; a discipline that introduces speculative intellection into domains where only hearing and performing are necessary. All this can be understood. There is an historic animus against theology—all theology—that makes its introduction into Jewish thought suspect and precarious. Analysis of the historical opposition to theology in Jewish life would take me far afield, although to many of you it would be a most engaging polemic. Yet I am not interested in defending Jewish theology against antitheologians. There is no gain to such an enterprise, for Jewish history can be employed either to abuse theology or to support it, to deny it an appropriate place in Jewish intellectual history or to so inflate its past glory as to have the effect of substituting some form of neo-medievalism for the theology appropriate to the present moment of our lives.

The task that I set for myself today is a limited one: I wish to explore the grounds of theology as a discipline of thought, to consider the appropriate rigors and checks upon theological thinking, as well as the scope of theological freedom. These will be formulated as general reflections, neither exhaustive nor comprehensive, but rather eductive and allusive, drawing out from my own method some of the principles I have come to regard as decisive markers of theological method rather than of theological madness. In the second and final part of this essay, I should like to apply the general rubrics of theological thinking to the demands of Jewish faith and history: to adumbrate what I take to be the unique forms of Jewish belief and to suggest how theological thinking may be employed to articulate them more profoundly.

It is scarcely possible to speak of theology in general, for the God one pursues and seeks to understand is a God already discovered, and the experience of discovery is either utterly particular and individual or else the result of having passed through that education of the religious sensibilities that is the consequence of traditional formation and instruction. In neither case is the theologically pursuit separate from the experience of a particular history of faith. Where theology is spoken of in general, what is really at issue is philosophy of religion. Within the scope of philosophy of religion—a discipline that concerns itself with the foundations and noesis of religious sensibility—theology becomes an exemplification of religious sensibility in the process of self-clarification. To the extent that religion is an object of philosophic study, the religious experience becomes central; the object of that experience, however, remains conjectural. Philosophy of religion does not begin with God and as often as not does not end with him. Theology begins with God and as often as not does not end with him. Theology begins with God and returns to him, though it ends with man. The directional vector in theology is from God to man, since theology begins where the philosophy of religion ends.

Theology, as Jews or Christians understand this discipline, is not to be confused with metaphysics, although as often as not metaphysical argument may be introduced into the elaboration of categories that regulate the experience of God. What is primary to theology is that the experience of God be prior to the interpretation of the experience; that a relation exists between the person of the theologian and the God of theology; moreover that belief is not independent of an historical context and modus of articulation. Presumably for this reason theology follows from and does not precede the experience of belief. Presumably, as well, theology works upon the materials given by God to belief, and though it should refine and winnow the grounds of belief, it does not supply those grounds.

I have always regarded theology as a nonspeculative discipline. This is only to say that theology does not conjecture its object but is given it. Theology begins at that moment in the life of the believer when the materials of faith—the teachings received, the experiences undergone, the scriptures assimilated, the historical events endured—are no longer self-confirming. This is perhaps an obvious point but worth regarding, since versions of this interpretation are used by those hostile to theology to support their opposition. If indeed it is the case that the experience of faith can be so overwhelming, claiming the entire life of the believer, inspiriting his action, and forming and sustaining his commitments, his need for theology can only be regarded as the mark of an attenuation of faith. Theology, in such a view, is a falling off from faith, a diminution of belief, a call for reason to supply better justification for the life of faith than the sufficient attitude of complaisant piety. If the believer knows in faith that the world is fashioned by God, that history is destined by him, and that man will be redeemed by his merciful salvation, it seems irrelevant, indeed impious, for theology to explicate further what faith already regards as self-evident.

What such a view fails to account for, however, is that faith, no less than theology, cannot occur in the absence of history. The believer also occupies a time and space. Even when Kierkegaard speaks of the believer making himself contemporaneous to the Incarnation, severing the ligatures of history, in order by that miraculous suspension of historical time to experience the depths of his inwardness, his particularity, his existential nexus with his salvation, he does not deny the historicity of faith nor does he burn out the roots that the believer has sunk deep into historical time. Kierkegaard denies history its secular dialectic, but he affirms that the experience of faith is always *heilsgeschichtlich,* an event within sacred history, the history of filled time, time penetrated by God. The believer experiences the reality of God within his situation and the situation of the believer is as much an appropriate subject matter for theology as is the God that belief affirms. In this view, theology is appropriately a method of establishing the senses in which what God says of himself and of man and what man says of God and of his own situation may be correlated. The believer makes an address out of his situation. What is the situation of the believer? To the extent that the believer believes, it is his concern that the object of belief be relevant to the demands of his situation. The situation of the believer, no less than the situation of the nonbeliever, is exhaustingly human. The willingness of the believer to undertake that program of thought which pushes life to the limits, and subjects it to the at times searing critique which leaves him muddled and in despair; what elicits such crises of existence in the believer but leaves other persons content in their relative disorder remains for purposes of this discussion a mystery. We may acknowledge, however, that if for Plato philosophy begins in wonder, faith begins in wonder turning to despair, becoming, if you will permit, suicidal. The experience of faith is a passing beyond the limit of situations—despair, guilt, anguish, and the intimation of death. This is true for us, but as well for Abraham, Isaac, and Jacob. The existential categories do not change; history continues to unfold; the concatenation of circumstance alters; the application of the enduring categories of existence vary, but the condition of man which lies at the vortex of history is identical now as then. Faith begins and ends with feeling, with the extension of sensibility beyond the perimeter of consciousness, from the apprehended to the intuited, from the presence of the felt to the feeling of presence beyond the transmissible range of sentience. Conceptualization may intervene, forcing primitive (or primordial) notions to descend from the cortical imagination to the antennae of the sensorium, giving back to the world the wonder that the world first bestowed upon it. Within this circle of feeling, the life of faith can unfold. There is no requirement for thought as such. The believer need never think, and it is no derogation to faith if he forces thought from himself. Feeling and primordial conceptualization will be sufficient to provide him with necessary teaching, with appropriate pieties, with deeply held moral and quite possibly mystic maxims or convictions. In other words, faith has no need of thought, surely no need of consecutive thought, much less systematic thought, and even less of theology or theological method.

The obligation of thought is optional and it arises only where the believer believes but is not clarified. The project of clarification is infrequently the conscious objective of thinking. Men think, think prodigiously in fact, but rarely set for themselves the explicit task of thought which is the task of clarification. They arrive at conclusions of thought either prematurely or not at all; they affirm *some* thing, some life principle early on, intuiting a structure in the world that accords with the unfolding biographical order of their lives, and rest firm with it, only occasionally, if ever, significantly altering it or converting assumed conclusions from one received teaching to another. Man is too often, then, a creature who gives up thinking, rather than a creature who perseveres in thought. He is a creature who mistakes the ongoing defense of *having once thought* for the enterprise of continuing to think. This is obviously dangerous, for such an attitude toward the world concludes in either sterility or fanaticism, if not both, for the fanatic is surely boring and sterile, and quite possibly a menace.

If the task of thought is the task of clarification, to the extent that thought clarifies the life situation of man, thought is never completed nor is the situation ever finally clarified. Thought always puts to itself issues that exceed its already funded wisdom and for this reason thought pushes beyond its own conclusions. I see no reason why this enterprise should not continue until death. If thought puts to itself the question of the ground of thought, however—that is the question of the ultimate justification for the task of clarification—it asks a question for which it is desperately unsuited. How shall it be that a consciousness that can compass but the smallest range of experience and distill from the field of its exposure even less, garnering for the memory such a miserable harvest on which to feed in the winters of its loneliness, how shall it be imagined that such a consciousness will be capacious enough to draw from the limits of its purview enough to persuade it that it is illuminated; that it is harmonized with the world; that though it strains to think, the world about which it thinks and the self to which it wishes to be reconciled shall provide it with clarification respecting its ultimate ground? What I am speaking about here is the desperation of finitude in all its aspects before the task of clarification.

The thinking man may philosophize, but his philosophy, like the serpent who consumes his own tail, is bound to turn upon itself. Philosophy may clarify the philosopher, the self may achieve its own identity in thought, but for the philosopher to reconcile his own self with the world, to pass through the dualities that naked thought posits in the world, to avoid the madness that comes out of dualism, he may either retire into silence (where speech gives out before wonder) or he may surrender to that impossible possibility which is that the ground of existence must be posited beyond the reach of empirical reason, beyond the palpable evidence of the senses, beyond the natural world, beyond the categories by which human thought is only human.

The pursuit and discovery of God are for the thinking man who has set himself the task of clarification both a misery and a joy; a misery for he knows that his language is false, his gravity imponderable, his silence a gesture of helplessness. He cannot speak of this God except in terms that the philosopher, as much imprisoned by his finitude, will regard as foolish and meaningless. Every statement that such a thinker makes to the philosopher is bound to be winnowed by the language of translation, to be compromised and eroded. Wittengenstein was right to recommend silence in the face of the mysteries, but then Wittengenstein was uninterested in theology, whatever the mysticism of his temperament.

Our problem is different, for though we may recognize the discontinuity between the language that philosophers employ and the fateful language that theologians improvise, we still feel beholden as thinking men to require that our theological language be more than apologetic, that it do more than simply interpret our historical preferences, our intellectual atavisms, our sectarian discourse. Theology is not simply defending the God of Israel before the God of the Church, or discriminating biblical epistemology from the rigid monisms of Eastern religions. It is not only the conversation of believers with believers, a method of establishing a viable—even if not common—discourse among the faithful. If it were only that theology was the unraveling of a higher circularity to lay over the circularity of ordinary thought, the highness of the one and the ordinariness of the other would be at best rhetorical, without real meaning or profundity.

Theology is, however, a discipline related to that of philosophy, employing many of the same procedural devices and many of the same rigors of correction and confirmation; theology is as related to the factual situation of man as is philosophy. The task of clarification has proceeded from the hard rock of finitude (against which the despair of philosophy breaks itself) to the assertion of a reality, an existence whose givenness is postulated to thought, whose very opacity, difficulty, comprehensiveness, and totality is so extreme as to compel the normative categories of thought to be modified. The affirmation of God, however much it be an affirmation that is constantly destroyed and reborn (and we may recognize that for the believer and theologian this tension of loss and rediscovery is endlessly repetitive), confronts not a thinker who is also a man, but a man who thinks in order to comprehend his humanity. Since the thinker's primary reality is his very own reality in all its personal, social, and historical complexity and individuality, theology is not a concern abstracted from the concrete particularity of his own life. There can be no general truth about the world and man, unless that general truth be first a truth for the man who thinks and defines it. The situation is *my* situation, the finitude is *my* finitude, the consciousness is *my* consciousness. Only after the world has been made mine can I give it back to others; only after I am justified can I share that justification with others; and only after God has become mine can I set myself to showing him forth to others. My absurdity, my irrationality, and my predicament must first be dissolved by the theological affirmation before the solvent role of God can be made a general reality who bestows his gifts on all man and all the world, before God can be, all to all, himself always *The All.*

II

The Jew who thinks about being a Jew is not simply a man thinking about being a man. One question, at least, has been resolved. It may well have been resolved *illicitly* (and there is surely a sense in which it has been resolved *prematurely,* but no less conclusively): the man who has decided that he is a Jew must address his questions of the universe and his questions of himself from a rather different perspective than if he were born of a different history. The Jew thinks out of a complex situation, and that situation is defined and modulated by Jewish shades and specters, by Jewish sentiments and experiences, and by events and conditions that have happened to Jews as a result of being Jewish. There exist Jewish facts, if only because Jews have been involved (whether directly or accidentally is irrelevant) in their occurrence. This is the factuality of Jewish existence; it is the natural phenomenology of Jewish experience, the bracketing, discrimination, identification, and denomination of the Jewish about the Jew. Yet clearly the Jewish about the Jew will not enable him to identify himself amid the clutter of experience that history has assigned to his condition. It will enable him to know who he is like, to what body of history he is *comparable,* to what order of man and society he *belongs,* but it will not enable him to know who he is. The Jew extrapolated from the riot of natural humanity and assigned history is little more than an historical creation and, as such, relative, perishable, and mortal.

There is no reason why the Jew should not be relative, perishable, and mortal. He may, like other men, be content to die and pass away. If he wills his mortality or irresolutely surrenders to it, however, he ignores one aspect of his natural situation and historical conditioning that is a primary source of the exasperating legacy of paradox in Jewish existence: the continuing and ongoing opening toward transcendence which has been a mark of Jewish endurance, continuity, and immortality. The Jew who reflects upon his Jewish existence uncovers the living shoots of transcendence that lie buried, hidden, overwhelmed by the rich humus of mortality with which Jewish existence—surely in our time, but as well in all times—has been covered.

Transcendence is not imposed. Transcendence is a directional valent of mundane existence. It is a domain, a province, an unfilled and contentless "nothing"; it is not, however, a mere emptiness, that is an emptiness unrelated and discontinuous with the busy occupation of immane existence. It is a projection of immane existence, a thrusting out of and beyond the conditions of nature. It is "empty" only in the sense that it is not filled by nature, however much our natural existence alludes to its content, suggests it, and indicates it. Transcendence is not equivalent, therefore, with the supernatural. Where transcendence is an epistemological gesture, a "nothing" that surrounds and buffers the heavy atmosphere of everyday life, supernature is a filled emptiness, a substantial presence that is at the superfices of transcendence. In effect, we transcend toward the supernatural. The supernatural is a goal of transcendence. It is not objective, not demonstrable in an orderly and reasonable enterprise of confirmation, but it is seizable in the imagination. The world of the supernatural impinges upon the world of immane existence, touching, interpenetrating, sinking roots into our world.

There is no thing, no creature surely, that is natural or supernatural *as such,* whose domain is below or above, immane or transcendent. Any such artificial classification denies the vitality and energy indispensable to living realities. All of our usage of the terms natural and supernatural is artificial. It is usage to aid the classifying impatience of thought. Things are regarded as natural if their causes, however complicated and reticulated, can be isolated and scrutinized by the observer. Yet the web of causality, though it be scrupulously analyzed, is insufficient to encompass the total life of any object in nature, for the ultimate causality is inaccessible to the percipient. If we were content to describe as natural that which we, as human observers, may fully comprehend we should be obliged to regard much of what we commonly consider natural to be unclassified, possibly even unclassifiable. It is at this juncture—the moment at which our patience thins and our methods of description become boring and inadequate—that we desert nature and assume the attitude of art. The imagination invariably begins where nature, secret and inarticulate, baffles or tires ratiocination, when the labored inquiry ends and novelty withers before the eye of the now impatient observers. At such moments, if we are capable, we begin to complete nature for itself, imputing to it a borrowed life.

The borrowed life of the imagination, wherewith objects acquire an involvement and interconnection that reason cannot justify, is the beginning of that addendum of the natural that, though by no means superior to nature, is surely beyond the natural. This is the thrust of transcendence. The natural object still lies before us: unbidden and unyielding, simply there, obstructing or confusing us, awaiting our response (whether it be the response of the Zen poet who simply looks and sees, respecting a presence and consciousness he assumes, but cannot confirm, or whether it lies before us waiting to be moved out of the road that we may pass through). Whatever our response, it is the infuriating silence of nature that compels us to regard the natural as so much ours to conquer. Were nature able to answer, to rebuke us, to convince us that she does, indeed, praise God, but never die, we might be more respectful of her unresponsiveness. Yet the opposite is the case: we regard nature as we would wish to be regarded—with awe, with reverence, with wonder, and with terror. But we are not regarded with such mute solemnities. We are the creatures who love and destroy, who handle and create, but we are not awesome or revered. Indeed, it is only when a man ceases to live for other men that he becomes a figure, totem, or image, an object of reverence or terror. This cannot occur when he is simply a man. When he is a man, his very distinctness from nature obliges other men who do not regard him with reverence or terror to regard him as natural. The most inexplicable dimension of man—the modus of his feeling and action—is what others regard as most natural. For we say of a man in passion or in jealousy that it is his *nature,* given his past, the accidents of his life, the determinants of his ancestry; in effect, we make natural in man that which is already beyond the domain of the natural. Such a man no longer acts within the canon of nature and reason; he is already the mutant of the imagination, the beyond-nature, the fantasy that skeins his interior world. Yet we call him natural—this crepuscular man. What, then, is it within men that is comforted by the reduction of experience to the natural? Do we not make nature into the unnatural, the antinature, by insisting with such rigor upon an assessment of nature that is coterminal with our capacity to isolate and reduce it? It is as though we come to life—in this Occidental world of trust—duty-bound by some obscure law of haste on to death to get as much of the fathomable out of the way so that we can get on with the enterprise of living with the unfathomable? Yet in precisely this way do we achieve the ridiculous posture of having removed from our worldly and irrelevant nature precisely that dimension of our own being that is like that of nature—incommunicate, solitary, unyielding, silent, and interior. We make nature into the fully caused, into the known and knowable, and in doing so, we separate ourselves from the same matrix of flesh, bone, and tissue that makes us like to the very organs of nature. We assume that nature is unconscious and that, being unconscious, it is external, static, without history and connectedness, and finally without a meaning for us, except as it gets in our way or as we pretend that the Uncreated Creator uses the power of nature to chastise *our* rebelliousness, as, for example, with Noah's flood, the searing storm that leveled Sodom and Gomorrah, and the flood of Lisbon.

It is my conviction that the thoroughness with which contemporary Jewish thought has dispatched the idea of the supernatural reflects less an examination of the real problem than a perfectly legitimate rebuke upon an excess in dogmatic theology, both Orthodox Jewish and Christian. The dismay with which any new thinking about the supernatural is greeted betrays, however, not a valid and authentic demurral to an impure and dangerous idea, but a bona fide dissatisfaction with the theology of miracles and wonders which is the hallmark of both a naive and hallucinatory literalism and a device of nineteenth-century theology that wishes to retain literalism without bibliolatry. Both objectional doctrines were literalist, but both were marked by an inversion of language and thought which I have tried to avoid. Their arguments were characterized by an identification of God with the supernatural and by an authoritarian emphasis that poured truth and grace down from above upon truculent and rebellious creatures. My contention, quite the reverse, is that the supernatural is an implication of nature, that it is an intuition nourished and evoked by the incommunicate silence of the natural; nature, narrowly understood, and man, regarded here as natural. Moreover, what we intuit out of the natural about the supernatural, the experiences of wonder, fascination, and terror (indeed, the preliminary categories by which Rudolf Otto indicated the presence of the Holy) are preliminary to the intuition of God. God is the eventuality of the supernatural. He is there beyond our intuitions, but he is not there without them.

The presence of God at the limits of our access to transcendence and our intuition of the "beyond-nature" is (thought having pushed us beyond its capability and competence) an affirmation of belief. We say "there is *this* (*this* presence, *this* being, *this* ultimate reality, *this* God) which enables *that* (the resistant, intractable, obscure, dark-light world of things and selves) to cohere. God enables us to cohere.

It is now, at this point where the *man* in the Jew has found it possible to suspend thinking *only* as a man and to begin thinking as a *Jew* amid his humanity, that the natural man (having located the direction of transcendence) can begin to let the action of God (his mercy, grace, loving kindness) begin to work within him. Nature having touched to the uttermost hem of the supernatural can allow the divinity within that dismal, despairing, hopeless emptiness fill him. The natural preeses beyond itself to despair (that is, the despair of unknowing); it surrenders to unknowing enters the "dark night" of which all mystics speak—a metaphor for the condition of desperate ignorance—and there identifies a frail connection between the emptying of the self of all knowledge, the abandonment of knowledge, the perfect unknowing that enables the process of knowing to be renewed and the being whose existence it renews. It is the passion of thought and the desire to know that presses us to the limit where thought cannibalizes itself in despair, where knowing ceases, where the emptiness of the self is undergone and the fullness of God may commence.

Obviously my argument is circular: faith assumes all along what faith seeks to find. True. But then I have not pretended to write as other than one who believes in what he has found; moreover, believing in what I have found I do not believe that it can be found *only* by myself (for that would be to say that all men make their own gods, and religions are simply consensual agreements to pool fragmentary visions) or that I brought into existence what I believe and it will perish when I die. It is my persuasion that we think ourselves to the limits of thought and find at the limits an order of existence that both authenticates and nullifies the enterprise of thought. Both authentication and nullification are indispensable, for the authentication without nullification would render belief suspect and nullification without authentication would make thought gratuitous. We are creatures who think. We can do no other. We are as well creatures who must acquire the aptitude to suspend thought at the limits, for otherwise we would only *think*—we would lose the capacity to imagine, to dream, to prophesy, to create. Thinking and nonthinking, the natural enterprise and the supernatural vacuity, the thrust to the limits and the gifts of God are all of our portion.

The limbo is past. The man who thinks to the limits and meets himself on the way back is a different man than he who journeyed forth; the man may have been a natural Jew—a Jew conditioned by a history and an experience, but the man who returns is no longer conditioned by a natural history and a natural experience. The history and the experience are now different. This is to say only that the intuition of the medium of transcendence, the emptying of self into the emptiness of the supernatural, the taking on of the new self in faith, the coming to believe in God makes a difference to the inherited and instructed history and experience of the old Jew.

This language will probably bother everyone. It bothers me a little. I can already hear the voices whispering against its mystagogic implications, its dubious Christianizing theology of baptism—old Jew, new Jew. Yet let us look for a moment at our actual historical situation. This theology of renewal, with its obviously mystic epistemology, would be unnecessary if the conventional dogmatics of Orthodoxy worked. If there were an unbroken, majoritarian consensus with Judaism, a consensus that maintained an undefective line of continuity from Sinai to our day, we should have only to speak of more and less pious Jews, of more and less believing Jews, of more and less faithful, instructed, and obedient Jews. We can no longer. We can speak only of a community of believing (more or less) and unbelieving (more or less) Jews—and surely the numbers of those who do not believe in the institutions of Judaism (more or less) are vaster by far than the community of those who believe and observe something, anything, of what historically identifies the Jew as a creature covenanted to God. Obviously there is a broken circuit in Judaism. The vertical ascent to faith which intensifies the way of knowing into the vision of God no longer necessarily or by definition intersects the horizontal course of historical Jewish experience. There are Jews of whom it may be said the historic Jewish experience—the natural experience of the Jew—is absolutely meaningless and irrelevant.

How shall such Jews be redeemed to their vocation in Israel? It cannot be accomplished (of this I am totally and absolutely certain) by a renaissance of Jewish culture, language, civilization, nationality, indeed, by any and all devices and disciplines of natural Jewish existence. Jews cannot be returned to Judaism by Jewish education. Jews can be strengthened, deepened, and intensified in the action of belief by Jewish instruction, but the presumption of such efficacy is that they already or still perdure in faithfulness. They believe, however unknowing they may be of the axioms or penetration of that belief, however flaccid and contradictory its posture; but they believe, and given the rudiments of belief, Jewish education may be availing. All of my thinking is directed not to them, however (although it might as easily be directed to them as well), but to those who no longer believe, who have never believed, who do not raise these questions of themselves from which belief may follow. It is for them that the argument I have been developing is relevant. Moreover, such Jews coming to wonder before God are *converted,* however much they may be virtually and mystically present within the House of Israel from the day of their birth. (A theology of the virtual and invisible Israel may still our despair at the defections of our fellows and brothers, but it cannot restore belief to the unbelieving.)

These reflections must come to an end somewhere. They can go on, hopefully will go on, to the exposition at some future time of a theology of renewal, but the present is all that I can manage. It is hoped only that if it is criticized that it be better criticized than earlier Jewish attempts in our generation to think theologically have been. It must be understood that refusal to think about theological questions within Judaism is no longer possible. Not only is it not possible, it is dangerously irresponsible. With pathetically few exceptions, there is no Jewish theology in the world today; there is no Jewish theological thinking; where it is found, among younger thinkers here and abroad, it is regarded with suspicion and contempt. Jewish thinking, about God, man, and the world; about the connection between historic Jewish experience and the experience of all mankind; about the vocation and destiny of the Jewish people as it relates to the task of mankind—all these are primary Jewish questions for which there are sources in our traditional literature. These questions must be asked and answers must be offered by Jews thinking as Jews— and to think in this way requires that Jews employ all the resources of the tradition; but thought has its own canon and its own history, and Jewish thinkers who value only what traditional Jews have thought rarely examine the canon of intellectual history as such. They think, but their thought is shrill, reedy, predictable, and finally marginal. There must be a new beginning in Jewish thinking. Without it, Jews may well survive, but much beyond the immediate, visible future, Judaism cannot.

LIFE AMID THE PARADIGMS
OR THE ABSENCE OF
A JEWISH CRITIQUE OF CULTURE

I

It is uncertain to me as I begin writing these remarks whether there is truly an absence of critique in the regard that Judaism casts upon culture. It is surely the case that the critique that has become familiar in the Christian world—the standards that are layed over culture by the absolute character of Jesus as Christ—has no relevance to the order of Jewish criticism. Indeed, it may well be my discovery that the critique that Judaism devises in antiphon to general culture is structured from sources that are hardly recognized as sources of judgment, that the Jewish critique precisely because it is not formulated with the familiar emphases of Christian judgment is not seen by Christians to be judgment nor by Jews to be criticism.[1] It may come to be the case that the Jewish judgment upon culture—both secular and Christian—will be quiet, indeed, even silent, but that nonetheless in that silence the voice of the judging God may be discerned.

But I cannot be certain of this outcome until the work is done. Indeed, I may find unexpectedly that the apparent absence of a Jewish critique of culture in modern times is in fact the consequence of an older

Journal of the American Academy of Religion 54, no. 3 (fall 1986): 499–519. Permission granted by Scholars Press.

conviction that Judaism has nothing to say to general culture, that general culture is anathema to its teaching, that it is—given the framework of its conception of the religious undertaking of mankind—irrelevant what falls outside that framework, that heteronymous culture, grounded as it is upon principles, procedures, and acts that only tangentially and secondarily depend upon religious auspices, is some form of derangement and defect. And all this despite the erroneous persuasion of some critics that we must regard Kafka and Freud (sometimes even Karl Marx) as Jewish critics of culture, a notion that seems to me particularly dubious since their command of the sources of Jewish insight is so precarious that their most profound judgments are self-judgments, autobiographic partialities introjected into the whole of culture. The sheer negativity that their critique of culture yields is wholly accurate to the paucity of their Jewish premises and not wrong for that limitation, but surely dubious as evidence of something transparently Jewish.[2] (It is becoming a national pastime of intellectuals to speak about the Jews with a claim upon knowledge that derives either from a haphazard and inadequate command of the sources, obligatory citations from standard works of Walter Benjamin, Jacques Derrida, Ernst Bloch, Hannah Arendt, or Gershom Scholem, or a loosely fabulated suite of constructions that work over the rabbinic literature or classic Jewish literature as though it were something that could be easily whipped into presentable shape with a minimum of bother with the primary sources or the great scholarly achievements of late nineteenth- and twentieth-century students.)

My original impetus to undertake these remarks was the conviction grown up in me over several years that Judaism had failed general culture by having formulated no terms of criticism nor any dialectic strategy for shifting from its holy principles to the public domain where culture thrives. I had begun in the belief that Judaism was barren before culture. However in the course of thinking about the terrain I intended to examine, I was stunned by the recognition that such an attention may well be off the authentic course of Jewish praxis, irrelevant to its own nature, and disruptive of its primary care and solicitude for this world.[3]

These brief autobiographic asides upon a personal ambivalence and indecision are not without their methodological centrality. There can be no significant hermeneutical development unless the thinker sets forth at the very beginning the context that prompts his inquiry, the first scintilla of care that inaugurates the investigation. Inquiry (and hence our human thoughtfulness) begins first and always in a kind of derangement in which the issue is projected as though it carries with it, immanent in its title, an animadversion to the outcome. The thinker is first aroused. It is only after his arousal that the thinker begins to reflect. But true thinking cannot know the outcome until the thinking is completed (and even that outcome is not complete until the thinker ceases to think forever). The thinker may have hoped that the title he set at the beginning of his exposition would be the final title, bearing within its short formulation an anticipation of the outcome of thought, but such a procedure is notoriously dangerous.[4] It encourages a corrupting rhetoric, since the thinker is oriented toward an audience he has not yet met and begins to create an investigation designed to delight or irritate an audience whose composition he can hardly know and to whose needs he should be supremely indifferent. This predicament of thinking toward a public reminds me of the tale told of Hannah Arendt, who was attacked by a critic who inquired of her in the discussion period following a lecture of what she was thinking when she made a certain observation. She replied, I am told: "Sir, I was not thinking. I was reading. I did my thinking weeks ago."[5] Her reply is not merely jocular and irresponsible, but rather a profound indication of the differentia that must be established between the thinker who thinks and is observed thinking by an audience for whom the thought is fortuitously intended and the thinker who reads thought, but knows full well that such thought is now past, completed and finished in an antiquity that may be only several hours old, but is nonetheless absolutely sealed off from the flow and movement of the present in which the text is read aloud.

II

The caveats I have just set forth are terribly important, although I do not believe their importance will become evident until the very end. It is certainly clear that the religious response to culture can hardly be conducted as an academic address. By its very nature, as I have explained, the audience becomes an object and any hope of introducing the dialogic principle into our exchange is foresworn. Therefore, it is only natural that I should try to construct my observations by a gathering of the cultural artifacts of this century, hoping, bleakly I confess, that by some phenomenological congregation I shall be able to display before you the predicament rather than eliciting it from your own recognition of our shared situation. Such a dull method prescribes the annotation of anthropological data, identifying cultural materials, configurations, attitudes that detail our culture and having them in view to pass judgment upon them. But this is not what I am after. I have no wish to lock horns with culture over some triviality that would result in the disarming of Jewish criticism by revealing its unsophisticated approach to cultural artifacts, nor could I possibly develop in the compass of this hour an adequate phenomenological selection of cultural elements which are susceptible of this or that mode of Jewish critique.

Let me turn the question in a Christian direction, even if briefly, by inquiring what is it that is addressed when religion speaks to culture? How does one make certain that when culture is confronted by religion that religion is not used as a rhetorical cudgel for beating up culture (an undertaking easy to accomplish, being the regular subject matter of preaching and sermonics where the audience's silence and indifference protect the speaker from close scrutiny)? Is it appropriate for religion to pass judgment upon all of culture or only upon those portions of the cultural matrix that aspire to the condition of the religious, e.g., those cultural events that take the sublime as the atmosphere of their creative aura? Moreover, in an unredeemed world, is it appropriate for religion to train upon culture the sights of transcendent judgment, when human beings undertake in the enterprise of cultural creation to formulate their autonomous contribution to the enrichment and growth of civilized community? But having said this it must be acknowledged instantly that religions which are in any way integrated with the cultures they address are not general or abstract social communities, but concrete, immanent, intimately bonded associations that make use of precisely the artifacts of culture they are inspecting. There is no such thing as general religion. There is no longer even Christianity or Judaism. Rather there are Christians and Jews who are self-interpreting, validated in their self-interpretation by regulative principles that are no longer administered by hieratic and absolute bodies that set forth and enforce the criteria of belonging. (Hardly any of us could avoid the fires of Calvin's Geneva or the Holy Office, although I am persuaded that there are more than a few who would willingly light those fires again.) It is not then that Christians and Jews are lonely creatures of faith in the modern world or not simply lonely creatures of faith, but rather creatures of faith who do and believe what is asked of them that they be confirmed as Christians and Jews. The objective criteria are proposed but cannot be enforced, despite the wish of the various religious communities to compel what is taken as tradition to be an unbroken and continuous passing of persuasion between the generations and the apodictic enforcement of the performance of identifiable religious acts, even though it is impossible to be certain of the actual beliefs construed within heart and head.

The religiously autonomous, whatever their wish to be part of the great tradition, cannot evade their freedom. It is one of the victories enforced by secular culture upon the religious (and in this respect culture, narrowly understood, emerges in our time as the replacement of the religious) that the numinous discovery is sought today not in prayer and liturgy (much less in the libraries of the faithful which are—as Andrew Louth has glossed them in *Discerning the Mystery*—the laboratories of theology),[6] but rather in heteronomous events of culture. In our day cultural events are besought as though they were occasions of revelation—the gravity, relevance, intimate address, disclosive power being pursued in the theater where middle brow dramas (one thinks instantly of *Equus and Amadeus*) are treated as solemn occasions or the operas of Robert Wilson, the theatricals of Elizabeth Swados, the music of Philip Glass, the films of the new German directors are construed as though they provide their public with a rush of the exuberant numen, despite the fact that such celebrated numinosity contains but a single (perhaps two) filaments that burn briefly, sputter, and go out. In all such events of culture where revelation is expected, the audience appears generally passive, riveted by the expectation of profundity, waiting happily, greedily to be either humiliated by big ideas or overwhelmed, to be told that art and beauty surpass their comprehension, that all they are is bourgeois consumers and that they—rather than the artists who purvey such compromised hype—are guilty of mediocrity. The truth, of course, as Adorno observed, is that the makers of culture (and not even here the oddly modern formulation "makers of culture" as though one could speak of single authors or artists who could be accounted the makers of the classical tradition or the Bible or the Renaissance) are collaborators with the bourgeois consumer. Both contribute to the rhythm from which cultural artifacts are configured. Not even the "pure"—if there are such—are unaware what fills the concert halls and theaters, what excites the boards of sponsoring foundations, what delights the skeptical custodians of the large emoluments that support cultural experiment. No, the makers cohabit cozily with the made and the artifact—dance, play, novel, painting, musical composition—is what is left over after the copulation of maker and audience is consummated with the willing voyeurism of press and television.

The odd proof of these generally unprovable assertions about what passes as high and inaccessible culture (each arguable, but also defensible) is the now generally accepted contention that in this century there can no longer exist the undiscovered maker of genius. Every artist, it is believed, has an audience, every composer a following, every writer a publisher. No one of talent, it is believed, can remain—as was commonplace in earlier centuries—undiscovered and unknown. No one need any longer go mad, sink into despair, disappear into the bush, to cope with failure. Ours, it is held, is the century of success where nothing of genius can be kept private; indeed, the very notion of privacy, of wishing to be unknown, of doing one's work sequestered, hidden away is regarded as proof of mediocrity and defect rather than of the considered choice to be hermetic, aloof, disengaged. The virtues of privacy and isolation, indeed the very excellence of the public failure that characterizes the achievements of artists such as Hölderlin, Kafka, and Schönberg is regarded as accidental and contingent, in no way constitutive of the achievement or a dimension of its essential nature.

III

All this, however, will get us nowhere. Such forays into the thickets of modern culture—its reality as mass culture or midculture or the culture industry—yield at best a display of commercial vulgarity in which traditional arrangements of values are reversed, success being treated as the marker of eminence; notoriety, publicity, fame becoming the proof and guarantee of importance; wealth, royalties, grants, awards the public recognition of excellence bestowed by generally unserious bureaucrats.

Indeed, Adorno (100–101) was once again correct in his persuasion that culture in the modern age does not occur by reason of a public embodiment of a private struggle of the imagination, but is managed, devised, pressed forward by administration.[7] In a phrase, culture does not emerge out of the combat and resolution of an imaginative tension with tradition, but is administered and wrought by committee.[8] This judgment is true, not alone of democratic societies, but of totalitarian societies as well. In Adorno's Marxist reading, free market capitalism and state capitalism both contain and control culture by administering its seed and growth funding, its distribution and dissemination, its rewards and, as well, its punishments.

And yet, what has just passed in my discussion—however its accuracy—yields nothing. These remarks qualify at best for another symposium, a special issue of *Salmagundi,* one more declamation where rhetoric prevails over thought. It cannot have authentic weight for the simple reason that it projects images of the debile estate of modern culture which in no way reveal the web of tradition that undergirds it. Such argumentation masquerades, displaying large cuts of familiarity and recognition, awareness of cultural procedures, a sense of on-the-scene fidelity and truth, and yet adds up to nothing more than the tricking out of subjectivity as though it were an absolute and objective viewpoint. It is a deceit; it is deceitful. And although I would still contend for the truth of what I spoke and the lamentation it sounded, I would still convict myself of a kind of intellectual sleight of hand, a verbal legerdemain which persuades by high language and elevated example rather than by thinking about the interactive nature of religion and culture.

The difficulties implicit in this kind of criticism of the cultural arts is not alone that it addresses only one dimension of the cultural complex, its aesthetic manifestation as an exemplum of administrative manipulation, leaving out of account the larger structure of culture that includes the works of the mind that are law, political and social theory, philosophy, and theology, but more importantly, that it borrows its religious focus from the assumption that the critic is a believer even though as believer, the mode of criticism is not religious, but psychological and sociological. Such evasive criticism does not assist in establishing a Jewish mode of criticism even if the critic is a believing Jew. It succumbs to the historicist fallacy of dramatizing a defect of cultural production and presentation as though such defect possessed a ontological status that was always and forever true. This is, of course, the difficulty posed by a phenomenological description of a cultural event—the critic is trapped by his subjectivity of understanding which, however percipient and shrewd, mistakes the truth of his understanding by forgetting the singularity and exclusiveness of his vantage point. Only when the critique of culture has its ground in a tradition that can yield axiological judgments that cut through the relativity of historical events is it possible for the critique to stand, to make claim to some form of absoluteness and objectivity, to be genuinely a critique whose principles claim and justify transcendence.

This predicament of judgment has been commonplace among Christian theologians of culture, but it has not been apparent among Jews. Jews, it would appear, have had no particular interest in culture, in the culture of the nations, in Christian culture, in cultures to which they had no access and of which they had little or no significant experience. It remains to be seen if all this is true of the modern situation.

IV

The notion that a theology should be timeless is a fundamental error. If anything, I think precisely the opposite should obtain. A theology must not be timeless, but time-full, cognizant and attentive to the events of history that have occurred during the life of its construction, reflecting if not terrestrial auspices then at least a sense that theology is a human production of understanding and must undertake to interpret events that have especial significance for the theological enterprise.[9] If every theological undertaking had not sought to take account of the time and culture out of which it came forth, if it did not address—even in the guise of timelessness—the dramas and alarums of the age out of which it spoke, there would hardly be need for the theological inquiry to be launched and relaunched as many times as it is throughout the ages.

There is certainly a classical Jewish theology—not one theology, but several, responding to earlier accounts of the most ancient experiences of the Jewish people, but then acquiring through the millenium from the Exodus to the start of the Common Era, a variety of elaborations and developments which find the Jewish people wandering, settling inhabiting a special land, developing a cultus and sacral system, backsliding into idolatry and recovering from idolatry, submitting its conduct to prophetic excoriation, being driven into exile and returning from exile, losing its temple and regaining it, only to lose it again finally, being suppressed and reviled by Hellenists and then by Romans, developing a legal tradition and a narrative fund of story and exegesis by which to refine and deepen its legal structure. And all this in the duration of a millenium and a bit from the going forth from Egypt to the codification of the Mishnah. But if all this is viewed as a completely commonplace historical evolution and development, it would hardly become the occasion for a theological treatment that produced at least two comprehensive literatures and numerous literary genres that compose the biblical canon and the Mishnaic redaction of the Jewish consensus regarding social, domestic, and liturgical law that established the groundwork of the great halakhic tradition.

The fact is that from the very earliest period of Jewish self-reflection, the Jews have been obliged to interweave their understanding of the God who summoned them from Egypt with a variety of historical occasions that compelled them to think and rethink their fundamental religious and social codex, to redefine themselves in the interest of continuing growth and development, to attend to new and emerging moral and social complexities that its biblical origins suspected but had never explicitly set forth.

Clearly, whatever God reveals, whenever God reveals, under whatever conditions God reveals, his medium is the event and the human experience of it. God is endlessly interpreting through the historical medium. The timelessness of God is a metaphor for a suite of theological assertions about God's nature which have little or no relevance to the issue of how God manifests himself. Whenever he is manifest, he addresses the human order with words or acts. These are the means of the divine incursion and the incursion scarcely creates history, but is the capstone or the zenith or the fulfilled language of an event already unfolding under auspices that appear initially to be causally finite, human, natural, and historical. It is then always the source of revelation and never its medium that confirms the level of discourse to be established. God is full of time when he addresses the people, but the fact that revelation is encased in the temporal does not mean that the ontological status of the source of revelation is infected by time.

Such formulations are metaphysical coefficients of dealing with the complex issue of Judaism and history. It has been contended most recently in Jewish thought that Judaism stands outside the domain of the historical. Franz Rosenzweig argued such a position as a consequence of his reading of the biblical narrative of the origins and unfolding of the people toward covenant with God and beyond into a life within the precincts of the *halakhah*. Devising his views only a few years after his return to Judaism, in the midst of the First World War, Rosenzweig was determined to rescue himself from a position which he initially regarded as a decisive in his repudiation of Judaism. He was first persuaded that it was Christianity which conducted the historical life and that Judaism seemed in his view shunted to one side, cut off from the mainstream of engagement, somehow eternalized, somehow moribund. If Christianity inherited the historical kingdom of ends and the processes of salvation by which humanity achieved them, what possible value remained to Judaism? This position was held unqualified in Rosenzweig's doctrine for several years and brought him to the border of conversion. It was only with the intuition of a different reading of the Jewish situation that his position altered, Christianity was reinterpreted, and his own return to Judaism confirmed. Indeed, trained as a historian under Friedrich Meinecke, Rosenzweig regarded history as the threshing floor of human enactment and *Erlebnis*. History was real; eschatology, however, was the domain of the nonhistorical and hence chimeric. The reversal in Rosenzweig's thinking emerged with his growing conviction that history was provisional, always incomplete and unfulfilled, even unfulfillable, never to be consummated nor transformed, whereas the eschaton as he understood its Jewish significance was not located at the end of history, but was always just outside history. Since eternal life and the redemption which eternal life signifies is not realized at the end of history but, as the blessing that follows the public reading of the Torah asserts, is "planted in our minds," history is denigrated, the fabrications and tossings of historical enterprise are rendered marginal, and the Jew into whose life eternity is already given need not worry about the historical at all.

It is no surprise then that Rosenzweig—having come to believe that history was irrelevant to the life of Jewish faith—should also pronounce against Judaism's care for creativity and culture. Judaism, as he wrote, "is alive only insofar as it is with God. Only when the world too will be with God, will Judaism be alive also in a worldly sense. That, however, will happen only beyond history."[10] Alexander Altmann is surely correct when he observes of this formulation that "the inevitable price Israel has to pay for being the people of the Kingdom is a loss of worldly creativity."[11] Clearly what is at stake in Rosenzweig's pledge of Judaism to the service of the Kingdom—a kingdom formed within the magic circle of continuous presentness before God and persuasion of God's unbroken presentness to the people—is a retirement from precisely the issues that define historical life in the twentieth century. Rosenzweig's persuasion was that the real life of Judaism is conducted within an eternal fire which the flowing waters of Christian history can neither reach, much less inundate and extinguish.

Rosenzweig's view of the ahistorical character of Judaism may stand as an altogether appropriate response to the German Idealist incorporation of biblical tropes of providence and the gathering Kingdom in the late Hegel and Schelling. Unlike them, however, Rosenzweig would have no part in a doctrine that believed that history drove forward toward divine self-realization. In Rosenzweig's view the imputation of process to the divine life was beside the point. God does not become. He is and moreover he is outside of history.

Such a view of history was possible until the holocaustal *tremendum* destroyed European Jewry.[12] It is hardly possible for a Jew to speak presently of a dialectic interaction of Christianity and Judaism as collateral instrumentalities of salvation. What Rosenzweig tried to salvage out of the remains of idealist optimism and historical ineluctability (his reading of the Johannine Age) has had the ground cut open beneath it. The destruction of European Jewry cannot be accounted a work of divine mobilization and hence a modality of the eternal will. The work of destruction was a work of culture, a culture emboldened by a formulaic mythologizing of the Jew and his assumed divisiveness. Notwithstanding its almost atemporal and unreal formulation of the Jewish danger to European culture, the *tremendum* must be accounted an accomplishment of the historical imagination. The *tremendum* of European Jewry was a natural-historical phenomenon, leaving aside of course a theology of the demonic which is not germane to this discussion. Indeed, it may be the case that it was a natural-historical suppuration of Christian and secular history, while Judaism remained inviolately beyond history, but it can be denied that the historical arm of anti-Semitism reached over the boundaries of the historical and plucked the Jew from his brave removal from history and returned him into its midst.

But having said this, is it possible to maintain in this day that Judaism and the Jews escape history and in the process of escaping history effect not merely a repudiation of the making of culture but a total indifference to its production and presentation? In one sense, surely, it can be maintained. The fundamentalist orthodox who stand utterly to the side of time, historical making, cultural pluralism, who regard the sole legitimate undertaking of Jewishness to be the study and observance of the *halakhah* (moreover a study and observance frozen by social norms and conventions defined several hundred years ago) can persevere in a vision of Judaism defined by theological canons that have absolutely no interest in the historical present or its immediate past. They care only for the gathering signs of the eschaton as interpreted by texts set down a thousand or more years before (indeed whether a text is biblical, rabbinic, geonic, medieval matters little to them, since what matters is the fidelity with which the text recalls and transmits the sacred tradition). There is clearly a living example of ahistorical life that thrives in the Jewish world. These orthodox fundamentalists, like fundamentalists everywhere, are dreadful theologians. They have virtually no interest in theology for precisely the reason that theology has always recognized, namely, that theology is thinking and fundamentalists are prevented by the power of their literalist fideism from inspecting the manifold contradictions they are emboldened to formulate as indisputable. For them it is no issue to be outside of history—to hold with a creation fashioned less than six thousand years ago, to teach the laws of sacrifice in anticipation of a miraculous restoration of the temple and its cult, to hold with a literal retribution that perforce inculpates the six million murdered as a mysterious portion of divine punishment. These mentalities, despite their lack of subtlety and grace, are nonetheless an authentic expression of an extremism that clarifies the actual territoriality of every religious community. As extremes they set the boundaries, but they clarify the center as well.

The fundamentalist's conduct of life as a discipline of ahistorical intellectualism became for Franz Rosenzweig a theological discovery that released him definitively from an idealist rendering of the progress of providence and reason. It could hardly have been understood by the conservative leaders of German Jewish Orthodoxy that what was their normalcy was Rosenzweig's theological *novum,* that their indifference to the workings of the Johannine spirit had become for Rosenzweig a successful maneuver for stripping Judaism of the requirements for cultural creativity and historical relevance.

In the aftermath of the *tremendum,* Jewish thought once again turned, repudiating the withdrawal from history and announcing, in Emil Fackenheim's formulation, a return of the Jew to history. The occasion for the Jew's descent into history was the destruction of European Jewry, but the occasion for his redemptive restoration was the formation of the Jewish State. How is this turn possible? Rosenzweig's position enjoys a kind of structural purity that accords well with the facts of European history. The Jews as believing Jews did not really participate in European history. They were present, witnesses through the apertures of the historical, poised to recognize and interpret, but hardly significant dramatic personages in the unfolding of European events. They were in Rosenzweig's view not simply ahistorical bystanders, but voluntary, conscious, self-determined nonparticipants. Although the natural Jew might well have wished to put on a uniform and fight the wars of liberation, attend the universities of the emancipation, produce poetry and plays in the foreign tongues of the street, they were—with few exceptions—shunted to the side of the arena. But this was not enough for Rosenzweig. Forced to the side of history, the Jew contemplates his destiny and pronounces it good. He elects to remain where he has always been—a contemplative creature, a reflective who breaks his days assaying his relations with the *halakhah* he is bidden to study and obey (obedience preceding study, although study filiates the law, determines its unfolding, formulates its instruction, and characterizes the facticity of its performance). Such a life in the center of the law and its intellectual documentation allows no sphere of justification to any undertaking not directly empowered by the law. Law is obedience, not fulfillment; attention and study, not completion. It is a continuous working toward and before God. There is no time that remains over from the feasting of study to attend to the arts and disciplines that constitute culture. What little has been left over by the concentrated working of the Jewish religious imagination has produced only ornamentation to study, lyric formations that concentrate the energies of the soul in poetry, song, decoration, but hardly primary works of creativity. While the Christians were building their cathedrals and carving their saints, the Jews were continuing to do what they had always done: make texts, not create texts, but make them by the painstaking elaboration of previous texts, incorporating tropes and formulations that existed before, attending to their nuance and correlation with the practices of the day, and pressing out new meanings, *variora,* refinements, as well as novelties and innovations that cohered with their precedent. The fact that the working of the Jewish textual imagination had little contact and interaction with the world of Christian culture did not however mean that the Jewish preoccupation was intentionally hermetic, obscure, and secretive. Part of the sense of discovery that held Rosenzweig in thrall was that he came upon the domain of Jewish study and textual making as a fully assimilated German intellectual who was obliged by the original form of his reversion to Judaism to go through Christianity on the way back. He discovered what he took to be the ahistorical charater of Judaism because he stepped into its charmed circle out of the thrashing life of Christian and secular ambition. He entered a world that had no time limits, no borders and boundaries marked by temporal goals and spatial obligations, no structure of alternatives, no temptation to do something else, no reward for autonomous genius, no picture of the temporal kingdom of celebrity (nor for that matter any guarantees regarding the eternal kingdom). The reward, the promise, the gift was in the ongoing process of winning a clearer sense and understanding of what it was that God required of the Jewish people that it might be liberated from the bondage of Egypt. Eternal promise confronted eternal paradigm.

Was the Rosenzweig reading of the Jewish condition effaced and nullified by the *tremendum?* Has the Jew been compelled back into history by the destruction that nearly obliterated him and by a redemptive reading of political events that yield that parlous national complexity, the State of Israel? It is a theologically dangerous position, more dangerous even than the view that leaves the Jews outside of history. If God wrought the *tremendum,* it is plausible that God would have a hand in the redemption. But if God is responsible for the *tremendum,* I would agree with those who urge that we be finished with such a God. And if God remains as uninstructed as his creatures in imagining that territory creates justice, then it seems hardly desirable that the divine politician be accredited.

V

The impasse is this: there can hardly be a Jewish response to culture if the Jewish imagination is constrained to work outside the domains of the historical where culture and its artifacts are formed. On the other hand, those who would insist that the best is to be ascribed to God and the worst ascribed to the deceits of mankind leave themselves open to a selective and ultimately subjective reading of the historical experience. In other words, I remain undecided whether the Jewish experience is historical or ahistorical, whether our ontological formation is shaped by history or whether we are not an epiphenomenon to be accounted for by

non-Jewish history, our personages, movements, settlements, wanderings, ideological affirmations and denials a portion of our natural disposition among the nations, but hardly participatory in the central drama of
our reality which is not to mature, to prosper, register and appraise progress in the familiar terms of historical growth and historical degeneration.
Are we eternal and hence unfrangible whatever the world does or are we
now for the first time since the destruction of ancient Israel returned to
the scene where world history unfolds?

I have thought for some time now about the curious formulation
that appears in the Mishnaic tractate *Pirkei Avot* (the Sayings of the
Fathers) 5:25 to describe the repleteness and plenitude of Torah. There,
in a formulation ascribed to the obscure Rabbi Ben Bag Bag, it is written:
"Turn it, turn it, for it contains everything." The usual reading of this
passage is that it offers a celebration of the comprehensiveness of Torah,
taken here to mean not only the decretals and narrations of the Hebrew
Bible, but as well the whole of its elaboration in the Mishnaic canon, and
the conversations of the rabbis that constitute the matrix of Oral Law.
But, for a moment, let us speculate the curious language, "turn it, turn
it." This inaugural clause is usually not interpreted, since the full weight
of the apothegm falls on its conclusion. Turning of the text comes to
signify the endlessness of the document, its incompassability, its fullness,
and plenitude. But I should like to wonder about the process of turning
the text. It is as though we could take the numerous folioed writings that
compose the rabbinic canon and hold them in our hand like a globe, like
a universe. And we turn this universe of learning and by the process of
turning aspire to come to the understanding that it contains everything.
But turning is clearly a metaphoric action. It is surely not turning as such,
but study alone that turns the pages of the tradition. And though we
begin to turn it as though it were a globe, alluding a cyclicity and recur-
rence that sheds light as it is turned, in fact we are asked to begin at the
beginning and by studiously turning the pages of its text come upon
everything that it is needful to know that we become sages and obedient
servants of God. But let us press the image a bit further. If at the same
time that the apothegm alludes the infinity of the text and adjures us to
a turning that catches all light, there is the implication that no single
aspect of the text contains everything (although there are kabbalistic observations that suggest that every single letter of Torah contains by implication all wisdom, but that only by patient following of the entire text
can simple mortals come upon the whole of it).

The skein of the Torah is its wording, its language that installs its
textuality and enforces the enterprise of study as the means of disclosure

and revelation. The linguistic surface that guards the complexity of meanings is not without the conditioning of historical experience. There is biblical Hebrew whose subtleties are myriad—suppressed syntax, sprung rhythms, future tense to be understood as past, negations that conceal affirmations; and later, Aramaic, a street language that acquired in the course of centuries a syntactic precision which could be interwoven with Hebrew expression to form a language that adduced the example of social and political conduct in classical Jewish society, supplying a technical vocabulary that enabled the rabbinic sages to elaborate refinements and interpretations of legal practice; Hebrew returns, broken open by the speculations of the medieval philosophers and legists, allowing further access to the dramas of the historical life of European society, the Arabic Kalam, and the philosophy of the ancient Greeks. The languages that preserve and disclose Torah bear the impress of historical events—presenting the Jews in controversy with their neighbors, interpreting economic and social habit, elaborating the ultimacy and uniqueness of their God.

The language that we are required to turn over and over in order that we may glimpse the plenitude of Torah is a language fashioned by the historical experience of the people. The historical language of the Jews was its culture, but curiously the historical language was the skein, the covering, the surface whose meanings were all concealed. Only by consecrating a life of study, hearing words of Torah constantly, by the road, at table, in lying down and every rising up, was that historical texture penetrable to its decisive core.

If then we may introduce a way through the maze of contrariety that holds us undecided between the historical centrality and the ahistorical marginality of the Jewish experience, I would formulate it this way. History is preeminently the husk that guards and protects the Jewish paradigm. The historical condition of language and textuality is the screen fashioned over centuries for both concealing as well as protecting the paradigmatic example of Jewish experience.

Exodus from Egypt is one pivotal paradigm; the wanderings and murmurings are modulations of the text; the coming to Sinai and the making of the Golden Calf; the binding of the covenant and its reassertion and public reconfirmation several times in the subsequent history of the people are elaborations of this principal paradigm of liberation and consecration. But there are other primal paradigms. God is one, unique, uncompassable at the same time that he is passionate, engaged, jealous, angry, loving. Another paradigm that underlies a whole range of biblical narrations, each of which has the purpose of clarifying that God may well be a God of the philosophers principally for philosophers, but the God of Abraham, Isaac, and Jacob for ordinary Jews. God delivers himself of words; he speaks through messengers and annointed servants; rarely does he speak directly without mediate vocalities; sometimes he kills because his power is uncontrollable, sometimes he raises up, elevates, and bestows new names in celebration. But always his principal manifestation beyond sheer presentness is through language that is declaratively gestural and physical and sometimes through gestures that are unspeakably raw and direct. The speaking God is a paradigmatic and primary Hebrew adventure. The covenant itself is paradigm precisely because the details of the contractual understanding between God and the people are not set forth but are implied and extrapolated by the employment of collateral texts found elsewhere. No less the Sabbath—the ordinary Sabbath—and the *Shabat Shabaton*—the Sabbath of Sabbaths which is the Day of Atonement—appear paradigmatically suffused with eschatological meanings that describe the interruption of daily time as well as manifesting the frozen time of death gathered into the eternity where redemption and resurrection take place. And, finally, the black paradigm of destruction and Exile occurs repetitiously throughout the Jewish experience, but is never documented and historically annotated without the introduction of tropes and analogues that transform its occurrence from historical episode into metahistorical instruction and judgment. Personages are paradigmatic (Abraham, Sarah, the Patriarchs, Moses, Aaron, the Prophets). Historical agents are employed paradigmatically to evade causal constructions of history (Pharoh, the Assyrian kings, the Hellenizers, and the Emperors of Rome). And lastly, biblical salvations and biblical resurrections ground the paradigms that enrich the Jewish eschatological imagination.

I have purposely avoided being systematic at this juncture. The ideas are too fresh, perhaps too unsorted and unrefined for systematic ears, but they remain transmissible and I hope intelligible. Nor do I imagine that I have really exhausted the range of possible paradigms or settled the connection between paradigmatic structure in the biblical text and its elaboration beyond into rabbinic and postrabbinic usage. Neither should it be thought that any paradigm will do, that any formulation that underlies the definition and clarification of a primary experience is paradigmatic. The paradigm is something remarkable and unfamiliar, even estranging, but not less critical for being the stuff that lies beneath language, at the core of experience, defining a center and radiating influence through the generations, supplying Jewish literatures with their interior logic and unanimity, providing those who break themselves upon its linguistic obduracy with the justification for their assiduousness.

The Jews wandered in the desert for forty years. We have little proof of the historicity of this event other than the assertion of the biblical narrative; however the biblical narrative is not history, although it employs certain devices of historical exposition—it seems to have a forward thrust (although it often repeats itself and doubles back); it converts the historical similitude into the occasion for moral urging and communal consecration; it tells us many things that we may presume are facts; and then it amazes us with wonders and signs that are most uncharacteristic of historical exposition. The wanderings in the desert lay the foundations for the paradigm of homelessness. Over the course of nearly three millenia the Jews have transformed this narrative of wandering in the desert into their very own, proper paradigm of exile and diaspora. Had not the Exodus itself been accompanied throughout the dispersion of the Jews with analogues and correlates that spelled out its enduring significance, the Exodus would have remained an unexceptionable historical event in the early history of the Jews. It would have been possible, as faith and religious community strained and waned to enforce the secularization of these discrete events, to interpret the Exodus as a remarkable but still typical episode of early history, marked by elisions in the narration, lacunae, incompletions, and inadequacies of historical telling. And so the Jews were led out of Egypt. And so the Romans were encouraged to depart Rome and colonize the provinces of the Empire. And so in wars of conquest and expansion, the Arabs spread across the narrows into Spain. Leadings forth and settlements, wanderings and conquests—these are not unusual events in the political history of peoples.

What remains unusual in the biblical narrative is that the Bible has no particular interest in instructing us in the atmospherics of biblical history. We acquire no sense of biblical time that accords with our own. We enter a biblical world that does not breathe the air of origins and causalities. The Bible indites events; its choice of language alludes but rarely completes; it knows in what it is interested and it very often excludes consideration of precisely what arouses the curiosity of the centuries of its readers. It employs the machinery of historical linguistics, but the machinery is devised and runs on different principles of energy and purposiveness than the normative rules of historical depiction and evidence. Clearly this is the case because the Bible is setting forth paradigms of all civilization even though it is riveted to the description of the steadfast behavior and backsliding of one people only. It is the intention that the Bible instruct Jews most particularly, but not insofar as they are unique or peculiar in their own right but only by virtue of God's preferment. None of the premises of the text are rational, much less reasonable. God acts precipitously and is infrequently outraged, one suspects with himself, for having been so unpremeditated and cavalier in his election of the Jews.

The paradigm is slowly formed and out of the paradigm, its grounds elaborated, its implication spelled out by commentary and continuous turning of the text, it acquires resonations and echoes that effect the transformation of what would have remained a remarkable historical leading forth out of one land toward the precarious conquest of another into a primary unity that contains all the essential modalities of divine promise and human dereliction. The Jews are the specific subject matter of God's action; this God whose name is no name is the specific divinity whom the Jews halfheartedly believe and disbelieve, follow and repudiate, trust and deceive. And so a piece of specific Jewish history in the course of its usage and elaboration acquires a paradigmatic employment and significance that has the effect of slowing down temporality, heightening mysteriousness and distantiation, stripping from the event its surface of historicity in order that its manifest content as paradigm might be disclosed.

What then does this mean to us? Are the Jews a historical people? Are they locked like all the nations within the causality of history or do they fall outside its structure and purview? The answer is neither the one nor the other, but something I have proposed as a means of sidestepping the extremities and effecting a kind of reconciliation. Of course the Jews are a historical people because Jews are not always or even consistently God-obsessed. Jews have natural, social, political lives that hardly raise the question of divinity. Although that natural life is governed by the jurisprudence of equity, torts, and legal arrangements that spell out Jewish privileges and Jewish obligations, the tasks defined by Talmudic law scarcely cover the manifold complexities of modern life. Today, with the exception of the quasi-theocratic State of Israel, Jews live in obedience to the sundry laws of the sundry nations. The natural life of the Jews is not significantly different from the natural life of other citizens. The change is rung only when the question is asked regarding what positions the Jew before God. When the Jew asks the question of purpose, ultimate hope, final meaning. When the language of finalities and *teloi* is explored, the natural Jew ceases to be of interest and the Jew situated among his paradigms emerges to the forefront. It is then that Jews return to worry the text, to probe it, to be bathed and suffused by the enterprise of considering it—even in its banality—to be more profound and true than any other literature. It is at such moments that the Jew confronts the paradigmatic core that is swathed—hidden and guarded—beneath its historical sheathing.

The paradigm has no history in ordinary time because it is quintessential history; history construed outside of time, endowed with timelessness and primary narrative power, conceived and set down in an atmosphere that throbs with time, that seems to be history, that tells of human actions and divine interventions, that proposes mythic extremities and yet remains curiously unhistorical, disinterested in the issues of cause and origin, dominated by only the personalities of the great God and his loyal servants and all-too-human loving and betraying people. In this rendition, the argument may be concluded: the Jews are not a historical people (Rosenzweig is right), but the paradigms of Jewish consciousness have a historical life—they alter, acquire clusters of new significance as later events confirm and modify their reach and application. The Jews, severed from history by the governance of paradigmatic life, enter history only insofar as the events that alter them from beyond the reach of their interior life are in turn reshaped and reshape the primary paradigms.

All Jewish history written from the perspective of the nonparadigmatic is perforce non-Jewish history, obedient to schemas of rationality and lucidity that derive their principle of interpretation from the already secularized vantage point of philosophic inquiry. Even a masterpiece such as Yosef Yerushalmi's little volume, *Zakhor,* derives its power from having established its point of access at the very borders of entrance into the paradigms. Yerushalmi scrutinizes memory and the ardor of memory by threading the memorial canon through the interpretation of the historical process. He provides us with a reading of the historical husk, but not of the paradigm itself. The power of Yerushalmi's inquiry is that it almost vindicates the victory of the Jewish imagination over modernity and modern culture, but is itself so tempted by the thirst of modernism that it risks making of modernity something it cannot become, a new paradigm.

In sum, the crucial question remains: can there be a history of the paradigms other than through further literary or liturgical creation? Can the history of the paradigm (which is itself nonhistorical) be written that does not at the same time explode the paradigm and, by exploding the paradigm, explode the Jew? The paradigms can never be flattened out and read like a linear text. They can be set forth and exhibited by art; they can be tracked by historical science; but they can never be rendered true or false by any formal epistemological investigation. They stand as ontological foci of the Jewish experience and are only interpretable and understood by the elaboration of new analogues and resonations.

VI

In conclusion, we return to the question with which we began: the absence of a Jewish critique of culture. There is no question but that many Jewish writers and literateurs undertake to employ what they construe as Jewish principles to interpret the culture of the modern world—to supply a theocentric judgment upon the heteronomous productions of the culture industry. Such critiques have a kind of marginal, journalistic utility that prove to be illuminating or flat as the writer is inventive or pedestrian. But finally whatever such critical assessments accomplish they are not in any profound sense or in any true sense Jewish critiques of culture. The existence of a Jewish critique of culture cannot be other than secondary, even beside the point, to primary Jewish reality. That this is not the case with Christianity must be acknowledged. The Christian is always under the judgment of Jesus Christ and it matters little what judgment is passed upon the world, there is enough ambiguity in the Gospels and the Patristics to allow for judgment to be rendered, for the *saeculum* to be assayed and adjudicated, for normative principles to be extrapolated from the theological reading of the Christ to enhance any conservative or any progressive, any loving or any hating, any victorious or any despairing cultural sign or event. Culture can be hidden in the folds of Christian civilization and vindicated and criticized, as Christopher Dawson proposes in *Religion and Culture,* or submitted to the absolute criteria of the church incorporating the person and kerygma of Jesus as Christ insofar as it defines the proper Christian function of art, music, and architecture in Paul Tillich's *Theology of Culture* or employs the Christ as his historical person and teaching are manifest in Christian tradition in H. Richard Niebuhr's *Christ and Culture.* But such utilizations as enable a rich speaking of the Christian Church about culture are denied to Judaism. Church and Christ bestride history at its center, interpreting what is pre-Christian and judging what is post-Christian. The Christian exegete can always pretend to objectivity, can always employ the closed system of the absolute viewpoint given him by revelation in Jesus Christ. The Christian can be or not be part of culture as he chooses, as he chooses and as culture allows.

None of these free options is open to the paradigmatic core of Jewish life. There may be a unified field theory of Jewish events that enables the natural Jew of affections, civil obedience, and historical adaptation to be at the same time the student of supernatural and paradigms that enlarge and contract so slowly as to appear to moult outside of time. The paradigms are the grasp the Jew maintains upon the *eschaton*. The fact that the ancient paradigms acquire through the centuries additional modalities and manifestations—the Exodus both producing as well as being enlarged by later displacements and wanderings; the prophetic judgment and destruction producing as well as being enlarged by later destructions; the first revelation, "I am God," becoming the source text for the whole literature of *halakhah* that has no truth or justification other than "I am God." These primary paradigms that roll through civilizational time, gathering later resonations and readings—unlike the judgments passed by Christian interpretation—cannot alter culture. They are even irrelevant to culture. But they are alongside culture as valences whose reality sometimes contradicts culture, sometimes vindicates culture, but are always intrinsically indifferent to it.

NOTES

1. The elliptical style of these opening remarks is genuine rather than rhetorical since it is the case that as I began to compose this essay I was not yet persuaded of the direction the exposition would take. There are—as the reader becomes aware—two false starts, the first methodological and the second compromised by subjectivity masquerading as absolute. Only after these false starts does it become possible to strike out in a correct direction.

2. I have a most specific group of Jewish and non-Jewish purveyors of such misinformation, but this observation would stand even if it were, as the logicians say, an empty category, "a class without members." There are enough members although each exemplar of my stricture would deny vulnerability to the charge.

3. The "original impetus" to which I refer was genuinely the first inspiration to this essay. I was persuaded that Judaism had actually failed modern culture. As attentive readers will realize, I have totally reversed that judgment.

4. The title of the address underwent at least three changes as the direction and goal to be reached shifted and at last settled.

5. This tale is not apocryphal as its truth is attested to by Professor David Tracy of the University of Chicago, who was present. I used a version of this story in my novel, *An Admirable Woman* (1983), which is construed by poor readers as somehow a fiction about Hannah Arendt. It would have been so much easier if there had been several exemplary women who emigrated to the United States during the Hitler years. Unfortunately there was only one Hannah Arendt. I have created in Erika Herz another. Now there are at least two.

6. Andrew Louth, *Discussing the Mystery: An Essay on the Nature of Theology* (Oxford: Clarendon Press, 1983), 45ff. Louth's book is a stunning work whose wisdom, moderation, and equable argument regarding the relevance of hermeneutics in Christian theology proved very instructive.

7. T. W. Adorno, "Culture and Administration," *Telos* 37 (1978): 93–111, esp. 100–101.

8. Cf. as well the illuminating discussion of Jay: (111–60).

9. This is not the same as asserting a renovated teaching of the kairos, since what is contended is that theology (which is a human discipline of understanding) informed by revelation should be filled with time, not that the moment of its disclosure is itself a kairos. The idea of time filled and kairos are different from each other, although not quite so different from each other. They are complementary and mutually regarding notions.

10. Franz Rosenzweig, *Briefe* (Berlin: Schocken Verlage, 1935), 311–12.

11. Alexander Altman, "Franz Rosenzweig on History," in *Between East and West: Essays Dedicated to the Memory of Bela Horowitz,* ed. A. Altman (London: East and West Library, 1935), 202.

12. I cannot delude myself that my introduction of the term *tremendum* to replace both holocaust and *shoah* has caught on, but I continue to use the term to allude to a refusal of finite and clear language. The *tremendum* signifies a monstrosity that refuses rational inquiry and discourages the near-hysterical overload that has become too frequent among Jewish (and some non-Jewish) interpreters. It is enough I think to employ a counterlanguage to Rudolf Otto's description of God as *mysterium—tremendum.* See, A. A. Cohen, *The Tremendum: A Theological Interpretation of the Holocaust* (New York: Crossroads, 1981).

THEOLOGY

Theology in Judaism is an intellectual discipline with a continuous history but a discontinuous tradition. Despite the unbroken production of works either partly or wholly concerned with the asking of theological questions, the issues they have raised have not always been considered central or even germane to the conduct of Jewish religious life.

The classical rabbinic literature is clearly marked by the consideration of theological questions—the nature, person, and manifestation of God; the relation between God and history, evil and freedom, redemption and eschatology—but answers to such questions were not regarded by the tradition as either decisive to the acceptance of God's dominion or useful in the clarification and interpretation of Jewish law and practice. We can reconstruct the assumptions and worldview of the rabbis and thereby devise for them a virtual theology, but we have little reason to believe that we accomplish more by such an exercise than the exposition of their theology as we construe it. The classical tradition either regarded theology as secondary to the elaboration of the halakhah—its assumption and presupposition, so to speak—or else distinguished its own mode of speculation so radically from the Greek and Hellenistic tradition of which it was aware as to have pass as theology what the Western (Christian) intellectual tradition, more cognizant of its Greek than of its Hebrew roots, might not consider theology at all. Rabbinic theology may well be a unique genre that depends upon a different canon of evidence, even an original logic, surely a different arrangement of speculative priorities than was common among the Greeks and their Christian legatees. It remains an ongoing predicament of historical interpretation whether to regard *aggadah* as the literary form par excellence of classical Jewish theology. Clearly, the *aggadah* is the authentic mode of Jewish theologizing, but whether it yields an internally coherent theology is debatable.

It may well be the case that the rabbis undertook to deal with theological questions in a manner so inapposite to the discourse made familiar by Christian inquiry that Jewish thinkers are obliged to construe the discipline of theology differently. Clearly the halakhah is grounded upon assumptions about the nature of the created universe so distinct from Christian parsings of the formulas of dogma that, ab initio, whatever may be termed theology in Judaism must be differentiated from its more familiar Christian manifestation. It may then follow that the Jewish understanding of theology is skewed by a prudent unwillingness to have its method confused with that of Christians, who have, over the centuries, preempted theology. Jews cannot, for that reason, assert—as is so often done with an almost cavalier unsophistication—that theology is not a proper mode of Jewish inquiry. Theology is, after all, a scrutiny of the language and an interpretation of the ultimate reality that is God.

Heuristic considerations aside, the rabbinic tradition surely concerned itself with the formulation of normative beliefs insofar as these reinforced the obligatory demands of halakhah. Insofar as belief in providence, reward and punishment, the coming of the Messiah, and resurrection of the dead constellate a rabbinic system of hope that confirms and solidifies normative practices and supplies an ultimate justification for obedience and performance of the *mizvot,* one may speak of a virtual rabbinic theology. Moreover, it is correct to regard the halakhah as itself the embodiment and expression of theological conviction. The formulation of Jewish beliefs independently of halakhah is in some respects appropriate to their formal nature, namely beliefs that entail no correlative acts (as in those of eschatology), while in other respects, as for instance in the ordinances governing prayer, theological conviction is collateral to and complementary with the performance of halakhic obligation.

At the very outset, what may be recognized as a consistent characteristic of Jewish religion (and presumably then of any Jewish theology that would elaborate it) is that the relation between the Jew and God is manifested in a complex and interconnected structure of acts, beliefs, gestures, and words. The rabbinic Jew scarcely questioned the provenience, presence, and providence of God; they were the presuppositions out of which classical Judaism lived. It is correct then to argue that for the rabbinic Jew—insofar as the rabbinic Jew conducts life within the settled delineations of Torah—the theological care for clarification and definition of first principles of belief hardly exists. The rabbinic Jew does and hears as the tradition affirms that God authorized acts and instructions. It matters less that such a Jew understand the God who lies behind the law; rather more important is that the logic and implication of the law be explicit and clear.

The discipline of theology emerges to the forefront only in the historical situation in which the bond of practice and obedience and the assumed persuasiveness of divine justification have to whatever degree eroded. The erosion—whether acknowledged or not—begins with the challenging assault mounted by the formulation of Christian belief during the patristic age. It matters not at all that few if any talmudic sages afford us evidence of their discomfiture in the face of Christian challenge. What is known is that many Jews of the Roman and Hellenistic Diaspora did succumb to Christian suasion, proof at least that the fortress of halakhic faith was not impervious. Christianity, unlike rabbinic Judaism, cannot, however, help but be theological, since its message is not contained within a structure of acts and instructions but is rather a series of assertions about a bizarre drama of salvation that require belief and the acquiescence of the intellect.

Theological reflection among rabbinic Jews is thus always posterior to acts; for Christians, however, it is always prior. All Christian sacramental acts incarnate prior beliefs, manifesting them as mysteries. All Jewish beliefs interpret and elaborate the mystery of acts themselves, determining finally that many, even those regarded as critical, derive their justification from no rationalization, no human logic, but merely because they are the will and ordinance of God.

The Christian assault upon Judaism during the apostolic and patristic era, accompanied by the diffusion of gnostic permutations of the substance of Greek philosophic inquiry, left its mark upon rabbinic Judaism principally in respect of the latter's increasing reluctance to engage in theological confrontation and debate. In the few theological encounters that did occur (recorded only by their Christian protagonists, as in the celebrated dialogue of Justin Martyr with the Jew Trypho), the Christian imputes to his Jewish interlocutor an interest in organizing his confession of faith in both logical and systematic order, always grounding assertion, however, upon scriptural warrant. Even more so in the case of those encounters between pagan and Jew recorded in the Midrash, the effort of theological crystallization and the offering of summations of Jewish belief and intention derive their power and authority from biblical texts.

The Bible has always been the foundation upon which any Jewish theology grounds itself. It is the first document of divine generosity toward mankind and, although not the last (since any enterprise of the human hearing of God may be counted an instance of ongoing grace), to the extent that human hearing wishes to stand within the continuum of such audition, it makes first appeal to the warrant of its most ancient revelation. Such a tradition of hearing beginning in ancient times was pursued, virtually unbroken, through the Middle Ages. It was one thing, for example, for Saadiah Gaon to undertake an interpretation of the foundations of knowledge and understanding, but quite another when such philosophic curiosity collided with explicit scriptural announcement. The philosophic undertaking can proceed independently of theological noesis only so long as piety does not require its contradictory contention to return to Scripture for correction. Where contradiction occurs, as in the discussion of the eternity of the world or its creation ex nihilo by divine will, or in matters relating to the abstract and negative character of man's knowledge of God's attributes when contrasted with the vivid anthropomorphism of many biblical texts, the task of philosophic theology is to develop a language of distinction that preserves scriptural integrity while at the same time proposing to reason a theory that accords well with the most exquisite and delicate of divine gifts—man's ability to think coherently.

Jewish theological language during the Middle Ages, although employed in the creation of many of that era's most intense pietistic and mystic works (in which terminology shifts from epistemological groping to ontological postulation), survived and remained influential principally in its nonmystical formulation. Whatever the reason for the suppression of the contrarational current of medieval Jewish thought, it appears that the major thinkers who continued to be read as sources of instruction to postmedieval Jewish thought (including our own) were preoccupied principally with establishing coherence and complementarity between substantive Jewish beliefs and the skilled employment of reason rather than with the transmission of a normative mythos of the divine-human transaction.

Clearly, whatever we shall first begin now to learn of theology from Gershom Scholem's interpretation of the mystic tradition in Judaism will require a double rinsing of our mythological tradition; first, to ensure that the relation of the biblical mythos and theology is clear, and, having accomplished that, to devise a language that enables the mythos to be made public, namely to radiate discourse, to enhance lucidity, to check its list to obscurity, and to insist that its findings be compassed—even if they cannot be absorbed—by both reason and Scripture. Since Jewish mysticism was not a doctrine of solitary contemplation but an esoteric excursus upon the fundamental problems of the universe and Jewish existence within it, such mysticism can never become more than a curiosity unless it can be rendered public, its internal logic and interior drama translated analogically, and its findings properly subsumed and ordered to prior and more conventional realities of Jewish thought. The temptation of the inexperienced to make Judaism esoteric before they have mastered its exoteric concreteness is one against which we need to guard.

The theological language that was strained through the meeting and response of Jewish thought to the early challenge of the Enlightenment (*Haskalah*) can be summarized thus: God remained the absolute and unsurpassable reality, whose creation had established the human community and inaugurated the historical antecedents that gather and swell into the Jewish people, congregated in Egypt and led forth to covenant and revelation; revelation supplied that people with a law that defined its civil independence as well as autonomous ritual crystallized in the temple cultus and subsequently destroyed by historical misfortune. In the dispersion to which the Jews came, the practice of the law and the ongoing deliberation of its implication became the normative praxis of Jewish existence. Theological speculation slumbered, the annotation of Jewish history remained episodic or was elevated into a transhistorical mythos, and a complementary mystic tradition emerged to supply a wholly original narrative metaphysics to Jewish existence.

For the enlightened among the Jews, emancipated and free access to European culture augured the imminent end of classical Judaism, the only task remaining being that of documenting its course in order to provide the archives with an accurate summary of its achievement before its demise; on the other hand, those without conscious interest in Jewish religion began the work of national rescue and regeneration based no less patently upon the assimilation of secular ideologies of social liberation to the tasks of Jewish revitalization. For the one, Jewish theology was merely the history of Jewish ideas whose sway and significance had ended; for the other, Jewish theology consisted of a body of notions about the universe that were either obscurantist and benighted or else available for transformation into the secular language of Zionist politics and social vision. Only two sectors of Jewish life continued to deal with the reality of God: the committed Orthodox of Eastern Europe, for whom the panoply of Enlightenment—Bible criticism, modern science, Jewish historiography—implied a radical assault upon the halakhah and its observance, and the new Jewish thinkers—Salomon Ludwig Steinheim, Naḥman Krochmal, Solomon Formstecher, Hermann Cohen, Leo Baeck, Martin Buber, Franz Rosenzweig, et al.—who attached themselves to one or another aspect of the theological problem and undertook its renovation.

In broad strokes, the issues of historical theology that carry us up to World War II can be set forth: Hermann Cohen argues the case for construing Judaism as the moral religion of reason that Kant had sought and had denied Judaism exemplified; Martin Buber imposes upon Judaism a metaphor of dialogue by which to describe the ontological grounding of revelation whose authoritative content he nonetheless rejects; Franz Rosenzweig extends the terrain of phenomenological ingathering to describe a Jewish metaphysics that successfully interprets classical texts in such a way as to harvest a conceptual framework of creation, revelation, and redemption that all but strips the Jew of historical reality. In the same era in which these major theologians are at work effectively severing the connection of the Jew to history by making of history either a temptation or a myth, the great Jewish historians—Simon Dubnow, Salo Baron, Yehezkel Kaufmann, Yizhak F. Baer, and others—are defining a Jewish historiography of event and causality in which theological ideas are exhumed but appear hardly decisive. The alienation of theology and history is virtually complete at the time of the advent of Hitler and the destruction of European Jewry.

It cannot be speculated what Cohen, Buber, and Rosenzweig might have thought had they survived the Hitler era and been agile enough to entertain its grotesque implications. Cohen was long since dead, Rosenzweig had died young, and Buber, vaguely undertaking to deal with the Holocaust, proposed a refurbishing of such millennial notions as the *deus absconditus* and "the divine eclipse." Among younger postwar theologians, the Holocaust is either represented as such a great mystery that nothing theological can be said that is relevant, or else it is treated as a historical *novum* from which we may derive moral imperatives and messianic hopes but hardly theological clarity.

It is contended, moreover, that there can be no Jewish theology in this most terrible of centuries unless it is prepared to ask: What do we know *now* about the creator God in whose universe such horror is permitted? It may well be the case that the appropriate reply of classical traditionalists is that nothing can be asked about God's nature, that he keeps the mystery to himself, that we are obliged only to persevere in serving him. To this the reply has been made: Why continue then to serve such a God? If the traditional God is he who cares and is merciful, so much for the value of his scriptural promises. If it is said that all who perished—stressing the children, as Emil Fackenheim has done—were sinners, so much for the divine understanding of sin. And if, as is also done by some religious Zionists who enjoy hearing the rustle of the messianic wind in the establishment of a Jewish state, the birth of Israel is to be credited to divine redemption, must not the Holocaust be ascribed as well to God—and, it might be added, is even that excellent, but beleaguered, state worth six million Jewish lives?

All of the foregoing perplexities are intended to illustrate the difficulty of standing with the classical agenda of Jewish theology: a God of absolute authority and perfect understanding, all-powerful and cognizant, creator, revealer, redeemer according to his own will and council, lawgiver and instructor to a nation of imperfect creatures, offering free will but reserving the privilege of intervention, using history to correct and instruct by both action and passivity. This theological description remained possible so long as the predicament of man remained one that philosophers and theologians could address in personal, existential terms, where loss of trust and erosion of faith were predominant, where Jews could still think of leaving Judaism for Christianity as an issue of personal decision, indeed where the task of theology was construed as the instruction of private conscience, the clarification of religious understanding, the turning of personal knowledge from egoistic preoccupation to the divine object of contemplation.

If, however, such a God no longer exists or, as is suggested, never did exist, the task of theology is not optional and secondary to Jewish tradition, but unavoidably primary. Without addressing He Who Spoke and Created the Universe as though he were new to us, as though everything that had been thought about him was now demonstrably implausible or morally inadequate, the Jewish religious enterprise (and no less that of all theist religions) must be abandoned. It is not enough for believers to believe, although there will always be those who continue to keep faith long after it has ceased to be true, and any faith, all faiths, may be sustained with uncritical tenacity; one suspects, however, that as faith becomes increasingly fanatic, as politics replace belief with an ideology that tests the truth of God only with successes won by power, it is hardly likely that such a faith will long survive (indeed, it may be questioned whether civilization will long survive).

It has always been the starting point of my own method of theological inquiry to acknowledge in faith that God has told us *that* he is (this is the starting point of theology in faith); God has disclosed his name in order that he may be addressed and worshiped, itself the starting point of prayer and blessing; God has revealed his Torah that may be served according to his will, itself the starting point of obedience; God has revealed the promise of futurity and redemption—that he will be with us when he chooses to be with us, this theophany asserting the mystery of his historical presence. He has left to us, however, always and most particularly, the ascertainment of his nature. We possess the who of God's person and the how of his intimacy, but we know little of his nature. To that question he turned his back to Moses at Sinai and symbolically refused to us any guarantee that the compliments paid his nature by traditional theology are justified. All that needs to be believed in order for us to allow our God to survive the Holocaust (along with a remnant of his people) is that his infinitesimal uncontrol be acknowledged to be as much a treasure of uncertainty to God as it is a kingdom of unknowing to man, that God can do almost everything, but not everything, that man's freedom is not simply a gift, but an indispensable surd of the divine nature, and that man's very existence reflects upon and corroborates God's limit. The primordial nature of God is inexhaustible, but the consequent, effectual nature of God—the God of acts—has dire consequences for historical life. Both natures must be explored again as if starting over.

Put as an assertion of faith from whom theology must begin its reflections, the classical conception of God was a working out of the entente between Scripture and philosophy. As long as the universe held that sustained both faith and reason, it was possible to abide with the definitions the classical tradition devised. The modern understanding of God was a working out of the entente between philosophy and history; as long as the universe held that permitted the dialectic of their enraveled dominions, it was possible to abide with the tension produced by their definitions. Both universes—the classical and the modern—are irretrievably gone, plundered by cruelty, still threatened by annihilation.

The God of Israel is worth the undertaking, and the time is now to build again upon the wreckage of previous understandings. The God who will endure—who has endured, who still seeks us—may well prove to be less imperious and authoritarian, but may gain in credibility and truth what he has lost in unconditional absoluteness.

RESURRECTION OF THE DEAD

Belief in the resurrection of the dead (*teḥiyyat ha-metim*) is an explicit dogma of classical Judaism, reaffirmed and elaborated by Moses Maimonides, treated by Ḥasdai Crescas as a "true belief" (rather than as a fundamental principle of Judaism), retracted to a more debatable level of deduction by Joseph Albo, and all but lost as a central teaching ever since the close of the medieval discourse. Nonetheless, despite its fall from the dogmatic eminence in which it, among other beliefs, was regarded as a sine qua non of rabbinic eschatological teaching, resurrection continues to be affirmed in the traditional liturgy. Introduced as the second blessing of the Eighteenth Benedictions (the *Shemoneh Esreh*) recited during the *Amidah* (lit., standing prayer), it asserts that God keeps faith with those who lie in the dust and will, according to his mercy, raise the dead, restore them bodily, and grant them eternal life.

Bodily resurrection, that is, resurrection of the flesh, the reunification of soul to corporeal individuality, became a cardinal doctrine of rabbinic Judaism, making its appearance in "proto-pharisaic theology" in the fourth century B.C.E.[1] Despite the aristocratic hostility of Ben Sira (Ecclus. 10:11; 17:27; 41:3), it was further refined by the Book of Daniel (Dan.

12:1–4) and collateral apocalyptic literature and ultimately consolidated as pharisaic doctrine. Even earlier than these apocalyptic formulations of resurrection as an assertive teaching of Jewish eschatology is the famous passage in Isaiah, shown by Yehezkel Kaufmann to be of eighth-century B.C.E. Isaianic authorship: "Oh, let Your dead revive! / Let corpses arise! / Awake and shout for jou / You who dwell in the dust!— / For Your dew is like the dew on fresh growth / You make the land of the shades come to life" (Isa. 26:19).[2]

Among the characteristic popular sentiments of those who live in the twentieth century is the oft-heard wish that life not be prolonged unduly, that beyond strength and lucidity there is no value to life. Coupled with this rejection of the ability of medical science to prolong length of days without comparably guaranteeing the quality of life lived is the collateral, albeit ironically expressed, hope that there be no life after death, no on-going immortal soul, and surely no reunified flesh and spirit as offered in the promise of resurrection. It is enough, one thinks, to have survived this century's warfare and genocide and the pressures of an increasingly inhumane society and to have come in fullness of years beyond even the "three score ten and if by reason of strength four score" (Ps. 90:10) augured by Scripture. What is it then to believe that even beyond these generous years God offers to the just the eternal life of reconstituted and ensouled flesh as the End of Days? How is one to take this promise, and to what end is it believed to be offered?

The underlying presupposition behind the doctrine of the resurrection is that eternal life in the presence of God is indeed an immense and unmerited generosity. Resurrection, as described by the tradition— whether in its popular and anthropomorphic mythology as an almost Oriental banquet or in its more austere promulgation as eternal study in the supernal yeshivah whose director, guide, and spiritual master is none other than God himself—is a meaningful gift not only to those who in this life have thirsted for God and whose thirst has not been satisfied. We no longer have a communal consensus that stakes the value and reward of life upon the certainty of the living God. Indeed, millions may be obedient to Torah, believers according to their lights, but nonetheless lack that obsessional attentiveness that made God-talk no less common-place in the markets of medieval Europe than discussion of the price of bread. Not everyone in the Middle Ages was devout or, for that matter, aware of the provocative disputes that arose in Spain, Provence, and France about the writings of Maimonides (notably his views on resurrection), but many were—despite their lack of scholarship—constantly aware of God's weight and pressure in their lives.

The resurrection of the dead strikes us in its formulation as a portion of Jewish eschatological teaching as unpersuasive in the invariable way in which an alogical, antirationalist assertion inevitably fails: Its poetry is too coarse. It cannot be demonstrated except in the respect that theology may ratify, and thereby assent to be self-evident, any doctrine that has the warrant of scriptural revelation. But even if one accepts the Maimonidean principle that one (or two) citations in Scripture are quite sufficient to confirm a teaching based on Scripture, it does not help; even assuming a fundamentalist theological method, Scripture denies a vitality beyond death with no less clarity than it affirms it. Indeed, Scripture is hardly the place to go when one wishes to form a consensus on the more vague issues of Jewish belief, especially those that relate to its eschatology. It offers too many views, and despite exegetic methods of distinction and analogical reasoning, the contradictions within Scripture are sufficiently bold and asseverative to militate against reconciliation. Moreover, even if one were to secure complete scriptural clarity, the miracle of resurrection would be obliged to ground itself upon yet another miracle, divine revelation. Whatever it might commend to faith, it could not commend to reason. Indeed, if immortality of the soul ceases to be a major doctrine in the Jewish philosophic agenda after Kant's demolition of the argument in its favor in Moses Mendelssohn's *Phaedon,* how much more so the resurrection of the dead, which relies less upon Greek philosophic modes than it does upon parallel notions of the afterlife common in ancient Egypt and Persia?

The observation that the poetry of doctrinal resurrection is coarse grained does not apply to the second blessing of the *Amidah,* which is, if anything, exquisite, drawing as it does upon the extraordinary metaphor of Isaiah, in which the light dew that vivifies the parched earth of summer is construed to be the dew that restores the dead to life. Rather, what appears to be coarse is the intellectual hedging that begins with Saadiah Gaon's almost mechanistic account of resurrection[3] and is succeeded later by Maimonides' novel but unenthusiastic tergiversations on resurrection, culminating in his *Treatise on Resurrection,* in which *tehiyyat ha-metim* becomes an adjunct of the terrestrial reign of the Messiah, followed by a second death and subsequent spiritual immortality in the World to Come (*Olam ha-Ba*). Few indeed among the philosophers rise to the enthusiasm of that nascent kabbalist the thirteenth-century poet-mystic Meshullam ben Solomon da Piera, also known as En Vidas de Gerona, who boldly asserts: "I believe in resurrection when the body and soul will arise and the bones will come to life again."[4] For the most part, the Jewish medieval philosophic tradition squirms to uphold resurrection, since it is rabbinic dogma. At the same time, contradicting as it does the whole care of Jewish philosophy that its doctrine be made pure, intellectually coherent, and nonmythological, the resurrection of the dead—whatever its values to the popular imagination as both carrot and stick with which to reward and punish—remains a doctrinal embarrassment.

What remains profoundly unclear is why thinkers as eminent as Maimonides among the Jews and Avicenna among the Muslims struggled so mightily to veil their theological disdain of bodily resurrection, apparently constrained to do so not only by an overriding consensus of the faithful, but also by those who guarded orthodoxy against heretical opinion.[5] What is there about the doctrine at once so appealing to general sentiment and so disquieting to reason?

Indeed, the more one thinks about the matter of the resurrection of the dead, the more one is obliged to wonder at its theological persistence and its mythological power. Why does it endure? Few indeed are those who continue to imagine the earth is flat, or that God created heavens and earth less than six thousand years ago, or that the sun stood still at Jericho. Despite even the willingness of the most profoundly committed believers to interpret the odd science of ancient Scripture, there is no concerted effort to expunge the explicitly literal formulations of Jewish liturgy with regard to resurrection. The blessing stands and is spoken thrice daily. it may be claimed that although it is spoken, it is nonetheless disbelieved, but this may be doubted. Any formula of faith spoken persistently and over millennia may be questioned, but the willingness of the faithful to speak it even with an attitude of skepticism indicates that it strikes a chord so deep and acoustically inaccessible that its resonance remains deeply personal and inarticulate. It is, therefore, to the teaching of resurrection as a profound structure of the religious consciousness that we now turn.

Our undertaking is not to supply a different doctrine to replace the eschatological drama of bodily resurrection, but—quite the contrary—to set the matter of resurrection into the situation of modern man and the modern world. To do this, we must recognize the agonized longing of man to evade death without integrating it into life, thereby avoiding the passion that illumines all the great modern partisans of resurrection in the flesh such as Søren Kierkegaard, Miguel de Unamuno, Franz Rosenzweig, and Lev Shestov. Viewing death as an unnatural, however commonplace and pervasive, conclusion to the ongoing striving of self to create, endure, and transform has caused the hope of resurrection to become an extension into eternity of the conviction that anything as miraculous as the existence of each single creation cannot be allowed to perish by an economic, unprofligate, and ceaselessly imaginative God. Otherwise put, God has better uses for life than to create it and then to condemn it to an unransomed death.

The principal difficulties that the idea of resurrection presents to a theological tradition of reasonableness is that it wrests from God a promise that distorts the accepted characterization of his nature and behavior. The pressure in the Jewish philosophic tradition is to make God's ways compassable to reason, his behavior orderly, and his care for the world persuasive to the good and the holy, rather than eccentric, irrational, or capricious. A capricious God harks to paganism; a reasonable God is one who makes his Torah the model of conduct, whose just and merciful nature commends morality for its own sake without need for the baited hook of resurrection. Of course, it could be argued that all of the promises of eschatology are baited hooks—the coming of the Messiah, the kingdom of God, the World to Come—no less than resurrection. Each element of the eschatological skein of hope is grounded upon a miraculous bringing to pass. And if these are miracles that can stand in faith, why not resurrection, which is not a promise of a communal restoration or a transformation of the order of human society, but a guarantee of God's mercy upon flesh and spirit? Resurrection in the flesh is a miracle that God works for the individual, and its consequence—given its emplacement within the messianic era or, for some, within the kingdom of God—is both a supernatural judgment upon the life completed and an assertion of God's immense and unpredictable love. What fails within nature and dies is restored in the kingdom, transformed, strained of the agitations of flesh, and purified by miraculous grace.

"On that day the Lord shall be One and His name One." This promise of the messianic reintegration, part of the *Aleinu* (lit., it is upon us) recited at the conclusion of prayer services, bears striking resemblance to the Christian assertion of apocatastasis, expressed in I Corinthians 15: 26–28, where Paul—the mystic who had never seen his redeemer in the flesh—asserts: "The last enemy that shall be destroyed is death. . . . And when all things shall be subdued unto him . . . that God may be all in all." The Christian analogue of resurrection is brought forth here not as proof of our own, but rather to suggest a currency of argument that extends beyond the theological into a domain where metaphysics alludes to the greatest of mysteries. The presumption of the *Aleinu* is that until the very end, the finale of the universe before its transformation under God, the consciousness of God is rent, his person still distinguishable from the seal of his name. However, in the very last, when God ends the created order and supplants it with a perfection it has not known, the finality of death, the end of terrestrial consciousness among creatures, is overcome by the same overcoming that ends division within God. God is reunited, his name rejoined to his person, his being now one and indivisible; for us, creatures in an imperfect universe where with all striving of consciousness to assert life, to press the claims of its eternity in the vivacity and intensity of life's enactment, death is now conquered and God bestows upon the dead a unity analogous to that which he has won for himself—a unity of illuminated consciousness and perfected flesh.

Resurrection remains a mystery, scandalous to reason, obnoxious to those with a deficient sense of the deep mythos of consciousness, embarrassing to thinkers who believe divinity reasonable and sufficient. For this thinker, the task of faith is so immense and unsatisfied, the pain of consciousness so extreme, the presence of death so constant that the conviction of resurrection—even if it must be kept a private belief shared only with God in prayer—is so overwhelmingly gratifying, so true to what one still loves about God (his unpredictable generosity no less than his unpredictable disengagement) that is it held by us as a doctrine in trust, neither pressed upon others nor denied by ourselves. Samuel Hugo Bergmann, the philosopher, captured this appeal of the doctrine in summarizing his beliefs on his eightieth birthday, in 1963: "I believe in the Holy One, Blessed be He, creator of the heavens and the universe. Secondly, we know from this that the world is not subject to blindness. . . . Thirdly, I do not accept the reality or actuality of death. Our lives are possessed of a significance entirely different from that which we usually ascribe to them. . . . I am saying here that people will live after death and will have to account for themselves. . . . Everything we do here on earth has an eternal, cosmic meaning."[6]

NOTES

1. Louis Finkelstein, *The Pharisees,* 3rd ed., 2 (1962), 747.

2. See Yehezkel Kaufmann, *Toledot ha-Emunah ha-Yisraelit,* 3 (1), 186ff.

3. Saadiah Gaon, *Book of Beliefs and Opinions,* Samuel Rosenblatt, tr. (7), 264–89.

4. Daniel Jeremy Silver, *Maimonidean Criticism and the Maimonidean Controversy, 1118–1240* (1965), 189.

5. Joshua Finkel, "Maimonides' Treatise on Resurrection: A Comparative Study," in Salo W. Baron, ed., *Essays on Maimonides* (1941), 119.

6. Eli Shai, "Samuel Hugo Bergmann: A Partial Portrait," in *Ariel* 57 (1984).

ESCHATOLOGY

Eschatology signifies the doctrine of the last and final events that will consummate the life of man and the cosmos and usher in the "day of the Lord." Such a definition, broad and general as it is, encompasses a considerable variety of classic Jewish belief and undergirds the language of the prayer book insofar as these convey teachings regarding the life that succeeds death, the coming of the Messiah, and the establishment of God's kingdom. Eschatology reflects a constellation of Jewish hopes and expectations for God's working the miracle of the end as he wrought the miracle of the beginning. Eschatological speech, as it appears in the traditional prayer book from the numerous formulations of the *Amidah* to the declaration of the *Aleinu* to the recitation of Maimonides' Thirteen Principles, reflects a coherent movement of Jewish conviction and elicits a credal reflex that, as often as it is obediently delivered, remains nonetheless obscure.

There is a thoroughgoing Jewish eschatology, but there is certainly no normative clarity as to the meaning or intention of its formulas. The promise of the gift of eternal life, the transformation of history, the bringing of the nations to the worship of the God of Israel, the emergence of the messianic personage, the apocalyptic end of time and nature, the promulgation of divine kingship and sovereignty, the ransoming of the dead and their restoration to physical and spiritual vitality—all these represent elements of eschatological teaching. However, as the formulae of eschatology become elaborate and replete with allusions to biblical sources, apocryphal and apocalyptic emphases, Gnostic byways, rabbinic elucidations and metaphors, and medieval speculation and modern reformulation, it becomes ever more explicit that despite the insistence of the tradition that there is a core of dogmatic affirmation that constitutes the Jew's dream of promise fulfilled and expectation gratified, the eschatological teaching is a muddle. There is profound disagreement with regard to the interpretation and reception of the belief in life beyond death. Some thinkers speak of two resurrections, some of spiritual resurrection alone without need for bodily vivification, and yet others formulate a naive and gross teaching of bodily transfiguration and paradisal gratification. No less is the disagreement over the doctrine of the Messiah, who is seen by some as entailing only a political ransoming of the Jews from subjection to the nations (with the malign consequence that often contemporary Jews believe that the establishment of the State of Israel coincides with the beginning of messianic restoration), while others continue to maintain that the Messiah is a person specially endowed by God and anointed to leadership of his people, and yet others hold that the Messiah is not a person at all but a mood of universal ethical regeneration. The apocalyptic end of time and history, the great mystical orgy of ruin and consummation, the triumphant emergence of the avenging God succeeded by the God of victorious compassion is—even more than the preceding notions—fraught with difficulties and stubborn unclarity.

What does it all mean? What need is there for an eschatological doctrine? Why is it indubitably a portion of the teaching of historical Judaism? And how may its tenets be submitted to judgment and refinement so that its essential intentions may be clarified and set straight? Rather than analyze the specific eschatological thought of Israel, this essay addresses the question: Why eschatology? Why teachings regarding the End of Days and fulfillment beyond our years and the implication of such a rich working of the theological imagination?

Eschatological teaching, grounded in the hope that God will ransom, redeem, and reward the faithful while bringing evil under final judgment at the End of Days, clearly implies ethical resolutions as these are entailed by the doctrines of providence and reward and punishment. Since it is taught that the Jew should not do the will of his creator out of crass desire for reward, there can be little conviction that doing the will of God and observing the Torah with a clean heart and an obedient spirit will be rewarded. Moreover, what reward could God give to obedience in this life, in the midst of living, when the task is not yet done nor the full course of life completed? God does not reward in the midst of life; indeed, it is surely questionable whether God rewards contingent service and its finite human performer at all. (The evil surely prosper and the holy and obedient are still brought low with suffering.) However much the simple believer may wish to espouse a belief in meticulous reward and punishment, the evidence of this world is hardly conclusive. Murderers too often die of old age and their victims remain dissolved in the lime pits of concealment. The belief in some kind of accurate distribution of rewards and punishments (moral accuracy on the part of God being a critical aspect of such distribution) is hardly possible. There is always disequilibrium and imbalance in God's administration of rewards and punishments, with the consequence that we take refuge once again in a noetic fog where God's intentions remain impenetrably hidden. Unfortunately, then, providential compensations and divine settlements do not help us much in understanding the source for the development of eschatological teaching.

At the core of most interpretive definitions of the ethics of eschatology is a sense of the universe as a mathematical composition in which the analogues of the human condition are devised out of systems of rectification and mathematical models of restored equilibrium and balance. God's equation is expected to work: divine promises are expected to be honored; however, if they cannot be honored under conditions where freedom and voluntary choice obtain, they are reserved by God until this life (and this world) have come to an end. In the age that succeeds our own, then, in the era beyond human life when freedom has ceased to be an ontological obstruction, God is able to exercise the power that during the days of man he was obliged to check. In other words, the displacement of divine compensation from the time of this world to the World to Come is a subtle revindication of a divine omnipotence necessarily challenged by the demanding reality of freedom and a reassertion that in the time of the *eschaton* (which is beyond time) God is once again alone and all-powerful. The content of eschatological teaching is formally a repostulation of a divine fiat that acknowledges no human opposition or human contrast; it reaffirms at the end what was present before the beginning of creation.

How do we know the promises of eschatology? By what combination of divine and human potencies are the teachings of eschatology woven together as a skein of hope laid over the disappointments of unrequited longing and unrewarded service? This is the hardest of difficulties. It would have been sufficient had there been a divine mechanism for acknowledging in the midst of life or even at its end that a person's work was remembered and loved by God—if only God had reserved a miracle of self-disclosure to each of those who had lived and prepared to die. But there is no machinery of approbation and appraisal. No man dies knowing for certain the worth of his days. Into the silence of God man puts forth a suite of hope that ratify and confirm the workings of a life, the faith that history will be clarified, that good works will be rewarded, that life will be restored, that the just will live into eternity in the presence of God.

And yet it must be asked if these hopes for salvation beyond the days of our life are truly what we project them to be. Without a sure continuity of consciousness between the living and the dead revived, there is no real resurrection. Without the certain knowledge that the self regenerated by divine love remembers and is identical with the self that has died, the reward to self is chimerical. Without a sure persuasion that the cruel and unmerciful are actually damned to a torment of absence from the living God, there is no punishment that has any theological vivacity or appropriateness. Even then the Messiah—he who comes to restore the Jewish people and establish the conditions for reforming the human stock in preparation for the kingship and reign of God—is thin hope except insofar as this hope lives upon the passion for an ultimate vindication of millennial suffering and depletion. The Messiah is believed in wholeheartedly, since without the promise of his advent how can we justify the unparalleled suffering of the Jewish people? The coming of the Messiah is proof then not of the victory of God (which takes place between time and eternity), but of the faithfulness of Israel, who has been given every reason to defect and did not.

To deal with questions such as these (and there is a vast structure of questions, each holding itself intact and erect by implying its dependence upon other elements of the structure), it becomes necessary to probe beneath the questions rather than to inquire about their objective coherence and consistency. Any eschatological doctrine can be made coherent and self-sufficient; however, without a curiosity about the nature of human trust and hope that is the nonrational presupposition out of which such doctrine emerges and from which it derives its self-conscious authenticity, it is hardly possible to make such doctrine both true and believable. Even eschatology must stand upon the foundations of the fundamental inquiry into the ground of the self and its placement before the presentness of God.

Theological argument in this century has pursued several lines. One line of argument has undertaken to ground the initial movement toward faith, that is, the first urging to go beyond the sufficiencies of the empirically self-grounding self toward a rock that lies outside the self, upon the acknowledged fact of man's terror of death and the inability of philosophy to remove the sting from dying. Other theological explorations have made the discovery that every interaction between human beings is ontologically defective unless the presence of an eternal Other or an eternal Thou is set down in its midst. Still another line of argument has undertaken a critique of the idealist tradition, arguing that reasonableness and the schemas of reason at best organize programs of abstraction that have little efficacy in ordering and containing the outbursts of unreason that periodically inundate human life. In each argument an epistemological insufficiency is made the occasion for an ontological corrective: A failure of human knowledge is overcome by a preliminary intuition of another order of being that addresses, compensates, and completes the epistemological defect.

The opening of awareness to an ontological source outside the self through which the self secures its ground becomes the starting point for the quest to God. God first appears to faith not as promiser or savior, but as source of life, the God who creates and sustains. As such God is set against the reality of man's dying, and however utter the reality of death, death does not lose its power to command into life, to shape life not by the putative evil of dying (for death is no evil), but by the simple fact that death is an ontological surd, a simple zero, a negativity that passes no judgment. Death stops life, nothing more. The various ascents of the self confirmed out of God toward the incorporation of the eternal Thou in human interaction or the turning of God toward a critique of human knowledge (or any of the other methodological staring points for faith) are interruptions that compel the attentive to stop and scrutinize, to think deeply, to put into question settled assumptions, to open ways of incertitude, to formulate a metaphysics of finitude, and so forth, all with the intention of opening the being of the self to being itself, and beyond even being itself to the holy ground of being who is called God.

Eschatology originates in the very beginnings of belief in God. Indeed, it is argued that the constellation of hopes that makes up eschatological teaching is given as the first gift of faith, given at the same instant that belief takes itself beyond the self-grounding of the self to a grounding that has its source beyond the self. The only risk of faith is the first. Everything afterward is a consequential unraveling of the self and the enravelment of God into the self, a dialectic that is mandated by the opening of the self to the ultimate Other and the authenticating movement of the Other from mysteriousness, hiddenness, and abscondite distance to presentness. Indeed, it is perhaps here in the personal intimacy of the divine-human encounter that the divine indifference to history (which leave it vulnerable to such uncontainable cruelty as we have experienced in this century) may be located.

God begins working at the beginning, and the response of man out of his equally mysterious—but imponderably finite—freedom is to go forth out of finite being toward being itself, toward encompassment, toward expansion of the minute kingdom of the self grounded now by the Other, toward visionary hopes for a universe grounded by the Other, toward fundamental reordering of empirical being, toward a redemption that turns and actively reorients creation. It is this procedure that is the drama of eschatological hope. It is no mere psychological projection, but an ontological dream that grows forth from the ground of man's first beginnings in belief. All eschatological teaching is directed toward an enhancement and confirmation that the finite being that gives itself to being and to God is justified, solaced, even rewarded, surely ransomed from history, indubitably redeemed into being, and given the sureties of divine presentness and eternity.

II.

MODERN JEWISH THINKERS

Introduction

Paul Mendes-Flohr

For Judaism to be spiritually and intellectually engaging, Cohen held, the presuppositions of classical Jewish belief must first be "theologically reconstructed." Cohen's conception of this endeavor was inspired largely by the German Jewish thinker Franz Rosenzweig (1886–1929), whose uncompromising affirmation of theistic faith—refracted through the categories of divine creation, revelation, and redemption—was supplemented by an equally unyielding adherence to rigorous philosophical reflection. Cohen was also drawn to Rosenzweig as a kindred soul who prefigured his own intellectual and spiritual biography. Like Cohen, Rosenzweig was a *ba'al teshuvah*, a repentant Jew who returned to his ancestral faith after having seriously considered conversion to Christianity. Halting before the baptismal font, Rosenzweig—like Cohen—sought to reappropriate Judaism theologically.

Rosenzweig would remain an overarching figure in Cohen's theological universe. But there were also other Jewish religious thinkers from whom he drew inspiration and guidance. Indeed, at the outset of his efforts to reclaim his spiritual inheritance, Cohen sought to establish a tradition of modern Jewish theology that would not only legitimate his own project, but also provide the conceptual grid to articulate the issues he would address. The first fruit of this effort was his volume of 1957, *Martin Buber,* followed in 1962 by the far more comprehensive study,

117

The Natural and the Supernatural Jew. This latter book not only explored the leading exemplars of modern Jewish relgious thought—from Moses Mendelssohn to Rosenzweig—but also set the most insistent theme of his theological writings, that the Jew has both a natural and a supernatural destiny.

Since the Enlightenment, Cohen avers, Jewish thought and imagination have with ever increasing measure focused on the "natural" Jew enmeshed in immediate social and political concerns. Cohen feared that this understandable attention to the interests of the natural Jew, abetted by the secular attitudes and biases of the modern period, has led to the neglect of the "supernatural" Jew, the Jew of the covenant, conscious of his or her transcendent responsibilities. Accordingly, the urgent task of contemporary Jewish religious thought, he believed, is to develop a strategy to reintegrate the natural and the supernatural Jew; otherwise the prospect looms that, while the Jew may survive, Judaism will perish.

Hence, in his writings on Judaism, Cohen notes that "my concern is less with Jewish history as such, with the works of the Jewish mind, with the identification of its peculiar cast and accent, its spirit and force, than with a specific phenomenon: the Jewish mind as it has thought and continues to think about its supernatural vocation." Yet, Cohen insisted, supernatural vocation cannot come at the expense of the natural Jew. Although the modern experience has been fraught with ambiguous, indeed, profoundly ambiguous, fortunes for Jewry, it has also served to teach the Jews that they cannot ignore the real world in which they live, that is, the actual historical world. The Jew, Cohen argued, therefore has an obligation to live in history and holiness—in time and eternity—as a single, indivisible task.

Cohen, hence, criticized Rosenzweig for detaching Jewish spirituality from history. Despite his admiration for the great German-Jewish thinker, Cohen could not accept his proposition that Jewry was essentially an ecclesiastical community, sequestered in prayer and study, blissfully indifferent to the quotidian rhythms and woes of the secular world. Cohen objected to Rosenzweig's premise that as a metahistorical community illuminating eschatological hopes beyond temporal ambitions and conceits, Judaism would be restored to its pristine vocation, and as such engage the mind and soul of the contemporary Jew beholden to the allure of modern culture.

> It is questionable whether Judaism can be restored—whether Judaism can be "smuggled into" general culture, as Rosenzweig thought, if general culture is really unnecessary and authentic Judaism is obliged to be indiffer-

ent to it. Rosenzweig's cure tends, it seems to us, to further debilitate the patient by sundering precisely those connections to the real world, man, and God which he had so painstakingly reconstituted. The metahistorical community . . . may perish for lack of involvement, dedication, and responsibility to the whole of culture. It is here that the strong, however innocent and disarming, moralism of Hermann Cohen and Leo Baeck would have been a valid tonic to Rosenzweig's image of the paradigmatic holy community.

As a corrective to Rosenzweig's purely supernatural Judasim, Cohen sought a metahistorical community involved with history and dedicated and responsible to the whole of culture—a supernatural Judaism that acknowledged its role in the natural, mundane world of history.

From this perspective, Cohen was drawn to Buber's search for "the Holy within the concrete," the pansacramental life of dialogue. He could not accept, however, Buber's antagonism to the traditional forms of Jewish piety and the rejection of prayer and *mitzvot* as irrelevant to true service to God. Nor could he accept Buber's Zionism, for *galut* (exile) would remain for Cohen an essential condition shaping the Jewish spiritual sensibility. Here, again, he expressed an affinity to Rosenzweig.

One may view Cohen in the development of his own theological position as moving dialectically between Buber and Rosenzweig, as well as between other religious thinkers that emerged in Europe, particularly in Germany, in the nineteenth and twentieth centuries. The essays in this section, which span nearly thirty years of Cohen's thought, chart the dialectical sweep of his writings on these thinkers, each of whom gave varying emphasis to the natural and the supernatural Jew, respectively. Cohen regarded these thinkers as having existed in an existential and ideational continuum—and thus in effect as constituting a modern tradition of Jewish religious thought. With the advent of American Judaism in this century, however, Cohen felt that "the continuity is broken. There is no chain of succession which binds the traditions of European Jewry to the traditions of American Judaism, no neat lines of transfer and influence. . . . Whether the Jewish genius for religion will display the tensility, urgency, and creativity to make Judaism something more than a boring legacy of conservation remains to be seen."

Until American Jewry comes spiritually of age, it will have to look to European masters of modern Jewish thought for guidance and inspiration. More than their respective conceptions of Judaism, these masters provide a model of the type of serious, engaged theological reconstruction that Cohen felt was urgently necessary for the renewal of Judaism.

In the past, traditional Jewry stood under the tutelage of the rabbinic sages, the *talmidei chachamim,* who embodied the preeminent values of the community. Today, the community, at least the vast majority of its members, who no longer can gain their orientation from those values, requires a new type of guide. Cohen urged us to look to the noble band of modern European Jewish thinkers—from Moses Mendelssohn to Franz Rosenzweig—as exemplars of the earnest, urbane, and intellectually exacting theological discourse that will allow posttraditional Jews to integrate themselves anew into the spiritual landscape of the tradition, and to continue—as one of Cohen's few true partners in theological discourse, Abraham Jehoshua Heschel, put it—Israel's "quest for God."

Revelation and Law:
Reflections on
Martin Buber's Views on Halakhah

I

The "relational event" in which man confronts the reality of God is indeed the center of any genuine religious experience. There can be no doubt that Martin Buber has discerned a fundamental structure which contemporary Jewish thought must reperceive and emphasize. The existential fact, by its very nature, however, indicates an order of truth not so easily grasped by intuition. The meaning of the "relational event" presses us into the assessment of the substance of revelation. It is therefore of critical moment to ascertain whether the meeting with God is structurally identical with revelation, in which case the revelation at Sinai is rendered indistinguishable from the experience of the *baal teshubah;* or whether the "relational event" is posterior in time, structure, and truth to revelation, in which case its value, however real, is rendered tenuous without the complementary acknowledgment that Sinai is enduringly normative.[1]

The struggle of Jewish theology is to establish the bases and purposes of halakhah as the way of God. It is impossible to consider with seriousness any religious answer which does not meet the reality of the law. If the "relational event" of God and man is one that exists beyond the pale

Reprinted from *JUDAISM* 1, no. 3 (July 1952): 250–56.

of a revealed teaching, its pertinence to Jewish religion is rendered questionable.

Unfortunately, Buber has not afforded us a *locus classicus* from which to derive his conception of revelation. His reflections on revelation are scattered throughout numberless essays. At the risk of failing to perceive some critical nuance, I shall attempt to summarize his treatment of the problem.

Revelation, Buber contends, may be understood in three possible ways. (1) To conceive of revelation as but the aesthetic consciousness, rapt in the mythopoeic fancies of past ages, surrenders God's speech in history to the relativizing passions of the modern age.[2] It is on such grounds that Buber rejects it. (2) To receive revelation as a supernatural event "severs the intelligible sequence of happenings we term natural by interposing something unintelligible."[3] Buber regards the consequence of such supernaturalism to be an inevitable dualism, which thrusts God out of the totality of life into an abstracted domain of religion.[4] (3) Revelation, rightly conceived, is to be recognized as the response of man to the given of his experience. The event, even the natural event, is experienced as revelation when it is capable of transforming the receiver. Revelation is accounted the gift of God when, through its hearing, the entrance of man into life is radically altered.[5] The Bible is to be understood, therefore, as the relational meeting of Israel and God, as the community of Israel addressing its eternal Thou. The task of Israel is seen as that of reconsecrating itself to the Thou, of constantly recalling itself from the abominations of the object-world into the service of its Thou.[6]

The heart of revelation, according to Buber, is located in the dialogue of Presence and apprehension. It is not possible to speak of an unalterable center, a fixed middle point, in the movement from creation to redemption. "The revelation at Sinai is not this mid-point itself, but the perceiving of it, and such perception is possible at any time."[7] It is thus impossible to authorize revelation. Revelation cannot be frozen into the life of tradition. It can be seen only as the repetitive consciousness of its believers, each drawing out of himself the capacity to see it anew, to hear it more deeply, to fix its command to him with clearer direction.[8]

Buber's conception of revelation certainly has its profound appeal, for it succeeds, where the arid literalism of much Jewish thought fails, in bringing Israel before the Bible itself. Yet this conception seems to me to raise many questions and difficulties, and it is to these that I would like to turn.

II

It is significant that Buber does not adequately explain the apparent fact that God, according to the Bible, is capable of treating the community of Israel as a manipulable object. The perfect Thou, to whom the I of each creature ultimately turns, is capable of chastising with seeming heartlessness, of brutalizing His people with tyrannical leaders and corrupt seers, of sending His people into endless captivity. Where, then, is the Thou of meeting and responsiveness manifest? I am not here dealing with the problem of evil, for a more pressing question is involved. God is Thou, not because Israel has met Him as Thou, not because Israel has, at a past moment of its history, addressed God with wholeness of intent, but rather because God has revealed Himself. Revelation is deeply autonomous. It is neither the labor nor the fruit of the divine-human relation. The issue of relation comes after and without necessary connection to the reality of revelation. The revelation cannot, as revelation, be diagrammed in relational terms. Being autonomous, having purposes that elude the apprehension of His creatures, God can work the seemingly monstrous. Moreover, if the experience of relation within time is used as the reference by which time is seen before eternity, there is great risk indeed of destroying the eternity of the divine Thou.

It would be foolish to deny that man speaks out of his situation to God and that God responds in terms adequate to the situation. God indicates to the patriarchs the specific task which they are bound to fulfill. He does not offer thereby a statement of historical purpose. The commands to the patriarchs are distinguished by a repetitive emphasis upon activities within and conditioned by space—movement, travel, the purchase of land, the building of sanctuaries. The single line of generalized statement is the assertion, frequently reaffirmed, that the patriarchs shall inaugurate a great people whose service will be to the eternal God. It is only with Sinai, however, that the history of persons and the purposes of God are commingled. It is through revelation, in which content can only at our peril be separated from form, that God manifests Himself at Sinai.

The patriarchs were met by God. It is somewhat difficult to believe that every meeting was desired. God can compel the attention of man, forcing him to hear with the outer ear. God not only hears the pleading voice and answers. He can speak; He can disclose, He can reveal, He can make himself heard. He does not, however, coerce acknowledgment and belief. The reality of revelation is here, too, prior to the relation of meeting. Revelation is the call to meeting, but it is not identical with the meeting itself, as Buber insists.

The notion of revelation which Buber unfolds[9] indicates the legitimacy of this criticism. The identification of revelation with meeting permits Buber to state that the essence of revelation is that "a man does not pass, from the moment of the supreme meeting, the same being as he entered it."[10] But surely it is not inconceivable that revelation may bring about no such transformation. Revelation is surely in some sense independent of the structure of apprehension. When the content of revelation is appropriated as *mine,* God is truly met.[11] If we deny the primary significance of content in revelation, it would be possible to affirm that whatever God did at Sinai is irrelevant to the fact that it was God who did it. What God in fact said, each "And He spoke," is surely of equally profound value as the single statement, "And God descended." The form of revelation, the Presence of God, may actually be of less pressing importance than the assessment and appropriation of His objective disclosures.

"Man receives, and he receives not a specific 'content' but a Presence, a Presence as power."[12] Buber continues this formulation with an indication of the threefold reality which the Presence of God confirms. The reality of relation, "the inexpressible confirmation of meaning,"[13] and finally the assurance that this meaning is one to be released into *this* life, are, Buber believes, contained within the meeting with God. It is noteworthy, however, that with the exception of the meeting itself, each of the other two aspects is possible only on the assumption that there is something verifiable in faith or experience about the content of God's revelation. Presence as power will yield neither meaning nor "worldliness," unless *what* God says is acknowledged as a primary reality. To derive meaning and relevance from the content-bare Presence of God is difficult, if not impossible. It remains a fact that the biblical description of God's incursion into time commences with words of specific content (Ex. 19:3–6). As meeting is contingent upon revelation, so meaning is dependent upon content.

The content of revelation indicates the manifest reality of Presence. It is God speaking commandments of history for history out of the fullness of eternity that constitutes the wealth of revelation.

The role of meeting is to be found in its personalizing function. Each man appropriates the content for himself. But even though no man may receive the word of God for himself, the House of Israel has received the covenant. The act of meeting is the act whereby each man accepts for himself the word of God; notwithstanding, the word has already been received. The person, as person, can reject the word or meet it; yet for all time, as son of Israel, he must know that the law has been accepted for him.

Revelation is the act of God whereby He has disclosed the way and destiny of Israel. Meeting is the act whereby that destiny, that way, and its divine source are drawn into the inner life. The former is possible and valid for God without the latter, though its fulfillment cannot come until the latter is consummated. Both must ultimately join for salvation to be realized. Revelation is preeminently the disclosure of divine intention. As such, it is rich with content. The task of man is to take it from God, with indescribable delicacy of hand, so as to avoid shattering its divinity.

III

Once the possibility is denied that revelation discloses content, once the reality of revelation is restricted to its formal, numinous dimension, the halakhah is inescapably voided. Buber is not averse to writing that "just as the meaning itself does not permit itself to be transmitted and made into knowledge generally current and admissible, so confirmation of it cannot be transmitted as a valid Ought; it is not prescribed, it is not specified on any tablet, to be raised above all men's heads."[14] His reasoning is thoroughly consistent. If revelation is addressed to the receptivity of the "single one," its meaning is beyond historical transmission, its confirmation eludes the prescription of commandments. The generalizing function of revelation is thus neutralized. The sealing of the covenant carried by revelation is rendered inconceivable. Buber's argument rests here, as previously, upon the identification of revelation with meeting. If revelation is but the meeting of God and the person, clearly no commandment requiring universal obedience can possibly be forthcoming. The individual carries to God his inadequacies and doubts, his perplexities and longings. He receives in return the assurance of divine concern, sympathy, and understanding. The Presence is indeed confirmed in the heart of the seeker, but the seeker is not impelled thereby to normative conduct. The tradition of commandments in the halakhah can therefore be interpreted only as the illicit deduction of imperatives from the deeply private encounter of the "relational event." The uniqueness of meeting, the varying structure of dialogue, the differences that separate seeking persons one from another, render any generalizing statement of conduct spurious, and perhaps, to use a harsher word, idolatrous. Halakah is thus the misconceived projection of attitudes characteristic of false relation,[15] a rupture of the meeting between God and Israel.

The commandments are not, however, rational imperatives; nor do they offer themselves in the disguise of the "valid Ought." They are, to the extent that we acknowledge the ineluctable spirit of divine truth and will in the halakhic portions of the Bible, full expressions of God. The commandment becomes an external "Ought" only when its inner freedom has been sapped by the life of habit.[16]

To disobey the commandments is not to betray the moral law. It is to desert God, to rebel against His authority. It is sin, but not therefore moral wrong. The moral law has been, in the history of the West, variously constructed on natural or rational grounds. It is a very different matter, however, when God proclaims the commandments, projects them without any suggestion of reasonable ground or social function, without allusion to any raison d'être. In such case, the holiness of God alone validates the law. The commandment is not a rational "Ought," because a man may conceivably reject the claim of the commandments, whereas no man conscious of his reasonableness can repudiate the fruits of his own reason. To reject the commandments is to reject the will of the eternal One, who notwithstanding our "likeness" to Him, is yet other than we. To reject the imperatives of reason is to reject what is wholly ours. Law can be conceived as the "Ought" only when, as with Buber, the relation of law and revelation has been severed. The law then becomes the product of obscurantist religiosity which the modern spirit can with justice renounce. It reflects an essential betrayal of man's meeting with God; it cannot be the consequence of man's struggle to appropriate the explicit content of revelation.

It is of course true that the Bible is the record of dialogue, but we are not given thereby the principles wherewith to disentangle the revealed word from the received interpretation. The miracle of revelation is the entrance of God into time; the truth of revelation is the word of God sealed into the language of time. The quest for the true law—that is, the quest for the true authority and divine will—is begun aright when one seeks to extricate revelation from the documents of encounter. This is not to deny the relation of the I and Thou, for such relation is of ultimate pertinence to the individual, being his dialogue of appropriation; nor is it to denigrate the Bible. The Bible is all from God; yet His word is channeled through the mouths of men. The word is one which, in virtue of generalizing beyond the individual, is a statement of eternal purpose; the meeting is disclosure of personality, both God's and man's. Revelation is God's effective commandment to history.

IV

The historical dimension through which revelation is properly seen uncovers a further problem of perhaps greater seriousness in Buber's thought—the problem of time. Buber has written that the relation of an I to its Thou is achieved in the present. This present is not, however, a point, a simple moment. It is the "real, filled present"[17] which exists only insofar as actual presentness, meeting, and relation exist. "The present arises only in virtue of the fact that the Thou becomes present."[18] Every moment wherein the Thou is spoken becomes a kairos, a center point, for the I, since relation to man and relation to God are contained within it. In contrast to the present of the Thou, the world of It, of things, is of the past. This is to be understood, however, in perspective. Obviously, an act of cognition, an experience, a feeling, a using—all in the world of It—occurs to a subject in some present moment. It is not past in fact, but in meaning. A world experienced as a mere multiplicity lacks a filled present, for the intrinsic richness, foreboding, and consummation realized in the I-Thou is lacking. Man accumulates the world of It; he stores it, labels it, and dispatches it into the darker realms of the remembered past.

Buber notes that the tragedy of existence lies in the fact that the meeting of I and Thou is fated to pass. The Thou will become an object again. The most poignant love, the most dedicated piety, suffers loss. What, then, is the relation between man's dealing with the It and his meeting with the Thou? Is there total discontinuity between the experience of objects and the meeting of subjects? Clearly, the Thou will be different for the having of a past. Every Thou is both particular and general. The Thou is not an abstract essence; it is full concreteness. The Thou is the individuated "image of God." This is otherwise suggested when Buber interprets the much disputed phrase in Exodus: *Ehyeh asher ehyeh*. This phrase is understood by many to mean, "I am that I am," in the sense that YHVH describes Himself as the Being One or even the Everlasting One. Buber criticizes such an exegesis, saying: "that would be an abstraction of a kind which does not usually come about in periods of increasing religious vitality; while in addition, the verb in the biblical language does not carry this particular shade of pure existence. It means: happening, coming into being, being there, being present, being thus and thus; but not being in an abstract sense."[19] The past, the intermediate faltering from the present fullness of the Thou, must contribute value to man's speaking again. The woman loved and lost, but loved again, is something new for having been lost. This is not adequately accounted for in Buber's analysis. There is the tendency to make the fulfilled present static.

The consequences of this difficulty for Buber's conception of law and revelation are far-reaching. In the effort to draw the Thou of God into

the heart of life, Buber exhibits a strange contrariness. Where once the
world and time were for God contemplated in love, drawn into eternity,
fixed before His gaze, judged before His immutable throne, they have
now become the point of fixity before which God moves. Where once
time was real before the mark of eternity, eternity has become an accessible dominion before the "filled present" of time. Time has been sealed
into the inner life of meeting. It may be suggested by contrast to this
view that God is not in time, nor time in God, but eternity is time drawn
into the equanimity of God.[20]

The immense struggle to release inwardness into the world, the effort
of Hasidism to redeem evil, is misconceived when the role of revelation
and law in Jewish tradition is misconceived. Inwardness without the law
of God, sanctification without the benediction, is the forsaking of eternity
for the vulnerable fortress of time. The crisis of halakhah is met in the
tension of time and eternity, of history and messianic redemption. Since
all man knows of God is what God has spoken and what man believes,
it is only too easy to draw God out of eternity into time, to make of God
the Thou before the struggling I, to abolish the objective word in the
attempt to appropriate it as one's own. Whatever the magnificence of
Buber's conception of I-Thou, the whole reality of relation between God
and man can be seen as meeting and encounter only if it has been forgotten that God is, whatever our formulations, mysterious, inaccessible, unpredictable. God can be counted on, but not accounted for. To annihilate
the law, the single instrument by which time and eternity, the profane
and the holy, the ordinary and the unique, are locked together is either
to lead man into the mystic way of self-evaporation or to render God
submissive to the demands of life relations. Time is not static before God.
It is not only from the present of our relations that we learn. To make
the I-Thou into the antithesis of the object world, into its suspension,
denies to the I the opportunity of making of its past a Thou, of redeeming
it of evil by having learned from it its mistakes.

The halakhah is the way by which Israel's path through creation is
signaled. It is the means of ultimate reference, through which the spirit
is turned to its source and guided into its task. It does not permit us to
overlook the fact that the separation of the holy and the profane, the
pure and the impure, the good and the evil, is essentially arbitrary. The
rest, that which falls out on the other side of all distinctions, is the area
of risk that no man is free wholly to exploit or wholly to ignore.[21] The
Hasidim knew of the other side, the side of risk, the side neither touched
by the arbitrariness of commandment and prohibition nor consumed by
victorious evil. This is the side into which the commandments lead us,

the commandments being neither the instrument whereby we flee from evil nor the amulet by which we are guarded from its poison. It is the area in which we are compelled to seek sanctification. The error is to imagine that without law the struggle can be waged. Without the seal of revelation, without the means whereby inner demand and living deed are compelled, each Jew would be cast into the desert of human groping unprovided with the power to withstand its blandishments of despair.

NOTES

1. Martin Buber, "The Man of Today and the Jewish Bible," *Israel and the World,* 93ff.

2. Buber, op. cit., 97.

3. Buber, ibid.

4. Buber, ibid.

5. Buber op. cit., 98f. "He who takes what is given him, and does not experience it as a gift, is not really receiving; and so the gift turns into theft. But when we do experience the giving, we find out that revelation exists. And we set foot on the path which will reveal our life and the life of the world as a sign of communication."

6. Buber, op. cit., 89; "What Are We to Do About the Ten Commandments," op. cit., 85–88.

7. Buber, "The Man of Today and the Jewish Bible," op. cit., 94.

8. See Buber, *Two Types of Faith,* 62–65, where his conception of heart and intention in relation to Torah is explained.

9. Buber, *I and Thou,* 109–12.

10. Buber, op. cit., 109.

11. Cf. Franz Rosenzweig, *Briefe,* Letters, 398, 413, 435.

12. Buber, op. cit., 110.

13. Buber, ibid.

14. Buber, op. cit., 111.

15. This real, however false, relation is designated by Buber as I-It; see Buber, op cit., 12–14, 35–39.

16. Buber, "The Education of Character," *Between Man and Man,* 113.

17. Buber, *I and Thou,* 12.

18. Buber, ibid.

19. Buber, *Moses,* 51f; *The Prophetic Faith,* 28–29; "Faith of Israel," *Israel and the World,* 22–23.

20. *Des Angelus Silesius,* ed. Wilhelm Bolsche, 177; "Im Grund ist alles Eins. Man red't von Zeit und Ort, von Nun und Ewigkeit. Was ist denn Zeit und Ort und Nun und Ewigkeit?"

21. *Hasidism,* 44–46.

The Jewish Intellectual in an Open Society

There are two traditions of the Jewish intellectual: one is ancient, the other modern; one enjoyed an illustrious patrimony and achievement and only in our day has come on ill-fortune; the other began in dialectical tension and counterpoint to classic Judaism and only in our day has defined itself in alienation from classic Judaism; the one was religious, indeed philosophic, in posture; the other is not only secular, but bemused by religion and, what is more surprising, indifferent, if not bored, by speculative philosophy. The "ghetto" of the religious despises the "ghetto" of the secular as theologically illiterate and un-Jewish; the conventicle of the secular regards that of the religious as parochial, conservative, and out of date. The fact that the religious are energized and, to a degree, unified by their dedicated hostility to and incomprehension of the secular Jewish intellectual is not recognized by them. The fact that secular Jewish intellectuals derive much of their self-definition as Jews and intellectuals from their spirited and deliciously painful disaffection from the community of traditional Jews is equally ignored. Without the palpable pressures of the other, both ghettoes would be obliged to function with different criteria of cohesion and membership; both would be

Reprinted from *Confrontations with Judaism—A Symposium,* edited by Phillip Longworth, 17–34. London: Anthony Blond, Ltd., 1967.

compelled to ask different questions of themselves; both, in effect, might be constrained to end their ghettodom. It is ironic that the gentile Christian world which was responsible for the original ghetto is no longer responsible for the perduration of the Jewish ghettoes of the present day. The Jews, however, *are*—both the traditional and the secular. They need each other, and the radiant warmth and reassurance of their own circle and their own malaise to guarantee their existence. They need to pinch (and occasionally mutilate) the flesh of their own to know that they are yet alive. It is a pity.

I

The Jewish intellectual is a modern phenomenon. Neither the Sage nor the Scholar needed to be intellectuals. And it is the Sage and the Scholar, not the intellectual, who is the beau ideal of Jewish tradition.

Max Scheler in his essay, *Vorbilder und Führer,*[1] distinguishes between the relationship of a subordinate to a leader and the relationship of the emulator to the model. The former relationship is explicit, formalized, conscious—the soldier knowing the responsibilities and obligations laid upon him by his commander, the employee recognizing the tasks and objectives defined for him by the executive. The relation of subordinate to leader is partitive, incomplete, a fragment out of the whole of life. It is not a total and absolute relation, engaging the whole man in subordination to a complete ideal. It is a public and real relationship, involving neither mission nor destiny, neither considerations of perfection nor salvation. But the relation of the emulator to the model is rather more mysterious: the model is unconditional and the service it demands is unconditional. The model is perfect, although the model may have ceased being a living reality, indeed, may never have existed. No matter, the model, by definition, is already incorporated into the world of myth, beyond time and the conditions of history. The *living* prophet is not yet a model (witness the extraordinary disbelief and petty politics which surrounded the careers of Isaiah or Jeremiah), but the prophet of tradition, already enlarged by faith and imagination, is transformed from actual man into paradigm. The model works upon the unconscious within man, eliciting from him responses of service, piety, and belief. The model creates, Scheler suggests, an a priori complex of demands to which the emulator responds, straining to define a compatibly ideal response. The model comes into existence in order to supply the historic man with an order of expectation and excellence. Of necessity, the model is conservative and transhistorical, invested as it is with qualities that bind it to values existing outside of time and place, outside of historical change and the requirements of expediency.

The model Jew is the *talmid chacham,* the disciple of the Wise. This is not to say that the *talmid chacham* should not seek to become in his own right a proper Sage, a maker of Law, a normative interpreter of the Sacred Tradition; or that he should not aspire to become a *zaddik,* "a wholly righteous man" who brings to such perfection the virtues of traditional knowledge and traditional piety, that he may—in and by his own person—effect the reconciliation of heaven and earth; or that he should not seek, as it has been suggested Maimonides sought in the closing years of his life, to become a prophet.

The Scholar and Sage, the Righteous Man, the Prophet—these are the models of Jewish tradition. They are paradigmatic persons, for they incapsulate all the perfections of a sacred tradition. They are normative, rather than rare and exceptional occurrences, for it is to them that the pious Jew should turn, when defining for himself the task of his own life. Moreover, they exist an have existed; they can be named and their lives narrated; they have influenced and continue to influence. But they are still models, for there are no rules or guides by which to be instructed in achieving what they achieved nor are there manuals and directions for their imitation. They are *not quite* human models and therefore not quite real: they are finally beyond time and history, caught up in mythology, legend, hagiography. It is known when such exemplary sages and saints, Rabbi Akiba and Rabbi Hillel, Maimonides and Jehuda Halevi, Rabbi Elijah Gaon of Vilna and Rabbi Israel Baal Shem Tov, lived and died, with whom they were conversant, and by what influences they were formed, but the whole of their lives is still clouded by mystery—and not simply mysteries which additional information might some day dispel, but mysteries that are essential to the awe and reverence with which they are regarded. They are paradigms to Jewish tradition, a priori models whom God, not man, created.[2]

The model of the Jewish Sage and Saint, the classic source and progenitor of the contemporary traditionalist, was first defined by the Hebrew Bible and rabbinic literature. The Bible is regarded by traditional Jews as a record of the meeting, encounter, and covenant of God and a People whom he chose out of all the peoples of the earth to bring near to him, to raise up from historical insignificance and educate, that it might—in attendance upon his instruction—become, in its own collective person, a paradigm to all the nations of the earth, in turn instructing them, setting for them an example, bringing them near to the single and unique God, the Lord of time and history. God is the sublime object of imitation for the Jew and in his imagination all the virtues to which he aspires are ascribed to God: God is seen by the rabbis as a studious and learned God, attending to the study of Scripture and its Commentaries, conducting in paradise a vast Talmudic Academy to which all those deserving and undeserving in the House of Israel are assembled in study and contemplation; as a pious and observant God, donning his phylacteries and saying his prayers, attending to feasts and festivals, remembering to say kaddish and pay his obsequies to the great among his favored dead; and a Lord of history, conspiring to raise up Israel from the dust, to renovate her conscience, to bring forth from her midst the Messiah, whose name he has known since immemorial times before even the world was created. If, then, such a God reveals his truth—showing forth in the person of his perfect imitators, his Sages, Saints, Heroes, Martyrs, the order of his perfection, displaying in the counsels of the Torah the laws and requirements of his realm, is it not clear that those who would wish to be faithful to his covenant with them should bend their years to the study of his work, to the understanding of his demands, to the fulfillment of his expectations?

The Jewish Sage is then the narrow gauge of the Jewish intellectual, the primary source out of which the Jew in the "Jewish" intellectual emerges. The intellectual in the Jewish "intellectual" has other origins and roots (of these we will speak shortly), but what is retained by the modern Jewish intellectual as the forgotten root of his *Sehnsucht* and unsureness is the classic root of the "Jewish" in his experience. The Jewish Sage was not hermetic, however. It is repeatedly emphasized in the rabbinic literature that the rabbis were fully aware of the alien and competing intellectual and religious traditions of the ancient world, familiar with pagan doctrines and teaching, concerned to refute and to bear witness against them.[3] The intellectual confrontation of Jew and pagan was a testimonial of truth against untruth. Although the rabbis of the Babylonian and Palestinian Talmuds used the device of parable and homily to counter the characteristics polytheisms and dualisms of the ancient world, they rarely, if ever (in this they are very much to be contrasted to the Greek-educated disciples of Jesus of Nazareth), attempted to employ the disciplines of Greek philosophy to demonstrate the truth of Torah.

The continuity of tradition from the Sages of the Talmud to the era of Jewish emancipation was relatively unbroken. There are of course innumerable subtleties which can be remarked, modulating the pristine independence and autonomy of Jewish intellection, but these represent inescapable accommodations to the pressure of life in the Diaspora rather than a fundamental revision of Jewish archetypes. Philo of Alexandria sought to exhibit Jewish truth in the vestments of neo-Platonism; Saadya Gaon, attempting to combat the insurgent heresy of the Karaites, employed Muslim rationalism to provide Judaism with a philosophic basis for demonstrating the claim of natural reason and thereby vindicating the Oral Law whose validity Karaism had contested; Bahya ibn Pakuda employed the insights of Sufi mysticism to lay out a system of duties imposed by God upon the interior and the public man; Yehudah Halevi, perhaps the most exquisitely arrogant figure of medieval Jewish thought, though radically contemptuous of all Christian and Muslim influence, was nevertheless fully conscious and responsive to challenges posed by Christian and Muslim philosophy; and of Maimonides, it cannot be doubted that the mode and discipline of his argument was shaped by his profound knowledge of the peripatetic tradition, culminating in the argumentation of al-Fārābi and the criticism of the Muslim Kalam which he defined.

The tradition of medieval Jewish philosophy from Isaac Israeli through the post-Maimonideans Hasdai Crescas and Joseph Albo was indubitably a tradition of the intellect. The intellect, however, was the faculty of apprehending truths which revelation had anticipated, but had stated in a form and with an authority distinct from, though not incompatible with, the parallel exercise of reason. Indeed, for many Jewish philosophers of the Middle Ages, the task of philosophy was coeval with the task of extending the range and applicability of Torah to the exigencies of daily life. Philosophy sophisticated the Jews' understanding of the groundwork of revelation, while the commentaries and codes systematized the regimen and discipline of obedience to the revealed commandments. Maimonides, the paragon of medieval Judaism, assumed both responsibilities of the Jewish Sage: he had attended to the task of philosophic understanding and apologia in his *Guide for the Perplexed* and had supplied to the generality of Jews a systematic compendium of Jewish law, the *Mishneh Torah*.

The emulator of the model, contributing as he did historically to the elaboration and sophistication of the model itself, was surely sage and saint, a man of intellect and piety. But he was not an intellectual as we employ this notion nowadays, for he did not regard the judgments of intelligence as autonomous and independent of the deposit of revelation and the discipline of Torah. The intellect, too, submitted to God. There can be no intellectual in the modern sense in biblical, rabbinic, or medieval Jewish tradition. There was none, although there was a fair company of extraordinary human beings, among the most spiritually gifted the world has seen.

II

The Jewish Sage could continue to define the model of excellence for Jewry only so long as the conditions of European culture were favorable—that is, favorably hostile and unyielding. The social institution of the ghetto, the *Juderia* and *aljama,* afforded the Jew an insulated environment, which, however, open to the ravages of Prince and Bishop, was still set off and protected from the irrational depredations of burgher and peasant. Jewish life in the ghetto, though no more halcyon than life of dependents anywhere during the Middle Ages, was still privileged. As *servi camarae,* in the usage first employed by Frederick II, the Jews were better off than Christian serfs—protected by the local Prince, granted rights and self-determination and local autonomy, succored and bid for. Medieval Jewish life was a preeminently religious life, a life girded by Torah, piety, worship, and study. In such a world the Sage and the Zaddik could continue to hold dominion.

The Jew was an accidental beneficiary and victim of the rise of nationalism and the diffusion of the spirit of enlightenment throughout Western Europe in the eighteenth century: *beneficiary* in that the irrepressible logic of revolutionary egalitarianism would not help but include, and therefore, however reluctantly, liberate the Jew,[4] and *victim* in that the price demanded for the Jew's free entry into European society was self-divestment of all those irrational legacies which rendered him separate, distinct, and autonomous within European society. Everything that the Jew had been in order to withstand Christendom and endure as a living rebuke to Christianity was now being asked by a less militant and unsacerdotal society as the price for admission to its world. The Jew was not unaware that what was being asked was that he cease to be a traditional Jew. What the Christian was not aware of was that he was not prepared, just yet, to complete his half of the bargain. The Christian was not ready to give up traditional Christianity, although he had already begun to transform it from an urgency for which he was prepared to go to war against his neighbor into a social utility whose viciousness and snobbism increased almost in direct proportion to the degree to which he had ceased to believe in it.

It is against this background that one can draw a provisory, but basic, distinction between the movement of enlightenment and the movement of emancipation. Though they are connected, indeed interdependent, movements, they arise from differing impulses and requirements.

Many Jews desired enlightenment who had no interest in emancipation—they sought enlightenment the better to serve the classic preoccupations of Israel (Moses Mendelssohn, Nachman Krochmal, and Samson Raphael Hirsch are among these—though vastly different from each other)—while others sought enlightenment that they might be liberated from the confinements of Judaism (Solomon Maimon, David Friedlander, and many members of the original German Society for the Culture and Science of the Jews). The forms of enlightenment were various and the movement for enlightenment pressed forward supported by many different and otherwise incompatible allies: by communal leaders such as Cerf Berr and his descendants; by ambivalent, satiric, and self-hating writers like Heinrich Heine and Ludwig Börne; by salon keepers like Henrietta Herz and Rachel von Varnhagen; by second-rate Kantian philosophers like Marcus Herz and Lazarus Ben-David; and by enthusiastic but ungifted Hebrew poets and journalists like the *Meassefim*.

The impetus to enlightenment was undoubtedly connected with the desire for civil emancipation, but few Jews considered civil emancipation to be as crucial as the social rehabilitation of the Jews. The Enlightenment, dependent as it was upon the intellectual resources of French and German philosophy and the increasing disengagement of European intellectuals from the doctrinal disputes of Protestant and Catholic Christianity, was turned toward making Judaism viable in an increasingly open, if not yet free, society.

The modern Jew who succeeded the age of Moses Mendelssohn (1729–1786) was a European according to nature and history and a Jew according to God. It was, however, patently impossible for one to be a Jew according to God without sustaining the vision of God's intimate connection with history. The God of Israel became, therefore, in the post-Mendelssohnian era a confessional God and Mendelssohn became, as the contemporary scholar Yehezkel Kaufmann has called him, the Jewish Luther, who sundered the living connection of faith and the people in order to return the people to the pristine condition which preceded its involvement in world history.

Mendelssohn wanted the Jews *out* of history. History was transconfessional and Jews and Christians were to become—what he believed them to be—sectarians bound to a moral law. But such a reform and reversal could not be achieved without devastating consequences. One consequence was that the interconnection of the faith of Israel and the people of Israel ended. Henceforward one's culture was that of one's nation and language and one's faith was directed toward an ahistorical God. It is no surprise that the earliest reformers, those directly inspired by the orthodox Mendelssohn—Israel Jacobson, Jacob Herz Berr, Abraham Geiger, and Samuel Holdheim—should have rejected the personal

Messiah, denied the sacrality of the Holy Land, abandoned the Hebrew language, and transformed the historical monotheism of the tradition into an ethical idealism, little different in concept (though less elegantly formulated) from Kant's *Critique of Practical Reason*. The messianism of the Jew disappeared and the new European messianism—culture, emancipation, and equality—was substituted.

The thought of Moses Mendelssohn was quickly forgotten and his descendants soon converted to the humane reasonableness of Christianity. But Mendelssohn, the exemplar of Jewish culture, survived and proved influential. Clearly the influence of Mendelssohn the thinker derived from the fact that his thought was unintentionally political. This is not to say that Mendelssohn was a politician. It is rather that the accent and emphasis of his thought—its sublime and admitted ignorance of Jewish history, its disastrous separation of law and teaching (those two inseparable senses of the concept of Torah), its uncompromising commitment to the superiority of natural reason over revelation—gave birth to a modern phenomenon, natural religion. And it was natural religion which served most particularly the political ambition of the Western, and subsequently the Eastern, European Jew for civil emancipation. The thought of Mendelssohn is undistinguished; but the political impact of a *Jewish* thinker who represented the cultural ideals of an already secular humanistic intellectual class was enormous. Mendelssohn made credible to Europe the existence of rational Judaism and the possibility of the de-Judaized Jew.

Traditional Judaism, by and large, never countered the thrust of Mendelssohn. Although for a century after his death, the polemic raged against Mendelssohn and his epigones, it was a hopeless and inept polemic. It had neither the argumentative power nor the versatility which earlier medieval apologists had employed in defense of classic Judaism. Samson Raphael Hirsch (1808–88), practically alone among Western European orthodox, waged war against the reformers but his tactic was fatally compromised by the fact that he sought to use the same intellectual source—the historicist rationalism of Hegel—to humble his opponents. It didn't work. The polarization begun by Mendelssohn was completed by the end of the nineteenth century. The Jewish community was radically split and the split was by then widened to include political commitments which supplied a vivid and demanding ideological opposition to religious conservatism. Secular Zionism and the varia of Marxism provided the Jew with instruments for dealing with the status quo of religious traditionalism and political conservatism: on the one hand, to get the miserable Jew out of Europe altogether, and on the other hand, to destroy the social and economic conditions of European life which impoverished both Jew and Gentile, forcing the one to humiliate himself before the threatening cudgel of the other.

The historical logic of the secular Jew was powerful. By the turn of the century the Western European Jew as politically emancipated and, if not (or ever) quite socially acceptable in Gentile society, he could at least put on the habiliments of middle-class mediocrity and present its suitable credentials. The poor were still about, Yiddish was still spoken, Zionism was still a cause, Socialism was still and ideology, revolution still a dream. The secular Messiah had yet to come. The religious Messiah, if he had come, had also gone, unheralded and unnoticed. Jews were out of the enforced ghetto. Henceforth, it appeared, if they were going to return to a new ghetto, it would be one of their own devising, one for which they opted, which they formed and populated to meet the requirements, no longer of Torah, but of *Yiddishkeit*.

The de-Judaized Jew had consummated the paradox of the emancipated Jew. Obviously the Jew wanted to collect the rewards of enlightenment and emancipation. Quite equally, enough Gentiles regretted that history had entered into such an unpleasant bargain with the Jew. Enthusiasm has its limits—egalitarian enthusiasm as much as any. But a de-Christianized Christendom could not make an effective case against a de-Judaized Jewry. The religious mythology of the Jew had therefore to be transformed into a racial and national mythology, religious anti-Semitism to give way to racial anti-Semitism, and from the Dreyfus Affair to Auschwitz there would be a straight line.

III

The nineteenth-century Jewish intellectuals who elaborated the "survivalist" ideologies of modern Judaism—*Wissenschaft des Judentums,* political and cultural Zionism, cultural autarchy, the Hebrew renaissance, the various forms of messianic Socialism—were, by and large, still working against the pressure and insistence of commanding traditional models. However, when one estimates the activity of Leopold Zunz and his circle, the extraordinary Moses Hess, or later, that of the poets Bialik and Tchernichovsky, the historian Simon Dubnow and the essayist Ahad Ha-Am, or the German neo-Kantian philosopher Hermann Cohen, one is obliged to recognize that for these thinkers (regardless of how little they prayed, how little they observed, or how obliquely they regarded theological questions) the center of their life was the Jewish People. The Jewish People was for them, as it had been for their ancestors, the primary bond of identity. The Jewish People was source and bearer, legator and legatee, conduit and destiny. For them the question was: of what? bearer, sustainer, conduit of what? For some, of pain and suffering to be assuaged—by courage and hard work, by redefinition and consecration to political and revolutionary goals or to the building of a new land. For others, of the most profound moral and ethical truths which, quarried from superstition and ritualism, would renew all mankind.

These Jewish intellectuals could not conceive of their function as intellectuals independently of their existence as Jews. This is not to say that they did not try, that for many bringing to union the power of their own conception with the unavoidable fact of their Jewishness was not a struggle unceasingly fought. It is not imagined that these were content and fulfilled intellectuals—that would be nonsense. What is being suggested is that for them the nexus of intellect and the people had successfully replaced the sundered bond of faith and people. The Jew could no longer regard the certitudes of faith as sufficient to accommodate the requirements of a larger culture for which political and social ideologies had already replaced theological allegiances. The Jews became proper Europeans, but insisted as well that Europe be fitted into the Jewish scheme of things: that Europe accommodate itself to the Jewish requirement to stay alive as Jews.

All this is now past. Such Jewish intellectuals, such intellectuals for whom being Jewish was as destiny as well as a fate, have by and large disappeared. They have disappeared and they have not been replaced. This is not to say that there are no longer Jewish intellectuals. What would the world be without them? No. There are *new* Jewish intellectuals and these are no longer simply *Jewish intellectuals*. They are *Anglo-Jewish* intellectuals and *American Jewish* intellectuals. This is not intended ironically. It is, of course, the case that Hermann Cohen was an astonishingly nationalistic German and that the Eastern European Jewish intellectuals often wrote as masterfully in Russian and Polish as they did in Yiddish and Hebrew. But for Hermann Cohen, son of a cantor from Coswig and Professor at the University of Marburg, the issue was finding the link which would inextricably unite Goethe and Kant with the Bible and the rabbis; while the autonomist Dubnow, for example, dreamed of building in Lithuania, Poland, or Russia a Jewish community which would be intimately conversant with the best thinking in non-Jewish intellectual and cultural life. For those late nineteenth-century Jewish intellectuals, there was a struggle against compartmentalization, a disinclination to build a dualism into their intellectual life, to separate out, for example, their equivalents to Blake, Donne, and Wordsworth as "real literature" and leave the medieval Spanish and Provençal Jewish poets, or the Kabbalah and Chasidic mystics to a restricted shelf, tolerated and smiled upon, but implicitly regarded as inferior.

There has surely been self-hate among Jews for centuries. Not everyone has regarded it as good fortune to be elected by God. Very few Jews have managed persuasively to regard it as good fortune since Hitler. But never before have so many intellectuals of Jewish origin, regarding themselves as Jews, writing as Jews, with bits and pieces of Jewish information sticking to them like flies to flypaper, been as abysmally and totally ignorant of the Jewish world, of what Jews have been historically, of what they have believed and thought, of how they have regarded themselves and their surroundings, as now. The new Jewish intellectuals seem able to get away with practically anything, to use the safe weaponry of public history—a macabre rhetoric at best—to terrorize the opposition into silence and cow the Establishment (both English and American) into imagining that it is a most powerful intellectual elite, capable of making and breaking reputations in the cultural and academic world with the same ease with which it is thought the homosexual confederation can destroy reputations in the arts. It is unnerving, particularly because it is both true and it works.[5] It is almost as though the slogan were "*épater les goyim.*"

Even here, in the assessment of the new Jewish intellectual, what was observed of those earlier postemancipation generations of secular Jewish intellectuals obtains. They are still working against the pressure of the classic sacral models. Still Sage, still Scholar, still Prophet; but Sage, Scholar, and Prophet become ideological postures. They are no longer archetypal models, serenely indifferent to the coming and passing of historical crises and events. The new Jewish Sage is totally immersed in history. He is the man who knows more about what goes on behind the Iron Curtain than the Russians do, more about Chinese Marxism, more about Fidel Castro and the Cuban Missile Crisis, more about everything—even though, by and large, he is not professionally occupied with the making or effectuation of government policy, indeed pretends to disdain such occupation. The new Jewish intellectual, the new Jewish sage and prophet, is the expert, the man who knows how the institutions of society work, what can be expected of men and what has to be dragged out of them. He is still a Jew, but like a latter-day sharpened version of the *maskil* in Yiddish fiction, he is more cynical, and somehow, to my view, less humane. It is the Jewish Sage as *Aparatchik.*

What I have briefly described above is about as far as the process of alienation can come. Jewish alienation is not, as some Jewish writers in England and America seem to suggest, an alienation from the history of the American or English people: distance from that stable, traditional, conservative Anglo-Saxon culture of which the Jew was not a creator, from which for centuries he had been excluded; or estrangement from that fluid, violent, madly moral and wildly dangerous America which is always a frontier culture somewhere, at some time. Surely it is alienation from that, but, finally, does it matter that Jews find it unconvincing to write novels about non-Jewish manners or a social ambience to which they have no entrance, in which they enjoy no mobility? The alienation that hurts is not alienation from Gentile history. It is rather that in the process of exploring the superficies of non-Jewish society Jews felt themselves obliged to lose contact with their own.

The Jew cannot become "authentic" to Anglo-American culture, not because the culture continues to decline him, but rather because he comes trained in atavisms and neurasthenic defenses which create a prepared arcanum into which to retreat at the first sign of being misunderstood or not understood at all. Alienation is a pathetic defense for being unprepared to be taken seriously. The jettisoning of Jewish baggage—the simple disinterest in matters Jewish—is a perfectly acceptable act if the act is *all,* if one expects nothing more in return for having performed it—neither sympathy and compassion over the miseries of historic prejudice nor the continued enjoyment of that almost totalitarian mystique of the unfathomable *Yiddisher kopf.* There is no reason why Jews shouldn't be neurotic, why they shouldn't be alienated if they want to be, why they shouldn't hope unreasonably for something in return for the fatal accident of Jewish birth, but equally they should be prepared not to have their way any longer. I would think Gentile philo-Semites would be getting tired of the unproductiveness of the conversation.

Having belabored the new Jewish intellectuals (whom I think I have made clear I find either boring or dangerously technocratic), the Jewish Establishment is equally a dead end. The Establishment, precisely because it is established both in Britain and the United States, is meticulously predictable. It is not simply that it is conservative and hence predictable; rather it is that it has so totally accepted and delights in its embourgeoisement that its intellectual enterprise and imagination—the rarity that it is exhibited (as in the famous appointment or lack of appointment of Rabbi Louis Jacobs)—becomes so embarrassingly artificial and parti pris as to be quickly regretted and withdrawn.

The present-day Jewish scholar, Talmudist, historian of the tradition too often regards his calling (those many that I know) as hopelessly inescapable—a true calling once, a mistaken, passed over, forgotten calling now. During the early part of this century when Jewish scholarship could be found all over Europe, when scores of archival collections were intact and hospitable to Jewish learning, when every major Jewish community in Europe had its rabbinical academy and its ration of distinguished rabbis and teachers, when, indeed, there was joy in the travel to learn and the delight of "holy conversation," the activity of "*Torah-lernen*" was still considered a revolutionary enterprise. It was understood by the Jewish scholars of that time that the credibility of their devotion to Torah depended upon a theology of creation, revelation, and redemption. Regrettably they, those older scholars, Zecharia Frankel, Soloman Schechter, Louis Ginzberg, among others, rarely discussed theology. They assumed it. They assumed that God had done all that Scripture affirmed of Him. Their questions, by and large, were what texts illustrated the Divine action? what did the texts mean? when were they set down? what traditions did they reflect? The historical-critical method of scriptural exegesis which overwhelmed Judaism in the nineteenth century continues to overwhelm Judaism to the present day.[6]

This is not to derogate the enterprise of scientific scholarship, the preparation of reliable editions of classic texts whose language and syntax had never before been properly examined and set forth. The work of Jewish scholarship is crucial, but the retreat of the scholar into the cocoon of scholarship, leaving the living Jew to the rhetoric of preachers and rabbis and the periodic psychic baths of professional fund-raisers, is self-defeating.

IV

There is no in media res, no third force between the Jewish scholar on the one hand and the new Jewish intellectual on the other. It is however a third force which is so desperately needed, not only that a parlous truce be established between them but rather that a communication be entered upon which will have the purpose of renewing the valid vocation of Torah for the scholar and enable the Jewish intellectual to make an educated decision respecting Judaism. The third force is the unaligned believer, the Jew who is neither with the party of the institution nor with the dernier cri of the intellectual. Perhaps what is needed is a recovery for the contemporary Jew of what Franz Rosenzweig had been for the German Jews of his generation.

Franz Rosenzweig (1886–1929) is appropriate to the issue of contemporary Judaism, for he was at one and the same time a heresiarch and a disciple of the Wise, a near convert to Christianity and in the closing years of his short life as student of the Talmud, a translator of the Hebrew poetry of Yehudah Halevi and cotranslator, with Martin Buber, of the Hebrew Bible into German, a founder of an adult education seminary in Frankfurt am Main, a Hegel scholar, and a theologian whose *Star of Redemption* is the major achievement of modern Jewish thinking. I regard Rosenzweig as a personal model, moreover as an appropriate model for contemporary Jewry. There were for him no settled issues, no final resolutions, no capitulations to an inherited orthodoxy. The question of Judaism was raised by Rosenzweig as a fresh problem, as an almost unheard-of, improbable claimant to human attention.

Rosenzweig plotted the argument carefully. The triumph of Christianity was no longer a certitude. Even Christianity was problematic, for it had never succeeded, despite its apparent domination of the West, in retrieving the world from paganism. And, to the extent that Christianity had won, it had won only at the price of paganizing itself. The church no longer missionized the actual pagan as had the Petrine Church; nor did it any longer baptize with the Pauline sufficiency of faith the interior pagan whom the Renaissance had produced. Both the Petrine and Pauline Churches had perished. What succeeded them both—in the time after Hegel—was the universality of the Church of the Holy Spirit, the Johannine Church. The modern church was no longer in submission to the Holy Roman Emperor or to the authority of the secular state. According to Rosenzweig modern nationalism is the "complete Christianizing of the concept of peoplehood."[7] The split which Luther enforced between the pure inwardness of faith and the external world, independent of the authority of the spirit, removed Christianity from the control of the world. Hegelian idealism made the Protestant error into an objective truth—spirit can really, it would appear, generate the world out of itself. The moment paganism comes to reassert the primacy of the individual, to initiate the Christian soul into freedom, the Pauline power of faith is dispersed by the free spirit of Johannine universality.

There is no question but that Rosenzweig constructed the history of his times. Despite the artificiality of his periodization and his often cavalier dispatch of traditions and ideas he despised, his was no casual historicism. Always he was concerned with laying out for himself the route of his passage back through philosophy, European history, Christianity, to Judaism. Rosenzweig was characteristically dissatisfied with partial turns of the soul, fitful and mixed allegiances. Each life decision was accompanied by a transformation of his vision of the universe, each stage of his life shaped the next and was carried forward, dialectically incorporated into the next, until it, too, was refashioned and transcended toward the final goal. As life had a destiny, so he believed the convictions which energized life had a destiny. The particular life was not a disinterested and uninvolved appendage of the universe, but its agent. Judaism was to be located in the universe against the background of philosophy and Christianity. If Hegel ended philosophy, if the Johannine Church was post-Hegelian Christianity, then Rosenzweig the Jew was no simple respondent to events, but a providential occasion for a new beginning.

Franz Rosenzweig is then an imitator of a model. What is proposed is that it is indeed possible and desirable, that between the extremes which imbalance contemporary Judaism a third option, in emulation of Rosenzweig's position, be described: radically alone and individual and yet wholly immersed in the urgencies of history; open and present before the claims of both Christianity and revolutionary Marxism and yet temporizing both claimants by making the antipolitical impotence of historical Judaism into a positive instrument of politics and reconciliation; compelling Judaism to make itself a witness to the non-Jewish world, to the un-Jewish world, to the world that doesn't even know that Judaism exists. It is, in effect, to charge Judaism with the burden of an almost Erasmian revolution, a humanist counterpoint to both Christianity and Marxism, which avoids both traditional obscurantism and the tedious litanies of Jewish self-hatred, which exposes not simply what is best in Judaism (as a one-among-many good and suitable doctrines), but what is unqualifiedly best, precisely because its concern is to afford the world a vision totally disconnected from the instrumentalities of power, sacerdotal or secular. At least, this is the direction of my own humanism, no less messianic for being humane, no less conservative for being apocalyptic, and no less original for being tied in all things to the archetypal Jewish Sage, Saint, and Prophet.

NOTES

1. Max Scheler, "Vorbilder und Führer," *Schirften aus dem Nachlass* (Berlin, 1933); *Le Saint, Le Génie, Le Héros,* translation by Émile Marmy (Fribourg, Egloff, 1944), 33f.

2. It is possible to shade the differentiations between the model, the paradigmatic person, and the archetype, but for our purposes, given the overlapping these concepts enjoy, I have not feathered their distinction. Clearly, however, all these are to be distinguished from Max Weber's idea of "charisma." The charismatic leader is natural, deriving his authority from within and imposing it upon a community his person has formed and disciplined. Weber understood "charisma" from the perspective of an already secular sociology of knowledge. His analysis, for example, would require that Saul felt himself deserted by Samuel (and hence lost his charisma) and that Jesus on the Cross felt himself foregone by God (and hence lost his charisma), whereas for our analysis the action of God (the a priori necessities of the model) was decisive, and the responses of Saul and Jesus secondary. Cf. Max Weber, "The Sociology of Charismatic Authority," from Max Weber, *Essays in Sociology,* translated and edited by H. H. Gerth and C. Wright Mills (New York: Oxford University Press, 1946), 245–52.

3. Indeed, the Sages of the Talmud strike me as exhibiting more liberality of intellect and generosity toward their enemies than do their successors in this most liberal age, when the destruction of character and reputation seems a commonplace of intellectual polemic.

4. Witness the fascinating argument of Christian Wilhelm von Dohm's decisive pamphlet, *Über die burger Verbesserung der Juden,* published in 1781, long before any formal move had been made toward political emancipation of the Jew and the even earlier (and logically impeccable) conclusion of John Locke's *Letter Concerning Toleration* (1689), both of which argue for the civil emancipation of the Jew as part of the humane toleration to be expected of an increasingly open, nonecclesiastical society. Cf. Jacob Katz, "The Term 'Jewish Emancipation,'" *Studies in Nineteenth Century Jewish Intellectual History,* edited by Alexander Altmann (Cambridge: Harvard University Press, 1964), 1–25; Arthur A. Cohen, *The Natural and the Supernatural Jew: An Historical and Theological Introduction* (New York: Pantheon Books, 1962), 17–19.

5. "It is true and it works." The evidence for this assertion is not had to come by. However, it would require a careful and judicious examination of the role the Jews play in the communications industry in the United States and Great Britain. I have neither the energy nor the competence to undertake such a study. To do so cavalierly might well yield an unintended (and certainly unwanted) support to the conventional claim of the anti-Semite, for to the anti-Semite the Jew has always controlled whatever he did not. Obviously there is no reason why Jews should not be powerful in any industry in which they function. The question here is whether or not the power they enjoy has resulted in the creation of an "in-ghetto," a ghetto in which, for the first time, the Gentile wishes to be invited, little knowing that what he will find there are all of his own artifacts, carefully laid out, organized, sifted, and understood "better than he ever did." It is my observation that such a ghetto, in fact, exists and only the "right Gentiles" are invited to enter.

6. The Jewish Theological Seminary of America, the institution responsible for the training of rabbis for the Conservative wing of American Judaism and itself the center for the historical-critical study of Jewish sources, has yet to teach the Pentateuch to rabbinic candidates with scholarly apparatus. It is simply not taught at all. The Prophets and Writings, yes, for these represent—presumably—some order of "secondary" revelation. Actually it may be surmised that this is the way the Seminary compromises to placate the Orthodox. Not very much unlike the theological pusillanimity of the Chief Rabbinate of the United Kingdom.

7. "Die Vollendete Christianisierung des Volksbegriffs." Franz Rosenzweig, *Briefe,* edited by E. Simon and Edith Rosenzweig (Berlin: Schocken Verlag, 1935), 686. See also Alexander Altmann's essay, "Franz Rosenzweig on History," *Between East and West,* edited by Alexander Altmann (London: Leo Baeck Institute, East and West Library, 1958), 194–212. Cf. as primary references on Franz Rosenzweig: Nahum N. Glatzer, *Franz Rosenzweig: His Life and Thought* (New York: Schocken Books, Inc., and Farrar, Straus & Young, Inc., 1953); Steven S. Schwarzchild, *Franz Rosenzweig* (London: The Education Committee of the Hillel Foundation, no date); Arthur A. Cohen, *The Natural and the Supernatural Jew,* op. cit., 120–48.

Franz Rosenzweig's The Star of Redemption: An Inquiry into Its Psychological Origins

I

How to speak of *The Star of Redemption?** What is it? Most evidently it is a book in the precise sense in which Franz Rosenzweig himself thought of books: a prologue to life. The most renowned philosophers and theologians of course wrote books, only books, and of them we say, not without disparagement, that they mastered theory, but too often exhibited little or no capacity for life.

It is no less the case that Franz Rosenzweig was contradictory in his estimation of *The Star of Redemption*. To some he wrote that it was a Jewish book, that it had to be published by a Jewish publisher, that ideally its only true existence would be in the Hebrew language; to others he described it as a general book, a work of demolition and reconstruction, a proto-Jewish book at most, a prolegomenon to Jewish books, and therefore like all books, half-live, half-dead as the thinker who *only* writes books is half-live, half-dead. No wonder then that *The Star of Redemption* concludes with the phrase: Into Life, signifying that thought was complete and now life could begin.

It is not the case that the thinker is half-dead, half-alive, that the work of thought is preliminary to life, that a book is only a means of

Midstream 18, no. 2 (February 1972): 13–33.

tying off the damaged arteries of existence, in order to permit by focus and concentration the healthy blood of perception to course out with vitality. A book of speculation is a creation and as creation it is mediate to existence, already experienced with less than satisfactory structure and control, an existence anticipated which will enjoy the benefit of the clarity wrested from internal argument. A work of thought is a creation. It is unusual to think of works of philosophy, much less works of theology, as works of art, but it is as a work of art—with qualifications which I will elaborate—that I wish to regard *The Star of Redemption*.

The thinker is first of all a living man. This is certainly the case with Franz Rosenzweig. It may not have been the case with other thinkers. In fact one suspects that it is not the case with other thinkers. There are certainly thinkers who think as an excuse for life, and those thinkers are at pains to prove everything, to demonstrate that their theorems and postulations account for all their experience, that nothing significant is excluded and whatever is excluded is either vulgar, base, or irrational. They, too, construct their metaphysics to accommodate their old experience of the world, their primal pleasures or dissatisfactions, their prerational encounters with the terrors and joys of existence. They may hide their past from us, but they cannot hide from us the fact that they had one, and however much it may be irrelevant to the confirmation or disproof of their theory to conjecture the dramatic turning points in life, which set them in the direction of their formed views of reality, we can be certain that they had such turning point.

When, in July 1921, Rosenzweig undertook to write *Understanding the Sick and the Healthy,* a popular book to explain the argument of *The Star of Redemption,* he had in mind, already well elaborated in courses offered at the Frankfurt *Lehrhaus,* the idea of common sense. *The Star of Redemption* is common sense and if it is regarded as a recondite, obscure, forbidding interpretation of the world it is misunderstood. It was conceived by Rosenzweig as an exegesis of what a living man would encounter if he opened himself to the ultimate questions, if he undertook the project of asking reality to explain itself.

II

There are two incidents which are crucial to an understanding of the conception and creation of *The Star of Redemption*.

The first was the impassioned discussion that occurred on the night of July 7, 1913, between Rosenzweig and Eugen Rosenstock-Huessy, in the presence of Rosenzweig's already converted cousin Hans Ehrenburg.

The second was his lonely participation in the service of the Day of Atonement in Berlin on October 11, 1913, a service which was intended to mark his departure from Judaism and the Jewish faith and in fact resulted in his reconversion and return as *baal teshubah.*

These events, recorded in every discussion of Franz Rosenzweig, are given enormous weight and significance and indeed they deserve them. The first event was defined by the power of the argued word, the word spoken which denies all relativity, beginning as it does from the confession of faith. Rosenstock-Huessy confronts his friend and admits that—despite his academic prestige and dignity as professor of medieval constitutional law—he is, in fact, a man of faith, that he believes in the reality of revelation, that moreover revelation, the self-revelation of God to man, is for him the principal source for the human understanding of love. He confesses to an absolute conviction, a conviction which debars all relativity, all "as if" mediations, all secondary considerations of logic, ethics, or history. Rosenzweig is backed to the wall, and struggle though he does, he is like Jacob and the angel, wrestling not to defeat God, but to win from him a blessing. By morning he joins in the confession. He asserts that he is no longer capable of espousing any relativistic doctrine; that he is beyond history and historical adaptations and that Judaism—as purveyed to him—is dead; that he is now joined to the Johannine church of the spirit in which Rosenstock-Huessy and other thinkers like him believe; and that the only way open for a believing man, living in Germany, in the midst of the new era of hope and possibility, is as a Christian. He resolves. There is the joy of fellowship. Hans Ehrenburg, more particularly than Rosenstock-Huessy, feels confirmed, having left Judaism for the church only four years before. Rosenzweig resolves to leave Judaism—as a Jew, however, not as a pagan—and therefore despite the pained and angered rejection of his decision by his mother, attends the New Year services in the synagogue of Cassel and is left unmoved; only by chance is he in Berlin for the Day of Atonement. There he is illuminated.

III

Franz Rosenzweig was an only child, born on Christmas Day 1886 in Cassel into a milieu of stolid, conventional prosperity. His father, Georg, was a very successful manufacturer of dyestuffs and a man highly respected for his civic spirit and good works. His mother, Adele Rosenzweig, was a woman of great charm and energy, possessed as Nahum Glatzer writes, of "an intuitive understanding of everything noble in life and in letters."[1] Their home was a social center of Cassel where prominent officials, civil servants, and communal leaders gathered for social and intellectual exchange.

The environment of the Rosenzweig home was indistinguishable from the bourgeois refinement and comfort described so warmly by Thomas Mann in *Buddenbrooks,* resting upon a foundation of work, cultivation, and money. The world of the emancipated German Jew was not much different from the society of the enlightened German Christian, but for the fact—as Rosenzweig noted many times in his use of the one Yiddish word that stuck in his consciousness until the time of his conversion—of the *rishis* of the Gentiles. Despite social compatibilities and interactions, Gentles were presumed to hate Jews and Jews to be continually on their guard against Christians.

The presumption of Gentile *rishis* was certainly underscored to young Franz by his grand-uncle, Adam Rosenzweig, a beloved but ambiguous figure for him, who lived in the Rosenzweig home. Uncle Adam, who died in 1908, retained more than a nominal Judaism. He wore a skullcap for one thing, but lived nonetheless in the assimilated Rosenzweig home, a witness to a reality remembered, lived, but untransmitted. Uncle Adam was the immediacy of the Jewish world as Franz was to experience it for many years until that fateful Day of Atonement. But Uncle Adam was more than a living remnant of the people; he was also a man who understood all culture, who was able, not despite but because of his Jewishness, to be as well a source of German culture to young Franz. It was through Uncle Adam that Rosenzweig made the acquaintance of the German culture of the postemancipation era, and no less the earlier legacy of Geothe, Dürer, and Rembrandt. It was the same Uncle Adam who, on the day of Franz's first departure for school in 1893, in the words of his schoolmate, Joseph Prager, "seized him in both arms, shook him violently [by his school satchel], and said emphatically: 'my boy, you are going among people for the first time today; remember as long as you live that you are a Jew.' "[2]

Let us assume for the moment that Joseph Prager has remembered the incident accurately and has transmitted to us Franz's actual account of the event; what is implied here? At the very least there is a curious employment of language. "You are going among people for the first time." The outside world is people (*die Leute*). The world at home is presumably Jews. Jews are in some sense not people. Or, as Adam Rosenzweig would perhaps have explained, Jews are Jews, not people, who are Gentiles. Otherwise put, Jews are safe at home, but not among the Gentiles. Or yet more strongly argued, the security one feels at home bears no relation to the conduct of the world where the *rishis* of the Gentiles (people) obliges one to remember always that one is a Jew, that being Jewish can never be escaped, that—and here Adam's faith is revealed—the implied imperative is: one must never wish to escape. It is certainly an ambiguous episode in the life of a six-year-old boy. Within the Rosenzweig home, the place to which Gentiles came to eat, drink, converse, think aloud in the company of Jews, where Jewishness was not the issue, but general German culture was all-important, one can imagine the deference, perhaps servility, undoubtedly respect and ease with which Gentiles and Jews interacted. Young Franz would have had no reason to suspect that the world would not be like his home.

We could assume an easy transaction between home and world which would have neutralized the shock effect of Uncle Adam's paranoid assault were it not the case that Uncle Adam's nephew, Georg Rosenzweig, was an unreassuring emissary to the world. If one acknowledges that it is the role of the father to interpret to the child the content of the world beyond the home, to report on its risk and danger, and to exhibit to the child the way and means of dealing with it (all healthy and unanguished devices, one might hope), again we might assume a blunting of Uncle Adam's warning. But this was not the case. Although only little is known about Franz's relations with his father, much is implied.

Every child has periodic dissatisfactions with his parents, but usually after death memory closes over dissent and a picture of warmth is retained. Not so in Franz's case. Shortly after his father's death, on March 19, 1918, Rosenzweig acknowledged in a letter to Hans Ehrenburg his estrangement from his father:

> My mother is surprised to learn from the recent letters that my lack of rapport with Father was taken so seriously by my friends and acquaintances. I am not. It always troubled me, and when our relations improved during the war (partly *because* of the war, through the simple, *undemanding* concern with survival) I was very happy indeed. They would have gone on improving. Outward success, which would have come with time, would have satisfied Father's need (a need, after all, very easily satisfied) to be "proud" of me. . . . Nevertheless, I can't reproach myself for what happened earlier; our natures were too different. It wasn't merely a question of "social" vs. "unsocial" (if it had been, I would have been obviously in the wrong), but it had to do with Father's lack of direction in his activities. This made him a remarkable *man,* but estranged me from his actions. I have always admired him (you will remember how once as a freshman I worked in the office for three weeks; I pretended that I did it in order to

learn how a business operates; actually I did it simply in order to see him at work), but could never become interested in what he was doing. The fact is that in his hands everything turned into a "piece of business," never into a subject. Once one has been bitten by the mad dog of the *idea,* one is no longer interested in anything but subjects. It wasn't the theoretical man defending himself against the practical man—I needn't tell *you* that this is a false dichotomy; especially toward the last. Father came to know my practical side—a practical side so strong that anyone knowing it might never suppose that I had also a not inconsiderable theoretical talent, but might think my true vocation lay in the realm of organizing and propagandizing. . . . Rather, it was the man possessed of ideas defending himself against the father who grappled indiscriminately with whatever came to hand. I shall always be grateful that toward the very end my own obsession and his grappling converged in one of my "subjects," which he converted into one of his "pieces of business."[3]

The mature assessment of his father was underscored by an earlier letter—the only letter preserved in the *Briefe* which is addressed to his father. This letter confirms the suspicion that Rosenzweig felt himself profoundly at odds with his father. After wishing him greetings on his birthday, Rosenzweig goes on to apologize for the "hateful scenes between us" of the previous year, but then expands on the fact that his father "has the capacity to forget what he wants to forget," whereas, "I forget nothing easily."[4] The apology becomes an apologia. Matters are left where they began: stubborn and intransigent opposition. It is not inappropriate to guess from this inconclusive evidence that Georg Rosenzweig was a distant, formal, apparently undemonstrative father, capable of cutting himself off from the disagreeable without confronting it. There is every evidence from the quality of feeling demonstrated in Rosenzweig's many letters to his mother that she preserved the domain of feeling and administered its distribution.

Georg Rosenzweig was all business, rectitude, rightness. One can justifiably surmise that in Georg Rosenzweig one is dealing with a not unfamiliar type, bourgeois self-righteousness, constantly validated by power, money, and good works. One is not surprised that when Franz was eleven years old, bearing home a report card attesting to the highest grades in the school, his father should offer him a *reward.* Not the memory of a hug and kiss, but a reward, to which, not uncharacteristically, Rosenzweig replied, "I want a teacher with whom I can really learn Hebrew."[5]

Franz's request is unusual. Why a Hebrew teacher, of all possible rewards? A familiar ambivalence is suggested: to be a Jew is dangerous;

it exposes one to Gentile anger and opprobrium. Georg Rosenzweig, apparently cold and distant from his son, is nonetheless the medium of contact with the world in which successful management and control and the making of wealth are a means of triumph over the Gentile. But there is besides him Franz's mother: warmth, tenderness, feeling for the noble and excellent, patroness of arts and music, from whom Franz inspired to learn music, languages, the appreciation of the arts. Last but not least is mysterious Uncle Adam, who is a blood relative of the same father and yet so unlike him, a synthetic union of the astringency of his father and the passion (not warmth, but passion) of his mother. What is more truthful than to acknowledge that in the request for a proper Hebrew teacher, a *melamed*, young Franz is expressing both contempt and longing, the wish to wound his father and the wish to please him, to show to his father a different way, another reward, but equally to exhibit to his father the surfacing wish to exceed him, to replace him, and—does one dare to admit it of our saints—to "slay" him using God's language as the instrument.

At the end of his adolescence Franz Rosenzweig is formed. Formed, but not completed. This is critical. By the end of one's teens, the whole man is present in that complex of strengths, gifts, confusions, which one regards as youth. We are all aware that the formed man is virtual within that seeming inchoateness. In the letters and *témoignages* of that period a number of articulated characteristics are apparent: Rosenzweig is, as he observes of himself later, regretting but bidding farewell to it nonetheless, a prodigy. He is a child prodigy, incredibly intelligent, swift of mind, omnivorous in his taste for culture, but as yet incapable of focus and definition. He studies violin, drawing lessons, examines musical scores, frequents the art museum of Cassel where Rembrandt's painting of The Blessing of Jacob is to be found, studies the Bible in Zunz's redaction (a further family legacy since Samuel Ehrenburg, the grandfather of his convert cousin Hans, was a colleague of Zunz in the theological institute which he directed), and vacillates between the study of medicine, philology, history, and science.

The world is open to Rosenzweig. But he has not forgotten Granduncle Adam's admonition never to forget. He does not forget. Quite the contrary. He begins to exhibit a familiar pattern, the wish to distance himself from those who remind him that he must never forget. The signs of specifically Jewish self-hatred manifest themselves. He writes from the University of Göttingen on October 22, 1905, on the occasion of a "mixer," at which a Jewish fraternity sought to pledge him, that: "The people as individuals were nice-looking, cheerful, and well-mannered. Very few typically Jewish-looking young men, some of the handsome racial type, about half without marked traits. The prevailing tone exactly the same as among Christian students, which is meant neither as praise nor censure. Even the beer-drinking code showed no trace of the Jewish esprit. It was just the opposite. After this test, racial anti-Semitism seems to me more senseless than before. These people are, at least at their present age, as completely 'German students' as can be imagined."[6]

As individuals, his fellow Jews are attractive and indistinguishable from Gentiles, but taken in aggregate the question of comparative physiognomy is raised, and the Jews pass, although not without uneasiness. Rosenzweig is expressing his own racial ambivalence and his wish that he could escape Uncle Adam's warning. He silences this wish by a rather typical response which makes the Gentiles stupid for their racial anti-Semitism, and which affirms that Jews either as individuals or in aggregation are indistinguishable from non-Jews. They even drink beer like Gentiles. They pass. They are not loathesome. Does one fail to recognize that young Rosenzweig is informing us that he has deep suspicions that the Jews are recognizable, that they are visible and different? He is afraid. He is one of them. He is noticed. He can never dissimulate.

Not long afterward Rosenzweig writes in one week a series of letters which underscore the psychological current we have been describing. These letters detail several themes which must be regarded as associated, not alone in this exposition but for Rosenzweig who wrote them: on January 28, 1906, he writes about the endurance of friendship, the unconscious sharing in all the mutations of the friend which debars absence and distance from undermining coparticipation. A few days later on February 1, he observes that the bourgeoisie of Germany are overprotected, coddled, and therefore weakened, whereas the true individual must always refuse such nourishment in the ambition of growing strength and independence. On February 5 he reads Nietzsche's *Thus Spake Zarathustra* and comments: "Who can possibly be a disciple of Nietzsche, base anything on him? He is a scaler of heights and therefore lonely. Who dares follow him? Who has enough conceit for that?" And on the very next day he describes a dancing party in a letter to his parents in which he fascinates and then humiliates a young girl who was attracted to him. He mocks her by declaring his love for her while at the same time giving "her a glimpse of a mind dissatisfied with God and the world." At a critical moment he abandons her on the floor and "escaped to the landing where I ran into Hans (Ehrenburg) and doubled up with laughter in his arms."

It was about Hans Ehrenburg that he wrote when he spoke of enduring friendship and it was in Hans's arms that he doubled up with laughter. The lonely Zarathustra, the ambivalent Jew, the ambivalent sexuality of the ambivalent Jew, the search for true friendship, the humiliation of the woman, the repudiation of the father, dissatisfied with God and the world.

It is with reference to this early period of Rosenzweig's maturity that one can begin to describe the Jewish embodiment of the interior conflicts to which we have already referred. But, before we can undertake this description, it must be pointed out that the devising of an objective referent for interior conflict is one of the primary means by which the creative personality lays off upon the world the alarums and complexities which, in less creative persons, are either dissolved by routine, postponed until transformed into more complex and less accessible neurotic patterns of behavior, or held frozen as characterological formations from which ressentiment, hostility, antagonism, frustration, and dissatisfaction might ultimately arise. How else to explain the phenomenon of the sexually impotent Jewish anti-Semite, all of whose friends or lovers reflect the apposition of the hated self? An uncreative dissolution of conflict. No art, certainly no theology; rather a life founded upon resentment and anger, the drama of self-punishment, the spectacle of public self-embarrassment and humiliation. Without the gift, without the formative presence of Uncle Adam, without the indulgent love of Mother Adele, the paranoid terror of Uncle Adam combined with the coldness, perhaps even the hostility, of father Georg, could well have turned young Franz in directions out of which not creation, but manifest self-destruction might have issued. It will be clear that the possibility of self-destruction was not so distant from the borders of Rosenzweig's consciousness as to be discounted out of hand. The narrowly averted conversion to Christianity (whatever the existential truth of religious conversion), would have been in Rosenzweig's case a self-destructive resolution of conflict. But Franz Rosenzweig had genius and the gifts which inform genius with duration and the character to persevere in the fulfillment of both.

"Why does one philosophize?" Rosenzweig asked himself in 1906. "For the same reason that one makes music or literature or art. Here too, in the last analysis, all that matters is the discovery of one's own personality."

A few days earlier, in a joking but nonetheless philosophic mood,

Rosenzweig noted in his diary the meanings which Judaism had to him. They were predictably self-indulgent and narcissistic. The delight in Judaism lay in the pleasure of molding it himself, forcing the material of the Jewish world to his own ends. Judaism was simply the religion of his fathers and that was the whole of its ethnic claim. He admitted to the enjoyment of certain Jewish customs, "without having any real reason for doing so." This he regarded as its essential metaphysical claim, for Jewish custom, he acknowledged, is Jewish dogma. "I like to think in biblical images" is regarded by him as the indulgence of myth-making. And lastly the eudaemonist objectives of religion are satisfied not by religion at all, but by his belief in Plato.

A quip, a jest it would seem, this light sally into the interpretation of religious existence. But not far from the truth, for what is apparent is that at no time does Rosenzweig believe that religion is ethics; moreover, as he says in the same entry, religion "can never base itself upon ethics. Ethics has its origin outside of religion. . . ." What is shadowed here is the sense that reestablishing just relations between father and son, between son and the world, between natural Jew and natural Gentile is not an issue of justice, not an issue of ethics. The primal warfare is in the fabric of the universe. But more than this, the decision to exclude ethics from religion, to inflate religion with the metaphysical, the metaethical, the metalogical, with dogma, with the people, with the language of myth foreshadows the structure of *The Star of Redemption.*

By the end of 1906 and the beginning of 1907 other preoccupations begin to emerge in his thinking. There is for instance the lovely triad of themes (October 8, 1906): "Better write / than read. Better write poetry / than write. Better live / than write poetry." The process of interiorization, still lacking content, but no longer without form, is becoming explicit. It is what Bergson describes so tellingly in his Bologna lecture of 1911 on philosophical intuition as the negative valent of creative intuition, the telling to the self of *what* is not, without the affirmative clarification of what the real object and enterprise of thought and life are.[7] The process of creative intuition proceeds by way of negation, the psyche turning away from the unsuitable options of the world toward those which, now contracted and defined, become the occasions for creative employment.

It is during this time, 1907–08, that Rosenzweig exhibits his anxiety about death. By this time Rosenzweig must have known enough of Jewish history, enough of the *rishis* of the Gentile world, enough of the significance of Uncle Adam's warning, to know of several species of death— those distant and those unconsciously present, death by loss of one's

natal name, death by mutilation, the parricidal wish and the self-punishment which blunts it, and not least the expectation that one or another
of those whom he loved, loved deeply, but nonethless ambiguously,
would one day die. It is a wonder that in his comments about death in
1907, a few weeks before his twenty-first birthday, he should deny reality
to death, affirming that "physiologically speaking, man (i.e., man as phenomenon) is dead all his life. As for man as noumenon, such a thing as
'death' (cessation in time) does not exist, since noumena are timeless.
Man as phenomenon, body and soul, does not die since he has been
dead from the start, man as noumenon (the personality) does not die
since he has never lived (in time)."

A very strange formulation. What then is man? He is neither dead
nor alive. He is a book. He is a book writing itself, like Kant, from whom
the language of noumenon and phenomenon derive. It is not possible
that young Rosenzweig, now approaching legal manhood (the ineffectual
Jewish manhood having long since come and gone, for Jewish manhood
in such cultured households could not mean what it meant among Jewish
peasants, the assumption of genital responsibility and ritual self-control
and discipline), would undertake to distance himself from his father, to
deny both the real father and his divine magnification?

This is the time preliminary to the conversion crisis, to the period of
religious search and religious resolution. Two months later, on February
27, 1908, Uncle Adam died. Death did not happen. It was not a psychological problem, not a metaphysical question suitable for genius notebooks, but a feared fact, a reality.

Only slightly later Hermann Badt, an ardent Zionist, visited Rosenzweig during the summer of 1908 and observed that Franz's morning
levée was of such protracted and ritual proportions that he inquired of its
significance; to which, in Badt's words, Rosenzweig replied with "a long
lecture that was half-serious, half in fun. Indeed he said the moment of
daily reawakening from nightly death was for him the greatest and holiest
moment of the day. It was impossible ever to dwell too fondly on this
daily renewal, one must taste it consciously in every detail. . . . He said
that he alone is truly blessed who is able to experience consciously this
daily reawakening but also in the moment of death to remain conscious
and make the step from this world to the next with his senses intact."[8]

At this juncture of Rosenzweig's psychological history one discerns
the gradual shifting of interior argument from the self to the plane of the
world. The argument about man, the living dead, the timeless essence,
begins to wither and in its place further marks of the Bergsonian negative

intuition appear; for in a letter of May 1908, Rosenzweig writes that "history is psychological 'materialism' stated more generally, materialism of events, while true materialism is ontologial. Where the latter says that everything exists in space alone, the former says that everything exists in time alone. Values should be rescued from history as well as from science; both space and time are coffins."

Space and time, the interior scheme through which the Kantian man perceived the world, were dismissed as coffins. This could mean that Rosenzweig continued to think of physiological life—life in extension—as death, and noumenal life—life beyond time and space—as fantastic and unreal. Clearly, however, a crisis was anticipated, a crisis already animadverted in the intensification of such compulsive ritual as his daily staring down of death.

Throughout the letters and diaries of Rosenzweig's university years there is the constant undercurrent of dissatisfaction, the self-recognition of difference from others, intellectual difference in that he was enormously brilliant and contentious; emotional difference in that he was immensely sensitive and self-critical, constantly submitting himself to moral tests; and social difference in that he was a Jew. The wish to concentrate these differences into a single formulation which would have the value of focusing his genius without diminishing it is certainly evident. At the periphery of this wish to ontological concentration, there is his growing preoccupation, with death—his own—and single-minded preoccupation with religious questions, beautifully disguised by wit, irony, and high culture.

The disguise is penetrated and the struggle of Franz Rosenzweig to come to terms with himself, with his authentic conscience, and with his passion to tell the truth, even if it is hurtful truth, is revealed on the occasion of the conversion to Christianity and subsequent baptism of his beloved friend and cousin Hans Ehrenburg during the fall of 1909.

The conversion of Ehrenburg was the first turning point, but unlike the pivotal events of his all-night discussion with Rosenstock-Huessy four years later, followed by his wholehearted acceptance of Judaism and Jewish identity, the conversion of Ehrenburg served him as a foil to confront his parents with his dissatisfaction with them. We cannot regard the letters of this period (and undoubtedly the many heated, but unrecorded, direct conversations which he must have had with his parents) as being really about Ehrenburg. Ehrenburg was a justified cover to the real issue being fought out. Undoubtedly the conversion was socially embarrassing to the bourgeois Rosenzweigs, who regarded their Judaism with the same pride and dignity as they would any heirloom of the family—to be ad-mired at a distance, to be brushed off for fall use and covered against spring cool and summer dampness. An honored heirloom. Had Ehren-burg not been an intimate of the family, an intimate of their only son, a son of whom they undoubtedly had formed their own doubts and anxie-ties (for Franz was continually warning them in subtle ways that he found their Judaism insupportable, that he had no affection for national solidar-ities and group loyalties per se, that religion had nothing to do with ethics, that his studies of Judaism were no different from the studies which any historian of modern thought would have undertaken), we would not regard the exchanges about Ehrenburg's decision as more than family gossip. But clearly they were more, and his family was justified from their own perspective in showing concern. The Rosenzweigs were beginning to lose touch with their son. Franz was consciously distancing himself from their time-bound, space-worn values in order to define his own.

The project of maturation, however one wishes to understand this, entails the psychological murder of one's parents. The murder if consum-mated in the imagination and realized by the separation, discrimination, and independence of the child, is a murder from which rebirth follows, the rebirth of the parents as friends (or strangers), the rebirth of the guilty murderer as an independent spirit who can now love and be loved unharmed by the guilty wish to be other than his beginnings. The deci-sion to be mature (that is, to be other than one's beginnings) is the para-digm of revelation in the psychological development of man. Every man finds a different excuse, a different occasion, a different moment at which to declare for maturity, to kill the parent symbolically and, in gaining life, to return life to those slain loved ones. It takes time, much time, and there are those who never bring it off—who remain entrapped by the unclarity of dependence and never leave, too frightened of the wish to slay, too terrified to consummate the separation even in imagination— and there are others who make the break, but do so with such pain and guilt that they are crippled by self-imposed punishments.

Rosenzweig was to experience both modes—the mode of separation by symbolic slaying and the experience of profound guilt (not without indication of serious cycles of depression and elation, humiliation and joy) which followed it, issuing at last, following the death of his father, in a sublime transmogrification, the writing of *The Star of Redemption,* which was offered as a periodically presented gift from the vulnerable son in the trenches of the Balkans to his grieving mother.

IV

The conversion of Hans Ehrenburg started Rosenzweig on the course of self-confrontation and separation from his parents which was to conclude in 1913 with his decision to become himself a Christian followed by his decision to become what his parents were unable to be, a *believing* Jew.

The first moment of the process was defined in outraged defense of his cousin Hans: "it would have been best if Uncle and Aunt had had their children baptized or circumcised at birth, but it's better to repair the omission belatedly than not at all. Because I am hungry, must I on principle go on being hungry? On principle? Does principle satisfy hunger? Can being nonreligious on principle satisfy a religious need? Or can the empty notation in the registrar's office, 'Religion Jewish,' satisfy a religious need? If I am given the choice of an empty purse or a handful of money, must I choose the purse? Again on principle?"[9]

A few days later he writes once more from Freiburg, "We are Christian in everything. We live in a Christian state, attend Christian schools, read Christian books, in short, our whole 'culture' rests entirely on a Christian foundation; consequently a man who has nothing holding him back needs only a very slight push to make him accept Christianity. In Germany today the Jewish religion cannot be 'accepted,' it has to be grafted on by circumcision, dietary observances, and Bar Mitzvah. Christianity has a tremendous advantage over Judaism; it would have been entirely out of the question for Hans to become a Jew; a Christian, however, he can become "[10]

And a month later: "It doesn't rest with the children but with the parents, and religious instruction is of no avail, at least to us, without a religion that is seen, heard, tasted, and visibly exercised upon the body."[11]

The issue was squarely put to Rosenzweig's parents: it is your task, not mine. Judaism is parental obligation not filial duty. If it has ceased to be the one, it is because it was never the other. Implicit in this argument of Rosenzweig's was the honest recognition that religious atavism is unavailing, that the complaint of desertion and dishonesty is false since the first responsibility to the child is the witness of the parents. Already in this vigorous dissent from the "heirloom" Judaism of his parents is the inchoate recognition of what was to be central to Rosenzweig's own Judaism: not loyalties, sentiments, affections, nor paranoid distrust of Christians and Christianity, but a founding of community upon deeds, acts, and performances which can never be overwhelmed by the buffetings of history.

Rosenzweig had begun, by means of his polemical defense of his cousin Hans against the social outrage of his parents, to describe the ambit of authentic Judaism and authentic Christianity, a Judaism he could not yet accept for himself without first having tempted himself to the edge and brought into the open the manipulative control which his mother exercised upon his freedom by the giving and withholding of approval and which his father exercised by inaccessibility.

The next three years can be described as a troubled interlude, an emotional hiatus during which the issues of Rosenzweig's personal identity were being forced into the mold of intellectual argument. These were the years during which his studies of history with Friedrich Meinecke, his readings of Hegel, and the development of his excellent study *Hegel and the State* took place. But it was also the time between his first meeting with Eugen Rosenstock-Huessy, a Christian of Jewish origin, who was professor of medieval constitutional law at Leipzig, and his going to that university as a student in 1913 expressly to avail himself of Rosenstock-Huessy's influence. They had met at a conference of young historians and philosophers at Baden-Baden in 1910, and it was as a consequence of this conference, which looms large in Rosenzweig's correspondence of these years, that the beginnings of his revulsion against absolute idealism in philosophy and objectification in history can be found.

Rosenzweig adored Hegel, was fascinated by the enormity of his pretense to omniscience, but found himself always outside the system. He, the living subject, was personally omitted from the great mechanism of the Hegelian vision. He was outside as individual thinker; he was outside as thinker with a different view of reality, with a debunking mistrust for historical truth; he was, moreover, outside as a German who was neither Christian nor Jew. His position became no position other than that of critical distance from *all* positions. Such a posture was insupportable to someone as intellectually honest as Rosenzweig.

No wonder that Rosenzweig should come to Leipzig to be near Rosenstock-Huessy, that they should become inseparable, that the philosopher of "Speech-Thinking" (that is, speech as revelation), should confront Rosenzweig with an alternative to conventional philosophizing and conventional historiography. Rosenzweig was desperate to have a resolved point of view and, issuing from the resolution of point of view, an articulable personal identity which would enable not only the truth of the world but the much more desperately urgent truth of the self to be espoused.

Rosenstock-Huessy, a slightly younger contemporary of Rosenzweig, had become a Christian when he was sixteen years old. By the time of their meeting, he was an accomplished academician, a published author, already formulating the early drafts of his first major interpretation of "Speech Thinking," *Angewandte Seelenkunde,* which mightily influenced Rosenzweig's *The Star of Redemption.* Rosenstock-Huessy, with impassioned address, confronted Rosenzweig with the ambiguity of his uncommitted Hegelianism. Rosenzweig was behaving like an intellectual, whereas Rosenstock-Huessy was thinking like a believer.

The joining of the issue on the fateful night of July 7, 1913, has been described by Alexander Altmann as "the most decisive and most far-reaching event in Rosenzweig's inner life. It produced a crisis from which after months of struggle the new Rosenzweig emerged."[12]

Rosenzweig himself described the centrality of that encounter in a letter to Rudolf Ehrenburg. In that night's conversation Rosenstock pushed me step by step out of the last relativist position which I still occupied and forced me to take an absolute standpoint. I was inferior to him from the outset, since I had to recognize for my part too the justice of his attack. If I could then have buttressed my dualism between revelation and the world with a metaphysical dualism between God and the Devil I should have been unassailable. But I was prevented from doing so by the first sentence of the Bible. This piece of common ground forced me to face him. This has remained even afterward in the weeks which follow the fixed point of departure. Any form of philosophical relativism is now impossible to me."[13]

The change brought about by that evening of conversation entailed a complete reversal in Rosenzweig's mode of encountering the world. The philosopher is able to contain the world, to draw the world into himself, to make himself the fulcrum of the world. It is the philosopher's reason and the philosopher's argumentation which establish the world for him. The philosopher holds the world still in his categories so that he can endure it. But the thinker who cannot make himself the center of the world, who cannot bear the role of being divinity to his own creation, is forced outside his categories to the acceptance of the world as given.

Rosenzweig held one thing in common with Rosenstock-Huessy: he believed in the power of the word. In a sense that was the undoing of his relativism and the making of his theology. He believed in the power of the assertion that "In the beginning God made heaven and earth." Believing that speech was the cornerstone which sustained beginnings and ends, life and death, creation and redemption, he affirmed an unassailable premise outside himself on which to found his view of the universe.

The primacy of the knower is diminished always by the degree of absoluteness ascribed to the known and if, indeed, the known be God the knower is overwhelmed by him.

Another way of expressing this insight is to suggest that Rosenzweig intuited a resolution to his already documented parricidal conflict. By separating the living father from God, by granting to God the role of creator (not of judge) he was able to contain his own aggression, and in a certain sense to make that fantasied aggression beside the point. Being forced to belief in God, he was able to neutralize his wish to be done with his own true father. He resolved his father by accepting a creator God, a God who speaks, who is distant but still speaks, communicates, expresses himself in revelation to his creatures, and most particularly to this one of them, Franz Rosenzweig. The silences and incomprehension which separated him from his real father were now given metaphysical status in that God is solitary and incommunicate in himself, but in creation God is speech.

It may be suggested at this point (but could only be confirmed by a broader study) that Rosenzweig's rejection of philosophy and his adoption of "faith based on revelation" is a more acceptable resolution of conflict for the personality checked by a regnant superego than for one whose conflicts are withdrawn into the omnipotent ego and reformulated as the fount of perception and knowledge. A thinker who affirms, as did Rosenzweig, that speech is prior to thought, that philosophy is absorbed by revelation is certainly different—not alone in doctrine but in personality—from a thinker like Descartes, who makes thought prior to self and self a deduction from thought.

The nighttime conversation of July 13 provided Rosenzweig with the terms of his "New Thinking," his own formulation of the significance of Rosenstock-Huessy's "Speech Thinking." "Revelation breaks into the world and transforms creation, which is the Alpha of history, into redemption which is the Omega. Philosophy has a pagan quality. It is an expression of the Alpha of creation, of pure nature to which God has given freedom—even against himself. But as revelation comes into the world, it gradually absorbs philosophy, deprives it of its pagan elements, and illuminates it with its own light. The Omega of history will be realized after the element of creation, the world's freedom has spent itself. Then God, who allowed the world to be the Alpha, will again be the First and the Last, the Alpha and Omega."[14]

The recognition that history was absorbed by revelation means that history is no longer absolute. Hegel is "the last philosopher," because, to

Rosenzweig, Hegel reflected the consummation of the pagan philosophical mind. In this context Rosenzweig also joined himself to the position of Rosenstock-Huessy that the third period of Christian history signaled by the French Revolution; by the absolute idealism of Fichte, Schelling, and Hegel; by the paganic Christianity of Goethe which is beyond class and creed, had begun. The Johannine Age was the free spirit of God among men.

The last contact with a natural resolution of Rosenzweig's wish to separate himself from his father, from the conflict which Uncle Adam Rosenzweig had first defined, from the ordinariness of ordinary Judaism which nonetheless makes absolute demands upon loyalty (loyalty understood as loyalty to one's own, to one's parents in fact) ended with the realization that the individual does not dominate God, that God's standpoint is not man's and freedom prised from the universe is not freedom given by God. To recognize that God the Father is different from one's natural father, that loyalty to Him may sometimes mean disloyalty to one's generative father, that the *real* Father is eternal, the temporal father an illusion, enabled Rosenzweig to polarize God the revealer to himself, the thinker, to set in opposition once and for all his conscience (which forbids him the fulfillment of his parricidal wish without yet resolving it) and to subdue the philosopher's ego which would continue, without success, the struggle to assert its claim over and against the temporal father.

Rosenzweig solved the problem of his aggressive wish to humiliate his own father and with him his pedestrian social religiosity (which had become well established as the symbol of fatherhood) by means of a détente, a formal detachment, a surrender which divided him from his parents, allowing them to live on unslain, but allowed himself the privilege of transcending them to achieve a higher rung of self-identification.

Rosenzweig first tried to save himself by affirming Christianity. But that way would prove too much, too unreal, too irresolute. Leaving Rosenstock-Huessy that July night he affirmed later—two days in fact after he had resolved to remain a Jew—that he had no choice at that time but to become a Christian. If it was the Johannine Age of the spirit, if all things German were Christian, if Germany was, as he and many others believed, the home of authentic culture then what could a free man do other than become Christian? Nothing bound him to his home. He undoubtedly saw himself (no differently than he had earlier seen his cousin Hans) as a child of nature without religion who desperately needed one. Despite the fact that he had nominal contact with Jewish life, it was a life congealed and formal. Uncle Adam was dead, but even Uncle Adam had demonstrated that it was dangerous to be a Jew. Who could help young Rosenzweig to remain a Jew?

Rosenzweig returned home from Leipzig for the High Holy Days which began on October 2, 1913. He attended the services in Cassel and was unmoved. His letters home in the previous months were full of forebodings and warnings. He had resolved to become a Christian, but he had resolved nonetheless that he would become a Christian not as a pagan, but only as a Jew, passing from Judaism to Christianity without an intermediate lapse into paganism. A strange formulation, for Rosenzweig was surely by that point in his life, Jewishly speaking, pagan. Pagan in all things but the flesh. He was Jewish according to the flesh (and in that sense Jewish according to God), but in matters of observance and ritual behavior already pagan. The fact that he was circumcised (whereas Hans Ehrenburg had not been circumcised) was critical. He was a Jew in the flesh and he had survived that divine incision, healthy and undiminished. His was a struggle transposed from God the revealer and God the creator, to God in the mind and God in the flesh.

A few days after Rosh Hashanah of 1913 he came to his mother, New Testament in hand, and she anticipated his wish: "You want to be baptized?" Rosenzweig replied, "Mother, here is everything, here is the truth. There is only one way, Jesus." His mother asked him: "Were you not in the synagogue on New Year's Day?" He answered: "Yes and I will go to the synagogue on the Day of Atonement, too. I am still a Jew." His mother affirmed: "When I come in, I will ask them to turn you away. In our synagogue there is no room for an apostate."[15]

Rosenzweig apparently did not announce his intention to his father first. He addressed his mother. He undoubtedly expected more understanding and compassion from her. She was sensitized to his nature. He sought once more to reject his father through her. He employed his mother as conduit for his anger with the Jewish God, his dissatisfaction with Jewish constriction and convention, his refusal of the bourgeois ways of the Jews. But Adele Rosenzweig was more than equal to her son, more profound in her pride, and revealed to Franz on this occasion something most mothers would be reluctant to affirm. It is more commonplace for a mother to ask, employing the authority and assumed anger of the father, whether her son has discussed this decision with him. Or she might have disclaimed knowledge about such matters, but assured her son nonetheless of his father's anger. Or, if her relations to her son were more seductive and hostile to her husband, she might have said, "Anything you want if it makes you content is approved by me, but your father will be outraged."

Adele Rosenzweig, however, loved her husband very deeply. There was no wish on her part to pit father against son in order to assert her claims upon Franz. Adele Rosenzweig adored her son, honored him, delighted in him, but not to the exclusion of her own self-esteem, her own pride. She would never deny herself (and by implication the pride of her husband) by acceding without struggle to her son's wish. She stood up to Franz. She warned him that, despite his insistence that he was a Jew (and thereby unconsciously honoring Uncle Adam's command to him—which had the form of a command of revelation as later developed in *The Star of Redemption*), as an apostate he would die not alone to his father but also to her. God would refuse him and the doors of the synagogue would be shut. His terrestrial father would surely refuse him, withdrawing even further from affection toward his son. But, more horribly, his mother, the loving beloved, would withdraw that love and he would die, declared dead by order of her unsubmissive pride.

It is not clear why Rosenzweig left Cassel to pass the Day of Atonement in Berlin. It is told that he went to see a friend. One surmises however that more was at stake. The visit to a friend is surely an excuse. Rosenzweig could not risk the possibility that what his mother threatened would transpire, that she would stand forth and demand that he be cast from the synagogue. He did not risk it. Instead he went to the synagogue for the Day of Atonement, a small synagogue, an Orthodox synagogue in Berlin, and there he passed the Day of Atonement. We know nothing about what transpired, but we can guess from certain themes which recur in *The Star of Redemption* and in other writings. Rosenzweig discovered the liturgy of Israel as a felt liturgy, a liturgy which actually enabled humble men to be pulled out of time into the rhythm of eternity, a liturgy which exalted the mundane to the eternal.

The Star of Redemption is one of the most exquisite evocations of the power of liturgy and liturgical gesture. Liturgy becomes the dance of the soul in gravity, able to move out and over time to the eternal, able as well to move on the plane of the human, joining believer to believer in community, and able finally to raise up the community to God. Is it any wonder that Rosenzweig made so much of the single obeisance of kneeling which takes place during the Avodah service of the Day of Atonement, when the entire congregation prostrates itself as the Hazzan speaks in replication of the High Priest the ineffable name? The *Aleinu* prayer becomes the prayer for redemption and the redemption and restoration occurred on that crucial day for Franz Rosenzweig.[16]

Rosenzweig left the service resolved to remain a Jew. Several weeks after, in response to a letter from his mother which indicates that she had perhaps weakened in her resolve to repudiate her son, he affirms even more strongly his decision to remain a Jew. And lastly he transmits that decision to Rudolf Ehrenburg in a moving letter which recounts in full the history of his thought from the night with Rosenstock-Huessy to his decision to remain a Jew. "I must tell you something that will grieve you and may at first appear incomprehensible to you: after prolonged and I believe thorough self-examination I have reversed my decision. It no longer seems necessary (*notwendig*) to me, and therefore being what I am (*in meinem Fall*) no longer possible. *Ich bleibe also Jude* (I shall therefore remain a Jew)."[17]

V

The intervening years from 1913 until the commencement of his writing of *The Star of Redemption* during August 1918 exhibit the consistency of resolution and redefinition which one would hopefully expect to be the outcome of such traumatic origins. What is always magnificent about the manner in which genius deals with interior conflict is that it pushes itself toward the employment of the materials of the conflict, their reordering and redirection, with the consequence that the terms of the conflict are elevated into paths of construction and creation. Only the mock artist or the artist whose pathology disallows creation fails to employ the materials of his past.

The years from 1913 onward were a time of preparation. The decision had been made. And the decision was psychologically efficient. It enabled Rosenzweig to maintain himself within the circle of the family, to preserve his relations to his mother, but, most importantly, to at last conquer his fear of his father. He raised himself beyond his father. He thought himself beyond the position of his natural father and henceforward until his father's death would be able to conduct his father toward him, to make of his father the uncomprehending disciple of the son. Georg Rosenzweig was induced by his son to establish a foundation for Jewish learning at the instance of the great philosopher and fellow *baal teshubah*, Hermann Cohen. Franz employed an even more renowned father than himself to instruct his natural father in service to the Jewish people. A not uncommon reversal.

Rosenzweig was now free of his fear, and the work of his life could commence. The materials gathered during those years—the meeting and friendship with Hermann Cohen, the renewal of contact between himself and Rosenstock-Huessy which resulted in their extraordinary correspondence on Judaism and Christianity, his enlistment in the German army in 1915, and his assignment to an antiaircraft battery in the Balkans which gave him the opportunity during his periodic leaves to make contact with the Sephardic Jews of Yugoslavia and the Jews of Eastern Europe—were experiences whose value could be integrally focused in creative activity.

VI

The question to which we turn now is the most decisive: how does the thinker transform the materials of life, the promptings of that rich storehouse of dreams, fantasies, and wishes which is the unconscious treasury of men, the reminiscences and assimilation of truths won from conflict with others—with parents, with friends, with the world—into a work of art which achieves the intensity and passion reflected in *The Star of Redemption?*

Of course it is not always the case that the work of art expresses the resolution of conflict. It is no less commonplace for the work of art to transpose the conflict, intensify, exaggerate, condense it in such a fashion as to make the underlying, unresolved conflict less terrifying, more bearable. The horror of reality was not dissolved by Nietzsche's *Genealogy of Morals.* Quite the contrary, ressentiment became a principle for the understanding of culture. No resolution, only transformation into dogmatic principle. No less the case with Sören Kierkegaard, who encapsulated the dilemmas of his complex masochism into theological formulations which made loneliness, estrangement, anguish into categories of existence. And no less the case with Rainer Maria Rilke, with August Strindberg, with Simone Weil—the perceived enmity of the world was translated either into unearthly beauty or into unearthly pathos.

A more direct example is that of Ludwig Wittgenstein, the renovator of the logic of language, a speech-thinker of a different order, who concluded his *Tractus* by affirming that his propositions are elucidatory in this way: "He who understands me finally recognizes them as senseless, when he has climbed out through them, on them, over them. (He must so to speak throw away the ladder, after he has climbed up on it.) He must surmount these propositions; then he sees the world rightly. Whereof one cannot speak, thereof one must be silent."[18] A terrifying vision of reality, a vision which nonetheless Wittgenstein maintained to the end of his life, holding that all that which was most dreadfully profound—God, morals, beauty—were the domain of silence. Thought could be cut to the bone of truthful proposition, the utterly limited truth of proposition, but feeling was all that mattered; and of the domain of feeling there could be no speech. Where the speech thinkers first begin to speak, Wittgenstein maintains silence. We do not judge the one by the other. They are both correct. Indeed Rosenzweig knows they are correct for he too argues that the fullness of the liturgy is silence.

The Star of Redemption is a masterpiece of modern theological thinking. It could not have been written earlier than it was—not earlier in the life of its author, not earlier in the history of thought. It was absolutely contemporaneous to that other masterpiece of clarion theological thinking, Karl Barth's *The Epistle to the Romans* (first published in 1918). There, too, Karl Barth is insistent that his book be not only read, but heard. The use of spoken language, to be heard as written, is an ontological condition demanded of the reader, who no longer reads, but stands open before the word. The author is a medium of the word—he is the mediate revealer, for he transmits a corrected understanding of modern man, corrected insofar as he dispels the presumption of philosophy to tell the truth about God, man, and the world, as objects whose definitions are possible only because the thinker is the centrifugal eye of the universe, defining God as the origin of world, world as the place of man, and man as the knower of God. Philosophy absolutizes the position of the omniscient knower. Theology yields place to the Word, and once perceived the Word is the *relatum* which links God, man, and world; creation, revelation, and redemption. To link is, however, not to demonstrate, as philosophy in its Hegelian moment would contend. God cannot be derived from man; nor man from world; nor world from God. The All is independent of everything, and only revelation makes knowledge possible.

The initial act of *The Star of Redemption* is to undermine the anxiety of death which Rosenzweig had earlier banished by philosophical decree. Death is no longer unreal, no longer to be incorporated and expunged by denial of its power nor declared chimeric in the imagination. It is utterly real and it is in the fear of death that man begins to ask questions of the encompassing All which embraces him and his world. Philosophy—self-arrogating—may dismiss the fear of death as a debilitating anxiety, but from the standpoint of the individual man, who begins the inquiry without the answer, death and the fear of death are his starting point.

The opening book of *The Star of Redemption* is intended to force the viewpoint of the individual man, the existent man, the man who knows most deeply that thought cannot deny death, that the fact of death is presupposition of knowledge. Where Hegel would dissolve death in transcendence, Rosenzweig begins with human anguish before death, which is the positing of the essential nothingness to which all things return and from which all things can be rescued. At the very beginning is the temper of faith, the belief that the honest man, undrugged by philosophy, can contend with death and the dissolution of inherited certainties in the trust that a new foundation can be established for right understanding.

The complex language of Part I of *The Star of Redemption* is purposely intended. Rosenzweig is concerned to show that the elements of reality, God, man, and world, cannot be extruded from dualism. They are the protocosmic elements, the elements which can be contemplated by thought and defined independently of each other but cannot be vivified, obliged to interaction and movement, except by transforming conceptual entities into living realities.

As the reality of death introduced the decomposition of philosophy and the establishment of the grounds by which metaphysics (God), metalogic (world), and metaethics (man) could be extrapolated from the tension between the All and the Nothing, so the language of creation, revelation, and redemption is commenced by a discussion of the real miracle. Here again one cannot help but feel that embedded in this moving account of the meaning of the miraculous—the miraculous as it is given to the seeking man—Rosenzweig is making reference to the traumatic occasion of his all-night confrontation with Rosenstock-Huessy. The miracle of speech at the base of the New Thinking which consumes the introduction to this second part of *The Star of Redemption* arose out of his meeting with Rosenstock-Huessy in 1913. It was from that meeting that the germinal cell of his theology (the *urzelle* to which he referred in a subsequent letter to Rudolf Ehrenburg on November 18, 1918) derived.

Revelation is the miracle which discloses the figuration of the word in creation and its fulfillment in redemption, which unfolds to man the prospect of created reality and its completion as world, which signals the self-unfolding of the divine in freely loving and foretells the return of the divine into the divine, which is the self-reconciled God. Revelation is the miracle which brings God, world, and man together, which binds creation to redemption through the medium of the word. Creation from the view of revelation is the protocosmos, the diminuendo of reality, and redemption from the view of revelation is hypercosmos, the crescendo of reality.

But there is still man, the man who is addressed by the prospect of fulfillment, who dreams of redemption, who cringes before death, who encounters the panoply of the world—its arts, its passions, its imagination—with anxiety and forboding, knowing that these, too, speak the language of creation and redemption. He is not a man outside history. He is amidst history. He is the historical man who begins life at a given moment and whose life ends at a moment not yet given. Who is that man? He is a Christian man. He is a Jewish man. These are the only two. The others, those who are of other faiths, are remote from the drama, examples of accentuations and misconstructions, partialities, and defects. Rosenzweig is not concerned with the history of religion as history. It may be said that if, for Kant, space and time were interior modes which made cognition possible and therefore essentially unreal as objective categories, the same may be said of Rosenzweig's use of history. History is unreal—it is real only in the sense in which it may be said that a living man who dies has a definite history (history as measurement of time), but not insofar as history is at the center of the tension between God, man, and the world. History is not a medium; it is a mode of measurement (a spatialization of time). The real life of man is conducted on the road to eternity, when God is restored to God and the created universe—man and world—brought to completion. Given Rosenzweig's biography, it is inconceivable that he should have done other than to establish the parallelism of Christianity and Judaism, the indispensable presence of both teachings in the economy of the universe.

Christianity is a religion of becoming, a turning of the pagan out of a false metaphysics of knowledge into the true understanding of the way toward God. The Christian is a man always on his way from paganism to the truth of God. For this reason, as Rosenzweig made clear in his letter to Ehrenburg following his acceptance of Judaism, there is no way for the Christian to the Father except through the Son, but for the Jew mediation is beside the point, for the Jew is always with the Father, the Jew lives in the eternity set down in the midst of the people; and is consequently the paradigm of redemption. The Jew lives eternity and for that reason history is irrelevant to the Jew. The Christian must struggle with history, combat its paganic relativities, in the effort to make himself whole through time. The Christian, not the Jew, unfolds through history, but it is the presence of the Jew amid the nations that exhibits to him the goal, the goal of perfect intimacy with the eternal.

The enormous power of *The Star of Redemption* is that it released Rosenzweig from the grip of irresolute despair; it silenced once and for all his estranged distance from his natal environment, contained his articulated disappointment with his father, restored him to an objective love toward his mother, and most importantly kept faith with the truth of his Uncle Adam.

In the life of man there is a primal drama; a drama of exquisite complexity which, with a small cast of characters, unfolds the spectacle of all life—the will to love, the fear of love, the will to aggression, the control of aggression, the wish to slay and the containment of murder, the wish to achieve mastery without destructiveness. The perception that man is a creature whose mechanisms have been exposed and laid bare to scrutiny, exposed and examined for the first time by another man (one Sigmund Freud) does not make Freud the creator of man, nor does it diminish the achievements of men to understand that they are men, sublime in rare cases, complex in all, miserable in some, but nonetheless men who reenact all the ancient dramas of the race.

The work of theology, not unlike the novels of Dostoevsky, or the paintings of Paul Klee or Piet Mondriaan, are exhibitions of the drama of the unconscious rendered explicit by the work, subject to examination and scrutiny as the creator-artist gives us the clues and signs of his complexity. All art presses toward clarity. It is only a life in bondage to dependency that is unclear, for the unrealized self hangs onto others for its own authentication. That is not the way of the artist. The artist makes the work and the work carries the power of the life. It is no invalidation of the profundity of Rosenzweig's view of God, man, and world, of creation, revelation, and redemption, of Christian and Jew, to understand that these are bodied forth—enfleshed, so to speak—out of the confusions and dilemmas of growing up. The mature man is born out of the child, and it is to the lasting honor of genius that the complications of youth and maturation give up the prodigious achievements on which future lives, future humanity, and future art can build. What else is the instruction of the grandeur and misery of man? That others might live.

Into Life.

NOTES

All references to and discussion of *The Star of Redemption* are based upon the first English translation of this work, by William W. Hallo, published by Holt, Rinehart, and Winston, New York, 1971; 445 pages; $10.00.

1. *Franz Rosenzweig: His Life and Thought,* presented by Nahum N. Glatzer, New York, 1961, xxxvi. All quotations from letters not cited from the *Briefe* are from here.

2. Glatzer, xxxvii; Joseph Prager, "Begegnungen auf dem Wege," in *Franz Rosenzweig, Ein Buch des Gedenkens,* Berlin, 1930, 39.

3. Glatzer, 69–70; *Franz Rosenzweig: Briefe,* ed. by Edith Rosenzweig, Berlin, 1935, 293.

4. *Briefe,* 52–53.

5. Prager, Joseph, loc. cit.

6. Glatzer, 2; cf. also *Briefe,* Nov. 4, 1906, p. 30, for a reference to the racial characteristics of his philosophy professor, Jonas Cohn.

7. Henri Bergson, "Philosophical Intuition," *The Creative Mind,* N.Y., 1946, 126f.

8. Glatzer, 17; Hermann Badt, "Erinnerungen," *Franz Rosenzweig, Ein Buch des Gedenkens,* op. cit., 46.

9. Glatzer, 18f; *Briefe,* 45.

10. Glatzer, 19; *Briefe,* 45.

11. Glatzer, 19f; *Briefe,* 46f.

12. Alexander Altmann, "Franz Rosenzweig and Eugen Rosenstock-Huessy," *Journal of Religion,* Oct. 1944, p. 161. Also cf. Harold Stahmer, *Speak That I May See,* New York, 1968, 152.

13. *Briefe,* 71–72; Stahmer, 152.

14. Altmann, loc. cit., 261f; Stahmer, op. cit., 153.

15. Glatzer, op. cit., 25.

16. Mrs. Rudolf Hallo, the widow of Rosenzweig's distinguished colleague at the *Lehrhaus,* confined to me that when her husband sought to return to Judaism after his own disenchantment it was to the same Berlin synagogue that Rosenzweig took him for the Day of Atonement.

17. *Briefe,* 71.

18. Ludwig Wittgenstein, *Tractatus LogicoPhilosophicus,* London, 1933, 189.

Martin Buber and Judaism

Death seals with finality even the most fluent tongues, but death only begins the work of silence. Posterity accomplishes what death has begun: passing the whole work in review, determining what is enduring, what insubstantial, what lives beyond the reinforcement and polemic of the life and what dies with the death itself. So it has come to Martin Buber, the centenary of whose birth is recalled. His mouth was stopped by death and so for more than a decade has been the resonation of his work. Never particularly popular among his own constituency, always more highly regarded by others than by his own Jews, he was nonetheless one of the most influential Jews of our time. It was he, as much as any other, who gave initiative and vitality to the cultural and spiritual Zionism of the early part of this century and it was his writings and discourses prior to the First World War which motivated young Jews of Western Europe—principally the constituency of German-speaking Jews—to reinvest the enterprise of Jewish life with a significance and value which the ideology of assimilation had virtually denied it. He was a moving and evocative rhetorician, a stylist who mastered cadence and interval, whose dress and gesture were as carefully chosen as his language. He was an immensity

Leo Baeck Institute Yearbook 25 (1980). Reprinted by courtesy of the Yearbook of the Leo Baeck Institute and its editor (1970–1992), Dr. Arnold Paucker.

and a presence. Any who knew him could not forget him; however, to retain his person in memory is not the same as to read him, to study him, to be transformed or converted by his work. It is the work rather more than the presence which has effected the eclipse of his reputation since his death and which augurs a restoration to life of that part of his reputation which deserves to endure.

I

What then is alive and what is dead in Martin Buber's conception of Judaism? To determine this with any degree of credibility requires that I first take a stand respecting the measure, the criterion by which contemporary Jewish intelligence approaches and passes judgment on its past.

The generation of German Jews which came to maturity during the first two decades of the century was (to the extent that it was Jewishly self-aware) molded by the Enlightenment and the Emancipation, either enmeshed and snarled by the illusion of German receptivity and cultural accommodation or else critically self-distanced by the recognition that the lines of intellectual influence went more directly from the Jewish philosophers of the *Aufklärung* to Hermann Cohen's virtual identification of German humanism and Jewish prophetism than it did to mystical epistemologists like Franz Rosenzweig, apocalyptic litterateurs like Walter Benjamin, or revisionist historians like Gershom Scholem. I have no doubt any longer that the Enlightenment and Emancipation as it unfolded—not in its essential conviction, but in his historical ideology— devastated the vitality and interior certitude of Western European Jewry, depriving it of both spontaneity and continuity, while successfully persuading it that the gains were greater than the cost.

The initial impulse of Martin Buber's return to Jewry, signaled by his youthful Zionism, his turning away from the Stefan George *Kreis,* his critical volte face from Nietzsche (whose *Thus Spake Zarathustra* he had translated into Polish as a young man) was no simple crisis of assimilation. I have always been immensely curious about Buber's childhood and youth—although available information regarding his youth in the home of his paternal grandfather Salomon Buber is lean and not quite persuasive.[1] Buber was raised in Galicia. He was by natal determination a Polish Jew, an *Ostjude.* Although he knew German early, he also knew Polish, Yiddish, and, of course, Hebrew, which he had mastered as a young boy, studying Bible and *Midrash* under the aegis of his eminent grandfather. It is the case, however, as Buber attested in a famous letter to Franz Rosenzweig,[2] that shortly after his bar mitzvah he ceased all formal religious observance, never being seen even once, as Scholem noted with some amazement, in any Jerusalem synagogue during the thirty years of his residence in Israel.[3] And yet, after a period of seven years, during which he wrote poetry, read Nietzsche and Schopenhauer, absorbed the somewhat hothouse atmosphere of prewar Vienna romanticism, he returned not to religious Judaism but to Zionism, not to a Zionism of territory, but to a Zionism of holy space. Deriving much impetus from the work of Ahad Ha'am, with whom Buber was in communication, the framework of his Zionist formulation derived in considerable measure from heating up, inflaming so to speak, the rationalist assumptions of Ahad Ha'am's cultural Zionism,[4] driving those assumptions from their grounding in Jehudah Ha'Levi's concept of Israel as "supernation" and Maimonides' rational nation to occupy inellectual territory which he reclaimed from a transformational reading of Nietzsche, Feuerbach, Dilthey, and Simmel, all of whom had sought to reconstitute the image of the whole person, the healthy spirit, the integrated man whose life is openness, whose medium is spontaneity and truthfulness, whose goal is relationship.

The diagnosis of the ailing Jew that Buber proposed in his famous Prague lectures of 1909–1911 I entailed a series of critical estimations and judgments, which despite numerous refinements and alterations, remained virtually unchanged throughout his life.[5] The Jew was, in his view, a fractured spirit—vulnerable to the assumptions of bourgeois optimism, European materialism, cultural deracination. Whatever the gifts and talents of the Jew, they had been placed at the service of a world which at best manipulated them advantageously and at worst corrupted them. In such a view, the Jew was merely a shadow of himself, a spectral presence that reminded and underscored his intrinsic marginality and historical irrelevance. And yet, Buber reminded his hearers, the Jew of the present had deeper roots than those he had sunk in the shallow soil of Western culture. Those roots were the existential substratum of his contemporary predicament, for hard as he might try to evade the biblical past, the Jewish historical travail, or the arena of the mystical tradition, which effected their translation into the intimacy and directness of ordinary life, he was still their creature. Western culture—precisely the same Western culture—owed a profound debt to exactly the Jewish roots the Jew was trying to cut away. Buber's polemic in these lectures was profound and shattering. It is a justifiable contention that these *Drei Reden über das Judentum* were the single most impressive document of Jewish renewal in the fading years of Wilhelminian German culture. Buber called for renewal—an honest recognition of the free spirituality of Jewish sources, a search for the natural ethos of Jewish self-integration, culminating in a call for the establishment of a Jewish spiritual center in the renewed land of Zion.

At that juncture in Jewish history, Buber's was a perfectly plausible dialectic of rejoining the Jew to the Jewish community. Although Buber, already at this early date, had begun to inveigh against the petrifactions of orthodoxy, the dry-as-dust Talmudism of the schools, the weary attention to the details of Jewish mundaneness, it was an antinomianism less objectionable to disaffected young Jews than was the stern literalism of Jewish Orthodoxy. It worked, and worked profoundly. New centers of Jewish study were convened, new leaders made their appearance, Jewish books were published, the *Jüdischer Verlag* was founded by Buber and his associates, lectures and symposia multiplied, and it became clear, as we now recognize, that the solid strength of the first significant aliyah of German-Jewish intellectuals, teachers and converts from the bourgeoisie, was made ready to leave for Palestine in the aftermath of the First World War.

No one denies to Buber the preeminence of his leadership in this period. He was the inspired publicist of Jewish renewal, documenting that renewal by the evolution of his own intellectual materials—moving as he did from the translation and editing of Christian and Eastern mystics to those of Hasidism, leaving behind Jakob Böhme, Meister Eckardt, Nicolas of Cusa, Lao-Tzu, for his famous compendia of Hasidic tales, retellings and reworkings which enabled him to extend to Hasidic sources a cultural imprimatur already stamped by him upon materials of the international religious spirit. It was as though Buber had found in an authentic Jewish source the exemplification of personal preferenes which enabled him to persevere as a Jew, not only without ressentiment, but with joyful celebration. The fact that his reading of Hasidic sources has been virtually destroyed by the critiques of Scholem and others,[6] who have shown that his view of Hasidism as uninfluenced by the Kabbalah unformed by traditional normative Judaism, and disengaged from eschatological and apocalyptic interests is on all three counts false, does not detract from the invincible charm, tenderness, and love with which Buber recounted the Hasidic tales, infecting them with his own self-enchantment while encouraging all the Hasidic masters to sound finally like Buberians. Scholem's own confrontation with Buber on this point late in is life echoes a particular kind of horror and pathos, for all that Buber could say to Scholem's critique was that a whole life—his own—had been wasted on his misreadings if Scholem were correct.[7] It was a not untypical response and one, coupled with others that Buber has naively recounted, which discloses a disappointing streak in Buber's character, healthy pride verging on the illusion of omniscience.

II

The outbreak of the First World War marked a stasis in the development of Buber's thinking about the Jew and Jewish destiny. He was bonded to a formulation of personal religious enterprise in which the principal distinctions of his argument marked off the creative from the formed, the productive and future-orientated from the dead past, the history of Jewish Diaspora as one of alienation, timorousness, and capitulation, and the new future in Zion as one which augured new beginnings, the recovery of deeper realities, the meeting with God on an ancient soil that nonetheless remained eternally young. He had, to his view, succeeded in formulating his primordial Judaism—a Judaism not of essence, but of eruption; not of constituted forms, but of continuously fresh and innovative outburst and encounter. The Buber of the prewar period had employed a vocabulary assumed from German philosophy and mysticism and carried it with him like a bronze mirror into the dark places of his Jewish past, where whatever buried light it contained would flash upon its burnished surface, illuminating resemblances and corroborations. Buber knew what he wished to find in Judaism even before he had undertaken the search. What he found he always knew existed. It was there awaiting only his bidding to be renewed, as though the magic words were his and the resting princess of the ages needed only to hear those words to come alive once more. The vocabulary was already described in the *Drei Reden,* but as well in his little mystical tractate, *Daniel* (1913), and no less elaborated in his early writings on Hasidism.

Judaism was not a history of unfolding and emergence; nor a history of unresolved tension between internal dialectic and obdurate reality, between the wish for reasonableness and the passion for prophecy; nor between the stubborn givenness of the Law and the spinning dreams of the imagination, but rather a permanent state of warfare between the settled, the conventional, the organized, the institutional, the law and the administration of law, the priests, legists, and rabbis and the Jewish underground, the heretical, the spontaneous, the untrammeled and unconfined, the aggadists and storytellers, the mythomane and the mystic. With such a view it is no wonder that Buber's reading of Jewish history should have but few mountain tops, few valleys, and endless plains, flat and arid, under continuous cultivation but producing stunted and crimped crops. The peaks were the prophets, the kings of Israel, Jesus of

Nazareth, and, with ambivalence, kabbalists and Hasidim; the valleys were the gnostics and the demonic antinomians, Sabbatai Zwi, Jakob Frank, and Spinoza, and the plains, those endless plains, the ordinary history of Jewish traditionalism and endurance. Clearly a personal, an uncompromisingly personal, reading of Jewish history and one which, not surprisingly, received a more affectionate response from non-Jewish readers than from Jews. It was a reading which treated Jewish belief not as a continuity of tradition whose sense of *kehillah* and unity arose not from the common travail of survival and the shared espousal of a historical faith, but from the wish to achieve an enriched personal identity, an exalted experience of personal value and meaning.

Buber's appeal in the days before the First World War is easily understood against the background of the Wilhelminian German bourgeoisie. That age—drearily conservative, patriotic, smug and self-assured—found many Jews ill-at-ease with a historical faith which employed an ancient liturgy and custom, a foreign language, a bond of suffering coupled with the grim and often despairing historiography of *Wisenschaft des Judentums*. It was no wonder that Jews ran from Judaism, but it is no less a source of wonderment that they ran to German *Kultur*. Buber's critique both of bourgeois Western culture on the one hand, and the polemics of German Orthodoxy and Reform on the other, in the interest of an integral cultural Zionism of self-discovery and creativity struck home. It was a critique which elicited response precisely as long as the teacher was able to maintain the coherence of his teaching and the clarity of his acts. It was a teaching held together by the power of the teacher, by the authenticity of his word and deed.

The First World War and its aftermath and Buber's interpretation of both had a shattering effect upon that coherence. In the opening issue of *Der Jude,* which Buber founded in 1916,[8] there appears the first of many editorials which were to be published over the next eighteen months in which Buber gave his support to the war and the justification of its being fought to victory by the German *Volk*. Buber's arguments—in measure limned by Hermann Cohen's no less distraught essays on *Deutschtum and Judentum*—turn on the conviction of the mighty authority of German culture and the sense of its beleaguerment by Anglo-French civilization.[9] How Buber managed to construe support for the war as part of the legitimate espousal of *Der Jude* remains something of a mystery since in all other respects that remarkable periodical maintained an aloofness to the world beyond Jewry and Jewish preoccupations. Nonetheless it is the case that Buber wrote in September 1914 in a recently uncovered letter to Hans Kohn:

Never has the concept of *Volk* been such a reality for me as during the last weeks. A sincere and great feeling also prevails among the Jews. Among the millions who have volunteered were Karl Wolfskehl and Friedrich Gundolf . . . I myself, alas, have no prospect of being accepted; but in my own way I shall try to contribute. . . . Addressed to anyone willing to accommodate himself to these times are the words of John: "He that loveth his life shall lose it." If we Jews really felt, thoroughly felt, what this means then we would no longer need our ancient motto: "Not by might, but by spirit"—might *(Kraft)* and spirit *(Geist)* would become one. *Incipit vita nova.*[10]

What is remarkable about this passage and the subsequent argument which broke out between himself and his socialist mentor, the remarkably heroic Gustav Landauer, is that Buber employed the whole of his *Erlebnis* mysticism to underscore his reading of the war. The war binds Jews together in a transcendent cause and even though (as he acknowledged) Jews face each other over the trenches and indeed kill each other, their mutual suicide is justified by the fact that they are living real life, avoiding shadow life and insubstantiality, but sharing the challenge of a consummated risk. Although Buber tried to keep himself distant from a simple racism, from mere patriotic jingoism, anybody examining the letters and documents of the period will find that Buber carries to war the doctrine of his *Daniel,* turning such passages as, "the nameless spark . . . through which the deed from being the experience *(Erlebuis)* of an individual becomes an event given to all," into a justification of the combat.[11] Precisely this language of sparks which ignites the kinesis of which Buber talks frequently in *Daniel* (to transcribe the movment from potentiality to act) dominates his political journalism of the period. How Buber could have argued in "Die Losung" (The Watchword)[12] that despite the fact that Jews kill each other, "they are nonetheless fighting for their Jewishness," remains something of a mystery, although it is absolutely coherent with the predominant vagueness of his metaphysical thinking. Buber is always, to my mind, magnificent when he is interpreting a text, for one can then perceive the matrix against which the scalpel rubs—there is something to compare with the exegesis. But when Buber tries to lift from himself and others the incubus of bourgeois morality, by holding onto the bars of abstraction as he ascends the ladder toward the transcendent, he continuously risks a disappearance into abstract cant and ecstatic effusion. It is no wonder that when Landauer replied furiously to Buber's editorial, Buber claimed that he was misunderstood. Landauer disdained this new person—"der Kriegsbuber"[13]—the "war Buber," as he called him—and particularly attacked Buber's famous lecture on "The Spirit of the Orient and Judaism,"[14] claiming that its attempt to link the creative power of the ancient world with the contemporary German is flagrant and wholly unjustified nationalism.

Buber rethought his war years' doctrine, recognizing that there was a dangerous and corrupting link between his Erlebnis-mysticism and nationalism which demanded revision. It came after the war. Moreover it saved the moral credibility of Der Jude and cleansed in some measure Buber's own tarnished reputation. But that revisionism—the re-editing of certain of Buber's books to remove offending passages and the shift in Buber's teaching from Erlebnis to Begegnung mysticism and the philosophy of dialogue only served to shift doctrinal emphasis, to clarify and make explicit dimensions of Buber's philosophic doctrine which had been made obscure by his first wartime attempt to give it concrete application. The fact is that in the aftermath of the war when it might have been thought the time had come to put behind him the hated Diaspora, the desiccated Jewry of the alien exile and turn toward Zion redivivus, Buber—who had trained his generation—stayed behind. It is easy to understand why Buber stayed behind from 1933 to 1938, but it is difficult to understand why this early and progenitive Zionist inspired others to leave while he elected to remain another generation.

III

The publication in 1923 of Buber's most famous and undoubtedly least read work, I and Thou, marks a significant advance in his emergence from the murky teachings of Daniel—teachings which had prompted the linguistic theorist, Fritz Mauthner, to describe the Buber of those years as an "atheistic Zionist,"[15] intending by this acute and not wholly untrue assertion that the grounds of Buber's mysticism were not God nor any theologically grounded teaching, but rather a conception of the polarity and struggle which each person reflects in his coming into relation with the world and otherness. Each individual, in Buber's Erlebnis mysticism, either orientates himself to the world, mastering the means of manipulating the real by constraining it with laws of order and institutions of control or else, by the modes of actualization (or Verwirklichung—realization), effects a seizing of that unity which removes duality, partitiveness, the split character of things. The cognitive intuition of this early mysticism of experience—that all things are manifest in separateness, but that the world is finally one and that only through a descent and submersion into that unity is the fracture of the world mended—is a teaching which can be held without a divinity. It is akin to a Zen insight, a wisdom of healing and reconciliation which requires no God, no creation nor revelation, redemption into the unity of actualization being sufficient.

It was a weak teaching for Jews precisely because there was nothing remarkably or palpably Jewish in its presentation. Although it was reinforced by his early telling of the Hasidic tales, Buber had in this early work succumbed to the temptation of all wise men, which is to imagine that wisdom is general, indeed universal, stripped of the skin of particularity which marks any specific wisdom as having antecedents and sources that make for the discrimination of Jewish, Christian, or Zen truth in precisely the same way that it makes for Jewish, Christian, or Zen mysticism, rather than mysticism in general. Methodologically it was a shallow doctrine; metaphysically it produced more confusion— particularly as Buber manipulated its language during the war years— and needed to be superseded. It is this supersession he believed he had accomplished in *I and Thou,* a work which no longer turns on the explicit usage of *Erlebnis,* but transfers from epistemology to ontology the basic categories of his teaching, shifting the language from fluidities of perception and cognition to fundamental attitudes of being. Man is the creature who can address the world with two modes of speech—he can construct the world as an It, reifying nature and persons in such a way as to manage and contain them, draining them of life, compelling them to submit, or else as a Thou, wholly present in meeting, fully acknowledged and regarded. Every man is possessed of this twofold attitude toward the world, but the inborn Thou of every creature is now grounded in the eternal and unconditioned Thou of God and the It of the world is now the silence of nature. This short work, full of difficulties and compelling formulations, stands every test of time as a work endlessly suggestive, drawing together lines of reflection and argumentation which had preoccupied the German tradition from Schelling, Hamann, and others to Rosenstock-Huessy and Ferdinand Ebner, while no less attempting to effect through the life of dialogue a response to the despair of Kierkegaard.[16]

The rhythm of Buber's work reached a metric evenness with *I and Thou* and from that work to the end of his life, each new book and each new reworking of an old book was a continuous effort to make the materials of historical faith and traditional belief cohere with his intuition or else be cast to the sidelines of life and relevance. For a thinker who had, throughout his life, maintained an ambivalent connection with the mysterious and the wonderful, Buber's thought allowed for precious little that was unresolved, whose essence remained unplumbed, for the mystery that appeared simply, nakedly, and without interpretation.

It is absolutely logical that with the completion of *I and Thou,* Buber was armed with the means of interpreting Judaism and the Jewish world. The life of dialogue originated preeminently with ancient Israel for "Israel has understood—or rather, lived—life as being-spoken-to and answering, speaking-to and receiving answers."[17] The God of monotheism is a divinity translucent in all things. Whereas the pagan makes of each thing he grasps a little god, dividing the world into small principalities of power, the ancient Hebrew saw through all things to the eternal Thou that is its source. The eternal Thou, above all, is not idea, not a logical premise of our coherence and integrity, but is unitary person, nearing and approaching in dialogue, vanishing and eclipsed by confusion— always Thou, despite the mixed propensity of man to make of Thouness an *objectivum.* From such a criterion, it is possible for Buber to vindicate his critique of historical religion, of Jewish religion most immediately, for the living Thou struggles against the veils by which the hardened spirit of man wishes to conceal him. All ritual, all formal prayer, all law and observance, all institutional structure are human means of keeping the Thou in place, so to speak, under the human thumb.

It is no wonder then that Buber's conception of the creation is notably defective, confined to the analogy of the creative rather than to the exposition of the *bereshit* as such; no less wonder that Buber's doctrine of revelation draws virtually no distinction between the Sinaitic and the prophetic, indeed cannot, precisely because the content of the revelation at Sinai is specific, while the inspiration of the prophet is always the call to turning and renewal. Clearly Buber can impose upon prophetic revelation his pneumatic exegesis more readily because the prophet comes to God with a trained ear—one already familiarized by a history of the People hearing, but Buber's insistence that Mosaic revelation is of the same order, that all revelation is the same, is to mistake what historical religions cannot fail to accredit—that the revelation to the prophets returns the People to its task while the original revelation constitutes the People in the first place and makes known to it its task. The fact is that in Buber's thought it is the ineffaceable human propensity to deafness, to the construction of the world as a hoarding of dead things, to the speech of reification and the fabrication of the It, that conserves for him the hope of redemption and the continuous challenge of conversion and renewal. The speaking of the Thou is a creative apprehension of self-unity and a willingness to open oneself in trust to the world—that therapeutic ontology inspires, heals, and renews. The fractured world of loving service and backsliding, of miscreant kings and provocative prophets, of heart-felt service and stiff-necked prideful disobedience—the systole and diastole of biblical rhythm—leaves open the future of redemption to an ultimate optimism. Buber's doctrine of the Messiah, for me the weakest link in an otherwise thin but delicately wrought chain of argument, is as Scholem has observed from his own impregnable citadel, not "revolutionary" at all.[18] The Messiah is as Buber has written:

> the fulfiller, he who at last fulfills the function of the viceregent, through whose agency the ordering of the people under YHVH's leadership will be realised. He is anointed to set up with human forces and human responsibility the divine order of human community.[19]

The Messiah and the messianic order is linked to creation as its consummation; it is the ontological gloss of creation, that which fills the black holes of creation, ransoming its lostness and deprivation, bringing it to consummation. Messianic Judaism in Buber's view is not defined simply

> by the belief in a unique event at the end of time and in a unique human being as the centre of this event. The certitude of the collaborating force which is accorded to man connected the end of time with present life.[20]

The Messiah completes what each man undertakes to do in the fullness of the Thou.

IV

I cannot hope to have compassed all the relevant aspects of Buber's thinking regarding Judaism. I have specifically omitted discussion of his remarkable work of translation, both of the mystic literature and of the Bible, since my language is not German and I cannot hope to appraise, except at second-hand, what Rosenzweig called the impossible undertaking of translation; nor have I taken issue with Buber's interpretation of the Law and traditional Jewish institutions, since this is better done by those whose commitment to the Law is more complete than mine. I feel myself obliged however to raise a number of critical questions regarding Buber's teaching which are implicit in the exposition I have offered of his principal doctrine. I would like to divide these remarks into three parts: first, a consideration of what I take to be Buber's defective, indeed romantic, notion of evil; second, Buber's refusal of the historical; and third, Buber's religious anarchism.

It is exceedingly difficult to speak of evil in this age and to Jews. And yet to acknowledge this is enough. We are obliged to speak of evil, to understand it as the mountain we cannot scale and to recognize as well that the rock and earth of which it is composed we walk upon no less surely. There is no man who is innocent of evil or its existence, who can speak of it in our time without sickening intimacy, and who, perceiving it, feels nonetheless helpless before its face. The evil is so monstrous. I say all this because I have no intention of challenging Buber's sustained and unbroken doctrine of evil—a mild and I believe pathetic vision—in the aftermath of the holocaustal *tremendum.*[21] Buber did much before the full weight of the axe had fallen. His essay "The Land and Its Possessors," his open "Letter to Gandhi," is a masterpiece of ethical clarification, making clear to the Mahatma what no one else could have dared say, that Gandhi had no understanding of the situation of the Jews of Germany or the Jews of Palestine, that he spoke from the assurance of the soul-power of hundreds of millions and knew nothing of the state of beleaguerment which was that of the minuscule Jewish people.[22] Buber could understand suffering and human pathos, but his notion of evil remained without persuasive substance.

It is clear that Buber's conception of evil must be distinguished from a personalist doctrine of sin. The sinful man projects the *imitatio dei,* but misses it. He strives but turns himself back, falling away from the image before which he stands, repents his sin, and strives once more. This is the condition of ordinary creaturehood before the Lord who projects his will and makes plain his way. But of evil—the turning away from God which is principled and oppository, wholly constrained by a law of otherness and what Kierkegaard has called "shutupness,"[23] Buber takes account, but late account, the concept of evil occupying significant weight in his thinking only after his interpretation of the rebellion of Korah described in his *Moses* (1940) where Korah's repudiation of the humility and instruction of Moses is described by Buber as a demonic misconstruction.[24] We move beyond sin to wickedness, beyond wrongdoing to evil, beyond even miscreancy to the demonic. There is a virtual pressing to the limit of radical evil, but Buber draws back, struggling to maintain the narrow ridge where the dialectic achieves paradoxically, radical evil amenable even at the last to the optimism of redemption. In the volume of essays, *Pointing the Way* (1957), Buber's discussion of Hitler in his essay "People and Leader" declares that Hitler has come forward to assert with finality the condition of "the man without conscience." And even for Hitler Buber has a Jewish analogue, Jakob Frank, who was not simply a wicked man, but incarnate wickedness.[25] This seems, on the face of it, an accounting, a reckoning with the reality of ontological evil, evil which is an order of being, but it suffers in my view, as all of Buber's ontology suffers, from being tied to persons. The personalism holds up the image of the conscienceless man as a modality of instruction—evil, even evil is a pedagogue, pointing the way of ultimate rebellion, warning and guarding those who have in their hearts the mixed imagination of the twin inclinations of ordinary humanity, to do good and to sin, but such a pedagogic intention, however much it is a heroic struggle against dualism, against twin kingdoms of God and the devil, sacrifices too much for the equanimity of a monistic resolution. We are not able any longer to enjoy the ancient luxury of an ultimately victorious divinity.

The array of history—not merely the array of persons—compels us to acknowledge a kingdom of evil fabricated from the lives of inattentive persons. Persons who sin by turning away, by unclarity, by decisionlessness, by protestation of unknowing and innocence—all these innocent sinners of the twentieth century, formed by the unity of terror, by the threat to life which ends without resurrection and consummation beyond death—all these innocents are of the machinery of the kingdom of evil. Substantive evil (that metaphysical constellation) and ontological evil (that metaphysical abstraction) yield place to a demonism which has no place. What we are obliged to recognize (which I am persuaded eludes Buber) is that the reality of evil, its immensity, its capacity to overwhelm, engulf, and transform the innocent into its servant derives from the factuality of historical evil, evil as the kingdom of events, not personal deeds.

History was always for Buber the medium by which myth is echoed through the ages—its outer shell is the constellation of persons and events, actions and upheavals, but its interior meaning is to be limned through the predominant and formative mytos of culture. Biblical mythos is supervenient to history, supplying it with its implicative significance because it affords each historical witness with the criterion by which to appraise its meaning and self-referential relevance. History is then part of the dialogue between man and God—it is, despite its obvious circumstantiality, always of the portion of *Heilgeschichte,* endlessly inseminated with the divine, aborted, and come to birth, but always the medium through which God and man meet.

> What we are permitted to know of history comes to this: "This in one way or another, is history's challenge to me; this is its claim on me; and so this is its meaning as far as I am concerned." This meaning, however, is not "subjective" . . . It is the meaning I perceive, experience, and hear in reality . . . It is only with my personal life that I am able to catch the meaning of history, for it is a dialogical meaning."[26]

The predicament of such a treatment of history is that the historical as such is never as real as what it conceals and echoes. The murder is not simply murder but meaning; the devastation of nations and peoples, not simply that, but also an echoing of ancient trials and turbulence. Such a view of history makes it impossible to deal with the historical as such, for it lends itself too readily to a kind of reflexivity and pacifism, a modus of patient hearing and awaiting, until the right hour for each man, the right moment for the deed. Buber insists that his doctrine of history is not subjective, but the charge of subjectivism with which he dealt all his life and which he never succeeded in dispelling holds here as well. The charge of subjectivism is in one sense unfair, since objectivity is a robber of human passion and commitment which the real requires ever as much as it requires clarity and precision. Objectivity, subjectivity—these are the obligatory terms of argumentation. The dialectic of persons and events requires that judgment catch hold of the publicly received and held as much as it succors its roots in the internal life of understanding. The difficulty of Buber's teaching on the nature of history is that the inner core of history, its echo of the archetypal myth and its resonation within the continuous hearing of man, leaves history without a criterion by which to appraise its unfolding. History stretches from creation to redemption. It has no center. Its center is everywhere that a man stands open before it. Revelation is no center for Buber, since revelation to become a fixed center must have meaning and content, but as Buber had stated repeatedly, the content of revelation is within the *vaydeber* and not within the *naaseh v'nishma*. God reveals in speech, but what God says is altered by the hearing. The Thou is always Thou, but manifests itself differently to each I. There is no permanent I; there is only eternal Thou. History can have no center but the promise, no guideland and hence no *ceasura,* no Thou shalt, only Thou.

It is against this background that one may speak of Buber's religious anarchism, a criticism leveled most ardently and profoundly by Gershom Scholem, whose knowledge of anarchism is no less intimate than Buber's, although it takes its point of departure from a different manifestation of the religious reality.[27] And is religious anarchism a criticism? There are many today who would regard Judaism as overdefined, overlegislated, overparticularized, for whom shattering the shells of historical incrustation would be a service, not a defect. In part I would share with them, feeling often that it would be best if Judaism were to enjoy an age underground, bonded to heretical enquiry and dangerous speculation, but I would recognize nonetheless that it demanded no less a clear and responsible reading of its public, historical manifestation. Buber is surely wrong in thinking that the best ages of Judaism were when everything was being sown and nothing reaped. Surely reaping, that is consolidating and holding fast, making the way straight and safe, is as indispensable as the endangering enterprise of those who dare to face the abyss and do not shrink from its vastness and its threat. Buber was all too comfortable on the mountain peaks, alone with the eagles, when most of us are obliged to live not in the cracks, but in open spaces, the flat plain of history where the prayer of the ordinary, the candles and *kiddushim* and fasts of ordinary Jews are recognized for what they are—holding the sane center of tradition. Buber was all too often contemptuous of the simple way, thinking of the center as a narrow ridge between paradoxicalities. The center is, in truth, a large, broad, and grand highway of immense way stations and spiritual hostels, while beneath the beating hooves that bear us from life to death, it is natural that pebbles, rocks, a multitude of pedestrian obstacles require the endless effort of surmounting. The anarchism of Buber's religious thinking is a measure of its vision and its intolerance—its celebration of dialogue and its hostility to those who would speak through other's words and texts, through the history of descents to ordinariness as well as the climbing to the peaks.

Martin Buber was a romantic pedagogue fated to be misunderstood and misconstrued, while he talked ceaselessly to his people, making his word and the sequence of his books into the tradition by which his own anarchy would become code and be transmitted. He was not content with leaving a gnomic work, a single document, nor was he satisfied to say as another said, *"Into Life"* at the conclusion of his solitary theological preamble. Rather Buber thought of his teaching as healing doctrine, a modus of therapy by which broken spirits would be made whole, Jewish broken spirits, but also Christian broken spirits, for Buber spoke not from the center of Judaism, but Judaism was at his center; he spoke not out of being a Jew, but being a Jew was contained by him. He was larger than what he was able to teach and so he taught over and over again in the effort to fill his own lineaments. His person and his presence exceeded his word, however much he would have wished the word to echo within the narrow determination of person. This complexity ensures that insofar as Buber addresses the human spirit which may be Jewish he will endure, but insofar as he addresses the Jew as Jew, he must be constantly revised or qualified, or forgotten.

NOTES

1. Buber, who was not reticent about the currents that bathed his intellectual and spiritual growth, obviously confided little to his first biographer, Hans Kohn. There is scant reference

to his parents, his reminiscence of them and their divorce, or his youth in the household of his paternal grandfather, Salomon Buber. The awe and respect Buber felt toward his grandparents is palpable in the few letters he addressed to them (cf. *Martin Buber. Briefwechsel aus sieben Jahrzehnten*, I, 1897–1918. Heidelberg 1972, 152, and the moving letter to Salomon Buber of 31 January 1900, 153–54), but one feels deprived of an intellectual autobiography of those lonely Galician years. Cf. Hans Kohn, *Martin Buber. Sein Werk und seine Zeit*, Hellerau 1930, "Ursprunge," 13–18.

2. *Martin Buber. Briefwechsel aus sieben Jahrzehnten*, II, 1918–38, 141. Cf. also Gershom Scholem, "Martin Buber's Conception of Judaism," *On Jews and Judaism in Crisis*, New York, 1976, particularly 133–34 for discussion of Buber's views of *halakhah* in the light of his biography.

3. Gershom Scholem, "Martin Buber's Conception of Judaism," loc. cit., 129, although several lifelong Jerusalemites whom I have consulted contest this statement, they are hard-pressed to recollect more than one occasion on which they observed Buber in a synagogue.

4. The earliest recorded contact between Ahad Ha'am (Asher Ginzburg) and Buber appears in their correspondence where Ahad Ha'am writes to Buber from Odessa during July 1903. Obviously Buber's Zionism was formed of several elements, not the least being the personal influence of Herzl and Weizmann, but its intellectual stimulation derives in greatest measure from Moses Hess and Ahad Ha'am as Kohn indicates (*Martin Buber. Sein Werk und seine Zeit*, 14–16, also 43–45).

5. Martin Buber. *On Judaism*, Nahum N. Glatzer, ed. New York, 1967, which contains Eva Jospe's trans. of *Die Drei Reden über das Judentum* according to the revised text of 1923. It contains as well Buber's controversial essays, *Vom Geist der Judentums*, Leipzig 1916.

6. Gershom Scholem, "Martin Buber's Interpretation of Hasidism," *The Messianic Idea in Judaism*, New York 1971, 227–50. Also Scholem's essay, "Martin Buber's Conception of Judaism," loc cit. As well, note Jerome Mintz's modest footnote in his *Legends of the Hasidim*, Chicago 1968, 2 n. 4.

7. "If what you are now saying were right, my dear Scholem, then I would have worked on Hasidism for forty years absolutely in vain, because in that case, Hasidism does not *interest* me at all." Gershom Scholem, "Martin Buber's Conception of Judaism," loc. cit., 166–67.

8. Originally conceived by Buber as a project to be undertaken by himself and Weitzmann in 1902 (the original propectus for *Der Jude* appears in Hans Kohn, *Martin Buber, Sein Werk ud seine Zeit*, 296–300), it appeared under Buber's editorship as a monthly from 1916 to March 1924 when Buber relinquished editorship to a board. It was published thereafter as a series of *Sonderhefte*, concluding in 1928 with the publication of an issue consecrated to honoring Buber's fiftieth birthday. Cf. the author's introductory essay to *The Jew: Essays from Martin Buber's Journal Der Jude (1916–1928)*, University of Alabama Press, 1980.

9. Hermann Cohen's *Deutschtum und Judetum* appeared in two installments during 1915 and 1916 and is included in *Hermann Cohen's Jüdische Schriften*, Bruno Straus, ed., Berlin, 1924, II, 237–318. A small selection from Cohen's essay, trans. by Eva Jospe, appears in *Reason and Hope, Selections from the Jewish Writings of Hermann Cohen*, New York 1917, 176–89. Jacob Klatzkin's extended reply to Hermann Cohen, published in *Der Jude* (II, 245–52, 358–70) appears in trans. in my reader, *The Jew. Essays from Martin Buber's Journal Der Jude (1916–1928)*.

10. Paul Robert Flohr. *From Kulturpolitik to Dialogue. An Inquiry into the Formation of Martin Buber's Philosophy of I and Thou*. Ph.D. diss., Ann Arbor 1974, 136; also 206 n. 2. Flohr discovered the letter in the Jerusalem Martin Buber Archive, 376/1 (Correspondence between Martin Buber and Hans Kohn, September 30, 1914).

11. Martin Buber, *Daniel, Dialogues on Realization*. Translated, with an introduction by Maurice Friedman, New York, 1964, 115 (with minor editorial modifications).

12. Martin Buber, "Die Losung," *Der Jude*, I, Heft I (April 1916): 2.

13. Martin Buber, *Briefwechsel aus sieben Jahrzehnten*, 1897–1918, I, Letter No. 306, 433–

38. Cf. as well the excellent discussion of the controversy and its aftermath in Paul Robert Flohr, *From Kulturpolitik to Dialogue,* op. cit., 143–49.

14. Martin Buber, "The Spirit of the Orient and Judaism," *On Judaism,* 56–78.

15. Cited by Scholem in his essay, "Martin Buber's Conception of Judaism," loc. cit., 149. It is quoted by Scholem from a letter of Mauthner's included in Gershon Weiler's essay, "Fritz Mauthner. A Study in Jewish Self-Rejection," in *LBI Year Book VIII* (1963), 147.

16. Cf. Harold Stahmer's important study, *"Speak that I may See." The Religious Significance of Language,* New York 1968, were the theories of Hamann, Rosenstock-Huessy, Rosenzweig, Buber, and Ebner are carefully examined.

17. Martin Buber, "Spinoza, Sabbatai Zevi and the Baal Shem," *Hasidism,* New York 1948, 95.

18. The controversy between Scholem and Buber is set forth by Scholem in "The Neutralization of the Messianic Element in Early Hasidism," *The Messianic Idea in Judaism and Other Essays on Jewish Spirituality,* New York 1971, 176–202. Cf. also the discussion of the controversy in David Biale's important book, *Gershom Scholem, Kabbalah and Counter-History,* Cambridge 1979, 148–70. Also, Scholem, "Martin Buber's Conception of Judaism," loc. cit., 160–61.

19. Martin Buber, *The Prophetic Faith,* New York 1949, 153.

20. Martin Buber, "Spinoza, Sabbatai Zevi and the Baal Shem," *Hasidism,* 112f.

21. I first used the term *tremendum* to evoke the Holocaust in my lecture, *Thinking the Tremendum. Some Theological Implications of the Death-Camps.* The Leo Baeck Memorial Lecture 18, New York 1974. The term has been employed by me as indicative of a fundamental ontological structure in the lectures given at Brown University during April 1979, to be published under the title, *The Holocaust as Tremendum,* New York: Seabury Press, 1981.

22. Martin Buber, "The Land and Its Possessors," an extract from Buber's reply to the criticism of Jewish claims in Palestine put forward by Mahatma Gandhi. *Israel and the World,* New York 1948, 227–33. The full text appears in Martin Buber's *Pointing the Way,* New York 1957, "A Letter to Gandhi (1939)," 139–47.

23. Sören Kierkegaard, *The Concept of Dread,* Princeton 1944, 110ff.

24. Martin Buber, *Moses,* London 1946, "The Contradiction," 182–90.

25. Martin Buber, *Pointing the Way,* 148–60.

26. Martin Buber, *Israel and the World,* 78–82.

27. "To put it bluntly, Buber is a religious anarchist and his teaching is religious anarchism." Gershom Scholem, "Martin Buber's Interpretation of Hasidism," loc. cit., 245. As well see the discussion of Scholem's own religious anarchism in David Biale, *Gershom Scholem. Kabbalah and Counter-History,* 94–100, *passim.*

III.

JUDAISM AND CHRISTIANITY

Introduction

Paul Mendes-Flohr

Franz Rosenzweig once remarked that he preferred the medieval theological *disputatio* to contemporary interfaith dialogue. The former, which pitted reluctant representatives of a beleaguered Jewry against Christian clerics in debate about doctrines that divided their respective faith communities, were at least substantive and often brutally honest. Interfaith dialogue, however, for the sake of engendering good feelings and liberal consensus is theologically vacuous, the lines of division tidily ignored or camouflaged. But the theological differences between Jew and Christian, Rosenzweig contended, are ever so real; the challenge to both Jew and Christian is to confirm each other's humanity while holding firm to the faith-experience that divides them, and indeed must.

Cohen endorsed this position. He concurred with Rosenzweig that the well-intentioned but ultimately ephemeral emotions produced by liberal discourse do little to heal the scars wrought by the bitter experiences of the past; that the studied avoidance of theological and doctrinal disagreement hardly serves to remove misunderstanding. Cohen also concurred with Rosenzweig that, despite the humane concerns prompting the liberal conception of interfaith understanding, it hardly dignifies the humanity of the Jew and Christian, for it denies or minimizes the essential ground of their humanity, namely their respective faith commitments. "In the century of emancipation," Rosenzweig once observed, "the Christian ignored the Jew in order to be able to tolerate him, the Jew ignored the Christian in order to allow himself to be tolerated." The sorry consequences of such a studied indifference were manifest not only in its failure to remove the trammels of mistrust and enmity, but also because it often encouraged the Christian and Jew alike to regard Judaism as a hindrance to the Jew's humanity.

Accordingly, Cohen was intrigued and inspired by Rosenzweig's courage to declare unabashedly that, from a Jewish perspective, Christianity is ultimately based on a "fiction," and that if necessary the Jews would crucify Christ again. As Cohen pointed out, this was not an admission to the canard of historical guilt for the crucifixion. Rather, it was a bold and proud assertion that there were real and profound theological issues that separate Jew and Christian, and that the Jew was obliged to oppose—passionately and unhesitantly—Christian claims. Such considerations emboldened Cohen to stand virtually alone and declaim the fashionable reference in American discourse to the so-called Judeo-Christian tradition.

Cohen's initial offensive against this putative "tradition" came in an essay of 1958, "The Jewish-Christian Contradiction," the first selection in this section. He developed this critique more fully a decade later in his famous polemical article, "The Myth of the Judeo-Christian Tradition," in which he traced the history of the idea of this alleged tradition from its roots in the Enlightenment to the present, when it had been self-consciously revived in the wake of the Holocaust with the intention of distancing Christianity from the tragic events of those years. By invoking a *tradition* of concerns and sensibilities supposedly shared by Jews and Christians, the painful memories of Christianity's ancient enmity toward Israel were conveniently erased. Ever eager to gain acceptance, Jews quickly adopted the "myth of a Judeo-Christian tradition." This exercise in cultural amnesia, Cohen opined, is not only an affront to those who refuse to forget but also to those who take Judaism—and its claims about the nature of existence and human destiny—seriously. Such a Jew can be indifferent neither to Christendom's past mistreatment of Jewry nor to Christianity's fundamentally different views of the meaning of existence and human destiny. The reverse is equally true; Christianity cannot be indifferent to Judaism's contrary claims. "The dialectic is real, the conflict authentic, the historical enmity consequential."

Cohen pointedly appended to this observation a rhetorical question, or rather a plea: "But need the history that comes [as a result of the theological enmity] be as brutal as it has been? Is there not a way of conducting the dialectic of enmity with a passion constrained by human civility . . . , [can we not] confront each other without denying each other's humanity?" He boldly posed this question to his Christian colleagues in the afterword to his essay, "The Holocaust and Christian Theology," in which he delineated what he regarded to be the most exigent issues facing Christianity in the aftermath of the Holocaust. Christianity, he held, must unflinchingly address this question should it succeed, as it urgently must, in reconstructing its relation "not alone to the Jews but all mankind."

Cohen fervently believed that theological differences, indeed, theological enmity, need not diminish our appreciation and solicitation of each other's humanity. Thus, in rejecting what he deemed to be the moral and theological scandal of a Judeo-Christian tradition, Cohen called for affirmation of a "Judeo-Christian humanism"—a humanism that would acknowledge that our humanity may also be expressed in our differences about what the Protestant theologian Paul Tillich called matters of ultimate concern.

THE JEWISH-CHRISTIAN CONTRADICTION

In the ancient Good Friday liturgy of the Catholic Church, in the midst of incessant pleadings for all conditions of men, the following prayer is made: "Let us pray for the unbelieving Jews: that our God and Lord will remove the veil from their hearts, so that they too may acknowledge our Lord Jesus Christ . . . Almighty, eternal God, who does not withhold Thy mercy even from Jewish unbelief, heed the prayers we offer for the blindness of that people, that they may acknowledge the light of Thy truth, which is Christ, and be delivered from their darkness: through the same Lord, Jesus Christ. Amen."

Not alone in receiving the attentive solicitude of the church, the Jews are thus singled out for unique compassion.

Needless to say, I am under no illusion that the Catholic Church would alter its liturgy to conform to the reigning unbelief of contemporary culture. But that she should continue, in this age of "tolerance" and religious disinterest—a time when religion has become increasingly popular as it has become increasingly vulgar—to ask God's mercy on the unbelief of Israel is a fact I find extremely significant.

I find this fact particularly significant in view of the equally pertinent

Worldview 1, no. 2 (February 1958): 3–5. Reprinted by permission of the Carnegie Council on Ethics and International Affairs.

fact that Israel also maintains a liturgy of prayer on behalf of the unbelieving nations of the world. And these presumably include the nations in
Christendom. Two prayers in the liturgy of Judaism come to mind immediately—not prayers attendant upon specific events or crises of faith, but
generaly daily, and repeated prayers.

The former of these prayers affirms that God never rejects His elect,
that He will deliver His people from the midst of nations, that through
Israel's unity the nations will come to worship and glorify Him alone;
while the second prayer, the better-known *Alenu,* reaffirms the conviction
of God's unity and prays that the world will be united under His dominion, that idolatry will wither and pass away, that "the inhabitants of the
world may know and acknowledge that unto Thee every knee must bow,
and every tongue swear; before Thee, O Lord our God they shall kneel
and fall prostrate; and all of them shall willingly submit to the power of
Thy kingdom."

The prayer of Good Friday and the prayers of the synagogue, though
directed to the same unity of belief, are obviously incompatible. And
their incompatibility points toward profound differences between the
Christian and the Jewish approaches to history and world problems.
Where the Christian, with prophetic casuistry, reads Jewish hopes as
having already been fulfilled, the Jew affirms that, pretensions to the
contrary, idolatry persists, the nations are in unbelief, and only at the end
of days will God's elect be fulfilled and history united under the dominion of heaven.

Where Christianity assumes fulfillment, Judaism denies it. Where
Christianity affirms the completion of history (or at least the accomplishment of that instrument whereby history, in God's time, may be completed) Judaism insists upon the open, unqualified, and unredeemed
character of history. In sum, where Christianity asks that Israel remove
its veil, Israel insists that it is only delusion which imagines that the veil
is removed or removable until a true Messiah appears to redeem the time.

These theological differences, fundamental and irreducible, have
been obscured in our day. At first glance it would appear that such obscurity is preferable to the bitter and rancorous relations between Judaism
and Christianity which prevailed in previous centuries. We must, however, draw certain crucial distinctions before we succumb to the goodwill
which dominates the present moment.

Goodwill may be profound or superficial—it may arise from the endless resources of human love or it may be the hypocritical gloss of human
beings who don't care. It is essential to maintain, against the superficiality

of contemporary Judeo-Christian fraternity and brotherhood, the fact that Judaism and Christianity divide profoundly. This division is not repaired by the impermanent cement of sociology or the religious ignorance of contemporary man.

Judaism still asserts that history is not redeemed. Christianity still maintains that it is. This is a fundamental and irreducible disagreement, which divides Judaism and Christianity to the end of time. But this difference is not without consequences for the conduct of world affairs. If the world is unredeemed, there is no normative principle against which to judge world order other than one which takes into account, fully and deeply, the unredeemed character of that order.

The Christ is, from the Jewish point of view, no guide to "the world"—because the Christ vanquishes "the world": "I have overcome the world." In this sense, the anarchism of the *Philokalia,* Father Zossima, and Dorothy Day are of a piece. History—"the world"—exists only to be rejected—it no longer conditions the saved.

The obvious fact that history *does* exist—in spite of the insistence of Christian radicals that its conditions be transcended—is, for the Jew, empirical evidence of a high order that history is not yet marked with the transforming power of the divine. For him, the only principle which can be used to judge history is one which asserts that history is still open—that its time has not come, that however closed from the vantage point of the Creation, it is open from the perspective of its end, consummation, and transfiguration. Where Christianity (in what I take to be its authentic forms) has made the possibility of a new salvation redundant, Judaism must keep it open, because history bears the seed of the true Messiah.

Where Christianity seems to be pessimistic about history, such pessimism is to my mind a betrayal of its own self-definition: there can be no real pessimism if there is a church, a saving act, a divine intervention that has articulated the basis of reuniting fallen man to his source in God. Christianity should be optimistic.

Judaism, on the other hand, which seems imperturbably optimistic (such optimism is a consequence of the incredibly shallow "me-tooism" which characterizes Judaism on the American scene), should be fundamentally pessimistic. Its pessimism arises from the fact that it has two tasks: to call out to the world's smugness and satisfaction, to unsettle history, to probe its idolatries, its arrogance, its sureness, and at the same time to guard against false hope, caution against deceiving apocalypticism, protect its trust from the disillusionment of false messianism.

Judaism has, I would contend, betrayed itself. Such betrayal is, however, neither a new nor a compelling phenomenon in Judaism. The destiny of Israel is self-betrayal and repentance—an endless rhythm of stupid backsliding and regeneration.

Judaism has just passed through a century of backsliding. The transparency of the German-Jewish symbiosis ended in tragedy; the American-Jewish symbiosis (although, God spare us, not yet ended in tragedy) repeats the conspicuous pattern of historical Jewish backsliding. It is no wonder that the Jew should backslide in the Diaspora—for the Jew tends to live in two spheres: one, in which he is bound by supernatural ties that never yield to history or to nature; two, in which he is natural man, subject to the temptations of man—the passion for acceptance, wealth, comfort—all the vulgarity of the human order.

There is unending tension between his natural inclination and his supernatural vocation. The cultural symbiosis that he has forged between Americanism and Judaism is precarious. There is no need to document this. Will Herberg and others have exhibited how tenuous is the adjustment, how narrow the ridge he walks, how yawning the abyss. The natural man dominates; the supernatural vocation is suppressed.

The medieval confrontation of Judaism and Christianity is singularly unbefitting our time. It came to pass under conditions of the most grotesque and contrived caricature. Characteristic of both Catholic and Protestant images of the Jew was the conviction of his living death. The Jew, having died with the advent of Christianity, must be either ghost or devil to survive so persistently. It never crossed the consciousness of Christian theology that the survival and, what is more, the continued development of Judaism had providential significance for the Jew in opposition to Christianity.

The role which Christianity can perform in the face of contemporary Judaism is to revive the tradition of *adversus judaeos*. As I have tried to indicate, there is considerable basis and motivation for the relocation of religious polemics in our day: if Christianity is true it must be urged in the face of Judaism. It cannot, however, be urged as it was in days past. The triumph of Christianity over Judaism in the Middle Ages was a triumph *faute de mieux*. The Jew was the victim to be treated as Christendom chose—one day succored with kindness, the next day thrown to the flames.

Were this possible in our day—and the secular state has not made this completely impossible—it would accomplish as little now as it did then. The classic form of *adversus judaeos* was unhistorical, because it did not recognize the fact that it opposed only a construction, a theological abstraction. How many were the works of Christian apologetics written without the vaguest knowledge of *Jews* or Judaism, fabricated, without historical qualification, out of the ancient and questionable polemics of the Gospels? The *Jew* was little addressed. As the literature indicates, many such apologetic works were written to comfort some unlettered divine who was suffering at the hands of a more skilled Jewish dialectician.

The new form of *adversus judaeo* must meet the crucial question of the Jew: what is the evidence of the world's redemption? Construe evidence as broadly as one will—whether it be the evidence of history or the evidence of the spirit—the Jew remains outside Christianity in the conviction that the redemption of the world is a chimera, that what it promises it does not fulfill.

At this moment in history, religion has been singularly unproductive. Every meeting that I have attended of religious people seeking to articulate bases of common action in a thermonuclear age reduces itself to self-congratulatory platitudes. (I must, in conscience, exclude the seminars of the Church Peace Union, which are remarkably sophisticated, productive, and imaginative.) What becomes clear is that the reach of constructive theology falls short of contemporary events.

Protestantism tends either to talk of peace in terms that would frighten the most ardent Machiavellian or else to replay the record of World War I pacifism; Roman Catholicism strikes me as moving in an atmosphere of moral casuistry—beautifully statistical and well balanced, but utterly remote. Protestantism tends toward either the moral realism of Niebuhr or sentimental pacifism, while Roman Catholicism tends toward an arid rationalism.

The contribution of a revised *adversus judaeos,* or as this is, a *contra christianos,* to the crisis of modern history would lie in the relatively unexplored territory of contemporary statecraft and political theory. There is a prevailing tendency to leave problems of political theory to the experts, whether such experts be professional scholars or professional statesmen. The assumption on which we operate, as Henry Kissinger has observed, is that politics is so totally adventitious that its theory can no longer be articulated.

This assumption demands that human beings trust the prudence of politicians. Having no choice, no control, no principles in terms of which to charge politics with obligations, we abdicate. Needless to say, the willingness to repose confidence in experts creates the preconditions of the authoritarian state. It is evident that the moment the people debar their own intelligence and judgment from competency, they have granted the pretensions of the state to omnipotence and wisdom. We need not delude ourselves, the state—whether democratic or totalitarian by law—will always accept the mantle of omniscience and superior competence. At the lowest level it makes life easier for the state to operate without criticism. There is also a dangerous temptation to carry the egregious burden of statesmanship from simple paternalism to tyranny.

The contention of the Jew in the face of contemporary history is to mistrust its solutions and, in considerable measure, to charge Christianity anew with the burden of proof. If the culture of the West is Christian—as Christopher Dawson, Martin D'Arcy, and other distinguished Catholic theologians assert—there is need to show forth the fabric of that Christianity. If history, however, is shot through with the demonic—as Bultmann, Tillich, and Niebuhr would argue—it must be shown in what sense Christianity functions in the world at all.

If, as the Jews says, history is unfulfilled, and creation is yet open before the end, the Jew has an obligation, perhaps more profound even than that of the Christian, to join issue with history, to ready it for the end. The mere fact that the Jew has no investment in the historical order places upon him, more profoundly, the burden of shaping it.

In essence, my own position is that Jewish messianism does not depend upon the reformation of the temporal order, the transformation of man through extraordinary, but fundamentally terrestrial, means. The crude materialism of early Jewish messianism has been and will continually be purged. It is only the community that can hope to affect society and the state, only the community, preoccupied with the *facta bruta,* not the dialectical abstractions of the human situation, that can hope to affect the total order of power. The community—the family, the religious fellowship, the labor union, to take random examples—alone can hope to restructure primary human relations and ultimately affect the exercise of power.

In the last analysis, however, only the passion of man to seek God and know Him can supply any abiding source of strength wherewith to alter the demonic use of power in history. The turning of history to Him who transcends it comes only by the effort to rethink the foundations on which history and power are based.

Christianity is characterized by hope. Judaism is characterized by trust. The hope that what is believed has come to pass and will be justified is Christian hope. The trust that what is not yet, but is yet readied, will come to pass is Jewish trust. The joining of a fulfilled hope and an unfulfilled trust, in mutual encounter with the obduracy of man and the unyielding order of history, is still to be tried. At this juncture, no advent of community, no opportunity for fresh discovery, can be turned aside by either the Christian or the Jew.

The Myth of the Judeo-Christian Tradition

How can it be that Christianity, regarding itself the successor and completion of Judaism, should have elected to take into itself the body and substance of that Jewish teaching which it believed to be defective, which it regarded itself as having in measure rejected, in measure transformed, in measure repaired and fulfilled? How can it be that Judaism, the precedent in principle and progenitor in history of Christianity, should have remained not only independent of but unassimilated by the doctrinal vision and historical pressure of Christianity?

This is a conundrum, but it is not without solution. Orders of existence can remain contiguous without coalescing, parallel without overlapping. But to speak in this way of Judaism and Christianity is not quite accurate, for terms like contiguity and coalescence properly describe the disposition of objects in space, whereas the essential character of the Jewish and Christian connection is that of a relation in time, and not in time alone but in filled time, time in which events are numbered. History is the medium in which Judaism and Christianity are sustained. There is, therefore, in addition to space *and* time, the nexus of events, priority and succession, formation and influence, human passion and persuasion.

Reprinted from *Commentary* 48, no. 5 (November 1969): 73–77. By permission; all rights reserved.

Jewish and Christian time is impassioned time, time in which destinies are elaborated and consummated. Such time is the time of salvation. Jews and Christians in the first century, Jewish Jews and Jewish Christians, Jewish Jews and Gentile Christians, related less to one another as persons than to one another as bearers of the Word, as legatees and transmitters of saving truth. They could not but regard their simple flesh and their uncomplicated spirits as vessels of the Holy Spirit, the instrumentalities through whom God worked out extraordinary designs and expectations. Theirs was a personalism, but it bore less resemblance to the existential personalism with which we are today familiar than it did to the historical realism of the Bible, in which persons were immanent expressions of the divine-human tension. Biblical anthropology discloses more about God than it does about man. Biblical man, confronting himself, addressed God. He worked by a devious deduction, believing himself to be an extrusion and exemplification of the divine intention, and hence valuing his own action both inordinately and inadequately, for in his behavior he was both the bearer of the ultimate intention of creation and a hopelessly frail, limited, inconsequential thing: thus, the numerous psalms in which man is ranked little lower than the angels and in the same breath derided and derogated. Man was person and paradox—person because God had made each man unique and irreplaceable, and paradox because every man was in himself the crossroads and meeting ground of the failure and distortion of creation.

I say all this to suggest that the Jewish and Christian relation was in ancient times much too serious an engagement to become, as it has become in our time, an assumed tradition. The ancient world expected a redeemer. The Jews expected a redeemer to come out of Zion; Christianity affirmed that a redeemer had come out of Zion, but that he had come not for Israel alone but for all mankind. Judaism denied that claim, rejected the person of that redeemer, called his claim presumption and superarrogation, and denied his mission to them. (Indeed, as the Synoptic Gospels make abundantly clear, Jesus of Nazareth regarded his mission as being first and foremost, if not exclusively, to the Children of Israel, though, as theologians have come to teach us, Jesus did not understand either his own or God's will as well as St. Paul understood both.) That same redeemer, unheard by most of Israel, rejected by its Jerusalemite establishment, was tried as an insurrectionist and brutally slain.

It matters therefore not at all in my view that much of Jewish and Christian doctrine is confluent, for in what does that confluence consist? That Jews and Christians affirm an unconditional, universal, and unique God, single and undifferentiated; that that God is believed to have created man, set him in the midst of an ordered nature, appointed him to a destiny of service and trust, brought near a single people—selected arbitrarily, but nevertheless unambiguously—to be His own and to bring His teaching to all the earth. These affirmations respecting the creation, the covenant of God with His elected people-servant, the revelation of His teaching, and the promise of redemption—these truths, schematic, loose, general, archetypal, connect the vision of Judaism and Christianity. But this connection is a philosophic formulation of what in the order of faith pulsates with irrationality, passion, intensity, sharp disagreement, fissure, and the abyss of historical enmity. I suggest in part therefore that the Judeo-Christian tradition is a construct, an artificial gloss of reason over the swarm of fideist passion. But this, too, is not enough. What is omitted is the sinew and bone of actuality, for where Jews and Christians divide, divide irreparably, is that for Jews the Messiah is yet to come and for Christians he has already come. That is irreparable.

It is true that Jews have made concession to the faith of Christians, acknowledging alternately—with charity or animus—that Christians and Moslems are closer to the purity of the Godhead than are pagans and idol worshipers, but this is only to reaffirm that ultimately Israel, employing the artifacts of Christianity and Islam, will bring all of mankind to the divine teaching of Sinai. It is equally true that intertestamental theology and the early church fathers recognized the force of Israel's refusal of Jesus as the Christ by developing the doctrine of the Second Coming, recognizing as they did that the end of days had not come to pass as promised, that the transformation of time and history anticipated in the immediate aftermath of the Crucifixion had transpired only in the eyes of faith, and that for the public, unconverted eye there could only be the promise and persuasion of the time yet to come when Jesus would return in glory, to consummate Israel, and to reintegrate Israel and the church.

But in the meantime, between the times, between the promise of the synagogue and the promise of the church, what of *those* times? For those times (two thousand years of them have nearly passed), what ensued was mainly the pavanne of death, where faith throttled faith, believer tormented believer, and the impotence of man before the magnitude of his believing overwhelmed mercy and love. We can learn much from the history of Jewish-Christian relations, but the one thing we cannot make of it is a discourse of community, fellowship, and understanding. How then do we make of it a tradition?

It is curious to observe that in historical periods in which it may well have been proper to speak of tradition, men did not speak of tradition.

They recognized an order of receipt and transmission, a body of sacred and secular learning which defined the substance of divine revelation and humane instruction, but they did not regard the tradition as something outside of them, as an external datum, ordered, preserved, objectified. Tradition was interior and hence did not require sanctification and obeisance; it was active, *traditio,* the carrying over and forward of something which was supported and sustained. Only when *traditio* was used in the sense of *receptus* or *redactio,* as something defined, ordered, or enacted, was it understood in the sense in which we now use the term. The datum received or redacted, the Word of God, finished, closed, sealed into Scripture and hence terminated as a document, describes not the end of tradition, but the beginning of tradition. Before the redaction of the Hebrew Bible, there was a biblical tradition which kept alive the hot coal of God's word, passing it carefully, circumspectly, but intently and with seriousness from generation to generation, reviving and reawakening it, quickening and intensifying its power. And when that tradition ran the risk of splintering, it was set down, redacted, and sealed, and the tradition ended—only to begin again as rabbinic tradition, which in turn was accumulated, transmitted, developed, argued, lived, until it too became so vast, so sprawling, so subtle that it demanded redaction. The requirement of man to remember his achievements, to behold his works so that they might congratulate him is the impulse to redact the living, spoken, transmission of the word into its written, dogmatic, authoritative form.

Tradition is *living* when there is genuine tradition, the spoken word and the heard word surpassing the written word. It is the need to supply the spoken word with an adulterate preservative that compels us to conserve by writing. The most pristine traditions are bardic, epic, poetic, and never written. This is really only to say, as the Rabbis recognized, that in the Prophets and Writings God spoke, no longer directly but through the medium of His saints and prophets, and in the postbiblical literature God no longer spoke, but what was heard was an echo of his speech. This insight reverberates in the tale told by a Hasidic master who described the generational difference between himself and his teachers by explaining that when the Baal Shem Tov, the founder of Hasidism, had a difficult task to perform, he would go to a certain place in the forest, light a fire, and meditate in prayer; his successor knew the place in the forest and although he no longer lit the fire, he still remembered the Baal Shem's prayer; his successor no longer knew the prayer, but knew the place in the woods; and he, in his generation, all that he could do was to tell the story. In our time many of us no longer even have the enthusiasm to tell the story, believing perhaps that the story itself has become meaningless.

It is, indeed, this sense of intrinsic meaninglessness which is quite possibly a significant aspect of what has come to be regarded as the Judeo-Christian tradition. Despite the intensity and seriousness with which Jews and Christians engaged in murderous polemics from the first century until the late nineteenth century (and even today the thesis has been argued by the French historian, Jules Isaac, that Nazi anti-Semitism was a secular radicalization of the anti-Jewish impulses of historic Christianity), the debate was always qualified by the commonly held conviction that the manner in which a man composed his relationship to God was central and primary to his existence; that this relationship was constitutive, and therefore ontological, in character; and finally that it was a relationship which could only be regarded with absolute, albeit often dreary, seriousness. It was also believed that society and culture, being expressions of the relationship between man and God, could only endure and express their fidelity to God if they were religiously homogeneous, unmarked by dissent, disagreement, divisiveness; hence it followed that any community within the larger society which denied the prevailing and enforced homogeneity of doctrine, upon which the society's very life was believed to depend, should be either forcibly converted, driven out, or slain. But in addition to all this, there existed between Jews and Christians an order of ignorance which, even with the modest exceptions of German and Italian humanists, remained complete and impenetrable until the age of the Enlightenment. Jews regarded Christians as at best second-best, and at worst execrable idolaters; Christians regarded Jews as at best worthy of conversion and at worst deicides and anti-Christs.

Theological fratricide, however, cannot simply be deplored, although it is presently the easiest thing in the world of religion *to* deplore. The endless parade of Jewish thinkers addressing Christian audiences and rehearsing with calm and fluency the corruption of Christendom, alongside the equally sincere and passionate late-flowering recognition by Christian thinkers of the enormities which Christianity has inflicted upon the Jews, makes for a kind of rhapsodic, communal suffering which is finally purgative but not really illuminating. At the same time that I would recommend that we be done with the enumeration of massacres and the exhibition of Jewish scars, I would also suggest that we can learn something by reflecting on the order of seriousness, unanimity, and ignorance upon which this historical fratricide depended. And one thing we can learn is how the idea of the "Judeo-Christian tradition" began and why it has become in our day a myth which buries under the fine silt of rhetoric the authentic, meaningful, and irrevocable distinction which exists between Jewish belief and Christian belief.

I have indicated that the notion of a Judeo-Christian tradition did not come into existence during that period which enclosed the seventeen-hundred years of the origin, expansion, consolidation, and withering of Christian power. As long as Christianity could keep the enemy without the gate and was able to maintain a species of homogeneity and community which was for all intents and purposes unassailable. In that period Christianity engaged Judaism in debate less as a testimony to the openness of communication than as a theatrical exhibition of its power. There was no discourse, for none was felt to be needed. The argument had long since been decided by God and confirmed by the witness of the Church Triumphant.

The break in this pattern of no communication and antidialogue and the transition from a closed and homogeneous society to an open and fragmented society may be traced to the extraordinary revulsion through which European society passed during the century-long wars of religion. The wars killed in the millions, but killed, it was recognized, not for the sake of the Kingdom of God, but in order that principalities and potentates might retain inherited power and continue to exercise it. It was an insane time—a time, not a little like our own, in which millenarianism, the sense of doom and apocalypse, and eschatological expectation flourished. But out of that massive occlusion of wasted life, out of mountains of corpses, there came a revulsion on behalf of man which survives to our time. If the community of the religious, as an analogue of society, could yield such desperate and hopeless folly, then religion was the enemy of man, and the notion of God and his faithful was an enormous delusion and reservoir of unreason. The effort of the *philosophes* was both to debunk the irrationality of religion and to construct a civil society grounded upon the neutralization of religion in the public domain.

The critique of religion undertaken by the Enlightenment was profoundly antimythological. Aware of the luxury and opulence of ancient myth, and delighting in the aesthetic vitality and energy of its vision, the philosophers of the Enlightenment nonetheless had no doubt that ancient myth was against reason, and against common sense. But most particularly the Enlightenment was persuaded that the myths of religion produced fanatical narrowness, political repression, and social discord. In the view of the Enlightenment, sectarian religion was the enemy and

Christianity was the primary example of sectarianism. It could not be helped that in the attack on Christianity Judaism should suffer, for Christianity depended upon Judaism for the internal logic of its history. Early Christianity had sought to polarize itself to Judaism; the Fathers of the Eastern Church (and to a lesser extent the Latin Fathers) set the ministry of Jesus Christ in opposition to the teaching of the Hebrew Bible, expunging the Gospels of their Jewish roots, cutting off the church from its involvement in the fortunes of the synagogue, turning Christianity away from the Jews and toward the pagan world. The *philosophes* now recalled Christianity to its dependence upon the Hebrew Bible. The obscurantism of Christianity—however much it may have been enhanced and reticulated by the original doctrine of the myth of Jesus Christ—depended upon the Hebrew tradition. It could not be otherwise, then, but that a "Christo-Jewish tradition" should come to be defined and characterized as one of irrationality and fanaticism.

But if the Judeo-Christian tradition is initially a construct of the Enlightenment, it was not at that time a myth, for what the Enlightenment set out to destroy was, in fact, accurately perceived. Religious fanaticism—growing upon the soil of exclusivities, narrow sectarianism, doctrines of the elect and the damned—contributed to repression, nationalism, and war. In the assaults leveled by that Jewish precursor of the Enlightenment, Spinoza, in his *Tractatus,* and later by Voltaire, Diderot, and D'Alembert, the Hebrew biblical writ was perceived as a unit which, despite eccentric theological divisions and disagreements, produced in Christianity a religion to be opposed. The Christian religion depended for its essential theological groundwork upon the religious vision of the Jews and, for that reason, the Christo-Jewish legacy was both affirmed and opposed.

The nineteenth-century revolution in biblical studies begun by the German school of scientific higher criticism inaugurated the second phase of the history of the myth of the Judeo-Christian tradition. In response, it would seem, to the position of the Enlightenment, it became the concern of Protestant biblical scholars to disentangle Christianity from its Jewish roots, to split off the Christian experience from that of Judaism, and at the same time to naturalize the humanity of Jesus. It became commonplace in this movement of thought to demonstrate that what appeared to the light of Reformation theology to be most generous, humane, and charitable in classic Judaism was really a contribution from outside, whereas indigenous biblical Judaism was violent, self-righteous, obsessionally paranoid. The Hebrew biblical tradition was acknowledged, but its nobility and excellence had been taken over by the church, and what was left over to postbiblical, rabbinic Judaism (the Judaism of the Jews) was legalistic, ethnocentric, spiritually defective. From this movement of nineteenth-century thought emerged a species of hypostasis which envisaged the benighted Jew of the Old Testament, struggling along with a half-truth, in bondage to a hopeless legalism. On the one hand the genius of the Hebrew Bible was commended; on the other hand Christianity was set in superior condescension to the traditions of Judaism which survived, like ruins, the advent of Jesus Christ. The Judeo-Christian tradition was acknowledged, this time, by Christianity, but by a Christianity anxious to demonstrate that what had been correctly denigrated by the Enlightenment was, in fact, the teaching of the ancient Jews whose additions to and alterations of the pure Hebrew vision corrupted the source of Christianity.

The higher criticism of the Hebrew Bible became, as Solomon Schechter called it, "the higher anti-Semitism," designed to meet the critique of the *philosophes* and of German idealist philosophy by demeaning the Judaic element in Christianity. Whatever truth there is in the scientific criticism of the Hebrew Bible—and there is considerable truth—the ideological impulse was corrupt. The Judaism which survives the onslaught of Protestant higher criticism is buried under a mountain of historicist formulations, while a pure, virtuous Kantian Christianity—freed from Jewish accretion—is defined.

The social consequences of the de-Judaiznig of Christian theology could not be more evident than in the pitiful inability of the Protestant (and to a slightly—but only slightly—lesser extent, Catholic) churches to oppose German National Socialism. It is precarious to make considerations of ethics irrelevant to concerns of theology, to split off the task of living in the world from the pursuit of grace, to make, as many twentieth-century Protestant theologians have made, questions of ethics irrelevant to faith. Among the leaders of the confessional churches, only Dietrich Bonhoeffer in Germany and Karl Barth at its borders inveighed against the capitulation of church to state. The theologians of the nineteenth century had, indeed, succeeded: the ethics of the Hebrew Bible were winnowed by the Gospels and the ethics restored to Christian conscience were ethics for the "between-time," when history awaited the return of Christ. The purge of Christianity of its Jewish elements was disastrous. If that was Judeo-Christian tradition—in the spirit of Wellhausen, Kittel (and even most recently Bultmann's *Primitive Christianity*)—the world could not abide it again.

The renewal of the doctrine of the Judeo-Christian tradition, this time liberated from the ressentiment of Protestant defensiveness and Catholic hauteur, is a postwar phenomenon. Christianity has had a bad conscience and Jews seem justifiably content to pique it. Unfortunately, the penance which some Christians seem willing to perform and which some Jews seem anxious to exact, whatever its personal value, does not legitimate the creation of a "Judeo-Christian tradition." Clearly it is not denied that both religions share compatible truths. There is a common sacred history; the ethical values to which appeal is made are similar; the eschatological vision overlaps; the normative institutions of both faiths are analogous. Christianity is, as Christians describe it, the younger brother to Judaism and, as Judaism describes it, the daughter religion. The felt need, however, to spin from such compatibilities a "tradition" suggests the presence of something else.

It is an apparent truism that the concept of the Judeo-Christian tradition has particular currency and significance in the United States. It is not a commonplace in Europe as it is here; rather, Europeans since the war have become habituated to speak of Jewish-Christian amity, to define the foundations and frontiers of community, to describe and, in describing, to put to rest, historic canards and libels. In Europe they are not addicted as we are here to proclaiming a tradition in which distinctions are fudged, diversities reconciled, differences overwhelmed by sloppy and sentimental approaches to falling in love after centuries of misunderstanding and estrangement. I need not speak at length here of the religion of American secularism, that uncritical Jacobinism which is neither fish nor fowl, and certainly neither Christian nor Jewish. Suffice it to say that such secular religiosity is correctly perceived by both communities to be dangerous; it is the common quicksand of Jews and Christians. And it is here that we can identify the myth. Jews and Christians have conspired together to promote a tradition of common experience and common belief, whereas in fact they have joined together to reinforce themselves in the face of a common disaster. Inundated institutions have made common cause before a world that regards them as hopelessly irrelevant and meaningless. The myth, then, is a projection of the will to endure of both Jews and Christians, an identification of common enemies, an abandonment of millennial antagonisms in the face of threats which do not discriminate between Judaism and Christianity; and these threats, the whole of the Triple Revolution—automation, the population explosion, nuclear warfare—these are the threats which evoke the formation of the myth.

The threats are real and desperate, but patching over will not, in the long run, help. Patching over can only deteriorate further what it seeks to protect. The Judeo-Christian tradition is an eschatological myth for the Christian who can no longer deal with actual history, and a historical myth for Jews who can no longer deal with the radical negations of eschatology. The Christians must learn to depend upon the Jew who says salvation has not yet come, to interpret for him what happens when power collapses, how men shall behave when the relative and conditional institutions of society crumble, for the Jew is an expert in unfulfilled time, whereas the Christian is an adept believer for redeemed times *only*. The Christian may come to depend upon the Jew for an explanation of unredeemedness. The Jew, on the other hand, must look to Christianity to ransom for him his faith in the Messiah, to renew for him his expectation of the nameless Christ. This is the center of a true Jewish-Christian nexus, what might be called a Jewish-Christian humanism; but the possible lineaments of that humanism are scarcely to be glimpsed in our times.

THE HOLOCAUST AND CHRISTIAN THEOLOGY

The request has been made that I particularize proposals to assist Christian thinkers in the reconstruction of their relation, not alone to Jews, but to all mankind in the aftermath of the Holocaust. This request implicitly acknowledges the force of the deconstructive argument of my primary text. What is wanted now is some guide to renovation and restatement of the Christian message. On the face of it such a request strikes me as an encouragement of both arrogance and pretension (dangers to which all theologians are liable by the nature of their enterprise). I am inclined to ignore the specifics of the request, having performed sufficiently by tracing the historical discontinuity of Israel and the church, and indicating the moral and spiritual consequence of having regularized that discontinuity as a doctrinal presupposition of Christian interpretation of the Jew.

At the same time, however, as I am aware of the trap toward which such an inquiry leads me (not that the questioner desires to entrap me), I am tempted by the opportunity to elaborate further the implications of my argument. The argument *in nuce* is that the Christian community was

Reprinted from *Judaism and Christianity under the Impact of National Socialism, 1940–1945.* Otto Dov Kulka and Paul R. Mendes-Flohr, eds. Jerusalem: The Historical Society of Israel and the Zalman Shazar Center for Jewish History, 1987. Reprinted by permission of the Zalman Shazar Center for Jewish History.

rendered unable by its own ethical quietism and interiorized concern for the salvation of single souls and ecclesiastical communities to recognize that the threat posed by National Socialism was the predictable consequence of its having turned away from the Jews toward the Greeks. My contention—evidence for which continues to mount and multiply—is that the Christian turn toward the Greeks was not the exercise of a historical preference—a mere peripety of events—but a theological longing to escape from the persuasive mundanity of Jewish ethical and liturgical practice and to embrace a salvational scheme that virtually annihilates the relevance of history.

Irony of ironies that Israel should conduct a life-affirming covenant for two millennia and more virtually stripped of general historical relevance (an apparent nonperformer on the stage of world history), while Christianity—despite having doctrinally annihilated history—should have pursued the interregnum between Crucifixion and the Second Coming wedded to the machinations and deceptions of historical power. The church denied Israel reality but practiced a dialectical manipulation of its "nonreality" as the ongoing symbol of theological teachings against which it fought, heresies it condemned, sectarian movements which it battled to destroy. The Jew—although unreal—was always present among Albigensians, Cathars, Anabaptists, secretly Judaizing the church, constantly invoked as the demonic subtext to lapses of Christian orthodoxy. Of course it is contended by certain Jewish thinkers that Judaism is a religion that stands outside history, that its circle of faith is closed and locked from the inside, that its marking of the calendar with lunar strokes of a sacred time (ignoring the nations' calendrical domination by the sun) ruptures the familiar links that the natural Jew enjoys to public space and secular time. Such a reading of classical Judaism and its traditional descent is bonded to a view of the Hebrew Bible which regards it as a sublime and epic transcription of divine speech and therefore without value as a historical document. I think such a view extreme, although not without importance as a counter to the familiar literary-natural reading of the Bible as an ancient historical narrative. The origin of the Jews as biblically redacted is a dipolar phenomenon: there is the evidence of the Bible collateralized by the information transmitted by the stele and papyri of the ancient world; there is also the Word of God, that is, the manifest and overwhelming plentitude of an active and agitating divinity.

In short, Judaism continued to be a presence among the nations, a historical *absurdum* and perplexity, despite the conclusion of the church that its relevance ended with the drama of the life and death of Jesus the Messiah. The decision of the early church to read the continued survival of Jewish religion after the destruction of the Temple in 70 c.e. as an epiphenomenon, a mistake and error (and therefore a genuine byway of history), obliged it to undertake the Marcionist deformation of classical Judaism. Either it had misunderstood the intentions of God insofar as the Jewish people survived the time when its final destruction was appointed, or God continued to maintain a privileged covenant with his people that made the promise of Christianity (whatever its truth and value for the Gentiles) irrelevant for the Jews. Either alternative was requisite if the identity of the God of the Jews and the God of Jesus was to be maintained. However, if it was determined that the God of the Jews was bifurcated, that the God of creation was different from the God of redemption, that the God of illumination could be separated from the God of benightedness, it could then be claimed that however the Jews might endure, their endurance was henceforth without sacred significance, all light having fled from the Jews and settled upon Christendom.

The Marcionite heresy (heresy principally because of Marcion's insistence that Christians neither marry nor procreate—preferably male Christians should castrate themselves—with the ineluctable consequence that the Christian faith would have died out in the absence of the *paroussia*) lies for the Jews in its radical polarization of divine creation and redemption. It was hardly known among the Jewish contemporaries of Marcion what consequence would follow from the polemic generated by his attack. Clearly, anti-Judaism acquired a new and potent following among the Greek and Syriac fathers who followed in his wake, attacking Marcion as a heretic, but now also attacking Jews with a hitherto uncommon virulence and vulgarity.

It would follow then from this argument that Christian conceptualization of the Jew, Jewish history, and Jewish religion is built upon assumptions of exegesis that inculpate not only the Jews, but also the creator God to whom Israel attends. It also means that the God of the Christian is only the same God of Israel insofar as the church reads back from salvation to creation, reconstructing the God of the Jews where he is serviceable to Christian faith, but removing from him those attributes and acts that enable him to remain the bright God of Israel. The Christian removes from the God of the Jews those professions and acts that fail to prophesy and announce Jesus of Nazareth. The God of halakhah is clearly weakened; the God of ethical obligation binding the individual in service to the historical community is debilitated (since original sin is now introduced as the ontological deficiency of everything not granted the grace of Jesus Christ); and the God of a future kingdom, an unfulfilled messianism, an imperfect and unredeemed history, is undermined by the Christian belief in his own salvation.

The Holocaust of this century is either a work of God or it is not. If it is a work of God I concur that to continue to believe in God's great mercy and justice is more than a self-deception; it is a tragic misplacement of our meager human intelligence and capacity for faith. If the Holocaust is not the work of God, it follows that God does not do all things, that his capacity is in some sense contained and limited. The limitation of God's engagement with history was—I have always felt—indicated by the malign structure of earlier historical events that have beset the Jews, but until now it was never possible to constellate all such adventitious events and summations in so short a period of time. It took centuries for the Jews to pass judgment upon the Exile from Jerusalem, the pogroms of medieval Ashkenazic Jewry, the expulsion of Jews from England, France, and Spain. The doctrine of *kelipot* devised by the *Zohar* and elaborated by Lurianic Kabbalah to supply a reading of evil which involved God (but did not accuse him) was formed nearly two hundred years after a devastating event that concretized its conceptualization. The historical memory usually plods toward crystallization; it rarely races to judgment. In our day, however, the compression of time and space, the extraordinary detail of document and record allowed the Jews to learn within the space of one generation what had occurred during the Holocaust. It falls then to theology—not to Jewish praxis, liturgy, or halakhah—to provide an understanding of the Holocaust and the God who fashioned a human creation by means of whose obsessive genius it was wrought. Such an understanding obligates the concern, not only of Jews, but of Christians. This not simply for the reason that those who engineered and worked the Holocaust were nominally Christians from an ostensibly Christian nation. Such an argument would be insufficient to engage more than the conscience of Christians, an ethical entailment of limited authority. Rather it is that the God who judges Jews judges Christians as well, that the God of Israel is the God of Jesus Christ, that the God of creation is the same as the God of redemption. And that Marcion was not merely a heretic, but was unable to read Holy Scripture correctly. If, then, the God of the Jews is placed in the jeopardy of Jewish scrutiny and disbelief, the God of the Christians is also placed in question. Jews and Christians have been brought together by the Holocaust to confront their same God and each other with a mighty asking now as never before.

At this juncture I return to the request with which I began these remarks: What is it that this Jew asks of Christians, both taking their stand against the background of the Holocaust, both communities of faith thrown by the self-same historical event into a turmoil of question that addresses the very depths of their faith? The consequence of the questioning may result in a twofold renovation for Christians: that Christian enmity against Judaism must henceforth be explicit, open, theologically illuminated by the rancor of the Gospels and Epistles, rather than dark, implicit, covert (with the corollary that Jewish anti-Christianity must have the courage to be no less open and explicit), and that Christians must approach their own sources of testamentary literature, liturgy, and theological documents of the past with a suspicion that they contain and transmit a view of Jews and Jewish events that is triumphalist and derisive. Both these enterprises of admission are not simply stands taken in civility. They are stands bound and bonded to theological truth. Hence they are obligatory, not optional. And yet both modes of renovation seem to be in contradiction to each other: how, it will be thought, can theological enmity be justified while at the same time espousing a critical hermeneutic of suspicion? Both can be held, despite their apparent contrariness, since they are dialectically related: the epistemology of suspicion serves to refine and clarify the nature of the enmity, while at the same time shearing from it the excess layering of theological rhetoric that transforms an argument concerning truth into a rhetoric where power and force become instrumentalities of persuasion.

As I have argued elsewhere, theological enmity may assert its claim out of the circle of faith (indeed *must* assert such claim) since any believer *must* believe that he receives the benefits promised by his faith and that others, who choose not to pay the various prices of membership in the elected community, must be denied them. Enmity is the human consequence of both belonging to the elect and seeing countless others who do not belong, who apparently thrive in their unbelief, and who must nonetheless be denied some portion of the promises made to the elected and saved. Such theological enmity is the psychological detritus of true faith.

It is one thing to acknowledge that Christians will have enmity toward Jews and Jews will have enmity toward Christians by virtue of the imputation of salvational hubris of which Jews accuse Christians and the accusation of profligate disbelief with which Christians belabor Jews. However, when such theological enmity draws in support of state authority and either Jew or Christian is made to suffer in the flesh punishments which only God has the right to enforce, theological enmity becomes human enmity, issues of transcendence are made political, and civil brutalities that we have witnessed through centuries to our own day are not only encouraged but rendered unavoidable. The Holocaust is to be blamed upon human beings. However, its ultimate source in the secularization of theological teaching and the use of political machinery to enforce what only God speaking as God can require is its ideological origin.

Theological enmity is the contest of beliefs, not the contest of power. The way in which that enmity can be assured of its theological continuity irrespective of the temptations of power and force is by making certain that the hermeneutic of suspicion is in place at the same time. Suspicion must winnow teaching, liturgy, and doctrine with rakes of iron, curing and currying them, breaking loose hardened clods of dogmatism (even fanaticism) which speak with a certainty that transgresses the wholly human and invades the prerogatives of God. Anybody who would say, for instance, that "God does not hear the prayer of Jews" is trumped by a deeper error than bad rhetoric; such a speaker presumes to know and hence to speak as God, itself the greatest idolatry. Any church, moreover, that confuses its conviction of the presence of the Holy Spirit in its deliberations with God Himself commits a comparable transgression. God is always vaster than any of His manifestations, and even where a terrestrial declaration is sanctified by the authority of the Holy Spirit, it is already so mixed with human stuff as to be no longer a pure expression of God. We cannot afford to misremember that the moment anything leaves God—any truth, any insight, any formula of faith—it becomes party to man and is liable for all its transparency as divine truth to the risks of human misunderstanding.

Is more possible as corrective than simply a new method of speech? Am I really asked to propose that Christians rewrite Christianity or that Jews refashion Judaism in order to smooth the theological ground upon which Christians and Jews must walk? I think not. The Christian Testament is and must remain a mixed text for the Jews since it is not inspired by God speaking to the historical community of Jews. But no less the oral tradition which is the posterior canonic literature of the Jews—the rabbinic method supplying the Jews with the right way of reading Holy Scripture—can mean little more to the Christian for whom the rabbinic literature is unavoidably postlude. Both communities are historically locked by their literatures and by the stands those literatures require. But to be locked by tradition is only negatively freighted language for what is otherwise understood within each community as faithfulness and loyalty to one's ultimate conviction.

The critical task is not the remaking of either community of faith—a hopeless undertaking in general, and morally unsupportable as well. The critical task is rather that of obliging each community to scrutinize the social, moral, and political consequence of being locked into a system of truths that not only denies the truth of its competitors, but has frequently inspired those with a popular plurality of adherents to take measures to contain, to suppress, and sometimes—as in this century—to obliterate its competing opponents. (An ironic commentary on this most obvious, but neglected, of observations: I listened quite recently to an eminent Roman Catholic Islamist describing to me in an escalating rhetoric of hatred his interpretation of the actions of the Jewish people of Israel against the Palestinians, the nucleus of which is that Jews with power are tyrannical. The irony consisted not in the evaluation of the truth or falsehood of his claim, but rather in the fact that he cast the Jews in the same role vis-à-vis others that the Jew of history would have cast him as both Roman Catholic and Islamist.)

The matter of moment is how to build into the structure of faith a fail-safe mechanism that warns us that a decline of language is about to begin, that discourse willed by the care for truth is about to yield to debate powered by the desire for triumph. The latter always leaves a residuum of animus which, even if it is not intended that civil discord should result, awaits a future moment to be animated and released as hatred and violence.

The fail-safe mechanism (dubious as one is bound to regard all such devices) may well be installed in that intermediate realm of language which is no longer liturgical and not yet secular. For example, consider the reinterpretation of the Jewish guilt for deicide introduced by the Vatican Council. How can it be, one wonders, that Paul VI, preaching during Easter services thereafter should again denounce the guilt of the Jews. Clearly liturgy demands formula; all liturgy, in fact, is formulaic speech and is understood and received as such. Preaching, however, is not formulaic speech except if the preacher be poorly equipped to speak from heart and mind, and resorts to formula as a means of winning acquiescence. The guarding against the use of formulaic speech when the speaker is giving advice to the congregation is an obvious beginning for reconstruction.

The application of such a principle is widespread. Not only in preaching, but in catechizing the faithful, instructing their morals, clarifying their confusion, writing about the Word of God, and transmitting God's speech in the language of mankind—all these instances require the guard against liturgical formulae. What is at issue here is that any public address by a Christian (and by a Jew) must exhibit care for the freighted language of Scripture and the authority of liturgical formulae by refusing to employ them as though they were devised for the guidance and direction of natural creatures, prey as they are to the temptations of anger, frustration, envy, and competitiveness, all of which lead to a subversion of theological formulae and their employment as modes of secular coercion and suppression.

The speech of God to the church and the speech of God to the synagogue entail claims that distinguish and separate both communities. Even if a believing Jew never conceptualizes, much less feels, the power of the faith of the Christian, and the believing Christian never knows the reality of the Jew, the church is negated by the faith of the Jew and the belief of the Jew is derogated by the faith of the Christian. God has ensured their differentiation and has supplied each with a language of faith and celebration that ensures the separation of the two communities until the end of time and the coming of their means of redemption and reconciliation. As surely as Jews are instructed not to rush the End, Christians are warned not to speculate over the Apocalypse. What is God's deserves to remain His alone. But what is given over to humankind is a care to maintain what God has distinguished. If it is granted that Israel and the church are divinely ordained communities and the one has not disappeared for the sake and glorification of the other, their endurance—despite the trials and adversities of history—must be accredited to a quickening spirit which is God's grace. Jews continue to exist less because they have struggled to survive (though they have surely done that) than because God has not yet done with the Jews (this, a mystery of believing). And if this is the case, the suspicion, the mistrust, the caring quizzicality with which Jews are required to question any mundane institution (whether church or synagogue) follow from their not daring to speak God's language as though God were speaking.

I have always been delighted by the instructive traditions of the ancient world: the habit of Egyptian sculptors always to leave one portion of a Pharaonic statue incomplete in order to remind those divine rulers of their mortality, or the even more portentous habit of the emperors of Rome to be followed during their triumphal processions by a fool on a donkey calling out to them their faults and miscreancies to check their hubris and caution them against excess and boastfulness.

There is no basis for hope that Christianity's return to the Jews out of the thickets of Hellas will promise a new beginning for theological discourse and the grounding of a renewed care for the Jewish-Christian nexus unless the cautionary morality I have been arguing for is its psychological presumption. Nothing can be done to ensure that man shall be little lower than the angels until human beings begin to act upon more than their self-interest, to accommodate a sensibility of charity, to will a reduction in the abrasiveness that erodes civility in the commonweal where all of us—Christians and Jews—live out the social and moral implications of our theologies.

Franz Rosenzweig and the Crucifixion: An Historical Episode in Judeo-Christian Communication

Each time I bring myself to consider the substance of Christian belief, I find myself recalling an amazing passage from an undated letter written by Franz Rosenzweig during October 1916 to his friend and theological interlocuter, Eugen Rosenstock-Huessy. The first time, many years ago, that I referred to this letter in the company of Martin Buber and Nahum N. Glatzer, both of whom I was accompanying to the Jewish Theological Seminary (New York), where I was then a fellow in medieval Jewish thought, I recall Professor Glatzer smiling ironically and remarking that the existence of the letter should be kept secret. He added that its substance would only give confidence and support to those who, in their unknowing, hated Jews and the Jewish religion. Since that time, the correspondence of Rosenzweig and Rosenstock-Huessy has been translated and published,[1] and the letter is now public property, but its contents are still unremarked.

My contribution to this theological conversation regarding Christology and the estate of Jewish-Christian communication will be to quote Rosenzweig's letter in extenso, to set forth its historical context and mood, and finally to introduce a free commentary on the issues it raises.

Unpublished manuscript, 1983. Estate of Arthur A. Cohen.

What does the Christian theological idea of Judaism mean for the Christian? If I am to believe E. R.'s [Eugen Rostenstock, later to become Eugen Rosenstock-Huessy after his marriage] letter before last (or before the one before the last?): Nothing! For there he wrote that nowadays Koenig and he are the only people who still take Judaism seriously.[2] The answer is already on the point of my pen—that it was not here a question of theoretical awareness, but whether there was a continual realization of this theological idea by its being taken seriously in actual practice. This practical way, in which the theological idea of the stubbornness of the Jews works itself out, is *hatred of the Jews*. You know as well as I do that all its realistic arguments are only fashionable cloaks to hide the single true metaphysical ground: that we will not make common cause with the world-conquering fiction of Christian dogma, because (however much as fact) it *is* a fiction (and *"fiat veritas, pereat realitas,"* since "Thou God art truth") and, putting it in a learned way (from Goethe in *Wilhelm Meister*): that we deny the foundation of contemporary culture (and *"fiat regnum Dei, pereat mundus,"* for "ye shall be to me a kingdom of priests and a holy people"); and putting it in a popular way: that we have crucified Christ and, believe me, would do it again every time, we alone in the whole world (and *"fiat nomen Dei, pereat homo,"* for "to whom will you liken me, that I am like?").

Clearly this extraordinary text is multivalent, formed and layered critically, although installed in Rosenzweig's lengthy letter as a swift and piercing, admittedly proud and passionate, espousal. Here is a Jew who turned away from Christianity in interlocution with a Jew become a Christian, formulating the most radical historical admission a Jew can make. Yet the ostensive admission, the admission intended to shock his friend (since it is couched in a rhetoric of building and ascendant formulae, introducing Latin alongside German renderings of critical affirmations of the Hebrew Bible that had become liturgical tropes), concludes with a self-vindicating confession that not only he—the single Jew, Franz Rosenzweig—but also the collective "we" to whom Rosenzweig is lately joined, would crucify a pretender Messiah again as had been done two millenia before. The interest surely is not mere bloodthirstiness or cruelty, but rather theological service, a service to truth. This is the naked significance of the text.

We must assume (and the text clarifies it) that Rosenzweig is not insensitive to what he has acknowledged. He refers to his willing responsibility for the Crucifixion as a formulation "in a popular way." He means by this that the popular analogue to Jewish intransigence, stubbornness, refusal of Jesus as being the annointed Son of God, the Christ, has meaning only in the context of crucifixion. The Jews were not passive before the promulgations and formulations of the Disciples. Rosenzweig presumes that they were well aware of what was being asserted of Jesus of Nazareth, and that they (not merely a part of the people of ancient Palestine, not only those among the politically conservative Sadducean faction or the aristocratic social elite close to Pontius Pilate, but all of the Jews of that world, wise and ignorant, instructed and illiterate—to the extent that they were Jews in the flesh and constrained by their intimacy with the life and expectation of Jewish trust) would have voluntarily participated in the Crucifixion *as a theological action,* indeed, as the first concrete historical enactment of what was in that day the single radically constitutive Jewish dogma (virtually unformulated as dogma because received in the gut of the people and hence available to all, learned and unschooled) that God is a unity beyond parsing, "that He is One and His Name One," and "to whom will you liken me that I am like?"

Rosenzweig admits openly, powerfully, without embarrassment and evasion what centuries of Jewish apologetics had patiently devised as a misconstruction of history. Yet Rosenzweig, not unaware of the historical inaccuracy of the Christian accusation of deicide against the whole Jewish People (itself now acknowledged by Roman Catholic and Protestant churches), argues nonetheless in 1916[3] that what is historically untrue is still theologically indisputable.

The theological centrality of the Jews in the enactment of the Crucifixion is thematically critical because the issue of Christianity and its theological claims can never be a minor issue for Jews.[4] It is not that Christianity is wrong, false, mistaken, a system of fictions and untruths, but rather that Christianity presented itself to the Jew twenty centuries ago not as a church of power, wedded to the historical, joined as an administrator of culture and civilization in the West with all its deputations and princes and potentates, but as a simple community of disciples and a single Master, a humble community, a small, intimate conventicle of dissident Jewish believers who made a rather crucial assertion about their Master—granted an assertion made beyond his life and in the face of his resurrection—that he was the Messiah and King of Israel, no, more than these, as the early church quickly defined it, *the* Son of God.

The Christian faith would mean nothing were the Son of God to rise up, flourish among his small band of believers, and die in bed. History may tolerate such bourgeois destiny, but God could not. Moreover, Christian theology would find itself deprived of a critical exemplum. The very first requirement of a challenge reality as considerable as the events of the life and death of Jesus of Nazareth is that these events be promulgated by theology as facts. Less important that their status as novelty be proclaimed than that their occurrence is fact. Part of the assertiveness and comprehensive pretension of theology is that what it understands must be affirmed as carrying universal implication. The Gospels had to speak of "Jews" as a totality. They could not devise a partitive and qualified language. The revelation of the evangels demanded a total, uncritical, universal language. For their part, the Jews could only respond with an equally total and universal denial. Centuries of talking past each other did not, however, mitigate the efficiency of direct action. What is all the more remarkable then about the exchange of letters between Rosenzweig and Rosenstock-Huessy (the most sustained and riveted communication between a Jew and a Christian about the substance of their faith and belief) is that only a century earlier it might have led to civil charges of blasphemy with disastrous consequences for both interlocuters—the one for his naïveté in discussing such matters with a Jew, the other for his blasphemous arrogance toward Jesus Christ.

Yet we may sense in Franz Rosenzweig's formulation something rather more perilous and daring than a break in the Jewish silence of centuries. Rosenzweig is undertaking in this letter a theological initiation—the first precarious steps toward a Jew-Christian who can speak of himself as he does in the earlier letter of October 4, 1916, "as pre-Christian Jewish racial material. In my capacity for suffering and in my craving for it, the Jew comes out. I forge together German and Jewish gifts and possessions in my attempt to become a Christian."[5] Rosenzweig is quite aware that it was the strenuous, unrelenting battering administered to him by Rosenstock-Huessy that drove him over the summer of 1913, culminating in the nightlong dialogue of July 7, 1913, to affirm that he would become a Christian. Rosenstock-Huessy was more concerned with elaborating the absolute standpoint of his calendrical reconstruction of time with smashing Rosenzweig's relativism than he was with converting Franz Rosenzweig. Rosenzweig, always sensitive to nuance, understood that there was no way of avoiding the implication of Rosenstock-Huessy's assault. As he had written during 1909 to his parents, having already plowed his consciousness and opened its furrow too receive the seed of faith: "we are Christians in every respect; we live in a Christian state, attend Christian schools, read Christian books, in short, our whole civilization is fundamentally Christian."[6] Rosenzweig determined following the conversion experience of July 7, 1913, to become a Christian, but only after having lived as a Jew. This determination culminated in his passing the High Holy Days of 1913 in a Hasidic synagogue in Berlin, alone, unsponsored, anonymous. He concluded that sacred liturgy restored to Israel, persuaded, as he wrote his parents, that there was no longer any necessity to leave Israel in order to find God. As he would later formulate it in *The Star of Redemption,* the Jew is always with God and has no need to wander in search of him. That wandering and seeking, that would become in his mature theology the historical role of the Christian.

In the present exchange with Rosenstock-Huessy, what is striking, even overwhelming—more overwhelming in my view than the daring theological formulations that Rosenzweig delivers—is the intimacy and nakedness of the communication. What is at stake is not theological formulation, but living and speaking truth. It is this more than anything else that I find invariably lacking in the generality of ecumenical conversation between Jewish and Christian interlocuters. Such discussion invariably turns upon modes of theological language rather than upon the confessional and self-disclosure in which Christian seeks the help of the Jew, Jew the help of the Christian. The operative content of theological help is different than that of theological correctness. As Eugen Rosenstock-Huessy put it admirably in his introduction to the German publication of his correspondence with Rosenzweig:[7] "the letters are entirely free from any consideration as to whether they would do good or harm." That is to say, their formulation is free of all apologetic defensiveness or anxiety about the reception of specific language (such as the one cited here to which Rosenstock-Huessy made no subsequent reference, presumably regarding it as unexceptionable). This is possible because the interlocuters are known to each other, known in that deepest fundament of human respect and mutuality of honoring that enabled them out of the same and different sources to love each other as neighbors. The ground of their intimacy was an ethical rigor by which each took the other as truth-telling and, beyond their capacity for truth, honored their ability to name, to speak, to use language with humane caring.

At this juncture I would return to the argument I proposed more than a decade ago in my book of connected essays, *The Myth of the Judeo-Christian Tradition* (1970).[8] In that book I argued for the significance and clarification of Jewish-Christian enmity. The essential thesis is, I think, not only as true now as then, but perhaps truer now than then, precisely because nothing has changed, but the languages of evasion have become more subtle as theological sinuosity (that is, the granting of this or that to Jewish suppliants, the offering of this or that bone of candor as full fare to the Jewish hunger for rectification) has become more devious. I argued then that the real task of Christian and Jew is to make clear the nature of their theological enmity, its origins, structure, and constitution, but having effected this clarification, to offer from each side their enmity to God as an admission of historical finitude. As long as we Jews exist, we are a reproach to Christian faith (but of no especial significance to human beings who are Christian); as long as Christians exist, they are a challenge to Jewish incompletion (but ought be no threat to human beings who are Jews). The dialectic is real, the conflict authentic, the historical enmity consequential, but need the history that comes be as brutal as it has been? Is there not a way of conducting the dialectic of enmity with a passion constrained by human civility (indeed, is not civility the single contribution that secular pluralism makes to the religious conflict, that we confront each other without denying each other's humanity)? The curse can be hard to bear, but brutality is harder still and from murder there is no pardon. It is not God that compels us to murder. The devolution of civility into barbarism is an historical determination that arises out of our own sin and corruption. The enmity of argument remains utterly real, but such enmity cannot be conducted in imitation of the model whose possibility Franz Rosenzweig and Rosenstock-Huessy demonstrated.

The instruction of Rosenzweig declaration of faith to his Christian friend is horrendous and proud. It makes an indubitable theological affirmation. Indubitable from the Jewish side and by and large unarticulated only because Jews have found it easier not to think and to turn the other way. Jews, by and large, live among Christians, but bother very little with Christian faith and history. (This might be termed civil indifference, a socially acceptable but theologically unserious mode.) At best, when they do think about Christian belief, they regard Christianity as a congerie of strange and disquieting doctrine; at worst, when they regard Christians they find them generally unequal to their profession, wanting by reason of an extreme teaching considered more crushing, more demanding, more insistent than any Jewish "legalism" could ever be. We laugh (or at least I laugh) at the Apostolic notion of the "burden of the Law." The Law is light—albeit demanding and punctilious—when set beside the law of *agape*. Better that I be contentious with a discipline that makes me obedient and wary at every moment lest I transgress and fall into error and rebellion, than that I trust that grace writes the lines of the heart. The Jew is always paying attention; it is required. The Christian, particularly the Christian in a non-Christian world, has so much time between service that his mind wanders, and when the Christian becomes obsessive the temptation is to retire from the world completely or, adhering to it ferociously, to become simplistic even while remaining evangelical.

The Myth of the Judeo-Christian Tradition concluded with an essay, "Theological Enmity and Judeo-Christian Humanism,"[9] in which I devised the groundwork of a liturgical commonalty intended to embody the natural correlatives of a theology of hope. Both Jews and Christians in their concern for human beings have need of the Holy Spirit, whether the Holy Spirit be the teaching voice, the *bat kol* of Rabbinic times, the gift of grace. The bringing into our midst of the Holy Spirit is a task, not alone of prayer in singleness and within our historical liturgies, but in the formation of a liturgical expression that can serve as the natural coefficient of our shared humanism. The Jew need not learn to hear the Christian speak of the Christ come nor must the Christian learn to hear the Jew speak of the regency of Torah; but both must come to hear in each other the sounds of truth—that the prayer of the Jew is not alone for the Jew, but for all humankind; that the prayer of the Christian is not only for the faithful in Christ, but for all creatures. It is the commonality of human suffering that is the commonality of Christian and Jew; and there must come a means of expressing that shared experience and its implication. Such a liturgy must be a means of purgation—putting to rest the anger that has been the history of Jews and Christian—and a liturgy of hope, making appeal to God for the wisdom and forbearance to join together, beyond the temptations of power and divisiveness, to serve creation. Upon one thing the supernatural Jew and the supernatural Christian agree: the magnitude of creation and the excellence of its creator. Out of such agreement the natural Jew and the natural Christian are enabled to form an authentic community, a viable consensus, a meaningful cooperation that issues into a Judeo-Christian humanism.

NOTES

1. Eugen Rosenstock-Huessy, editor. *Judaism Despite Christianity*. The "Letters on Christianity and Judaism" between Eugen Rosenstock-Huessy and Franz Rosenzweig. University of Alabama Press, 1969.

2. Dr. Eduard Koenig was professor of Old Testament at the University at Bonn and had published about 1916 a book called *Der ewige Jude* that makes the irony of their reference clear.

3. Rosenzweig was fully aware of the critical reworking of the Gospel interpretation of Jewish participation in the Crucifixion set forth by such historians as Heinrich Graetz and such theologians as Leo Baeck, as well as in the writings of his teacher Hermann Cohen, Martin Buber, and other contemporaries.

4. If Jewish religion be regarded as an ahistorical phenomenon, nonparticipatory in history as such, Christian faith would have to be considered a theological novum of undeniable relevance. If Jewish religion, no differently than others, responds to the welter of culture and its course, the history of Christianity has had indubitably traumatic consequence for Judaism and its endurance.

5. *Judaism Despite Christianity,* 104–5.

6. Ibid., 29–30.

7. Rosenzweig, Franz. *Briefe*. Schocken Verlag, 1935, 638–39.

8. Cohen, Arthur A. *The Myth of the Judeo-Christian Tradition*. Harper & Row, 1970. Schocken Books, 1972.

9. Ibid. 189–222, particularly 217f.

IV.

THE HOLOCAUST

Introduction

Paul Mendes-Flohr

Cohen was wont to note that theology, or thinking about God, and believing in God, though intimately related, are not identical processes. Thinking about God means to engage in the reality of God; using an image from Heinrich von Kleist's *The Marionette Theater,*[1] in which one goes around Paradise to see if there is a hidden entrance at the back, Cohen pictured theology as trying to curve around God, and after being graced with fresh insight, returns to the realm of experience and belief. In thinking about God, we seek to construe, or rather struggle to understand, from hidden, less obvious angles, who it really is whom we celebrate and love in believing. Theology, Cohen held, brings us to the borders of belief.

Where those borders are, thinking can never know for certain. Indeed, the borders are constantly shifting. For if belief is more than a mere formulaic and catechistic reflex, it leads one to an encounter with the living God in history; invariably, the believer must perforce become a thinker who asks how a living God could bear to dwell in our often tormented world. It is Cohen's conviction that history affects God as much as it affects us.

Theodicy—the justification of seemingly inexplicable human suffering in the light of God's rule—is thus an inevitable aspect of authentic faith. For contemporary Jews, Cohen held, theodicy today perforce takes

231

the form of the harrowing question, "Where was God in Auschwitz?" As Cohen testifies in his "Autobiographical Fragment: The Holocaust" (the third selection of this section), this question had tormented him since his childhood.

It was not until the 1970s, however, that Cohen himself would dare address this question directly and comprehensively. Previously he had only perfunctorily considered the Holocaust in his theological writings. Not that he had hitherto been insensitive to the tragedy. On the contrary. Even before he affirmed the God of Israel and the Torah, Cohen was deeply tormented by the horror that befell the Jewish people during the Second World War, as he testifies in his "Autobiographical Fragment." The pain was there, but he did not integrate it into his worldview as it crystallized in his youth, nor later into his emerging theology as a believing Jew. Cohen, of course, was not alone. Postwar Jewish religious thought as a whole responded to the Holocaust with, so to speak, a delayed reaction. As Cohen himself noted in 1981:

> Thirty-five years have passed since the closing of the death camps. The first decade was passed in defining the language of formal description and formal judgment. . . . The second period saw the rescue of a literature, the beginnings of the controversies of interpretation, the publication of fictional accounts of the camps and autobiographic documents. . . . It is during the third decade and out of the fourth that a new moment in the assimilation of the historical reality began.

It was only then, after more than four decades, that Jewry first seemed ready to ask the question of why. Cohen undoubtedly bore personal witness when he observed that it was now realized that "it is not enough to deal with the reality of the death camps viscerally, with passion and anguish, with guilt for surviving. . . . It is simply not adequate to *feel* this enormous event. One must live with it." Living with the Holocaust meant for Cohen—and for other post-Holocaust Jewish thinkers—that a Jew was required to enquire after the meaning of the event. This meant allowing the Holocaust to challenge one's belief in the God of meaning, the God of creation and the source of life.

The first major, albeit oblique, response Cohen gave to this challenge was in his epic novel on the inevitable failure of messianic ambition, *In the Days of Simon Stern*. His first direct theological exploration of the subject came in his Leo Baeck Memorial Lecture of 1973, "Thinking the Tremendum." In this seminal lecture, he argued that the theological imagination that confronts the Holocaust is ultimately obliged to consider the question of radical evil—the possibility that evil is not simply a consequence of human failing but that it has an ontological status; it is thus fundamental to the very structure of existence. This possibility—raised with monstrous ferocity by the Holocaust—ineluctably leads to a radical questioning of the biblical conception of God as the ever-benevolent Creator and Sovereign—omniscient and omnipotent—of the world. To Cohen's mind, all traditional theodicies (invariably appealing to human sin, personal and collective, duly punished by divine judgment) prove hopelessly inadequate, if not offensive, in the face of the Holocaust.

Concluding that a rehearsal of the old theodicies would not do, Cohen thus decided upon a fresh rethinking about God, in which not only the traditional theistic conceptions but also the doxic-laden language of theology would be radically reviewed. As a result of this deconstructive journey, most fully pursued in his book *The Tremendum* (1981), he arrived at both a radically revised theological vocabulary and a modified conception of God. In the face of the Holocaust and "the *tremendum* of evil"—a neologism introduced by Cohen as the negative image of the *mysterium tremendum* or terrifying mystery of the Divine Presence—Cohen maintained that God could no longer be conceived of as the all-mighty and all-knowing Ruler of the universe. God's rule is seriously limited by the evil reality of the world. Yet, Cohen insisted, God exists and is still worthy of our adoration, obedience, and love.

Notes

1. See the essay in section seven, "The Sufferings of Heinrich von Kleist," and the selection in section five, "One's Own Text," from Cohen's novel *An Admirable Woman*.

Thinking the Tremendum:
Some Theological Implications
of the Death Camps

There is something in the nature of thought which is alien to the enormity of the death camps. There is something no less incommensurable in the reality of the death camps which repudiates the attentions of thought. Thinking and the death camps are opposed. The procedures of thought and the ways of knowing are confounded. It is to think the unthinkable, which is not alone contradictory but hopeless, for thought entails as much a moral hope (that it may be triumphant, mastering its object, dissolving the difficulties, containing and elucidating the conundrum) as it is the investment of skill and dispassion in a methodic procedure. The death camps are a reality which, by their very nature, obliterate thought and the humane program of thinking. We are dealing, at the very outset, therefore, with something unmanageable and obdurate—a reality which exists, which is historically documented, which has specific beginnings and ends, located in time, the juncture of confluent influences which run from the beginnings of historical memory to a moment of consummating orgy, never to be forgotten, but difficult to remember, a continuous scourge to memory and the future of memory and yet something which, whenever addressed, collapses into tears, passion, rage. The death camps

The Leo Baeck Memorial Lecture, #18, 1974, 3–23. Reprinted by permission of the Leo Baeck Institute.

234

are unthinkable, but not unfelt. They constitute a traumatic event, and like all decisive trauma, they are suppressed but omnipresent; unrecognized but tyrannic; silted over by forgetfulness, but never obliterated; rising like a shade in dreams, allusions, the imagination to plague consciousness without end.

Nearly thirty years have passed since the closing of the death camps. The first decade after the revelation of the murder of the Jews (and their no less misfortunate but unsung confederates, the Gypsies) was passed in defining the language of formal description and formal judgment. It was the time of the statistical accounting, the development of an accurate historical language, the numbering of the victims, the definition of the grammar of genocide, and the no less wall-eyed, benumbed dealing of judgment to the accused, the trials, the executions, culminating in the Eichmann trial of 1961. The second period saw the rescue of a literature, the beginnings of the controversies of interpretation, the publication of fictional accounts of the camps and autobiographic documents, by the quick and the dead, from Chaim Kaplan, Emmanuel Ringelbaum, André Schwarz-Bart, J. P. Steiner, Elie Wiesel, Katzetnik, Pyotr Rawicz, to mention but several among countless others. The task of this literature was neither to astonish nor to amaze, neither to exalt nor to abase, but to provide a vivifying witness to the mortal objectivity of the statistics.

It is during the present and third decade, now drawing to a close, that a new moment in the assimilation of the historical reality has begun. Another generation, those who knew not, has grown up—a generation that knows the birth and struggle of the State of Israel, but knows nothing directly of the Hitler years and the immediate shock of their ferocity. To this generation the question of meaning has become critical. It is the generation that sees upon its flesh the scar without the wound, the memory without the direct experience. It is this generation that has the obligation, self-imposed and self-accepted (however ineluctably), to discern a meaning and an instruction from the historical, not only lest the events recur, but more importantly that, if they do, they never recur in the same way. To achieve this prophylactic sense, this preventive vision, is the task not alone of energizing memory, hearing the witnesses, attending to their words and warnings, but is a task of thinking. It is not enough to deal with the reality of the death camps viscerally, with passion and anguish, with guilt for surviving and abashment before the enormity, with rage and anger, sublimated, as Jewish anger has always been. These are not enough, nor are they even sufficient. It is simply not adequate to *feel* this *tremendum.* One must live with the *tremendum,* and living with it requires that it be perceived accurately (to the extent that accuracy is possible about events as charged as these), clearly (to the extent that looking into the charnel house can ever be unclouded and precise), and distinctly (to the extent that it can be confronted as a constellated phenomenon which both does and does not indict all of Western civilized history, all of Christianity, all of silent humanity, and most of all, the history and faith of Israel). There was a time when it was understandable that one's reaction to the asking of the meaning of the *tremendum* was the fervid wish that it had none, that it implicated nothing beyond itself, that it described an historical horror, but that it did not tear apart the fabric of the larger universe where men create, make art, think, love, ransoming the human from the mud and muck of the concrete and particular. That time is past.

We are in the third decade. The distance between our selves and the events of the *tremendum* has grown. The survivors persist, most in private communication with their memories, most silent; others vigorously, often desperately, trying to bridge the chasm which opened beneath them then, thirty years ago, talking to us well and badly, convincingly and shrilly, patiently and irritably, superior to us and supercilious, guarding as they do a body of uncommunicate images and imaginings or else vaguely and mystically, floating beyond us, palpable ghosts and specters of a world we never knew. To the side of the survivors have come, however, in recent years, other aides and interpreters, the thinkers. It is as someone who is trying to think about the *tremendum* that I address you this evening. My observations fall into two general and primary categories: thinking about the historical and thinking about the meaning of the historical.

The predicament one faces at the very outset is that the procedures of traditional thought afford us very little assistance. Historiography is a patient accumulation of relevant information with a view to describing and interpreting events. The Dutch historian, Pieter Geyl, made it abundantly clear in his ongoing argument with Leopold von Ranke that history may be value-free, but that historiography is never so. History is not simply telling what happened. The historian always tells what happened from the historian's point of view. Geyl, writing of Napoleon while detained in a privileged concentration camp throughout the war, showed how European historians of Napoleon and of the Napoleonic era—Taine, Quinet, Sorel, and others—constructed Napoleon who was true to some facts, but not to all, accurate to part of the reality, but not to the whole, and in the process a liberal Napoleon, a reactionary Napoleon, a bourgeois Napoleon, a middle-class or an elitist Napoleon rose and fell. The facts were all there, but historians select. When a work of history refuses to select, when it has no point of view, it cannot construe history. Instead, it retires into chronicle and accumulation, telling all and obfuscating everything. Historiography must always select and combine, reconstruct and pattern, establish causalities and coincidences. One judges the acuteness and probability of truth by the ability of the historian to contain more of the reality, to reconcile its living contrariety and dissolve its palpable confusion, rather than by whether the story it tells is what one has all along believed or wants to believe. Great historiography renovates familiar readings of history and however parti pris, whatever its loyalties to one or another ideological movement or doctrinaire position, the great history declares its patent.

Traditional historiography does not help our dealing with the *tremendum* of the genocide of European Jewry precisely because the reality exceeds the causalities. Nothing before, not the French revolution, not the unification of Germany, not the emancipation of the Jews, not the rise of capitalism, not the teaching of contempt according to Gospels and church fathers, none of these, causalities though they may be, achieve more than a gloss of the enormity—explicating this or that figure in the Nazi movement or interpreting this or that current of mob psychology or popular ideology, but leaving intact and unexplained the singularity of a machinery conceived and constructed to destroy a whole people.

If historiography is not a satisfactory tool, are there not other disciplines of inquiry, the investigation of the psychological and linguistic conceits of the perpetrators and their victims, which will assist us? Is it not relevant to understand the modes of deviance which released the psyche and language of a civilized society from the bonds of morality to the development of which its own traditions of *kultur* had so profoundly contributed? What allowed, such a course of inquiry might investigate, the degeneration of German speech over the length of a half-century from the rich, imbricated, responsible pursuit of truth into the garbled, vulgarized German authorized and distributed by the Nazi press, Nazi literature, and official bureaucratic speech?

Such an inquiry would be illuminating, but ultimately ineffectual, since the debasement of language and the traducing of the psyche, dependent as it is upon the organ of speech, is a process observable in varying degrees in every Western language. Germany is only a case of more so and earliest, but there is little doubt that the same has been true in the Soviet Union, and one notes that even the *New York Times* often prints news which is not "fit" to be printed. The debasement of language, the stripping of its subtlety and moral intention is a procedure which began in the West long before Hitler and continues after he is gone. It will help us to explain a kind of cauterization of conscience by the use of metaphor and euphemism to understand that in official Nazi language the extermination of Jews was precisely that—the disinfectant of lice, the burning of garbage, the incineration of trash, and hence language never had to say exactly what acts its words commanded: kill, burn, murder that old Jew, that middle-aged Jew, that child Jew. Language created its own rhetoric of dissimulation, and a conscience which was no longer required to hear accurately, a result not unique to Nazi Germany, but, indisputably, an efficient aspect of its discipline.

The point is that whatever we may learn from history, linguistics, psychopathology, political science, or social anthropology about the conditions which preceded and promoted the death camps or the behavior of oppressors and victims which obtained within the death camps is unavailing. All analysis holds us within the normative kingdom of reason and however the palpable irrationality of·the events, the employment of rational analysis is inappropriate. I do not feel the calm of reason to be obscene, as some critics of the rational inquiry into the *tremendum* have described it. It is not obscene for human beings to try to retain their sanity before an event which boggles sanity. It is a decent and plausible undertaking. It is simply inappropriate and unavailing. Probative reason, dispassionate reason have no place in the consideration of the death camps, precisely because reason possesses a moral vector. To reason, that is, to evaluate, is to employ discernment and discrimination, and reasoned discrimination entails the presence of a moral ambiguity and its resolution. There is no possibility of regarding the *tremendum* as standing within the parsings of moral judgment. It is not simply that the death camps were absolutely evil. Such judgments do not help. It is not enough to pronounce them absolutely evil. Absolute evil is a paradigm. There is little to which we can point in the history of men and nations which is absolutely evil, although the criterion of that abstraction has helped moralists to pronounce upon the relative evils of history.

The relativity of evil in the temporizings of moralists rarely entails the exposition of the relative good. Relative evils do not complete themselves by the description of relative goods. Relative evil is measured in the mind against absolute evil. Of course, such a logic of moral expedience has an ultimate reckoning. If it is too commonplace for men to release themselves from the paradigm of the absolute, it is even easier to excuse transgression—the erosion of moral sensibility (that human ether in which the conscience breathes) is clogged and stifled; men rationalize and justify so long and so well that the time passes quietly, unobserved, when they should have stopped and shouted, "no, not this, not this."

But, of course, it is hard in a shouting and busy world, continuously assaulted by interests and needs, for any single man to be heard crying against the flood. In such a time, the recognition that there are absolute evils abstractly described, and formulated in commandments whose very authority guarantees transgression, has not prevented us from accumulating a mountain of small evils which, like the bricks of the Tower of Babel, might one day reach up and pierce the heavens. The point of this is to suggest that moral convention, a pragmatic regimen of norms and *regulae* of behavior, have authority only so long as the absolute evil of which they are *exempla* remains abstract and unrealized. When the absolute evil comes to be, the sphere of the moral and immoral ceases to be efficacious. Can one doubt this in the politics of the twentieth century? Until the end of the eighteenth century the political theory of Europe centered about philosophies of law, right, duty, and freedom. It was understood that the relation of citizen and state was somehow a moral relation, that the citizen was a person educated to freedoms and informed by responsibilities. In our time, such language has virtually disappeared from public debate and inquiry. The language of politics is not that of moral interaction and representation, but the calibration and weighting of power, influence, need, and control in such fashion as to guarantee for one's own constituency a larger and measurably greater security both for and against uncontested aggression. Questions of right and law, of justice and equity have virtually disappeared as criteria for social and political action. The consequence of all this—the process of the demoralization of the political—is the irrelevance of the absolute and the utter, as the adjectival thunder to the nominally relative. What men once called murder, barbarism, cruelty, or sadism is simply useless rhetoric. Not one of us can summon these words with the authority with which John Milton or Voltaire might have uttered them and few can hear the English rendering of the Hebrew prophets with little more than a recognition of their immense eloquence. Words no longer command us precisely because they no longer reflect concepts and convictions which directly agitate conscience.

If this analysis is correct, it will be readily understood why I have come to regard the death camps as a new event, one severed from connection with the traditional presuppositions of history, psychology, politics, and morality. Anything which we might have known before the *tremendum* is rendered conditional by its utterness and extremity. At this juncture, let me remark why I have chosen the word *tremendum* to identify the death camps and why, most particularly, I have not and cannot refer to Auschwitz as the name by which to summarize and transmit the reality. Auschwitz is only one among many sites of death. It was not even the largest death camp, although it may well have claimed the largest number of victims. Auschwitz is a particularity, a name, a specific. Auschwitz is the German name of a Polish name. It is a name which belongs to *them.* It is not a name which commemorates. It is both specific and other. And, if my perception is correct, what occurred then, from the time of the conception of the "Final Solution" until the time that surreal idealism was interrupted, is the transmutation of chosen persons into chosen people, of the scandal of Jewish particularity and doggedness into the scandal of Jewish universality. What might have been, until the time of the "Final Solution," a controversy about the particularism and insularity of Judaism in contradistinction of the dogma of nationalist anti-Semites who wanted a Jewry divested of Judaism and Jewish identity, a theological reform which wanted Jews rehabilitated by Western humanism and *kultur,* or a Zionism which wanted Jews tied both to self-determination and Socialist class-consciousness in the struggle against Jewish temerity and timorousness, became in the death camps the brute factuality of the universal. Not the individual Jew, not the martyred Jew, not the survived Jew—not a Jew by any name or fortune—not such a Jew of particularity was chosen. Jew, simple Jew, nominative universal describing and containing all mankind that bears that racial lineament until the third generation of ancestry, became chosen and was universalized. The death camps ended forever one argument of history—whether the Jews are a chosen people. They are chosen, unmistakably, extremely, utterly.

The uniqueness of the death camps, that which makes them a novelty in extremis, severed from all normative connections to historical precedent and causality, imparts to them a phenomenological simplicity. The death camps are a reality quite literally sui generis, and insofar as their reality is concerned, it is not necessary for us to perform phenomenological surgery, to bracket them, to excise their connections from the welter of historical conditions, to clarify the standpoint of perception in order not to confuse their manifestation with that of any other seemingly comparable phenomenon, like the social institution of the prison or the army. Simply defined (and the simpler the better for our purposes), the death camps were constructed to fulfill one purpose: to kill the greatest number of Jews at the least possible cost in money and material. To the side of Jews were added Gypsies, another "degenerative and infectious race," and the work was undertaken and, by war's end, almost completed. It was a task pursued with lethal self-sacrifice since, quite clearly, as many historians have noted, the war effort of the German army was severely impaired by the preference given to the transport of Jews. The simplicity of the phenomenon is no less its enormity. To kill Jews, any and all, defines the reality and clarifies its uniqueness. In the long history of "the teaching of contempt," in Jules Isaac's telling epitomization of the Christian doctrine of the rejection and humiliation of the Jewish people, the church never undertook to kill the Jews. Certainly the church had the opportunity; it did not have the intent. As Professor Yosef Hayim Yerushalmi pointed out recently, the anti-Jewish massacres of medieval times were "principally the work of the mob and the rabble" and, as he elaborates elsewhere in the same remarks, were often interrupted and contained by the appeals of cardinals and popes, rather than being the outcome of their direct instigation. This is not to say that Jews and Judaism were beloved to the church. It is merely to indicate what should not be forgotten, that the practice of the church was as ambiguous toward the Jews as was its theology. It acknowledged that Judaism was a *religio licita,* a legally permissible religion, even though a deluded one; that it worshipped the true God, although inadequately; that it was a primary faith, although one humiliated and superseded. The most telling observation of Professor Yerushalmi in this context is his ironic suggestion that had the church not rejected the Marcionite heresy, that which specifies the distinct and unrelated dualism of the God of Creation (that of Hebrew scriptures) and the God of Redemption (the Jesus of the Gospels), the Jews might well have been destroyed. Precisely because the church did not disdain its origins, did not repudiate the God of Israel, the Jews survived. Indeed, the novelty of the death camps is further underscored. The medieval tradition of anti-Semitism was *contra-Judaeos,* against the faith and the belief of the Jews, and, only by inference, against the people and the ethnicity that sustained that faith. The older traditions of anti-Semitism, those that stretch back into Roman times, the rage of Apion and Manetho, the confusions of Tacitus and others, signify an uncritical perception of the Jews as a political unit, a religious commonwealth that refused Rome, not allegiance, but moral capitulation. The ancient Jews annoyed Rome less because they were different than because they regarded that in which they were different to be superior to Rome. Perhaps there, well before Christianity, the seedbed of racial contempt is to be found, the ultimate historical ground of Sartre's contention in *The Anti-Semite and the Jew* that the anti-Semite chooses to make himself nondescript, to attach himself to the solidarity of the miserable mob, to make himself mediocre precisely because he cannot make himself individual. The anti-Semite takes upon himself the vulnerability of the state, the difficulties of an abstract, national pride and whatever there is, out there, that offends against the few values that give him identity, those he calls the menace of the Jew. Of course, Sartre's analysis is undergirded by historical assumptions with which we would take issue, but what seems to me most profound in his inquiry is the perception of racism as an instrument of insulating and aggrandizing the empty man, or, as is more appropriate to the anti-Semitism of figures of undeniable weight and influence—figures such as Marx, Bakunin, and Kautsky, to name but three revolutionary intellectuals whose anti-Semitism reached grotesque proportions—their anti-Semitism was a means of interpreting their ressentiment, their unreasonable contempt for the slowness, the intractability, the stubborn obduracy of the old order which refused to cave in on schedule.

State-instituted racism and racial anti-Semitism is a modern phenomenon, whose origins may lie in the classical tradition which knew no efficient distinction between the political manipulation of religion and the religious validation of the state. In the Middle Ages, the doctrine of the two powers, the king and the bishop, in continuous tension and embattlement, the king warring to win the loyalty and the blessings and benefices of the church, and the church using the weapons of popular agitation and excommunication to manipulate the powers of the king, maintained a healthy imbalance in which the Jews, *servi camerae,* bond servants to both crown and cross, were more often maintained as financial and political intermediaries to their disputes than cast into the fires of either. All this delicate tension dissolved with the victory of the secular state, the state which could conceive, administer, and propagate throughout its realm quickly and efficiently, employing the press, the clergy, the law, the army, and the civil service as instruments of disseminating policy. If that policy were racist, the Czars could with ease send the Black Hundred into the streets; it could distribute the Protocols of the Elders of Zion; the army could condemn Dreyfus and hold the government ransom for his condemnation; and National Socialism could institute the program of ultimate anti-Semitism, the death camps.

What must be understood is that the irrational phenomenon of racism can still be made intelligible—psychologically, socially, historically. Any Jew reading Graetz's *History of the Jews* before 1939 would, I think (seduced as he might be by Graetz's eloquence and narrative gifts), regard his summation of the many hundreds of pogroms, massacres, and riots which fill his pages as being antiphonic and unremarkable: 9 Jews were slain, 11 Jews died; 157 Jews were thrown into the moat and perished; 411 Jews were burned; 31 Jews died at the stake; 1 Jew died from his wounds. Indeed, the familiar litany of Jewish history until the death camps was predictable—whatever the violence, Jews died. The history of the Jews could be read as the history of Jewish dead from Ibn Verga's *Shevet Jehudah* until the beginning of the era of the death camps. The fact that the numbers were compassable, variant, incidental, rising and falling, great or few, without apparent pattern or consistency enabled us to regard Jewish history as a continuous narrative of Jewish lives being paid for Jewish life. Throughout it all, it could be said that Jews died *al kiddush ha-Shem,* in sanctification of the Name of God, as martyrs to faith, although undoubtedly many there were who were ignorant Jews, Jews without faith, even assimilated and unconscious Jews, killed no less as Jews, ennobled no less as martyrs.

The death camps changed all that as well. We are given a fixed number. We deal with a single inconceivable enormity, one figure of six million, that has neither grown nor varied, remaining a stationary imponderable. It is no less clear that the Jews who died cannot be called martyrs. This is not to say that they are not martyrs; it is only to say that the theological implication of such a martyrdom is as catastrophic for one's conception of God as it is trivializing of one's notion of martyrdom. If the reality is inconceivable, if we cannot encompass the decision of one people to congregate and destroy another, attended by the complicity and inattention of all the rest of mankind, equally inconceivable is any language of compensation or heroic transfiguration. The human beings who died are not made more sacred nor more innocent by being called martyrs; indeed, in martyrizing them we dismiss them, having given them their histrionic due. The only people who have the right to call the dead in the camps martyrs are those who believe in the sanctity of martyrs and are willing themselves to be martyrs. I know such people and I believe them when they speak of the martyrs of the camps, but I also know that very often they separate out from the company of those martyrs the no less murdered Jews who were nonbelieving Jews, Jews without *mitzvot,* even assimilated Jews, Socialist Jews, Jews with changed names and non-Jewish identities. It will not do to call them martyrs just yet.

I have come to the point in my remarks when the hopelessness of this inquiry seems insurmountable. I have done everything I can to make the death camps not only unique, incomparable, sui generis, but, more to the point, beyond the deliberations of reason, beyond the discernments of moral judgment, beyond meaning itself. It is precisely for this reason that I have used one unexplained term throughout this lecture, employing it conspicuously, but never defining it. I have spoken of the death camps. That is clear. A factual phenomenological description, a phrase almost neutral in its factuality. But I have also used the term *tremendum*.

Quite recently I had occasion to reread, as I do frequently, Rudolf Otto's magisterial essay, *The Idea of the Holy* (Das Heilige). That essay, a late product of German idealism, an early achievement of phenomenological analysis, is turned to the investigation of our knowledge of the holy. The holy is not simply a cognomen for God; it is not God's other name, a name among many names, standing alongside Merciful or Judge. The holy is the dimension of God's presence. The presentness of God is his holiness. Rudolf Otto, using the Hebrew Bible, with a sovereign control and a warming love of its nuance and texture, elicits from that text revelations of the presence of God which are astonishing. Indeed, astonishment, surprise, and amazement are the very terms by which Otto underscores the shattering perception of God's nearness. God is near, Otto indicates. God is present, Otto evinces, but God is not for those reasons any the less terrifying and unfathomable. It is for this reason that Otto describes God in a single phrase as the *mysterium tremendum*—the utter mystery, the enormous mystery, indeed, the terror-mystery, for *tremendum* has as well not only the aspect of vastness, but the resonation of terror. The phenomenology of the holy begins with the perception of the terror-mystery of God and radiates from there, qualified, moderated, and textured by the traditional modes of mercy, love, and justice, until the utter God becomes the Father God of *Tatenu,* until the shattering presence becomes the still, small voice, until the terror-mystery becomes a God with whom men can coinhabit the universe.

The terror-mystery of God, the *mysterium tremendum* of divinity has always, in the phenomenology of religion, been offset and contested by under-divinities, potencies, and dominions in the universe which loath such ultimacy. The perception of the demonic coexisted with the perception of the holy. Indeed, part of the terror-mystery of God is that his manifestation in whirlwinds and at seas, in fires and in floods was often perceived at the outset as the work of his opponent, his demiurge, his particular devil. No wonder that God, in his *magisterium,* often appears under the aspect of his terror. The ferocity of God appears to resemble the demonic. It is no less the case if one listens, as the text unfolds its narrative, that what begins in ferocity ends in a bird with an olive branch and a rainbow. The terror-mystery of the holy becomes the love-mystery of the holy and the terror dissolves into grace.

This is one reading of the aspect of the holy as *mysterium tremendum.*

But, let us put the case that we of the modern age no longer can deal with the holy, cannot perceive it, do not, justifiably one would think, authenticate its presence, but most contrary and fractious, regard ourselves as alone and autonomous in the universe, unbounded by laws except as conventions of power, unhedged by moralities except as consent and convenience dictate, is it not the case that in such a civilization all that was once permitted to the infinite power of God and denied to the finite and constrained power of men is now denied to the forgotten God and given over to the potency of infinite man? Caution: I am not proposing in this yet another gloss to the familiar discussion of Faustian man compacted to the Devil, with all its attendant critique of technology, machine-culture dehumanization. The argument here is different. It is the proposal of a counter to the *mysterium tremendum.* It is the human *tremendum,* the enormity of an infinitized man, who no longer seems to fear death or, perhaps more to the point, fears it so totally, denies death so mightily, that the only patent of his apparent indifference is to build a mountain of corpses to the divinity of the dead, to placate death by the magic of endless murder.

I call the death camps the *tremendum,* for it is the monument of a meaningless inversion of life, to an orgiastic celebration of death, to a psychosexual and pathological degeneracy unparalleled and unfathomable to any man bonded to life. And of the nations and cultures of the West, is there any so totally committed to life, to the choice of life and its enlargement as a system of conduct and behavior as that of the Jews? The Jew may well be the ideal victim because of his mere persistence, his sheer endurance, his refusal to die throughout four millenia until the *tremendum* was a celebration of the tenacity of life. Every Jew who has left Judaism for Christianity has invariably—and the literature is astonishing in its confirmation of this perception, from Paul to Tarsus to Boris Pasternak—argued that the old Jew is dead, that Judaism has no more life to speak, no more novelty to contribute, nothing vital and energetic any longer to transmit to the species. The Jew is, in such literature, construed as though dead, whereas no less clearly it is necessary to mortify Judaism in order to rationalize and excuse its abandonment. The living Jew must become the dead Jew in order that the non-Jew be saved. The covenant with life must be severed in order that the divinization of men and their proof against death be confirmed.

Martin Buber has written in a passage often cited that there is no caesura in the history of the Jews, no midpoint, no intermediation, no gap to be filled by the Holy Spirit, no descending dove of grace, no yawning time waiting for the divine incursion. Most specifically, in this teaching, Buber was addressing the absence of penultimate messianic moments. "In our view," Buber wrote, "redemption occurs forever, and none has yet occurred. Standing, bound and shackled, in the pillory of mankind, we demonstrate with the bloody body of our people the unredeemedness of the world. For us there is no cause of Jesus; only the cause of God exists for us." Buber tried to deal with the *tremendum* on several occasions, always obliquely, always *b'derech agav*. He spoke of our times as the eclipse of God, times when between men and God a veil had been dropped, a veil of confusion, obstinacy, or demonism through which the Word of God could not penetrate. He believed until the end of his life that God continued to speak, but that no man heard. Moreover, he continued to believe that God's speech was his action, and that not hearing that speech was, in effect, to destroy the efficacy of God. God spoke and created the world. God spoke and the people covenanted themselves to his service. Six million died and God's speech was not heard. Not enough. Moving rhetoric, but unfortunately not theology, not thinking. It has to be tougher than that. It has to be more than the eclipse of God. It has to be more than the death of God. It has to be more even than Nietzsche's madman proclaiming that "we have slain him." Not enough. And we know that now.

Buber's assertion that there is no caesura in Jewish history is accurate insofar as it concerns the eschatological vision of the perfecting and redemption of history, but wrong insofar as it misses the underside of history, the corrupting caesura, the abyss rather than the heavens of the historical. For the holy, there may be no caesura, but for the unholy, its name is caesura. The discontinuity of the abyss is precisely what insures that it is both caesura and *tremendum*. The abyss of history is, in this view, also a gap in normal time, no less a gap, no less a decisive gap than would be the messianic redemption. In the time of the human *tremendum,* conventional time and intelligible causality are interrupted. In that time, if not redemption, then the demonic tears the skein of events apart and man (and perhaps God no less) is compelled to look into the abyss. The Jews, for reasons no longer curious, have looked into the abyss several times in their long history. Tradition counts the destruction of the Temple and the obliteration of the Jewish settlement in ancient Palestine as one abyss. There was a caesura. The abyss opened and the Jews closed the abyss by affirming their guilt, denying the abyss, and assuming the culpability of the demonic. Not the "beyond reason," but the "within providence" became the satisfactory explanation. The expulsion of the Jews from Spain is accounted another. There was a caesura. The abyss opened and the Jews closed the abyss once again, not only by reaffirming

their guilt, but more by transforming the event into an end-time of ordinary history and the beginning-time of mystic gnosis in which a new
heaven was limned and the unseen order became transparent to mystical
understanding. The death camps of the modern world are a third. There
was another caesura of the demonic. This time the abyss opened and
one-third of the Jewish people fell in.

It is not possible to respond as did the survivors of the first abyss.
We do not hold ourselves guilty. We cannot say, as an incomparably
stupid rabbi is quoted as having said of the Maalot massacre, that it
occurred because the school in which the twenty-four children were slain
contained twenty-four unkosher *mezzuzot.* That extremity of magical, tal-
ismanic thinking is hopeless, and all the degrees of talismanism up to the
doctrine of "for our sins are we slain" is insupportable. But that was an
old doctrine of providence, simplistic, but not without counterbalance of
innumerable Midrashim which saw quite clearly into the nature of the
mystery. The real point is that for our ancestors, whatever the deficiencies
of their popular doctrine, they lived in the presence of the *Mysterium
Tremendum,* the Holy God, and knew quite intimately the shudder and
trembling of his immediacy. Nor do we respond as did the survivors of
the second abyss. The kabbalistic transfiguration of the Spanish exile and
the decimation of Sephardic Jewry represented an overwhelming and
ingenious reinvestment of the historical process with a new significance,
one which was adept at reading the sign language of events and determining an arcane and previously impenetrable language of hope. The
third abyss is read, however, neither with guilt nor with hope.

To read the event with neither guilt nor hope is a pitiless conclusion.
It lets the event lie meaningless, unrescued, unransomed. The death
camps are meaningless, but they are also instructive. This is obvious, but
I do not wish to complete my discussion with a recourse to homiletics or
consolations. I could (and I believe it would be fruitful on another occasion) undertake to apply the analysis of Franz Rosenzweig to the ahistorical character of life within Torah in contrast with the holocaustal
normality of life after the death camps, but I am frankly not ready for the
personal implication of such an inquiry.

For the moment I must allow the brutal summation to emerge as it
must. The death camps cannot be transcended. There is no way of obliterating their historicity by overleaping them. Quite the contrary. If there
is no transcendence beyond the abyss, the abyss must be inspected further. The descent deeper into the abyss must take place; in a word, the
abyss must be *subscended,* penetrated to its perceivable depths. The task

of the excavation of the demonic is no metaphor. How can we regard the atomic bomb, or Vietnam, or the revelations of Solzhenitzyn's *Gulag,* if not as modalities of the abyss, excavations and elaborations of the human penchant to self-infinity, to the ultimate hubris which brings not only Jews, but all men to the borderlands from which there is no return for any.

It begins with the Jews and it can end with the habitable world. There is no way of making the genocidal totality of the death camps meaningful to the non-Jew as such, precisely because every Jew that has endured to this hour is a survivor in fact or an accidental survivor at least, whereas for the non-Jew the genocide of the Jews is an objective phenomenon which, on the face of it, by its definition appears to exclude him. The non-Jew would be slain only by having become a Jew (as occurred to many); otherwise he is able to contemplate but not share in either the fate of the victim or the perpetual unease of the survivors. This is a critical distinction which makes all effort of the Christian or the non-Jewish secular opponent of racism fail to understand what exactly the death camps mean to the Jews. For the non-Jew the death camps are still, so he imagines, a paradigm of human brutality, at least an epiphenomenon. For the Jew, however, it is historically real. The Bible commands that every Jew consider himself as though he went forth in exodus from Egypt. The grammatical authority of the Haggadah makes clear that this is no metaphor, whatever our wish to make biblical language metaphoric. The authority is clear: I was really, even if not literally, present in Egypt and really, if not literally, present at Sinai. God contemplated my virtual presence, then, thirty-odd centuries ago. The fact that history could not prevision and entail my presence is irrelevant. No less the case that the death camps account my presence really, even if not literally, hence my obligation to hear the witnesses as though I were a witness, to be with the witness as though I were a witness. It is mandatory that this real presence of all Israel in the death camps, experiencing the *tremendum,* enter the liturgy as surely as it entered the narration of the Exodus. Within us there is always hope and despair, and within faith that twin constellation must be honored, the hope extended by God to man and the despair returned by man to God—the dialectic most grimly enacted in our time.

Beyond all these considerations, we return again and again to break our head upon the *tremendum* of the abyss, a phenomenon without analogue, discontinuous from all that has been, a new beginning for the human race that knew not of what it was capable, willing to destroy and to be destroyed. We must create a new language in which to speak of this in order to destroy the old language which, in its decrepitude and decline, made facile and easy the demonic descent. When the preparations are completed, then the new beginning of the race which started in that quintessential perfection of the abyss must be thought (lest it be considered unthinkable) and redescribed (lest it be considered indescribable) and reconnected to the whole of the past, lest the abyss never be closed, and projected into the future, lest the future imagine it has no share in that past. In that way, first by separating the *tremendum* from all things and descending into the abyss, then by rejoining the *tremendum* to the whole experience of mankind as end point of the abyss and new beginning of the race, it is possible to link again the death camps, the *tremendum* of the abyss, to the *Mysterium Tremendum* of God who is sometimes in love with man and sometimes loathes him.

Autobiographical Fragment:
The Holocaust

When I was a child my family organized large passover celebrations, bringing together as many as thirty people to a gathering of the clan in honor of grandparents and family founders. It was ostensibly a commemoration of the Exodus of the Jews from Egypt three millennia ago. It was in fact a frequently rowdy jamboree marking the fortunate passage of Jews from Europe to the prosperity and freedom of the United States.

What religious values obtruded were inevitably suppressed by the exuberance of the children and the chattering indifference of the adults. I never enjoyed these Passover *sedarim*. I suspected even then that something was being lost amid the triumphant assertion of American success. These Passover feasts took place, if my memory serves me, during the early 1930s, at the depth of the depression, during the opening years of the coming to power of National Socialism in Germany.

And then I went away to boarding school. It must have been 1934. The curious school to which I was sent was a catchall for every imaginable domestic displacement: parent's day always saw not less than four parents per child, although there were several of us whose parents were absent, trapped in Germany, in flight to Mexico or Cuba. There were also the children of the secretary of the Communist Party of America and the

Forthcoming 1, no. 3/4 (1983): 27.

vice-chairman of the New York State Communist Party. It was during those early childhood days at Cherry Lawn School that I acquired my first sense of the political disruption of our times. I was young, but I was ludicrously precocious. I read everything I could about the rise of fascism, the crisis of republicanism in Spain, the outbreak of the Spanish Revolution. I wrote a small history of the Spanish Civil War. I gathered money for the International Brigade. The vice-chairman of the New York State Communist Party heard me speak at an assembly and invited me to address a mass meeting at Madison Square Garden to support the departure of the International Brigade for Spain. It must have been 1937. My parents fortunately forbade my becoming a public speaker. I remained content haranguing my school, writing histories and plays, collecting money for Spanish Relief (all of which was mysteriously stolen from the wooden box I had made in carpentry class).

It was during these youthful years that I heard Hitler speak on the shortwave radio. His voice reminded me of someone else, but notwithstanding the resemblance that I only identified years later, the terror it inspired was unique. I collected evidence of impending doom like a scavenger foraging for the simple food of confirmation. I was not even a teenager, but my life was unnerved. My hands trembled; they have always trembled. It does not help to be told that it is a secondary genetic characteristic, probably inherited from my mother. I was frequently ill, once fatally ill, but miraculously recovered. It seemed all of a piece. The body was willful and unreliable, but no less the world and its inhabitants.

What I am trying to suggest with economy and concision is that events as maleficent and total as the *Shoah*—what I call the *tremendum* of evil—register upon some of us, but do not necessarily register upon all. Such immensity enters a psyche that is prepared to receive it as one more brutal datum in an untrustworthy world. Others, those somehow fortunate in their ignorance, assimilate these events as a threatening potency. I was prepared. My childhood was no delight. I had already prepared to die when I was six and had survived. I left home for the wilds of boarding school when I was seven and did not return until I was thirteen. I was a stunted child with a large imagination and a mind that guarded the secrets of loneliness and vulnerability with a frighteningly mature ferocity. It was no surprise to me finally that there were Hitlers in this world. Hitlers, and Stalins, and Francos—large monsters and small, manipulating continents, draining small nations.

Was it a surprise then to discover that along with the threat of illness against my body and assaults against my notions of freedom, there was the wish to destroy me as a Jew? Not in the slightest.

I went with my father in 1942 to a solemn gathering at Madison Square Garden. Cantor Kwartin (or was it Berele Chagy?) opened the gathering by chanting *El Male Rahamim*. It was solemnly announced that a report had been received through the Joint Distribution Committee and the Swiss Red Cross that the first million Jews were dead. Chaim Weizmann spoke from London by telephone and mentioned for the first time that we were being murdered by "a conspiracy of silence." A telegram was read from Franklin Delano Roosevelt asserting that when the war was won the criminals would pay. And we all stood and said *Kaddish*. I held my father's hand tightly. We both wept. Twenty-five thousand Jews wept. I have never heard so many people cry before. Never before. Not since. And that was all we did. We wept. And the next day the *New York Times* reported the event on an inside page, a single column, surrounded by advertising. So much for Jews without power (but having said that, let me add that any people desperately in need of the succor and attention of the world's conscience is by definition without power—this is true for Jews, but also for other people). "Never trust in princes . . . all men are liars."

I grew up and I went to university. I studied briefly at the Jewish Theological Seminary. I began to gather for myself the literature of the *Shoah*. I saw the pictures and was numbed. I saw the murderers in the box at Nuremberg and I felt cold. Those were years in which I could not bear to hear the German language; to shake hands with any German (even German-speaking Jews); to imagine that I would ever have a German automobile (I have never, but it is now price not conviction that prevents me), a German appliance, a German book in my library. I spent all those years of the late 1940s and 1950s cauterizing myself, burning the wound in order that the wound might heal.

These wounds never heal. The skin never closes and mends. No art resolves such wounds. Not even art. Art may transfigure the wounds, but only if it escapes from the confinement of realism, from literality, from transcription. There is no art that can make the *Shoah* significant if it is bounded art. The fact that art may sometimes be made by the victims who perished or by the survivors who endured is no guarantee that as art it will be any more effective a means of organizing memory than the narrative imagination working from the analogies of pain and dislocation that a child—such as I was—worked through on the way to maturity. The means of art are not identical to the reality of events. Once brutality and murderousness leave the reservoir of history and begin to sluice their way through our unconscious, their force ceases to be the force of event and becomes the memorable or the suppressed memory. What we recall, as survivors or as kinsmen to survivors, is already transcription and record. When it comes to the borders of recollection, these events will be for some only the substance of nightmares, for others waking screams and anguish, for yet others the opportunity for bloated rage, for yet others the materials of art. Art is only one means of reconstruction and preservation, and all arts—whether plastic or verbal—can only allude to content. No language, even the language of those who will say accurately "I was there" is to be necessarily trusted, even when the speaker adds "and I should know." The "I should know" is an addendum. It might well be the case that the person who was there should know, but very often, as has been documented, what is recollected years after the events is already pallid beside the lived event recorded in picture or film. It is the event stripped by memory of temperature, odor, humility, searing flesh, suppurating wound. And so, though the event repels art, art approaches the event. With timorousness, with respect, even with fear (which is a reason surely why so little of the art wrought out of the extermination camps succeeds in moving us). But then, compound the ambiguity: who is to say that when we judge the art we are judging accurately, acutely. What we are judging is the art, not the event, and passing judgment upon the truthfulness of art is different than passing judgment upon the rendition of historical events.

We come then to the work itself, my own work, for example. I could not speak of the *Shoah* for many years. One of my earliest books, a celebration of the complexity of the modern Jewish mind, *The Natural and the Supernatural Jew* it was called, dealt with the *Shoah* obliquely, not trivially, but obliquely. The *Shoah* had already worked its effect upon me, but I could not face it. The fact of the matter is that in those days there were many truths I could not face and so my inability to face the *tremendum* of my people was of a piece with my inability to confront much besides. It is true to say that I had yet to make the *Shoah* part of my autobiography. I kept it away along with other brutalities, the real ones of my own personal life, to which the *Shoah* was a grotesque analogue. I had not yet grown up.

V.

FICTION

INTRODUCTION

David Stern

The position that this section occupies at the center of this anthology reflects what the editors believe was Arthur Cohen's own estimation of his fictional writing's significance within the corpus of his work in its entirety. What is beyond doubt is that Cohen never felt his two main bodies of work—the fiction and the theology—to be in conflict or contradiction. As he wrote (in "Aggadah and the Fictional Imagination," reprinted in section six):

> I underlie both bodies of work. I hold them together in some delicate suspension, not quite like the random suspension of particles in a magnetic field, for as a human magnet I have both will and intelligence and can determine more efficiently what rises to the surface and what is suppressed.

Which is to say that Cohen believed that, ultimately, the same vision, the same preoccupations and obsessions, empowered and moved both his fictional imaginings and his theological searchings.

From 1967 until his death in 1986, Cohen published five novels in addition to *Artists and Enemies,* his collection of three novellas, which was published posthumously in 1987. Of these works, *In the Days of Simon Stern* (1973) is the only one explicitly on a Jewish theme, the

257

messianic drama in the aftermath of the Holocaust. The other novels, though they all touch in one way or another on Jewishness, are more directly concerned with other subjects—the meaning of art, the travail of the intellectual life, and, perhaps most importantly of all, the relation of falsity to failure, of truth and authenticity to success. The fact that these, and not strictly Jewish themes, were the main subjects of his fiction should give us pause before we assume that Cohen's theological writings were also purely, or parochially, Jewish.

The choice of what to include in this chapter of the anthology posed special challenges because of the obvious problems in extracting independent sections or passages from their larger contexts in the novels. Rather than make selections from all of Cohen's novels, we have chosen self-contained passages from two novels, *In the Days of Simon Stern* and *An Admirable Woman,* and have reprinted one novella, *Malenov's Revenge,* in its entirety. These selections also seemed to us especially representative of Cohen's narrative imagination.

"The Legend of the Last Jew on Earth" (from *Simon Stern*) is perhaps the most astonishing piece of fiction Cohen ever wrote. Obviously inspired by both the Grand Inquisitor's Tale in Dostoevsky's *The Brothers Karamazov* and the speech (sometimes entitled "Before the Law") that the priest in Kafka's *The Trial* addresses to Joseph K. near the book's end, "The Last Jew on Earth" is told to Simon Stern by a nameless, Elijah-like visitor that Stern receives immediately before he undertakes his messianic mission. A compelling parable of Jewish obstinacy and perdurance, the tale is probably the fullest expression of what Cohen understood to be the Jew's supernatural vocation; it is also powerful testimony to Cohen's talent as a historical fabulist who could make his fiction relate theological truths.

The second selection, "One's Own Text," from *An Admirable Woman,* is one among several meditations on life and literature belonging to the novel's protagonist and subject, Erika Hertz. Erika, the memorable character that Cohen modeled upon such German-Jewish intellectual emigrés as Hannah Arendt, was arguably the fictional creation with whom he personally identified most closely, while the particular subject of this meditation, Heinrich Von Kleist's essay, "On the Marionette Theater," was (as we know from the remarkable essay, "The Sufferings of Heinrich von Kleist," reprinted in section seven), one of Cohen's own favorite texts. In that sense, this meditation may be said to be one of the more autobiographical confessions in Cohen's fiction.

The final selection in this section, the novella, "Malenov's Revenge," is perhaps the most disturbing fictional work Cohen ever wrote. The story of the doomed relationship between the great Russian modernist painter, Yevgeny Malenov, the founder of "projectivism," and his patron and epigone Joseph Karnovsky, the novella is an energetic, disjointed, and utterly disheartening tale of discipleship and friendship gone rotten. While the reader is bound to be impressed by Cohen's talent at evoking ever so accurately the world of European avant-garde art at the beginning of this century—its cafe life, its politics, its personal, professional, and sexual quarrels—what gives the novella its real power is Cohen's fearlessness in portraying the sad, disquieting relationship between two artists, one an authentic genius, the other no genius at all, as the former slowly but inevitably destroys the disciple's life. Although Karnovsky happens to be Jewish, there is little that is explicitly Jewish about this novella.

Increasingly in his fiction, Cohen turned away from the question of Jewishness per se to that of the life of the intellectual or artist, particularly that of the solitary genius, or near-genius (and Cohen was ever alert to the abysmal difference between the two); indeed, one might say that the solitary artist became a kind of figure in Cohen's work for what had earlier been embodied in the natural and the supernatural Jew. The difference between how the typological pair fared in the theology and how the character made out in the fiction is, in a sense, the history of Cohen's own life. In his theological writing, the natural and the supernatural Jew is an integrative ideal, the focus of a call to renewal. In the fiction, the two dimensions appear as two disparate albeit related themes—the demands of art and the bonds of friendship (or discipleship)—which cross in this story as though in a double helix, ultimately to intersect in a disaster.

The Legend of
the Last Jew on Earth

In the region of Catalonia, beside the rivers Ter and Onar, in the city of
Gerona, on the Calle de la Disputacion, which commemorated a long-
forgotten controversy between his kinsman, Rabbi Moses ben Nahman,
and the convert Pablo Christiani in the presence of King Alfonso and his
court in the capital city of Barcelona, there lived in our time the last Jew
on earth. He went by the name Acosta, a respected and honored pa-
tronym among Spaniards, but he was as many, if not all, Acostas, descended from secret Jews.

Don Rafael Acosta owned, as did many citizens of Gerona, a shop
that specialized in the leather goods for which the region is famous. He
inherited the shop from his father, who died when Don Rafael was a
young man; however, his mother had managed it with such meticulous
efficiency that by the time of his twenty-fifth year, when it was fitting
that his apprenticeship end and he assume control, it had grown to be
one of the most prosperous shops of its kind in the city, exporting cured
skins to leather fabricators in France and England and distributing
gloves, jackets, coats, hats, and other articles of leather made by house-
holders in the region to other parts of Spain and handicraft centers
throughout the world.

From *In the Days of Simon Stern*. New York City: Random House, 1973, 117–46. Estate of
Arthur A. Cohen.

Don Rafael became the director of a substantial business. His mother, now aged, her fingers gnarled by arthritis, sat in the study of their ancestral home, a stone house in the old quarter of Gerona, reading the Spanish fables in which she delighted, mending her son's clothing and overseeing Marietta, the cook, and Rosa, the maid, in the performance of their simple domestic tasks. Don Rafael had no interest in marriage or in the fathering of children, although he was aware that in his ancestral faith celibacy was not a virtue and a man without wife and children was accounted but half a man. No matter. There were none of his people about him in the market of Gerona and none remained in the ancient judería where he lived. He was unafraid of reproach or disapproving stares; his fellow Jews had long since disappeared, disappeared before he was born, and of their memory only tales and legends remained; with these he was well familiar because his mother read to him on the Sabbath of the miraculous Toledans and Cordobans of earlier centuries who had caused the light of Judea to burn in that farthest reach of the Mediterranean. He knew of all the saints and philosophers, generals and poets, legists and mystics who had flourished in the land of Spain and of their trials and torments at the hands of Almohades and the Holy Inquisition, and of the pogroms and desecrations, and of the ghettos, and of the fiery preachers—converts and Jew-haters all—who picked off, one by one, from the stock of Israel the finest branches and grafted them forcibly to the numberless trees in the forest of Christendom. But, as with his lack of interest in marriage and in the fathering of descendants, so Don Rafael had no interest in the ministrations of the Mother Church. He had mother enough of his own, security enough in his business enterprise, youth enough to enjoy its fulfillment, and he counted it possible that in his later years, like an aging prince, he might take to himself a young woman for warmth and pleasure, and perchance, in the natural course, an heir would issue whom he would legitimate.

The people of the city of Gerona, set down by God in a plain of the north of Spain where mountains and valleys were verdant and productive, where peasants worked and were fed by their land, and industry and effort were rewarded by crops and produce, were generally indifferent to the dogmatic exigencies of religion. Catalonia was at the crossroads between Christendom and Islam, the way station from the shrines of France to the shrine of St. James of Compostela, the political cat's-paw of Louis of France, Henry of Aquitaine, Roger of Sicily. But that was some time ago. In recent centuries Spain had settled into withdrawal; a half-century or so behind more industrialized societies, she was at this moment restored to a constitutional monarchy, a regal church, an agrarian prosperity, and an uncommon calm. Spain loved to be at rest. It was in this most serene and comfortable corner of that peninsula of inactivity that Don Rafael Acosta was born and lived.

In his fortieth year, at the time of this narrative, his mother was gathered to the blessed and shrined in the memory of her son at the abundant age of eighty. Don Rafael was alone in his generous and well-trimmed world, walking in his black suit of heavy wool and his broad-brimmed Spanish hat to Casa Acosta in the Plaza España of Gerona, taking his lunch in the hotel on the square, joining friends in the bar behind the entrance to the ancient cathedral for a glass of wine and conversation or a game of billiards before returning to his home to rest and eat a late supper of Spain. His was the simple and uncomplicated life of the commercial gentry. It suited his quiet manner and gentle bearing, his shy smile, which he covered with his hands, his black hair, which sometimes fell with youthful indiscretion over his forehead, his slim and erect body, which he bore with agreeable disdain. He was an excellent and unexceptionable man, and it was through no fault of his own that it came to him to enact the remarkable drama of being the last Jew on earth.

Don Rafael knew nothing of the world. That is the critical fact. The events of the larger world were quite simply irrelevant to him. Nothing beyond the precincts of Gerona engaged his attention, unless, of course, a famine in Uruguay or a pestilence in Argentina had destroyed so many hundreds of thousands of heads of cattle that the price of Spanish hides was forced by scarcity to unexpectedly profitable levels. Then Don Rafael would smile without covering his mouth and point to the newspaper in the bar behind the cathedral and announce the good fortune which was Gerona's through the bad fortune of South American cattlemen. It was a simple view of events and not unlike the view of most men. But aside from that, aside from the report of news that bore upon their lives directly and without the requirement of reflection, he and his associates and friends had no curiosity about the great world. It could not be known therefore or regarded with more than passing interest that in that year, Don Rafael's fortieth, the conversion of all the world to the Catholic faith had been completed. Assuredly, the cardinal archbishop of Gerona noted the event and delivered sermons about it, but his remarks were consigned to the back page of the Monday edition of the newspaper, below the results of the soccer tournaments and the corrida and it was hardly an event for prosperous burghers to note, perhaps least of all Don Rafael, who never read the *Noticias Religiosas,* and in fact was accustomed to avert his eyes in a millennial reflex at the sight of the person or picture

of the archbishop in his episcopal robes. It should be recalled, however—
and this he remembered much later—that his mother on her deathbed
had taken his hand and put it to her heart and demanded his promise
that until his own death he would not depart from the faith of their
ancestors. He had sworn and moments later she had died. The ancestors
of Don Rafael Acosta had come to Gerona in the time of Moses ben
Nahman, the Talmudist, the commentator, the grammarian, the mystic.
Moses had lived in fact directly across the road from Don Rafael Acosta's
paternal ancestor, who had come to Spain from the Muslim kingdom
of Fez in the early part of the thirteenth century. The Acostas were a
distinguished family, physicians and Talmudists, who served churchmen
and grandees with uncompromised dispassion and rectitude while never
neglecting the poor and sick among their own people.

It was at the time of the massacres of 1391, more than a century and
a half after the Acostas had come to the city of Gerona, that the family
publicly abjured the Jewish faith, renounced the ways of their ancestors,
and took upon themselves the outer garments of Christian worship They
appeared to serve the Lord of the Christians mightily, observing absti-
nences and vigils, attending mass with regularity, receiving the sacraments of the Church, giving obedience to its laws and regulations. What
was not known was that, foreseeing the possibility of just such times as
these, the old patriarch of the Acostas, Solomon ben Jehudah, had drawn
up and notarized a document, signed in his presence by all those of his
family, binding them forever (despite any and all derelictions which
might result from fulfillment of the commandment of our people, that
we live) to obey in continuity and to death the seven principles of the
faith of Noah. Moreover and wherever possible, they were sworn to the
observance of the Sabbath and the Fasts of Av and the Day of Atonement.
They were then commanded, even to the fiftieth generation of those who
might live, to return in fullness and faith to all the remembered observances of the House of Israel, to remove from themselves the deceiving
guise of the Other Faith and to obey the God of their fathers until the
time of the true Messiah—but this only when true service could be accomplished in peace, serenity, and without threat to life.

The family swore to this document, affixing their names, some seen
even in children's scrawl. The document was placed behind a vault stone
over the high fireplace of the reception hall of their home, and each year,
by candlelight, on the Sabbath preceding the Day of Atonement, it was
removed and read aloud. In more recent times there were none who
knew Hebrew, but no less faithfully the family gathered on what it believed to be the Sabbath before the fast (they had nowhere to turn for

accurate knowledge of the calendar, and during the nineteenth century, although the fires of the Inquisition had long since been banked, the spirit of Spanish intolerance remained pure and uncorrupt), and no efforts were made to recover and return these secret Jews. They withdrew the document, examined it in silence, swore an oath of loyalty, and returned the document to its hiding place. Correct Catholics—some of them, indeed (may they be spared in His mercy), believing Catholics—they nonetheless maintained this secret practice of ancestral obeisance. And so it continued to the time of the family of Don Rafael Acosta.

Change, in the guise of boredom and inaction, had come to the Spain of Don Rafael's parents. No longer obliged by law to be an *observant* Catholic, it being sufficient that one remain in the eyes of the world a Catholic, the father of Don Rafael began to educate himself in the practice of his ancient faith, obedient to the demands of his ancestor, Solomon ben Yehudah. He secured books of instruction in the Hebrew language and explained their presence in his home by the curiosity he felt for the life and times of the antecedents of his Christian Lord and Redeemer. In time he taught himself, his wife (a distant cousin whom he had married in her youth), and then his only child and son not only the language but the liturgy of the Jewish people. They were not meticulous in their observance, it being left to the declining years of his father and the fifteenth year of Don Rafael's life to learn by accident about the laws of the phylacteries (which they undertook to procure and don) or the *mezzuzah* (which they promptly affixed to their doorway, concealed behind an iron cross).

Don Rafael Acosta could not have known then that he was the last Jew in Spain—indeed the last Jew in Europe—that no Jew survived in the Holy Land, that all the crypto-Jews, proto-Jews, aboriginal Jews, the few hundred Samaritans who clustered on Mount Gerizah, the black Jews of Harlem, the Falashas of Ethiopia, descendants of the Queen of Sheba, were no more; that the small community of Japanese Jews, the Karaites of southern Russia, the Jews of New Delhi and Bombay, the surviving Chinese Jewish family in Shanghai had vanished, gathered up into the Holy Roman Church. But not these alone. Not Jews alone had vanished from the earth. Indeed, they had been the last to go. Some, to be sure—refusing the gentle advice of Franciscans and the hectoring Dominicans and Jesuits who had passed throughout the world in caravans of faith, distributing crosses and rosaries, instructing in the day and baptizing at nightfall—chose to die, taking poison or starving themselves to death in undemonstrative demurral. But they were few and their numbers were not reported. It was the case that after two thousand years of militancy and combativeness, what the Church had sought by sword fell to it now without effort.

It was a miracle of the Church Triumphant. Sikhs and Buddhists, Confucians and Shintoists, Taoists and Zoroastrians, Holy Rollers and Methodists, Adventists and Christian Scientists, Muslims of the Mutakallimun and Muslims of the Sufi, all these capitulated, singly, in family, in village, tribe, whole nations in an orgy of pacific espousal. Giant crosses played the skies of all the continents by day and night, radios offered masses and oratories of thanksgiving. The numbers of the recalcitrant were reduced gradually, with unapproachable tribes contacted and inundated by forces of missionaries. The tropical forests of Indochina, the tangled rivers of New Guinea, the green maze of the Amazon were all penetrated and their people converted.

The Reformed churches were the first to bow their knee to the holy pontiff, then came the patriarchs of the Eastern churches, then the Muslims of North Africa, the Near East and Asia, and then polytheists and pagans of Asia, and last, following the atheists of North America and Europe, came the picking off of the Jews, those wild fruits of the branch, the first flowers of divinity, the last witnesses to stubborn unbelief. It was done at last. The new millennium could begin. The reign of the child of God, the son of the Lord, the Lamb of Heaven, could begin, and ultimately, finally, at a moment that would still remain unknown the Parousia would come to pass. The Christ would return in glory, and the world would be judged. All believed that they would be saved, nature transfigured, and the age of renascent beatitude, at the end as it was in paradise at the beginning, would commence.

It so happened that a young priest from Saragossa, just returned from a triumphant sojourn among the tribesmen of the African grasslands, had taken his old mother and father on a tour of Spain. They arrived in Gerona late on a Friday afternoon and parked their battered car in the Plaza España before Casa Acosta. Don Rafael had been busy throughout the day. A convention of nurses had just completed its deliberations, and customers crowded his shop to buy presents for their families. It was late in the day and he had become accustomed to returning home early on the eve of Sabbath so that Marietta could serve his supper earlier than usual, depart, and leave him to a quite evening of reading in the Torah and examining the rare editions of Hebrew works he had begun to collect. He had closed the door behind the last nurse, a pretty girl from Valencia in honor of whose long black hair he had offered a ceremonial discount. He had already sent off his assistants and turned out the lights in the stockroom when he heard a knock at the front door. He determined to ignore it, but the knock continued, followed by a low, muffled but insistent call for help followed by a plaintive *"por favor."* Annoyed, Don Rafael unlocked the door and opened it. The young priest from Saragossa stood before him.

"Sir," he said directly, "my car refuses to start. Would you be kind enough to push me into the street? Perhaps then I can encourage a passing car, if one chooses to come at this hour, to assist me further."

"There will be no cars at this hour. Not for two more hours. Those that come now are all rushing to go home. I doubt that even our gracious Geronans will stop for you, Father."

"You may be right. The problem is my parents." He motioned to an old couple seated erect, unsmiling, as though Egyptian dead, in the backseat of the vehicle.

"Indeed," Don Rafael commented. He thought he might show hospitality. It did not matter that it was the eve of the Sabbath. The young priest would not know or care. He seemed pleasant enough. He would bring them to his home and call Garaje Jaime to assist them. By ten o'clock they would be off and he could retire to his study. He proposed that the priest and his parents return to his home for supper. The priest smiled appreciatively, and after a brief and virtually inaudible consultation with his parents who even then did not speak but inclined their bodies slightly in an unspecific nod of acknowledgment, the proposal was accepted. Don Rafael called his housekeeper to inform her of his guests and arranged with Jaime to send someone to pick up the keys to recharge the battery of the old car. It was done.

His guests were left in the darkened drawing room of his home. Rosa, the niece of Marietta, served them sherry while he rested. At eight o'clock a light supper was served. It had not been customary in his family for a large meal to be offered in honor of the coming of the Sabbath. The festive meal, as always among working Spaniards of the provinces, was at noontime. A simple soup, a fish turned in oil, and a salad were sufficient. And wine.

The priest (he had introduced himself and his family as Mendoza, his own name being Don Xavier Maria) was curious, but not astonished, to find Don Rafael seated when they entered, a small black-velvet skullcap pushed to the rear of his head, almost indistinguishable in the twilight. The priest, peremptory as is habitual to his vocation, made grace without deferring to Don Rafael's wishes, crossed himself, as did his parents, and commenced to spoon the soup, unaware that Don Rafael had not responded "amen" to his benediction nor, for that matter, crossed himself. Don Rafael pushed back the heavy oak chair, rose to his feet, poured wine from his drinking glass into a small silver thimble cup and incanted quietly, but without haste or embarrassment, the kiddush of sanctification, sat once more, broke off a piece of bread from a small loaf which stood before him and blessed it. Not until he was about to lift his spoon to begin his meal did he become aware that his guests were motionless, no longer eating, their faces ashen with incredulity. Of a sudden the old lady began to cross herself rapidly, hitting her forehead, shoulders, and chest in a frenzy of movement. The old man began to shake, one leg striking the table repetitively. Only the priest remained unstartled by the scene, though he regarded it as curious. He turned to his parents and with a gesture of his hands he calmed them. He turned to Don Rafael who had watched their consternation with amused confusion.

"Who are you, sir?"

"I, Father?"

"Yes, my friend."

"I? Indeed you must know. I am the proprietor of a leather shop in the Plaza España of Gerona, called Casa Acosta. I am the Acosta. Don Rafael Arturo Moyse Acosta of Gerona. Born in Gerona. And, with the grace of God, to die in Gerona in this house."

"I see. Yes. Quite so. But, tell me, Don Rafael, what was that rite you performed?" the priest demanded, wagging his finger theatrically at the silver thimble cup and the bread.

Don Rafael was abashed at the priest's unexpected rudeness, but he replied. "That rite? Oh, Father. You must know it well. It is the ancient ritual from which the Eucharist of the Church arises. Wine. Bread. Blood. Body. You must know?"

The priest frowned and a tie appeared over his left eye, a slight irregular spasm. "I know of no such rite. Indeed, there were a people, the Jews, who until recently practiced such a cult, but they are either dead or converted."

"Indeed," Don Rafael replied.

"Completely. Yes, the last of them were baptized eighteen months ago. I, personally, was responsible for administering baptism to the remaining forty Jewish families of Fez, Morocco, two years ago while on my way south toward the tribes of the grasslands. I am finished with them now. Every Jew and every Bantu who came into my way has been baptized."

"In that case, Father, I must disappoint you. My family came from Fez more than seven hundred years ago. I am, if you will, a Spaniard from Fez, and moreover I am a Jew. It may well be that I am the last Jew on earth." Don Rafael began to laugh. The very idea seemed so witty, so preposterous, there was nothing left to do but laugh. He laughed a good while, his face reddening, his hand steadying the skullcap upon his head.

The priest frowned. Anger replaced curiosity. "I do not believe you, Don Rafael Acosta."

"Believe me, what?" Don Rafael replied, his laughter subsiding.

"That you are a Jew."

"But, of course I am. I am, as regards the world, unobservant Catholic, a not unusual phenomenon in Gerona. No self-respecting Spaniard would go to church—that is for women and old men and parents of priests. I was born a Catholic of visibly Catholic parents. But my father and mother were both believing, practicing, devout Jews. I am as well. And now if you will excuse me for a moment. I should like to call Jaime."

Don Rafael rose from the table and left. The remainder of the meal was served, but Don Rafael's guests ate no more. The mullet in white wine did not please them, nor the salad, nor the fresh fruit. They were, permit me to say, thunderstruck. Don Xavier sat at the table without speaking. His mother suggested that he lead them in a decade of the rosary, but the young priest demurred. Something more drastic was called for.

Don Rafael returned to the table after it had been cleared and coffee and walnuts served. "It's done. Fine. The man from the garage was just here. I gave him the keys and he will drive your car here when it is repaired. There will be no charge. Hospitality, particularly Sabbath hospitality, is always complete."

"My dear Don Rafael, I do believe that what you said is correct."

"What, Father?"

"That you are the last Jew on earth."

"No, my dear Father, I was joking. I was teasing you. That's quite unfair. My apologies."

"No. No. You don't seem to understand. In all likelihood what you are saying is true. You are the last nonbeliever in the world, not simply the last Jew on earth, the last nonbeliever, the last non-Catholic."

"But if you wish you can regard me as a believer. I was baptized. It's there, as you would say, even if it can't be seen. It's only that I don't believe a word of the Catholic faith, not a word. I am a Jew, and that's quite enough."

"Quite enough for whom?" The priest spoke with solemnity.

"For me, of course. For me. Nobody demands more of man. I am a decent man, a good Spaniard. I support the government, endorse its laws, contribute to charity. It is only that I am stubbornly pledged to my ancestry."

Don Xavier did not persist. It seemed hopeless. His host seemed to have no interest in his anomalous situation. He was without curiosity, dull, unimaginative. It seemed irrelevant—more, wholly uninteresting to him that he might in fact be the last Jew and the last non-Catholic on earth. It was pointless to contend further with such proud and indomitable ignorance. The priest broke off the conversation, thanked Don Rafael for his hospitality, and left as soon as the car was brought. He did not neglect, however, upon arrival at his hotel that same night, to address a letter to the cardinal archbishop of Gerona, the Most Reverend Pedro Fernando Corazon y Iturbe. His letter read:

Most Reverend Father,

It is my duty to inform you that in your midst there is one, Don Rafael Acosta, proprietor of Casa Acosta on the Plaza España of your city, who remains, despite the visible triumph of the faith, recalcitrant and unconverted. He is, dangerous enough, a lapsed Catholic, having admitted to me that he was baptized at birth, but, more grievous than this, his heresy is not that of natural ignorance or libertinism with which we could more easily contend, but of active devotion and fealty to his ancestral faith, that of the benighted Jews.

There are, you are aware, no longer Jews in our world, may the mercy of the Lord be praised. He is, I feel confident to claim, the last. But it is not simply that he proclaims his faith (I witnessed at his table this evening the performance of antiquated rites which gave me and my aged parents who were the inadvertent victims of his hospitality a shiver of mortal terror) from the fount of simple ignorance. With such ignorance we have proved in recent years we are more than capable of dealing. It is rather that he, who bears upon his brow the waters of baptism, by giving allegiance to a dead belief, actively despises our truth. If he remains unrepentant he will corrupt others. Knowing as we do that the ways of truth are encumbered with thorns and stones, we cannot risk that one, even one, active unbeliever be allowed to thrive, lest his presence infect others who find the path of salvation hard.

I urge you to take action.

If for any reason you wish to contact me, I am shortly to return to my family home in Saragossa, where I am available at the Church of San Xavier, after whom I am named.

I am a priest of the faith recently returned from our missions in Africa.

Yours respectfully,
Xavier Maria Mendoza

Don Rafael, on the other hand, did not think further of his evening with the family of Mendozas. He had found the meal tedious, the priest ill-mannered and ungracious, and his parents superstitious peasants. Once they had left he drank coffee in his study until midnight, reading quietly from his father's Bible the portion of the week which tells the story of the righteous convert, Jethro, who was the father of Zipporah, who was the wife of Moses, who was the father of all our people.

The following days were uneventful. Twice Don Rafael observed that a middle-aged man in a black suit and white straw hat stood across the street from his shop, smoking small cigars, but he imagined he was an idler who fancied himself elegantly turned out and stood about to attract the attention of the girls promenading the Plaza España at noontime. On the fifth day his assistant, Pablo Henriquez, motioned to the idler and said laughingly, "We are being spied upon, Don Rafael."

"Who? Where?"

"There, across the street. He is there during the comfortable hours, but when I arrive early in the morning to open the shop, there is another, a bald, fat man who is relieved about eleven by this one."

Don Rafael shrugged without interest. "I don't understand, but if it continues I will see to it. I am well known and respected in Gerona. Why should anyone spy on me?"

The following Friday, when he arrived at the Plaza España to have coffee in the café which was directly across the square from Casa Acosta, he noticed a small crowd gathered before his store. He hastened toward the crowd, and pushing through, saw to his horror that the front window of the shop had been broken. Pablo and his fellow assistant, Benito, had begun to hammer a wooden beam across the window and clean away the glass, but the shock of this vandalism left Don Rafael stupefied.

Don Rafael called the police and the alcalde. An inspector from the Police Department, with whom he often played billiards, arrived and explained apologetically that he knew nothing of the culprits, that, indeed, he would be vigilant in pursuing them, but he added as he turned to leave, "You may well have brought this upon yourself, old friend." Were it not that he knew this man's wife and children, having bought them ice cream each time they came into his shop, he would have lost his temper, perhaps even have struck the inspector. As it was, his rage increased and tears of frustration came to his eyes. He closed shop for the day, sent his assistants home, and sat in the darkened interior, occasionally stroking the finely tooled display cabinets, their stomachs decorated with carved flowers, their feet golden orbs covered with Empire ivy.

Nothing happened during the remainder of the day, neither telephone calls nor further visitations from the police. The inspector did not return. The mayor, who had once dined in his home, did not respond to his call.

Don Rafael was upset—gloomy, to be more precise. He had never experienced vivid fantasies of enmity or persecution, but the days which followed provided him with fuel enough for a furnace of suspicion. The window was only the beginning. One night the shop was broken into and all the cabinets of ladies' purses and the glass counters with men's wallets and watchbands were overturned. Nothing irreparable, nothing broken, nothing stolen, but hours of restoration and inconvenience. A few days later a drawing of a Jew in sackcloth, his head surmounted by a medieval conical hat, a sign around his neck proclaiming Marrano, and the flames of a bonfire searing his bare feet appeared in whitewash on the vitrine of the shop. A curiously scholarly insult, Don Rafael thought. He did not immediately discern its source. A leaflet—Benito and Pablo gathered up fifty of them scattered in the wind that circled the plaza— denounced Casa Acosta as the purveyor of cheap, synthetic products, the leather imitated, the prices inflated. Business did suffer. The other merchants commiserated with Don Rafael, whom they liked, but professed ignorance of the origin of his misfortune. The harassment continued for a month—vandalisms, insults, graffiti, obscenities. Benito quit Don Rafael's employ claiming a nervous stomach. The matter was grave. To be sure, Don Rafael was not indifferent to the situation. How could he be? But he was ineffectual. He telephoned the Perfectura several times daily, but each time the jefe was unavailable and the duty officer answered him with bored rudeness. He wrote a dignified letter to the Alcalde of Gerona, but Don Francisco did not reply. It seemed hopeless, and Don Rafael, by now in genuine torment from many sleepless nights and undigested meals, contemplated leaving Gerona, even leaving Spain.

On a Thursday afternoon, nearly five weeks after the original visit of the itinerant priest and his parents, a limousine bearing the coat of arms of the Episcopal Diocese of Gerona appeared before the door of Casa Acosta. The chauffeur, a sinewy Spaniard with thin, dry lips, presented him with a letter, signed by a Monsignor Siguente, the personal secretary of the cardinal archbishop, requesting the presence of Don Rafael in extraordinary audience that afternoon, in fact in fifteen minutes. The chauffeur, without so much as an "Excuse me," went to the rear of the shop—indeed as though he knew it—and brought Don Rafael his suit jacket and topcoat, which hung in a small wardrobe in the wrapping room. Don Rafael followed the chauffeur to the limousine, entered and sank back into the refined comfort of the ancient Mercedes. The car started off, up across the bridge into the old city of Gerona, up the backstreets toward the cathedral and the palace of the cardinal archbishop. It was not a long ride. Six, perhaps ten minutes. The car stopped and the chauffeur opened the door for Don Rafael. Don Rafael hesitated. It was not that he was frightened. He had been to the palace many times, during the annual blessing of the city, at Christmas time when the cardinal saluted the merchants of Gerona, and indeed at the investiture banquet of the present cardinal. He hesitated then not from nervous unfamiliarity. Rather he dimly understood that perhaps not the *jefatura,* not the alcalde, not even the few envious merchants of the Plaza España were responsible for his misfortune, but the cardinal himself, and if the cardinal, the whole of the Church. He struggled out of the car. The chauffeur walked ahead, his hand beckoning him from behind to follow. Damned impudence, Don Rafael thought. He was led through a dark vestibule lined with heavy furniture and bust portraits of the archbishop's predecessors, men with lean jaws and small eyes or else jowls cushioned with flesh. They ascended two flights of stairs to an antechamber where a young priest sat in semidarkness writing entries in a large vellum-bound volume. The priest jumped up, looked at Don Rafael with a smile, rang a small hand bell which must have been concealed in the palm of his hand, the vast oak doors before which they stood opened.

Don Rafael entered and the doors closed behind him. He stood alone in the darkness. A voice from within another chamber invited Don Rafael to enter. He did, advancing four steps through an archway into the room, which appeared to be a library, for there were tiers of shelves lining the walls although few books could be seen.

"Come closer," a small voice proposed. "You will not be able to see me, unless you come closer." Don Rafael advanced hesitantly. "Closer still. I am not well. Nor am I an easily visible man even if I were." Don Rafael walked toward the voice and saw a very tiny priest, who sat on a low divan covered in red damask. A single light from a lamp shone upon the table to the side of the divan. In the peripheral light which barely included the priest, Don Rafael could see a man of considerable age, his face a map of rivulets and creases, his skin the color of wheaten wafers, dotted with brown grain. "Do sit next to me, my son." Don Rafael sat upon the divan and clasped his hands before him. "Do you know who I am?"

"Your Eminence?"

"Not quite. I am no white eminence. Grey, black, scarlet perhaps, but no public eminence in the panoply of the world." The old priest chuckled. "No. I am a priest pure and simple (I am Father Espinosa), but my responsibilities encompass the Society for the Propagation of the Faith, the Secretariat for the Promotion of Christian Unity, and until recently the nearly moribund Holy Inquisition. Note well that I have said 'until recently' and 'nearly moribund.' It would appear you intend to revive me."

Don Rafael did not understand, although he remembered well from history books the cruelties of the Inquisition. But no one had been burned in Spain since the eighteenth century.

"Father, I do not understand you."

"You will understand me terribly well, my son. Do you smoke?" The priest withdrew a packet of cheap cigarettes from the pocket of his soutane and offered one to Don Rafael. Don Rafael waved it way. He was becoming unnerved.

"Help me then, Father, to understand why I am here, why I am being persecuted."

"Are you a Catholic, my son?"

"The truth, Father, is this. I was baptized a Catholic as were all my family, but we have never practiced nor believed the faith. We are Jews descended from Jews who in this good Spain of our times are able, without giving public offense or disgrace to our friends and neighbors, to honor what we believe."

"You are a lapsed Catholic?"

The phrase came to his head, "Canonically speaking."

"In a word then, you are a Catholic in mortal sin."

"No, Father, I am an observant and believing Jew who, through the habit of centuries since our forebears were driven from this land, has been obliged to appear to be what he is not. I am the sole surviving member of my family. I am not married. My parents are dead, may they rest in peace. I am all that is left."

"Precisely!"

"Precisely what?"

"Precisely the point. You are all that is left anywhere, my son, anywhere in the entire world."

"I don't understand."

"Technically we could ignore you. We could say to ourselves, 'This peaceful church has good Catholics and bad Catholics.' We could say to ourselves quite simply that you are a bad Catholic—no sacraments, no communion, no prayers and benedictions. That would be all right under certain circumstances—if you lived, say, in Zanzibar or Tanganyika. But here in Catholic Spain it is a different matter. And in Catholic Gerona, founded even before the time of Rome, an ancient city of the faith, to have in the midst of Gerona, in the bosom of Spain, in the heart of the West, in the innermost ventricle of the heart of Christendom, not only a lapsed Catholic, but a believing Jew—no, my friend, that is quite a different matter."

Don Rafael clearly did not understand the priest. He smiled in dumb incomprehension. Father Espinosa shifted his inconsequential weight; his feet, hidden beneath him, covered by his soutane, appeared as small protuberances seated in red-velvet high-heeled pumps. They peeked out at Don Rafael, caught the light, and shone. The priest observed Don Rafael's curiosity. "My small feet," he said, lapsing into reverie. "My gazelles, I call them," he went on, first addressing them and then Don Rafael. A curious fellow, Don Rafael mused. "A different matter, my son."

"What? Which?" Don Rafael had lost the conversation. Feet. Shoes. The endearments of Egypt.

"We have returned, my son. From reverie to reality. You have not understood me, have you?" he said, extending his bony hand, white flesh, to pinch Don Rafael's leg. "Are you awake to my meaning?"

Don Rafael became dizzy; a small pain, hidden at the base of his skull, moved out of the moraine of buried impressions and memories into the whole of his head. He asked for water. A bell tinkled and a pitcher of water and tumbler appeared. He requested an aspirin. It was produced. He saw no one, but hands reached around him out of the darkness to set down what he had requested.

"Are you quite restored?" Don Rafael nodded. "In that case, let me continue. It should be clear by now. You are, my friend, not alone the last Jew in Gerona, the last Jew in Catalonia, the last Jew in Spain, the last Jew in Europe, but in fact the last Jew in the entire world. The very last." The priest struck his knee with two fingers. It was not an emphatic gesture, but it was emphatic enough.

"I see now," Don Rafael murmured. "Clearly now. It is for this reason that I am persecuted. First that priest and his family, and then the humiliations done to me and my establishment. Yes, I see."

"Those torments embarrassed me, I assure you, Don Rafael. I have put an end to them. Our Lord, the cardinal archbishop, is a peasant from Asturias, adamantine, to be sure, but somewhat crude. I persuaded him to put an end to harassment. He listens to me. No, no. There will be no further persecution." The priest stopped for a moment and sucked on his lower lip. He swallowed hard and his throat clucked. The moisture gathered from his lips (like a bird sipping dew) was quite enough. "If you do not mind, it will all be satisfactorily completed when you sign this document." He took a letter from a drawer in the secretary which stood at the head of the divan and handed it to Don Rafael. "No, no. No need to read it now. It is perfectly clear. It is simply a document of faith, precise and crisp. By the regulations of canon law you must be genuinely free to examine it in quiet and contemplation. To submit to Christ is a choice of will. The will must not be constrained. I would not think to have you sign it here in my presence, under the constraint of my inquisitorial authority. No. No. You must have time and leisure to reflect. I think our interview is concluded."

Don Rafael took the paper, folded it, and put it in his pocket. "By tomorrow then. Let us say, three o'clock in the afternoon. At the cathedral. Tomorrow. You will return with the document, executed, notarized, if you please, and we will hold a small celebration for the last Jew on earth." The priest laughed. Don Rafael left the presence of the priest and descended to the small plaza before the episcopal palace. He thought to return by foot down behind the Arab baths, the long way, circling back to the small *rambla* of the city by way of Calle de la Plateria to the avenue at the center of which Casa Acosta had stood for more than one hundred years. But that was not to be. As he reached the bottom of the steps the same Mercedes hummed to a stop before him, and the chauffeur, this time with cap in hand, alighted and hurried around to open the door for him. He had no choice but to get in and be driven to his home. When he reached the door to his house and reached up to put his fingers to the parchment of the *mezzuzah* concealed behind the iron crucifix, both had disappeared and in their place a minuscule ex-voto had been attached. He entered the house, and a painted statue of the Virgin, illuminated by a halo of colored lights, affronted his eyes. The living room was a garden-house of white lilies, and where, before, the pictures of his family had addressed their love to his eyes now hung St. Francis being visited by the stigmata, St. Sebastian delirious in his pain, St. Stephen beheaded, and others and more in the ecstasies of their martyrdom.

Don Rafael did not even turn the pictures to the wall or order them covered. He let them be. He stared through them, indifferent. He took his supper as before. He made his blessing and he said his grace and he thanked God that he had been permitted the honor of this season and its trial and he went quickly to his room, not daring or even caring to ask Marietta, who had waited anxiously for his questions, as to how these disgraceful intrusions had come to pass. It was not her fault. Nor, he reflected, was it his. The maladjustments of fortune, the woundings of time.

It was nearly midnight when he emptied his pockets and took out the momentous letter. He sat back in his tufted chair, his bare feet cold upon the stained-wood floor, and poured himself a drink of brandy and then opened the letter. It read:

> I, Don Rafael Arturo Moyse Acosta, known to all as Don Rafael Acosta, resident in the most Catholic city of Gerona in the region of Catalonia, submissive to the grace of her protector and lord, the cardinal archbishop, the Most Reverend Pedro Fernando Corazon y Iturbe, do hereby declare in the presence of all the multitudes of Christendom that I abjure, deny, refuse, hold in contempt, anger and dismay, repudiate, reject and despise the congeries of errors and the magnitudes of untruth which are, have been and ever more shall be in the memory of man to the doctrines of the Old Church, the dead Synagogue, the withered limb of Christ which by this act I do cut off. Though I am baptized into Mother Church I have wandered with her ungrateful recusants and though I was availed the instruments of my salvation, I blunted them and cast them aside for useless and deceitful teachings.
>
> I am penitent. I implore the mercy of the Church and I repent my waywardness. In love and in faith I ask to be released from my sin, to have imposed upon me any penance the Church in its mercy deems fit to cover my stain.
>
> I, Don Rafael Arturo Moyse Acosta, the last Jew on earth, ask to disappear.

For many hours he sat and watched the paper in his hand until the letter wavered and disappeared into blackness. He read it no more. The paper passed from his sight, and the reverse, printed as images are printed in our brain, upside down for storage in the recesses of memory, was retained. He slept that night in his chair, and in the morning, cold, his feet icy, a sniffle in his nose, a huskiness in his throat, he pulled himself up before the sun and bathed himself in its winter rays. He said the morning prayers as he had said them many thousands of times before. He wrapped himself in his phylacteries and wound the knot of unity around the middle finger and draped his father's silk prayer shawl over his eyes, and resplendent before the sun, sang out the praise of God and the abundance of his manifold compassions.

The morning hours passed and at eleven he returned to the shop, avoiding the chauffeur whom he saw lounging before the house. He went down into the cellar, and through an underground passage which let out into the street three houses away, walked quietly to the Avenida, where, as was his custom, he took his coffee.

The noon hours came and the shop closed for the afternoon siesta. Don Rafael did not leave but ordered a soup and fish to be sent in. He waited and he thought. A desultory reverie. He rolled back the skin of the *merluza* and uncovered its skeleton embedded like a fossil in tender white flesh. Skin flayed from bones. A taste and it melted; his jaws worked slowly. He chewed long and distractedly until there was no flesh between his teeth and he bit his lip and cried out.

The shop reopened. An old lady bought an ivory comb in a tooled black leather case. Don Rafael sat in the rear of the shop and sipped his coffee, already cold. He knew the letter of recantation by heart and its words blew through his mind like rain-soaked winter leaves. At ten minutes to the hour of three, the Mercedes came to the corner of the Plaza España and stopped; its driver, now dressed in gray garbardine and black puttees, approached the vitrine, rapped and crooked his finger. Don Rafael rose and pulled on his overcoat. His assistant stood by quietly, averted his eyes, and busied himself with a feather duster when Don Rafael nodded his goodbye.

The paseo was quiet. A German couple was drinking coffee at the Montana Bar, but otherwise the shops were closed, the usual throngs of strollers were absent. The Mercedes turned around and passed to the rear of Casa Acosta into the narrow street which ascends through the Old City to the cathedral square. The car moved like a lizard, scuttering forward and stopping suddenly to avoid an idling pedestrian. As the car mounted the cobbled streets Don Rafael became aware of the numbers of people moving, it would appear, in the same direction as he. The last street before the cathedral square was packed with people; the car—the only car—moved with difficulty, but the chauffeur never sounded his horn. People stepped aside and the car passed through.

The automobile entered the square as a light rain began to fall upon the bared heads of the multitudes, the thousands of Geronans, top-hatted dignitaries, choristers in black satin and white lace, the bishops—there were eight—in rose gowns, the papal legates, and high above them, at the top of the fifty-eight steps of the marble staircase that ascended to the doors of the cathedral, his Eminence, the cardinal archbishop of Gerona. At his side, holding his arm, was the withered priest, Father Espinosa.

The door of the automobile opened and Don Rafael stepped out into the warm rain. He looked about him, and dazed by the assembly, turned as if to reenter the car, but a chamberlain approached, and grasping him firmly by the elbow, pressed him to the base of the stairs and sternly whispered, "Go up. The cardinal awaits you. No nonsense now." There was nothing to do but obey. Don Rafael put his right foot to the first pediment and hesitated. The leg abandoned him. It tingled with electric-ity, benumbed. Don Rafael struck his thigh with his fist. The leg moved and he followed. Slowly he rose up, catching sight in furtive sidelong glances of old friends, Marietta, Pablo and Benito, and unmistakably the young priest Don Xavier Maria Mendoza.

A dozen steps from the top, Don Rafael hesitated. Those near him pressed forward, hands outstretched, thinking he would now retreat. He smiled. He was calm. He continued on his way. The last step brought him to the level of episcopal authority. The Te Deum began, the church doors swung open, incense floated into the rain, photographers discharged their flash bulbs, radio technicians adjusted the bank of microphones that stood to the rear of the cardinal. The old priest limped to his side and spoke, "The world awaits you. Speak the recantation and then hand the document to the cardinal and kneel before him." Don Rafael bowed his head in salutation to the cardinal and moved toward the microphones. There was silence but for the gentle patter of the rain. Don Rafael passed a hand lightly over his forehead and touched his eyes in a gesture of friendship toward himself. He paused and breathed deeply. He began, "I believe in one God, Father Almighty, maker of heaven and earth," and he paused, "and . . . and . . . that is what I believe, that is the only belief I share with you." Cries: "No, no." "And the rest that I believe is what I have learned from my father and my father's father and all those in the generations of fathers which stretch back in the history of time to Moses, my first master . . . And so much more, if you would like to hear about it."

Don Rafael paused. He would have continued and told the history of the generations of Israel, but he was not allowed. The microphones went dead, the crowd pushed forward in a mass up the stairs and Don Rafael, shielded by the cardinal, who stepped forward to protect him (and for his solicitude was slapped in the face by a hysterical woman), retreated to the sanctuary of the cathedral.

Don Rafael surrendered to the darkness of the cathedral. The great doors had shut behind him, the shouts of the crowd had disappeared, even the bishops and Monsignori who had crowded the chancel, staring back at him and murmuring in consternation, had vanished. He was quite alone. It must be sundown, he thought, for the rose window of the west wall shone purple. His mind was empty of thought or, rather, it was full of so many thoughts he could not settle upon one. The effect was the same—vacuity and apathy.

"It was brilliant," a dry voice crackled from behind him, a voice placed so close to his ear that he felt its breath upon his neck. He had no need to turn. He recognized the ancient priest of the Holy Inquisition,

Father Espinosa. "Brilliant, brilliant. The opening of the Credo and no more. I congratulate you." The priest applauded and Don Rafael heard the measured beating of hands behind him.

"Don't mock me, Father. I staged nothing. In fact, Father, I almost went on—the whole Credo, by rote, just as I had learned it from the Sisters when I was a child, but that wasn't possible. I'm sorry, Father."

"You are a trouble, my son. Why couldn't you have been cooperative? Trouble for us, annoyance, irritation, and such an ordeal for you. Oh dear me." The priest was unhappy. "I'm not a young man, you must have gathered. And now all this exertion in my closing years. I had other projects for the end of my life. A visit to the monuments of the East and then retirement to a monastery for some restful meditation, and bleaching of my soul. And now this." The priest sighed. "You won't reconsider, would you?" Don Rafael said no. "I thought not. Well then, what to do? His Holiness telephoned. He was vexed. Do you realize that all of Spain and most of Europe, perhaps even Africa and Asia, heard your ridiculous broadcast? All of Christendom, all of Christendom. Oh dear." The priest cracked his knuckles nervously.

"I am sorry to have been a trouble to you, Father. But it had to be this way. You do understand, I'm sure. I might have signed the paper"—remembering it now, he handed it over his shoulder to the priest—"and gone on as before, masquerading my feelings, but that display you staged out there was intolerable. A humiliation. I just couldn't."

"Yes, yes, to be sure. A little overtheatrical, but then the Church is rather theatrical, don't you think? All our plainsongs and chants, our symbols and allegories, gold braid and lace, liturgical artifacts and mysterious bells, all these devices make the faith a bit spectacular. I find it exhilarating, however. The range is so extraordinary, from austerities that verge on the morbid to such ecstatic opulence. You don't agree. I know. You like your little desert visions, your bleak little vision."

"I'm tired, Father. A trying day, very trying. If you don't mind—and thank you for chatting with me—I'll be going."

Don Rafael rose, nodded distractedly toward the high altar, and went toward a side door at the apse of the cathedral. Three officers were waiting and took him into custody. That Sabbath eve he was flown to Rome. Father Espinosa was on the plane, seated in the tourist cabin, reading his breviary and sipping brandy, while Don Rafael and his captors dozed in the forward cabin.

Don Rafael was taken to Vatican City and turned over to an officer of the Swiss Guard who conducted him to an apartment. A very beautiful suite of rooms, from all reports. A week passed during which Don Rafael saw no one excepting a doctor who certified that his body and mind were sound. He was allowed to think. In the meantime the preparatory secretariats of the Council, those charged with developing its agenda, awaited advice from its listening posts throughout the world as to the effect of Don Rafael's stubbornness. They were not slow in coming. First off, it was headline news everywhere: LAST JEW SAYS "NO" (one paper had it as "No thank you"); JEW BELIEVES ONE GOD ENOUGH; SPANISH JEW DENIES CHRIST; and a thousand variants depending upon whether the paper was a *Le Monde* or an *Osservatore Romano*. By week's end there were reports that a small group of Tibetan Catholics had fled to the mountains to renovate a lamasery, that a former sufi in Cairo had mutilated himself during a trance, that an enclave of Sonora Indians had reinstituted the peyote ceremony, that two missionaries had had their brains eaten by supposedly pacified headhunters in New Guinea, and quite near to home in Abruzzi a shepherd boy claimed to have seen a bearded man with stubby horns coming down a hillock, carrying under his arm two engraved plaster tablets. There were now fifty or more Abruzzians awaiting the reapparition of St. Moses.

It was determined therefore that Don Rafael had to be made an example to the faithful, lest an incident of disease become an unchecked plague.

Eleven days from the evening of Don Rafael's arrival in Vatican City, Don Rafael was accompanied by a papal chamberlain in formal attire and a contingent of Swiss Guards to a chamber buried in the gloom of the Vatican. There an assembly of examining bishops had gathered to query him and hear testimony from others. Three bishops in imperial purple, a deaf cardinal, and Father Dominic Espinosa.

Don Rafael enters.

PRESIDING BISHOP (*To Don Rafael*) Do be seated. (*Motioning to a fauteuil covered in yellow silk which stands to the side of a long fifteenth-century Spanish mahogany table*) Are you comfortable? Excellent. We would prefer you not to smoke. The cardinal archbishop of Turin is deaf, but we will hear for him and (*pausing*) his eyesight tells him more than most of us hear. (*The others smile thin smiles*) Yes, now, what have we here? (*Shuffles some papers, puts on eyeglasses, but peers above them in a curiously affected manner*) Ah yes. You are Don Rafael Arturo Moyse Acosta of Gerona?

DON RAFAEL Yes.

PRESIDING BISHOP Good. Well then. Now what?

FIRST BISHOP (*Pinching his chin*) You are a Catholic?

DON RAFAEL Only in a manner of speaking—

FIRST BISHOP What manner is that?

DON RAFAEL A speaking manner, as I just said. If someone says to me, "You are a Catholic?" I say, "Most certainly," if it seems likely to end the conversation. I don't enjoy talking about religion. I prefer keeping religion to myself.

SECOND BISHOP To yourself, indeed. My dear man, religion is a matter of public record, like birth, marriage, and death.

DON RAFAEL True. For those purposes I am a Catholic. But, otherwise, since God observes the workings of the heart, its intentions, so to speak, I am not.

FIRST BISHOP And for those obscure regardings, what are you?

DON RAFAEL Must I say?

PRESIDING BISHOP Of course you must. Are you embarrassed?

DON RAFAEL Afraid, not embarrassed.

PRESIDING BISHOP What is it then?

DON RAFAFI Jew.

PRESIDING BISHOP Jew what?

DON RAFAEL I am a Jew.

PRESIDING BISHOP How so a Jew?

DON RAFAEL I am a Jew in the flesh. I am circumcised. I am a Jew in the spirit. I await the Messiah. I am a Jew by nature and profession. I am patient.

FIRST BISHOP A Catholic and a Jew. A hippogriff, a gorgon, that's what you are. A bastard, a corruption, that's what you are.

SECOND BISHOP To be blotted out.

PRESIDING BISHOP (*Rapping his episcopal ring upon the table*) Now, now. Please. (*To Don Rafael*) Do you realize the seriousness of the charge against you?

DON RAFAEL What charge? I don't understand. Why am I here? Why do these gentlemen—your colleagues, sir—speak to me in such a strange and insulting manner? I have done nothing to offend them other than—I gather—exist. I endure and my endurance is an offense. Well, then, that's that.

FIRST BISHOP That is not that.

SECOND BISHOP Most certainly not that.

FIRST BISHOP You cannot remain both "this" and "that."

SECOND BISHOP You may become "this."

FIRST BISHOP You cannot remain "that."

PRESIDING BISHOP In other words, to translate these grammarians, you must resume your life as a Catholic and cease to be a Jew.

DON RAFAEL I don't understand at all. One Jew in all the world and you fuss. It's quite foolish. I'm no competition. I don't even want to compete. I wish only to exist. I don't ask anything from you—no charity, no attentions, no favors. I want to be. That's what I am—a being who wishes to be, to continue in his ways, to live out his life. I don't preach. I don't argue. I don't parade my beliefs in public. I am a private man.

FATHER ESPINOSA Not quite. True. You *were* private, but you are no longer.

DON RAFAEL That's your fault.

FATHER ESPINOSA That may be, but fault it is not. You are an impediment. Were you undetected, persistent in your ways, private, as you say, the damage would be no less grievous. Do you imagine the offense is mitigated by privacy? The scandal is to God and it would be enough that He is scandalized, that because of your persistence in unbelief, the belief of others is compromised. No, no. I can see that you are *no* theologian. But we are. We are meticulous theologians. And the precision of our belief demands from us no less pure and undeviating logic. You are the last unbeliever and a Jew unbeliever at that. For that reason you are the first as well. You are unique. You *must* be converted. Do you understand, my dear friend, what your persistence does to this world? It alone prevents us from bringing the Kingship of Christ to the earth.

DON RAFAEL (*Softly*) All by myself?

PRESIDING BISHOP All by yourself.

FIRST BISHOP Does that please you?

DON RAFAEL (*Softly*) No. I am frightened.

SECOND BISHOP As well you might be.

DON RAFAEL No, not pleased at all. What's to be done with me?

FATHER ESPINOSA Recantation as before. But this time very public, exceedingly public. His Holiness will receive your petition in the Sistine Chapel. He will raise you up into redemption.

DON RAFAEL I understand your predicament, but no. I do not wish to rejoin the Church. I decline the privilege of saving the world. Saving the world is your job, not mine. I didn't ask to be a Jew. I didn't ask to be a man, or a Spaniard, or a leather merchant. But I am all of these things. And what I am by providence, I elect to remain. I will be all of these to the end of my life and I will be these faithfully.

PRESIDING BISHOP Well, Fathers, you've heard him?

CARDINAL (*Draws a finger over his throat and gurgles*)

PRESIDING BISHOP Please, your Eminence.

FATHER ESPINOSA We have no choice. He must be punished.

DON RAFAEL Severely?

FATHER ESPINOSA Severely.

DON RAFAEL How? How will I be punished?

FATHER ESPINOSA Humiliation.

The session came to a close. Don Rafael was returned to his rooms. Father Espinosa remained behind and continued to converse with the bishops, who called upon him to describe the implications and consequences of Don Rafael's stubborn refusal.

"My friends," he began, "we are at a curious impasse. It is ironic that now, at this moment in time, as we draw close to the return for which, as believers, we have waited nearly two millennia, our way should be—as Saint Paul previsioned—blocked by the Jew. I shall not fatigue you by reciting the historical miscreancy of that people. To be sure, they did not by their natural proclivity and disposition disdain our Lord or impede the dissemination of His Word. What they opposed, what they denied, they did as if by the implanting of God. He who made hard the heart of Pharaoh that He might rescue His own hardened also the hearts of Israel, that she might wound and slay her savior and remain until the end a people adjudged and condemned.

"We care not that from that time until this the members of that small society of supernatural criminals became the wards, chattels, property of the realm to be fatted or starved, contained or expelled, indulged like children or murdered like men, according to our wishes. We did not count it a certainty throughout that long vigil of time that a day would come—as it has now come—when the sweet air of the end would be in our nostrils. Throughout that vigil we threw down her altars, drove her sons forth, and slew her graybeards. Israel cannot torture forth the last drop of His blood and we cannot destroy Israel. Yet Osiris grows up from his own entrails, dies, and returns, forever unto ever again, year by year. We are regenerated and so is she. Ah yes, God hardened her heart and God keeps that hardness resolute, congealed, obdurate, and though we kill, kill, kill, she is there again.

"But now as Saint Paul foretold, the time of the last harvest is come, the gathering in of the gleanings of all our fields. There is one left, one from amid all the peoples of the earth, the last unbeliever, the last Jew.

"The world is reconstituted. The body of the New Adam, until this moment a nervous and puny thing, lying exhausted upon the straw pallet of the world, is healthy and intact, but for this tie in his cheek, this wart upon his thumb, this boil upon his thigh. This last Jew is the sole blemish of the New Adam.

"Having said this, let us counter our own argument. True, we are, in this Holy Church, the vicarage of God, conducting man through the treacherous narrows and shoals of his life, and it is we, with the timbrel of charity and the drum roll of hell, who have brought all dissent to confess its folly before Saint Peter's throne. But we, we, too, are mortal (whatever our virtues and our grace), and though we are already in the forecourt of the Kingdom we are as distant from the supernal throne as infinity and eternity. It is finally up to God. Would we save the world without God? We would not. We cannot. It is one thing to praise ourselves for having drawn together the appendages of the world, for having made of the disjected members of our species a single body, but without the breath of the spirit, of what value is all this quantity—of what value is it that untouchables and princes, muzhiks and headhunters, Eskimos and pygmies, know a bit of catechism and cross themselves—of what value? No. No. The breath must be kissed into this dumb Adam.

"The Russian theologian A. S. Khomiakov told us in former times of the vitalities of *sobornost*. That noble amateur believed that a congregation of the faithful is numbered not by head count but by heartbeat. Not ten or a hundred or millions but two or three who speak the name of Jesus Christ in purity of heart. There—in that small bedraggled company—is the truth. We, by contrast, are confronted by the reverse of the situation of our Russian friend. We have, not two or three, but one; and this one, in palpable good faith, simplicity, clarity says no. I decline, he says. I confess only the old, wasted inheritance. So there, he says. The New Adam remains blemished. No unanimity to the Visible Body. No concord to the Invisible Body.

"We have a recourse. Let Don Rafael die. Now that would settle everything. A touch of poison, an overdose of pills. Done. An expeditious resolution. (I see some of you like that. Dear me. You do not understand.) Expeditious, but completely misguided. We may deceive men, but we cannot deceive God. No. We cannot be the hand that holds the dagger hilt. We must proceed otherwise. We have already received—did you realize?—a petition from India with more than a million signatures calling for Don Rafael's speedy conversion. In America cenacles of worshipers are dedicating unceasing prayers to the Blessed Sacrament importuning intercession that the heart of our impenitent be melted. And, last but not least, for here is the clue to our decision, the Japanese—remembering well the martyrdom of their own Jesuit missionaries and the veneration they now offer their relics—have asked that Don Rafael be brought to that island for a tour.

"They write and I excerpt the letter of the bishop of Kyoto: 'Most excellent Fathers,' etcetera, etcetera, etcetera (here note), 'unbelievers in the past were employed by us, as living examples to the faithful. By the witness of their materialism, errancy, and sensuality we demonstrated most graphically the virtues of the Faith. The evidence of the unbeliever was good for the believer. Now there are no more unbelievers, but the loss of unbelievers does not make believers perfect. Think not all Christians good Christians. Far from it.' Etcetera and so forth. (Now, pay attention!) 'If, however, you would bring through our land that last unbeliever, parade him as our old lords paraded their captives through all the streets and let the faithful see with their eyes the damnation that awaits unregenerate sinners, it may revivify and cleanse their faith . . .' and so forth.

"Your murmur approval. Splendid. Right. Put into the language of theological argument (for we will have to defend our course before the Holy Father), it is this. We are One but for one. We have all power—the power of unanimity. But who knows what power *is* and who *has* power? If one can do everything, one is, insofar as man is concerned, already a god, however much he fails of divinity.

"The predicament of power is that it is mindless. Power has no intelligence of itself. It receives its instruction from outside. Everyone is charmed by the story of Sisyphus and his rock, but no one respects the mountain upon whose surface his heroic folly was dramatized. The mountain was the real power, and were it not for the labors of Sisyphus it would not be known how truly immense, difficult, hazardous its abraded incline really was. The mountain is the raw totality of power, but it is the subborn stupidity of Sisyphus that gives the power meaning. Our recalcitrant Jew—more than all the believers of Christendom—makes real the power of Christ. Don Rafael is the irritant that makes the Body of Christ move. He, my friends (forgive my ecstasy), perhaps even more than the return in glory which we await, is the harbinger of the Kingdom of God."

It was decided then and there. Don Rafael would be displayed to all the world, toured, paraded, exhibited as a specimen, and at the conclusion of his international tour, returned to Rome, and there, during the hour following the last of the daily masses, brought caged into the square before St. Peter's and left—guarded, to be sure—to be stared at and loathed by deputations of the faithful.

The tour proved miraculous.

In each land of the world a procession was organized, and in imitation of the custom of ancient Rome, the cardinal or bishop of the realm led the procession of penitents through the streets, his vestments gleaming in the sun or sparkling in the rain, and beside him, his hands cuffed, his legs hobbled, hopped the figure of Don Rafael Acosta, his body draped in rags, his face begrimed with ash, upon his head a dunce cap on which was written in the language of that nation: The Last Jew. Somehow, Don Rafael survived. His eyes, blinded by dust, his flesh blistered with the wounds of rocks and the beatings of enthusiasts who broke the ranks of the police to switch him or punch his back, his legs a pulp of sore flesh, he was returned to Rome early in the fall of his captivity. Although he was given little encouragement an energy consecrated by will pressed him constantly back into life.

One morning, the week before Christmas, Don Rafael was brought in his cage into the square of St. Peter's. The bells tolled his appearance, and a crowd of pilgrims surged and heaved to catch sight of him. Children sat upon their fathers' shoulders, nuns trained their binoculars toward him, others stood on camp chairs, straining for a glimpse. Within the cage, his head drooping upon his chest, his black beard falling in snarls, wild and untended, upon his shirt front, Don Rafael shivered from the wind. He was feverish. At a moment before the hour of one, when the guards would return to draw away the cage and bring to an end the appearance of the day, Don Rafael commenced to speak. At first his words were soft, lifting upon the wind and flying upward, unheard and lost but to those few who had commanding positions in front of him. Gradually the crowd grew silent and his voice dropped from the register of birds crying against the elements to the resonant address of one who speaks to his fellow creatures:

"The time of my life comes to an end. I am still a young man, but my life is fulfilled. I did not think it so. I fought against death, but I can restrain it no longer. I have known this for some time now. It is hard to go on telling oneself that there will be a deliverance, waiting, waiting daily for some miraculous hand to reach down and release me from my misery, return me to my beloved Gerona, restore me to my friends and to my livelihood. How could it be, I thought, that God should not pity me and show me mercy? Who am I, I said to myself, but an ordinary man, extraordinarily unfortunate? Why should I be elected for such torment? I was not the first Jew. Why then should I be the last? I suffered all that I have suffered—all indignities and outrages—softly, without public tears (but do not think that I did not cry privately, cry and beg, and call to my mother and father for help—I did), certainly not with temper or anger. What would my anger have brought me? Your contempt, your jeering? I had no need of them. Were I to have railed against you, I would have died long before this, long before I could understand what makes you so hard and cruel, and God so silent. The two of these must be understood together—your cruelty and God's silence. Now I understand them.

"I am an ordinary man. I have explained that. But I am an ordinary man with an unordinary quality. I am a Jew. Now that fact—being a Jew—could be ordinary, like being a man, but it would require that you permit it to be so. It cannot be treated by you as something exceptional, bizarre, suspicious, uncanny, or else by regarding it as such you oblige us ordinary men to behave as though we *were* very special. You make us extraordinary by deciding that you cannot cope with us. So much for you, but what about God? Why does He not rescue me? Why did He not rescue all of my brothers who, like me, have said no to you? Why?

"I shall now tell you. Because He accepts your verdict. No. More than that. He decided upon it long before you did. He decided we were extraordinary from the very start, as witness all our prophets and teachers and visionaries. Why rescue *us*? Rescue poor people. Rescue ordinary people. They need rescue. Save them, Lord, before us. To rescue us is to deny who we are, to make us ordinary.

"And now, do you know why Jesus died on the cross and was rejected by the Jews? It was because He asked God, 'Lord, why have you forsaken me?' Had He not spoken these words He might well have died—no less died—but I will tell you something, all the Jews would have believed in Him. 'He is surely a Messiah,' they would have said, because He says nothing, calls for nothing, asks for nothing. He knows that God is with Him. I know that God is with me, now and forever. You are not yet saved, but I am ready to die."

Don Rafael Acosta closed his mouth and died. He died and was buried, and in the aftermath of his death, there came those who believed he was their ransom and redeemer, and those people, like our beloved Don Rafael, were again called Jews.

ONE'S OWN TEXT

Each one of us, I have come to believe, has a text written with oneself in mind. It can be a text familiar to everyone, but still addressed to only one or two in each generation. Most people may receive only a fragment of their text—an allusion to a principal need or an obsessive fantasy, an island idyll or an immensely handsome man; nonetheless, it is still *their* text since it is the fulcrum of their dreams.

Artists, poets, philosophers are not given their text, but must go in search of it. Searching for their text, in fact, is precisely what makes them artists, poets, philosophers. Were they given their text with their youthful dreams, they would be satisfied so early that little would be left unresolved to compel them to the pursuit that agitates their inquisitive passion. No. We must search for our texts. Usually, we do not find them early. In our novice days, when we are still limbering the muscle of our talent, we attach ourselves to fragments of the text, words out of context, words not yet reshaped by the imagination. These words we may come upon by happenstance in our casual reading or hear in conversation or find by accident in dictionaries—searching for one word, our eyes fall upon another. We overhear our reality when we are young, but in middle

From *An Admirable Woman*, 178–84. Boston: David R. Godine, 1983. Estate of Arthur A. Cohen.

years if we are lucky we find our texts and then, having entered into age, we are able without fear and without confusion to pass the most pleasured time, unraveling its significance, living its consequence, and drafting interpretations as the bequest of ourselves to future times and to others whose text it will, in turn, become.

My text was embedded in another. Of course, I had read the Book of Genesis. I had read it in fact many times, but I was not aware then that my text was Genesis 3, which narrates with incomparable brevity the story of the sin of Adam and Eve and their exclusion from Paradise. I became certain this text was mine many years after I had closed my copy of the Hebrew Bible for the last time. I had come upon my text almost casually. Uncle Salomon had told me the story of the embarrassed Adam and Eve and the insinuating snake. He had made me laugh with his telling, imitating the snake with a hiss, and solemnly miming the Lord God as he calls out for his disobedient children. My uncle Salomon had not really understood the gravity of the tale. He had made it seem, like so many other Bible stories that he told me, a dramatic invention, and a lean and bare one at that, rather humorless considering the absurd situation of Adam and Eve. However, had it not been for Uncle Salomon's dramatic rendition of such Bible tales, it may be doubted that I would have carried the text around inside me for as long as I did. (It is possible, you see, that one can mistake one's own text, and failing to identify it, adopt another not intended. Such mistakes can prove catastrophic. Since the way of tragedy is that of necessity, it may be argued that choosing the wrong text is binding oneself to the ineluctable through whose strict and unyielding fabric nothing of the light of one's proper freedom is allowed to shine.)

I became certain that the Genesis tale was my text when the stolen copy of my volume of Heinrich von Kleist arrived at the apartment during the spring of 1963 after Martens's death. The superintendent brought me the package, neatly tied, my name written out in imposing majuscules, the stamps of the Federal German Republic announcing its general origin, since the sender had omitted his name and address from the outside of the package. I took it that he did not wish the book returned even if it did not find its destination. I thought that correct. It had belonged to no one but myself, and having been stolen from my library and having made its way (by what devious route I cannot imagine) from Berlin, where it had occupied a position of some honor in my small collection of literature, to a bookseller in Köln, where it was rescued from the ignominy and misunderstanding of being shelved somewhere between Klabund and Klopstock and was sent back to me, I instantly regarded the book as possessing an endowment, a kind of magic (aura I should call it) which other books did not possess.

I opened the book carefully and noted, remarkably for me, that I had written my name on the flyleaf—evidently in my eighteenth year, since my handwriting had just begun to exhibit that stepping out into assertion that marked my passage from adolescent shrinking to uncertain pride. And so, I had acquired a volume of Heinrich von Kleist's collected works that contained the writings of his very last years. I began turning the pages of the volume, hunting, I suppose, for some additional message this belated homecoming might carry.

It all became clear when I arrived at the little essay *Über das Mario-nettentheater* which Kleist had written in 1810, about a year before his suicide. The little text occupied six and a half pages in my edition. In its margin I had written the dates on which I had read it, something extremely unusual in my habit. I had, in fact, studied the little essay four times. I read it aloud once more and noted the date, 26/4/63. It was only when I finished reading the last page that I noticed I had lightly underlined the concluding exchange between the essay's interlocutors, the question posed by the interrogator to the principal ballet dancer of the local theater whose ruminations on the mysterious grace of the marionette provided the pretext for Kleist's reflections.

Alluding once again to the dancer's earlier reference to the predicament of the fallen creatures of Paradise, the interrogator asks: "Does that mean we must eat again of the Tree of Knowledge in order to return to our state of innocence?"

The dancer replies: "Of course, but that is the last chapter in the history of the world." I had scored *this* passage years before.

What Kleist had described contained the secret ambition of my life, yet another confirmation of the epiphany of Paris that I described earlier. My life task had been until that moment and remained confirmed thereafter to understand the unspeakable loneliness of human consciousness—the shared faculty of awareness whose every detail defies camaraderie.

The genius of Kleist's little essay lies in its spirit of resignation and hope. The curious interrogator encounters his friend, the principal dancer of the local ballet company, whom he has observed in rapt contemplation of the performance of a troupe of marionettes that has been set up in the marketplace.

How can it be, he wonders, that such a professional dancer should be enchanted by these manipulated creatures? His misunderstanding is initially challenged by the dancer's assertion that the marionettes are performers of perfect grace to whom no human dancer can compare. However manipulated, the manipulation of the master's cord is but a submission to the wooden dancer's perfect center of gravity which allows arms and legs to move in balance and harmony, needing to touch ground only to reaffirm the earth's existence, but not to provide the marionettes with any necessary firmament. The marionettes exhibit the purity of natural grace, their sense of gravity always intact; no human dancer, contrived and reflective, needing decision and reminiscence of choreography, can achieve any comparable perfection. The human dancer does well to think upon the marionette since he *can* intuit and comprehend its wooden perfection while, however desperately he desires it, he *cannot* grasp the perfection of God. The marionette is always telling the truth of its being, whereas the human dancer—always an imitation of the whole—covers his inadequacy of affectation, shifting the soul from its true gravity through an artifice of technique which serves only to confuse and obscure.

The interrogator is unpersuaded, regarding the dancer's approval, no, celebration of the marionette as a conceit, a verbal fireworks, a mere excuse for bad dancing, or worse, false humility since he is himself the finest of dancers. It is then that his dancing friend confesses the despair he guards. And what is that? It is the despair of knowing the fall of mankind. Human dancers cannot dance pure, their souls in order, their spirit correctly situated, since they are fallen into self-consciousness. The misconception of the dancer—and by extension all of us—follows from our having eaten of the Tree of Knowledge.

"But Paradise is locked and bolted, and the cherubim stand behind us. We have to go on and make the journey around the world to see if it is perhaps open somewhere at the back." The grim interrogator laughs in disbelief. (I did not laugh nor have I ever laughed at this passage. Moreover, I am convinced, the interrogator did not laugh in high spirit, but rather with grim acknowledgement of our entrapment, his thin lips nearly closed, his teeth grinding, his laugh more like a groan.)

And so, the desperate paradox of the human: we are perfect *before* self-consciousness and we are fallen thereafter. Our condition before knowledge is innocence (some might say stupidity and ignorance, but they do not understand what is meant by the Tree of Knowledge). At the same time, we are creatures who mime infinity and for us to be innocent is to be deprived of that which resembles the God in whose likeness we are made. Therefore, we pursue knowledge and lose grace, lose purity of heart, lose innocence. Whatever we do, whichever horn of the dilemma we propose to adopt, we mortally wound ourselves.

We can, however, flee the dilemma entirely by proposing to reenter Paradise by stealth, by going the long way of history and hoping to find at its back another route of entry. We are not assured that there is such an opening. Or rather, we are assured that the opening exists, but only at the end of history, at the very end.

Genesis 3 is most certainly my text. I learned from it the deviousness of the historical way, the only weapon in fact that we retain in our struggle against being less than we are—that is, marionettes of perfect grace—and aspiring to be more than we can manage, that is, divine.

Malenov's Revenge

ONE

It never occurred to me that Joseph Alexander Karnovsky had been murdered by the great painter Yevgeny Mikhailovich Malenov. Moreover, the means by which Yevgeny Mikhailovich eroded the life of Karnovsky, his benefactor and patron, is so odd, so original and unprecedented, that when I came across the documents that revealed his carefully annotated plotting, it took me many months to assimilate my discovery and to determine its accuracy and truth. Finally, in the end, I concluded that Malenov had destroyed Karnovsky as surely as if he had shot him through the heart.

Before proceeding, however, to recount Malenov's history, his entanglement with Karnovsky, and the formation of Malenov's decision of "diabolic revenge" (forgive me for tergiversating, but even as I write the phrase "diabolic revenge," I am obliged to insert it between quotation marks, less to suggest that I am lifting this phrase from a Malenovian source than to underscore the ambiguity I feel about its employment at all. Did Malenov revenge himself on Karnovsky? and, if so, did second sight constitute his "diabolic means"? or did Malenov only supply the

From *Artists and Enemies*. 127–74. Boston: David R. Godine, 1987. Estate of Arthur A. Cohen.

conditions that enabled Karnovsky, with his own aberrations and ambition, to seize the opportunity, so to speak, to *murder himself*—and that not suicide, which is a voluntary act, after all—clearly self-murder, quite unintentional, involuntary, desperate, necessary, fated as if by another hand), I must tell you something about the voice that speaks here so emphatically, for it is I who organize and dispense this narrative.

I—my name is Isaiah Wolff—am not a principal in these events, although I appear a number of times, marginal and in the shadows. Nonetheless I am critical to the narration—a linchpin, moreover, because it is I who discovered that Malenov wished to destroy Karnovsky and in fact succeeded two years after his own death, when Karnovsky was found in his studio surrounded by his finished canvases overpainted in black, dead of what was medically determined (although metaphorically described) to be "cardiac explosion."

All perfectly straightforward, you may think. No, you won't think that at all. You will say: "Curious, bizarre, but no murder." And I, who had known Karnovsky for many years and had sold him all the books, photographs, gallery announcements, exhibition catalogues, personal correspondence, posters, newspaper and magazine cuttings, museum handouts that documented the life and work of Yevgeny Mikhailovich Malenov (items, I might add, that Karnovsky later received in abundance following Malenov's death), would have concurred with your disbelief, until it became my task to appraise the archive of Malenov-Karnovsky papers for purposes of a testamentary bequest Karnovsky had made to the Museum of Modern Art following his own death. Karnovsky's executors, his lawyer and his accountant, chose me because they had been coming across my name for years in Karnovsky's annual account records, each year the sums growing as the prices fetched by every scrap relating to Malenov's life and works commanded increasing prices to purchase and even higher prices to sell. (For example, a simple postcard that Malenov wrote to his friend Naum Gabo when he left the Soviet Union for Berlin in 1926 I bought for a modest sum and sold to Karnovsky several years later for $60—a photograph of a Berlin café, Die Florelle, with the following Russian text: "Not the Stray Dog, but it will have to do and the tea at least no flies in it. See you soon. Yevgeny." Amusing, intimate, but not an important document. And yet, given the fact that Yevgeny Malenov rarely wrote letters, much less such casual communications as postcards, $60 turned out to be a quite reasonable price.) I thought I knew everything there was to know about Malenov: his mournful celibacy, his second sight, his curious essays about the messianic hope of projectivism (a position he shared with his sometime colleagues and infrequent friends Kazimir Malevich and Piet Mondrian, although Malenov's messianism was of the Russian strain, saturated with references to his beloved Saint Sergius, the baleful eye of the apocalypse, and petty allusions to the shopkeeper mentality of Jews, whom he both loved and feared), his contempt for most painting "merchants" (his term for art dealers), as well as his occasional lapse into pedophilia, a preoccupation he indulged vicariously through the gathering of a substantial collection of photographs of naked children ("beyond eight they are already mature"), which he examined principally during the years when he felt utterly abandoned and alone, and then only at night, when the moon was a sliver of orange, and its nauseous light streaked his bedroom, and he reinvented his childhood in the countryside near the village of Gradiesk in the Ukraine.

I was amazed by Malenov's melancholy, his self-doubt and no less monumental certitude, his mad religiosity, his pedophiliac amusements and passion for dancing the fox trot, but I never thought him capable of murder. He seemed so conventionally a genius—that is, a worker with such absolute pitch and profundity—that I, with the habit of the world, rationalized and excused all the rest of his anomalous conduct as quite fitting, suitable, "to be expected of genius" (an American accommodation to comme il faut), and never thought him the worse for being simultaneously a misanthrope, a religious fanatic, and among the warmest and most tender of human beings. But that was my illusion. I had no idea, therefore, that Malenov could harbor such a deep resentment, annotating the details of each provocation and interpreting its gravity and significance by construing every seizing, prizing, mandibular gesture of the insatiable Karnovsky as one more move by his adoring disciple to despoil him. Persuaded by the voluminous Malenovian archive of diaries, scraps of screed, notations of implied insults and indirect humiliations administered, Malenov believed, by his wickedly competitive patron, it was not surprising that the conception of revenge was installed as a blood ruby in the crown of Malenov's program of accomplishment from almost the very beginning, when Malenov first met Karnovsky in Berlin during the late 1920s. Not surprising, but nonetheless wholly unpersuasive, for Malenov's revenge upon his fellow artist and patron requires a reading of Joseph Alexander Karnovsky's character wholly at variance with my own.

I will set down the facts and try my hand at an interpretation or two, but the ultimate decision will have to be made by the reader, who constitutes a jury of one to pass judgment on the issue of the crime. I do not know; I cannot be certain.

Two

The Russian community of Berlin, a mélange of exiles and itinerant revolutionaries, often gathered during the late 1920s at Die Florelle, a large café in shouting distance of the Kürfurstendam.

It became customary after 1921, when Die Florelle opened (and was discovered by the considerable Russian-speaking population of Berlin to be fortuitously situated near the most frequented public thoroughfare in the city, not far from the popular emigré nightclub Die Blaue Vogel, around the corner from an efficient travel agent who specialized in bookings to the Soviet Union, three blocks from a street of moneychangers and small banks, a kiosk that dispensed hot borscht and meat pastries, and two restaurants devoted to Crimean and Georgian cuisine), for the left side of the café to be crowded with revolutionary sympathizers, comrade members of trade commissions, visiting Soviet poets, artists, and ideologists, while to the right of the central service area glared antirevolutionary social democrats, aristocrats and nobles and exiled members of Lenin's bureaucracy, as well as landscape painters, lyric poets, and angry journalists. The infrequent German who strayed into Die Florelle, unaware of the ideological combat of its habitués and their seating arrangements, was sometimes caught in the crossfire of insult and the occasional stream of hot tea thrown with screams by one or another enraged partisan of left or right.

It was generally the case, however, that Die Florelle was calm. It was regarded by the principal agents of both the revolution and its opposition as an oasis in the mined terrain of postwar German politics, and, despite the excitable character of its clientele, partisans of all extremes thought it wise to keep Die Florelle clear of violence so that its patrons could be counted, identified, and even surreptitiously photographed. At the front of the café, looking out toward the broad avenue where flaneurs ogled and sniffed throughout the day, was a single row of tables—not more than sixteen, it appears, if the photograph before me that I found among Malenov's mementoes is not deceptive—separated by a narrow walking space from the packed and jumbled partisans of left and right. That single row was regarded by Die Florelle's clientele as confirmation of its management's neutrality. There, at those sixteen tables, sat tea drinkers and chess players who claimed political unaffiliation (what the Soviets inimitably called *smenavekovtsy*). From time to time, their neutrality compromised by the discovery of an acquaintance in one or the other camp, they disappeared into the passionate embrace of left or right, surrendering their privileged position near the café's vitrine to yet another visitor, who took up transient residence at the front tables, awaiting in turn persuasion or relapse into ideology.

The manager of Die Florelle, the complaisant Carlo Zuchotti, born in the Ticino, raised in Zurich, and now café owner in Berlin, was superbly indifferent to politics. He stood beside the double doors, a clutch of menus in his hand, waiting to see who would push through the doors into his café. It didn't matter whether it was a weary count dressed in riding clothes, just off from teaching young girls horsemanship, or a consumptive artist from Vitebsk, or a communist journalist such as Ilya Ehrenburg. Carlo Zuchotti was indifferent. He smiled, assessed his guest's relative prosperity, and led him to a table appropriate to the cut of his suit and the quality of his boots. He concerned himself with social notes, not politics. It was for this reason, perhaps, that he made the mistake of conducting Yevgeny Mikhailovich Malenov to a central table in the file of the *smenavekovtsy,* the uncertain and undecided. Yevgeny had insisted on such a table (he wished to keep his eyes peeled for the arrival of a dear friend he had arranged to meet there at 2 P.M. precisely), and Carlo Zuchotti, imagining that Malenov's pointed index finger marked an assertion of political neutrality, seated him at a front table commanding a view of both the boulevard and the sector occupied by counterrevolutionaries. For his part, Yevgeny Mikhailovich, suffering from a tenacious head cold, wished to be seated at a table swimming in warm spring sunlight.

As though in duet, a baritone voice called out from a table of flanneled emigré intellectuals seated near the rear of the café surrounded by other members of the declassed nobility and anti-Bolshevik intelligentsia, "Yevgeny Mikhailovich. My God. You, here, now," at the same instant as a rose-lipped voice, throaty with tobacco, gaily shouted in antiphon, "Beloved Yevgeny, at last." Both speakers stepped into the neutral area where the waiters circulated and disappeared into the moil, and both reached across to seize Yevgeny's weary hand. He smiled, distracted, uncertain to whom to turn. He half rose from his table, embraced Masha Dmitrievna, and, reaching around her somewhat chunky amplitude, shook hands with the tall, lanky young man in his early thirties whose drooping mustache and watery gray eyes suggested breeding and exhaustion. The salutations done, Masha Dmitrievna nodded brusquely to Captain Nikolai Alexandrovich Plakhov, late of His Imperial Majesty's Horse Guard, and both seated themselves at Yevgeny's neutral table. They knew the rules—unspoken and most certainly unenforced, but nonetheless clear by custom. It was understood that politics were to be avoided at the neutral bank of window tables. They could be alluded to, animad-

verted as screens to insult and humiliation, but they were not to be
openly discussed at the tables of the uncertain and undecided.

"But you are uncertain, my dear? Do you still preserve your neutrality?" Masha Dmitrievna inquired, a blue fingernail scratching at a crumb
of cake left behind on Yevgeny's table. Captain Plakhov scowled, but she
was a beautiful woman, after all, he thought. What she lacked in tact and
diffidence she more than compensated for with radiant black eyes and a
mouth of almost criminal sensuality.

Yevgeny Mikhailovich was not well that day. He explained later that
he sometimes found his mind suddenly overcast, as though a cloud had
befogged him or an iron vise, like a medieval instrument of torture, had
settled around his forehead, electrifying his eyebrows, which in such
episodes he believed to be aflame. He felt a weight, a bitter constraint
that prevented him from thinking normal thoughts at all. During such
bouts of physical oppression and incandescence, he came to await—after
the battles of denial were done—an insight of premonitory vision, so
startling, so terrifying that he had no way to dealing with it except to
surrender to its instruction and do its bidding, whatever it was. It was a
tradition, after all, that ran in his family. Like his great-aunt and a second
cousin, Yevgeny Mikhailovich possessed second sight, unpredictable, for-
tuitous, and for the most part not at all prophetic. That is to say, Yevgeny
Mikhailovich saw into a future that was already past or, to be more accurate, he knew of an event's occurrence in advance of all notification, and
these gifts of illumination, bridging space and time, allowed him to take
measures of self-protection or self-advancement well before he had been
given eyewitness reports or detailed information. He saw into the future,
but his seeing could not alter events or forewarn their participants. He
was always just on time. But then, that was miraculous gift enough. For
instance, he had awakened one cold morning in Moscow several years
before, absolutely persuaded that his younger brother, then a boy of sixteen (later killed during the civil war), was in great danger. He dressed
quickly and hurried to the telegraph office to send a message to his family, living at the time some fifty versts from Novisibirsk. Late that day he
received a reply from his father: SASHA PULLED FROM BENEATH THE ICE IN
SKATING ACCIDENT STOP HE WILL LIVE PRAISE GOD FATHER. It turned out that at
precisely the hour of seven in the morning—the time noted on Yevgeny's
telegraphed message—the boy had had his skating accident. A peasant
driving sheep to market had seen it happen; quickly he unwound a rope
coiled around his waist, threw it to the boy, and pulled him to safety. But
such episodes of second sight always left Yevgeny Mikhailovich with a
terrible headache and in a mood of such despondency that he was unso-

ciable for a month. He often wrote of the "heavy burden" imposed on him. "So much for so little," he once complained. "At least, if I were prophetic—" But he never completed his blasphemy.

There were other incidents, less dramatic but no less exemplary. He was warned in second sight that such and such a collector would not show up to purchase a painting; that his dog, Petka, had died of old age; that his apartment building was aflame, but that the blaze had been put out before it reached his studio. All these episodes settled upon Yevgeny a mood of constant attention to omens and alarms, hints and allusions that everyday occurrences thrust before him, demanding appraisal and estimation. Fortunately, most were barren of hidden meaning and revelation.

Masha Dmitrievna had entered Yevgeny Mikhailovich's life one evening late in the winter of 1925, after a meeting of the artists of UNOVIS, who were planning an exhibition to celebrate the anniversary of its founding. Yevgeny, seated in a corner of the artists' clubroom, drinking a fruit juice while everyone else was drowning themselves in vodka, was stroking a vagabond cat who had ambled into the gathering and had slowly threaded her way from legs to laps, rubbing against them and rising to each crooked nail that promised scratches of affection. With Yevgeny, the black cat came home to serious and considered adoration; his strokes were rhythmic, his purring confirmed her own, his whispered endearments (barely overheard by Masha Dmitrievna, who had singled out Yevgeny for attention early in the evening's proceedings) to the nameless animal movated to a crescendo: "O yes, Nadezhda, yes, sweet Lazar, ah, Kazimir, ah, ah, Kazimir, yes, Alexander, yes, yes, old puss Popova."

"What are you doing here, Yevgeny Mikhailovich?" Masha Dmitrievna inquired, somewhat belligerently, irritated and confused by his insistent nomination of each of the artists of the day as sobriquets for the purring black cat.

"And why not?" Yevgeny replied, without looking up.

"What do you mean, 'Why not?' You have to be a party member, don't you?"

"Not at all. Never, in fact. An artist is enough. A teaching artist, more than enough. And who cares anyway? Let them hang the pictures upside down, my own included, for all I care."

Masha Dmitrievna snorted contemptuously. "With yours it wouldn't matter." She thought to insult him, but he was indifferent.

Yevgeny smiled. The truth is that in most cases his work could indeed be hung upside down, because the pictures had no sides, no top, no bottom, no right, no wrong. They were cuts of the universe and, to his mind, infinite, able to be hung on the ethers of space and to fit in, blended into clouds and rushing wind, immense black, deep blue, indifferent to bourgeois space and domestic architecture.

"What are you doing here, Yevgeny Mikhailovich?" Masha Dmitrievna now repeated, poking a ringed finger at weary Yevgeny Mikhailovich, whose head had suddenly begun to ache.

"Plakhov, do me the kindness of expelling this Cheka agent. I couldn't stand her in Moscow, why should I tolerate her in Berlin?"

"Cheka? Never! Independent always. A private operative," Masha Dmitrievna replied, her eyes flashing with anger.

"Nobody is independent in the Soviet Union," the captain replied, rubbing his hands on his sweaty jodhpurs as though to clean them before pushing Masha Dmitrievna.

"You would know? How would you know, you czarist lackey?"

"Plakhov, please, lift her up and throw her out. Hurl her into the heavens."

Captain Plakhov stood up and pointed arrogantly to the sector of Die Florelle where the revolutionary cadres had put down their glasses of tea and were wiping their mouths, waiting with excitement. The counterrevolutionaries, pent up and ferocious, were shifting in their seats, positioning themselves for something brilliant and decisive. How they wanted to deal the Soviet Union a great blow. "Go to your comrades, you spy agent, you viper villain, you Cheka whore."

"Oh, Plakhov, not that. She's not a whore, I believe," Yevgeny remonstrated at Plakhov's extremity. "Torturer, traitor, cesspool, viper's den, perhaps, but not a whore. Much too pretty to make it business." Yevgeny was watching Masha's eyes, closed with fury, her purple eyeshadow obliterating her pupils.

At this precise moment of insult and acrimony a young waiter, unaware of the brewing conflagration, was stepping deftly over legs outstretched into the open space that separated the Reds and Whites of Die Florelle. He balanced a tray laden with cakes and coffee. Masha watched the waiter approach, and her crooked smile expanded into a wicked grin as she lifted the tray from his upturned fingers and overturned it on Plakhov. Her rage gave way to gales of laughter, and the Red contingent of Die Florelle burst into shouts and applause. After a stunned moment, the counterrevolutionary Whites each reached for the nearest to hand; instantly a barrage of bread slices covered with jam, dishes of sticky kissel, tea (with and without pots), demitasse spoons, metal ashtrays flew through the air as attack and counterattack transformed the negotiated decorum of Die Florelle into a street battle. Not a fist was raised, no bodies made contact, but words and implements found their targets or slammed harmlessly against the café's walls, leaving behind blobs of cake and splatters of dribbling compote. Amid the festive battle, Captain Plakhov, straightening his tie, wiping glazed fruit from his jodhpurs, and smoothing down his hair, already matted with drying mousse and whipped cream, turned to Masha Dmitrievna and with an open palm smacked both her cheeks, bowed, and fled the café. Masha Dmitrievna, an instant earlier shrieking with joy, now dissolved into humiliated weeping.

Only the occasion and cue of this pandemonium subsided into silence while the din rose above him. Yevgeny Mikhailovich was gripped by his tormenting adversary; a vise of pain settled about his temples and crept out toward his eyeballs. He groaned inaudibly, swallowing his anguish. His guest was an hour late. He was not coming. He had already forgotten Masha Dmitrievna and Captain Plakhov. Who were they? he briefly thought, as he heard the door slam behind Plakhov and observed Masha Dmitrievna collapse in tears. What is this pain? Yevgeny wondered, forgetting as he always did its source and significance. Brain tumor? Stroke? Arthritis of the temples? He invented ailments and catastrophes. He would die momentarily. The pain rose and swelled his head like a melon; he pincered his temples with his forefingers and groaned again, this time aloud. Suddenly, it all cleared, and before his eyes the fog lifted and a path through his confusion became visible. As in all earlier episodes of his remarkable visionary sight, Malenov saw a complete scene, an augury of an event already in process or almost completed: a room furnished with the artifacts of worldly comfort, plush and stuffed, solid, heavy tables and cabinets, and remarkable pictures, including one, he recognized, by himself—painted when he had been a futurist. At the door, two men framed in a bluish-gold light stood talking. One extended his hand to the other in farewell, a strapped suitcase at his side. The other clasped the extended hand in both of his. On the table lay a mountain of manuscripts, papers, drawings, and painted canvases. Suddenly, Malenov recognized the personages of his vision. His beloved friend whom he was to have met at Die Florelle at 2 P.M. precisely, the painter Kazimir Sevenerovich Malevich, was leaving the apartment of his acquaintance, the sculptor Alexander von Riesen, and rushing for the railroad station to return to Moscow. Yevgeny Mikhailovich knew for certain that he would never see him again, knew that Malevich was returning to dissension and hostility, knew that he would leave behind the masterpieces of his youthful years, a hoard of crucial manuscripts, a bundle of canvases, knew that in seven Malevich would succumb to illness and die, and knew that for a generation or more his name would be obliterated in his homeland and forgotten in the West.

(All of these visionary anticipations suggest, indeed, that Yevgeny Mikhailovich enjoyed some degree of prophetic sight. But I cannot be certain. He claimed for his second sight only a victory over space, not time. Yet these assertions about the future and fate of his friend Malevich appear to be both genuinely prophetic and accurate. Curiously, Malenov dated this passage in his diary in a hand different from that in which he wrote the entry. Moreover, he wrote in parentheses after the date, "Vision of a vision. Written years later when everything is confirmed." I have no way of knowing whether Yevgeny is congratulating himself on the accuracy of his second sight or fleshing out a simple clear sight with facts he learned much later. Either is possible. Yevgeny hardly invented himself; he was a genius and needed no shamanic myth to improve it!)

The battle of the cakes and teapots subsided. Every table was clear of implements. Signor Zuchotti screamed at his customers in German and Italian, interspersed with such vivid Russian curses as he had learned from his more outspoken clients; the waiters began to swab the walls with damp cloths; the shouting gave way to good-natured laughter and squealing. Amid this subsiding clatter, Yevgeny Mikhailovich, his hands gripping his painful head, lurched to his feet, bellowed like a wounded beast, and rushed toward the glass doors. Wrenching them open, he looked back briefly, a vacant and uncomprehending smile on his face, and fled into the sunlight.

THREE

Ever so briefly, even at the risk of confusing the reader or boring the most avid enthusiast of narrative, I must tell you a little, a terrible little about the battles within Soviet art that thrust Kazimir Sevenerovich Malevich and his curious doctrine of Supremus to the forefront, leaving slightly behind (his footsteps almost crossing over and filling up to the narrow instep those of the older and more famous practitioner) Yevgeny Mikhailovich Malenov and his projectivist vision, whose architectonic schemes (which he called utopics) were soon enough to be hailed as the successors to Malevich's ideas. Malenov was to become a world hero of art, transcending the ideological culture he loathed and had left behind.

Think of it this way. First the world was a richly painted drapery hung before an unexplored space, filled with figures, nature in glow, transfigured color. Then, it was thought that way lay behind the drapery had somehow to be insinuated onto the stage: light came from within the painting (as well as from the sun behind the artist), and its rays broke up the surface of the image, fracturing its space, splintering its angles, making simple creatures all legs and arms, all planes and angles, all colors of a dizzy rainbow. But then these curious Russians, annoyed that heavy industry and artillery shells, chemical formulae and electrical generators, textiles and rubber boots should all come from the West, determined that at least a native poetry and a private art should claim a Russian progeny. They began as early as 1910 to look at Western poetry and painting, to drift in and out of Western studios, examining what the West had decided to throw away (Vladimir Tatlin, for instance, scrutinized the contents of Picasso's studio) and returning to Russian to make a new art. Vassily Kandinsky came back from Germany to teach and train. The poets Velimir Khlebnikov and Alexei Kruchenykeh collaborated with, among others, Kazimir Malevich to make illustrated books that cost only four kopecks but trained Russian eyes to affix words of poetry to their visual icons. A topsy-turvy time. Artists painted themselves green and blue, wore spoons in their lapels, drew red triangles on their cheeks, dressed in castaway clothing and dined on caviar—all to make an impression, to strike up an acquaintance with the bourgeoisie, loathed and envied as the bourgeoisie always is.

The point is this: in the absence of a long tradition of their own, it was easier for the Russians to become Soviets and make a new art. They had nothing to lose by becoming inventive geniuses and writing unintelligible manifestos that caused untalented hearts to skip a beat, that gave employment to ten nighttime laborers of the poster-posting guild, and that later provoked quizzical looks, scratched heads, creased foreheads, dubious pouts, and, and in their train, miserly mimes without gift who paraphrased the same, repeating it until its slogan, "Anything fills space since space is empty," sounded more and more ridiculous, although at first scrutiny it had seemed saturated with oriental sagacity and aesthetic nihilism.

Four

Yevgeny Mikhailovich flung himself into a taxi turning the corner in front of Die Florelle and, although never informed of the address of Alexander von Riesen's apartment, gave the driver an exact street and number. A half hour later, panting with exhaustion, he stood before a door marked by the discreet, minute, engraved *carte de visite* of the German artist. He rang urgently, tattooing his anguish with a suite of stabs at the button, whose answering sound he could not hear. After what seemed a decade of silence, the door opened a crack and a shrunken old woman, her gray hair raised into a bower that overwhelmed her tiny face, looked at him crossly. "Malevich?" Yevgeny shouted, thinking her deaf as well. She winced before his assault.

"*Kein Malevich hier. Er ist zuruck nach Moskau gegangen.*" She scrutinized him once more and slammed the door.

Yevgeny rang again and, failing to rouse her, began to bang at the door with his fist, even to kick the door. But no reply. Malevich had left Berlin. No message. No farewell. The only Russian artist he secretly adored had vanished. Yevgeny Mikhailovich was alone, abandoned in the West. Like all Russians overcome with emotion, he began to weep. Once again he had seen a future, already past.

FIVE

An incomprehensible sadness flooded his body. Yevgeny Mikhailovich lay on his uncomfortable bed in the room he had rented near the tram station. Malevich had left without a word of farewell, and the moon flooded Yevgeny's room with a silvered grimness that signaled war and battle. Yevgeny wanted to banish the moonlight. It was not an orange moon, heated by the summers of the Ukraine, but a moon compromised by coke fumes, sparkling a little with silver as though a particular lunar effort had been made to harbinger the full moon. Yevgeny lay naked upon his bed. His tears had stopped, and he had made himself a disgusting glass of tea with hot tap water. His stomach had stopped exploding. Yevgeny withdrew the album from beneath his papers and returned to bed. He stroked its cover, mounted in birch bark he had stripped and fashioned into a binding. (Malevich no longer loved him.) The first pages were innocent, hiding from the inquisitive the ignominy of his private fantasy. An ordinary scrapbook, clippings from the press, documents from the classroom, disused ration books and identity cards. He turned those pages rapidly. At last, the first of his delights. A naked child at the beach in Odessa. He had taken the photograph himself. She stood at the water's edge, a crooked finger pointing out to sea, her tiny alabaster buttocks smiling, although the face that looked over her shoulder toward the camera was pensive and withdrawn. Another: a boy of seven, half-dressed, a naval jerkin, naked loins, a tiny member like a button. And then, clipped from newspapers, little children in various states of amusing undress, holding furry kittens, laughing with nothing funny in view, small flesh like kneaded dough, rosy, smooth, hairless, indistinguishable as to sex for the most part, the precious simplicity of undifferentiated nature, childhood before the rage begins. And at the conclusion of the gallery, fifty pictures, clipped, mounted on black blotting paper, and the very last to which Yevgeny came, the very last to which no further need be added, a photograph of a naked boy, his head shaped like a dunce cap, the straggly hair long about his ears, and bright happy eyes turned upward toward a large bearded head that reached down, obedient to the little hands that held his ears, pulling the head toward puckered lips. It was Yevgeny and his father. One summer day behind his natal wooden house, among the goats and chickens. That flimsy joy of childhood, frozen now into a pastiche of remembering other children, other joys of naked unknowing.

For some years now, amid his dark times, Yevgeny Mikhailovich had rescued himself by finding an image for his album, pasting in one more dream-saturated recollection of an irretrievable moment of contentment. He knew perfectly well that he was called a pedophile; he was often caught out mooning about schoolyards, watching the little children walk home, holding hands, their strapped books over their shoulders, little dresses, little uniforms, and high-buttoned shoes. He sometimes photographed them, his eyes stripping them of their clothing until he could see their lucent flesh and observe the modest ripples of their energy. But it was no ordinary perversion, this love of a lost time. Eros was no winged creature in hot pursuit of some nubile Psyche. He took no pleasure from this recollection, no pleasure, no tension, no release. It was so infinitely sad that he likened his album to a breviary and his recollections of sun-drenched love near Gradiesk to the saying of a litany of loss.

Six

Yevgeny Mikhailovich Malenov could not afford much wood for the small stove that supplied the only heat in his room in the Prenzlauer Berg quarter of Berlin. He had arrived a year earlier, in May 1926, from Moscow. To be precise, he was in self-imposed exile from the Soviet Union. Betrayed by his uncomprehending colleagues, removed from his position as a teacher of painting theory at UNOVIS, denied access to the preferments and sinecures that came with subscription to the triumphant ideology of art as the instrument of revolutionary process and material fabrication, he decided he's had enough egalitarianism. One day, therefore, Yevgeny Mikhailovich requested permission to travel abroad to meet with German artists at a congress of revolutionary aesthetics that had been convoked by a splinter group in the Black Forest. Although the ministry regarded his petition as curious, they recognized and approved of some of the names on the invitation Malenov had presented to substantiate his request for travel documents, and after three weeks of deliberation his exit permit and passport were ready. Normally, these would be accompanied by authorization to the central bank to release sufficient gold-backed currency to facilitate a traveler's passage to the West, but Malenov had no bank funds. Instead, he kept his cash—an insignificant amount— hidden in a metal alms box he had stolen several years earlier from an antique store that fronted Leningrad's Neva (he had always wanted a metal bank as a child, but the only one he coveted cost fifty kopecks, which his father had thought extravagant). Yevgeny Mikhailovich intended to buy his ticket and as soon as possible thereafter convert the rest of his funds into gold, no matter what the cost, as he was persuaded that paper currency would soon become worthless, banks would fail, and as usual the poor would suffer.

Against the prospect of starvation, he kept the gold wedding band that his father had given his mother a generation earlier and a pair of silver candlesticks that had been left to him along with two cows, several goats, and the worthless contents of a peasant's wooden house when his parents died of influenza during the terrible winter of 1918. Although his family had maintained a religious home, all that remained of traditional piety was an icon of Saint Sergius, to which Malenov had impiously tacked a photograph of his father and mother, regarding them as holy martyrs, no less saints and intercessors than their beloved starets.

Yevgeny realized that his departure from the Soviet Union had to be efficiently masked as simple travel. He was too famous to risk advertising his departure. His closest friends among Soviet artists—Kazimir Malevich and Vladimir Tatlin (themselves raging enemies of each other)—would each construe his defection as a betrayal, neither regarding it possible that he could be friend to the other, but that of course was Malenov's way of negotiating the perilous rapids of Soviet life, sluicing through narrow channels to the sides of which rose sheer and impassable walls of ideology. Friendships took place deep down in the narrow passageway between ideological escarpments, and there, racing against the current, human beings were frequently dashed to death against the implacable stony sides. Malenov avoided extremity by learning early to keep silent and do his work. Careful attention to the ideological battles among the futurists before the revolution and between the constructivists and the naturalists in its aftermath had shown him that the most reckless and endangered were not the artists but the theorists. It was immensely precarious for the artists to set forth their ideas, to supplement their paintings with their prose. He preferred the view that artists should conduct their public careers without tongues or, if they insisted on talking, restrict their interpretations to the weather, the availability of firewood, or the quality of herring. It was not that Malenov was a coward. Not at all. If one judges by the considerable body of notepaper filled with Malenov's unpublished writings—essays in many drafts, undeclaimed manifestos (besides his celebrated Projectivist Manifesto), copies of Malevich's most famous work, *The New System of Art*, and the brief excursuses on Suprematism that Malevich hung on his initial admiration for Cézanne, all annotated in Malenov's tiny hand, which, even had they been discovered, would have proved undecipherable—Malenov was anything but a coward. It was not that he had opinion and was too scared to set it down. It was that he had opinion but thought it prudent to avoid misinterpretation. The prisons were already filling with the misunderstood, and he had no intention of contributing himself to penal reformation. Rather, he thought it wise to emigrate, to leave the country with as much as possible and virtually nothing at all. He filled two large suitcases with finished canvases wrapped in oilcloth (more than forty pictures), a sheaf of drawings, his notebooks stripped sheet by sheet from their gluebacked spines and, turned face up, used as wrapping paper for his clothing, stuffing for his shoes, lining for his overcoat—in a word, some hundred sheets of theory concealed as junk and detritus. He left behind most of his belongings, virtually all of his books, a dozen works of art by other painters (consigning all these to his landlady, to whom he promised one day to send instructions for shipment), and late on the evening of May 7, 1926, traveling light, he took the train from Moscow, arriving in Berlin some fifty hours later.

For all his apparent unworldliness and inability to marshall power and influence in the society of the arts he had left behind in Great Russia, Yevgeny Mikhailovich was persuaded without compromise or uncertainty of his immense talent. (His notebooks from the period, which I studied carefully after they came into my hands for appraisal following Karnovsky's death, were abundant in their assertion of his genius. It was not uncommon for Malenovian sentences to begin, "Praise God, but my genius does not allow for so and so," or "Genius tells us with the help of God that thus and so is the case"—"genius" being for Malenov little more than a substitute for the personal pronoun. However, unlike most people's assertions of their sovereign ego, genius meant for Malenov something haughtily impersonal, as though seated upon his brain were another creature, not of his own devising or instruction, who pronounced as Genius through the medium of Malenov. One presumes, although there is no independent authority for this, that Malenov's conviction about his genius resembled the workings of the Holy Spirit in the ancient seers of Israel, whose prophesies he continually underlined and indeed lifted for his own proclamations.) In the throes of making art, Malenov believed that his spirit lived outside his body, that the canvases he wrought, although consciously tacked to the walls of his room, were painted by him under the influence and direction of his own divinely appointed daimon, and that what was made, although exhibited and sold under the name of Malenov, was to be attributed to an exalted spirit (also named Malenov) who took up residence within him whenever he was agitated to make art.

Though he felt constrained to ascribe his genius to another, Malenov had, unfortunately, no one but himself—in all his terrestrial mundanity—to blame for his exceptional poverty. He had never, he confessed years later, really thought about how he would support himself when he arrived in Berlin. He did not expect that his train would be met by hordes of enthusiastic collectors, but neither did he imagine that the collapse of the German economy would leave artists totally without means of support, as they were when he arrived. Moreover, he was not aware that the kind of art to which he was committed was virtually without precedent in Germany, even among those nominally associated with interest in pictorial space and architecture. For the first months, therefore, he did little more than keep himself going, doing odd jobs of proofreading for a Russian-language publisher, washing dishes in restaurants, once securing a commission to design a book jacket. From each payment, having set aside enough money for his frugal habits, he extracted enough to buy wood and tools with which to build stretchers for his small canvases, and pigment powders with which to mix his paints. For months he hardly made a picture; each day was consumed rushing after bare subsistence, with neither time nor energy remaining when the day was done to do more than fling himself on his bed and sleep.

By midwinter of 1927 Malenov had exhausted his resources. His little alms box was empty, and the gold ring and candlesticks had been pawned for a pittance. He was quite literally near starvation, and his rent was overdue. It was time, he persuaded himself, for a miraculous intervention, a sign that grace was renewed and his genius reaffirmed. It had to happen; it had always happened before. Sitting in the corner of the cheap bar where he had gone to drink a beer before returning to his room, Malenov reviewed the events and occasions in his life when, down and out, he had been rescued suddenly, unpredictably—miraculously, as he believed. Such a time had come again. He spoke silently to his parents and Saint Sergius, drained the mug before him, put out his few coins, and left. So preoccupied was he with his prayerful beseechings, Yevgeny Mikhailovich almost tripped over the figure seated before his room on the top step of the second floor of the rooming house. At first he was frightened. He had read of murderers hiding in stairwells (Raskolnikov instantly came to mind), but the voice that spoke quietly to him, calling him by name, reassured him.

"Malenov?" it repeated. "You are Malenov, are you not?"

"Malenov. Yes. I'm Malenov. Who are you? What are you doing here? How did you get in? How did you find me?" The questions spilled out, confused, still frightened. Nobody had ever come to Malenov's lodgings, certainly not such an elegantly dressed, odd gentleman as now rose to his side.

"I have been waiting for you here for more than an hour. Please, may I come in and then I will answer all your questions?"

Malenov unlocked the door, entered the room, and switched on the single light that hung from a cord over the bed. The odd gentlemen followed behind him. There was no chair. Malenov pulled out a stool from under his worktable and invited his guest to be seated on the bed. It was chilly in the room. Late October. Malenov opened the grate to the metal stove that stood against the wall, pretending to stoke the coals, although it was clear that nothing was aflame and there was no coal in the metal pail beside the stove.

"Please, don't trouble yourself. I will keep my coat on. We can talk without a fire. . . . And now to your first question. My name is Magnus Fingermann. I was born of German parents in what is now called Leningrad. (It will be easier for both of us if I speak to you in your own language.) I returned to Berlin shortly after Brest-Litovsk. I had no interest in your revolution. I hope that does not bother you, but I am frank with my opinions. On the other hand, I have great interest in the new art you are making, particularly in *your* new art, my dear Malenov. I am by vocation a connoisseur; I live as an art dealer, a private art dealer who buys and sells the occasional masterpiece that falls my way and no less occasionally takes an interest in a neglected artist, whom I help to bring to the public's attention. I become such an artist's agent, and I retain a commission from everything of his that I sell. It is a simple arrangement. Because I am not married and my needs are modest, I make a living sufficient to preserve myself and my habits even in these increasingly dark days."

Malenov instantly recognized that his prayers had been answered, the intercession accomplished, the miracle wrought. He would have hugged this Fingermann, except that he did not believe it was Finger-mann by himself, unaided, who had found him; rather, the larger power in the universe who supported his genius was to be praised. He vowed that as soon as Fingermann left, he would light a candle before the icon of Saint Sergius that hung over his bed.

"And you know my work?" Malenov inquired diffidently.

The odd man, his large head wobbling precariously on his slight and subtly deformed body, examined Malenov carefully before answering. "I know your work very well and for many years now, since the early days in Russia when you were near the Jack of Diamonds group and later when you broke away from Malevich to begin your own experiments. Yes. Yes. I most certainly know your work. And you have been here now for nearly six months and you haven't painted, you haven't sold a picture, and you're starving. Oh yes, my dear fellow, I have been following you closely. May I see that stack of pictures turned to the wall?"

Squinting suspiciously as he always did when asked to show his paintings, Malenov moved toward the pile of pictures and then stopped and asked again, foolishly, but with a peasant's incredulity: "So you want to see my pictures, eh? All right." Silently, Malenov turned each picture, lifted it in his hands, held it before the curious Fingermann, and after a minute lowered it, replaced it against the wall, and lifted another. Exactly an hour later the odd Fingermann had purchased four paintings, paid for them in cash, and arranged to return the following day to discuss details of their relationship.

No sooner had Fingermann left Malenov's shabby quarters than Yev-geny, overwhelmed with good fortune, threw the banknotes into the air with an exuberant shout and saluted Saint Sergius, whom he took to be transformed from grave saint into smiling benefactor. Yevgeny Mikhailov-ich was saved, starvation averted, genius reaffirmed. In deference to such an immense good fortune, Yevgeny took up his brushes and worked the entire night, struggling to effect a new balance between a floating promontory he had launched into a blue-white ether and a series of proportional geometric forms that tipped from its plane. It was a difficult conception because it involved all his notions of a post-Newtonian space combined with visions he had entertained of the Third Rome of Moscow that would harmonize the universe and lead it to perpetual peace. Every-thing Malenov made in art had two meanings, it now appears: one acces-sible to the reading of aesthetic judgment (plainly a public, exoteric significance); the other, metaphors and reminiscences of the great wis-dom of Sophia (heralded by Vladimir Soloviev and given theological definition by the ex-army officer A. S. Khomiakov and the churchman

Sergei Bulgakov, whose religious retreats Yevgeny had secretly attended), defining an esoteric mishmash.

In the days that followed Malenov met often with Magnus Fingermann, who promised him exhibitions and installations, public celebrations and testimonials, magazine articles and interviews, patrons and connoisseurs. Alas, Yevgeny Mikhailovich believed every word. It seemed only right and fitting that his genius should be honored. The work was brilliant, after all. And it is true that certain things did happen that might not have happened without Fingermann's enthusiastic support and enterprise. Herwarth Walden would never have come to see Yevgeny's work and selected two pictures for an exhibition of the new Eastern European art at his Der Sturm Galerie, nor for that matter would László Moholy-Nagy have invited him to travel to Dessau and hang his paintings in the student foyer of the Bauhaus (Yevgeny was nervous about submitting his work to student perusal and declined the invitation, impolitely, with a postcard). But beyond the four pictures that Fingermann had purchased that first night, in the months that followed only a half-dozen drawings of no particular importance were sold, and these to a textile manufacturer who extracted permission to adapt and reproduce them on bedroom wallpaper.

Yevgeny Mikhailovich needed money to buy materials and maintain a minimal existence, and still he was always short. Fingermann, pure good will, undiminished enthusiasm, although himself a miracle, was unable to work miracles. By the end of 1927 Malenov was again near the edge. Again the rent was due, and although he still had enough money to see himself through for about a month, he was on thin ice.

"We need to make an action," Fingermann announced late one night, after Yevgeny had spent an evening watching him perched on his mechanical high chair swiveling his tiny body into majesty by raising himself three feet off the floor. "Yes, an action," Fingermann repeated in reply to Yevgeny's silent incomprehension and wrinkled forehead. "A public event, a crossing of swords with the establishment, a gesture so bizarre and ridiculous that you will be noticed—whether for good or ill does not matter."

"I am no fool," Yevgeny blurted gruffly, "no fool, and nothing I do is allowed to be foolish. Genius, thanks to God, does not permit it." Yevgeny huffed and snorted, blowing the words out his nose rather than through his large and generous mouth.

"You do not understand, my dear fellow. Not at all. I should never wish you embarrassed. Never. Nor humiliated," Fingermann emphasized, as though embarrassment and humiliation were inseparable insults.

"What I crave is an event whose panache and brilliance is so palpable, so immediate, that artists and public alike will rush to salute you, will admire you, will invite you to champagne dinners and flock to your dreadful studio just for the honor of having met you." He paused, almost rhapsodic in his enthusiasm, whirling himself up and down on the oiled mechanism of his high chair. "And, of course, I will be there, in the wings, so to speak, talking you over with museum directors and collectors, selling a picture now and then, arranging exhibitions not only in Berlin but throughout Germany, even France and Italy. But what kind of action? That's the question. What kind?"

For more than a half hour they remained silent, drinking vodka, smoking black tobacco, pacing and swiveling by turn. At last, as though Yevgeny's daimon had bifurcated, separating like a paramecium into two, each with a whole nucleus of genius, Yevgeny shouted aloud and Fingermann struck his forehead. Yevgeny shouted, "Projectivism," and Fingermann cried, "A bombing raid." Indeed, the one had conceived the text and provocation, the other its method of delivery. It was agreed that Yevgeny Mikhailovich would set down his radical conception of a new space that he called projectivism, whose ultimate consequence would be the remaking of cities in free space (which he called utopics), and crystallize its doctrine into neatly articulated points, fleshed with rhetoric and underlined with tantalizing imagery. The resulting manifesto, printed with a reproduction of one or more of Yevgeny's drawings, would be loaded into an airplane; four major cities of the German art world would be bombed with projectivism on the same day; two hours before the event the press would be notified by telegram where the manifesto would be dropped and advised to hold open their afternoon editions to accommodate the news.

PROJECTIVISM: *The New Utopia*

The Black Square of Suprematism was autobiography. It was shot into the clouds, but fell to earth. Constructivism collected the pieces of the Black Square and tried to make housing out of them. Projectivism will make the New City. Its program is the Painted City.

PROJECTIVISM is no longer communist. It has left the Socialist Empire. It is living in a rooming house in East Berlin.

PROJECTIVISM is not only a new art, it is not only a new architecture, it is not only a new urbanism! PROJECTIVISM is the future of mankind.

The art of the past is about self and selfish. The art of the past is about subject and subjectivist. The art of PROJECTIVISM is beyond self and subject.

It is the teaching of the new Utopia, and the practice of its teaching is called Utopics.

The constructivists want art to be made rational: theirs is an art for technocrats.

PROJECTIVISM is beyond the mechanomania of the constructivists. We will build a new city of man upon this earth because we will bring down the heavens to earth. The forces of the ether, the vectors of universal planes, the directional signals of light, the beacons of the stars—these will be the elements of the new art. We will project into the universe and, bending, all light and energy will return to earth. Constructivist art is beyond Newton; PROJECTIVIST art is beyond Einstein.

PROJECTIVIST plans for the revolution of art are already devised. PROJECTIVIST cities are under construction in the mind of genius.

PROJECTIVISM is planning its revolution in a rooming house in East Berlin.

—Yevgeny Mikhailovich Malenov
March 11, 1927

It could not be foreseen that such an outrageous text would produce such an immense impact on the populace of the cities where the hundred thousand leaflets were dumped, but Frankfurt, Hamburg, Munich, and Berlin were not tranquil cities in the spring of 1927. Germany was in disarray, militants of all parties and persuasions could gather riot strength in a matter of hours, speeches rang over airways. Sedition was commonplace and sedition was everywhere, but it was no longer clear what constituted sedition—the legally empowered authorities of Weimar were considered as seditious as its extreme enemies on the right and the left. Who, then, was this revolutionary madman that drafted down on them at midday, carrying an unintelligible doctrine that floated into consciousness the promise of mass housing (an end to unemployment, some concluded), the guarantee of a new utopia, the assurance of a noncommunist revolution—and all out of a rooming house in East Berlin?

Fingermann had planned it well. The newspapers had been informed; the radio stations conducted street interviews, impressions were formed of the metropolitan vision of Yevgeny Mikhailovich Malenov, and by late in the day the block in front of his cheap quarters in the working-class district of Prenzlauer Berg was jammed with the mob, with curious oglers and bourgeois enthusiasts, with police on horseback and agitators in leather coats, all wanting to see Malenov.

Fingermann was enthusiastic. Only Yevgeny Mikhailovich was unaware of the extraordinary excitement that his manifesto had generated.

He had delivered the text to Fingermann more than a week before its airborne descent, and although Fingermann had tried several times the day before the action to see Malenov—sending him telegrams and hand-delivered messages—Yevgeny was painting in solitude. As was his habit, he had tacked to his door an announcement informing visitors that he was at work and not to be disturbed; however, with a conspicuous indifference to confusion—his mastery of German did not yet encompass the law of contradiction—the announcement read: MALENOV IS PAINTING. NO ONE IS AT HOME.

Until that portentous afternoon during the second week of March, when the action had taken place, no one had bothered to read the messages Malenov tacked to his door. For more than a week, Malenov had not left his room. Supplied with tea, stale buns, tins of soup, and condensed milk, he had worked furiously either painting or writing, sometimes writing on his paintings, sometimes drawing on his notepaper, frequently trying to collage manuscript to canvas, in order to produce an integrated document of the projectivist universe he was in the process of creating. Whenever a telegram was slid beneath his door, he cursed the intrusion of "art merchants" like Fingermann; whenever he heard the landlord's wheezing cough in the hallway, he cursed the existence of landlords. He wanted nothing so much as to be left alone in total silence, submissive to his daimon, working ferociously, living without substantial food and sleep, as if disembodied, so to speak, an astral genius, Malenov.

At last, taking courage, Fingermann mounted the stairs to Malenov's room, behind him a pair of cynical newspaper reporters assigned to track this latest phenomenon of apocalyptic Weimar enthusiasm. Fingermann knocked on the door. No reply. Malenov later claimed that he was sleeping, that he had just gone to sleep after thirty hours of work. Fingermann banged louder, accompanying his thump with the shouting of Malenov's name. Silence. A shoe dropped to the floor. Fingermann resorted to a melodious threnody of raps and bangs. The door was at last thrown open, and Malenov, dark and enraged, stood before them in his long underwear, screaming at Fingermann in Russian. Fingermann tried to control Malenov's anger, pointing nervously to the two journalists, who grinned broadly at this apparition. "Another madman," one whispered. Fingermann denied it. But Malenov, hearing the insult, began in a rapid mixture of Russian and German to celebrate madness in general and his own in particular.

He began, "*Da*. I am mad. Absolutely mad. And who wouldn't be mad living in a mad country?" The journalists began to pay attention, an exchange developed, a conversation ensued, and the journalists, first amused, ended amazed, as this remarkable man seated on his bed in his underpants began to describe the predicament of German civilization with a telling particularity and observation, showing his paintings as examples of health and cure, supplying quotations from his manifestor and unpublished writings to document the visionary ferocity of projectivism. After nearly forty minutes the journalists had enough copy and decided to leave, after persuading Malenov to throw open his windows and salute the thinning crowd below. Shouts of "Hurray for housing" greeted his waving arms; smiling Malenov withdrew, closed the windows, pushed Fingermann from his room, and went back to bed. He slept for nearly eighteen hours.

By the following Friday, when he awoke, two telegrams shoved beneath his door by the landlord announced the sale of five paintings to a Swiss collector and a German industrialist; a commission from Alexander Dorner of the Kestner Gesellschaft to make two lithographs for his museum; an invitation to a conference, Architecture and Pure Plastic Painting; and a long extract from one of the interviews that had appeared that day in the *Tagblatt* under the headline, "Yevgeny Mikhailovich Malenov: Visionary Painter and Utopian Architect." The text was all wrong, but it was respectful and generous. Malenov had definitively emerged from obscurity. Although never a celebrity—that dubious estate would overtake artists some time later—Malenov was never again unknown. There would always be someone in the entourage of the arts who would know of Yevgeny Mikhailovich Malenov, who could identify his doctrine and describe his imagery, who knew where his paintings fit in the scheme of modernism.

All this attention did not secure for Malenov a reliable income. He continued to live, as he once put it, "from foot to mouth," displacement with more than an element of truth, since as often as his hand lifted fork to face, it had first to push out of the way the arrogance of foot, which declaimed, spluttered, enthused over his utopic schemes and dreams. Unworldly, indifferent to the machinery of the world, content with little beyond subsistence, wanting nothing more than the acknowledgment of his vision and its efficacy, eager only to get on with the work of incarnation that would show forth the supreme harmony of his genius, Malenov paid little attention to Fingermann's antic claims on his behalf. The more Malenov withdrew into work, the more Fingermann undertook to agitate the recognition of his genius, dogging journalists, sending out photographs of the artist in his "studio of poverty," as he named it, borrowing pictures and failing to return them as promised, arriving hours late at restaurants to which he had bidden Malenov appear for dinners with enthusiastic collectors (Malenov would arrive only to discover that no reservation had been made and no collectors had appeared), wearing Malenov out with endless complaints about his lack of gratitude and appreciation for his efforts on Malenov's behalf.

Malenov was wearying of Fingermann. One day he appeared at Fingermann's home in a fashionable quarter of Berlin and demanded to see him. A butler tried to prevent his entering until he had been announced, but Malenov pushed him aside and strode through the living room to the study at the rear of the house overlooking a charming flower garden. It was late April, and sun streamed through the house; Malenov envied Fingermann the riches that enabled him to buy a portion of the sun. Malenov pushed open the glass doors that sheltered Fingermann's spacious verandah from the rest of the house and found Fingermann lying on the floor looking about him at his gallery of masterpieces—Cézanne, Renoir, Picasso, a Kirchner street scene, Otto Dix, a large Schiele—but where were the more than twenty Malenovs that he had carried away over the past months?

"Where is Malenov?"

"Ah, Malenov, it is you? Why weren't you announced?" Fingermann asked languidly, undisturbed by the appearance of the bullheaded Malenov.

"I choose to be unannounced. How would someone announce a Malenov to a Fingermann?" he snarled.

"Ah, my dear genius, you seem disturbed. Why are you disturbed?" Fingermann inquired, placing joined hands behind his head and raising himself a few inches from the floor.

"Where are Malenov's paintings, Fingermann? I have come for an accounting and settlement."

"Your paintings, my dear genius, are no more. They are all gone. Sold for a song. I am tired of you, Malenov. You are a genius, but like all geniuses you don't produce enough. You think too much. You talk too much. You paint too slowly. I have gone back to the masters. I am finished with living artists. Too much work for a small fellow like Fingermann."

"Then pay me the song."

"What are you talking about, dear Malenov? What song?"

"You sold them for song. That's what you said. Give it to me."

"An expression, dear fellow. I sold them for practically nothing—even the industrialist from Zurich (actually, he makes ladies' hats) paid me so little it was hardly decent taking the money. But if you insist. There, on the desk, there's a pile of banknotes. Take them. They belong to you. It looks like more than it is. Take the money, dear fellow, and go away. I'm enjoying the sun."

There was an instant during which Malenov imagined lifting little Fingermann and throwing him through the window into the garden beyond. His rage was luminous, but it passed as quickly as it had been ignited. He had no intention of wasting his years paying for the crime of murdering an art merchant. Too foolish, too disgusting. Instead, he determined to annihilate the presence of Fingermann, to gather up the moneys due him and without another word to depart. The red of rage had already diminished. Only the tips of his ear lobes remained bright. Indeed, he had passed beyond rage into a equanimity of such supreme indifference that he was unaware that as he returned from the desk (where he had seized the money and stuffed it into his overcoat), he had stepped on the recumbent Fingermann as he passed out of the verandah. He heard Fingermann scream with pain, but he was unsure from where the cries had come. He had almost fractured Fingermann's shoulder, but he could not remember how it happened when it was reported to him months later.

SEVEN

Malenov, depressed, wandered the streets of Berlin after he left Fingermann's apartment. The depression was as large and ill-fitting as the threadbare herringbone overcoat that enveloped him. (Depression, anxiety, alarm, fury rarely seized Malenov with an explicit declaration of their origins and force. He was generally unaware of his psychic states, rushing speedily beyond intimate pains and dislocations to a metaphysical conclusion that snared him in appraisals of his own energy and production. Everything he felt—all his longings and disappointments—rarely turned upon the deceits and corruptions of others. Finally, it was always *his* fault for not doing enough work. Saint Sergius glared at him, the Third Rome exposed its rotten beams, all the young naked delights of his album of regrets suddenly frowned. It was Malenov's fault if the world worked awry, if the Fingermanns among dealers turned out to be feckless charlatans.) Malenov wandered the streets in the spring sunlight, returning home at dusk, trudging up the stairs of the rooming house. Upon his bed the landlord had placed a letter with a neatly typed address. Malenov assumed it was from Fingermann already, an explanation, an apology perhaps. But he had no further interest in Fingermann. He had been cheated, but it hardly mattered. Genius, he believed, was not restricted to a few works; it could create again and better. He lay down on the bed and heard the letter crinkle beneath his buttocks. He removed it and, as he passed it before his face, bunching it into refuse, he noticed the Soviet stamp and the return address. He shouted with joy and tore it open:

> Dear old friend. I am coming to Berlin for a big exhibition of our new art that will open at the Lehrter Galerie end of March. I will see you there, no? They have a beautiful work of yours that I sent from my own collection. With sincere warmth, Malevich.

Malenov overflowed with happiness. He did love Malevich, love and honor Malevich, honor and celebrate Malevich, celebrate and occasionally borrow from Malevich. Projectivism was, he admitted years later, a spark of the Supremus ignited on the anvil of his own genius. Malenov leapt from his bed and dashed out of the rooming house, found a taxicab and headed for the Lehrter train station, where the gallery was located. The small gallery was already closed for the night, but he saw his painting hanging beside others less distinguished; it was a radiant composition of 1923, in which a rectangular lozenge of orange floated off a gray-white scaffolding into an immense sea of powdery black. He had forgotten the painting and he adored seeing it again, even if it was lit by a poorly powered night lamp that stood in the center of the forlorn and empty gallery. Malenov was paralyzed before the vitrine and did not notice that an attractive woman in her mid-thirties was attentively watching him, waiting for the opportunity to speak. After twenty minutes, Malenov heaved a sigh and broke out of his delirium of pleasure.

"Herr Malenov? It is you, isn't it? I am so glad that you finally came to the exhibition. We've been trying to find you for weeks. It was only now, with Malevich's arrival and your press interviews, that we learned your address and have written inviting you to come. And here you are at eight o'clock in the evening, more than an hour after our closing."

The pretty girl, with lips painted like sticks of cinnamon, sweetly hummed her greeting. Malenov turned and in a kind of reverie, still delirious before his painting, nodded to her, as if to query her identity.

"Fraulein Kammerer. Francine Kammerer. The Lehrter is my gallery. Let me tell you. The exhibition is a great success. Your very original publicity stunt quickened interest; attendance has been much greater than we had anticipated." Malenov wasn't quite certain to what she referred, but he smiled radiantly at her attention. She reopened the gallery, walked him through the exhibition, and took him for supper in a café around the corner from the station. At the very end of the evening, Malenov remembered his old friend. "And Malevich, dear young lady. Where can I find Malevich?"

"He is out of the city. He insisted on visiting the Bauhaus in Dessau. I told him that I had called and that the school was closing for Easter holidays, but he went nonetheless. He said Kandinsky was enough reason. All of you Russians are so incredibly stubborn. It doesn't matter. He will be back tomorrow, he promised me."

"And his address?"

"He is living with von Riesen. I don't have the address written down, but here is the telephone number. Riesen has installed a telephone. It is probably easier to send a telegram, but then without the addresss? No. Try the telephone or come by tomorrow in the late afternoon. Malevich is usually here at that time."

Malenov watched her write the telephone number of von Riesen. A small, sinuous hand, each letter and number embellished like a baroque woodcarving. She did it unself-consciously, without pretension. Clearly, it was the way she had learned to write. Malenov watched her with smiles of appreciation. A lovely woman, he thought. Dare I fall in love with a grown-up? He suddenly blushed; his reverie of love had frightened and embarrassed him. He turned to Fraulein Kammerer and stumbled his apologies. "I am sorry. Rude and vulgar. Rude and vulgar. I must go now." He snatched the bit of paper from beneath her pen and fled into the night.

The following morning Malenov fell into the center of an unfinished painting. He worked steadily throughout the day into the evening. It was almost ten o'clock when he remembered that he had promised to go by the gallery in the late afternoon to visit with Malevich. He tried to call from the corner café, but the gallery was long since closed. The next day was Sunday, and everything was closed. By Monday he had totally forgotten the gallery in the Lehrter train station, the exhibition of new Soviet painting, the charms of Francine Kammerer, and Kazimir Malevich. He had promised himself that he would take a holiday in springtime, before Easter, a walking holiday in southern Germany, and he set off by train for Munich. He planned to be away for more than two weeks, hiking in the woods, sometimes sleeping out of doors, once or twice perhaps finding hospitality in a cheap inn or the haybarn of a peasant. He adored hiking, although Bavaria was completely different from the Ukraine, where flat surfaces, undulant with waving stalks of grain and corn, predominated. In southeast Germany, hills and mountains, valleys and ravines compelled the traveler to watch his step lest he fall off into a charging river or tumble from a rock and break a leg.

Malenov was always excited by the dangers of nature. Nature was for him a metaphor of his painting; it supplied atmosphere and tone; form was in the brain; the painting was reality. One morning he trudged out into the countryside carrying a large sketchbook, his pockets bulging with colored pencils and crayons; he crossed a field, dodging cow droppings, and descended a narrow path that approached a rocky wall that sheered off to a river below. Swollen with the runoff from melting mountain snow, the river careened over jagged rocks and monumental boulders. Jamming his feet into the trunk of an uprooted fir tree that fronted the chasm, Yevgeny began to draw the wall of rock on the other side. Amazed by the geological strata that formed this outcropping of the mountain range in the distance, he devised a pattern of colored surfaces, shading them to suggest their interconnectedness and linkage, gradually erasing the sharp lines that marked the actual divisions of nature, until hours later what had emerged from his concentrated reading of the landscape was a Malenovian abstraction. It could have been executed in his Berlin studio, although Malenov insisted that this first drawing of what became a suite of images would have been impossible without the suggestion supplied him by that sheer wall of layered stone, the dashing river below throwing spume into the air, and his increasingly panicked attempt to get it all down before the light changed. The original drawing was rectangles and projectiles as before, although the palette had moved downward from the ether colors that Malenov favored for his heavenly ascents to the earthy tones of ochres and umbers that enriched his transcription of the essence of this animated abstraction he called nature.

When he returned to the small inn where he had been settled for the last days of his holiday trek, the innkeeper greeted him warmly: "Ah, painting our scenery. May I see?" Malenov opened the sketchpad and watched the innkeeper, crestfallen and confused. "But what is this?"

"The canyon and the river outside town."

"I've never seen this before."

"It is there most certainly. It seems, sir, that you look but you don't see." Malenov was content with his day's work. He laughed when he accused the innkeeper. Usually, he growled. The innkeeper was nonplussed; shrugging his shoulders, he went off to make Malenov his afternoon grog of hot wine, lemon, and cinnamon.

The following day, although it was now early May, a spring storm descended on the village, unseasonable winds shattered the calm of the valley, and an enormous tree was dislodged and fell into the roadway, cutting off the village from the dirt road that joined it to the small Bavarian hamlets that clustered the mountain range. Yevgeny Mikhailovich awakened with a chest cold of such magnitude that his coughing shook the quiet of the inn no less than did the battering storm winds. He remained in bed for nearly a week, tended with soups and suspicion, for his execrably accented German, clearly Slavic in origin, unnerved the conservative women of the inn as much as his odd drawings of the surrounding mountains and valleys, which he tacked to the walls of his room, annotating them with titles in Russian while describing in German their complex abstract vocabulary with such banal simplisms as "Mountains and Rivers" or "Prehistroic Bavaria." The mother of the innkeeper, a shuffling woman in her seventies, muttered to herself about Yevgeny's German, persuaded that his drawings were spy codes for a Bolshevik invasion of southern Germany. She mentioned her suspicions to the local constable, who arranged to sneak into the room when Yevgeny was down the hall in the lavatory, but he found nothing suspicious about the drawings, although he declared with certainty that they were "not art."

After six days in bed, Yevgeny decided that he was recovered and appeared one morning for steaming coffee and hot rolls in the common room below, his scarf wrapped about his throat up to his nose, leaving only the smallest of apertures for the insertion of food and liquid. In the days that followed he stayed near the inn, walking down into the village square to introduce himself to the various tradesmen of the village, sketching occasionally, reading the out-of-date newspapers the innkeeper received by mail from Munich, until, in the third week in May, he announced one day at noon that he was prepared to leave, having already arranged to ride in the back of a horse-drawn cart that was about to set forth with cut wood for the trading center of Rosenheim, some miles away in a lower valley, from which he could catch a train for Munich. He paid the innkeeper, embraced the mother with eager enthusiasm, hugging her immensity with such ferocity that she cried out in dialect that he was assaulting her, tipped the young girl who cleaned his room, and, having packed his rucksack and strapped his sketchpad to his back, climbed up onto the mountain of cut logs and shouted to the young driver that he was settled and ready for the journey.

Yevgeny Mikhailovich did not return to Berlin until May 26 at dusk. He found many letters and local telegrams, inviting him to salons that were long since over and dinners he would never have enjoyed. There were two messages, however, from Malevich: "What has become of you?" read one, and the other, somewhat more plaintively, "Am I never to see you? Are you angry with your old friend?" Yevgeny retrieved the slip of paper on which Francine Kammerer had written the telephone number of the von Riesen apartment where Malevich was staying and rushed across the street to the local *bierstube,* where he phoned the apartment. An old woman answered. "No, Herr von Riesen is not at home. No, the large Russian is not at home. Yes. I will give them a message."

"Tell them to meet Yevgeny tomorrow afternoon at Die Florelle. Two o'clock. Yes. Two in the afternoon. Please promise to give them the message. Please. Please. You have it clearly? Yevgeny. Die Florelle. Two exactly."

But the old lady had hung up the moment he had begun to repeat his instructions. Yevgeny thought for a moment to call back to make certain that he had reached the right number and to give the message again, but he thought the old lady might well sabotage him if he called to repeat himself. Yevgeny contented himself with waiting ten minutes, dialing the number again, and, when the old woman answered, putting down the receiver. Yes, it was the same cracked and weary voice. He had reached the right number, he believed.

And the rest is known. Die Florelle. Precisely at 2 P.M. The battle of cups and cakes, the seizure of premonition and the precipitate dash for the von Riesen apartment only to discover that Malevich had left for Moscow, departing without ever having seen again his younger friend and colleague, the great successor to Supremus, master of projectivism, severe theoretician of utopics, then penniless and abandoned in Berlin.

EIGHT

Joseph Alexander Karnovsky disembarked at Hamburg early on a glistening January morning in 1928. He had departed three weeks earlier from New York, determined to search out and impress Yevgeny Mikhailovich Malenov. It is true that he did not have Malenov's address, but that seemed hardly an obstacle. He had accumulated a considerable collection of what he correctly called "traces of the Master," and had ordered them in such a way as to provide him with an only slightly blurred profile of his quarry: several photographs (all enlarged and retouched); reproductions of a number of Malenov's paintings; a brief biographical notice appended to the one gallery catalogue that had reproduced Malenov's work; three terse discussions of Malenov's oeuvre in otherwise uninformed comment on the postrevolutionary Soviet avant-garde; and, most significantly, a translation of the text of the Projectivist Manifesto dispensed over the major cities of Germany some months before, which mentioned that the artist lived "in a rooming house in East Berlin." The field was narrowed considerably, and Karnovsky was confident that if a New York art periodical had reproduced Malenov's manifesto, it had presumably been published previously by the German press, which would have elaborated the cryptic allusion to Malenov's dreary quarters with a specific mention of the street and number. He had no fear, then, that Malenov could evade him, much less would wish to evade him. Why, he reassured himself, would the painter want to avoid an ardent, a young acolyte, a potential disciple, particularly a disciple of some means (with more means to come) who only wished to aid and assist the Master, to learn from him, to profit from his presence, to assimilate everything, from the ideas of his art to such minor matters as how genius disposed of rejected drawings.

Karnovsky sat in the lounge car of the Hamburg-Berlin night train smoking thin cheroots and drinking brandy, watching his pleasant face glint and wink in the various mirrors disposed about the sofas and shiny mahogany tables with which the car was furnished. He enjoyed the salubrity of elegance, seated in the warmth of his floor-length beaver coat as the cold crept in and the air began to smoke with chill, smiling to himself almost triumphantly. He had crossed the ocean to find a genius in Berlin to whom to apprentice his own modest but swelling talents.

It had to be. It had to be, he kept repeating to himself, sometimes saying the words, sometimes seeing them before him like the dire warnings written on the plaster wall of Belshazzar's palace, sometimes outlining them with his finger on the befogged windowpanes that blotted the night lights of the countryside past which the train speeded.

It had to be. (What had to be? I wonder now. The victory of determination over obstinacy is the most that one can construe this phrase— repeated and underlined in Karnovsky's journal of his Berlin hegira—to mean. It had to be, one surmises, because it left out of account everything that was not controlled by Karnovsky's will and what he took to be the omnipotence of the largesse he wanted to bestow. He knew nothing about Yevgeny Mikhailovich Malenov. Indeed, in those early days of the maturity of Joseph Alexander Karnovsky, he hardly knew the details of himself. He had, as all attractive young men, a consoling naivete that imagined reality curling in fright before beauty and intelligence, the filling cheek, the open smile, the intense and passionate eye, the casually cut hair, long and short, rippled and straight, the generous mouth, all ornamenting an intelligence that organized these discrete items of masculine beauty into a face that was, indeed, passionate and intense, that bespoke intelligence, that was occasionally, in fact, very intelligent and always—in Karnovsky's case—somewhat frightened, somewhat calculating.)

Somewhat frightened, somewhat calculating. (Dare I say this with certainty about the young man of twenty-two who descended at 6:30 on the morning of a snowstorm that stalled Berlin for two days during early January 1928? Can I be certain? I worry about my temptation to pass such judgments on young Joseph Alexander Karnovsky. And yet it seems hardly possible to resist them. Item: he had boarded his ship, the S.S. *Intransigent,* as Joseph Alexander Karnovsky, but minutes later registered for his table assignment and deck chair as J. Alexander Karnovsky. Item: I found years later among his papers of the period a snarly and contemptuous aside about the ancient origin from which his English name was expanded. Our Joseph Alexander thought his biblical antecedent boring and punctilious and preferred to retract him to a mere initial, focusing his favor instead on Alexander, whether thinking of the Great Alexander or considering the liberal czar of all the Russias who had freed the serfs and perhaps facilitated—through many permutations and misjudgments—the flight of Karnovsky's parents and himself from the Old World to the New, I do not know. Moreover, it didn't matter. In those days, he preferred being a bright Alexander to acceding to such a stern monitor as the ancient Joseph.)

A porter rushed forward to seize Karnovsky's valises. Karnovsky was exhausted; he had passed the night in an almost somnambulistic contemplation of his destiny, flitting between various schemes and dreams of his future, reviewing his coming to be in this hour, abroad in the world, fled from the comforts and securities of domestic succor—his father's scrutiny of his enterprise, his mother's bourgeois dismay at her only son's seduction by the world of art. Karnovsky had already left behind several snakeskins of permutation upon the beds and bureaus of his family apartment, passing through moultings that had jettisoned without apology all his father's commonplace expectations for his son.

Markus Israel Karnovsky, a tea importer of renowned connoisseurship, had been a principal purveyor of Russian and oriental teas to the family of the czar and the nobility of the Russian Empire. Wisely, Markus Karnovsky had never sought to capitalize on his mercantile involvement with the aristocracy to petition permission to live in St. Petersburg, with the result that when the revolution occurred, he was far from the scene of early hostilities and near enough to borders of escape that he could prepare wisely and well his departure from the embattled nation. He quietly sold his several shops, happily accepting losses and smiling cheerfully as the new owners fleeced him, each month converting cash into gold and jewels with a calm and deliberation that belied the financial debacle he had accepted as inevitable. A man of forty-eight with a nervous wife and a fourteen-year-old son would do well—he counseled

himself—to move slowly, without attracting notice, condensing his holdings to a few treasures that could be sequestered and smuggled across
borders. He knew that inevitably he would come to the attention of the
Red authorities for being a merchant and tea supplier to the czar's family
and to that of the Whites for being, despite his indifference to matters
of nationality and religion, a Jew of Odessa, an acquaintance of Jewish
nationists, Yiddishists, Hebrew poets, and rabbinic scholars, all of whom
made a practice of requiring Markus Karnovsky's advice in the mixing of
their breakfast teas and special decoctions.

During the summer of 1919, with the war between Reds and Whites
already raging, Markus Karnovsky arranged an unpretentious holiday for
his family at a small Black Sea village near Ovdiopol, on the Rumanian
border about twenty miles from Odessa. He had already negotiated the
sale of his apartment and its furnishings, making certain that the documents of sale passed between intermediate friends to the gentile physi-
cian who was eager to expand his practice and improve his social
standing with the purchase of the Karnovskys' spacious apartment. They
fled safely from Odessa, carrying little baggage and what might be taken
for a holiday pannier, all jewels hidden in bottles of jam or pressed behind the anchovies of pitted olives or stuffed into silver bugle beads that
decorated a peasant blouse his wife had made for the occasion of their
flight. They arranged one morning for a young sailor to take them for an
idle day on the Black Sea and then, beyond the sight of land, to make
sail for the nearest settled habitation in Rumania, the small city of Sulina,
where one of the mouths of the Danube disgorged into the sea. All the
way across, Markus Karnovsky distracted himself (while his wife groaned
from seasickness and worry) by instructing young Joseph Alexander in
the mysteries of sums and subtraction. His wife was irritated with his
meticulous instruction, her anxiety mounting as the gentle sea swelled
and rolled the fishing vessel down the coast toward Rumania and the
young sailor, unaware of her nervous condition or the momentousness
of their escape, sang songs to himself in a language the Karnovskys were
certain was not Russian.

The lights of Sulina were matted by the distant gloom; the fishing
vessel turned in toward shore, deposited the Karnovskys on a rocky
beach, and abandoned them. They trudged in to the highway, found an
inn for the night, presented themselves and their papers at the police
station the following morning, and secured the travel documents necessary for them to proceed to Constanta, where they boarded a freighter
for Istanbul. There, two weeks and one day after their flight from Odessa,
they embarked for New York City. The migration of the Karnovskys was

wrought by energetic flight and bribery, a jewel here, a gold coin there, a family moved from the misery of war-torn Russia (where in time what assuredly awaited them was impoverishment and death) to the principal metropolis of the new world, which in their unsophisticated imaginings they had not thought larger or more dense than Odessa, that two-story, wood-and-stone city of southern Russia.

The Karnovskys settled down. They learned English; they refused to forget Russian; they read Russian books; they declined to read Russian newspapers and magazines; they had no interest in politics or historical events; they cared only for what Mrs. Karnovsky called "culture," which included Markus Karnovsky presenting his thick Russian accent accoutered in velour hats and soft alpaca jackets. No rebuke to Markus Israel Karnovsky; he did his best with what he was, with what he knew, with what he construed his future in America promised. He devised and he dreamed, always taking into account the indefiniteness of his wife, who fluttered and sneezed over his arrangements, caring more for the proprieties than for the substance of events, and his growing son, who mooned and affected very long hair and sad eyes.

The Karnovskys did not think of themselves as immigrants, certainly not as exiles. They were "sojourners," and when they came upon the word and mastered its subtleties, they described themselves as such. They had left Russia behind because its atmosphere had lowered and become inhospitable, but their indifference to events was so ingrained that for Markus Israel Karnovsky the mention of his middle name became sufficiently discomforting that he dropped it entirely. They were not Jews in exile or wanderers from a nation of wanderers; they had come to New York because it was no longer possible for them to be tea merchants to the noble houses of Russia. That was all there was to it. (And, let me make clear, Markus Karnovsky was not intent on wealth or power; he thought of dealing in tea the way other merchants thought about fine wine or antiques. His was a calling, indeed a vocation, that required for success an incredibly sensitive nose and an astute and uncorrupted palate, fingers that felt boding staleness in the slightest crackle of a leaf, and a knowledge of the scores of variations that marked out the teas of China and southeast Asia from the black teas of Russia, varieties that alluded to smokiness or the aroma of burning fall leaves, that promised a loosening of catarrhs or a tightening of flabby chins. The tea merchant was a born homeopath, one step from professional medicine, akin to magician and alchemist, but also unsentimental trader and merchant, who mixed and blended, branding his name on certain teas as being his very own.)

Within a year of their arrival, "Karnovsky Selection" was inscribed in elegant serifs on fine boxes and metal containers sent forth to such distant and exotic places as Denver, Portland, and San Francisco, across the nation back to the borders of the Pacific amidst which the many tea-growing lands were situated. In time Markus Karnovsky branched out, acquiring on his staff a pepper expert and a master of herbs, buying contracts that ran into the tens of thousands of dollars, speculating on growths and deliveries, buying up and selling short, taking delivery of rich cargoes and selling their contents to large food shops and new conglomerates that produced tinned soups and seasoned vegetables. In time—that is, near the end of the 1920s—the House of Karnovsky had become one of the best-established importers in the nation, with a staff of thirty tasters and sales personnel clustered around the mahogany tables in the inner rooms, where annually the tasting of the new teas would be conducted with solemn formality in the presence of Markus I. Karnovsky, a figure of portly solidity, now bearded and framed in fur lapels.

Despite his preoccupation with tea, pepper, and herbs, Markus Karnovsky did not neglect the education of his son. On Saturday mornings he walked with Joseph Alexander through the park, from their apartment on West End Avenue toward the reservoir, stopping beside the bridle path to mark out with his walking stick mathematical problems that he wished his son to solve and simple French sentences into which he had installed an error that he required his son to catch and correct. No reward for success nor punishment for failure, he believed. Simple performance, that was all. He was surely unaware that wresting a smile of satisfaction from him became so important to the uncertain young man that when he failed—as happened, if not frequently, at least some of the time—and Markus Karnovsky's eye clouded, a furrow of consternation appeared, a bit lip, a clucking sound of disapproval (all involuntary), the ensemble of grimaces and sounds struck deep into the heart of the young aspirant, who shook his head with horror that he failed and was often inconsolable for several hours beyond the moment, refusing to release himself from the judgment of worthlessness with which he assailed himself. "He wants so little of me," the young boy said to himself, "and even then I fail him." Had it crossed his mind that his father had spent little more than a brief hour's walk on Saturdays in the company of his child, a mathematical mistake or a brutalized French construction would not have weighed so heavily. But that was not the case. In time, what began as the wish to give simple pleasures and rewards to his otherwise preoccupied father became a monumental struggle to impress and overwhelm him (and perhaps, sotto voce, to strangle his instructional chords). He loved him so much and yet remained so unsatisfactory a loving son that he found it hard to imagine loving anyone else, loving another, loving a woman, settling finally some years beyond this adolescent interregnum with attending to himself only, loving himself—if such muddled and ungratifying self-love could be called loving.

Of course, there is more provocation and incident behind the introspection, self-enamorment, and nerveless certainty that finally emerged from the welter of beginnings as the grown Joseph Alexander Karnovsky, but too much detail would take me far off course. The misery of the Saturday trial by ordeal, for example, would have returned to the miasma of gestures by which most human beings conduct the work of the affections, had its implication of insensitivity not been confirmed by many other passages of formal rightness with which his father and later his mother conducted their relationship with their only child. Everything from the clothes Joseph Alexander wore and the amount of time he was expected to spend in earnest effort in the bathroom to the fixing of permissible times for reading and obligatory times for roller-skating (which was called a "healthy exercise") were fixed by what his father— remembering czarist times—called "Papa's ukase." Joseph Alexander was never asked to do anything; he was always told in a voice of peremptory loftiness, his father's voice swooping down on him from elevated heights where decisions were presumably made only after consultation atop Olympus. But if such examples fail to persuade us of the depth of injury sustained by the young man, think only on the grotesquerie of the following episode, underlined in red crayon in the recollections of childhood I found among Karnovsky's papers after his death:

> When I was nearing my fifteenth birthday, my father ordered me one day to make myself ready for my first trip to his tailors, where, I assumed, the passage from knee pants and cutaway jackets furled with a velvet collar would give way to a proper suit. Father ordered me to dress with particular formality for the visit to his tailors—"they are imported gentlemen like ourselves"—which I took to mean that he wished me turned out in shirt and tie. I presented myself as his breakfast concluded; the maid—a young girl of particularly striking attractiveness—was clearing the table. Father took one glance at my get-up and called me to his side. Reaching into his pocket, he withdrew his complicated pocket knife, one of whose gold appendages was a small but deadly scissor. "Your tie is improperly balanced," he declared sourly, and seizing the errant end, which drooped foolishly below the line of the front striped streamer, he summarily scissored it off. The maid giggled. I shook violently and then burst into tears. Many weeks elapsed before a large package was delivered from Father's

tailor. The suit intended had been ordered without my seeing it. *Hoc pater fecit.*

Enough then. You know Markus Israel Karnovsky sufficiently; since he plays a minor role in the events that follow and disappears to an early grave before J. Alexander Karnovsky has been four months in Berlin, it is enough to have briefly annotated the characteristics he exhibited as father. He somehow knew that he had failed as father, but always imagined that it was much more to the point of paterfamilias to serve both wife and son by a single, efficient enterprise: his vocation as expert on the various leafs and buds and fruits that constituted the mysterious world of teas and condiments. He never complained about his son; he took it for granted that he would never become an expert at anything. Indeed, he rationalized the success of the House of Karnovsky by believing that his own eminence would protect his son from the need to become eminent himself. It did not surprise him, therefore, that his son, having mastered languages and mathematics, later science and mathematics, and subsequently science and history, would refuse to become what his father had marked out as the only alternative to a vocation in tea. Joseph Alexander had no wish to become "a technical man," as his father called chemists, engineers, physicists, even astronomers and medical practitioners. The arts were exhausted by teas and herbs, wines and scents; the rest was consigned to the dominion of precision and exactitude, where the laws of the universe groaned. Since those laws were as recondite and untransmissible as the secrets of nose and palate, it was assumed that his son would become "a technical man." However, Joseph Alexander would have none of it. He began to visit museums when he was sixteen and never left off; when other boys rushed from school to the playground, he began to draw, compelling himself through pens and pencils to combat his father's decision regarding the life he had selected for him. By the time he had spent two years at Columbia University, enrolled in engineering but preferring to ignore its requirements in order to audit lectures in the history of art, it was clear to the father that to oblige his son to become "a technical man" was to risk driving him from home or, worse, mangling his spirit. Markus shouted at Joseph Alexander, berating his stupidity and arrogance, contending passionately that "the new world is a technical world," and artists would be crushed, but in the end he accepted the inevitable, settled on his son an allowance that varied as the yield on speculative futures in the black peppers of Madagascar determined, and turned him loose. Joseph Alexander, for his part, grateful for an income that ranged between $2,600 and $3,400 a year, depending on the fluctuations in his pepper endowment, rented an apartment in Greenwich Village, arranged his books on a windowsill, acquired a companionable alley cat, and spent his days drawing. In time Karnovsky decided to formalize his study of art and registered for courses at the Art Student's League. His father, before agreeing to pay the fees, conducted a scrupulous examination of the institution, even going to the length of pretending to enroll himself for beginner's courses, to test the manner of instruction, the temptations posed by live models, and the canons of legibility and imitation observed by its faculty. He wanted to make certain that his son would become a creditable artist, if artist he wished to be. At least, he imagined, let his son's studio be immaculate, his scenes and views bright and attractive, his dress and manner polite. To be sure of Joseph Alexander's acquiring such decent habits, he wanted to assure himself that the boy's teachers would be unexceptionable. After a month of close examination of the league's teachers and students, Markus Karnovsky reluctantly concurred in his son's decision and paid over his fees.

It is important to note that young Joseph Alexander Karnovsky (then approaching his twenty-first birthday) was not without talent. His eye was acute, his hand cunning, his sensibility—fresh and unjaded—receptive to enlargement. It is unclear to what vision he pinned his talent, but it was indubitable to his assigned teachers—a large woman with hair drawn tightly into a bun and an evanescently thin academic draftsman with a pince-nez—that Joseph Alexander Karnovsky, former student of engineering, was more exuberantly committed to making canny marks on paper that signified body and form than to casting sums and devising mechanical theorems. However, what might have satisfied his teachers, who regarded their teaching enterprise with indifference (believing themselves to be wasting time with the bourgeoisie when they should have been making revolutions of their own at home), hardly sufficed for Karnovsky. By the end of his first year at the league he knew perfectly well how to draw from life, to shade and hue, to adumbrate and allude in charcoal, pencil, and watercolor. He had even executed in oils—more to prove that he could than from any conviction about the work's importance—a large canvas depicting two nudes seated on gilt chairs, their bodies crumpled with weariness, each with a hand raised to a furrowed brow, one (the male) so foreshortened that he appeared to be suffering from collapsed lungs and advanced consumption, the other (the female) with breasts pendulous and sagging, an old woman, thickened at her hips, stockings falling about her ankles. They were not a cheerful pair, and, although the picture won a prize in the annual exhibition of the league and Joseph Alexander was able to present his father with a check for $25, he derived no pleasure from his ability to make presentable drawings, neatly considered, evocative, but finally second-rate. There had to be something more, a way of reconstructing the universe that would accord with his growing demand for an alternative that could efficiently challenge both "the technical world" vaunted by his father and Madagascar gold, as his particular peppercorns were collectively known.

NINE

Joseph Alexander's first whiff of the existence of Yevgeny Mikhailovich Malenov occurred fortuitously. He overheard a conversation—more precisely, he eavesdropped—one day while he stood in line at the white-tiled cafeteria on Broadway where students of the league usually gathered between classes for coffee. An elderly gentleman, clearly an emigré, was shouting in Russian to an old woman: "Projectivist Manifesto. *Kvatsh!* Lines in empty space, poking God." The man snorted, his hand trembling so violently that his tea sloshed over the metal tray he was carrying to a table at the rear of the cafeteria. Intrigued, Joseph Alexander followed the pair and seated himself just behind them. "What does it mean, Elena? What? *Kvatsh.* Double *kvatsh,*" the old man continued to growl. "I have read it carefully and not one word makes sense. And who signed it, you may ask, Elena? Who? None other. Our old friend, the Muscovite, Yevgeny Mikhailovich Malenov. Naturally! Malenov. Projectivism? *Kvatsh!*"

Alexander Karnovsky had noted the name Yevgeny Mikhailovich Malenov in his little sketchbook, opening to a clean page, where he wrote beside the name in giant Cyrillic majuscules, "WHO IS THIS?" Until that moment Joseph Alexander had had no idea that any artistic ferment accompanied the hue and cry of revolutionary Russia. When the Karnovskys arrived in New York from Odessa in 1919, although they continued to chatter in Russian at home, his father's interest in things Russian waned. They had come, after all, to America, and it was problematic enough to be Russian Jews without being thought communist sympathizers as well. But Joseph Alexander's interest in the artistic enthusiasm of revolutionary Russia was piqued by this chance encounter with Malenov's manifesto. He diligently searched the Russian-language press for mention of Malenov and found two references, both respectful—but inconclusive. It was in an issue of a German illustrated monthly, *Der Querschnitt,* which was gathering dust in the stacks of the New York Public Library, that he discovered a photograph of Malenov, seated on a straight-backed chair, a cane plunged between his open legs, his enormous peasant hands resting like chunks of cubed beef on its gnarled handle. Malenov stared out at the photographer like a guardian lion, a large body surmounted by a vast head framed by straight black hair that dropped down about his ears. Malenov's eyes, hardly visible beneath hooded eyelids, were particularly unsettling, at odds with his sharp, pointed nose and capacious mouth, clamped shut. Behind Malenov (which explains his aspect as guardian lion), rose a wall filled with unframed paintings of various magnitudes. Karnovsky sat in the reading room of the library and whistled aloud. Heads turned, but he continued for some moments to whistle with amazement. An attendant came to silence him. Karnovsky vowed to return the following day to vandalize the copy of the magazine, to slit the picture from the page and bear its leonine subject to his Village lair.

So this was Malenov. So this was Malenov's projectivist image. So these were the Malenovian visions—ellipses poised in space, hovering on the ether, borne on winds, each latticework of ellipses, perpendiculars, floating triangles, painted with what he guessed were serene shades of cobalt blue, cadmium yellow, roses and reds, light grays, desperate blacks, tribunals of space, revealing a new dimension of the universe, where ordinary things, familiar nature, conventional events were excised and a new space, a beleaguered time, an atmosphere void of history and humanity was presented for the contemplation of the metaphysical eye. This was the sublime art for which Karnovsky was searching. His heart surged, the adrenalin flowed like gushing sex, his head pounded. He was ravished by the sight of this score of miniature pictures—each less than postage-stamp size in the photograph—hanging on a wall behind a monstrous beast of an artist.

It was remarkably easy for Karnovsky to give up literal figuration and artistically plausible renditions of what the hoi polloi took to be the real, and to begin to refashion the universe as an abstract underpinning of line and shape overlaid with color. He had read enough philosophy to be aware that everyone uses abstract ideas but generally has no notion that they are speaking in abstractions. All language, he understood, was an agreement upon significance, settling on the heads of little words like *good* and *God* meanings that stripped them of all their richness and complexity in return for the easy possibility that human beings could invoke both without the requirement of even scratching their heads in wonder at what they meant. He began to believe that everything—every style and convention of the species—was marked by stupidity, ignorance, and compromise. It unsettled him to realize this, but did not bother him sufficiently to make such accommodation corrupt or capitulation to such shoddy employment invidious.

All these reflections had the consequence that Karnovsky vowed to become an abstract artist. He concealed this decision from his parents, showing them old drawings of street scenes and rosy nudes when they inquired after his work during their infrequent visits to his apartment. He had no wish (nor need, for that matter) to make his parents any more alarmed than they were already by his artist's life. His reluctance, indeed his fear, of disclosing his resolution to his parents was only slightly less bizarre than the fundamental fact that he had *vowed* to become an abstract artist, as though this, too, were an act of will.

Abstraction, of course, is a work of the mind, and at first it caused him no end of problems. He thought for a while that abstraction would arise before him with the same clarity and power as rain sweeping the streets or sunlight bathing a tenement. It was some time before he came to understand that everything finally was an abstraction of something else, not simply a reduction to elements, as naive thinkers imagine. Abstraction was not removing and simplifying, but actually a kind of adding, a putting on of different eyes. His first abstract drawings in the Malenovian mode were ridiculous, anatomies of line that treated everything like a skeleton. His hand was nervous; he used a ruler and red and blue pencils. The results were thin and neat, as though he were designing street maps and did not dare to get them wrong lest pedestrians lose their way. He was, you will understand, still trying to hold on to a notion of imitation, as though abstraction were merely a technique of easing confusion. One day, however, as he sat by his window overlooking Ninth Street between Fifth and Sixth Avenues, he noticed that the sun streaked through the old wavering handmade glass of his windowpanes, separating the light into bands of color. Thinking that the effect would disappear, that his eyes were playing tricks, he nervously arranged his pencils by his notebook and began to trace the bands of color. The light did not alter. It was midday, and the brilliant sun remained for many hours, the light separating invariantly into bands of pure color, striking a patch of floor and saturating it with beam mixtures that glowed, humming with new arrangements of colored lights. He worked quickly, suddenly freed from the constraint of representation, producing sheet after sheet filled with closely valued streamers of colored light, hastily rubbed, some narrow, others dense and deep. As the light changed, so did his reflection of its intensity. He was unaware of the passage of time, the light dulled and darkened into rich blues and purple blacks. Later, as rain overtook the sunlight, his sketches began to glower and gloom. He had made dozens of drawings, each filled with patterns of streaking light, the color analyzed and weighted, the drawings no longer resembling anything but a cool eye and a contemplative brain joined to fingers that moved the pencils quickly over the cream paper. He had rendered the light as cuts and patches of color; he had made a suite of abstractions. Granted, they were not yet beautiful; the drawings were not held by a formal counterpoint and drama that communicated fluency to the colored lights. But they were indubitably genuine abstractions, conventional notions of reality having given way to transformation, light become color, color become motion, motion become rhythm, rhythm achieving an intensity and contrast that promised a new way of seeing.

It was done; Joseph Alexander had made himself into an abstract artist and he adored the nomenclature, calling himself an "abstractionist" from that afternoon on, announcing that evening in a bar on University Place, where he sometimes went for a drink before supper, that he had done something new that day. To himself, he confided that he was ready to find Malenov and begin his apprenticeship to a master.

TEN

As we have established, Joseph Alexander Karnovsky arrived in Berlin during a snowstorm early in January 1928. To be precise, he arrived on Wednesday morning during the first week in the new year and went immediately to a small hotel, the Atlas, behind the Kürferstendamm, where he booked a modest suite. He had no idea how long he would remain in Berlin and determined to be comfortable during his stay. The manager of the hotel, her ring of keys jangling at her hip, conducted him through the apartment, prettily arranged with solid peasant furniture; a large eighteenth-century ceramic fireplace dominated the room, and pink, purple, and blue floral wreaths battled on the wallpaper. Karnovsky would have preferred the suite naked and undecorated, furnished with spartan severity, because he had come to believe that his newfound vocation as an abstract artist required a lean and disciplined atmosphere for work, but he announced, after reflecting some minutes, "I guess it will do. I'll have it by the month. In advance?" Frau Liebkind nodded and extended her hand. "Here it is," Karnovsky said compliantly, handing her a packet of small green and brown banknotes. "And now, Madame, could you direct me to the largest newspaper in the city? I need some information."

The manager knitted her black eyebrows, virtually joining them in a bushy assault upon her pallid complexion. "*Ja.* The biggest? It must be the *Berliner Morgenpost.*" Joseph Alexander set off at once, hailing a taxi and giving the driver an address not far from his hotel. By late morning he had found what he wanted: the address of Yevgeny Mikhailovich Malenov, back issues of newspapers that described in detail the bombing action organized by Magnus Fingermann (whose little head appeared in an oval inset that invaded a large photograph of Malenov's room in the Prenzlauer Berg), several interiews with Malenov, and additional commentary that Karnovsky found later in the Kunstbibliothek. By midafternoon he had accumulated enough new material to justify a leisurely coffee in order to study his trove of documents and extract from them odd details of Malenov's history—his fondness for cats, the recent walking tour of Bavaria, his icon of Saint Sergius, the death of his parents from influenza—which, he thought, subtly dropped into conversation, would help to persuade Malenov that he had before him a genuine enthusiast, a disciple without guile or deviousness, an ardent student of his life and work.

It was already too late to call on Malenov. Anyway, Karnovsky had decided that it would be more delicate and less overwhelming to send Malenov a hand-delivered letter, written on the notepaper of his hotel, the following evening.

Karnovsky had determined that only subtlety and patience would convince Malenov to trust him. He had picked up several odd clues during the course of his newspaper inquiries and concluded (erroneously, I believe) that Malenov was suspicious of the young, imagining them to be incapable of loyal affection, constancy, and good sense. Karnovsky decided, therefore, upon a less frontal assault, persuaded that geniuses like Malenov do not succumb to naked flattery.

"He has to be seduced," Karnovsky confided to his notebook. "If he believes that I need him desperately, that I will starve without his nurture, he will be less likely to regard my helping him as patronage. The Malenovs of the world, I am certain, hate patrons—at least such bourgeois and crass patrons as exist today." As Karnovsky regarded himself as neither bourgeois nor crass, his stratagems were carefully devised to avoid Malenov's confusing his goodwill with the suspicious maneuvers of someone like Fingermann, against whom Karnovsky had conceived an irrational dislike, regarding his looks as sneaky and his attitudes—quoted in interviews—as no different from those of a circus barker.

Above all, despite the absence of any admission of this fact in Karnovsky's considerable writings about Malenov dating from this period, Alexander was clearly afraid of Malenov, persuaded (as he was justified in believing) that Malenov would reject him. It would have gone so much easier, I am convinced, if Karnovsky had simply appeared at Malenov's lodgings and asked to study with him. Granted that Malenov had little or no experience teaching, but then most painters who have students hardly teach them. The master painter exists as example—everything he does reflects a kind of sureness and no less sovereign experimentation, which cannot fail to instruct the attentive student. The young painter watches the older as he prepares his canvas, mixes his paints, struggles for certain effects, and in the process of watching comes to understand painting as a necromancer's art, for what is put down hardly dries the way it first appears, and every painter has his special secrets. Had young Karnovsky gone to work for Malenov, stretching canvas, doing errands, cleaning the studio, serving him as indispensable assistant, he would have learned without being tempted to imitate. The problem was built into the procedure by which Karnovsky insinuated himself into his master's life. He could not accept their inequality and, failing to recognize the absolute and indispensable inequity that exists between master and assistant, was tempted from the beginning to lean too heavily on his teacher, to think himself entitled to receive the magic of the master without the requirement of first becoming a magician in his own right.

Eleven

Karnovsky's first communication with Yevgeny Mikhailovich Malenov was thrown into a corner with considerable annoyance. Malenov was once again at war with the world. His door displayed at least two announcements: the first declaring rather politely, for Malenov, his total unavailability and inhospitableness; followed by a smaller paper, neatly written in crabbed majuscules, that clarified the first: I AM METAPYSICALLY AVAILABLE (THAT IS, I EXIST), BUT I AM INACCESSIBLE. I PAINT ALWAYS. LEAVE ME ALONE. PLEASE. ALONE. "Alone" was underlined three times in a gradual of black, red, and blue stripes.

Malenov's landlord was indifferent to these front-door exhortations. He read them, laughed hoarsely, and pounded on the locked door with malicious ferocity. The door opened, and Malenov greeted him with a large red tongue projected with animus. "Button your pants," the landlord smirked, laughed again, and spat into his green handkerchief. "You artists," he muttered. "Who needs you?" He threw the letter on the bed, turned quickly, and slammed the door with renewed violence. Malenov almost wept with rage. The landlord's initial assault on his door had so startled his hand that the line he had been drawing quivered slightly. He now had to paint over the inch or so of canvas and begin again.

"Shall I feel sorry for myself? Do I have time? An indulgence," he answered, finally, and relaxed. He knew perfectly well that artists parade before others, conducting small scenes of petulance and temperament. It was required. He practiced on his landlord. The stuck-out tongue was one such. He had caught his profile in the mirror over the sink and winced. "Foolishness. And Malenov is never foolish. *Aargh.*"

Malenov told Karnovsky the following evening that he was exhausted. He hadn't read the letter until early morning of the next day when he awakened. The light had disappeared; he was painting amidst shadows, the naked electric bulb, which he sometimes shaded with a green-visored cap he had found in the market, threw grotesque shadows on the wall, but paintings like Malenov's thrived on internal light, light that glowed from the imagination, transformed by colors whose harmony and warfare bustled through the intellect before they were even mixed.

"Will the world ever be as wonderful as this?" he asked himself, observing the curious projectiles and spatial displacements he had wrapped in a shadowy penumbra of slightly roseate milk-white. "Never. It can never exist, because it only exists in my dreams," he answered himself, poking his brush menacingly at the window beyond which lived a billion or so people unaware that Malenov was reconstructing their universe. He stepped back from the easel and collapsed upon his bed. Hearing the paper crinkle, he withdrew the letter and threw it in the corner. It was only in the early morning, when he had awakened and had made himself a cup of strong tea, that he saw the letter on the floor and retrieved it. He was quite calm. He had slept deeply. "And what is this? Fingermann reborn," he grimaced. He almost tore the letter into bits, but restrained himself. After all, he had not heard much from the world for several weeks. His brief bubble had burst; he no longer existed; he was already forgotten. Who then needed him so urgently that a telegram-letter from the Hotel Atlas was required?

The message began in flawless Russian, the script somewhat cramped as though written by a young and inexperienced adept of his mother tongue.

> Honored Yevgeny Mikhailovich Malenov. I have come a very long way to meet you. In fact, dear sir, I have voyaged across the ocean from New York, to which my parents and I—fled from Odessa nearly ten years ago—have come and, so to speak, settled.
>
> I am a young painter. Painting is my life. That is the way I have chosen. So much so, Yevgeny Mikhailovich, that I can now say with confidence that painting chooses me. But I still risk losing my way. I have rejected the figure. I can no longer paint from nature. What happens with me is that everything I paint is imagined form, a working through ideas

that have no counterpart in nature but are nonetheless natural, because they are true.

In other words—and you above all will understand me—I am an abstract painter, a painter of new geometries and alternate spaces. But I am afraid that in my new country there is no one to teach me. Or to be frank, honored Yevgeny Mikhailovich, no one here is a master as you are. I do not need a teacher as much as a model—someone who will show me more than method and technique—someone, indeed, who is a kind of— how shall I put it—moral master of paint. And so I have come to Berlin to find you and to ask whether I might be of use to you, work for you, assist you in your great labor, and by my working for you, alongside you, under your tutelage learn indirectly what I cannot learn by myself.

Will you do me the kindness of meeting me for supper tomorrow evening at 8 P.M. in the lobby of my small hotel, where I will be waiting for you with warmth and anticipation. Of course, if you do not choose to come, it will break my heart, but I will be forced to accept your decision. I will not pursue you, you may be sure. I know how much you have already suffered from foolish sycophants and dishonest impresarios.

Do you need help, honored Yevgeny Mikhailovich? If you do, may I add—and I do so with embarrassment—I expect to be able to pay you well for allowing me to assist you. I know that my assistance will be unimportant to you, but your assistance to me (the very fact that you exist already assists me tremendously) will be more than enough reason to help you. Perhaps the $100 that I will be able to pay you each month will make life easier for you; perhaps you will wish to move your quarters; perhaps you would like a larger apartment with a well-stocked kitchen so that you can eat more than tea and rusks; perhaps having paint and canvas, colored pencils sharpened and at the ready, and new brushes will make it easier for you to be what you are already, one of the geniuses of modern art.

Please, dear Yevgeny Mikhailovich, come to dinner.

Yevgeny Mikhailovich read and reread the letter of J. Alexander Karnovsky—as the letter was signed—numerous times. He laughed as he read it; once he danced jubilantly until he fell exhausted on his painting stool, his eye entranced by an unfinished corner of one of the pictures he had been working on the night before. He attended to the corner, mixing an almost transparent blue that he applied with an infinitely patient evenness that belied the presence of a hundred strokes and a tremulous hand. Finishing the work, he remembered the letter and read it once more (regarding it first with his eyes as though it were a fresh and original discovery), then he repeated it aloud (evenly, like the application of paint, uinflected, flat, unpunctuated), and then again chanting it like a church choir, and lastly singing it like a lover's ballad. He was aware that there was something in the letter that eluded him, a missed beat, a slightly tinny note that he could not place. But he rushed from the apartment nonetheless and, drafting a reply at the local post office, cabled the Karnovsky youth that he would come to dinner that evening. His reply, so characteristic of Malenov's soul-baring demeanor, read as follows:

To my host, J. Alexander Karnovsky.

I dive to the heart of your invitation. Dinner. Dinner. Dinner. The prospect of a dinner delights me. Indeed, yes. I starve, you know. Of course, I starve. (But I think to myself. How much time you save starving, Yevgeny Mikhailovich. Less eating, less cooking. Less cooking, less waiting for water to boil. Less watching eggs until their shells crack and announce their hardness. And if no eggs to watch, none to buy in the grocery, where, once or twice even, I was forced to steal eggs in order to have something substantial to eat.) Of course, I agree to dinner (we will see, however, about the $100 a month—that makes me suspicious—not you, sir, but the *fact* of $100 a month, each month, every month—such money makes me suspicious). Yevgeny's stomach moans so loud it sometimes startles him when he works. Yevgeny is sick from starving. Yes? Yes, indeed, Yevgeny Mikhailovich is most certainly sick from starving. He is so happy to take dinner with young Karnovsky.

But then you write, "Do you need help?" I reply differently than I do to an invitation to dinner (in a good restaurant, I hope, where I can have borscht and pirogi, a piece of boiled beef with potatoes and more cabbage, good, yes, and beer, maybe a vodka? O wonderful invitation!). Yevgeny Mikhailovich does not want help. Help is help, sir. It comes or it doesn't. If I have to ask for it (which I am required to do since I am expected to answer the question you put: "Do you need help?" honored et cetera, et cetera), it is no longer what it starts out to be. It becomes instead conversation in the air. If I have to answer the question, the burden falls on me. I am compelled to please and supplicate. Rather than do that, I would tell you to put your offer back into your mouth and grind your teeth. I do not ask for help. (But for God's sake, young Karnovsky, take the trouble to read between these lines.)

It will interest you to know that I have thought a great deal about the time I have saved by not eating during the past six months. If I could make time into space and lay minutes end to end, my savings would not mount to the heavens, but I would have saved at least several miles of time. Counting up my daily savings: not less than eighty minutes saved each day. Multiplying, I gather for my art 560 minutes in a week—enough for a few drawings, enough for a small oil, also enough for a large headache and an irritable stomach, interminable dry belches and sour farts. And yet, with all this saving for art, I grow weak and tired. Perhaps it is not wise making virtue out of such a grave deficiency as food. I am a drought and a famine. How can I make utopics the glory of God if I starve to death? I long to meet you. 8 P.M. this evening at your hotel.

The letter was signed in full, the letters carefully written. It was not an afterthought, since the pen pressure was even and fluent, but Yevgeny Mikhailovich felt constrained to add to his identity the single word "Painter," as though Karnovsky had not known to whom he had written his letter.

TWELVE

J. Alexander Karnovsky had installed himself at a small table in the hotel dining room, separated by large potted rubber plants from the small lobby that fronted the street. He wanted to see Yevgeny Mikhailovich before he was seen. He needed to measure and appraise. (*Who is that large mass that has just shouldered his way through the glass doors? It couldn't be Malenov. It is not even twenty minutes to the hour of our appointment.*) Karnovsky needed a preview, a foretaste. (*What's he doing? He's thrown open a large bear coat, shivering with icicles. He's tinkling like a chandelier and melting sound into the carpet. He's left a small puddle at the desk.*) All afternoon, Alexander had paced his hotel room. He drew a little; he composed sketches and drafts of ideas as though already on Malenov's staff; he imagined conducting tours through the Malenov Museum of Abstract Art, of which, naturally, he was director, exhibiting his own work in a small gallery where disciples and epigones hung their second-generation reflections. (*Now he's talking to the desk clerk, wagging his large head from side to side; at last, he has removed his fur hat and, in a single gesture, wriggled out of the bear coat, which he has dropped in a heap on the rug, and thrown his hat on the pile. He's laughing uproariously. What's so funny? Could it be Malenov? The vast body turns; seizing his fur in an enormous fist, he lifts the wet and dripping arctic apparel and flings it on a smooth leather couch, slumping down beside it. Oh. God. It is Malenov. So large!*) Alexander couldn't imagine anyone so large. Not tall, although he was reasonably tall, but packed, congealed, massive, as though his body had been carved from an ancient tree of spectacular girth. He was a lumbering creature, with rounded shoulders and slabby sides like a well-padded animal. His hair—he remembered the image in the first photograph he had razored from *Querschnitt* months before—dropped down his head, matty, stringy, like flaps that obscured sound and interference, provided warmth and cover, and imparted to his head an effect at once formidable and childlike. Alexander lit one of his cheroots and drank off a glass of wine. He was suddenly unnerved; his heart stuttered, caught on the same beat; his lower lip began to quiver. So this was the great artist whom he had traveled from America to meet.

Malenov sat now in the lobby, leaning forward slightly, his head turning from side to side, watching every movement, expecting J. Alexander Karnovsky to enter from the street, to descend by the stairwell, to exit from the elevator, to emerge from the restroom, to materialize from behind a potted plant. Several times Yevgeny's eyes had passed over the face of Alexander Karnovsky, blinking nervously, but his glance continued to peregrinate the lobby, engorging a small dog that dangled from a leash tied to one of the rubber plants while its owner ate on the other side, narrowing to entangle a young man—much too young, Yevgeny muttered, dismissing him with a wave of his hand and refusing to tie him in the snares of inquiry—returning to Alexander Karnovsky, who answered a stare with fascinated curiosity, once half-rising to break the strain, but falling back, as there was still time before the hour. Yevgeny Mikhailovich belched and covered his mouth with the back of his hand; he reached into the side pocket of his threadbare jacket—a thin weave of indistinction and brown—and pulled out Karnovsky's letter, flattening it and laying it beside him on the couch, imagining that if the young American passed through the lobby, undecided as to who (although Malenov and the dog were the only creatures waiting in the lobby) had been the recipient of his dinner invitation, he would see the letter, understand instantly, and approach. And then, suddenly, the bells of the city began to strike the hour. 8 P.M. J. Alexander Karnovsky, dressed in gray flannels with a silk tie of conservative stripes, stood up from his table and calmly—so it appeared—walked from behind a rubber plant, his hand extended. "So you are Malenov, whom I have crossed the ocean to meet."

Yevgeny Mikhailovich remained seated. Too lethargic and disarticulated, he could not instantly come to his feet and seize the white hand ribboned with delicate blue veins that hung in the air before him. He let the hand remain extended, watching it intently, ignoring the face of Alexander Karnovsky. When the fingers began to curl and bunch, dropping with indifference to Karnovsky's side, it was Yevgeny who saluted him, lumbering to his feet, towering over Karnovsky, his mouth open, lips drawn back into a rigid smile of amazement. As little as Karnovsky had anticipated the immense Malenov, Malenov was startled by what he perceived to be Karnovsky's physical insignificance, his precarious slightness, the elegant, somewhat troubled features of face, his light complexion, his thin eyebrows. Karnovsky didn't add up to much. He seemed weightless. However, Yevgeny had seen the nerveless focus of the eyes,

black and ungentle, examining him rapidly with the precision of a professional appraiser who was expected to observe quickly and in detail anything of value that might fetch a price at the bankrupt's sale of personal
possessions. Karnovsky's small black eyes hardly flickered. They seemed
dead and yet they were alive, tugging at one of Yevgeny's ears, hooking
into Yevgeny's tattered shirt and frayed cuffs, dropping disdainfully to
Yevgeny's scuffed high shoes, whose laces were knotted at several places
where they had snapped. Alexander's eyes, hidden in deep sockets where
they swiveled in their clandestine orbits, conducted his brain over the
outcroppings of Yevgeny's face. Yevgeny knew that he was focused on
and observed; Karnovsky was certain that he had caught everything.

An instant of silence; traces of suspicion; the last shudders of fright;
and both burst into greetings that rose higher and higher until over-
arched by Yevgeny's fluted cry of hunger. "Aaay! I starve. I must eat. Now.
If you don't mind, young gentleman. I must eat. To the first business,
first." Alexander's face relaxed, the eyes rested, and the fair face shone
suddenly with warmth and generosity as he turned toward the dining
room and, with a wave of his arm, bowing like a master of ceremonies,
conducted Yevgeny Mikhailovich to a table set in a quiet corner of the
restaurant. A splendid dinner unfolded: a rich soup bubbling with hospitality, a platter of roasted chicken with specially cooked side dishes of
kasha and mushrooms, red cabbage and cranberries, a green salad with
cheese, and strawberry tarts. Vodka and wines. Eat and eat. Talk later
after stomachs were filled and Yevgeny lay slumped in contentment.

"And so, now, are you satisfied?" Alexander asked quietly when coffee arrived accompanied by a small dish of chocolates.

"Indeed. So much so that I thank you, young gentleman, for your
kindness." Alexander nodded. It seemed to be going all right. The bear
was sated.

"May we talk now about art?" Alexander inquired, moving his chair
back from the table and crossing his legs. "May we talk about art? That
is what brings me this distance, Yevgeny Mikhailovich. For nothing else
would I be impetuous enough to cross the ocean during winter. The sea
was malevolent. Monstrous waves and powerful winds. I stayed below
throughout the journey. Sick the whole time. Yes, a dreadful passage. But
it's all behind me now that I see you, Yevgeny Mikhailovich."

"Yes," Yevgeny grunted, snatching up a chocolate and dropping it
into his upturned mouth. "I see. Of course. And all to see *me*," he twin-
kled. "So, young man, what do you see? And what do you know about
me?"

Karnovsky gulped. The examination begins, he winced. "Too little,

I'm afraid, but I have done some work on you, rather more than you would imagine. If nothing else, I am ingenious.

Karnovsky described his first hearing of Malenov's name in the Broadway cafeteria. Malenov listened, trying to guess the identity of the old couple who had spoken of him so knowingly. ("Who could they be?" he wondered aloud.) Karnovsky proceeded to review the articles and essays, documents and photographs that he had accumulated. Yevgeny was impressed by Karnovsky's ingenuity. He was clearly useful. Of that Yevgeny was certain. Whether he was talented, a gifted artist, that was another matter and—Yevgeny readily confessed to himself—one considerably more ambiguous and even, perhaps, of less importance. It was unclear to Yevgeny whether he wanted Karnovsky to be gifted. (A secretary, an amanuensis, a body servant need have no comprehension of the master; indeed, for the performance of indispensable but modest tasks, the less critical the eye, the less judging the raised eyebrow, the less scrupulous and appraising the servant's intelligence, the more likely the work will be done promptly and without reservations.) But, already, Yevgeny Mikhailovich knew that he would have to compromise. The young man before him knew too much, was too worldly, too accomplished in the fashionable to be content to receive orders and be expected to obey them. Yevgeny was thinking to himself, half-listening to Karnovsky's artful quotation of passages from the press, already somewhat bored with the accomplished ventriloquism of his young acquaintance.

"And what does all this have to do with me? Yes. Yes. You know all about me, everything that they"—he waved dismissively about him, implicating the others ostensibly filling the near-empty dining room—"know about me: surfaces and exteriors. But I am not there at the surface. I do not hang on the body of the universe like a flesh pink or a wispy violet. You know that. I am more than all this press nonsense. Let's go see. Right now. Let's go see. We will go to my room and we will look at paintings. What do you say to that?"

Alexander Karnovsky was delighted. He signed the check, organized a pile of banknotes for the waitress, retrieved his fur coat from the cloakroom, and hailed a taxi at the entrance to the hotel. Twenty minutes later they were standing before Yevgeny's door, reading the memoranda posted for the importuning public. "These notices are serious?" Alexander asked quietly. "I find them frightening."

"They are meant to frighten. Surely. How else should it be? If we artists behaved exactly the way the world expected, it would destroy us. It is a Malenovian rule: never assimilate! Anything that the world asks you to do, consider whether it would not be preferable—on principle and even if it goes against self-interest—to refuse. There are, for instance, many times that I would love to be interrupted while I work. It goes badly. I am hungry and I stop to make tea. I hear shoe-shuffling before my door. I know it is someone who hopes to catch my attention—a journalist, a dealer, perhaps even a collector. They come all the way to this filthy slum; they climb the stairs; and what do they find on this door but another in a long train of Malenovian rebuffs: Go away. Malenov is not at home. Malenov is painting. Malenov is in a nasty mood and will bite you." Growling and gnashing of teeth. "Actually, the truth is that I am desperate for a human face. I am tired of my floating projectiles and empty space. But if I give in, if I behave like an ordinary bourgeois, I am doomed. Word will get out. Oh, that Malenov, it's all theater. I had a nice chat with him today. Dear fellow, even gave me a cup of tea. Oh, you say he's a genius. Not at all. Pleasant, ordinary sort. That's what they'd say. The myth would dissolve. I would go on making great paintings. It wouldn't affect my work, but it would be harder to get them to believe that what I'm doing here is desperately important not only to my salvation but to theirs. Yes, truly, my stay-away notices are meant to frighten off the packs of wolves that gather at my door, sniffing, scratching."

Karnovsky was impressed. Malenov had spoken to him privately, personally, revealing a hidden side, an unknown reason. He resolved to write it all down when he returned to the hotel. He would make a beginning at keeping notes and records, gathering the information he would need one day for a definitive study of the Master. The door was opened, the bulb tightened in its socket, and the green-visored light diffused a slummy hue. The bed was unmade, a candle burned before Saint Sergius, and paintings were stacked by the score against the wall. Yevgeny pulled out his stool and seated Alexander upon it. Without removing his coat, he began to show his work. Each painting was presented for several minutes, hung on a nail, bathed in the mean light. Raised up, each of the paintings was exposed in a kind of logical sequence as though the order had been planned, the continuity formulated as a strategy of presentation and conversion. The paintings unfolded the elements of the projectivist vocabulary, spatial forms, architectural masses, signs and symbols of the new grammar of affirmation and denial out of which Malenov conceived the universe to be fashioned: elements and devices, painted with a perfect simplicity and flatness, without narrative allusion or indication of similitudes, direct and uncomplicated colors on a white or black ground. Small, iconic pictures. And then as the paintings proceeded, the elements came together, several elements appeared within the same space, spaces embraced and coalesced, combined and passed through, shadow space, real space, objects projecting into infinite worlds where the Malenovian vision of reconstruction was to be consummated.

Three hours later it was done. It was past midnight, and the streets were silent. The taxicab that Karnovsky had ordered to wait, its lights extinguished, was the only vehicle below. Cold frosted the window-panes. Malenov no longer moved. He waited. Minutes expired while he waited. Karnovsky thought intently. It would have to be right. There would be no second chance from this genius.

"We both come from Great Russia," Alexander at last began. "I come from a different world than your own, but I know something about your world. Our worlds were never the same, although they touched and passed each other in language, in literature, in memories and affections. These paintings. They are like nothing I have ever seen. But they do remind me powerfully of something out of the tradition of Great Russia. Mostly the color. Where have I seen such remarkable silk colors, such amazing diaphanous blues, such rose, such grays as those from which you build your humane abstract spaces? The icon. The great Russian icon. It is as though you have taken all the miracles of the icon—all its eternal power—and retold them as stories of divine space." Alexander stood up suddenly and embraced Malenov, folding his arms around his shoulders. And then, mysteriously, he burst into tears. "I don't under-stand what you've done. It is a great body of work, so great. I will have to study it and learn. Will that be possible?"

On that unanswered question the evening ended. The two artists agreed to meet the following day for another meal, this time a luncheon, after which they promised to visit museums and galleries together. The education was fated to begin.

A brief extract from Malenov's journal, which I found under the date of their first meeting and had translated.

Today I met this young and not unappealing Jew from New York who travels the ocean to learn more of my work. He insinuates it that way. I am become a project of learning. Ha! My work is no problem to be exam-ined. If there ever was a problem in painting, my paintings have solved it. I have no doubts about my work. Why should I have doubts? If my achievement were recognized and celebrated, then I would have doubts. Othewise, as it is, I am entitled to be sure. I am so alone. Will this Karnov-sky make me happy? Or will he mock my loneliness and—when I least suspect it—rob me of my genius. . . . And do I take him seriously when he celebrates our icon? He, child of a race of iconoclasts, how can he understand our flat little depictions of sanctity? He is quite right, of course. My pictures owe a great deal to the icons—not their subject, but their application of paint and their frontality. But how can this young Jew understand all that? It worries me that he speaks of icons. Either he lies about his feelings or, worse yet, he has no feelings about the subject at all. And so his tears are lies and he tries to deceive me. I do not know. But be watchful, Yevgeny Mikhailovich. Be watchful. Enjoy yourself, but be watchful.

The following days were delicious for Master and his young friend, for Alexander Karnovsky and his new paternity in art. They were inseparable, meeting for a late breakfsat, trudging through the snow and observing the curious Germans, visiting museums, taking in the art galleries, seeing a Charlie Chaplin film, going to theater, eating meals and drinking wines, running into Fraulein Kammerer at Die Florelle, taking coffee at the Café des Westens, rummaging in bookstores, visiting nightclubs, dancing fox-trot with the girls ("I love the fox-trot and I'm also good—you don't believe me—at tango. Watch me, young Sasha"). By the end of a week, Alexander was allowed to call his teacher, now friend, Yevgeny, sometimes even Zhenya, most often Yevgeny Mikhailovich. He found calling him Master uncomfortable and vaguely unsettling, although he had done so repeatedly during their early meetings. But it was particularly discomforting to Alexander when he went to buy tickets or pay a check or hand change to the program seller or the cab driver. Yevgeny had no money, and here Alexander was calling this impoverished, unkempt genius Master while he continuously paid out money on his behalf. He wasn't sure what made him uncomfortable. If anything, the older should be attending to the needs and follies of the younger. Not the other way round. And yet here he was, a young man approaching his twenty-second year, fumbling for bills and scooping change from his coat pocket to amuse and recreate this unworldly, indeed unaware, artist in his early forties. However, it pleased more than it unsettled Karnovsky: he had a sense of his power and enforced it, buying more for Yevgeny than was required, certainly more than was asked for (a warm button-front sweater, a wool scarf, a new teapot and an assortment of Russian teas, a pair of fur-lined winter boots, and a book on Russian icons with a particularly marvelous reproduction of the famous icon of Saint Sergius on which Yevgeny's was modeled). Some of the gifts he bought when he was by himself, wandering, cut adrift, shopping, but more often he bought most cannily when they were together, admiring the displays in the great department stores. Karnovsky would observe Yevgeny's eyes coveting something, and the moment Yevgeny had gone off, attracted by another counter, Karnovsky would return, surreptitiously acquire, say, the black woolen scarf, wrap it, hide it behind his back, and, as the attendant pushed open the doors to shuttle them back into the winter of Berlin, Karnovsky would reveal the package, ceremoniously untie it, produce the scarf (or gloves or beaver cap), and present them to an embarrassed Yevgeny.

"Too much. It embarrasses me."

"What embarrasses you?"

"These gifts." He pointed to a chair at the table in the *konditorei* where they stopped for late afternoon coffee and counted off four items of vesture and garb, some still in their boxes, some already worn and frosted with snow. "It embarrasses me. No. I feel humiliated, Alexander." He became passionate and rapped the table with his knuckles to emphasize his unhappiness.

"It would be better, wouldn't it, if the arrangement were different? Yes. You know, I would prefer if you gave me gifts. Yes. I would really prefer it. But that will take time. These gifts, dear Zhenya, these are money gifts. They are of no importance. What you will soon give me—all the intangible gift of your genius—well, that will really be a priceless gift, an incomparable gift."

"Yes? So!" Yevgeny Mikhailovich fell silent, thinking about his incomparable gift. It almost made sense, the young man's logic, but he caught himself breathing with difficulty, a sudden constriction tightening his chest, and he touched his heart lightly.

A second week had gone. Yevgeny Mikhailovich hadn't painted since Karnovsky's arrival. Karnovsky, for his part, had stopped sketching and had begun writing voluminous entries in his journal, annotating Malenov's person, history, remarks and observations, his predilections and preferences in art, his ferocities and rages (rather more general and diffuse than his enthusiasms). On a separate page he noted expenses in order to satisfy, he claimed, mere curiosity. Karnovsky wrote every night with his final brandy and every morning with his waking coffee. And another day would begin, very much like the previous one. He worked exceptionally hard with Malenov. One night as he fell exhausted into bed, he realized for the first time that it had all ceased to be pleasure. It was without interlude, relief, interruption. No other person intruded. They were a most unlikely, inseparable couple, seldom out of each other's sight, seldom far from each other's ear. Sometimes Malenov spoke uninterruptedly, imagining aloud, re-creating the history of his youth or describing in detail the early adventures of the Russian avant-garde, recalling his arguments with Livshits, his fights with the Burliuks, his gambols, drunken, with Mayakovsky—all liveliness and wit. But at other times he plunged ahead into the snow, leaving Karnovsky behind, refusing to speak, clenching his jaws shut, while Karnovsky tried to relieve Malenov's sudden melancholy with the offer of a bunch of flowers or a plate of steaming pirogi from a street kiosk. Nothing had been resolved, no arrangements had been discussed, no program of association defined. It had to be faced. Rich though he was, with more than enough money to pay for the diversion of the Master, Karnovsky was fast approaching the point where something formal needed to be settled if he were to avoid having to cable New York for funds. He preferred not to deal with his father at this juncture. There would be time for that.

"The time has come, Zhenya. We have to settle something." They were seated in the dining room of Karnovsky's hotel having a drink before going off to supper. "Don't you think we have to settle something?"

"I don't understand, young friend. What are you talking about?"

Karnovsky was amazed. It was as though nothing had happened, as though more than two weeks of gift-giving and generosity had no significance (indeed, in one description of those weeks, Karnovsky referred in his journal to the absence of a "payoff"—the precise phrase). "Talking about? Am I mad, Zhenya? Am I going mad or already mad? I wrote you a long letter, my very first letter in fact. I said it all there. *Clearly!* I wanted to work for you, to collaborate with you, to learn from you. More than two weeks have passed since we met. We haven't traveled out of each other's sight for a minute. We are to all the world like odd—the phrase would be—lovers and yet we aren't lovers, surely, but rather acquaintances who have become friends, who having become friends must now become fellow workers in the cause of projectivism and utopics. No? Isn't this a correct description?"

Yevgeny Mikhailovich again felt a sudden tightness in his chest. He could barely breathe. He pulled at a button of his shirt and opened the collar, loosening the new striped tie that throttled his throat. "I can't speak yet, my friend. Give me a moment to breathe. I need to think. But continue, yes, continue. Let me hear all of it."

"The major questions," Karnovsky continued, "remain unresolved. May I assist in supporting you? How much may I give you each month? May I work for you? (Payment enough for my support.) Do you wish to continue to live here and work in Berlin? Do we live together? But even if we don't, you need more space, better space, proper materials, and, most important, Zhenya, most important of all, we need a program. How shall we bring you to the world?"

Yevgeny Mikhailovich flushed red; his temples began to pound. He groaned. He was convinced that he was about to have another visitation. He waited while his temples pounded and his head, streaked with pain, swelled and diminished, expanding his brains and crushing them beneath his weighty carapace. "Aaaaay," he groaned aloud. Several heads turned and frowned. Germans disliked public display. ("A noisy Slav," somebody muttered behind him from a table of stocky businessmen.) But nothing happened. The rush of terror washed through his body and drained away; his feet, once heavy as though the fluid of anxiety had pounded through his thighs, descended his legs, and caused his ankles to swell in size, now drained out into the rug through his fur-lined boots. Karnovsky was frightened. It was all embarrassing, these displays and tantrums. It reminded him of the little fits of his own childhood, childish demonstrations of terror. But here, before him, was a man he believed to be one of the great artists of the age, still unknown and unrecognized, but clearly a genius of modern art, who heaved in front of him and moaned as though an electrical charge had just coursed his body.

"Are you all right?" Karnovsky asked timidly after some minutes of watching Yevgeny's agonies.

"Nothing. Nothing at all. It was only," he paused and thought a second, "it was only that I thought I was beginning to see the future. But it was nothing." He did not explain, and Karnovsky, his own terror renewed, did not dare to ask. The conversation was definitively interrupted, and they went off to dinner. It was only much later, seated beside each other on a banquette in a spacious ballroom, watching elegant couples glide and whirl, that Yevgeny suddenly began to speak, remembering each phrase that Karnovsky had used hours before, addressing himself directly to the matter before them, as though the conversation had never been broken off.

"Indeed, yes, you have a point, Karnovsky. You have come a great distance to meet me. We have been, yes, yes, inseparable for two weeks. You are convincing. I have watched you carefully. You seem to be telling the truth. Not what you say. But what you do. You have been greatly generous with me and you have kept your distance. I don't think you harm me. No. I agree then. Let us find a nice studio, with a few rooms attached, and a small kitchen. Not much, but better than now. You will have a room for yourself. We will see how it goes. Yes? What do you think? By the way, does Karnovsky cook?"

Karnovsky was stunned, but he agreed. (January 21, 1928: "He has caved in—quite unpredictably. I thought it would take much longer.") The following day, they began to look for an appropriate apartment and found one on Sigmaringerstrasse in Wilmersdorf, not far from the Preussen Park, where of an afternoon they could sit, surrounded by trees and shrubs, and drink tea from a thermos. The rooms were spacious and well lighted. The largest, with solid walls and a parquet floor, became Yevgeny's studio; in the rear were two bedrooms, a narrow, sufficient kitchen, and a generous bath where Yevgeny sometimes took himself for an afternoon of hydrophilic indulgence. Nothing to do then but move in. The furniture was adequate, even stylish. Their landlord, an aging doctor who had come up from Swabia during the war to work in a military hospital, was now retired and living on the income from his small country estate. He was descended, he announced, from a convoluted line of Swabian aristocracy who, he insisted, were all inbred and, therefore, slightly mad. His eccentricity consisted in little more than wearing a moth-eaten woman's wig atop his own thinning hairline; he laughed at himself, but persisted. It bothered no one in postwar Berlin. He, for his part, thought the ménage of Yevgeny Mikhailovich Malenov and Alexander Karnovsky equally strange and, hence, never removed his woman's wig when he came to bring them their mail or deliver a package.

The first weeks were tense. Neither Yevgeny Mikhailovich nor Alexander Karnovsky had ever had a roommate. Each was hardly suited to living with another. Their ways were irritatingly dissimilar. Yevgeny Mikhailovich scattered papers and trash, dropped paint on the floor, never shut doors, endlessly chattered to himself, explaining the universe to each of his paintings, and allowed himself the luxury of large and expressive eructations. Alexander Karnovsky thought Malenov a peasant—coarse and vulgar like a peasant, but also strong and resilient. Yevgeny did not mind carrying out the garbage, moving heavy furniture, trudging up the three flights of stairs with baskets of vegetables and bottles of milk. Karnovsky, by contrast, was a cat, silent, gliding on felt paws (he walked about the apartment in his bedroom slippers), sitting in a darkened room accustoming his eyes to shadow and gloom, or else, unpredictably, bursting into song, playing tinny records of Chaliapin, Caruso, or Lucrezia Bori. But somehow they managed not to get on each other's nerves. They acknowledged their difference, spoke about it openly, admired the ingenuity of God for having brought such unlikely creatures together into an association of art and service. Their world composed itself, the Odessan Jew from New York, the Ukrainian from Moscow, seated side by side in a bright apartment in southwest central Berlin at the end of the 1920s.

Bizarre, but also idyllic, you might think. I thought so for a time, until I found an outrageous passage in Malenov's diary that referred to the tremendous argument that broke out between them on the 26th of April, 1928. Karnovsky's journal for that day, on the other hand, said nothing further than "A brief discord."

"The swine," Malenov's diary began.

> Now I begin to understand what is going on. I knew it couldn't be as simple as it seemed. Nothing as simple as that he loves and admires me and will do anything to serve my art. The swine! He saves everything I throw out. Everything. I thought it helpful of him to do the housecleaning, to dust the rooms occasionally, even—although not often—to make my bed, to pick up after me, to put my brushes in turpentine. I thought all of this an unexpected kindness. He did all this when I went out for a stroll or to visit Die Florelle. He said he would stay behind and keep house. Sometimes, I would return after several hours in the late afternoon and a large tea would be ready and we would sit in the last light and talk about painting. But all that nice nice was simply a trick, a way of putting me off guard while he collected my leavings, gathered up everything I wanted burned and saved it. Why, Alexander Karnovsky? Why do you save up my shit bits? If I don't want them, how dare you save them? It's all business, you think. Everything to do with Malenov can be made into business, you say to yourself. Well, I'll show you, young man, I'll show you.

It had come about this way. It is true—undeniably—that Karnovsky had been emptying the trashcans, salvaging bits of paper on which Malenov had drawn, even saving ends of canvas where Malenov had tried out the colors he had mixed. Karnovsky had gathered and sequestered, marking each drawing with the date of its disposal, noting the painting to which it pertained (because Malenov's paintings were never given titles until they were exhibited, the only way a sketch could be correlated with the finished work was by drawing on its recto a miniature of the finished work with which it was connected). During the three months that they had lived together before Malenov made his discovery of Karnovsky's oversized album, Karnovsky had removed and identified several hundred sketches, drafts, visual notes, and color swatches.

The day Malenov decided to check up on his colleague by going through Karnovsky's belongings, Karnovsky had decided to spend the afternoon wandering by himself in Berlin. That is what he told Malenov. Actually, he had arranged a luncheon with Francine Kammerer to discuss the career of Yevgeny Mikhailovich. Fraulein Kammerer had no idea that Yevgeny might be interested in an exhibition. By the end of lunch, it was arranged. Alexander Karnovsky thought it would make Yevgeny happy.

He rushed from Die Florelle to the house on Sigmaringerstrasse. He was eager to tell Yevgeny the news that the Lehrter Galerie would mount a major exhibition of Malenov's Berlin works, to open at precisely the time that tourists flood into Berlin during June. Francine Kammerer was enthusiastic. "It is so important to see his work. Even I hardly know it, but if Malevich swears by Malenov, who am I to say otherwise?" she said smiling. (Alexander Karnovsky watched her smile and shivered; a bit of lipstick clung to her white teeth, as though a drop of blood had fallen from a slow leak in her brain. It excited him oddly.)

Alexander quietly opened the door to the flat. He smelled smoke. Easter was just past, and Yevgeny had spent the better part of the previous week swooning in the Russian church; he always grew a beard at Eastertime, his gesture of mourning for his wounded and murdered God. It had turned warm, however, so what was fire doing in the grate? "Yevgeny," he called out, but received no reply. And yet he knew that Yevgeny was in the studio, sitting before the grate. He felt Yevgeny's lumbering presence like a black cloud hovering over a spring field. "Yevgeny," he called again as he opened the double doors into the studio.

"My God," was all he said. Yevgeny Mikhailovich was sitting in front of the fire, slowly ripping each drawing from Karnovsky's album and throwing it into the flames. "You swine," Yevgeny mumbled. "How dare you save what I throw out? Who are you to decide what is to be saved? Are you the artist? You swine. How dare you?"

Whatever it was that Yevgeny expected to elicit by his spring bonfire, it somehow failed. Alexander Karnovsky was neither humiliated nor abashed, nor was he stricken with guilt and apologies. Rather, he kept repeating a softly spoken American curse until Yevgeny Mikhailovich finally turned and, curious, inquired, "What is this 'asshole'?"

"You, Zhenya. You're the asshole. What do you think you're doing? Embarrassing me, trapping me in some secret activity, catching me out doing something you didn't authorize? Listen, Yevgeny Mikhailovich, you may be a genius, but you're also an asshole. Now, what that means, in case you don't know the expression, is that you sometimes have your brains up your ass instead of in your head." Alexander Karnovsky said all of this in a quiet voice. He didn't lose his temper; he never lost his temper. In fact, having heard reports of other episodes not unlike this one, I can suppose that Alexander Karnovsky expressed all his outrage in a conversational tone, without his cheeks reddening, without ever stamping a foot or pounding a wall.

Yevgeny Mikhailovich had imagined that, caught out, the young scoundrel would confess to something outrageous, but there was nothing outrageous to confess. Quite the opposite, as Alexander Karnovsky went on to explain. He saved all this random detritus covertly so as not to make Yevgeny self-conscious. He annotated and marked everything in order to provide the basis of a documentary archive, without which Yevgeny's work could not be correctly described in years to come, when all that would remain would be the work itself. Speaking quietly, his calm explanation punctuated by an occasional "asshole" of diminished annoyance, he eventually calmed Yevgeny Mikhailovich sufficiently that he stopped ripping work from the album and burning it. At last he closed the album, lifted it from his lap, and shoved it beneath the sofa. The one-act drama had come to a close: "Yevgeny is truly sorry. Please forgive him." Alexander went over and squeezed his neck affectionately.

(It was never clear to me, however, whether Yevgeny's description of this incident in his diary was made before or after Alexander Karnovsky's return. It seems hardly likely—given Malenov's psychology—that he would, in the midst of fury, take time to write even an outraged entry. Hardly likely. In that case, it must be assumed that despite his apology he remained enraged; that his suspicions once aroused were not so easily allayed; and that hours after the confrontation he wrote out his condemnation of Karnovsky. All this remains, however, my conjecture.)

Alexander decided not to tell Yevgeny Mikhailovich about his visit with Francine Kammerer of the Lehrter Galerie until the following day. Yevgeny was immensely pleased, though he did not dance to the news as was sometimes his habit when overwhelmed by the unexpected. But when Fraulein Kammerer arrived at the studio the following week to discuss the exhibition, make a preliminary selection of the works to be presented, negotiate terms, dates, Yevgeny was almost charming, his bullishness withdrawn, and he listened passively as Alexander Karnovsky raised all the necessary questions, made notes on their discussion, and served coffee.

"You choose well," Yevgeny announced generously as the afternoon waned to a close.

"That pleases me," she responded. "It is an achievement, this work of yours. It is the line between Russia and the West that has been missing. Nothing more is heard from Malevich, and Lissitzky is also back in Moscow (and not well, you know . . . his lungs)." She added ominously, "It's all up to you, Herr Malenov." Yevgeny seemed momentarily troubled; he resisted carrying the burden of modern art. Alexander Karnovsky was, however, delighted; the young woman seemed well able to appreciate his Master. "And the gallery would like to purchase in advance of the exhibition those three paintings," she stated matter-of-factly, pointing to three canvases that described the link between Malevich and the De Stijl paintings of Mondrian and van Doesburg. It was a wise choice. Those paintings, after all, now occupy a position of considerable importance in the collection of the Stedelijk Museum in Amsterdam, whose director bought them some years later to document the connection between the Soviet avant-garde and Western abstract painting. Yevgeny Mikhailovich for an instant seemed deliciously happy; a smile broke through his cloudy, overcast face, and he shook Francine Kammerer's hand with both of his, saluting her on her good judgment. (It seems an oddly sententious gesture, but if you have observed, as often as I have, painters suddenly overcome by delight amid their ongoing social ineptitude, it frequently turns out this way: the artist congratulating the collector on his intelligence, or prudence, or good sense, but really meaning, how good to make a sale, to have money to put aside, to be at last recognized by the coin of the realm.) They discussed the price, briefly, Karnovsky keeping silent but attentive, and when the price was settled and paid over, it was arranged that Yevgeny Mikhailovich would come to the gallery later in the week for a visit with Fraulein Kammerer, at which time the paintings would be delivered. An unbusinesslike transaction—this paying first and delivering later—but trust is always unbusinesslike.

"In the meantime," she concluded pleasantly, "keep those pictures for me. They are my treasures now."

Thirteen

Yevgeny Mikhailovich fell in love. Hardly credible. Everything we know about Yevgeny Mikhailovich denies it. Vast though he was, in the domain of sex he appeared stunted and diminished, restricted to his nighttime fugues of fantasy and voyerusim, staring at the album of his little delights, delights of both sexes caught in their wavering androgyny. He had never shown interest in grown-up women and yet (surprisingly to Karnovsky) he seemed suddenly overcome by Francine Kammerer. Yevgeny had first thrilled to her solicitude when they had met the year before at the Lehrter Galerie, but he had forgotten about her during his Bavarian holiday. It was only when they encountered one another by chance at Die Florelle and Yevgeny had introduced her to Karnovsky and they had shared a table and drank a musky pot of Lapsang Souchong together—brewed and stirred to perfection by the son of the master of teas—that Yevgeny thought again about Fraulein Kammerer, installing an image of her kindness and attention in his small cabinet of private images. During that second meeting, while Alexander was brewing and stirring, swishing hot water, and compelling their aging waiter to learn the methods for properly offering fine tea, Yevgeny had engaged Francine Kammerer in conversation, doing more than rumbling and growling, actually undertaking to speak sequentially about the new Russian art, looking, if not in her eyes, then just slightly above them to her lofty forehead, and in the course of their hour together agitating a perplexing unease that caused his hand to tremble as he helped her into her coat and bade her farewell. She smiled deliciously and thanked him for having struggled to explain himself in German. "I hope we will meet again." Yevgeny Mikhailovich, suddenly agonized by his forwardness, retreated into Russian, saying something unintelligible, and they parted.

Karnovsky, for his part, was disconcerted by Yevgeny's interest in the woman. She seemed unlike the girls he invariably chose when they went out to dance. On those few occasions, Yevgeny selected only tall and undeveloped young women, whose long faces, deadened with layers of powder, made them appear more like mannequins than agile and swift dancers whom he led ponderously through the required steps. Yevgeny danced poorly, despite his conviction that he moved like Valentino, but he conducted himself with a kind of gravity that pleased his partners, and they always presented themselves again whenever he appeared at the spacious dance hall. But Francine Kammerer was unlike Yevgeny's dancing girls, somewhat on the short side, with blond hair that she pushed back from her right eye with a red index finger. Whenever she talked, her blue eyes flashed comprehension and her white teeth, gladdened by conversation, were slightly parted; she was always attentive, ready to join in, to respond, to carry forward the interlocution. Francine Kammerer was highly intelligent and knew it. She understood her business and accepted both the responsibility and the embarrassment of being the owner of an important little art gallery that had enough sense to be ahead of fashion and not enough aggression to become rich.

Yevgeny Mikhailovich was obviously delighted by the explicit confusion in Francine Kammerer of enthusiasm and ignorance, familiarity and inexpertness. It relieved him of the tortures of silence and banality that always afflicted him during his dance tourneys, where he never knew what to say after the dance was over. He thought he was obliged to do more than offer his partner a glass of wine and pay her for her time; indeed, once, persuaded that his young partner wanted to engage him in conversation, he announced to her as he poured her a second glass of champagne, "You know I am Russian painter," to which she replied, "How splendid! Will you paint me? I've always wanted a little portrait to send my old mother." "Not portraits of people, but of universe," Yevgeny replied, and the conversation stopped as abruptly as it had begun. But with Francine Kammerer, Yevgeny had gone on and on. Karnovsky knew that Fraulein Kammerer was sympathetic to Malenov's work and he determined to test her interest, but he somehow feared Yevgeny Mikhailovich would waste time with her.

"We must thank Fraulein Kammerer for our food and lodgings. Yes?" Yevgeny announced after she had departed, putting all the money he had received for his paintings in Alexander's charge.

"It comes at a good time. My bank transfer is late again," was all Alexander replied.

Several hours later, Yevgeny burst into Alexander's room, throwing open the door and startling the sleeping young man. "I think I am in love with Fraulein Kammerer," he announced. "You think—maybe—it is possible? I don't know. I have never loved anything alive before." He beamed with pleasure. It seemed such a novelty, an incomparable prospect, a remarkable occurrence, unknown to the world, unfamiliar to others, and hence for Yevgeny Mikhailovich a phenomenon of unspeakable originality. "I must go out," he concluded. "I must find her. I must tell her Yevgeny loves her." He disappeared before Karnovsky, shaking with drowsy incomprehension, could reply. And it was more than an hour before Karnovsky absorbed the relevation Malenov had proclaimed (after all, he had been asleep with dreams of his own). In love? Malenov in love? And what would become of Karnovsky if Malenov went off after Francine Kammerer? Alexander became ill, promptly and disgustingly ill, vomiting what he was persuded was more than his last meal. His stomach ached from alarm, and he felt a certian soreness near his heart. He drank off a vodka to calm himself, but instead he became drunk, his head buzzing with fright, his stomach sour and turning with nausea. In love? How little Karnovsky mattered in such an equation, he complained. Just money. That's all he took himself to be—a source of money to be emptied and replenished. A damn Jewish banker is all he thinks of me. He began to cry with rage. He desperately hoped Malenov would return and find him beside himself with confusion and jealousy.

It is fortunate that Malenov never found out. Jealousy was well beyond the repertoire of emotions that occupied a central position in Malenov's life. Malenov was never jealous, certainly never envious. His estimation of himself was so well formulated and secure that he could regard the fortunate or miserable careers of others without drawing comparisons. If anything, Malenov's sense of the world was defective. Since he did not bother much with his own situation—taking poverty no less than well-being as an accident—he would never have understood why

Alexander Karnovsky suffered such anxiety because he, Yevgeny Mikhai-lovich, had decided—improbably, to be sure—that he was in love.

Malenov was gone for hours. When he returned, he entered Alexan-der's room and, thinking that he was awake, announced in a sober and careful voice that he had finally found Francine Kammerer at her apart-ment. "I have told Fraulein Kammerer that I love her. She smiled at me when I told her. She did not punish me for telling her I love her. Good, no? I think she loves me back. Yes? Don't you think so, Sasha? I gave her cheek a pat. Even a small kiss goodbye. I am so happy to love her. What do you think, Sasha?" He waited for several minutes for Karnovsky to answer, but Karnovsky was deep in a drunken sleep. "Aah, poor boy. He waits up for me and I come home so late. Tomorrow, I will tell him of love."

It went on like that for weeks. Yevgeny was besotted with Francine Kammerer. It never occurred to him that perhaps she was being uncom-monly generous and available because he had joined her gallery and she was engaged in all the details of exhibiting his work. Every day, he went by the Lehrter Galerie to speak with her, to take her for luncheon or for tea. She was always polite, always smiled, always answered his questions directly and without guile. To his professions of love and fidelity, she replied unambiguously that he was a great painter. The inappropriateness of the reply never struck Yevgeny. Quite the contrary, he believed that every time he said, "My dear Fraulein Francine, how much I love you," and she answered, "You are a marvelous painter, Yevgeny," that a logical synapsis had occurred, that the appropriate and correct reply to his love was celebration of his genius. It made sense to Yevgeny Mikhailovich. It even, one suspects, made sense to Alexander Karnovsky, which made him all the more anxious and unsettled. Yevgeny no longer worked; he had bought a secondhand balalaika on which he picked out moony Rus-sian ballads; he sometimes drank too much and curled up on the floor of his studio and fell asleep.

Alexander Karnovsky began to wonder why he stayed on. "Cut it, cut it," he shouted aloud in his room, but it was not easy to cut his losses, to cut his ties, to cut off and break for home. And, Alexander had begun to paint when Yevgeny stopped. There were so many hours now when Alexander was left to himself that he knew he had either to get to work or become hysterical. He began a series of black and red pictures, into whose undifferentiated ground he inserted letters of the Cyrillic alphabet, small verbal icons painted in contrasting black or white. (Severe little pictures of a certain handsomeness and indubitable derivation.) Alexan-der worked long hours on his suite of pictures. Once Yevgeny entered without knocking while he was working. Alexander tried to cover the picture, but was too late. Embarrassed, he stepped back and watched Yevgeny think about the canvases. At last, "Very good, but too centered. Even the universe is off its axis." That was all, but enough, quite enough. Alexander was not thrilled, but he was encouraged. He began to work even harder, deciding that it was best not to bother anymore about the ridiculous love affair of Francine Kammerer and the Master.

Karnovsky's work, in fact, began to go well. What made Karnovsky's little series of alphabet paintings intrinsically interesting was that he worked up the surface of the pictures to ensure a kind of textured complexity in which brush, trowel, even finger could be recognized. As well, Karnovsky began to mix up the Cyrillic alphabet so that the letters ceased to be read as simple words but rather as a jumble of marvelous shapes, whose literal meanings became the least arresting aspect of the whole. Clearly, Malenov's praise had been enough to excite him: the letters no longer sat on an invisible ruled line but seemed in some cases to be thrown at the canvas, in others to be falling off an unstated diagonal, and in yet others, like fat little creatures in a children's book, to be tumbling off a wall. Karnovsky worked every day, breaking in the afternoon for a stroll, sitting in the park near the apartment, or drinking cognac in a café. He continued to attend to Malenov, but his enthusiasm for documenting his every move had somewhat diminished, particularly now that those moves included trailing after a younger woman who, the Master had persuaded himself, understood his deepest soul. Karnovsky's reaction to Malenov's infatuation was profound, but hardly audible.

The week before Malenov's exhibition was to open, Alexander Karnovsky heard from home. He had written several times, brief notes, little more than reassurance that he was alive, that he had met his teacher, that they were working well, that life was promising. His mother wrote him every week, a detailed letter of meticulous unimportance; his father sent him clippings from the newspapers that mentioned the House of Karnovsky—one contained a photograph of his father tasting tea. It was the last communication he was to receive from his father. Shortly after that letter reached Berlin, a cable arrived announcing his father's illness. The message trembled with anguish: "DEAR FATHER HAS HAD A STROKE STOP I DO NOT KNOW IF HE WILL LIVE STOP BESIDE MYSELF STOP COME HOME MY ONLY CHILD LOVE MOTHER." Alexander had virtually no time in which to conjure the paralyzed and incoherent father who survives a stroke before another telegram solemnly confirmed the hour of his death. His mother was apparently distraught. The family lawyer cabled demanding Alexander's return to settle the estate and take up his responsibilities for the House of Karnovsky.

The telegrams arrived at the beginning and near the close of the day that Yevgeny Mikhailovich had rushed to the gallery early in the morning to supervise the arrival of his paintings from the framer, to plan their hanging with his Fraulein Kammerer, to be interviewed by a journalist, to rehearse a lecture on abstract painting that he was to give for a private audience of specially invited critics and connoisseurs the night before the public vernissage. He was not expected to return home much before eight in the evening. Alexander had agreed to prepare a buffet supper for a group of friends of the Lehrter Galerie, who were to come back to the studio for an evening with Malenov. But entertainments and soirées were not uppermost in Alexander's mind. His father was dying; his father was dead. He stared at the first telegram and tried desperately to suffer for his father. Without success. His eyes wearied of the effort to cry. No tears. His body seemed like stone. The second telegram was delivered in the late afternoon. Finality, and the distorting confusion of experiencing death without ever having understood tragedy. His father, relatively speaking a young man of fifty-eight, gone without a final word. Alexander dropped the telegram and, with the only mark of hysterical grief evoked by this sudden, premature, and first death of his experience, felt his body with a gentle hand, covering every surface of his chest, his stomach, his groin. And then, quietly, he wept, not in grief and mourning, but in anger.

Yevgeny Mikhailovich returned to the apartment surrounded by his new friends and admirers. The rooms were dark. He clapped his hands to announce his arrival, but there was no reply. He imagined that Alexander had devised some fête, some surprise, some theatrical invention to greet him and the friends of the Lehrter Galerie, but there was nothing, only a bulky envelope containing an advance against his expenses for the next six months and a brief letter of farewell:

Excellent Yevgeny Mikhailovich.

My father has died suddenly and I am recalled to New York. I have taken the afternoon train to Hamburg and will catch a ship leaving for New York tomorrow morning.

Forgive my sudden departure. You certainly have no need of a mourning son at this time. My presence could not be more burdensome to you in the midst of your success. The funds I leave you honor my commitment for the coming six months.

Paint well and think of nothing else, dear Zhenya. There is nothing else of any importance. I wish I could be as single-minded and total as you; it would make it easier to say no to my father's legacy, but unfortunately I am much weaker than I thought possible and, even though I do not mourn hs death, I am strangled by the power of what he leaves me.

Honoring you,
Alexander.

Only a few letters between Yevgeny Mikhailovich and Alexander Karnovsky over the succeeding months have been located. (There may have been others, but I doubt it.)

June 27, 1929 Berlin
Young Alexander. It has been a triumph. Dear Fraulein sells my work with great confidence and intelligence. The paintings fly from the Lehrter (nine paintings so far and the exhibition is open only two weeks). I am so pleased. And to good collectors, too. The Kestner Gesselschaft has reserved two pictures and many artists have asked me to make exchanges with them. Isn't that good? The press has been unusually attentive. I think they may be catching on.

But, you know, it is still a silly business. Today, I eat. Tomorrow, I get ready to lose weight again. That's the way it is.

I know, Alexander, I should have written you. I apologize. I should have said how sad I am at your father's death. But I did not know your father. How could I be sad? And you, how many times I heard you complain about your father's coldness toward you. I was not certain that sympathy was what was called for. Have I been wrong toward you? Tell me if I hurt you.

Your painting friend,
Zhenya.

July 19, 1929 New York
Zhenya. I have your letter. Don't worry about it. I think I understood your silence. It doesn't upset me. I am beside myself with work. My father's estate was not at all tidy. He kept his papers in a terrible mess. But it appears now that he was richer than any of us imagined. By far. Everyone advises me not to sell the business immediately. They say it is much wiser to operate the business for another year or two before trying to sell it. (There are at least three companies that have asked if it is for sale, which makes me suspicious about selling now.) To my amazement, my father left me in charge. He knew that I was ignorant about his business and cared little or less, but he still put me in charge. I consult daily with Mr. Salomo—Father's trusted adviser—who understands everything. Do you

think Father did this to trick me into submission? (Painting. What is painting?) It depresses me—all this worry about money and business. What do you think I should do?

Alexander.

September 24, 1929 Garmisch

Young Alexander. It is more than two months since you wrote me last. What am I doing here in the mountains? Recovering, that's what. Recovering from love. Clearly, Francine Kammerer does not love me. (I am finished with women. I was right to have been celibate all those years—not that I was not celibate with Kammerer. We did nothing but occasionally hug. Pinch was more like it. Pinch and squeeze. I was quite foolish about her. How little I understand about women. In this, so terribly an amateur.) She was never untruthful. I admit that. She thought I was a great painter. That was all there was to it. I was a great painter. She was a splendid dealer. I confused her loving my work with loving me. (She sold fourteen paintings. I earned much money. It will see me through the coming year.)

One day, she told me at dinner that I was becoming so possessive and demanding that it could not continue this way. I was horrified. "Where did you get the idea I loved you? I never said that to you, Yevgeny Mikhailovich. I said I admired you, that I admired your work, that I admired your art. But love, devotion, marriage, household living, I never gave you to believe that was possible. Now, did I? No. Never." I was beside myself. We were around the corner from the gallery having dinner. In a rage, I battered in the locked door of the gallery and went out the door with the six paintings she had left and my portfolio of drawings. She screamed for the police. They arrested me and kept me in custody overnight. I paid for the damage to the door. *Ein verruckte Kunstler,* was what they kept calling me. Yes. I am mad. Very mad. Anger and madness make for me a wild liquor.

Your Zhenya.

November 9, 1929 New York

Zhenya. It had to end that way. I was certain long ago. She was not for you. No woman can be, I suspect, unless she is prepared to obliterate herself taking care of you. Not that I was any improvement over a woman. Our living together would have come to an end no less decisively, although not as violently. It was a good fortune in at least this respect that my father died when he did. We were able to separate without a battle.

You did not answer my question. I asked you what you thought I should do? Do I have any talent? Should I continue to paint? Please address yourself to this when you reply.

Alexander.

January 1, 1930 Berlin

Sasha, straight away, yes, paint, paint, paint. Painting is not something you put on and off like your fur coat, a luxurious outer garment. Painting is all transcription, registering mental facts sensuously. There are days that I do not touch my paints, but I think of myself as painting nonetheless. Those days, I think painting (not *about* painting, but painting itself, and my body shakes as though I were actually making the movements that result in the mysterious passage of ideas from the brain to their forms to their colors). Sometimes, I imagine I am a tube of paint and want to squeeze myself all over the street. Those days are quite insane, almost pathological, but they are part of the process: you know, the more I think about painting, the more I realize that the first idea and the final painting are not what counts, but what goes on in between is everything. Painting is all process, thinking sensuously and out loud.

You have the talent, but you do not have the resolve. Maybe it is because you are young. Maybe it is because you are rich. Maybe because you do not understand the poverty of Saint Sergius. But let me tell you one thing, Alexander. Even if I were to tell you that you had no talent, if you believed me, *you would have no talent.* The issue of will and conviction is everything. What other people say is of no importance. So, paint and paint and do not be distracted from paint.

Your friend,
Zhenya.

There was no further communication between them for many months. They were in touch, to be sure, but there were no further letters. Yevgeny Mikhailovich sent Alexander every newspaper article, catalogue, casual mention that appeared in the European press regarding his work. Attached to these were little notes: "See, my old friend. They do not forget me," or "Several more for your scrapbook," or simply, penned in the margin of a newspaper article, "From Zhenya." Karnovsky never acknowledged Malenov's little packets of celebration. He couldn't. If he were to begin to write, he would have tempted an explosion of anger. And yet, he knew that Malenov was only partly to blame. It was simply that having found his Master, he had lost him again. His father had ultimately triumphed, imprisoning him not in the world of technology and science whose authority he had trumpeted, but snaring him in the coils of commerce. Every day, Karnovsky awakened to a three-piece suit and white shirt, to somber neckties and conservative overcoats. Every day, Karnovsky ordered from the hotel kitchen his juice and coffee and consumed them in the rented suite he had decorated with paintings by Malenov and Karnovsky. At the hour when he would have begun to work in Berlin, he descended in the elevator, entered a taxicab that awaited his appearance, and sped downtown to the House of Karnovsky. It was always the same: meetings with Mr. Salomo, the senior member of his father's staff, reviewing expenses and sales, conferring with advertising and marketing strategists, pretending constantly that he was fascinated and delighted by the aromas of tea and the redolence of spice. He loathed the enterprise, but succumbed to its aura of power and inheritance. An oil painting of his father stared down at him. Sometimes it glowered in the rain or sparkled in the sunlight, but it was always the magnificent founder, whose ingenious gifts of smell and taste had built a little empire of exotic commodities.

Karnovsky had no release. Mr. Salomo, occasionally sensitive to his fidgeting and inattention, would advise him to take the afternoon off and perhaps treat himself to a Broadway matinee; once, to Karnovsky's horror, he suggested that it was such a lovely day, perhaps he should set up his easel in the park and make a landscape. Karnovsky replied sourly: "I don't like nature as it is."

This dispirited young man was barely noticed in the conduct of the House of Karnovsky. He was allowed to come and go, to be present or absent at meetings, to approve or disapprove a decision of his subordinates; but whatever he observed, having evoked polite nods of approval or condescension, hardly mattered to the inexorable course of commerce. Mr. Salomo complimented Karnovsky if he said something approprriate or to the point. For the most part, he ignored him. Karnovsky never objected. For nearly two years after his father's death, Karnovsky accepted the regimen imposed by his inheritance. One day at luncheon with Mr. Salomo following a meeting with the firm's auditors, who had presented them with the figures for the year just concluded, Karnovsky suddenly interrupted Mr. Salomo's pleased recitation of their healthy balance sheet and confided that he had every intention of selling the company at the first opportunity. Mr. Salomo was horrified. The House of Karnovsky was his life, and his life, at sixty-eight, was hardly over. He protested, but Karnovsky was adamant. "I loathe this business, Mr. Salomo. Loathe it. Clear enough and unmistakable. I want to paint. Do you understand? I want to paint. That's all I want to do. Paint, paint, paint." Apoplectically overcome, his voice choked with emotion, he stood up from the restaurant table and fled.

The subsequent months made it easier for Karnovsky to abandon his father's company. Karnovsky's mother, increasingly estranged from living after her husband's death, passed through a massive heart attack and died three months later in a sanatorium. This signaled freedom for Karnovsky. There was no one to whom he had to explain his life.

Karnovsky never returned to the House of Karnovsky. It was arranged that he would receive papers from time to time for review and signature, but he never again set foot in the offices. And, as he said, he organized himself to paint, going about it with a meticulous assurance that surprised him. He had a lesson from which to begin, a reflection he had uttered in frustration nearly a year before: "I don't like nature as it is." Read this formula as an utterance of annoyance or pique with divine incompleteness, and only a portion of its profundity would reveal itself. Karnovsky was closing in on his own visionary breakthrough, a premise of reconstruction that would be as authentic and original to him as Malenov's projectivist architecture in space.

Karnovsky had not wasted time during his tea and spice days. It was hardly possible for him to paint seated at the vast desk beneath the portrait of the founder. Not possible at all, although once or twice he had sketched and drawn a notion or two; but it did not prevent him from shutting off his telephone, announcing to his secretary that he was taking a nap and didn't wish to be disturbed, and then removing from his desk his various treasured books: Paul Klee's *Pädagogisches Skizzenbuch,* Piet Mondrian's *Neue Gestaltung,* Malevich's various Russian and German treatises on the new theory of painting, but even more exciting because seemingly light-years from the world of art, books of meditation and philosophy from Plato's late dialogues, Pascal's *Pensées,* Burton's *The Anatomy of Melancholy,* Spinoza's *Ethics,* Nietzsche's *Beyond Good and Evil,* a gallimaufry of the wisdom literature of the West. He trained himself to read slowly, penciling in the margins delicately formed comments that alluded to his growing conviction that as an artist he stood outside the mainstream of world culture: he had stopped believing that the speeding racket of automobiles, the collapse of world economies, the starvation of the unemployed, the rise to power of idiot demagogues could possibly be influenced by daubing canvas with bits of paint. He had won out over commerce and technology to an appreciation of his friend Malenov's single-minded and, above all, private dream of a reconstructed universe. What could he do now but become a prophetic artist—like those whose works he coveted and whose essays of self-interpretation he considered the visionary literature of his century. He even, remarkably, allowed himself once again to be called Joseph Alexander Karnovsky, restoring to eminence in his private canon the ancient dream interpreter of the Nile, the old prophet Joseph, whose paternity in Israel continued to discomfort him with an unease and nervousness that he took to be absolutely appropriate to his time and century. What can one say of this Joseph Alexander Karnovsky? He had finally grown up to inhabit himself, his emotions and intelligence at last swelling to fill out the weightless grace of his face and figure. A line appeared on his cheek, crow's-feet crinkled at his eyes. They pleased him immensely. He remained a man alone, still without connections to human beings aside from the distant Malenov. But loneliness is bearable when despair gives way to energetic production.

FOURTEEN

I have tried with considerable diligence to reconstruct the six years that elapsed between Alexander Karnovsky's flight from Berlin and Yevgeny Mikhailovich's passage out of Europe to New York. The difficulties of such reconstruction are immense. They are, in a definite sense, unfathomable, because documentation is nonexistent. The bits and scraps that Karnovsky culled from art journals and critical press during those years set forth at most the contours of Malenov's considerable international reputation. Of Karnovsky's trials far less is known; virtually nothing that constituted the life of Alexander Karnovsky was preserved. Karnovsky was not writing in his journal about himself. Whatever he wrote—those few entries I was able to find for these intermediate and dark years—dealt with Malenov, only with Malenov. The single entry, for example, of October 21, 1932—a mere notation of fact accompanied by a clipping from a financial page that described the transaction—stated: "The House of Karnovsky no longer exists. I sold it today for 1.4 million dollars cash. It would have been more had we not been in the midst of a depression. They tried to persuade me to take stock, much more stock, but I am not interested in having to spend my years in consultation with idiot brokers and financial consorts, buying and selling bits of paper whose ultimate value is dubious. Better the cash. And now, God, let me paint." The little article that appeared in the New York Times stated the terms of the purchase by Consolidated Emporia, a food chain that added the House of Karnovsky to its portfolio of specialized food services. In the first annual report of Consolidated Emporia following the acquisition, the House of Karnovsky was listed in its schedule of divisions under Beverages and Condiments. So much for the vocation of Markus Israel Karnovsky.

It was during this period that I first made Alexander Karnovsky's acquaintance. He had telephoned my office and inquired whether by chance I had any materials relating to Yevgeny Mikhailovich Malenov. As it happened, I had nothing; indeed, I confessed politely that I scarcely knew the name. Karnovsky was only too willing to inform me. Several weeks later, I was fortunate to be able to buy a small library belonging to some Russian emigrés, one of whom was an unmatriculated student of architecture. His contribution to the family collection—mostly issues of fin de siècle Petersburg art journals and books illustrated by Bakst and Benois—was a handful of theoretical treatises on the new Russian art that included a little pamphlet hectographed in purple ink by Malenov, containing very early drawings of the basic Malenovian shapes and their permutations. My command of Russian was minimal, restricted to the alphabet, which enabled me to vocalize titles but hardly to read. I called Karnovsky and slowly pronounced the title of Malenov's first treatise (it was his *Elements of a New Utopics*). Karnovsky was enthusiastic, announcing the rarity of the work I was offering him at, as he put it, to my pleasure, "such a reasonable price." He visited me the following day to collect his purchase, and what began as a simple transaction was enlarged by conversation and lunch into an afternoon of confidences and intimacies. What do I confess about Alexander Karnovsky? I found him awkward and vulnerable, but immensely intelligent, serious, and appealing. His was a look of bewilderment that I have always found attractive—the kind of unsureness that is one minute covered with arrogance and another hidden behind a hand through which the low voice speaks, uncontrollably shy and melancholic.

As we approached the conclusion of our first luncheon, I realized that I had learned virtually nothing about Alexander Karnovsky. He knew who I was. That was transparent, and I had elaborated the history of my coming to deal in the rare materials of European art history—letters, manuscripts, prints and drawings, documents and photographs, illustrated books and obscure periodicals—but I had learned nothing of Karnovsky. Of Malenov I knew abundantly, almost too much, as I was now girded and tied by the cords of Karnovsky's judgment without being able to confirm it by personal encounter. There were no works by Malenov at that time in American museums. I was promised a tour through Karnovsky's collection, which consisted, he said, of some dozen paintings and drawings and a large album of preliminary sketches and drawings that he had accumulated in Berlin and taken with him on his departure. But my knowing whether Malenov deserved Karnovsky's unqualified enthusiasm (or whether Karnovsky deserved my sympathy, if it emerged that he had been duped by a minor artist) had little or no bearing on the phenomenon that, to my mind, seemed most remarkable. Not only the talent of Alexander Karnovsky but—in some mysterious and as yet indefinite sense—his life depended on the existence of Yevgeny Malenov. Malenov, whether he knew it or not, dominated and determined the life of his disciple and enthusiast, even though they were separated by thousands of miles. Speaking of Malenov, celebrating his genius, describing his personal eccentricities and boorish manners, his charming self-confidence, his oddities and peccadilloes was his young admirer's favored occupation. I grant you that it all began to weary me by the third of our meetings, since the only way to relieve Karnovsky's depression was to ask him whether he had had word of Malenov, at which point he would begin to dream aloud, his spirits lifting slowly, until after some minutes— orbiting—I was regaled with the aesthetic navigations of the genius, but it left me with little choice: depression or Malenov, hardly a rich and variegated social selection. He concealed from me completely that he, himself, was an artist, aspiring to greatness.

Boredom, I had come to realize, was one of the unavoidable by-products of being a dealer. Most collectors, I am persuaded, are obsessive acquirers whose passion is rarely accompanied by any fund of knowledge. Unfortunately, I had little to learn from my clients, which left me for the most part bored by them.

Karnovsky was something of an exception to my rule. He was undoubtedly obsessive, but his monotonous absorption focused on a single painter and was not involved in the least with either prestige or power, the twin monsters that inspire most collectors to pursue the prowl and hunt. Karnovsky never celebrated the prices at which he had purchased his treasures or compared his holdings with the purchases of others. Indeed, in the case of Malenov, nobody in the world of money and power really cared. Starvation was commonplace for artists during this period, and virtually every European artist of any importance did something else to make ends meet—designing furniture, printing books and leaflets, teaching, touring as performers, and with all, living scrappy and impecunious lives. (I have just learned, for instance, that the splendid collagist Kurt Schwitters began in Hanover by selling his little works for two and three marks and achieved great success in England twenty years later selling them for five pounds.) Malenov's situation was somewhat worse than most because he was an immigrant to the West, without proper command of any language except Russian, a visionary and utopian whose doctrine was transmissible but indisputably vague and romantic, who was without following, camaraderie, or support, cut loose from the great Soviet artists, who had by the end of the 1930s all returned to their homeland for the rewards of ignominy, humiliation, and death. At the same time, Malenov was immensely fortunate. He had Alexander Karnovsky—introverted Alexander, rich, handsome, dedicated, whose life and vigor were drawn like an infusion from Malenov's vitals.

During supper after the opera one night in October 1935 I remarked to Alexander—somewhat flippantly, I admit, since I suppose I had become enamored of the young man—that he should stop all this mooning and moaning about Malenov and simply bring him to New York.

It had been a wearying performance of an Italian melodrama, the soprano trailing twenty feet of white organza train like a royal gown when she was at most a celebrated courtesan, the tenor indifferently belting his tunes. I had nonetheless looked forward to the evening. I had not seen Alexander Karnovsky for nearly a year. He had been traveling—not to Europe, as I had thought likely, but to the Caribbean, where he had rented a house in Jamaica and tried to begin serious painting again; but he complained that the sun was too brilliant, the flowers too abundant, the undergrowth too lush.

Instead of paint, Karnovsky felt oppressed by the opulence of his life and had retreated into his books. Preparation, he called it. This was the first time he had spoken to me of his own work as an artist. I knew that he was rich (I had noticed the item on the financial pages), but I was unaware until that casual aside that he was also possessed of the same vocation as his friend Malenov. I confess I was stunned by the revelation, so casually inserted into his conversation. Perhaps he imagined—a not uncommon habit of the rich—that I had made inquiries about him and had found out everything that needed to be known. (The truth is that I had tried. I knew many people about town and am not uninterested in gossip. But unfortunately, practically no one had ever heard of Joseph Alexander Karnovsky, and those who had had never met him. He traveled in circles that did not overlap my own, a fact I found upsetting, but no matter. It was only when I brought up his name to a rather sleek and clever art dealer whom I met at a cocktail party at the Morgan Library that I discovered something about his background. Apparently, this art dealer had sold him a Malenov several years earlier—one that Karnovsky had recognized as stemming from the group of paintings exhibited at the Lehrter Galerie in 1929—and in the course of their transaction had learned among other things that Karnovsky was interested in philosophy and painting. The art dealer mistakenly regarded Karnovsky as a mere dabbler, neither a serious collector nor sufficiently rich to be cultivated. So much for making inquiries.) Seated before me at Longchamps, not far from the opera house, Alexander seemed hardly a painter, although admittedly I had readily consumed the cliché of long-hair artists, and Alexander's soft brown hair barely broke the collar of his tuxedo. In the midst of my effort to comprehend his casual disclosure, I was struck by the evident pain elicited by my proposal that he carry Malenov out of

Europe to New York. Instead of the long-faced, somber, even solemn Karnovsky to whom I was accustomed, he suddenly collapsed, as though my suggestion had plunged a knife into his amour-propre. Karnovsky first groaned, "No. Not that. Not now," and then, recovering from his first deflation, confessed to me that nothing could be more inopportune.

"I've been away from that vast ego for five years now and I enjoy the separation. No, Isaiah, I depend on it. I couldn't bear to have him in the neighborhood. Living with him was difficult, even impossible. I tried to work, but how does one work with a genius next door? Everything I made was covered with a Malenovian pall, as though he had invaded and occupied me. Such a succubus was possible in Berlin, because I didn't have the vaguest idea of what I was doing, but the last two years—Jamaica excepted (and that was as much a recuperation as anything else)—I've been hard at work, and since I came back to New York in May, I've made some objects I think first-rate. And several dealers think so, too."

"And you'll exhibit them?"

"In January, my first show. Isn't that wonderful? But if Malenov were here it would all start again. I haven't left off sending him money. I send. He receives. We don't discuss it. But I couldn't cope with him in the flesh."

"But, my friend, your obsession with him continues. You speak of nothing else. I didn't even know you made paintings of your own until now."

"Not paintings, sculpture. I make constructions out of wood. Sometimes I paint them. Sometimes I use different qualities and grains of wood that emit natural color. No need for paint."

"You should be very happy with yourself."

"I am. Perhaps for the first time, I am."

FIFTEEN

The first exhibition of Joseph Alexander Karnovsky's work opened in a serious Manhattan gallery toward the end of January 1936. It was a smart opening, well attended, voices modulated, the hum audible, the excitement controlled and well mannered. The major newspapers of the city reviewed the show, and all the critics praised it. Dorothy Miller of the Museum of Modern Art promptly came by the gallery and reserved a piece; several prominent collectors stopped in, and four works were sold during the first week. When the exhibition closed in early March, the reputation of Karnovsky, sculptor, was established. Karnovsky's dealer spoke of him now simply as Karnovsky; collectors referred to "my Karnovsky"; museum curators made diligent inquiries about the possibility of acquiring "a recent Karnovsky." Virtually every sculpture was sold, as were most of the pastel drawings that reflected process thinking about the issue of each construction.

By any standard it was an immensely successful debut. Many people knew Karnovsky as the son and heir to the so-called Karnovsky fortune in tea, and undoubtedly several of his father's friends who had observed young Karnovsky rise up to overshadow his father had acquired his works, but Alexander was indifferent to the implication of such commercial nepotism, precisely because nothing negotiable was to be gained by owning a Karnovsky. Indeed, in those days of the mid-1930s, art was simply the corona of society, and rich people acquired painting and sculpture in the same way that horse people acquire racing prints—art went with a certain level of ease and social self-assurance. The buying of art wasn't to be inspected closely, nor its motives questioned too intently; owning art was much like owning good luggage or well-made shoes: one didn't buy too much of it, lest its abundance send the wrong signals. Having a Karnovsky was daring enough—owning work by a Jewish artist descended from an Odessan tea merchant implied that amid a house full of odd French names and English watercolors, there was an American ethnic who did a sculptural turn. (At the opening, one lady was heard to remark: "How terribly contemporary!" Indeed!) The social chic of an art collection was still monitored far from the modest corridors of the Museum of Modern Art. A Karnovsky remained closer to Picasso than Picasso was to Velásquez. (Today, of course, it's all caught up. Karnovsky is still Karnovsky, but Picasso is an old master spoken of with the hushed respect accorded a bit of bedaubed canvas that commands a million dollars.)

Karnovsky's works were indubitably handsome. (That is the most that my unsophisticated eye can determine.) They were wooden structures built up of irregular boxlike rectangles mounting upward, with occasional interruptions as flanges projected out into space and way stations imagined by Fritz Lang turned at angles to the primary grid. They were not brilliantly fabricated. No matter. Already collectors understood that the difference between Karnovsky's art and carpentry lay in the formal power of the image and the appearance of fragility: the small nails could be seen, putty was artlessly applied to fill unwanted holes, the wood was rough and poorly planed, but the forms themselves—"architectonic but hardly architectural," as one critic put it—thrust dramatically up from their small, unpretentious black bases.

Is it any wonder that Karnovsky was unenthusiastic about the prospect of Malenov coming to New York? He was having his own success, a success perhaps grounded on imagery suggested and worked out in two dimensions by Malenov, but sufficiently obscure and unknown to the American public as to allow the passing of his own work into modest celebrity unmarred by the cavil of imitation. One critic, to be sure, writing for the French periodical *Art Aujourd'hui,* remarked of Karnovsky's work that he stood in a highly respected modernist tradition that stemmed "from Malevich and Malenov," but that observation suggested neither Karnovsky's borrowing from Malenov nor his transcription in sculpture of what Malenov had asserted in painting to be his projectivist vision. As far as Karnovsky was concerned, his work was original, fresh, and spontaneous. That was all that needed to be said, although surely his lack of enthusiasm about transferring his beloved Malenov from Berlin to New York brooded possibilities that were still unformulated, perhaps even unconscious. What if, I speculated, Karnovsky had in fact made use of sketches devised by Malenov for a suite of unrealized sculptures? What if Karnovsky had seen Malenov drawings and simply filled out their implied volumes in wood? What if, in short, Karnovsky was simply a transcriber who avoided the charge of outright thievery and plagiarism by concealing as sculpture what had been created as painting? But how was I to answer these questions? I was unskilled as either connoisseur of modern art or historian of its complexities.

During the late summer of 1937 Karnovsky received a pitiful letter from Malenov. It was the first letter Alexander had had from him in many months. Earlier in the year, at about the time of the opening of Karnovsky's exhibition, Malenov had written describing a commission he had received to execute a large mural in Stuttgart. He was not clear whether the commission was an official assignment or was financed by private sources. This is a relevant question principally because the American art press had already noted that the new regime in Germany was in the process of stripping from its museums and public collections every painting, sculpture, drawing, and lithograph that reflected, in the judgement of the authorities, the degenerate influence of the Jews and other inferior peoples, including notably Slavs by race and communists by politics. Listed among the Russian-born artists whose work was to be withdrawn from public view was Yevgeny Mikhailovich Malenov. When I brought this information to Alexander's attention, he was instantly upset. I observed his eyelids flutter, a sure sign in Karnovsky that something troubled him; when he undertook to comment on the report, he stuttered slightly, unable to find the right words to suggest both his indignation and his unwillingness to rise at that moment to the implication of the news. He knew that it was all over in Europe for Malenov, that his time of success and recognition was about to be eclipsed, but he was unable to bring himself to the obvious conclusion that what I had earlier proposed as challenge—that he bring Malenov to New York—was now necessity.

Malenov was again in need; Karnovsky was once more to become his succor and savior. Of course, succor and salvation had little do with uninterrupted financial aid. Karnovsky had promised Yevgeny Mikhailovich a hundred dollars a month and, throughout the years that had passed since they met in 1929, Karnovsky had delivered. Every month Karnovsky's bank had transferred by cable to a bank in Berlin the mandated sum, and every month, notified of its arrival, Malenov had appeared at the teller's window, presented his identification, and received a hundred dollars' worth of German currency. It was efficient and unemotional, a detached transfer, an impassive reception. It would have been much better, I think now, if the machinery of subvention had been more personal, if each month Karnovsky had been obliged to compose a brief letter and mail a check, if each month Malenov had been obliged either to ignore his dependence on the benefaction or to compose a note of thanks and appreciation. The enmeshment would have been more complex, but no less would the parties have been compelled to actually give and receive, to acknowledge and appreciate. When the fortunes of Malenov were rising, he could have suspended the gift, and when his fortunes sank, he would have been obliged to request that the money be renewed. The utter indifference of mechanical instructions—faceless bankers, impersonal tellers—routinized a personal gift and transformed a moral commitment and charity into the anonymity of an arrangement whose private dimension was elided. Karnovsky was allowed to forget what he was doing, and Malenov could ignore what he was receiving. Of course, the deep truth is that neither forgot. They occasionally chafed under the arrangement, but were too lazy and casual to call attention to the bondage of their relationship. The transfer of funds was an enslavement for both, and although they fulfilled the right regimen of charitable bequests, removing from generosity and receipt the risks of embarrassment that arise when gifts are made face to face—the proffered gift, the scraping receipt, the procedures of condescension and humiliation—the impersonality of their transaction proved, in my view, to be exceedingly harmful. The large ego of genius accepted the small sum of support, and burgeoning talent was constantly reminded by his monthly generosity of an indebtedness to his master that bruited dependencies and reliances more dramatic than mere money.

Unavoidable then that in the fall of 1937 the interests of Malenov and Karnovsky should collide. Malenov's need was reasserted at a time when Karnovsky's success required that the existence of Malenov be obscured. An inescapable moral dilemma, which Karnovsky was compelled to resolve. He did the right thing. Despite his reluctance, the historical evidence of misfortune could hardly be obscured. Malenov was in trouble; indeed, virtually all of the finest artists of Germany were in trouble, but Karnovsky had little interest in the generality of political misfortune. He could not help all the artists stranded by the barbarism of the regime, but Malenov he could help, and he could not close his eyes to that fact. Reluctantly, he opened his eyes and focused—even if narrowly—on the predicament of his teacher and master in art, Yevgeny Mikhailovich Malenov. With a weary shrug of capitulation, Alexander composed a telegram to Malenov: "HAVE LEARNED YOUR PICTURES WITHDRAWN FROM GERMAN MUSEUMS STOP IT'S ALL OVER IN GERMANY STOP COME TO NEW YORK STOP EVERYTHING ARRANGED STOP ALEXANDER."

There was no immediate reply. However, a month later, a letter arrived that explained Yevgeny's silence.

My dear friend. Your telegram came the day before my studio was broken into and paint poured over the floor. Many works were slandered. Cut into little pieces. Would you believe it, Sasha? I still do not. It is madness here. Many painters are quitting, going back to small villages and hiding out. Some take up house painting and bricklaying. This is no country any longer. It is a jungle. Yes. Yes. I will come. I don't know where I will live, but we can find something, isn't that so? I will pack up everything. (Francine Kammerer's gallery is closed. Her grandfather is a Jew. I didn't know that. Poor Francine.) Please, dear Alexander, send me funds so that I can leave. I have money to live on from day to day, but no money put aside for big moves like this. I am not sure that I can survive in your country, but I have to go on. The work is wonderful these days, the canvases larger, and I did a splendid mural for an architectural project in Stuttgart, which was to have been inaugurated last month. (It is canceled now. In its place someone has painted a tasteless tableau of thick-chested workers building houses and large-breasted pink women with hair as blond as cornsilk carrying cement. It is called *The New Germany Builds*.) But I have my own hopes to keep alive. I could surrender and die, but I cannot give in now. That would be too foolish.

Zhenya.

Sixteen

"It is exactly as I saw it."

Yevgeny Mikhailovich whistled with delight when Alexander Karnovsky threw open the door of the third-floor walk-up apartment on Sixth Avenue and 54th Street several hours after the *Berengenia* docked in New York on November 2, 1937. A large room, light and airy, freshly painted white, furnished with a large couch, dining table and chairs, a spacious worktable, bookshelves, a comfortable bedroom and bath at the rear, and a small, fully equipped kitchen. Yevgeny was presented with salt, bread, and wine to dedicate his new home, and the two friends, the painter in his mid-fifties and the sculptor entering his thirties, settled down to review the history of their separation. "Exactly as Zhenya saw it. First clear sight in many years and good one. On the deck of the ship in late afternoon, I saw this room. Exactly, this room! It must have been the day you signed the lease for it. Exactly. Same day exactly. I saw this room, filled with sunlight, radiant, walls white and pure. Oh, I will make such paintings here. I will make such paintings. I will thank you, dear Alexander. I will reward your trust."

It is hardly likely that Karnovsky would have fallen back into his predictably self-effacing demeanor before Malenov had he been able, early on, to bring Malenov to his studio, to show him his recent work, to elicit reaction to his newfound activity as a sculptor. Surely Malenov had learned that Karnovsky had had his first exhibition and that it had been immensely successful. Such news travels, and Malenov, despite his indifference to other people's success, would have been curious enough to have confronted Karnovsky's work, acknowledged its source in his own, and perhaps have been delighted by the progress of his young disciple. He might have stinted his praise or brought out this or that drawing of his own to document an option that Karnovsky had refused, but he would have willingly assimilated Karnovsky's dependence on his own achievement as his point of departure.

Karnovsky's failure to admit to his own work was a serious—I think, decisive—mistake. It set in motion the furious progress of anger and betrayal that was to follow. And yet, it is understandable. Karnovsky had not grown up with the kind of strength and assertiveness that Malenov dispensed so easily. Malenov's ego was so large and expansive that he could distribute in a day assertions and announcements of his genius that would take Karnovsky months to formulate. Karnovsky had achieved something important, but the knowledge that he was reworking in sculpture occasions and possibilities implicit in Malenov's paintings robbed him of the joy and pleasure his success should have brought him. The money his exhibition had earned was nothing beside his inheritance; the few Karnovskys now presented by museums among their new acquisitions were more than offset by the number that stood in entrance halls to summer homes in Southampton and Oyster Bay, mere condiments for the rich. Karnovsky was invited to parties and intimate soirées where the odd writer or painter turned up to amuse for his supper, but Karnovsky soon tired of this. He kept feeling that he was traveling with false credentials, that whatever he had demonstrated of his talent was siphoned from the profligate generosity of his master's genius, that he was still, despite his accomplishment, a beginner who had yet to find a voice of his own. His depression continued, his melancholy was revived, the presence of Malenov, now close to hand, loomed as a challenge to which he should have risen, a threat to his independence that he should have undertaken to combat. The day Karnovsky had sent his telegram of invitation, he was about to assemble two sculptures in his studio. They were as good as sold, his dealer told him and urged him to finish and deliver. Karnovsky looked at the pieces that night, but could barely see them through his gloom. They remained unfinished. By the time of Malenov's arrival ten weeks later, Karnovsky had convinced himself that he was untalented, worthless, and incapable, and had suspended work.

Moreover, the months that followed Malenov's arrival revealed something of which Karnovsky had not been aware. The discovery only served to consolidate his melancholy. He had believed for many years that no one in New York knew of Malenov's existence. Alexander occupied such a diminished world that he was generally out of touch with what transpired beyond its borders. He imagined that the absence of clippings, the failure of American magazines to contribute to his growing collection of articles and essays documenting Malenov confirmed that Malenov was unknown and unregarded. It suited his fantasy to think that America was still rude and unsophisticated. Although the Museum of Modern Art had opened its doors in 1929, and its sweep and influence were already regarded as innovative, the very notion of American connoisseurs passed him by. Europe was culture; America was commerce. This was the legacy of indoctrination in which his father had raised him, and he had accepted its stricture without examination. Such attitudes, unfortunately, comported with the manner in which Karnovsky did things: he was arrogantly rich, never counting his change or adding up a bill to check a waiter's calculation or examining the contents of a package to see that everything charged had been delivered; he never bothered to make certain that he had money in his wallet; he wrote checks, stepping into

banks and shops where, even if he was unknown, his letter of credit—
always in his wallet—was sufficient to insure that any Karnovsky check
would be honored. He was always out of touch, moving through the city
unawares, bumping into people he never saw, passing through reality like
a magician who pretends to walk through walls, except that Alexander's
misreading of solidity and substance was never willed or calculated to
elicit huzzahs of amazement from onlookers. Alexander Karnovsky simply didn't read the world accurately. What he took to be the world's
indifference to Malenov was more accurately a reflection of his own separation from the coteries that formed the art world and were generally
quite familiar with European developments, following Mondrian in Paris,
van Doesburg in Holland, and Malenov in Berlin.

It was to Karnovsky's considerable surprise, then, to discover several
weeks after Malenov's installation in his new studio that several American
artists had already come to call, that one of the curators of the Museum
of Modern Art had left his card and invited Malenov to a museum reception, and that Malenov—the absurdly unworldly painted he had abandoned in Berlin eight years earlier—had puffed out and expanded.
Malenov quite easily stepped out into the city, walking briskly down 57th
Street, cutting through the park, lying down on park benches to survey
the skyscrapers surrounding him, charging into crowds with an unfailingly correct apology for his bustle and rudeness, pushing aside obstacles
and obstructions that prevented his movement on subway platforms and
buses. Malenov had mastered the indifference of reality to precisely the
extent that Karnovsky had succumbed to it—the one persuaded that
talent and achievement could bend the real to serve him, while the other,
despite being efficiently outfitted with wealth and first success, still cow-
ered before the world, once again uncertain of any role other than the
enhancement and celebration of the importance of his older and more
accomplished friend.

The means by which Karnovsky undertook his program of enhancement was not, however, determined by a desire to see his friend independent and free, abroad in the land. It unsettled Karnovsky to learn that
Malenov kept company with painters who were indifferent to his eccentricity, who regarded the subtlety and power of his paintings as more
important this his execrably accented potpourri of languages—part English, part German, trailing off when words failed into a low rumble
of Russian—who were amused by his oversized overcoat bulging with
notebooks, a small box of pastels, and leaking pens that occasionally

stained through his jacket lining and left surreal shapes on his breast pocket.

Yevgeny Mikhailovich quickly became for his fellow artists the "bear" of the art world (the small art world that existed in those days), "bear" having come to signify not only the Great Russia from which he came but the aspect of massiveness, almost monstrosity, with which he wheeled through the city, his head lowered as if preparing to charge the unsuspecting and devour them.

Alexander Karnovsky was unable to revel in his friend's modest reputation. It was, I suspect, an authentic reputation, marked by the admiration of those who know what it is they celebrate—painting, the act of painting, the quality of paint, and not cleverness and novelty or the ability of painting to comment on this or that recognizable nomenclature of social vulgarity. Oh, these New York friends of Yevgeny Mikhailovich knew he was the real thing, the genuine article, a proper genius, who fashioned a mysterious universe of space and populated it with shapes that neither told a story nor narrated social muck. Yevgeny was a great painter, and younger painters knew the difference and admired him. They sought him out, invited him to their studios for comment, took him to tea and slipped him vodka in his water glass, loved him sober, preferred him drunk, but with everything respected the fact that he had survived, that he had fled Russia (but rarely spoke politics, which made it possible for even avant-garde radicals to tolerate him) and had already fallen in love with New York (which delighted everyone else).

Everyone, that is, except Alexander Karnovsky, who confessed to me one day that he was losing Zhenya.

"What do you mean by such an insane remark?"

"Just that. Just that. I'm losing him. He's on his own. He's off on his own. He doesn't need me anymore. Except, yes, sometimes to pay the bills."

But it was hard to interpret this last. It wasn't said with anything like the sneering bitterness such words imply. It was offered as fair comment, an extenuation of an otherwise frankly descriptive assessment: He's doing all right, but sometimes he needs help. To myself I had observed: And what did he need from you before other than money, and listen, young Alexander, who found whom? Who traveled to Berlin in search of a master and turned up Yevgeny Mikhailovich Malenov? The reversal had transpired, the upside-down version of the universe that is at the heart of all envy and all malevolence. All that any reversal requires is one act of superlative forgetting, dropping one critical, holding stitch from the fabric of the universe, and, pressured, the frayed thread can unravel the most carefully contrived and persuasive tapestry. What had he wanted from Yevgeny Mikhailovich? A lover? Bizarre, but possible, an authentic genius of no particular physical charm who could overwhelm and subdue him, turn him out of his virtually sexless and smooth neutrality toward a delicious perversity of sublimation, which might have enabled him to show his contempt for his paternity while submitting to its gender. But more. Denied by his history that indispensable species of trust and confidence that enables parents to die and allows children to survive and prosper, Alexander Karnovsky had devised an alternative route, a means of egress in art, which took him out of the kingdom of fathers and installed him under the authority of masters. A neat parallelism, but it hardly describes the reversal. How came it to be, then, that Alexander Karnovsky, one minute obligated to bring his master to New York, now chafed that the Master had come and was able to survive, no, thrive on his own?

A revealing example of Alexander's nervousness and unease before Malenov's fluent and unself-conscious mobility: Once, not more than three weeks after his arrival, Malenov visited the Metropolitan Museum of Art. He planted himself before a Renaissance painting dominated by a blue and pink sky lowering upon an Adoration of the Magi, and there he stayed for nearly three hours, quietly, transfixedly examining the painting. It was approaching the closing hour, and the guards, having observed him earlier, were by then persuaded that this monstrous enlargement of a man was going to do some violence to the little painting. As the hours passed and Yevgeny's nose approached closer and closer to the canvas, the number of guards observing him rose from one to four, and a small assembly of spectators filled a half-circle at the perimeter of the room, expecting something terrible, something vile, to transpire. At precisely the moment that one of the guards decided to approach and inform him of the museum's imminent closing, Yevgeny Mikhailovich whirled about and, tears streaming down his face, cried out: "How does a God settle among us?" No one understood his Russian interrogation, but no one undertook to pursue and question him. (He fled the museum and did not return for a month, when he appeared with a false beard, convinced that the entire staff of the museum was awaiting the next visit of the hysterical Russian, armed to the teeth and prepared to do battle.)

When Yevgeny Mikhailovich told the story to Alexander and myself that evening, we laughed until the tears came. We laughed; Yevgeny was finally persuaded to laugh, although he warned us that his next visit would be in disguise, but Alexander Karnovsky, although he had laughed, added: "Oh, dear Zhenya, you shouldn't go on such expeditions without telling me. I would have come with you."

Clearly, Karnovsky needed to regard Yevgeny Mikhailovich as somehow unable to conduct himself in the world—not as madman or dangerous, rather more as a genius incompetent, like those amazing defectives whose brain is stuck on an infinitesimally minute synapse and who, despite idiocy, are capable of adding in their heads immense columns of figures or recollecting dates going back to the beginning of history. And why this need? And even more so, why in New York, with an exaggerated insistence not at all evident during their Berlin months together?

One explanation, of course, is that during those early days, despite ample funds to organize and conduct his life with Yevgeny Mikhailovich, there was not much experience left over. Alexander could still dream paintings with an energetic will to make them; he could still regard Yevgeny as his discovery, his secret authority, his unknown master. He could pretend that everything he saw in Yevgeny's work and reconstructed in his own was an original creation. There was no one to gainsay his borrowings. Yevgeny would never comment, amused, perhaps flattered by Alexander's diligence and attentiveness, perhaps regarding his often academic translations of Malenovs as a legitimate device of pedagogy, even encouraging Karnovsky to find a vocabulary that would help transmit the Malenovian doctrine to others. Moreover, during their Berlin idyll, when neither could communicate efficiently with others, they were capable of bolstering each other's confidence and optimism without the need of checking their own judgment against a judgment being offered in a language foreign to both. But in New York, all the hermetic enravelment and self-infatuation that had characterized their life in Berlin before the advent of Francine Kammerer was dissipated by the commonplace directness of American speech and manners. There was no way that Karnovsky could prevent Malenov's entrance into the world. It was possible then, long ago, when Malenov was starving and Karnovsky was a rich aspirant, but by 1937 all the conditions had changed. Malenov was internationally regarded as a master; still poor, still uncelebrated by the coteries of fashion, he was nonetheless highly prized by the only world that mattered to him, fellow artists and utopians like himself.

Karnovsky, for his part, despite his reluctance to own up to the fact that he had stretched his talent to the limit and had accomplished the making of a body of work, establishing the foundations of a respectable career, still felt himself trammeled by his unspoken recognition that he was borrowing heavily on aesthetic capital he had not earned. In everything else immensely rich—itself a sufficient difficulty for a young artist—he had built his idiom on the transformation of ideas derived from his long and serious consideration of Malenov's painting. Where Malenov was quite willing to imply his utopian vision, Karnovsky was determined to formulate sculptural skyscrapers that signified heretofore nonexistent architectures. He was undeniably original, but he was not a genius, not a talent of first rank. He worked out the implications of premises he was unable to formulate. That was his achievement. It was also his curse and his predicament.

Several days after Malenov arrived, he asked Karnovsky whether he had been working well during the years of their separation. He admitted openly, indeed with considerable warmth and interest, that he was curious to see Karnovsky's work, to learn of its unfolding and development. They were sitting in the sun-drenched front room of Malenov's apartment drinking coffee Alexander had brewed. Dozens of half-opened cartons and broken-down suitcases lay about the room, and pictures were stacked against the walls, but Malenov was more interested in Karnovsky than he was in settling in. "All this can wait. Let's see what you do in art," Malenov asserted, waving dismissively to his belongings.

Karnovsky answered simply: "I've done nothing worth seeing."

"Oh," was all the comment Malenov made, and he jumped up from the table to show Karnovsky a box of Russian books that had arrived in Berlin with all the belongings he had left behind in Moscow eight years before. Karnovsky took this to mean that Malenov was perfunctory in his curiosity, that it didn't matter to him what his young friend had accomplished. Not true at all, as I discovered later from Malenov. The truth is that he was upset and alarmed by Karnovsky's self-effacement. It was so unlike the Karnovsky he had known, assertive, energetic, once prepared to work in a bedroom adjacent to Malenov's studio (certainly not the best of working conditions), but now, although completely freed from the wheel of necessity, apparently unable to make art. ("Something is wrong with Sasha," he admitted ruefully. "The whoosh has left him." Although I could not identify the rush of air that signified Malenov's *whoosh,* I took it to be an audible metaphor for inspiration.)

But it hadn't ended with Malenov's simple "Oh" of disappointment. Karnovsky put down his cup and tried to explain; almost stuttering, he admitted that he had left off painting and begun to make wooden constructions. He even drew for Malenov several little figures that suggested the complex structures he was undertaking to build, but all this description and allusion was after the fact. It was as though Karnovsky were trying to introduce Malenov slowly to the idea that his young disciple was not simply attempting sculpture, but had in fact exhibited some twenty of them, that the exhibition had occurred months before, that most of them had sold, that Karnovsky was already an independent, working artist. But he could not bring himself to admit this. It would be like a mere mortal admitting to a divinity that he had wrought something on his own, unauthorized and without permission, and now, confronted by divine curiosity, was guiltily trying to hide his creation. Such evasions and deceits are as deadly to human transaction (where it is hoped candor and trust would obtain) as they are corrupting of all relations between divinity and creature.

Malenov was perplexed by his young friend—even more deeply perplexed when Alexander concluded their breakfast conversation by laying his monthly stipend upon the table, this time in banknotes, resuming, it appears, the habit of giving that had characterized their earliest transactions. Malenov resisted picking up the money for several days. He put coffee cups, dirty plates, filthy paintbrushes down on the bills, hoping to soil and transform the banknotes into something else, but they did not disappear, although they were now covered with rings of brown and splotches of yellow and red. He began to hate taking the money from Karnovsky. He sensed that taking and receiving from his benefactor was beginning to work an insidious influence on both of them, compelling the one to silence and evasion, the other to an almost childlike dependence. Picking up a ten-dollar note, soggy with spilled soup, Malenov suddenly cried out: "I will give back all money. *All.*"

The following month, when he needed to fix a leak in the bathroom, he asked Karnovsky to call the owner of the building. And then regretted the request. "Why should he call that man? I will go to the landlord's office and introduce Malenov." But that was not as easy as it appeared. The lease for the apartment was in Karnovsky's name. The landlord would not have known who Malenov was. "You mean this is not my apartment," he asked Karnovsky. "Of course it is, Zhenya, but you weren't here to sign the document. I signed the papers. I paid the deposit and the security and the rent." (And so I ask, why didn't Malenov ask that the lease be transferred to him, even if Karnovsky were required to guarantee it? And why didn't Karnovsky propose the transfer and be done with it? But nothing as simple as this was possible.) It continued as before: Karnovsky paid and Karnovsky paid and Malenov vowed to pay back and nothing was resolved. It cost Karnovsky several hundred dollars a month, what with the stipend and the rent and extraordinary expenses such as a new winter coat, a reconditioned icebox when the old one burned out its coils, the replacing of a door that Malenov admitted kicking in during a fit of temper early one morning after a sleepless night.

Malenov had been constantly assailed with inquiries about his obscure enthusiast and benefactor, whom his American friends had seen at his apartment either preparing drinks and coffee or else sitting diffidently among them, hardly speaking. Malenov was unable to escape rumors of Karnovsky's work and exhibition. It was discussed by the painters he met at a gathering of the Association of American Abstract Artists, to which he was invited during the fall of 1938. A painter from Oregon, for instance, who wore a red-and-black-checked lumberjack's shirt that Malenov instantly coveted, had been pointed and direct: "You know, that friend of yours, Alex Karnovsky—the guy I met at your studio last week—he's making some good stuff. Not bad at all. But it all comes out lookin' like blown-up Malenov. And he's got some good moves of his own to make. Malenov, listen here, why don't you stop him taking a bead on your work and make him fire away at his own target for a change." Malenov didn't quite understand the painter's language, but he caught its sense. Karnovsky was admired, but everyone suspected him of trading on Malenov's ideas. In itself, that didn't bother Malenov. What bothered him was Karnovsky's unwillingness to bring him face to face with the work, to confront the situation, to be open and direct about his supposed dependency. If Karnovsky had had the courage to deal with his derivativeness, Malenov might have shown him the way out or, at the very least, given him his blessing to go on adapting. But Karnovsky's refusal to invite Malenov to his studio came to signify for Malenov that something was being concealed from him. Others knew Karnovsky's work—everyone else, in point of fact, except Malenov—and, for his part, Malenov regarded himself as the only person who was absolutely entitled to know what his young disciple was making.

The advice given by the painter from Oregon was excellent and to the point, but unfortunately it came too late. If all along there had been a stream of work flowing from Karnovsky, if the work had never stopped, and if the sculptures had continued to accumulate, refined, strengthened, governed by a critical eye that could mark the difference between the working through of new ideas—however clumsily realized—and mere rehearsals and rung changes on notions cooked and served by Malenov, it would have been possible for Yevgeny to check Alexander's fall into recapitulation of the ideas and images already proposed by his master. But Malenov could not tell Alexander what was going wrong and, more to the point, he had no interest in doing so. The Malenov journals make this clear. As well, they reveal something else: the guilt and embarrassment at being in Karnovsky's debt and the consequent reservations Malenov maintained about his disciple, his suspicion that by accepting so much over the years, he himself was being hobbled. Not that Karnovsky interfered with Malenov's art. Never. Malenov's art was always beyond manipulation and control. Indeed, as long as Malenov worked, Karnovsky raised no objection, never chafed, never complained that he was blocked and unproductive.

It was only when Malenov went out into the city without leaving a note of detailed itinerary tacked to his door that Karnovsky became anxious. "Where can he be at this hour?" he complained, seating himself before his door, awaiting his return. But Karnovsky was back in less than fifteen minutes, carrying a bottle of cream and six cakes filled with cheese in a little box. Karnovsky followed Yevgeny into the apartment. Malenov disappeared into the kitchen, and Karnovsky smelled coffee brewing in a saucepan (Malenov boiled it with egg shells and then strained the thickened mixture into a porcelain coffee pot.) Shortly, Malenov returned to the atelier, carrying a tray filled with cups and saucers, the cakes displayed on a blue plate, the coffee pot redolent with his concoction.

"People are coming to visit."

"Wonderful. Do I know them?"

"No. Not friends of yours, I think."

"Shall I stay?"

"Not a good idea. Very nervous people. They may buy something, you know. Best I do it myself."

"Oh. I didn't think I'd interfere."

"That's not the point, Sasha. You come here at all times, day, night. I never know when you come. No telephone. I am usually home working. Don't you think you should see me not as often? I feel you sometimes around my neck like a rope."

"You want a telephone? Tomorrow. I'll get you one."

"I hate telephones. I never want a telephone. Don't you dare telephone me in this room."

"What is it you want then, Zhenya?"

"Alone. I must be alone. You follow me like a sad animal. Yes. Yes. Like a small, sad animal. But you are a good artist and you have work to do. Go home and do your work. Let me alone."

Karnovsky left immediately. He got up from the sofa, pulled open the door, and left. He managed to reach the street, dizzy with confusion. He wanted to disappear; for an instant he even wanted to die. A taxi stopped in front of the building and four people got out, three women and myself. We had an appointment with Yevgeny Mikhailovich Malenov. As we approached the door, Alexander saw me and screamed, I thought melodramatically, "Traitor, traitor," and rushed down the street.

My friends, an Italian marchesa, her sister, and a friend of theirs, who were in New York after spending six months in Palm Beach, wanted to meet the remarkable artist. They had seen paintings of his at the Biennale a year before and, learning that he was now settled in New York, asked whether I would introduce them. I had arranged the meeting and had inquired whether Yevgeny would invite Alexander—a courtesy on my part, as I had no idea of the mounting tension between them.

I was annoyed with Alexander's little outbreak of pet. I thought it rude. He never even allowed me to introduce him to the charming marchesa and simply ran off down the street, shouting "Traitor." My friends were alarmed by the scene and, when they reached Yevgeny's flat, insisted on telling him of the meeting. I wasn't certain Yevgeny had understood their heavily accented English, but he did catch the marchesa's repetition of *traditore* and understood instantly that Alexander was infuriated by my presence at the gathering. The ladies were amused by Yevgeny, too amused in fact to take him seriously. He tried to interest them in his work, but after discoursing about his understanding of the universe for several minutes, during which their faces froze into polite incomprehension, he stopped, and I conducted the gathering through chatter and gossip for another half-hour, at which point we all left.

"Even you usurp me," Alexander shouted at me the moment he opened the door to my insistent ringing.

"You're mad and you know it. What kind of nonsense is this? Usurp you. Traitor-talk. What stupidity. If anyone is at fault, it's your friend Yevgeny Mikhailovich. I didn't keep you from being present. In fact, I asked him whether he would invite you, and he said he would think it over. It's between you and him. Leave me out of your little melodrama."

"Yes, yes. I know. He's getting tired of me. I don't blame him at all. He said I'm a noose around his neck. And he's right. Completely right. I'm terrified of him—terrified that he should see my work and recognize his own in every corner of what I made; terrified that if I own up to what I've accomplished, he'll tell everyone I'm a thief. What do I do instead? I stop working and follow him around like a concierge waiting for a tip. I disgust myself. I'm weak, goddamned weak, and I can't do anything about it."

"But you can. Show him the work. Invite him here and show him what you're doing. You told me the same story about your time in Berlin together. You were making your alphabet paintings in the next room, hiding them from him, and one day he came in unannounced and praised you, and from that day on you worked like a demon. Why shouldn't it work again?"

Alexander took my advice. More than a month passed, during which he hardly saw Yevgeny Mikhailovich. He never visited Malenov's apartment. Sometimes he circled the building, standing in the street, his eyes straining to see into the studio, to catch a glimpse of Yevgeny, but he never went up the stairs. Of course, he had written Yevgeny and apologized, but had received no acknowledgment. Yevgeny sulked every bit as strenuously as Alexander became pensive and melancholy. Their moods of rejection and unhappiness were immensely compatible. At last, however, after nearly forty days of this ridiculous separation, I persuaded Alexander to write and invite Yevgeny to his studio. When the letter was written, I took it from him and delivered it myself, handing it to Yevgeny, who opened it, read it, and said that he would come.

Both Yevgeny Mikhailovich and Alexander were happy that I was present at their reunion. It would have been impossible without me. They would have been unable to speak. When I arrived with Yevgeny Mikhailovich, Alexander had already had a drink of cognac, and Yevgeny dived for a bottle of gin, which he poured into a water glass.

"Well, I guess you want to see my secret work." Alexander laughed nervously and opened the double doors to the studio. He had arranged to borrow back from collectors several of his most severe and imposing sculptures, to which he added three new pieces that he had assembled and finished at four o'clock that morning.

Yevgeny Mikhailovich shambled into the studio, his large body stalking the room like a predator. But suddenly a look of calm came over him, his face relaxed, and he stood up erect before one of the largest of the constructions, a smile of delight kneading his features, filling them with his familiar warmth. "Amazing," he said at first and then lapsed into silence, moving slowly from piece to piece. Alexander stood behind him, trembling slightly, biting his lip. I remained at the entrance to the room where I could see them both and observe their remarkable confrontation. At last, "Amazing," again and then a flood of words: "Yes, yes, yes. I think you do something amazing, Sasha. Ha, ha, ha. I worry from other people you make sculpture out of me. No. No. What you do all your own. Malenov take no credit out of this. None at all. I think your work original, you know, something you make up out of Karnovsky. Very good. Fine. We show together, no? Good idea. We show together and put stop to all this nonsense about Malenov giving away genius to Karnovsky."

Karnovsky was overwhelmed. He took it all as it was offered. A superlative gesture of generosity from the older artist to the younger. Of course, I had listened closely to Malenov's testimonial and never once heard the words of praise that Karnovsky insisted he had heard. I heard words of amazement; I heard exclamations of originality, expressions of pleasure that Karnovsky couldn't be accused of being an impersonation of Malenov, but never an assertion that Karnovsky had made beautiful works of art. Karnovsky, however, was completely persuaded by Malenov's apparent enthusiasm and grasped him around the neck, hugging him with delight.

"May I give you one of these pieces, Zhenya?"

"You want to give Malenov one of these?"

"It would make me very happy. Yes. May I?"

"You need to make much more work before you give away. Save them for our exhibition. Later, well, later, you can give one to Malenov."

Malenov had interrupted the festival of their reunion with a reproach of realism. Not enough work to give it away. Keep working. Make lots of work. Then we decide if you're an artist, a working artist, or an uncommitted epigone who makes art from time to time whenever everything else becomes boring. Malenov still held the hammer in his fist and saw no reason not to bring it down, when it suited him, on the head of Karnovsky.

During the weeks that followed the entrance of the United States into the war, neither Malenov nor Karnovsky worked particularly hard making art. Both were agitated by the proximity the war assumed to their lives. After the fall of Kiev, Malenov was galvanized into fierce patriotism, inventing wildly imaginary wars in which his familiar spaces were filled with screaming projectiles embedded in circles of red. These paintings—the half-dozen he made in a burst of energy during the summer of 1941—were contributed to charity bazaars to raise funds for the Red Cross and to supply winter relief to the embattled Soviet armies. Once, overcome by reports of the devastating losses that afflicted the Red Army during the spring of 1943 at Stalingrad, Malenov even attempted to enlist, but was rejected with hilarity. Following his rejection, Malenov kept at Karnovsky to enlist, but Karnovsky—terrified by war and violence—avoided Malenov's challenge, knowing full well that in due course the draft would catch up with him and that there was no way of avoiding it once the notice arrived. Karnovsky was called up, reported for a lengthy physical examination, and was finally rejected after the doctor vaguely inculpated his heart in some irregularity. Karnovsky was so relieved at being refused that he paid no attention to the medical reason.

When the tide of war turned during early 1944, when the Soviets began their devastating drive against the invader and the Allies landed in North Africa and invaded Sicily, Malenov and Karnovsky felt they had been given permission to resume their work as artists and begin planning the joint exhibition Malenov had proposed almost five years earlier. They were encouraged in this decision by Karnovsky's dealer, who had agreed with enthusiasm to mount the exhibition, even proposing for it the publication of a catalogue that would document the work of each artist and annotate the collaboration and development of their complementary visions. It was agreed, without sufficient reflection on Karnovsky's part, that Karnovsky would write the essay about Malenov and Malenov would introduce Karnovsky.

The exhibition, scheduled to inaugurate the gallery's program during the spring of 1945, was prepared with exceptional care. Special walls were constructed at Malenov's suggestion in order that the gallery space acquire a labyrinthine aspect in which the viewer would be led through small rooms hung with paintings to interior spaces where Karnovsky's sculptures were installed. The placement of the temporary walls enabled a visal counterpoint, paintings offsetting sculptures, sculptures leading into rooms of paintings. There were, of course, many more Malenovs than Karnovskys. As hard as Karnovsky worked, he did not complete more than eight new constructions for the exhibition. Although Malenov visited Karnovsky's studio often during the working months that preceded the vernissage, Karnovsky never thought to inquire of him which works he was going to exhibit.

About a month before the catalogue was to be sent to the printer, Karnovsky asked to come by Malenov's studio to see the work he planned to show. He wanted, he said, to be able to write about the specific works intended for the show. Malenov temporized with Karnovsky's insistence. "Not necessary. You know Malenov's work better than Malenov. Write about the whole Malenov. Americans do not know Malenov. A general introduction is a better idea." Karnovsky readily agreed; it seemed the correct approach. Since the works shown at the exhibition were going to be listed on a separate sheet inserted in the catalogue, it wasn't really necessary for Karnovsky to see them. In fact, he never did see them until the day before the opening, when it was all too late. Every time Karnovsky visited Malenov in his studio in the months before the show, the walls were bare, work stacked in closets or covered with a tarpaulin in the corner. Karnovsky was without suspicion. He was still overwhelmed by Malenov's generosity.

The day the catalogue went to the printer, Malenov had not yet delivered his essay introducing Karnovsky. He promised to leave it at the gallery, but it never arrived. Finally, ten days before the opening of the exhibition, Malenov went to the printer and delivered his carefully written text, which, despite an occasional lapse of syntax that he urged the printer to correct, was in presentably decent English. No one saw the catalogue until it was delivered to the gallery the afternoon of the opening.

Even without the catalogue, however, Malenov had arranged surprise enough. He had allowed Karnovsky to install the exhibition, permitting him to arrange the forty pictures that Malenov insisted on showing in the small rooms that swept through the artificial rotundas greeted by the temporary walls where Karnovsky's wooden constructions were standing. Karnovsky was unnerved by some of the recent paintings Malenov had completed for the exhibition. They not only seemed to reflect visual ideas out of which his sculptures had come, but several alluded directly to the turning grid on which his architectonic structures were built, as though Malenov had devised a series of paintings after the fact to antedate and criticize Karnovsky's work. Although Karnovsky had situated those several paintings distant from his sculptures so that at least the untrained eye would pass over the analogy, it was hardly possible for him to ignore the similarity of painting and sculpture when he arrived late in the afternoon for the opening of the exhibition. To his horror, he learned that Malenov had spent three hours that afternoon virtually rehanging the exhibition in order to make unmistakable the dependence of the young sculptor on the master's work. Moreover, that horror was only the beginning. When the catalogue arrived, Karnovsky immediately turned to read the text of Malenov's introduction. It read with almost demonic subtlety and insinuation as follows:

> The relationship of Yevgeny Mikhailovich Malenov and Joseph Alexander Karnovsky has been intimate and profound since their meeting in Berlin in 1928. When they met, Malenov was already an artist of considerable reputation, well known in his native Russia, where he was an active collaborator with the great artists of the avant-garde, Kazimir Malevich and Vladimir Tatlin. Malenov left the Soviet Union for the West after losing his position as teacher of painting theory at UNOVIS. His work had been exhibited in all the major salons of the new Russian art both before and after the Revolution of 1917.
>
> What was Joseph Alexander Karnovsky before his meeting with Yevgeny Mikhailovich Malenov? He was a child of wealthy family derived from the mercantile bourgeoisie of Odessa. Like Malenov, Karnovsky was of Russian background. But the difference in their age at the time of their meeting was almost twenty years. And the difference in their education and experience was even more vast than is suggested by the difference in their age. Malenov was bursting with ideas; Karnovsky had only one idea: to meet Malenov.

Malenov will be indebted to the end of his life to the generous support that Karnovsky gave him. Without Karnovsky, Malenov would today be dead; without Karnovsky, Malenov's work would be unknown and Malenov would have surely starved to death.

But it is equally true that without Malenov, Karnovsky would not have been able to realize his ingenious constructions. In order to demonstrate this fact, Malenov has made especially for this exhibition a number of paintings that exhibit within the Malenovian idiom the three-dimensional undertaking that Karnovsky has so cleverly contrived. Malenov would not have made them as has Karnovsky, but then Malenov is a painter, and Karnovsky has learned his art out of the astute study of possibilities lodged in Malenov.

Karnovsky's work is more than an achievement. It is amazing.

It is a wonder that Karnovsky did not commit suicide that night. It is a wonder. I still marvel at it, but now, in retrospect, I have come to understand that Malenov's brutal assault on Karnovsky was simply preparatory to the bequest he had foreseen and had set in motion to bestow. He punished Karnovsky with the large fist. Indeed, the punishment worked. The little essay of introduction was sufficiently subtle and artful that all the critics and gallery visitors received the instruction. Those who observed the relation of painting and sculpture did not need to read the catalogue; those who read the catalogue hardly bothered with the work. The result was inevitable. Malenov overwhelmed Karnovsky, buried him under the double assault of his attack and the sheer number of works he offered. The critics—even those who had praised Karnovsky's first exhibition—now treated Karnovsky's work as a pendant to Malenov's. Many of the lengthy discussions of Malenov's oeuvre—excellently introduced and documented by Karnovsky's thorough and affectionate catalogue essay—concluded their discussions with variations of the following: "The exhibition also exposed eight new sculptures by Malenov's disciple, Joseph Alexander Karnovsky," or, "The catalogue essay on Malenov was excellently prepared by the young sculptor, Joseph Alexander Karnovsky, who showed some of his new constructions." No one was heartless enough to set forth the complex stratagem of subversion by which Malenov had undermined Karnovsky. They apparently felt it was sufficient to ignore Karnovsky, to relegate him to the role of mere disciple and praise his scholarship rather than his art. And for whatever purpose Malenov had devised his savagery, it was effective. Malenov sold many works and acquired a new and enthusiastic American dealer; Karnovsky sold one construction and lost an American dealer.

It might seem inevitable in the course of most human relations that an episode of such malevolence would destroy the friendship of Yevgeny and Alexander Karnovsky. Think again. Friendships are destroyed by cruelty and deceit only when friendships have been grounded in equity, when some equivalence has been settled, territorialities defined, boundaries and borders scrupulously adhered to until the hour of the fatal breach. But such equities had never existed in the friendship of Malenov and Karnovsky. As deeply as Malenov had felt Karnovsky's artistic dependence, his punishment was contrived to temporize and relieve the guilt of his own dependence on Karnovsky. To that time, Malenov had no identity that was not supported and vouched for by Karnovsky. He had no documents of emigration, no ration card, no lease, no official papers of any kind that did not carry the guarantee and authentication of Karnovsky. Karnovsky supplied Malenov with his principle of identity; Malenov supplied Karnovsky with his aesthetic. An equity in appearance, but not a genuine equivalence, because art had no public face or credibility, and everything that a human being could claim to be was defined by his face before the law. In that respect Malenov was nothing, Karnovsky everything. And Malenov determined that he would have revenge for his servile capitulation to Karnovsky.

SEVENTEEN

It is not believable to me that Malenov had foreseen the hour of his death. Indubitably, nonetheless, near the end of his journal, Malenov confirms it, and Malenov is dead, dead of congestive heart failure following a siege of neglected pleurisy:

> It is time to be done with all this huffing and puffing that is called life. I accept my end, beloved Sergius. I have nothing more to do. The work is done and I am bone dry and weary. How successful I was, throughout all my years, in fending off the scrutiny of others who might have seen beneath my bluster a soft and vulnerable heart that wept bitterly at its loneliness. I kept off friends and intimates to preserve my solitude. I understood clearly how disagreeable it was for Sergius to go off into the wilderness to found his chapel and then (even saints become famous), attracted by his piety, his fasts and austerities, his conversations with the Holy Spirit, to be suddenly inundated with disciples who wanted to share his understanding, to be conversant with his spiritual genius, to support and settle him despite his wish to be alone. It is all so strange, how God works with his saints. And so filled with confusion! Sergius wished to serve God alone, and God made his pieties so great and magnified his achievement so immensely that suddenly he was surrounded by disciples and was obliged to

leave off his pieties to feed them and to tend the beggars who flocked into his wildnerness to populate it with their own misery.

Have I done differently? Little Joseph Alexander, my unpious Jew from Odessa, came nearly full circle of the world to find me in Berlin, to make my wilderness habitable, to settle me in triumph, and in return to be nourished and fed by my gift. Is it any different? Am I not a new saint of the modern world, the only kind of saint bearable in the modern world—the end of bohemia and the beginning of celebrity—who wills his work to be his own, and the more he struggles to make it difficult and intractable, the more the world wishes to master it, to translate it into its own idiom, to suck out its indigestible marrow and consume it.

I would have been content to have had a small career of neglect, like Van Gogh or Gauguin, to have had few admirers and fewer buyers, if it could have been done without the waste that both those genuises expended in disease and madness. Their modernity began when they realized they had sold little or nothing in their lifetime. If we artists could have continued to be guildsmen as in the Renaissance, doing our work for the most part anonymously, giving employment to useful historians who could then have tracked the signs of our identity beyond our death, I would have been content. Let only one of my pictures carry a signature and all the rest be known as Pseudo-Malenov or the Master of the Utopic altarpiece, how nice that would have been! After one's death, all fame is useless, and before one's death, all fame directs the way to dying. It is so with me. I know that my time approaches fast, since I am come into the palace of fame and fame dwells like a vulture over my doorway.

I see my dying as clearly as I saw the apartment from which Malevich fled or the rooms in which Karnovsky settled me. I see into rooms, it appears. My deadly second sight is housebound, confined to quarters and domiciles. In those rooms I see the lines of my catastrophe. And it is in this very room where I sit now at peace writing out the details of my death that I observe the outline of my dying. Over there, I fall down on the floor near the window. I am too exhausted to reply to the knock upon my door, the persistent knocking that is Karnovsky come to call, his daily come to call, his persistent, relentless dogging of my steps for which he pays me monthly, that earns him the right, he supposes, to make my days unbearable, to keep me from my solitary pieties, from Saint Sergius, from my album of little treasures, from all the ministries of solitude that I have organized and put to work over a lifetime.

And, you, too, Karnovsky (though you did not intend to wear me down by your persistence), you will pay for having destroyed my solitude. I have also made preparation for your death. If all this comes to pass, I will have set in motion an inexorable plan. It is not, Sasha, that I am angry with you. Not at all as simple as that. It is that if I die (as I see myself dying), the balances in the universe will have been jarred. There can be no reconstruction of the universe according to my plans and programs if the foundations of the world shudder and groan from the tilt of your devising. If I die because of you, you must die because of me. The work is more important than either of our lives, and I would have you dead that the work of reconstruction can go on.

Enough of this. I have seen enough of this. And now it is to the sinew of the real, where bone, muscle, tendon stretch and turn upon a universal rack, that we must pay attention. It happens: it does not happen. But all will be ready if it does.

The day after Malenov wrote this entry in his journal, with dusk accumulating in Yevgeny Mikhailovich's apartment, Alexander Karnovsky brought me along for his daily visit. I had not seen Yevgeny for several months. I was pleased to be invited for their time of teacups and cakes; my own life had been sordid and boring. But it was unclear why Alexander had insisted on my joining him. It was less an invitation than a command. "You must drop everything and come with me to Zhenya's." The tone was so uncompromising that I succumbed instantly. Only later did I become curious about Alexander's invitation. Why now? Why me? Why the necessity of this moment? Nothing was anticipated, although everything transpired, indeed everything that I later discovered in Yevgeny's journal was set in motion that afternoon. Had Alexander expected it? Had he been forewarned? Was he also gifted with sight? No. Not at all. Karnovsky came close to philosophy and metaphysics, but he was not a spiritual man; sensuality at bay, that is the closet he came to the spirit. But all human beings, I conclude, have the capacity for being unpredictably unnerved. Something can rise up out of the prospects before us that baits our attention, sets us at the ready, makes us aware— even if insubstantially and fleetingly—that there is something that might happen, that is around the bend of light, hidden in the infinite rooms of time.

As we climbed the stairs to Malenov's apartment, Alexander confessed that he was apprehensive. "Thank you for coming, Isaiah. I needed someone else today. I feel it." I couldn't ask what he felt, as the door was thrown open and Malenov invaded the space to hug Alexander and swallow my hand in both of his. Before we could halt the progress of events, consume our tea, nibble at the toast, talk about the unseasonable cold snap or even comment on a vast new painting that covered ten feet of his wall, Malenov had begun to talk. The talk seemed rehearsed, as though it had been practiced over and over, learned and memorized.

"Before we talk of other things, I have something to say to you, dear

Sasha," Malenov began speaking his curious brand of chopped English, "about which I have thought now for nearly eighteen years. You have been more than helpful in my life. You have sustained me through all these years, good years and bad years. I think the time approaches—fast approaches, I am afraid—when my life comes to conclusion. No. No. Do not argue with Zhenya. You know perfectly well such things are not secret from me. I know they will come to pass. When remains uncertain. But now rather than later is undeniable. I propose to repay you everything that I owe you—the nearly forty thousand dollars that are due to you—by leaving you everything that is in this studio, all the paintings and drawings, all my books and records, all my journals and notebooks, in short, everything. You have wished to be my child and so you shall become my child when I am dead."

Alexander Karnovsky, to my amazement, was not surprised. He kept silent for several minutes, not fidgeting, implacably staring at Malenov. I found the silence like the eye of a tornado, of such immensity and power that it grinds out the living in a whirlwind. "Your figures are correct, however just beyond forty thousand," Karnovsky murmured in a low voice, removing a slip of paper from his pocket on which the precise sum had been noted. "Thank you, Zhenya. Nothing could move me more than to become your child of inheritance. But shall we make it legal?"

Malenov did not object; it had all been anticipated and accepted, even the cautious disbelief of Karnovsky's request. Malenov brought paper from his desk and, leaning on a small drawing board, began to write as Karnovsky dictated a simple testamentary document, naming himself as sole heir and executor. And then it became clear why I had been brought to this incredible afternoon tea. "Will you witness Malenov's signature, Isaiah? I will fetch that cleaning man we passed in the hallway. He will be the second witness." Moments later an elderly Italian, holding a crumpled banknote in his left hand, entered the apartment and put his signature beneath my own, printing his name and address below his nervous scrawl. It was done and witnessed.

"Legal, yes? I am finished, so to speak," Malenov added wryly, as he poured a fresh cup of tea and seized a cherry tart in his begrimed fingers. "You see the painting behind me. Very big, much bigger than the Stuttgart mural the barbarians cut up in Berlin. It may be my last great painting. Quite possible, you know. I've seen it all. My death, that is."

"Oh, stop, Yevgeny Mikhailovich," I exclaimed. "We are all going to die some day, but not just yet." (I never could bear conversations about dying. The only tradition I extracted from my family was their ingenious refusal to speak of death. Death was never final among my folk—it was always spoken of in the euphemism of travel, one minute here, the other out of sight in some other realm where we would all meet up again. My grandfather would leave the table enraged if even the word *death* were mentioned, and my father, until his own death not long ago, spoke of it as though it were an avoidable happenstance, occurring only because of some mistake or error of judgment. He was in the habit of speaking about the time beyond his death in the language of uncertainty: "If I die, Isaiah, you will have to take care of your mother." He did, and I am still caring for my mother. But at the time of these events, several decades ago, when I was a manuscript dealer in my early forties, I found it exceptionally difficult to listen to this bizarre Russian genius, discoursing genially about the time and occasion of his death. Particularly, of course, because I accepted that what he was saying was inexorable and bound to come to pass precisely as he had imagined it and, as I later found, set it down in his journal.)

"My death not important. Everything I wanted to make is done. This last picture is, you understand, kind of summation. See how red planes pass through black solids into blue ether. It's what I've always dreamed to build—vast planar platforms to launch projectiles into space. Malenov's space-travel architecture."

Karnovsky listened closely as Malenov continued his interpretation of the unfinished canvas behind him, once getting up from the sofa to examine a dense area of the composition where the black paint shone like polished ebony. He made no further reference to the testament, which he had simply folded and inserted in his wallet. It was all terribly strange. Alexander had never alluded to the vast sum that Malenov owed him. Indeed, I had never thought of Alexander's monthly generosity as a debt incurred, carrying the obligation of repayment. It was presented as a charity, I took it to be a charity, and yet, clearly, without relatives or heirs, the aging Malenov had conceived of the bequest as the single means he possessed of repaying his benefactor. I was not aware at the time, however, that the bequest carried with it a more insidious intent. Malenov knew that his reputation was continuing to rise, that his works—once valueless—now commanded international attention. With the war concluded and museums throughout Europe beginning the work of reconstruction, demand for master paintings of the century would mount, and the desire to bring together and aggregate holdings diffused by the European destruction would intensify. Of course, I did not learn of Malenov's malevolent construction of his bequest until several years later, but it seemed less surprising when I discovered it, given the cold, indeed calculating, manner in which Karnovsky had received it. He knew to the penny how much he had given Malenov; he was cognizant of all the requirements for preparing a legally incontestable document of bequest. It was as though simultaneously with Malenov's presentiment of his own death—his famous "second sight"—Karnovsky had been suddenly illuminated. Karnovsky denied it when I inquired, but he did acknowledge that during the days prior to Malenov's announcement he had been unable to sleep, had felt incredibly tense and apprehensive, and had—for reasons that he was unable to fathom—counted up not only the money he had given to Malenov but the number of paintings and drawings that he owned from Malenov's hand, as well as the quantity of documents dealing with Malenov that he had accumulated over the years.

EIGHTEEN

Alexander Karnovsky broke down the door to Malenov's apartment during the early morning of February 11, 1948, and found him collapsed on the floor by an open window, gasping for breath. He was near death. After his removal to a hospital, where an elderly doctor tried to make him comfortable, he expired. It is not clear whether he had opened the window and allowed freezing winds from the Hudson River to chill the apartment or whether he was ill before opening the window and then, weakened by pleurisy, had collapsed while trying to close it again. Whatever the sequence of events, because of his debilitated condition, his admitted weariness, the abscesses on his lungs and his overburdened heart, by the time he was found—apparently more than a day after his collapse—there was nothing that could be done to save him. Of course, had Karnovsky gained entrance to Malenov's studio the first time he had come by and listened at the door, hearing him pacing inside, hearing the indistinct cough (hearing the slow and somewhat dragging footfall uncommon for a man who always moved briskly and with resolution), he might have gotten to him in time. But Malenov, it must be assumed, had anticipated this and had resumed his habit of posting notices upon his door to discourage visitors: MALENOV NOT RECEIVING TODAY, MALENOV WORKS, LEAVE MALENOV ALONE. The piling of ordinance and warning had frightened away the postman, who had a registered letter for Malenov. A Swiss visitor who had wanted to speak with Malenov about a commission for a projectivist installation in a local museum had slipped his card under the door, but, obediently, had never knocked. Karnovsky, going by the apartment morning and evening, hoping to be admitted but each time finding the notice of admonition in place, hearing Malenov inside, persuaded himself that everything was all right, that Malenov was working on some large enterprise and did not wish—genuinely—to be disturbed. It hurt him, of course, that no exception had been made for him. (Once, he told me, several years earlier, when they were organizing and planning their famous joint exhibition, Malenov had written a notice for his door that read: NO VISITORS FOR MALENOV EXCEPT KARNOVSKY.) Karnovsky was an exception to all Malenov's rules, and if so then—once, even—why not now, when Karnovsky anxiously paced the hallway before his apartment trying to make up his mind whether to announce himself, to call out, or simply to repeat the low rapping that he had used in the past when he wanted to enter Malenov's atelier at the front of their Berlin apartment. But for some reason he had not knocked.

Or rather, I can guess the reason: ever since Malenov had nominated Karnovsky as his heir, their relationship had changed. For the first time, Malenov had ceased to be oblique with Karnovsky. Indeed, on one occasion he had dismissed a new construction Karnovsky had ventured to describe to him. "Sounds like a packing crate, not sculpture." Karnovsky laughed and persisted in his description. "Aach, Sasha, I do get tried of your making me into solids. One Malenov is enough. We don't need a half-Malenov called Karnovsky." It was cruel; it was intended to be cruel. Karnovsky didn't reply. Malenov had punched him in the stomach; he was winded. There was no reply. It was almost true. But why, suddenly, did Malenov begin speaking this way to Karnovsky? Of course. Now that Malenov had decided he was his heir, he had no further need to guard his tongue. He was quits with Karnovsky. The slate was clean, the scales balanced. Whatever bitterness Malenov had felt over the years when Karnovsky was accumulating the stuff and substance that was Malenov, a junior Malenov, a minor Malenov, there could be no confontation except by indirection. Malenov repaid Karnovsky all those years with slyness and slights, small reproofs and critiques, driving him away, but also recalling him as unpredictably. All those years he continued to receive money from Karnovsky—no, to take money from Karnovsky—and Karnovsky gave the money as forcefully as it was received. Karnovsky controlled the finances of Malenov and, consequently, controlled his movements. Every time Malenov wanted to take a holiday, to drive with some acquaintance up to Cape Cod for a week or take a train to Chicago to visit the Art Institute, he had to ask Karnovsky for something extra. Money was always around and abundant—banknotes were found after Malenov's death inserted as bookmarks in volumes he was reading (Malenov once explained he couldn't pay his gas bill because he hadn't finished a certain book where he was using a twenty-dollar bill to mark his progress), rolled with a rubber band among his underwear, hidden in the jacket pocket of his suits, flattened in his favorite pair of walking shoes—and yet never organized in one place where Malenov could find it. He treated money indifferently, casually, and yet he had need of it and knew when it was instantly required to fund an excursion. It was then, requiring fifty dollars, that he would touch Karnovsky for an advance against the following month, to which Karnovsky always replied, "No, no. I'm not a bank. No need for an overdraft. Here, take it. I have more than enough." And yet Karnovsky *was* a bank, a benevolent bank who was always beseeched the same way and always responded generously. An uncommon bank, but at last fulfilling one requirement of a bank's reality: there was a never-ending supply of money in the till, and Karnovsky was always willing to bestow it on Malenov.

Malenov obviously despised the fact that he could not support himself; even after a score of exhibitions, after the sale of several hundred paintings, after the praise and admiration of museums and cognoscenti, he was still broke, always poor, always a supplicant to the young man who was unfailingly generous toward him, but who wanted more than anything to become the new Malenov, replacing the visionary paintings with original sculpture, taking from the master as reconpense for his generosity a little bit here, a little bit there of the original genius that made projectivism one of the most controversial and argued doctrines of modern art. It was bound to end badly, and this despite the fact that both men admired each other, depended on each other; in the fatality of such hopeless arrangements of trust and mistrust, they were also committed to destroying each other.

Karnovsky sadly arranged the funeral for his dead friend. Testimonials and reminiscences were offered by representative figures of the European art world who had come in the course of war to settle in the United States, artists who had known Malenov in Moscow and Berlin, museum curators who had begun to collect him in Europe and America; and finally, reluctantly, unhappily, Alexander himself concluded the solemnities with a brief recitation of remarkable events in the life of Yevgeny Mikhailovich, episodes and anecdotes, most culled from his vast archive of Malenoviana, some, indeed those of greatest warmth and intensity, drawn from their own intimate but troubled friendship. The service—wholly without religious allusion—concluded with a pianist rendering Scriabin's sonata "Towards the Flame," Karnovsky's single concession to Russian spirituality.

After the service, Alexander invited everyone back to Yevgeny's atelier for a sort of festive wake. When the guests arrived, a long table was ranged with vodka, champagne, beer, and whiskies of all kinds, vast platters of salmon, whitefish, and caviar, trays of cold cuts, loaves of bread, salads, and pirogi stuffed with meat, potatoes, and vegetables. The party went on interminably, but by late evening all of the guests—the forty or so who remained to drink themselves into oblivion—were aware that Alexander Karnovsky was the new son and heir of Yevgeny Mikhailovich Malenov. It was a secret Alexander would have been well advised to keep.

A month after the death and cremation of Malenov, Malenov's dealer persuaded Karnovsky that a second and final joint exhibition of the work of Malenov and Karnovsky should be held the following season. Karnovsky agreed, although already he thought it unlikely that there would be enough time for him to make new work. He had ready several drawings that he wanted to translate into wood, and he had recently begun to use sheets of colored Bakelite to contrast with the graininess of ash and oak, but making art was not something you could start at eleven in the morning and then break for lunch to deal with matters arising out of the Malenov estate. He kept repeating to himself *ars longa, vita brevis,* but he had already reconstructed the meaning for him of this familiar Latin apothegm: art took a long time to make and his life was so short, the working day was so abridged, spans of uncommitted time were so infrequent that he was lucky if he had ten hours a week in his studio to work at sculpture. And ten hours was hardly enough time to consider oneself an artist, much less to make art.

Karnovsky tried: he tried profoundly to return to his work. He thought it a responsibility that he had to Malenov to continue making Karnovskys, to press the future of projectivism by insisting on its visionary architecture and demonstrating its possibility. He even organized a small collective of young architects to work on housing projects for postwar America and Europe that would incorporate projectivist principles in the design of urban spaces, treating highways and mass transit as systems of utopic grids, funding research that might yield a new and untried building material that could sheathe his new constructions. But everything that Karnovsky pressed forward in support of Malenov's principles diminished his own time and prevented him from attending to his own work.

It was under control for a while; Karnovsky did manage a number of hours alone. But as the time approached for the exhibition to open, it became clear that he would have at most one new sculpture ready for presentation. The rest would be Malenov, and, consequently, it fell to Karnovsky to choose which Malenovs would be exposed, to annotate the catalogue and provide an introduction. It tooks months of work, as everything connected with Malenov went slowly. Because Malenov had successfully built into his oeuvre a dimension of obscurity and confusion, there settled upon his heir problems of scholarship and documentation that were uncommon in the work of other artists. Malenov rarely signed his work, never titled it until it was exhibited, and dated it in the most bizarre of fashions: "Begun one night in the winter and finished several years later. YMM." Is that a date? What winter? Where? Later than what? The "YMM" passed as signature and authentication, but the anecdotal dating compelled Karnovsky to settle for approximate chronology based on internal evidence of the work—changes in Malenov's palette, shifts in the positioning of certain forms, introduction of the enlarged format, use of collage elements, all these variations in the scheme of Malenov's work were well documented by Karnovsky (he had, you see, put his ledgers of Malenov's working drawings and sketches to good use) and allowed him after weeks of careful examination to decide that a certain painting had been made in Berlin during the early 1930s or in New York prior to 1942 or in the period after their disastrous joint exhibition or in the season before his death. Many of the paintings Karnovsky knew firsthand, having been present when they were made and having reproduced and dated them in his notebooks. The real problems were the little pictures that Malenov had made but never shown to Karnovsky and, more serious still, the work done in Berlin from 1929 until his removal to New York. Many problems, many problems indeed. And all of them—precisely as Malenov had envisioned—fell on Karnovsky, robbing his own time of any concentration that might be considered private and saved for Karnovsky.

The exhibition of Malenov and Karnovsky opened in due course and was hailed by the critics as an opportunity to see the genius of the late Yevgeny Mikhailovich Malenov. The fact that Karnovsky had presented a new sculpture and included four previously unknown constructions that he had sold privately during the previous two years was completely ignored. Of course, Karnovsky's inheritance was discussed, and his enlarged responsibilites as the concierge of Malenov's reputation were duly noted, but Karnovsky the artist was never mentioned. Indeed, that was never discussed again. Karnovsky's dealer became Malenov's dealer and an even closer intimate and adviser of Karnovsky, but he never again asked about Karnovsky's work. Karnovsky the artist simply disappeared or, more accurately, was so confused with the fame of Malenov that one almost spoke of them as a hyphenated enterprise, the work of the one, the authority and scholarship of the other. The Malenov-Karnovsky oeuvre: the dead artist Malenov had made the work, the scholar Karnovsky annotated and exhibited it. For a time Karnovsky was able to bear the intrusion, delighting, in fact, that he was in a sense closer to Malenov in death than he had been to him in life, interpreting his work, defining its intent, formulating its ideology, supplying the world with the language of its exegesis. Karnovsky took upon himself the requirement of making Malenov legible and in the process not only supplied each painting with a history and documentation, but fitted it into a scheme of vision, invented by himself, and supported by documentation that no one could question. But all the while it ate at Karnovsky that he had been obliterated by the new eminence, that Malenov had installed himself in his brain and now weighed upon his heart with a pressure that had become unbearable. Indeed, the first time that Karnovsky complained of a savage pain in his chest—a pain of such intensity that it seemed to be ripping him open—he regarded it as such a fitting metaphor of Malenov's incision in his life that he waited until it passed and never pursued the matter. Not that anything could have been done to relieve the presence of Malenov in the lining of his coronary arteries. Malenov had obliterated Karnovsky, quite simply. By 1950, there was nothing left of Karnovsky that had not been recast by Malenov—all his imagination, all his energy, all his time was devoted to Malenov. And though the bright lights of wealth and money had not yet come to shine directly on the artist and his works, its angular and embarrassed radiance was sufficient that Malenov's unsold paintings and drawings had come to be valued at nearly a million dollars—a modest sum by today's standards, but vastly more than Malenov had earned during his lifetime, and an inheritance that in time would rival and ultimately surpass the considerable wealth enjoyed by Karnovsky.

Nineteen

Finally, the revenge was accomplished. Alexander Karnovsky, approaching middle age, was dead of an exploded heart. The medical description is precise and not unusual. It occurs some two thousand times a year in this country, but despite its relative mundanity, it is a heart disease of such complexity and suggestiveness that I am obliged to regard its occurrence in Alexander Karnovsky as a malign fulfillment of another's will, an intended murder, conceived by another, foreseen in the clear vision whose documentation I discovered and had translated, projected with an almost demonic persuasion into the life and person of another, and brought to pass two years after the seer's own death.

I have described how the last years of Alexander Karnovsky were beset with Yevgeny Mikhailovich—more than beset, encumbered and obliterated. Every day was given over to Malenov, every free minute was spent thinking out the consequence of a loan, a bequest, a sale, an exhibition, a catalogue, an essay, a critical volume, an offering at auction, an interview, an archive, a documentary center and library. What time would there be again for Karnovsky? No time. Never again a moment of time in which the name Malenov would not insert itself through the cracks in the structure of a thought, in the interlineation of a letter, in the syntax of speech, or—as is the case with an aortic dissection—in the transmission of blood to the heart.

Karnovsky's body was found on the floor of his studio at the rear of his hotel apartment. His feet were drawn up as though trying desperately to relieve the pain that tore him in two. Most remarkable is that a half-dozen of Karnovsky's paintings, made when he had lived with Malenov in Berlin, were obliterated by broadly painted black brushstrokes, as though during the frenzy that preceded the explosion an almost hysterical anxiety had seized Karnovsky and compelled him to assert during his last hours of life that he was no painter, that he had no further wish to compete with his master, that he surrendered to him in his final agonies and elected to destroy his past as artist. Indeed, this is further confirmed by the fact that one small maquette of an unfinished sculpture had been smashed with a single blow, and pieces of wood were strewn over the floor. Karnovsky had capitulated in the hours before his death, and Malenov victorious, seated in majesty before a wall of his works in a grainy enlargement of the photograph Karnovsky had cut from the German magazine nearly twenty-five years earlier, gazed down on the destruction that he had envisaged and accomplished.

A handkerchief clutched in Karnovsky's hand suggests that he had perspired profusely before the onset of the fatal attack; moreover, the muscles of his jaw were clenched in that tightly constricted vise by which some fight against excruciating pain. All the elements foreboding such a wild and uncontrollable cataclysm as aortic dissection were present: premonitory anxiety, drenching perspiration, excruciating pain; even a drop of bile vomited during the advent of the attack stained his chin. One can only hope that Karnovsky lapsed into unconsciousness as the tumorous blood-filled swelling ripped the aortic lining, tearing it open before a geyser of blood poured through its wall, drowning him in hemorrhage.

TWENTY

The Karnovsky bequest was enormous, involving gifts and benefactions of many millions of dollars, accumulated slowly over the more than twenty years since the death of his father. Karnovsky had been totally unaware of his investments. All these had been handled by his father's former adviser, Mr. Salomo, a man well advanced in years, who turned over to Karnovsky's accountant an impeccaby honest set of books. Karnovsky' only genuine life-interest had been Malenov, whose own records and documents were neatly ordered in eight filing cabinets located in a study abutting Karnovsky's studio. There, in that small alcove, Karnovsky must have sat at his worktable and pursued the study of the Malenov Codex, developing a complex system of archival filing that cross-referenced photographs of every painting with the large folios containing preliminary sketches and drawings, and with files of letters, documents, clippings referring to the work in question. That part of Karnovsky's research was complete at his death.

Incomplete, and therefore of striking importance to this narration, was Karnovsky's biography of his friend and destroyer. The manuscript had first undertaken to describe the complex Malenovian visual vocabulary, to document the sources of his metaphor (pursuing his language through Ouspensky, Bragdon, Steiner, Mondrian, Malevich; various non-Euclidean geometricians on the one hand and mystic theoreticians of the Third Dimension on the other; the vocabulary of the new urbanist architects and Soviet aesthetic theoreticians) and to relate them to Malenov's delirium in the presence of various Russian Orthodox theologians and verbal romantics. Karnovsky had carefully tracked the working of these ideas through the six hundred paintings completed by Malenov and the more than two thousand sketches, drawings, lithographs that Malenov had employed to trace the undergament of his universe.

Of proper biography there was little or nothing. Karnovsky had explained to me that Malenov's life hardly mattered. The life of an artist was in the work, he argued. Everything else was simply the excrescent bubbling of genius, hardly of importance except as a frame in which to insert the works, to establish their temporal sequence, the birth and transformation of ideas, the dismissal and recovery of visual notions. Malenov's life would come at the end, when the work of deciphering and explicating the painting was completed.

Evidently, Karnovsky was reading through the Malenov journals on the night of his self-destruction. The three thick volumes of letters and writings that constituted the personal memorabilia of Yevgeny Mikhailovich Malenov were piled on Karnovsky's worktable in the archival alcove. He had accustomed himself to using paper clips to draw his attention to a particular page to which he intended to return. The first two volumes were bulging with paper clips, sometimes flagging little pieces of paper on which Karnovsky had noted a remark or internal reference. In the third volume, however, paper clips were evident only throughout three-quarters of the sheaf of papers that made up the album of Malenov's final years. Moreover, at a certain point, the point in question, Karnovsky had affixed a paper clip, although the sheet on which Malenov's handwritten Russian entry appeared had adhered to the next page and two pages beyond. Only by steaming the sheets was I able to cause Karnovsky's profuse perspiration to be condensed; the pages were then freed and swabbed dry with cotton-tipped sticks. Clearly, as I reconstruct it, Karnovsky must have come, at approximately ten o'clock of the evening in question, upon Malenov's remarkable journal entry and affixed the paper clip, as would be automatic in the case of a Russian entry that required careful scrutiny and translation. His eyes dropped down the page, he turned it, and then, as he suddenly perspired, droplets of sweat fell on the pages, dried, and sealed them together. These were surely the last pages written by Yevgeny Mikhailovich Malenov about Joseph Alexander Karnovsky. They were, moreover, the last pages read by Alexander Karnovsky before the beginning of the attack that murdered him within two hours, thundering pain obliterating consciousness while the lining of his heart was breached by a tidal eruption of blood.

> Alexander Karnovsky.
> In all my life of second sight, I have never seen into the future. Everything that has come to pass in my visions occurred at the same moment as my seeing. I saw but I changed nothing, made nothing come to pass by having seen it. My sights were innocent. But I know from all that has happened during the recent years that this time it is different. As you have demanded of me that I pay up to you, returning in kind for the money you advanced, I determined to leave you everything after my death.
> My death is coming inexorably, sooner rather than later, I have no doubt. My obstinacy will make it certain when the right time comes to pass, but your death is no certainty, your punishment no inevitability. Until this moment! Now, I see it clearly. To destroy you, I give you what you desire—everything I have made, everything on which I have put my signature. It is what you want, but it will kill you. You will never make again a work of your own. All your own ambition will be silenced, and you will work only for me when I am gone. You think the Malenov inheritance will make you rich, famous, celebrated. It will do that most assuredly, but it will also destroy you as I know and have decided.

TWENTY-ONE

It is not my way to succumb to tales of demonic prediction and vengeance beyond the grave. We are modern men, without superstition,

after all. But this tale is so remarkable, its slow accumulation of understanding and anger so unparalleled, that one gives up rational renditions
of the real (which supply us at best with what reason governs) and enter-
tains, even with dismay, alternatives that can encompass more, enabling
such mysterious aptitudes as "second sight" and predictive visions to be
accredited, if only because what they envisage was accomplished. But,
having said this, there is a larger reading that I cannot fail to note. I have
survived some three decades beyond these events. I undertook to edit
and publish the manuscripts of Karnovsky about Malenov. Malenov's
undistributed work was passed by Karnovsky to me. I was named the
ultimate heir and owner of the Malenov oeuvre. Karnovsky bestowed on
me—along with a generous financial settlement—the labor that he did
not complete. It nearly destroyed me, as well. But I resisted; moreover, I
had never been a source of anger to either Malenov or Karnovsky, and
so, when I completed the editing and publication of Karnovsky's study, I
established a foundation and consigned all of Malenov's unsold work to
its impartial determination. I freed myself of Malenov and Karnovsky,
and I have continued to live my solitary and not unpleasant life to its
own gathering confusion.

I have told a sad story, a story of incommunication and loneliness,
in which two artists—the older master and the younger aspirant—
instead of learning how to speak the volumes they formed in paint and
wood, broke away from each other, shut themselves off in misunderstanding, frustration, jealousy, and anger, and, instead of learning how
they might love each other more wisely, devoted their misunderstanding
to projects of revenge and punishment. The truth is that both artists were
nearly pure, but they lived at the beginning of that vulgar time when
art is no longer understood apart from celebrity and money. Their own
proximity to that time of desperate confusion contributed more than
anything else to the destructiveness that was unleashed.

VI.

THE JEWISH IMAGINATION

Introduction

David Stern

One of Arthur Cohen's earliest projects, begun when he was a graduate student at the Jewish Theological Seminary, was to write a commentary on the Book of Exodus. Although Cohen never completed the project, he published one section of the commentary in an essay ("On Scriptural Exegesis," *CrossCurrents* 5 [1955]), in which he explained his hermeneutical principles. The Bible, he wrote,

> can be met with theology and philosophy, in the same way as the Masters of the Midrash met the Bible with ingenious question and speculative response. The dialogue is unbroken so long as the enduring partners to dialogue do not weary of the task. It is my belief that, more than mere biblical criticism, we must reconstruct our contemporaneity to Scripture. . . . The Bible is open to receive; for behind it, within it, God is speaking out to us, waiting, all too patiently, to receive us.

Reflecting Buber's teaching of dialogue, this passage espouses a stance that consistently characterized Cohen's attitude not only toward the Bible but to all Jewish literary tradition. That attitude was authentically dialogical, that is, truly committed to an exchange between the intellect and the imagination and to preserving the integrity of both partners in the exchange—the tradition and its modern recipient—without

407

compromising their individual characters. The danger of such dialogue, as Cohen knew well, was that, in making the Bible or Jewish tradition one's own, it is possible for the objective reality of the Bible and of the tradition to dissolve, as it were, in one's own subjective appropriation.

The first two essays in this section, "Jephta's Vow" and "Job and the Modern Imagination," both confront this problem: How to make the Bible into our own possession without turning it into a mere reflection of our poor selves? The solution Cohen proposed was not to ask what the Bible means to us, but rather, what we—particularly those who "are no longer sufficiently believing"—can mean to the Bible. Not incidentally, Cohen chose to ask this question of two especially problematic biblical narratives, and particularly to those readers who have lived through the horror of the Holocaust.

The same refusal to make an easy identification between his literary projects and those of the tradition characterized Cohen's own evaluation of the "traditional," "Jewish," dimensions of his writings. The final four selections in this section all address the question of the "Jewishness" of his fiction. The first three essays were originally talks or occasional notes Cohen delivered and wrote after the publication of his various novels. In defining the Jewishness of his works, Cohen did not doubt the fact that they were "Jewish"; rather, the question was, In what does their Jewishness consist? Cohen had no illusions about the untraditional nature of his novels. All contemporary Jewish fiction, he wrote, was at best "the prospect of aggadah." This was so because it was at best the recognizable formulaic medium—the traditional language, imagery, and thematic vocabulary—that had once made *aggadah* accessible to all Jews. The task of modern Jewish writers was now to reproduce a tradition of their own, with its own formulae. One instance of such a tradition lay, Cohen believed, in what he called the messianic epic, and it was this tradition to which, he also believed, *In the Days of Simon Stern* belonged.

The final essay, originally a lecture Cohen delivered at an international conference on Jewish writing since World War II held at the Rockefeller Foundation's Bellagio Conference Center, is more continental than Anglo-American in style and preoccupation. Organized in numbered theses, which range in form from epigrammatic meditations to traditional-like stories, the essay is in fact a series of juxtaposed reflections rather than a single, sustained argument. Indeed, as Cohen says in its final passage, the lecture is a series of sample-entries from his notebooks. In the same passage, though, Cohen also describes the entries as "in substance . . . all textual commentary," that is, quotations, allusions, interpretations, and reworkings of earlier texts. By characterizing the essay as a type of commentary, Cohen was doubtless trying to locate his own writing in another historically Jewish tradition. Cohen clearly had in mind Midrash, the exemplary form of commentary in classical Judaism, but he was probably also thinking of Gershom Scholem's observations (in his famous essay on revelation and tradition) on the centrality of citations in Jewish exegesis, and of Scholem's close friend, Walter Benjamin, whose greatest ambition (it is said) was to compose a work consisting entirely of quotations. In either case, Cohen's attempt to define his writing as commentary recalls his youthful ambition to write a biblical commentary. The difference between a traditional commentary of the sort he then sought to compose and the writings he actually produced are one sign of the distance that Cohen's own imagination as Jew traveled in the course of his life.

JEPTHAH's VOW

The last oratorio completed by George Frederic Handel toward the close of his life was based upon the biblical narrative of the career and passion of Jepthah the Judge. Although Handel is sensitive to the pride and fall of Jepthah, his tenderness is really extended to the faithful piety of his daughter, who was to suffer the consequence of Jepthah's outrageous vow. The aria which follows her immolation, "Waft her, angels"— supplicatory and confident though it is—is already a sentimentalization of the biblical narrative, for if there be biblical tragedy, the hero is not the daughter who bewails her virginity and offers herself up to the knife, but the folly and hubris of Jepthah, who bound himself in pride and was destroyed by it.

The narrative of Jepthah (Judg. 11–12:7), despite the insistence of many biblical scholars that it is derived from two independent sources, possesses an uncommon dramatic unity. Whether Jepthah's heroic accomplishments as Judge are recounted in order that the story of the sacrifice of his only daughter be unfolded or whether the narrative of his earlier career is recalled in order to supply the raison d'être for this fateful vow, clearly the tragedy of Jepthah is the heart of the narration. This is, as well, the way the rabbinic sources regard it. Considering Jepthah's

Published posthumously in *Conjunctions* 19 (1992): 313–15. Estate of Arthur A. Cohen.

career as Judge of Israel for six years (Judg. 12:7) to be of little consequence, the rabbis emphasize wherever his name is mentioned the stupidity, vanity, and ignorance of the Law which led him to his ridiculous vow and its execution. For the rabbis, Jepthah is an example of one who made an imprudent vow, moreover a vow which could easily have been absolved had the High Priest Pinehas not been so proud as to disdain Jepthah and Jepthah so vain as to be indifferent to the High Priest's counsel. For the rabbis, Jepthah is but the occasion for the homiletic exposition of a culpable and foolish leader.

It was the music of Handel which first directed me to the narrative of the Bible many years ago. Those early university years, when first I became a student of Aristotle's *Poetics* (a text I was to be obliged to read more than a score of times, accompanied as was often appropriate by the Orestes or Oedipus cycle) seemed extraordinarily relevant to the career of Jepthah. Jepthah seems a tragic hero, for he was, as Aristotle designates, a man of power and authority, more grand than those who would behold him, but no less vulnerable to those torrential claims of glory which annoy the gods and encourage them to chastise. Jepthah, like Oedipus, makes a vow, and his vow, flung before his multitudes, no doubt in the enthusiastic hours before he joined battle against the Ammonites, was that if God would deliver the Ammonites into his hands, "then it shall be that whatsoever cometh forth of the doors of my house to meet me, when I return in piece . . . it shall be the Lord's, and I will offer it up for a burnt-offering." Jepthah triumphs, the Ammonites are subdued, and he returns to his home in Mispeh and there comes forth from his house to greet him, "with timbrels and dances," his daughter, and the text adds with an extraordinary compassion and simplicity, "and she was his only child; beside her he had neither son nor daughter." Presumably Jepthah repented his vow, but it is his daughter who holds him to its letter, saying, "My father, thou hast opened thy mouth unto the Lord; do unto me according to that which hath preceded out of thy mouth." Having confirmed Jepthah in his resolve, she then pleads that he permit her a respite of two months that she might go into the mountain with her companions and "bewail her virginity." At the end of her seclusion the Bible speaks succinctly: "she returned unto her father who did with her according to his vow; and she had not known man."

It is simple and yet its naked simplicity is horrendous. Baruch Kurzweil, the eminent Israeli literary critic, in an essay on "Job and the Possibility of Biblical Tragedy" (*Iyyun* 12, no. 3–4 [October 1961]), does not speak of the story of Jepthah, although he considers the tragic possibilities offered by the stories of Cain, Abraham, Saul, Moses, Job. Kurzweil argues that the Bible, leaving no room for the possibility of an existence without redemption, does not offer the option of tragedy. Presumably tragedy is to be defined as fall without salvation. And there is surely truth in this, for the audience that reads Scripture (*not* the audience that views Dino de Laurentis and John Huston) in an attitude of belief *knows* that what was told there is part of the history of salvation, that even the irrational episode, the non sequitur, the unresolved ambiguity is part of an ongoing divine-human process, to be resolved, to be consummated. There is only tragedy for Kurzweil when the audience is moved to "pity and fear" by the similitude between their condition and the afflicted nobility before them. Tragedy is didactic, not redemptive.

Kurzweil's view of tragedy, of course, assumes that the Bible is all of a piece. Though not wishing to raise here the controversies that exacerbate biblicists, there is little doubt that the Bible is a complex document. Whether of a single hand or fashioned by many, it reflects the pagan underground of ancient Palestine as surely as it bequeaths the foundation of Jewish existence and salvation. I cannot help but regard the story of Jepthah's vow as testimony to that pagan substratum. God is present, but it is the God of *dike,* of a supervenient justice. God is offended and God punishes. It would have been sufficient had Jepthah been courageous, fought valiantly, judged excellence, for God would have delivered the Ammonites to him. But Jepthah exceeds the measured line which is border between the competence of man and the suzerainty of God and God smites him. He vows, and the logic of the vow, its inexorability, is carried to its conclusion. God retires and allows the working of Jepthah's price and Jepthah's self-arrogation to bring about his downfall. According to some sources, Jepthah dies an unnatural death: fragments of his flesh fell from his body at intervals and were buried where they fell, so that his body was distributed throughout the land. In *The Legend of the Jews* Louis Ginsberg says Jepthah was dismembered (Vol. 4: 46).

The grandeur and horror of the story of Jepthah's vow is precisely its tragic persuasiveness, for in this narrative a portion of a universe already sacralized breaks away and floats free from "sacred history." Or perhaps it is but a warning that God is sometimes stoney-faced, flinty, contemptuous of our condition.

I confess that I am comforted by the knowledge that there is this story in the Bible, that the story is told and never recalled again throughout Scripture, that the rabbis really ignore it, but that it is there— complete and unvarnished—a biblical story no different than a sequence of stories than run through the literature of the West. Think only of Piave's libretto for Verdi's *Ernani* (based on a play by Victor Hugo) and one can see the bathos to which vain vows can be brought. The prototype to all these is Jepthah's tragic vow.

JOB AND THE MODERN IMAGINATION

The enigmatic Borgés observes that the literary imagination creates its own past, invents its own history, and populates it with heroes and demons of its own devising. There is no longer an objective correlative to the imagination—or, put otherwise, the urgency of the modern imagination enforces upon its own subjectivity the properties of objective reality—substance, density, complexity. As it appropriates this and that, taking over from storybooks and chronicles, testaments and accounts the figures of fiction and history, it loses track of the definite lineaments and contours of the real and the fantasied. What is left often, as in a story of Borgés, or a calligram of Apollinaire, a collage box of Joseph Cornell, or a "ready-made" of Marcel Duchamp, is something which is no longer clearly what it appears—its "whatness" is no longer unambiguously art, its "thatness" is too palpable, its "isness" is so particular, so concrete as to be both terribly real and frighteningly transcendent. More and more we are obliged to make ourselves up as we go along. What seemed fixed—a given of our culture or an inheritance from our history—is rendered precarious by the necessity we experience of being always in motion, of being always open, pliable, responsive to the constantly sifting conditions of life.

Reprinted from *Congress Bi-Weekly* 36, no. 7 (May 12, 1969): 21–22. Copyright © 1969 American Jewish Congress.

As new Heracliteans, how can we regard such permanent achievements of the imagination as Odysseus, as the Preacher, or now, as Job?
Who are they—these epic wanderers, these sophisticated preachers,
these folk heroes? We make them into ourselves, we conspect them to
our own focus and narrow them to our own ground lens. They become
ours and they are lost to us, for what we end by seeing is not they, but
ourselves. And so we must ask of Job, who are we to him, what is it in
us that is accessible to him, and only thus do we make Job ours.

Job comes before us, as do all the shades and familiars of literature,
a survivor of centuries of exegesis and interpretation. When all is done
and considered, all the judgments and verdicts before us—as they are in
Nahum N. Glatzer's enormously subtle and judicious Reader[1]—we are
compelled to return to the text itself. Obviously we do not delude ourselves that rereading Job will enable us to see clearly what the writers
and interpreters miss. We miss as much as they, but we miss something
different, and something unique we catch. We miss the dark spots of our
own perception and we respond to the enthusiasms and exaltations
which are peculiarly ours.

Already in what has preceded I have indicated my stand in reading
Job. I can acknowledge the cogency and relevance of regarding Job as a
masterpiece of nature poetry (Robert Lowth, J. G. Herder), and I can
appreciate how the Jewish critics from the Middle Ages to our day (those
discussed by Glatzer in his precise, felicitous, and comprehensive essay
and those anthologized) have seen Job as a prism of the Jewish historical
experience and more as a homily on spiritual virtues, or how Christians
from the Greek and Latin fathers to Paul Claudel and Jean Danielou
consider Job "a holy pagan" (since it should be recalled Job was not a
Jew, but a pious Gentile of Idumea) who anticipates in his life and faith
the trials of Jesus; and I can bear the philosophic compassion of Josiah
Royce, the neat categorizing of Paul Weiss, the moving interpretation of
Job's theodicy offered by Emil G. Kraeling, the ever pompous Hegel, the
ever passionate Kierkegaard, the slightly fatuous G. K. Chesterton, the
outraged directness of Hayim Greenberg—all these in the two centuries
of modern times from which Glatzer selects the thirty-two writers anthologized. But I can become one with Job only if I can identify in myself,
however dim and imprecise, the correlation of the same disaster, trial,
combative speculation, and justification. Have I seven sons and three
daughters, or myriads of sheep, goats, and camels, or is my wealth and
power in the world like his, or would God think to report my presence
to Satan at an assembly of "the sons of God"? Surely not. I would lose

nothing like Job lost nor would my struggle or my faith be his. No correlation, no connection. If that were all.

Baruch Kurzweil, in an essay on Job (not included in this Reader), considers the question of biblical tragedy and concludes there is none. Although Kurzweil's essay is highly suggestive and profound, the error he makes is central to his thesis. Of course there is no biblical tragedy if the model of tragedy is Greek. In a universe populated by deities and moral perfections, the man obedient to excellences of intelligence and character must be humbled, for nature, family, or fortuity will periodically smash him. Oedipus, exposed to death as an infant, raised unknowing of his royal ancestry, returning to Corinth, resolving the riddle, must surely—given all this accident and ancestry—be trapped by the Fates. And so with others of the tragedies—setting themselves before the metaphysical limits will always aggravate the measure of the universe. Chutzpa is never amusing to the Greek. No wonder that Aristotle could extrude a didactic poetics from the materials of the dramatists.

But for the Hebrew the medium was not poetry, nor its lessons prudent. What the Greeks regarded as less reliable than poetry, the Hebrews digested as their staple. History was the record of inconstancy for the Greek and of meaningful action for the Hebrew. The individual could learn less from history than from drama, thought the Greek, since history dealt with unmanageable collectivities and ungovernable chance. But for the Hebrew, given the assumption of the historical, the personages of the myth became real—God was unique and absolute, man was always imperfect, finite, and compounded of good and evil. History, not drama, was morality; God, not gods; collectivities before individuals; actions, not speculation. Before God, all men fail. And without valid conflict, without the dramatic counterpoint of fallible man and obdurate universe there can be no pity and fear, no mimesis of excellence, no instruction from hubris. In a universe governed by God—even an incommensurable God, whose goodness is asseverated without proof—man cannot be tragic. He is always justified because he believes.

So Job appears to believing Jews. None fear Job or his condition if they are prepared, as, let us say, Rav Kook was prepared in the last months of his struggle with cancer, to affirm that even suffering was a joyful gift. Our own appearance to Job is different. We are no longer sufficiently believing. Too much has happened which we cannot compass, which we cannot fit even into Job's primordial assumption of a just and good God. To us, ab initio, the universe appears ambiguous, its creator ambivalent, His works both grand and deformed. It is a tragic universe: life is not only immediately questioned, but seems ultimately without justification.

The blasphemy which Job's wife counsels him to speak is not unappealing to us. It is righteous and angry. It knows that all this torment comes from He who is and nonetheless pronounces creation to be good. How come from Him such misery? Job incants a poetry of rage, loathing, contempt; he abjures the created, denies the felicity of things upon the earth, abhors the day of his birth, and pleads for death; he forswears the utility of knowledge and despises the moralities of the sanguine and the unblighted. What Job does until the very end when God affirms Himself once more is describe the tragedy of virtual unbelief, of an "as if" metaphysic in which all that had befallen him could not be if God were whom he believed Him all his life to be. God is as if not-God to Job. And then Job hears what his eye could not see. The riddle is not resolved, but God is once more in the whirlwind. Tragedy is dissolved and the restoration is brought to pass—the children, the cattle, the power. Job is returned to the world.

To us moderns, there is a more unsettling condition. Ours is not a setup, not a folktale, nor is our poetics of anger as magnificent or extravagant. It seems to us that all things Job says are to the point—his moralistic friends sound like second-rate preachers and teachers, and Elihu, a cold-blooded theologian. But after the rage is spent and Job recants before the voice, *our* rage begins. It seemed right then, at that time, for the silent God, the *deus absconditus* in the lifetime of the tormented Job to reveal Himself and justify impenitent Job. But we, millenia later, wearied by the attrition of single boils of unreason, confusion, and pain, to us no voice has come. To us only Eliphazes, Bildads, Zophars, Elihus speak—and no other voice.

The wonder of Job—the wonder so completely transmitted by this excellent Reader—is that of a double mystery. There is first the mystery of Job himself—self-contentment exploded into rage beyond the whine and whimper and banked by the reassertion of the ultimately Other, the God who gives no answer but Himself. That's the objective mystery of knowledge. The second mystery, more devious, is that this text, perhaps like Lucretius's *On the Nature of Things,* leaves us where we were, situated in our unbelief, but made serene by the certainty that for him, for them, for others, there is a satiation in the sheer enormity and grandeur of what remains unknown and silent.

NOTE

1. *The Dimensions of Job: A Study and Selected Readings.* Presented by Nahum N. Glatzer. Schocken Books. $7.95

Ferreting the Word

It is good to have one's work honored. But it is not decisive. Neither does it record the juncture or the separation between the writer and the world. The distances remain—the abyss which lies between the vision and the reality. Why the artist makes is a mystery. The artist hears the applause, receives the gifts of the world, smiling, accepts the honors and testimonials, and when all is done and the festivities completed, what is left to the artist is to go back to work. This is only to say what I have always believed: human culture finally does not care about the artist, but only about the work. When the world concerns itself more with the *persona* of the artist than with his work, it is a patent that the work has been misunderstood, that not the pain and promise of the work, but the drama of its maker has seduced his public. I am pleased then that you have seen fit to honor *In the Days of Simon Stern* and by implication to celebrate briefly its creator, but both Simon Stern and its author are already at work elsewhere.

The conclusion of *In the Days of Simon Stern* has been baffling to many readers. The compound of The Society for the Rescue and Resurrection of the Jews is burned out; the replication of the Second Temple is consumed in flames; the evil malefactor, Janos Baltar, has died in the flames; and Simon Stern has set forth into the world. Many readers have commented to me that they found this ending to be inconclusive, a predicament. It is as though having created the sense of the messianic vocation it is dissolved. I sympathize with my reader, but I must enter a strenuous demurral. The ending is precisely the point of my opening remarks.

In the tradition of the Jews a critical distinction exists between the work of redemption and the redemption itself, between the course of created time and space—history it is called—and the end of days, the *Aharit Ha-Yamin,* when consummated history and transfigured time and space shall be seen. I have no idea what the end of days looks like. I have not been there nor has knowledge of it been given me in more than the imagination, but I do know for certain that whatever is completed there—on the other side of history—is begun here, on this side of life. The redemption of history—that is, the disclosure of its inner life, the reading out of its meaning, the explicit articulation of its interior logic is a work left to the great synthesis of the end, but long before that in the cracks and fissures of time, human beings gather the energy and stand fast before it.

History is in my view a series of partial avowals and partial refusals of redemption. It is, according to the bare eyes of nature, meaningless, a repetition of cycles and patterns known since the archaic beginnings of man. "There is nothing new under the sun," the wise pessimist of Scripture reports, but the refusal of the preacher of Ecclesiastes to observe novelty in experience is the limit of his art and of his vision. From one point of view he was right. He cautioned men in an apocalyptic age from expecting the apocalypse. He warned culture that it had better be patient and courageous, for he observed no signs, no gathering speed, no vivid ellipses in the course of human society which boded that ultimate innovation which could be called redemption. Correct. But what the preacher had no wish to see—stoic Jew that he was—was that every human event has two sides, the side turned toward the quotidian and familiar, the regular and the ordained, and the side which is turned toward freedom and invention. Every moment, every event in our world, every person and every work has within it a logic of ordinance and the possibility of an explosive novelty. This is so because man is in my definition the creature of possibility. Not, mind you, the possibility of this or that, doing or making, but simply "possibility." Man *is* possibility and that is his freedom. He can rise out of the mud of his origins or he can founder and retreat into the mire. History—the scene of his unfolding toward the world—is thus rich with human possibility and every moment past and to come is rich in possibility. When possibility is tempted authentically by the future, it is an enactment which figurates redemption. When it is turned toward the past, holding it as a sanctum, a guard, a protection against the future, redemption slips further away and the idol replaces the living God of possibility.

If then I understand the decision of Simon Stern to go forth into the world, to go uptown, to discover that the beliefs of the nations are various, to insinuate himself into the world, to insert himself into the cracks in people's lives which they open unwittingly to redemption, he is continuing, in hope, to be a messianic bearer, a portent of tidings of joy. Obviously Simon Stern is not the Messiah. If I had thought of him as the true Messiah and wrote of him as fiction it would be tantamount to admitting that I did not believe in the Messiah nor hold out hope for his advent. It is precisely because Simon Stern is fictional, but real, a messianic messenger upon whom men can rely, but a partial disclosure, that I can believe in him as possibility. What I wished to show is that Simon Stern can persuade some people—Nathan Gaza, Fisher Klay, even Janos Baltar—that he is a collector of redeeming sparks, that he is an exponent of the complexity of the heavens and the earth, that he is a redeemer of them, that is to say, that he enables them to open their possibility to the world, some to create, others to destroy. That is enough for fiction. Secretly I have thought, long after *In the Days of Simon Stern* was published, that it would be marvelous if, having created him in fiction, I had also created a real, living person, that one day he would greet me and observe that unlike the Golem of Rabbi Löwe of Prague, I had created a person who had actually acquired life from me.

Now that is the paradox of art, the reason why art is both the attraction and the despair of Jews, why writers and painters are both admired and loathed by Judaism. You see, the artist cannot help but behave immodestly. Henry Matisse was once asked whether he believed in God and he replied, "Only when I paint." I understand that, but writing is the art of the Jews—less visual people than many. Jews believe in God when they speak, when they make singing words. Jews gave the world the idea that by words were the heavens and the earth created. Ever after the delicious sin of Jews has been to make heavens and earth with words, to ferret the word, to dig and excavate for words, to scan the heavens for words, to throw up the letters of the alphabet to create incantatory words, to make golems and saints from words, and even by the right words to bring to us and to men the true Messiah.

Aggadah and the Fictional Imagination

This brief note was written only the day before the ordinary year renews itself. My recent novel, *A Hero in His Time,* was about to be published, the date of its appearance falling on the Feast of the Epiphany, which, despite its Christian origins, pleases me. If creation is an act which occurs in the twinkling of an eye while holy scripture stretches the twinkling to six days and tradition obligates the rendition of that drama each week, is it not appropriate for a new novel written by a lapsed theologian to be published on a day which celebrates someone's epiphany, anyone's epiphany, even an epiphany mistakenly ascribed to a divine tic?

There is more than a little curiosity about the rites of passage which I have elaborated over the past decade, from the writing of books regarding Jewish religious thought to the writing of short stories and novels. Many times I wonder about the significance of the passage, its intent and its purpose. I quickly eliminate questions of fame and fortune, since neither have significantly altered nor been enlarged. The people, by and large, who have read my theological writing don't bother with fiction and fiction readers are so various that as many miss the point of a particular story as get it. Indeed their predicament is no different than mine. As a reader I often change my mind about the point of a particular passage in my writing. Nothing is univocal.

Reprinted from *Sh'ma* 6, no. 106 (January 23, 1976): 45–46.

I seem to be putting the emphasis on getting the point of fiction. Such considerations are secondary. Fiction is not simply a covert way of smuggling moral truths to the reader in the guise of story. Story is not guise, with all the implication of sleight of hand, nor is it disguise, with all the shadowing of paint and artifice that masquerade entails. Story is everything to me. Characters like Simon Stern or Baltar in *In the Days of Simon Stern* or Yuri Maximovich Isakovsky or Yasha Isaievich Tyutychev in *A Hero in His Time* succeed or fail as characters *only,* but they are not conduits of my voice, mouthpieces of unearthly messages and truths that one expects to hear through the lips of Japanese mediums conducting the lessons of the spirit world. In other words, wherever my fiction fails—when set alongside the cultural masters who are esteemed and regarded as the ideal practitioners (I acknowledge only a few of these— Saul Bellow, Walker Percy, I. B. Singer—and not even these without reservations)—it is a failure of persuasion, and the charge of such failure I find unacceptable. My competition is against myself, making it harder and harder to squeak through with a rough edge or a sloppy transition. In other words, I can look upon *In The Days of Simon Stern* and *A Hero in His Time* and a new novel, now in progress and too dangerously fetal to be disturbed by description, as gambles against myself, against the vision which underlies the fiction and such books as *The Natural and the Supernatural Jew.*

I underlie both bodies of work. I hold them together in some delicate suspension, not quite like the random suspension of particles in a magnetic field, for as a human magnet I have both will and intelligence and can determine more efficiently what rises to the surface and what is suppressed.

Fiction, I have come to think, is the prospect of *aggadah.* The *aggadah,* not simply tale or story, has a structural anatomy, as well defined by evolution as by entelechy. *Aggadah* is story with a purpose. It is always epiphanic, constellating an attitude which reflects the received tradition of thought and behavior and profiles the future. The technique of Jewish storytelling from Rabbinic to Hasidic times maintains specific metaphoric continuities which are unconsciously formal—the language of mansions, of father and sons, of king and servants. These social modalities enable the vertical relation of God and man to be dramatically enfleshed. No less the language of *aggadah,* employing the virtues of the masters of Torah to exemplify the conduct befitting the ordinary in Israel. The *aggadah* is a pithy, allusive literature; immensely concrete precisely because the symbolic language is familiar and available to all; in most cases the referent—the *nimshal*—requires no explication since the meaning is given as part of the method of telling. In this sense, the *aggadah* is formulaic (as Alfred Lord has shown, in his *The Singer of Tales,* the Homeric epics to have been), relying upon a cultural ambience and transmission to establish the assumptions and the implications of the tale, to fill in the lacunae of allusion and description which the novelist considers characterization and coloring. The *aggadah,* for want of a more elaborate documentation, is a formulaic fiction—the formula makes possible instantaneity of communication; the fiction, lodged in the imagination, is the core of its freshness and spontaneity.

The contemporary novelist, the Jewish in the novelist who is a Jew, is not availed by the formulaic tradition, as such. Perhaps only Agnon was helped by the gnarled roots he had sunk deeply into classic and traditional Judaism. The novelists, however, who work through Jews and Jewish experience in a language other than Hebrew are differently situated. The Israelis, even where secular, hear the overtones of Hebrew and, well educated, know the implication of its shadow and twilight coloration. They are able to trade in the associations of the language even though its substantive content may be closed to them because of the absence of personal belief. Certainly this is the case with Yoram Kaniuk, Amos Oz, and others who, not explicitly religious, are nevertheless saturated by the claims of an unconscious vocabulary which depends upon the neologism and invention of Hebrew from Mishnaic times through the Middle Ages. They are, like my Russian-Jewish poet, Yuri Maximovich Isakovsky (the heroes of *A Hero in His Time*), both trapped and liberated by fidelity to the word and the language of its articulation. A Hebrew novelist is better off as a Jew than a poet who is a Jew speaking in Russian. In neither case, however, does the Jewish Jew ipso facto speak for the urgencies of the spirit which come from God. The differences obtain nonetheless between the imagination infested by God and the imagination as play with the cultural diaspora.

The religious imagination which created the *aggadah* helps the creator of fiction only in those situations where the magnitude of the novelist's ambition runs parallel to the magnitude of the *aggadah.* I make no claim of timelessness for *In The Days of Simon Stern.* Those judgments are determined elsewise and elsewhere. What I do know is that at many critical junctions in that novel the writing ignited when either I was stunned by a memory (an *aggadah* quoted in Neusner's *Johanan ben Zakkai; aggadot* relating to the Messiah; recollections of *halachot* dealing with *soferim*) and began to transcribe for full orchestra what the *aggadah* had scored for the small voice; or when confronted by an objective requirement of plot and narration I invented within a classic model—devising the Parable of the Rose and its variant exegeses or elaborating the Purim *walpurgisnacht*. In other words I worked forward and backward, from the imagination sunk in culture to the imagination forging new beginnings beyond the determinations of culture. What aided me of course was that the theme of the book was so immense, so inexhaustible. The book sprawled, perhaps even fell flat on its face a number of times, precisely because its theme was so immense. God willing, I will write *In the Days of Simon Stern* over and over again and others will join me to write their own messianic epic. It is a story worth inventing and reinventing again and again.

In time, of course, if what I have described does occur and a messianic literature develops, or a literature of heroism and example, that literature, created out of the fictional drive to imagine a new time and eternity, will supply the language of our own formulaic tradition. When the formulaic tradition of modernity is born the time will have come to destroy it and start again. That process may take two thousand years more. But then again, in that time, the true Messiah may have come to save us from the pain of new imaginings.

Our Narrative Condition

The search to locate and identify the Jewish ingredient in the literary work is not as easy as some might think. It isn't a question of making Jewish matters positive, attractive, affirmative. All of these may in fact be the result of telling the truth, but they are not necessarily advantages accruing to telling the truth. It may well be the case that for the writer telling the truth about Jews and Judaism is for the reader telling lies about them. It may even occur that telling the truth may offend not only some, but most, Jews. When this happens what must be appraised—and it is most difficult to pin down—is the oral intention of the writer. Otherwise put, does the writer wish to tell truth or does he wish to harm? If the former, even a work critical of Jewish life and institutions may be a positive and instructive work; while if the latter, no amount of positive benefit that might result could justify the enterprise. It's a dangerous business telling the truth about a vulnerable people and an unknown religion. Inevitably as Jews we make a special appeal to consideration and care. It doesn't help our critical judgment, but it does serve to contain our anxiety threshold.

It is not sheer obtuseness therefore to confess confusion and ignorance when confronted by the task of describing what constitutes the

Present Tense (summer 1980): 58–60.

Jewish element in the literary imagination. I can make up something, but I would be hard pressed to demonstrate it. It may well be to our bizarre vanity as Jews that we can account ourselves more sensitive to this or that inequity of the world, to this or that injustice, but even here—assured as such self-contention might have been a decade ago, we find even here that *our* interests are another man's injustice, but having no choice in a beleaguered world we stand our ground, roused to defend our turf with all the animal instinct and animal faith that the world has always allowed itself but denied to us. As Jews, we were expected to behave better, more wisely, more forbearingly than all others, because we were Jews and without power to do much else. Mixed fate, mixed blessing, tragicomedy that we have had to come through the world's cauldron to a power of our own which must assert its own interests before the world, our jaw jutting out against the jaws of others, our justice against another's justice. And all the relativity of interest and special need now denies to us the vanity of affirming some natural transcendence of world contentions and pressures.

And so our literature, the proliferation of our literature amid the rivings of an unsettled world that no longer imputes to us transcendence nor requires it of us as our passport to survival. In olden days—that is before the past war and its Holocaust—Jewish literature was, forgive me, a puny thing. It was a literature of the folk, a folk literature that was authentic only in its jargon, in its Yiddish, in its Ladino, in its prenational Hebrew—a literature that set forth mythic configurations of Jewish existence amidst the nations. The other literature about Jews, written by Jews or others about Jews in the languages of the nations, were essentially without mythic configuration, except let us say as George Eliot conjured her Jews in *Daniel Deronda* or Dostoevsky imagined their accursedness in *The House of the Dead* or Fitzgerald or Hemingway of Wolfe despised Jews, or Jewish literary pedagogues set forth the condition of Jewish rites of passage into the American world or into French culture or into the German *volk*. The literary imagination in the secular tongues of prewar sensibility were about providing Jews with the encouraging means of coming to terms, of finding the niche, of breaking out of mythic bondages into "goydom." But all this has changed, for non-Jews as well as for Jews.

I believe that holocaust drew that demarcation factually long before the Holocaust came forth to abrade public consciousness. Writers pick up the nervousness of culture much earlier than most people. That's their humane job. It may well have been the case that when Saul Bellow's *Victim* and *Dangling Man* were published little was known about the Holocaust then in progress and just concluded, but it was surmised and known. It was known as suggestion, as premonition, as the promise of that old culture of hysterical nationalism, and Jew sensibility responded to it by being on edge. No longer mythic configurations nor solidifications of the promise of transcendence: Jews were no longer evidenced in fiction by the Passover seder obligatory in the Anglo-Jewish novels of the thirties. Nor, for that matter, were Jews depicted as the craven victims or the unscrupulous advocates of an aggressive and demeaning capitalism as was commonplace in the proletarian literature of the same era.

In the post-Holocaust world that we have come to know, there has occurred not only the legitimation of our historical presence as the surviving remnant but the authentication of historical energy as a political power. Despite our historical speckness, our miteness rather than our might, the Jews are assuredly a visible mote in the eye of the nations that cannot be obliterated (for we survived) nor ignored (for we continue to be productive as a self-acknowledging people). We no longer transcend as a vapor, as an ether, or as a wind, but we articulated in all our multifariousness. It is in this sense that we produce not a literature, but literatures, not a single point of view but many views, not a coherent doctrine but a congerie of doctrines. There is Judaism, but not a Judaic literature, precisely because the focus of the Jewish spirit is no longer held in place by the specific gravity of something which, in the past, would have been called Judaism in diasporaor the Jewish enclave amid the nations. That, too, seems to have changed with the Holocaust and the creation of Israel.

The *paytannium* of northern Europe during the Crusades were different in emphasis and vector than the passionate religious lyricism of Jehuda Halevior Ibn Ezra, but what bound together north and south, Ashkenaz and Sefarad was an intimacy of connection to a common and shared historical predicament, that of being cast adrift amid the hostility of the world. Jews could be absolutely certain in those Middle Ages of being an authentic religion, but a despised one. Christians and Muslims were absolutely clear about being the adversaries of Judaism, Israel, and the Jewish people. But today, with so much unclarity about the religious question, with so much theological dubiety, with so much faithlessness and unbelief, the Jew before the nations is no longer a man with a despised religion as much as he is a person with a point of view as unclear and as unknown as everyone else's. The Jew is no longer the wearer of yellow stars nor streaked with yellow cowardice, but a strenuous witness to something indefinably unquenchable about the human spirit. I am not sure how to describe this theologically (that is discursively), but I can exhibit it in fiction as an insistence about going on, about perduring, about keeping up humane battle even when notions of humanity sheer off toward fanaticism among some and supine patience among others.

And so with all this and despite the necessity of making clear in works of history, philosophy, and theology the univocal—but still narrow band—voice of Jewish clarity and religious humanity, the problem of literature looms large. Thee is no cloture on the Jewish imagination or—more accurately put—upon imagining with Jewish materials. Although there are some little historians of the Jewish moment who enjoy the academic expertise of fencing the land and determining which herds shall graze in what pasture, I should think precisely the truth of the post-Holocaust consciousness is that there is no longer a properly demarcated Jewish pasture: neither diaspora energy alone as George Steiner would have it, nor the ridiculous insistence of Jacob Neusner that the Holocaust was a European experience and hence not psychologically decisive for American Jews, or the recently stated view of a young critic—who talks and tapes more readily than he sets down for probative scrutiny—that the likes of Cynthia Ozick and myself are examples of American Jews who were devastated by the Holocaust and have somehow created a false sensibility by being neither survivors nor the children of survivors.

The truth is, however, that all Jews are survivors and the children of survivors from the earliest memories of the people. The Holocaust is an immensity (a *tremendum* I call it) of our experience precisely because it shattered the humanist assumptions of liberal Judaism, the preposterous assimilationist ambition of nineteenth-century Jewry, the small ironies and petty diversions of Jewish class and elitist factionalism, indeed, any and all inherited assumptions and prejudices of traditional Jewish life. We have been forced by the Holocaust—once again—as the first people of the human race to rethink all our premises as once we thought out and affirmed them in the beginning. The flood then, fire and gas in our time: we begin again.

That is the first work of literature, the redevising of the narrative condition of the people of Israel and the Jewish people. Once we told the story one way and at the end of the narration the great redactor (he whom Franz Rosenzweig called Rabbenu) hewed and cut the narrative to the compass of a text, permitting strands of many traditions to be retained, cutting with an axe and pruning with paring knife until, for many centuries, the seams were almost invisible, perceived not as braided strands, but as contraries forcibly reconciled. Today, enlightened, we can read the ancient text with the joy of knowing the imagination of God and man in combat to press out a single text and not quite succeeding. And in our day, in the fourth decade beyond our decimation, when the braided text is seen now in all its violence and contradiction, we begin to bring forth a literature in many languages and from many sensibilities, unconstricted by learning, nor gender, nor habit of mind, nor education—some, undoubtedly many (perhaps even most) indescribably second rate (that is, impatient with the process of getting there and consequently imitative and deeply unreflective) and others first-rate, but narrowly focused, given to the depiction of a class or a social sensibility or a special experience, and yet others, very few in number (and who they are I could not say, nor is it interesting at this juncture to know) who encompass all of us by the sweep and power of an imagining that conjures for us as Jews and gives to all of us as mankind.

We are too soon to be acclaimed for having given to the world a literature, but of one thing I am certain: we have the seismic faults, the pit in the heart, the long silence before the dawn to know that we draw upon the real stuff out of which literature comes, out of which the new narrative of God's walk upon the earth and conversation with creatures is born.

Myths and Riddles: Some Observations about Literature and Theology

> Myth is an answer in which a question is comprised; riddle is a question which postulates an answer.
>
> André Jolles

1. .Theology is a public discourse with a private language. In this it resembles literature. The difference between theology and literature—one difference, at least—is that most people presume to understand literature. Few bother to understand theology or, bothering, assume that its arcanum is purposely obscure, designed by theologians to warn trespassers off their preserve.

God, the unsophisticated believer seems to insist, is the simplest of beings and therefore unequal to the complexities with which theology belabors him.

I prefer the gentle and exceedingly simple formulation of Saint Sylvester: "God is like an onion. He is very simple and he makes one cry."

Let us pursue this metaphor. I do not bother to discover who is Saint Sylvester. He sounds to me like a Judaizer. Saint Sylvester's theological formulation is, after all, so monochromatic, so concrete, so lachrymose.

The onion is all of a piece, it is generally recognized. There is nothing different at its core than what appears at its surface. Nothing new is revealed if we begin to remove its layers. Nothing at all. We weep, however, as we pare away each layer. One thing, of course, does occur. With

Prooftexts 7, no. 2 (May 1987): 107–22. Reprinted by permission of the Johns Hopkins University Press.

each layer that we remove the onion becomes smaller. Is this the same with God? Is the image precise, much less respectful?

But we must begin, I am afraid, with such matters as God and onions. We are persuaded to do so less by the accuracy of God's diminishment with each onion paring than we are by the certainty of our tears.

It comes to mind, however, that even tears are inappropriate. The Psalmist always begins with tears and follows his lamentations with an overwhelming of tears, a transfiguration of confidence and hope. We dare not, as Kierkegaard noted, despair before God.

Unfortunately this is all literary theology, a parsing of personal estates, both individual laments and individual aspirations. The conjunction of literature and theology unnerves me. I doubt the propriety of literature—its usefulness, its consequence, its capacity to shake us awake, to compel our attention—to the God who shrinks as he is pared or who makes us cry all the harder as he becomes smaller.

2. I do not understand what is Jewish literature.

I have some fairly specific notions about what is Jewish in Jewish literature, however. It is "literature" that baffles me. I do not understand literature. It tends to be used as a salute and a congratulation. Much too general, like an anthem. There is, however, something terribly concrete and particular about the Jewish. It doesn't much matter whether the Jewish is a condition, a lengthy fatality, or an incurable estate of optimism. Whatever it is, the Jewish is identifiable.

It is chicken bones in the pocket of the poor penitent on Erev Yom Kippur. So says Sholem Aleichem. For no one other than a Jew would these specifics have any meaning. Only in English would such facts require a footnote of explanation, since it is possible a Gentile might read the story and not understand. But a Jew reading such a story with such an arrangement of fact, particularly a Jew who could read such a story in Yiddish, would be obliged to wince and to laugh. Or it might well be, "One day during the time of the massacre I was sitting in a dingy room, writing. As if the Angel of Poetry had confided to me: 'The choice lies in your own hands. If your song inspires me, I will protect you with a flaming sword. If not—don't complain . . . my conscience will be clean."[1] So writes Abraham Sutzkever in his *Green Aquarium*. For no one other than a Jew would these images have any meaning. And such a Jew would be obliged to feel the pain of Sutzkever's irony.

There is no doubt that Sholem Aleichem and Abraham Sutzkever are Jews. They would not know how to write properly with the hands of Esau, holding a smooth pen, with fluent ink, preparing clean manuscripts. Jewish manuscripts, I think, are constantly subject to erasures. (Except for scribal copying, which is, after all, copying. But that's another problem to which we will return. It will be seen there that even copyists have theological problems with mistakes.)

3. The modern Hebrew term for literature is essentially an abstraction of the Hebrew for "book." It is "bookness." *Sifrut* is the quintessential book, book as essence, book even as substance without accidents. Book as actuality. *Sifrut* does not allude to literacy, which in its archaic derivations comes forth out of *litteratus*, that is, marked with letters. A coat of many letters. Literature is a constellation of lettered culture. Hebrew seems to think differently. It presumes the letters were formed before creation and that at least one book was written. *Sifrul* requires only a single *Sefer.*

"Jewish book" is the proper formulation for the Jew, not Jewish literature. Jewish literature alludes to a culture formed of letters rigorously gathered out of their natural dispersion. The Jewish book is somehow always in place.

As I have noted, it is clear to me what defines the Jewish—a resonation and sound chamber of particular experience, which employs a considerable variety of images and metaphors that signify the experience of Jews. But not only historical experience, surely. There is no historical experience of the Angel of Poetry (or the Angel of Death also alluded to) or even of Yom Kippur.

The disordering gift of the imagination may well reside in the ability to take the historical experience, bare and unwinnowed, and leaf it with the language of perpetual and renewing myth or liturgy that enables it to endure long after the specific event has been forgotten. If literature is an art it may be said that literature lifts the event out of the dust and makes of it myth. We are so stupid that only with myth is the memory alive and vigorous. Events are forgotten and misconstrued, indexed and forgotten. But who has not heard of Troy or, if they know nothing of Troy and its ardents, who has not heard of Adam and Eve, or Cain and Abel, or of Joseph and his brothers? And is there any doubt that what they have heard is myth, and not only the myths of our origins and descent into history, but the myths of other nations and peoples as well? Myth is not all slogan (although it can be that too). It is a mnemonic of feeling and the source of the deepest loyalty. It is so easy to betray history and survive. It is impossible to do the same with one's own myth.

4. Some have written that it is impermissible to assimilate the destruction of European Jewry to the millenial memorial of the destruction of the Temple on the 9th Day of Av. They say (quite correctly, I believe) that there is nothing in these modern events that does not overwhelm the confines of the ancient tropes, rendering *them* distended and flattening these catastrophes of our own day by false similitudes. (Again I believe they say something that is true.) All events, as events, are incommensurable. No fact is like any other. It is the resemblance of the catastrophe to the unconditioned finality of the fact that makes catastrophes incomparable and unassimilable to ordinary historical memorializations.

It would be the same for redemptions as for catastrophes. Each fact of ransoming or restoration would be incomparable. Presumably what the "historical" mnemonics of Jewish liturgists and *paytannium* undertook was to establish "catastrophe" as a Jewish trope, and having caught the underlying rhythm, to make of each catastrophe a stanza, a quatrain of particularity, held to the center by an overarching similitude.

The resistance to regarding these modern events as yet a further extension and original elaboration of the classical trope of catastrophe rests perhaps on the no less significant conviction that the trope, despite all mourning for the wasted ancient Temple and for all our persuasion that every Jewish catastrophe until the present began on the 9th Day of Av, did little or nothing to avert the modern catastrophe.

It could be the case not that the trope is false, but that the trope is no longer believed.

Long ago I stopped mourning the destruction of the Temple. I have no wish to behold its rebuilding nor have I any desire (as did my teacher, Rav Avraham Schreiber) to receive instruction in the laws of sacrifice. Rabbi Schreiber wanted to teach me the laws of sacrifice since I bore the most exalted of Hebrew names and might indeed in that time of rebuilt temples become the High Priest of Israel. I defile myself daily to render myself unfit. I visit graves and fail to separate myself from my beloved.

And yet if it is the case that the ancient trope of tragedy is no longer believed, then with it into oblivion goes the whole of the liturgy which is a necklace of similar tropes responding to the other side of the same question. In the one God is enthroned in judgment; in the others God is enthroned in mercy. There would be little point to the liturgy of mercy were we not also confronted by the inculpation of history.

This is, of course, the real issue. Not that the catastrophe of this century is vaster than any other, but that the Jewish people had no choice. Without choice, without guilt. And without guilt, blameless except by the work of a cruel God. Or a God who couldn't help himself.

Or a God who thought creating the heavens and the earth and all the creatures thereon to be enough. Or a God who didn't invent history. Or perhaps no God at all.

Whatever we have made of these modern events the last thing we have made is a literature. All of the literary undertakings by which these events are culled reflect the overwhelming need to carve out from the granite of implacability a corner of ostensible sanity. Either a sanity that normalizes insanity. Or a manner of speech that institutionalizes sepulchral gravity. Or a rhetoric of injury that makes it impossible for anyone but the victim or the survivor to speak.

Which, of course, makes the victim and the survivor the conservator of correct interpretation and, in extremis, the legitimated moral terrorist empowered to silence everyone else who was a bystander. No Jew, however, is permitted to be a bystander. Every Jew is commanded to be a witness. This is an article of faith. Even if my eyes did not see nor my ears hear nor my voice speak, I am no bystander. Only a witness. This is what is meant by the community of Israel.

Each and every Jew who has endured until this time is in some way a survivor and is commanded to address the world as a survivor. The survivor who was not a victim must hear the testimony of the victims who survived, but since it is the survivor who will transmit the knowledge of the catastrophe from this generation to the future, not a single one is freed from the obligation to judge not alone the catastrophe but the whole history of the Jewish people that begins five thousand years ago and is carried through the fire to this season.

The laws of mourning are obligatory for every Jew. Not only victims, but survivors. Once this is accepted by victims, survivors who were victims, and survivors who were not victims, it will be possible for storytelling to begin again in Israel. It is hardly storytelling when the storytellers require that the listener know that what he tells is not a story. In such situations (and it is commonplace in many *recits* of survivors who were victims) storytelling fails to estrange the commonplace.

Rimbaud wished to disorder the senses. I would wish to estrange the commonplace. Tadeusz Borowski succeeded in this. He estranged the commonplace of the death camps by not being a Jew and thus he could begin on the very first day of his arrival at Auschwitz by hating the Jews among whom he was cast until in the end he joined them and they entered him.

The real predicament that all talk of Jewish literature confronts is that it must either assimilate these catastrophic events to the episodic history of Jewish life or permit these events to tower so monstrously that nothing else would be allowed. Everything else would be dwarfed. Or made trivial.

5. What I propose is that these modern events be made liturgic as quickly as liturgy becomes possible so that they can serve us henceforward as the highest rule of critical adjudication, marking off the authentic from the lying, the truthful from the deceiving, the unique and irreducible from all efforts at universalizing symmetries. The catastrophe—now that it is surely history—must become the halakhah of speech, that is to say, the law of truth.

Once it is the law of truth (which strikes down misrepresentation and falsification) it is possible to raise again the question of truth-telling.

Truth-telling (which is the thinker's art whether the thinker be a poet, storyteller, exegete, or inventor of ingenious ideas) entails the recognition that at all times and in all places the truth is not wanted. Truth-tellers are wanted, but not their truths. They are protected even while their truth is spurned.

Recall the astonishing argument of Leo Strauss, who documented the curious history of persecution and the art of writing during the Middle Ages and among Jews. Persecution, of course, meant everything from capital punishment to social ostracism. The argument of true philosophy during the Middle Ages required literary art as a means of exposition and self-protection. There was a language open and fit for the audition of right believers. For them the argument could be devised in common, exoteric terms, built from shared assumptions and unexceptionable beliefs. But since all were not philosophers (indeed philosophy was not considered among Jews to be a requisite to learning) if one were both learned in Torah and a philosopher, one had either to make philosophy subservient to Torah that the general public remain confirmed in faith or reserve for the hearing of the few those esoteric arguments that could be pursued for the sake of deeper and more subtle wisdom. Strauss suggests that for these reasons Maimonides prepared his more popular and universally acclaimed rehearsal of the Torah, the *Mishneh Torah,* while for the few he proposed his *Guide for the Perplexed.*

I have returned many times to Leo Strauss's argument. It struck me that there had to be something more to his thesis than what was apparent. The interlineation of a coded text, the device of the loaded phrase, the purposeful contradiction, the secret arcanum which only the astute, careful, and perspicacious reader would discover (realizing with his discovery that what seemed to reflect the safe course of exposition actually revealed a countercurrent of heterodoxy) were undertaken by the great medieval Jewish philosophers less in terror of persecution than in celebration of the extreme consequence of speech. Language, after all, made the universe and by language are we slain. Therefore all caution and care for words. What a man thinks should be guarded and protected lest his habits of fidelity and obedience be compromised by intellectual subtleties. And so the great Jewish philosophers (and Muslim and Christian thinkers as well) created a doubling of language which spoke with one voice the efficient truths on which society thrives and with another voice (more still and small) advanced theoretic truths which none but the speculatively gifted would discern.

6. An example of theological misprision.

Saint Sylvester never said that God was simple. He said rather that God was good. About God's similitude to the edible bulb of the lily family, no mistake. Nor that God makes us cry. But why Saint Sylvester thought that onions were good I have no idea. He was undoubtedly an early medieval. Onions made up much of the peasant diet. They grew wild, withstood cold, and flourished under the worst of conditions. But how far should I press Sylvester's metaphor?

God, of course, grows forth under the worst of conditions. But evidently I have never thought God good. (Scholem is reported to have remarked once of Judah Magnes: "He could speak of goodness and justice without making one split one's sides laughing.") I have found God to possess so many other qualities more outstanding than virtue that his goodness never came to mind. Moreover, his virtue is among the more dubious of his moral attributes, since virtue, unlike majesty, grace and serenity, is grounded in the human realm where goodness changes from generation to generation like the seasons.

I dislike the notion of God's goodness. A simple confession of indifference to his virtue. It makes no difference to my conduct that God is good. It makes a great deal of difference to my conduct, however, that God's nature is always simple. It makes a great deal of difference to my conduct that God makes me cry.

7. The defect of all written texts is not the fault of speech, but the condition of time. Everything that is decisive may be known (in fact has probably been known since the ancient world) but unfortunately what the mind knows in simultaneity it must ploddingly unfold in speech. Words, alas, must follow each other, one after another, for pages on end, holding hands like a line of blind men. What we receive, however, when we read is not the sequence of the words, but the undulance of time. We

come to the word requiring not sense, but time. Surely it is the presence of time that prevents us from anticipating, that requires that we await each revelation of the word patiently, the compels our recognition that everything upon which we depend for life and truth must be wrested by one understanding from another.

Since time is the atmosphere of words, it is time and our *sensus temporis* that introduces into language what is called style. Style is essentially language taking account of its temporal medium. In this respect all literature (even the most unworthy) verges upon the metaphysical, since in even the most foolish heads time blows, obliging it to hurry on, to set it forth, to make the text. It is only when the text is finished that the wind of time shifts directions. It begins then to blow in the reader's head and the process recommences.

8. It appears in the liturgy of the Days of Awe: "The enlargement of the heart is for man, but the gift of speech is from God" [Prov. 16]; ‏לאדם מערכי לב ומה' מענה לשון‎.

9. The natal fall into consciousness is twice described.

The first time as Plato devised it. An event of reminiscence (anamnesis) Plato called it. In such events of reminiscence we recollect through the promptings of instruction the fundamental truths we knew at birth and lost. The second time as a Midrash understood it. The Hebrew tradition proposes that mankind once knew all essential truths in advance of birth; however, lest man in his pride come to regard himself as either the equal or worse the rival of God in wisdom, the guardian angel of each child put a finger to the infant's lips at birth and all was forgotten. The origin of our labial depression is this angelic counter to our hubris. But I think there may be a third view which regards neither deep instruction nor angelic premonition. Let us imagine that the origin of our natal ignorance is that at the moment of coming into the world each child bit its own lip and crying out in pain announced that it knew nothing (and hence the punishment for excess need not begin). Forgetting everything in tears, however, was to begin a primary schooling in discontent.

10. Consider this tale, perhaps legendary, or even a riddle.

It is recounted that a printer, a Hasid by conviction, who lived in Podolia during the middle of the nineteenth century, was laboriously inserting metal letters into the matrix of a page when he discovered to his horror that many passages of the manuscript from which he was composing were misquoted. It would have mattered little had the passages of quotation been from ordinary secular literature, for the printer was also in the habit of printing the handbills then coming into use among the Jewish merchants of the town. But that was not the case. The passages in question were extracts from Holy Scripture. Indeed, the copyist who had transcribed the learned text had made numerous mistakes, and were it not for the printer's considerable learning they might not have been noticed. However, he did notice and he corrected the errors. This was the last page of the manuscript, and when he closed his shop for the night he was satisfied that he had saved the word of God from misquotation.

The printer returned to his home, concluded his supper, and retired to his study for several hours of holy learning before he went to sleep. As he was studying, however, it crossed his mind that all was not well in his printing shop and when he went to sleep he reported terrible dreams. Unsettled letters rose from the matrices that he had locked and made ready for the press and flew about the room, refusing to return to the pages from which they had loosed themselves.

The following morning when *Shaḥarith* was concluded in the Bet Midrash where the printer prayed, he asked a Jew more learned than himself and a confidant of the Rebbe whom he served whether he could interpret his dream. The learned Jew inquired what he had done the day before and what events had transpired. The printer then described the difficulties created by the mistranscription of Holy Scripture in the learned text he was setting into type. The learned Jew then interpreted the dream: "Perhaps," he proposed, "other passages of Holy Scripture have been misquoted by the copyist and set into type by an ignorant typesetter. Perhaps then the letters are angry and upset. Since it is known that the Hebrew alphabet was created before the creation of the world, those supernal and holy letters are offended."

The printer hurried to his print shop and inquired of the young apprentice who had been assigned to set the earlier pages of the manuscript, it being required only that the master printer set the last page of each manuscript in order that the typesetters, printers, paper handlers, and other workers in the shop could then gather and recite a *Kaddish deRabbanan* and toast *leḥayim*. The young apprentice, skilled though he was in the printing trade, was not learned in Torah. He admitted that he did not know if the earlier pages contained misquotations from Holy Scripture. The master printer, a Hasid by conviction, examined the pages and to his horror discovered not one but hundreds of misquotations from Holy Scripture. The entire book, with but the exception of the final page, would now need to be recomposed. The cost to the modest print shop would be exorbitant and his promise of a finished volume by Suk-koth would be violated. He cursed the copyist and thought to have him put in *herem,* but the copyist had already left Podolia and it was not known in which direction he had traveled. Vexed and angered, the printer allowed himself to think (in jest or in despair it cannot be known): "God can be such a careless writer." The printer was of course referring to the careless copyist, but in his anger had exaggerated, accus-ing God Himself (it would appear) of the copyist's mistakes.

It is no surprise that on the evening of his blasphemy a fire broke out in the wooden trays that held the little metal letters of the many type fonts that the printer owned. The corner of the print shop which held the trays of metal letters was destroyed. The metal of each little letter, heated by the concentrated power of the flame, flowed together and fused (it was reported). All that remained of the thousands of Hebrew letters was a giant *Shin.* All took this to signify the accusatory finger of God's judgment.

The printer, a Hasid by conviction, chastened by his ordeal still won-dered about its cause and meaning. His manuscript was full of errors, the completed matrices awaiting only the embrace of ink and paper now required recomposition, and the fire had destroyed all his fonts. The printer was nearly bankrupted by his misfortune. It was then that he determined to visit his Rebbe at his summer court in western Czechoslo-vakia. It took him two weeks to travel by coach and train. Arriving at the Rebbe's court in late afternoon, he was told that his visit was expected and he was given an appointment for two o'clock in the morning of the day of his arrival. He believed his fortune was changing. Ushered into the presence of the Rebbe he was left alone. All of the Rebbe's attendants and *gabbaim* were motioned to leave. The Rebbe bade the poor printer to speak and the printer told the Rebbe the story of the manuscript, the mistranscription of the holy words of Scripture, and the ensuing fire.

The Rebbe listened carefully. When the printer had finished, the Rebbe spoke angrily. "There is something you did that you have not told me." The printer denied this but the Rebbe insisted. "There is something you said that you have not told me." The printer denied this but the Rebbe insisted. "There is something you thought that you have not told me." It was then that the printer remembered his blasphemy and re-peated it. "I thought to myself that God was a careless writer. But surely the Master of the Universe knows that I meant the copyist." The Rebbe was very firm. "You have thought blasphemy against the Holy Alphabet which is like the sinew and muscle of God. Without the Holy Alphabet there would be no Torah and if God had not given the Torah to his people Israel, who would serve him and what then would be our God?"

The Rebbe prescribed a penance and the printer, a Hasid by conviction, departed. In time all was restored to him. But that is the way such stories usually end.

I hear this story and I think to myself: Is blasphemy any longer possible in this world of our making? Observe initially that there are presuppositions even for blasphemy. God must surely exist if it is God that is to be blasphemed.

(I recall being challenged many years ago when I was young by a Christian who had overheard me say the name of Jesus. In those days I believed that Christ was his family name. He demanded in his anger that I retract my blasphemy. He said [I recall exactly]: "Take back that Jesus Christ." He even lifted a fist to clarify how seriously he regarded my utterance. I answered him that I was only trying out a name that I had recently come to learn. He countered my frivolous but truthful reply by saying that my tone of voice suggested more than recent acquaintance. "You're committing blasphemy," he said angrily. I gave in. Since I did not know anything of Jesus Christ, my ignorance in those days was invincible. I had said the name of Jesus Christ as lightly as I might have invoked Hermes Trismegistus. A bit of anger, a bit of magic. But how could this be blasphemy? It might have been a blasphemy if, not a Jew, but a Christian had spoken the name with the will to erase it. But could it be blasphemy on the lips of a Jew who had no need or will to violate syllables of air?)

I read the tale of the printer and recalled my first encounter with blasphemy. But I put to myself this question: if it is a blasphemy for a Christian to speak the Holy Name of Jesus Christ in anger, what would be a comparable blasphemy for a Jew? I understand the Christian's rage with my Jewish unbelief. It is meaningless to me, but serious for him. The *logos* after all became flesh and the Son filiates the Father. Offend against the one and the heart bleeds.

It is, however, a common Jewish reversal to put the book before the world, the writing before the word, in effect, literature before theology. Jews cannot help themselves therefore if they blaspheme by their very existence against Jesus Christ. This is because Christianity requires that the *logos* precede creation and Jews require not *logos* (nor even *logoi*) but writing before speech.

The ultimate blasphemy for a Jew would be to deny that God is a writer at all, that his Torah preceded creation and was its archetype and that speech, far from being the vital, spiritual inscription of God upon the stem of man, is already a deformation. Bluntly put, a Jewish blasphemy would be to say that God is an exceedingly bad writer, indeed, no writer at all.

Had the printer said that God was an exceedingly bad writer, perhaps no writer at all, not only his print shop, but Podolia and even the whole world might have been swept by fire.

11. Jacques Derrida remembers betimes his childhood as an Algerian Jew and comments:

> As was the case with the Platonic writing of the truth in the soul, in the Middle Ages too it is a writing understood in the metaphoric sense, that is to say a *natural,* eternal, and universal writing, the system of signified truth, which is recognized in its dignity. As in the *Phaedrus,* a certain fallen writing continues to be opposed to it. There remains to be written a history of this metaphor, a metaphor that systematically contrasts divine or natural writing and the human and laborious, finite and artificial inscription. It remains to articulate rigorously the stages of that history, as marked by the quotations below, and to follow the theme of God's book (nature or law, indeed natural law) through all its modifications.
>
> Rabbi Eliezer said: "If all the seas were of ink, and all ponds planted with reeds, if the sky and the earth were parchments and if all human beings practiced the art of writing—they would not exhaust the Torah I have learned, just as the Torah itself would not be diminished any more than is the sea by the water removed by a paint brush dipped in it." (*Of Grammatology,* pp. 15–16)

12. There is much more. This is only a sample, but not a random sample. I have been doing this kind of work for more than a generation. I have many notebooks full of such speculations and notetaking. Their order here—seemingly random—is rigorous. But it is an unconventional notion of order and rigor. It is in substance, however, all textual commentary, although very often the original text is omitted or misquoted, perhaps even lied about and misrepresented. The original text is someone else's problem and since, as often as not, the original text is deformed in my rendition, it no longer matters whose text it is. In many cases all I know of the original text is my misrepresentation of its substance and all I remember of it is its savor and trace. I try to make every quotation my own. If, after living with a text for a long time, I continue to remember its author, I give it back. It will never become mine and I have no use for it.

There are several passages quoted in this text but only one is a real quotation. I have not yet decided whether I wish to own it.

NOTE

1. Abraham Sutzkever. *Griner akvarium un andere dertseylungen* [*Green Aquarium and Other Stories*] (Jerusalem, 1975). Translated by Ruth Wisse with introductory text in *Prooftexts* 2 (1982): 100.

VII.

LITERARY, ART, AND CULTURAL CRITICISM

Introduction

David Stern

Alongside his dual careers as theologian and novelist, Arthur Cohen led a third life—as a man of letters and essayist. Beginning in his twenties and throughout the rest of his life, Cohen wrote and published reviews and articles in virtually all of the important intellectual journals and literary magazines of the time. His subjects ran the gamut from culture to politics and were frequently polemical in character, particularly when he participated in such debates as the place of civil religion in America. What Cohen wrote about most passionately, however, was literature and art.

As an essayist, Cohen followed in the venerable tradition of the man of letters, a tradition well established in the American intellectual world in which Cohen grew up and lived. In many respects, though, Cohen more closely resembled the American man of letters' European cousin, the feuilletonist or cultural critic. For one thing, Cohen, like the best feuilletonists, was unabashedly eclectic. He allowed himself to cross disciplines and fields, drawing insights freely from art, literature, philosophy, theater, politics, and religion. He also wrote with a verve and elegance uncommon in academic and journalistic prose, though it was hardly popular or populist in tone.

The selections in this section all exhibit Cohen's unusual intellectual versatility and his virtuosity as a writer. The essays on Nathanael West,

Miguel de Unamuno, Franz Kafka, and Heinrich Von Kleist are important not only for their intrinsic merit but also because they give us some insight into Cohen's understanding of the figures who were in fact his models as a novelist and literary intellectual. Similarly, the essays on the Jewish painters of Paris and on Dada typography offer small glimpses of Cohen's authority and insight in the fields of twentieth-century art and modern design and typography.

Although none of the essays is overtly theological, the reader will nonetheless note Cohen's repeated return to theological and Jewish topics—in the notion of the holy fool in West's bizarre fictions; in Kafka's negative theological vision and insoluble hermeneutics; in the question of what is Jewish about the work of the Jewish painters of Montparnasse; and in the implicitly religious desire behind the urge to resuscitate the living word that can be seen in Dada graphics. To be sure, there is nothing truly surprising about this. As a theologian, Cohen was continually preoccupied with the question of culture, especially so because he believed that Judaism could not be indifferent to any manifestation of culture if it was to fully realize itself in both its natural and supernatural missions. What is more revealing is how, even when he was writing about a topic that was not theological, he nonetheless had the knack of revealing its metaphysical significance. Glimmering with intelligence and sensitivity, these essays, despite their occasional nature, are surely among Cohen's best work.

Nathanael West's Holy Fool

To neglect Nathanael West is to neglect a writer who has examined the possibilities of belief and the consequences of its absence in our age and our society. Like Dostoevsky, though lesser, he is a writer who expressed his concern with ultimate questions in terms of the fate of the "holy fool" in our world. The consideration which he merits does not, however, depend primarily upon the artistic merits of his novels. His work is admittedly uneven. This is often the case with writers who allow their style to follow after their passion, and the passion of West determined his mood, his care, his clarity, his brilliance. Where he is most angry, in *Miss Lonelyhearts* or *The Day of the Locust,* one would have to go far to find his contemporary equal. Where he is unsure and experimental, seeking out a mood or groping for tone—as in much of *Balso Snell* or *A Cool Million*—he becomes alternately obscure or bathetic.

It is not for elegance of style, therefore, that one reads West. But this is true of Dostoevsky as well. It is rather the kinds of passions these writers sustain that concern us. Nor is the comparison of West and Dostoevsky accidental, for West considered himself most profoundly a disciple of Dostoevsky. *Balso Snell,* for example, makes frequent references to

Commonweal 64, no. 11 (June 15, 1956): 276–78. Reprinted by permission of the Commonweal Foundation. Copyright © Commonweal Foundation.

Dostoevsky, even employing a character named John Raskolnikov Gib-
son. West's writing is filled with quotations from and allusions to Dostoevsky.

Dostoevsky, in a profound sense, provides the paradigm of West's
creative activity. It should not be forgotten that the Dostoevsky of the
novels (not the journalist, Slavophil jingoist, or representative of conservative politics) was a radical critic of human society, founding upon an
ultimate dialectical indecision an absolute critique of Western materialism. It is not possible to sustain the theological interpretation of Dostoevsky without severe limitation. Dostoevsky's concern was neither formally
theological nor particularly occupied with the coherence of theological
insight. The Christian passion which marks numberless of his characters
and colors the tone of his novels is counterbalanced by equally passionate
heresy, disbelief, and perplexity. Never a scoffer or skeptic, Dostoevsky
still took the mystery of human events as a token of God's inscrutability
and man's ineradicable freedom. The Dostoevskean hero is in some sense
a pilgrim of the dialectic, alternately forcing the contradictory moments
of the dialectic to the fore, submitting them to the life test, and falling
victim to their implications. So the experiment of Raskolnikov, Ivan, Stavrogin, Kirilov, Prince Myshkin, and the Underground Man.

It is surely the hero of the dialectic, albeit the modern dialectic, who
occupies the center of West's four novels: *The Dream Life of Balso Snell,
Miss Lonelyhearts, A Cool Million,* and *The Day of the Locust.*

Balso Snell, West's first novel, is self-consciously avant-garde. It was
written during West's stay in Paris from 1924–26, although it was not
published until 1931. *The Dream Life of Balso Snell* is a rambling, episodic, frequently disgusting pilgrimage of a poet through the innards of
the Trojan Horse, to which he has gained entrance. It is a pilgrimage
through a most unattractive unconscious, but one which nevertheless
defines a number of themes which recur in West's later writing. The
ascetic, the mystic, the cripple, the pervert all appear. The compassion,
which found more subtle expression later in *Miss Lonelyhearts* and *The
Day of the Locust,* is present, but unformed. Balso Snell is passive—
confronting with contempt and loathing the progeny of his dreams—
estrangement, the unloved, absolute suffering, the pain of the world. The
hero is unformed, since he reflects at best the detours of the unconscious.
There is no stand, only a tentative apprehension of themes.

Throughout West's work there runs a single-minded preoccupation
with the character of "the holy fool." This theme has a long history in
Western religious thought, an especial history in Russian religious

thought, and a unique history in the work of Dostoevsky. From the un-workable plan for a novel to have been called *The Life of the Great Sinner,* Dostoevsky developed *The Brothers Karamazov* and subsequently *The Idiot* and *The Devils.* In each of these, elements of the same dialectic emerge: the opposition of the perfect sinner and the perfect saint. Dostoevsky was sensitive to the difficulty of making such characters authentic and believable. Raskolnikov, Ivan, Smerdyakov, Stavrogin, Kirilov emerge on one side; Sonia, Alyosha, Prince Myshkin on the other. The conditions of the Russian world—poverty, oppression, drunkenness—were the elements of external relief. The protest was not, however, against the degradation of the physical and social world, but against the impoverishment of the inner life of man, the void of inner truth. The effort of Dostoevsky was to relocate the varieties of human feeling and authenticity, to restore the possibility of sanctity.

In West the problem of the holy fool remains, though its statement and nuance are different. America in the thirties posed different problems than Russia in the sixties and seventies of the last century. Unlike their Russian nineteenth-century counterparts, the American intellectuals and artists were already in rebellion and alienation. The objective order had witnessed the triumph of industrial bureaucracy, the dislocation of personality, the fragmentation of the social order. Dostoevsky was a prophetic novelist, anticipating what was to be in the objective order, as it had already emerged symptomatically in the inner life of man. There is no question but that the spirit of man records more quickly and sensitively what emerges but gradually in the social order. Man usually knows, long in advance of his destruction, that he is being destroyed. It is Dostoevsky's uniqueness to have ascertained the consequence of man's disorder and to have described it. He is prophetic in the same sense that we recognize Kierkegaard, Burckhardt, and Nietzsche to be prophetic.

West, on the contrary, anticipates nothing that is to come. It is his merit to have described with unbelievable clarity the destruction that has passed, the pestilence that has visited us and has been invited to stay. The power of *Miss Lonelyhearts,* the ineffectualness of *A Cool Million,* and the more elaborate structure of *The Day of the Locust* result from the fact that the deterioration of the American world, West believed, was accomplished. The savageness manifest in *Miss Lonelyhearts* could become more subtle and exploratory in subsequent novels; West could return to questions of form because there was no longer any urgency to the problem. As desperate as *Miss Lonelyhearts* indubitably is, it is perhaps more optimistic than his later novels. For by the time of *The Day of the Locust,* West's anguish had settled and become tolerable.

Miss Lonelyhearts, the male writer of an advice column, has a solution to the horror of the world: it is what he calls "the Christ complex." The Christ complex is precisely a complex, not a belief in specific documents of faith, not faith in any order of sacrament or scheme of salvation. It is a complex, a fixation of the mind, a conviction that only if Miss Lonelyhearts himself becomes the shoulders of the world, the bearer of man's suffering, the kisser of lepers, restorer of bodies, nursemaid to the suffering and distressed, will humanity be healed.

In *Miss Lonelyhearts* the primary text is taken from Father Zossima of *The Brothers Karamazov:* "Love a man even in his sin, for that is the semblance of Divine Love and is the highest love on earth. . . . Love the animals, love the plants, love everything . . . you will come to love the whole world with an all-embracing love."

Miss Lonelyhearts, however, does not love the world. He is disgusted by the world, sensuality, his own body and passion. The contempt for the physical is hazed by liquor and rhapsodized by that mental liquor of the ascetic deceiver, the egotism of suffering. He must force himself to love, to take upon himself more and more of the world's anguish even at the sacrifice of all of himself, of the sanity which enables man not only to love completely, but wisely. Needless to say, his "Christ-complex" destroys him, for it deludes him. He misrepresents the world and is martyr to his misrepresentation.

In *Miss Lonelyhearts* West attempted to make a statement of what happens to the holy fool in the modern world. He is not treated as a mad saint and revered for his sanctity and the divinity of his madness. He is misunderstood and destroyed. It is not that he is either saint or fool, for, in West's view, he is a victim of the world he seeks to love, fragmented by the broken world he wishes to mend. He misapprehends the world because he is not capable, as modern man is generally not capable, of maintaining any distance from the world, any perspective or quiet before it.

A Cool Million sees the holy fool from a different point of view. It was modeled, as Josephine Herbst, West's close friend, has said, after the Horatio Alger stories, all of which West read in preparation of the character of Lemuel Pitkin. Such a model gives the clue to West's satire, for Lemuel Pitkin is all fool, all externality. He is the perfect fool, for he is nothing that the world does not make him. As a result, all his suffering is physical. The spirit, empty as it is, naive as it is, wholly American as it is, is untouched. The hero, nevertheless, in spite of having nothing to lose, loses all—his teeth, his eyes, a leg, his scalp. He is imprisoned, tortured, beaten up, exhibited for public amusement, caught in riots, victimized by Communists, exploited by capitalists, and killed as martyr to a semifascist Americanism movement. What a ludicrous hero!

Nevertheless, A Cool Million extends the argument of Miss Lonelyhearts. It eliminates another possibility of statement. The holy fool can be an ass. When heroism is made the extenuation of externality, when it is simply a foil of the public world, political values, countermaterialism, or pronationalism, the hero becomes incredible. What West satirizes is the kind of hero that makes national histories—Washington at the cherry tree, Jackson at the redoubts of New Orleans, Davy Crockett and his mountain lion. These are the public, legendary heroisms that propel a national community into self-congratulation when all is rotting about it.

His last novel, his most ambitious novel, The Day of the Locust, is a modification of the character of Miss Lonelyhearts and Lemuel Pitkin. Homer Simpson, the central character of The Day of the Locust, is the final statement and defeat of the holy fool. God has disappeared from discussion as early as Miss Lonelyhearts, not to reappear. This is not to say that he does not manifest Himself in the virtues of West's heroes; but He is no longer present in Himself, nor is He any longer addressed, as He was in Balso Snell or Miss Lonelyhearts. Christ has vanished, but His impress is retained.

Homer Simpson, the clerk from Waynesville, Iowa, comes to Hollywood, with meager savings, to discover happiness, peace, the perfect death, only to realize the consummate waste and boredom of such ambition. Instead, Homer wishes to love and adore. It is his misfortune to meet Faye Greener, who will have him merely to gratify her lust for possession—no love to return, just to own him, even though he is unattractive and meaningless to her. He demands nothing but to be owned and protected. Love is compressed into the syntax of the American world—the syntax of possession and ownership. Homer is holy, for his love demands nothing but to be in the presence of the object adored. It wishes only that Faye be present. She can make love to others, only so long as she is there. Homer is fool, however, to imagine that mere satiety with presence can be focused in the temporal order.

West makes clear that the middle-class image of security always destroys itself because it roots itself repeatedly in the transitory, in the most flimsy of all values, the security of place. Faye naturally leaves him. Homer returns to the one place of security, what West, in psychological jargon, calls "the uterine position." Homer curls up into a womb-ball and remains as such until his climactic end. The novel concludes where Homer, wandering before a crowd massed in front of a Hollywood movie opening, is tormented by a little boy throwing rocks at him. This unmotivated cruelty shocks him out of the inactivity of his grief, and he tries to trample the child to death. The brutality of the riot that follows is unbelievable. The quietude of the bored, tired, cheated middle classes disappears and the brutality of the race emerges.

The holy fool is ultimately defeated. The saint can communicate only when there is a community to address, when people are at least bound by common affections and belief, when they share sources of feeling and devotion. The saint cannot speak when absolutely nobody listens. He may live and die, known to God, but such secret sanctity will not allow us to praise, witness, or follow him in his way. Miss Lonelyhearts, Lemuel Pitkin, and Homer Simpson are defeated by their self-deception about the world and their misapprehension of themselves. Underlying all is West's bitter conviction that there is no communication in our world. Man shares nothing with man. If man seeks to address his fellow, whether through the active pursuit of love or the passive submission to others, he is destroyed. West's conclusion is that the holy fool will always be misapprehended and destroyed as long as the values of the industrial American world prevail. Success, money, power—all conspire to cast out love, to freeze the heart, to dull sensibility.

West may be remembered by us for having attempted to make a saint and a fool a convincing hero of modern fiction. His failure to support the saint and fool in triumph, to bring him into the world as an instrument of redemption, is testimony to his honesty and limitation. Unlike the world of Raskolnikov and Dimitri, our world is not redeemed by the fidelity of inwardness and attentiveness of love. West obviously could not accept the Dostoevskean answer, however much he might have desired to. He could not believe that others could be saved when he himself was not, that others could sanctify passions when he did not, that others could win out against the domination of success when he saw so clearly that his career was constantly blunted and rendered uncertain by failure.

It may be that West's career is the triumph of unbelief. More likely it is the triumph of a realism which is aware that belief cannot survive unless man trusts its authenticity. Ours is surely an age that does not trust God and ours is a society, West makes clear, that does not permit such trust to re-emerge.

Miguel de Unamuno: The Inventor of Splendid Arguments with Death

At his death in 1936 Miguel de Unamuno was the most influential thinker in Spain, more renowned than his younger contemporary Ortega y Gasset and regarded by his own aficionados as the greatest stylist in the Spanish language since Cervantes. Upon learning of his death, that other extraordinary stylist of the Spanish language, Jorge Luis Borges (then a young poet), wrote the following brief obituary: "The leading writer in our language is dead. . . . He was before all else, an inventor of splendid argument. . . . He debated the I, immortality, language, the cult of Cervantes, faith, ethics, the regeneration of vocabulary and syntax."

The only debate, however, to which Borges's random catalogue does not refer is the principal debate, the argument that undergirds all of Unamuno's life and thought and gives to it a power most peculiarly Spanish and most thoroughly universal. It is Unamuno's contest with death.

The first three volumes in the series of seven that will constitute the Bollingen Foundation's munificent Unamuno benefaction, although reflecting his early, middle, and late periods, although dealing with the heroic folly of Don Quixote ("Our Lord Don Quixote," 1905), the tragic destiny of men and nations ("The Tragic Sense of Life," 1921), and the

New York Times Book Review 78, no. 50 (December 16, 1973): 19–22. Copyright © 1973 by the New York Times Co. Reprinted by permission.

struggle of Christianity ("The Agony of Christianity," 1928) have as their common theme the human struggle against death. Undoubtedly it is his preoccupation with death that has impeded Unamuno's reputation in the Anglo-Saxon world. Our tradition (whatever its pleasure in violence) is neither fond of death nor hopeful of resurrection; but Spain, a culture which has stylized violence, is overwhelmed with death and committed to resurrection.

Unamuno's superficial morbidity—his delight in the mystical paradoxes wherein death is transformed into life, where submission to death insures the promise of life, where the preparation for dying and the manner of death is the consummation of ordinary life and the viaticum for life everlasting, where Christs in agony abound and no hieratic Byzantine Christs nor elegant French crucifixions are to be found—is offset by an espousal of quotidian life which turns his *thanatos* into the most intimate and sensuous of life-affirming doctrines.

"Our Lord Don Quixote" (brilliantly translated by one of the editors of the Unamuno enterprise, Anthony Kerrigan) is a hymn to the divine folly of Don Quxote, a folly and a divinity Unamuno convinced himself he perceived more truly than the Don's creator, Cervantes. "I consider myself more Quixotist that Cervantist, and that I attempt to free Don Quixote from Cervantes himself, permitting myself on occasion to go so far as to disagree with the manner in which Cervantes understood and dealt with his two heroes. . . . The fact is, I believe that characters of fiction possess a life of their own within the mind of the author who creates them, as well as a certain autonomy, and that they obey an intimate logic of which the author himself is not altogether conscious."

Unamuno goes on—and the explication of the narrative of "Don Quixote" which unfolds, followed in the Bollingen edition by sixteen additional essays on the implausible logic and consequence of Quixotism—to set forth the essential premise of all his intellectual criticism: madness is reality, and historical objectivity is madness. This definition of the quixotic is obviously at variance with its received understanding. The chivalric vocation and undertakings of Don Quixote, continuously pragmatized by his sympathetic squire, are treated by Unamuno as the ultimate pilgrimage. ("I believe we might undertake a holy crusade to redeem the Sepulcher of the Knight of Madness from the power of the champions of Reason.") The potentates of reasonableness—the planners, the scientists, the politicians of the possible—are all denounced by Unamuno as betrayers of the spirit of the Don.

Those who make the quixotic the impractical, the chimerical, the hazy dream of better worlds are the real fools, for in Unamuno's view they strip life of the precise ingredient which makes it worth living, that it is a continuous struggle with death. Any means by which a man subverts the kingdom of death is a triumph for life and, in Unamuno's clever logic, for eternity. Time and history are death, objectively is death, futurity and planning are death. Life is *existir,* which in Unamuno's fantastical associative etymologies is a modality of ecstasy, the *ek-stasi* by which man stands outside of himself and becomes eternal in the moment, and not the ephemeral *estar* or the ontological *ser.* Don Quixote becomes for Unamuno the Spanish Christian pilgrim for madness and against death (a definition not at all uncongenial to his contending spiritual descendants R. D. Laing and Thomas Szasz). The Don exalts an unfamiliar sanity which other men call insane, a sanity which, parched by definitions, seeks the waters of eternal life.

Miguel de Unamuno, the quintessential Spaniard of bearded face and piercing, sad-eyes, was born in Basque country, in Bilbao in 1864, in the midst of the Carlist wars. He was born with his first paradox, mastering a language and producing a heroic literature to defend a quixotic Basque tradition which had no literature of its own and which, in familiar separatist logic, regarded Castilian Spanish as a foreign language.

After receiving his doctorate in philosophy and classics at the University of Madrid during the effete eighties he was appointed professor of Greek at the University of Salamanca in 1891 and became its rector in 1901, a position he held until his death, although often stripped of his post, twice exiled, and in the last months before his death on December 31, 1936, confined by the Fascists under house arrest. His life was quiet, domestic, serene, although his words were bitter, hectoring, contentious. He was (and he saw himself in this respect) a voice crying in the wilderness, like his beloved Don Quixote. He rarely traveled, except in Spain, and though he wrote "The Agony of Christianity" while in exile in Paris, he found Paris and the Parisians frivolous and unnerving.

"The Agony of Christianity," like every Unamuno work, is based upon an etymological turn of phrase. The agony of the Christ, the agony of the Christian man is an agon, a struggle. And with what does the Jesus of the Cross struggle and against what does Christianity make contest? With death. The Christian glad tidings of great joy is that Christ is resurrected, that Christianity triumphs over death and it inserts life into the dead. The agony is the death throes of men and, in no less dramatic manner, if the wisdom of Don Quixote is his sublime movement through death, the wisdom of Christ is that all men are able to become Quixotes. The argument of "The Agony of Christianity" is exquisite, but it is hardly an argument of the head.

What must be made clear at this juncture before readers dismiss these murky lucubrations as those of yet another proud irrationalist is that Unamuno is a poet, a marvelous poet. Of course the presence of a poet is no more consolatory to most readers than an out and out irrationalist. Both set the teeth of American culture on edge. But there is nothing to be done about it. If Unamuno is un-American, he is incredibly Spanish.

The passion of Spanish literature, what surrounds its intellectual history with an alien penumbra, is integrity. Integrity is not simply moral wholeness and consistency. The moral effect of integrity is consequential to an interior coherence which might better be described as integralist. The Spanish literary tradition, a fusion of three cultures, Christian, Jewish, Muslim, has no choice but to be integralist. It can't get rid of its constituents. Unlike other cultures it chooses not to deny them. It refuses to melt them or to pot them. It takes its language and its history for what it is (see Amerigo Castro's magisterial "The Structure of Spanish History" for confirmation of this line of interpretation), the integration of three languages and sensibilities, three diversities of race and ambition, three living cultures, which however much silted over with the visible patina of regal Christendom contains words, *docta,* custom, arts, and architectures which are present and procreative even though Jews and Muslims have all but disappeared from the peninsula.

Unamuno, the alien Basque, is unafraid therefore of what makes up Spain. He is Catholic, but the essence of Catholicism is the doubting man who needs to renew faith daily; he is modern man, but his traditionalism informs him that Spain's avidity to become industrial is a hopeless ambition, given the untechnical nature of the Spanish temperament; he is a classicist who sees beneath the fundament of Spain's triune culture, ancient Rome, ancient Greece and vivid paganism. The only hope then for Spanish man and culture is to transmogrify the elements, to reconceive Spanish personality as integrity. The drive is toward interiority, for there integrity is to be found.

The Spanish man works from within outward. He can sit at his cafe in the square of Salamanca and appear to contradict himself endlessly, but he is only conceding to the evanescence and imprecision of language. He can point out one thing one day and deny it the next, but he is still telling a coherent truth, which is that integrity holds truth to be more complex than language.

The struggle to tell truth through language requires that the poetic thinker or the thinking poet force himself to pretend to sanity. Unamuno was a sane madman, like Don Quixote, whom he claimed to know better than his creator or even like Jesus Christ, whom he also claimed to understand better than His Creator—the reason for this being that he, Miguel de Unamuno, suffered the consequence of their existence, whereas their creators only created them.

The difficulty of Unamuno's thought rests more with us, his readers, than with what he wrote. We want something other than what he allows. We want an argument with a linear unfolding, a systematic coherence, a persuasive rationality. This is so because most of us use language principally as a means of imposing structure upon the chaos of our feelings and perceptions. Rational argument, we seem to be saying, must be preferred to outpourings and dramatics because what else can be made lucid if not language?

Unamuno, of course, understood long ago what we are only beginning to find out, namely, that language is as parlous as the condition of the man who speaks it. Both are riddled with confusion, contrariety, constipation. But whereas we might, for that reason, give ourselves over to purgings of language (imagining thereby that we purge ourselves), Unamuno celebrated our chaos. He could do this because he believed that the chaos was more apparent than real. Man thinks his world is chaotic and for that reason, surrendering to it, flies off in all directions, but if one accepts, as Unamuno did, that the chaos is only the ministry of death and that the truth of life is to be found in the structures men build against their death neither the vagaries of language nor the ravings of the heart are any longer alarming.

The center of the argument underlying Unamuno's most famous book, "The Tragic Sense of Life," is that all truly human beings thirst for immortality. The thirst for immortality is not simply the passion for glory, for monuments of memory and recollection, but the real care to endure, to go on with life beyond the formal term of life. The curse of modern men and nations is that they construct fabrications of eternal life, artificialities and simulacra that appear as breakers against death, but are in fact so dishonest that they fail not only to represent eternal life but guarantee to death the final victory. The technology of modern culture, the bureacratiziation of spirit, the atomization of the person—all the means by which mass cultures have sought to organize power as the instrument for the perpetuation of the historical nation—are fated to kill, for the thin breath of living men is stifled by such enormity.

Unamuno's recommendations, the return to agonic Christianity, the vitalization of personal integralism, which, not unlike the Buddhism Unamuno admires, distinguishes between specious and ultimate reality, are hardly practical programs. But Unamuno doesn't care a fig for programs.

He isn't really interested in saving culture unless it cares first. His own sensibility is too proud, too autonomous, too solitary and monkish to really bother with what others think is important.

Miguel de Unamuno y Jugo de Larraza, to cite his full name, Miguel of Unamuno, Marrow of the Race, like the biblical Isaiah, giving himself and others prophetic names, names which suggest the shorthand of his vocation, has been dead now nearly four decades, but there are few thinkers in our time who are both as irrelevant and relevant as he. His irrelevance consists in the obvious fact that he didn't know what happened after 1936. He never lived to see the principalities and dominions of death hold sway over the face of the earth. But his vision of an alternative, perhaps the only one we have the eros of life refusing to succumb, has never been more relevant. His paradoxes give hope, and what is more splendid for literature than to give hope?

The Typographic Revolution: Antecedents and Legacy of Dada Graphic Design

It is fated that any discussion of Dada should betray its origins in contradiction. Whatever method of clarification one undertakes, whatever diction, syntax, tone one adopts, it is already at variance with an otherwise received notion of Dada's implacable opposition. Dada is contrariety, the chiaroscuro of culture, which teaches precisely by virtue of its refusal to submit to the lepidopterist's science of classification, preservation, and pin mounting.

It is always a delight to pass time amid Dada artifacts and it is precisely this delight which I find curious, the why of my continuous pleasure in the company of Dada books, pamphlets, announcements, manifestos, typographic ephemera, as well as the objects, collages, readymades and photographic preservations (the memento mori) of the movement. It is not simply a necrophiliac delight, for Dada is not precisely dead, although it seems ever more improbable that it will be revived or should be. The modest efforts made during the outrageous sixties consisted principally in the confusion of the reckless, provocative, and petutlantly aggressive with Dada nomenclature, using the latter to rationalize and excuse the former. It was not only an historical gesture but one

Reprinted from *Dada Spectrum: The Dialectics of Revolt,* edited by Stephen C. Foster and Rudolf E. Kuenzli, 71–89. Iowa: The University of Iowa and Coda Press, 1979.

which missed the point of the revolutionary demurral of that decade and betrayed the essentially anti-ideological conviction of Dada.

I

Preoccupation with the composition, placement, embellishment, elaboration of words, their constitutive letters, and their ultimate intention to address forcefully is most usually associated with the progenitive impulse of Dada. Regardless of misconceptions which surround the identification of Dada and its spirit, there is consistency in the identification of its typographic innovation. Every viewer of Dada manifestation is struck by the obligation its visual language enforces to compel the eye to see differently, to record linguistic ideograms rather than words, to absorb rhythms of type rather than the familiar linearity of lead which characterized traditional typography, to take note of oddities and directives which force the eye to settle upon the minuscule in a sea of throbbing majuscules, to discover meanings sequestered in hidden places, slogans printed upside-down or obliquely, or in circles—language biting its tail. Typography creates an assault which sometimes bears profound and jarring language in its train and other times is merely a vast fist pounding out a tickle or a caress, the meaning being wholly unequal to the massive fist. The very distension of meaning and typography—its internal dialectic and contrast—is evident and striking. Dada is not simply nonsense by accident (although chance and accident will play a significant and frequently overriding role in the development of its strategy); it is rather a nonsense which coheres, defined not alone by external forces and considerations, but shaped by internal vectors of talent, ego, neurosis.

It is received opinion that the printed page is recto-linear, that type is arranged in blocks, serrated as the eye travels, moving with order and sequence from line to line. Type is altered and arranged according to classical models of balance and equilibrium, convention requiring capitals and minuscules; occasional italics to supply emphasis and differentiation; white space to define borders, margins, and interruptions on the page. The convention of the page apparently dictates the movement of the eye; but from where, I wonder, does the convention of the page derive? By what aegis is the essential recto-linearity decreed and what wisdom determined that the eye is best served (and through the eye, the machinery of the brain, its cortical transfer, its mechanism of recording and memory) by such an orderly blocking and emplacement of language? If it is the case, as I suspect, that written language is the settled exposition of speech, the determination to annotate the voice, there is a clue. Written language may well be an abstraction of the spoken voice, a means of condensing into coherent sequence what flows in the rhythm of spoken song. Written language is the setting down of speech; it is an immensely abstract mechanism of inditing and preserving the content of vocal narration by means of a structure of ideograms and, subsequently, with orthographic conventions replacing ideograms, the whole range and exuberance of primary language—epic, saga, tale, myth by which ancient societies described their origins and destinies.

Speech was more holy and sacred than written language; it preceded all Scriptures and it was in fear of the loss of speech that written language was devised. What has always been recognized, the visible worm in the apple of mythology, is that no sooner is living speech set down—in effect formed into a codex—than the intention of the setting down to preserve the living speech is itself the instrument of its dessication and forgetting. Holy speech lives better in societies where the great myths are repeated aloud, where storytellers have the obligation—in many societies under pain of death—to repeat the story cycles annually and accurately. Consign those stories to text, make literature out of myths, define classics by formality and orderliness, and the living perishes.

Throughout the ancient and medieval world efforts were made to relieve the formal enunciation of sacred text and chronicled history by the employment of elaborate embellishment. The monks beautified the Word of God, the Hebrew *massoretes,* believing the letters of the alphabet were iconic gifts of God, themselves bearers of meanings unique and differentiated (the aleph signifying a dimension of the divine person differently than the beth or gimel), formed passages of Scripture or liturgy into elaborate creatures, birds, trees, mythic beasts, allowing the visual assertion to address the eye before the letters and words of which it was composed had been made legible. It could not be mistaken that the story of Jonah was being told by a man fashioned of Hebrew letters emerging from the mouth of a similarly constructed fish (see plate 1).

In other words, the rhythm of voice which had been suppressed in the formal abstraction of written language was renewed by the demand upon the eye to perceive meanings in advance of reading them. Sight was being compelled to fabricate out of letters more than settled and sequential meanings. Note, as well, that very often in such manuscripts and later in the printing of words where meanings enforced visions (as, for example, in the cruciform printing of Robert Herrick's poem "The Cross" the traditional page was violated, margins were pierced, white space invaded, various weights and fonts were employed, and familiar case arrangements

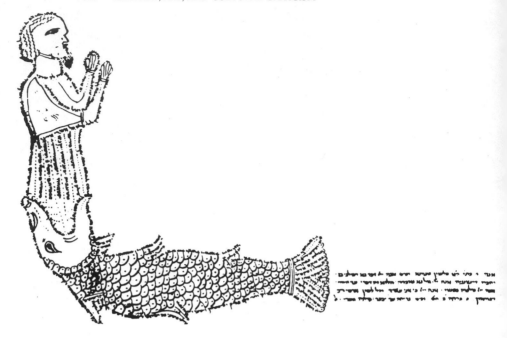

Plate 1: Hebrew scribal ornamentation of the
story of Jonah and the Whale.

of letters were discarded. There is little evidence that such penetrating
revisions of inherited typographic convention were undertaken by the
poet himself (unless the poet was also the scribe); it was more frequently
the enterprise of the inventive typesetter and printer (see plate 2).

II

The nineteenth century found the conventions of traditional typography violated more frequently, but violated without causing offense, since
the violation was committed not on behalf of high art and ideology, but
in the interest of a lower commerce of exploitation, publicity, and advertising. The placard, the sandwich man, the poster, the sign, the advertise-
ment, the leaflet, the broadside, prospectus, *prier d'inserer,* ticket,
handbill—all these methods of calling out, shouting, if you will, were
devices of circumventing traditional language, imitating the sound of
speech, and hence restoring to a kind of primacy the original spoken
rhythm which had been for millenia abstracted by written language. Advertising as a class of communication which incorporates all the specific

```
This      cross-tree    here
Doth      JESUS         beare,
Who       sweet'ned     first,
The       death         accurs't.
```

HERE all things ready are, make hast, make hast away ;
For, long this work wil be, & very short this day.
Why then, go on to act : Here's wonders to be done,
Before the last least sand of Thy ninth hour be run ;
Or e're dark clouds do dull, or dead the mid-dayes sun.

```
              Act   when   Thou   wilt,
              Bloud   will   be   spilt ;
              Pure   balm,   that   shall
              Bring   health   to   all.
              Why       then,       begin
              To    powre    first    in
              Some   drops   of   wine,
              In    stead    of    brine,
              To   search   the   wound,
              So      long      unsound :
              And,   when   that's   done,
              Let   oyle,   next,   run,
              To    cure    the    sore
              Sinne   made   before.
              And  O !  deare  Christ,
              E'en   as   Thou   di'st,
              Look   down,   and   see
              Us   weepe   for   Thee.
              And tho, Love knows,
              Thy    dreadfull    woes
              Wee    cannot    ease ;
              Yet   doe   Thou   please,
              Who    mercie    art,
              T'accept   each   heart,
              That    gladly    would
              Helpe,   if   it   could.
              Meane while, let mee,
              Beneath    this    tree,
              This    honour    have,
              To   make   my   grave.
```

Plate 2: Robert Herrick's poem, "The Cross."

forms I have mentioned is the medium that preeminently succumbed to transforming typographic innovation during the nineteenth century. Since its intention was thought to be vulgar, its means could be untraditional. Garishness of color, juxtaposition of bold wood typefaces, the use of illustrative cuts—pointing fingers and kicking boots—the mix of fonts, the stridency of exclamation points and underscorings, all these could be employed by the commercial arm of the reigning bourgeoisie to advertise a product and to sell it. Typographic novelty began, so to speak, in the marketplace, catching the accelerated pace of an urban culture, recognizing that as people had less time to stop, ponder, and appraise, the means of persuasion could no longer be the extended paragraph of explanation by which newspapers of the eighteenth century sold wares, but required rather the aggressive jamming of sensibility which advertising and publicity innovated.

The reason that we have all come to regard the typography and *mise-en-page* of Mallarmé's glorious poem, "Un coup de dés jamais n'abolira le hasard" ("A throw of the dice will never abolish chance"), published for the first time in London in 1897 in the periodical *Cosmopolis,* as so outrageous and daring is less, I believe, for the radicality of its typographic arrangement as for the fact that the muddied market had entered the drawing room. Commenting on the poetry of Mallarmé, P. O. Walzer (*Essai sur Stéphane Mallarmé,* [Paris: Editions Seghers, n.d.]) observes that "Mallarmé had pierced all the limits. Imagine ten pages of a periodical in which the words of a poem—instead of being prudently arranged verse by verse according to conventional formulas—are distributed apparently by chance throughout the pages, certain among them occupying a whole page by themselves." Moreover, examining the poem as it appeared in its more conservative redaction by Gallimard in 1914, the poem is not, like a dice throw, revealed by chance, but is rather arranged by chance. We witness then not the throw itself, but the aftermath and hence, given its arrangement (and I have examined the estates of the Mallarmé proofs and observed the care and precision with which Gallimard corrected the placement of type after Mallarmé's nephew, who had been charged to see the work through its first printing), one is struck by the previsioned unfolding of the throw—as though each phase of light which defined the visual spume left in the aftermath of the throw had been photographed by a futurist or painted like Balla's dog, each stage of the poem implicated by its predecessor and hence each roll of the dice upon the page implicated by its earlier trajectory, and hence each aspect of chance evolving not through spontaneity, but through the consideration of options and alternatives. The throw of dice is not truly a throw of dice, a roll in the face of chance, but rather a fixing of odds to which the actual throw is secondary (see plate 3).

What is splendid then about the *mise-en-page* of Mallarmé's poem is not that we are transfixed—as was Mallarmé himself—by the daring and dementia of the act (Mallarmé sent Paul Valéry a set of the corrected page proofs of the poem in March 1897 accompanied by a note which inquired: "Ne trouvez-vous pas que c'est un acte de démence?" ["Do you not find this an insane act?"]. And yet, as Mallarmé makes perfectly clear in antecedent mediations on the nature of the book, which he had written in 1895 and, indeed, in the preface which he appended to the poem itself, his decision to throw the dice as he did emerges as profoundly considered and adjudicated. Mallarmé wrote: "There is nothing new here

LE NOMBRE

C'ÉTAIT

ùsu flellairt

EXISTÂT-IL
autrement qu'hallucination éparse d'agonie

COMMENÇÂT-IL ET CESSÂT-IL
sourdant que nié et clos quand apparu
enfin
par quelque profusion répandue en rareté
SE CHIFFRÂT-IL

évidence de la somme pour peu qu'une
ILLUMINÂT-IL

LE HASARD

CE SERAIT
pire
non
davantage ni moins
indifféremment mais autant

Choit
la plume
rythmique suspens du sinistre
s'ensevelir
aux écumes originelles
naguères d'où sursauta son délire jusqu'à une cime
flétrie
par la neutralité identique du gouffre

Plate 3: Stéphane Mallarmé's poem, "Un coup de dés jamais n'abolira le hasard."

except the spacing of its reading. On an ordinary page of poetry written in short verse, the white takes up two-thirds of the page. I respect this proportion, but work for the redistribution of the white which replaces punctuation, and intervenes by effecting the transition from one image to the other, whether in order to mark the more or less direct relation of groups of words—a prismatic subdivision of an idea—with the central phrase." The white space is the silence which moves through the poem, and it is a silence immensely modern and profoundly signifying to us, indeed, as signifying as the words themselves. Imagine, if you will, what effect would be wrought were the same words thrown proportionally upon a wall painted white or against the side of a white building or the chalk cliffs of Dover. The whiteness would ultimately overwhelm the words until the white silence became a metaphysical assertion of such power as to all but obliterate the language which it surrounds.

The power of Mallarmé's gesture is then not its originality (since we note its calligrammatic antecedents in the middle ages, in English poetry, in Lewis Carroll during 1865, Gottfried Keller in 1867, and Christian Morgenstern's "The Night Song of the Fish" in 1905); it is rather that Mallarmé authorized the breakup of the classic page and made possible, not many years after its first appearance, Apollinaire's "Il Pleut" ("It rains"), which ran like rivulets down the page of Albert-Birot's *Sic*. Mallarmé's innovation was finally tame, but it gave a necessary permission for bourgeois culture to open the breach wider (see plate 4).

III

Two further precursors of Dada must be noted: the Italian futurists and the Russian cubo-futurists, both movements of independent impulse and origin, although it has been common in the West to regard Marinetti's 1914 trip to St Petersburg and Moscow as having set off the Russian experiment. This trumpeting of influence has been facilitated by accrediting a Marinetti trip to Russia in 1910, immediately after the initial impact of the February 20, 1909, appearance of the *First Futurist Manifesto* in *Le Figaro*. There is no persuasive evidence for such an earlier visit, nor does Benedikt Livshit's important memoir of the period, *The One and A Half Eyed Archer*—which describes at length Marinetti's visit of 1914—make any mention of an earlier descent.

It is the case, however, that at approximately the same time, two national traditions set forth to revise not alone the typographic page but linguistic sensibility. Primarily Alexei Kruchenykh and Velimir Khlebnikov and their friends in the Hilea and 41° groups, the Burliuks, Livshits, Maiakovskii, Ilia Zdanevich (later known as Iliazd), Kamenskii, and Roman Jakobson formed an enterprise of pressing behind the known and palpable meaning of words to their ulterior sound-meanings, their preliterate signification, and their unconscious linguistic depths. This urlanguage, which is called *zaoum,* produced a literature in which poverty of reproduction means (scarcity of paper and print) was coupled with the most intense imaginative invention. I would argue, in fact, that some of the most extraordinary and daring reformation of the traditional book came out of Russia during the period from 1910 to 1916. The first collective anthology, *Sadok Sudei* (The Trap of Judges), printed on the reverse side of colored wall paper was typographically conventional, although all the material in this collective was run-on without title breaks, the only indication of change of authorship being marginal annotations which serve the reader as a guide (see plate 5). More important to my argument is the fact that the poetry which is included by Elena Guro, V. Kamenskii, and Velimir Khlebnikov—even though conservatively set forth—is outrageously exuberant, indifferent to traditional poetic forms, and filled with neologistic experiment. Maiakovskii is correct in describing this early work as Russian futurism's "first impressionistic flareup." By 1913,

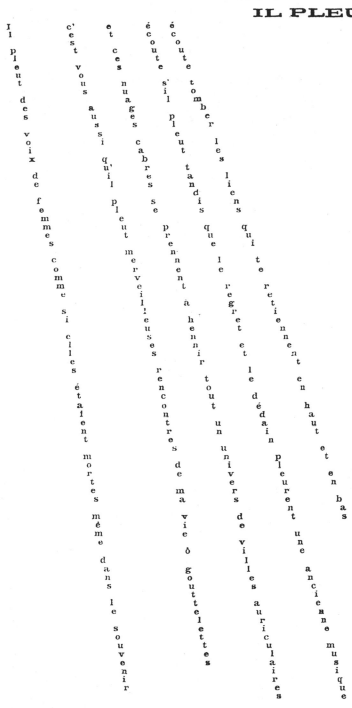

Plate 4: Guillaume Apollinaire's poem, "Il Pleut."

Plate 5: *Sadok Sudei (The Trap of Judges).*

when the second and smaller edition of *The Trap of Judges* appeared, manifesto had already come to the fore, personal freedom of creativity exalted, traditional poetic forms rejected, and language come under review and renovation. By 1914, when the unique volume of what was to have been a projected series, *Futuristy, Pervyi Zhurnal Russkikh Futuristov* (Futurists. First Journal of the Russian Futurists), appeared under the aegis of Kamenskii and David Burliuk, with Shershenevich actually in command, not only poetic and linguistic traditions were repudiated, but the familiar futurist typographic page made its brilliant appearance (see plate 6). On a single page, a poem of Kamenskii is presented framed by thin black lines, although subdivided irregularly like a madly cut pie into six irregular shapes within which different weights, cases, fonts are disposed—more than a dozen at careless count—forming a poetic impasto which is as brilliantly original as any invention of the Italian futurists. And lastly, merely to sample this phenomenon which is described in considerable detail by Markov in his *Russian Futurism,* Kruchenykh and Roman Jakobson (pseudonymously identified as Aliagrov) joined to-

Plate 6: Poem by V. Kamenskii.

gether with the artist Rozanova to create a book, *Zaumnayakniga* (The Book of Zaoum) in 1916 in which the text consists in letters rubber-stamped upon the page, sometimes in blue, sometimes in pink (see plate 7). The texts are marked by purposive misspellings of familiar Russian words, the employment of fragments of Kruchenykh poems that are wholly *zaoum*—that is, transrational poetry, sound poetry which echoes the roots of the language, but entail an open consciousness and a hearing cut free from the shorings of traditional patterns of language. Most striking is the fact that the principal word of literary convention, book (*kniga*), is misspelled in the title of the work in such a way as to provoke association with two other Russian words, those for "rotten" (*gniloi*) and "nit" (*gnida*).

Plate 7: *Zaumnayakniga (The Book of Zaoum)*, 1916.

By comparison with the poorly organized and depopulated circles of the Russian avant-garde, a movement which could not have numbered more than a few hundred adherents traveling from Odessa to Petersburg and Moscow, agitating against bourgeois culture, a modest precursor of the revolution, but one which the revolution ultimately would be obliged by its own totalitarian traditionalism to suppress, the Italian futurists of Marinetti and his circle comprised a cultural steamroller, humorless, aggressive, publicity-conscious, equipped with numerous publications and periodicals, sympathizers and street gangs, an aesthetic movement masking a nationalism redivivus. Although I dislike Marinetti and his movement, I am obliged to recognize that it forged from technological means devices of assault which were later to be reappraised and adapted by De Stijl, Bauhaus, and constructivist typographers. Marinetti's *Technical Manifesto of Futurist Literature* which appeared in *Der Sturm* in 1912 and was reported as well in the Russian periodical *Russkaya Mysl,* called openly for the destruction of the typographically harmonious page which Marinetti described as "monastic harmony, symmetry, equilibrious seriality of the page." Marinetti wanted instead words that ran like sound, words that were stressed like speech, growls that grew from small letters into screams (think forward to Raoul Hausmann's Dada book, *Hurrah! Hurrah! Hurrah!* in which the title word comes forth from a teeth-filled mouth outlined in white on a black cover until the hurrahs dominate the page). As well, Marinetti wanted various colored inks employed, up to twenty different typographical fonts to increase "the pictorial possibilities of the page," which, in turn, would augment the hitting power of poetry. Marinetti's "words in liberty typography," presented as spontaneity, was as rehearsed and manipulated as it could be, compositions for his first typographic adventure of 1914, *Les Mots Futuristes en Liberté,* being choreographed in detail, his type pages moving like a densely packed crusade of the insect kingdom assaulting a fortressed Jerusalem of the bourgeoisie (see plates 8–10). Marinetti was not alone—his example moved Boccioni in the review *Lacerba* as well as Soffici, Depero, Cagniullo, and others to a reconstruction of sound words on the page. The voice throbbed again; it sang in type and its melody, agitating and unnerving, alongside demonstrations, manifestations, declamations, and riots produced the futurist movement and forced bourgeois culture to pay attention.

IV

At last we return to the internal contradiction with which we began, a contemplation of dialectic, a speculation upon the contrarieties out of which Dada comes forth. All things for which we can find no appropriate accounting may not—by reason of their unaccountableness—be called Dada. Tristan Tzara blazoned: "Dada signifie rien." But if Dada signifies nothing, means nothing, it can be employed carelessly, carefully, indifferently to signify anything, everything. On the other hand, if Dada is the precipitate which remains after the political dynamism and aesthetic simultanism of the futurists, the concrete poetic imagination of the post-symbolist French poets, and the transrational inquiries of the Russian experimentalists have been exhausted, Dada would remain an international movement of an elitist and impoverished coterie of alienated artists, poets, intellectuals.

The truth is, perhaps, that Dada allows no definition because it both accepts and subverts all definition. All definitions are permissible, all explanations useful. This is simply a way of recognizing the obvious: it doesn't matter from where the light shines, nor the voltage it commands, something of the object is bound to be illuminated. Any definition works, even definitions which, at the outset, seem to be most outrageously inappropriate and false, but then it must be remembered that Dada has also been called fascist, totalitarian, communist, subversive no less than it has been called revolutionary, antibourgeois, anarchist and, no less, perverse, decadent, suicidal, anticulture. Dada has been called everything in anger;

Plate 8: Works from Filippo Marinetti's
Les Mots Futuristes en Liberté, 1914.

it has been named everything in celebration. Its adherents became its
enemies, its detractors became its publicists. If all this is the case, one
thing immensely important and profoundly understood from the outset
is that Dada is a denial of traditional logic: it suspends the law of contradiction; more than suspending, it violates it. Cutting it like a Gordian
knot, it denies the contradiction exists, because it is itself, in its gut,

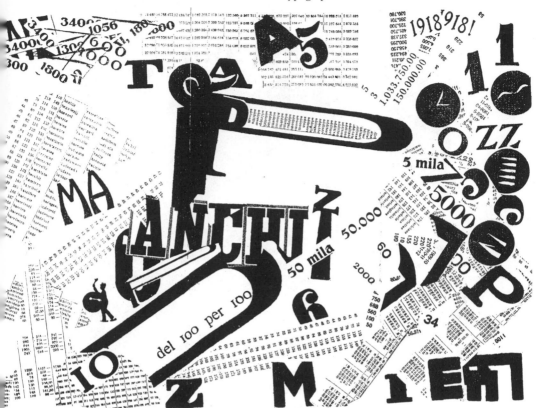

Plate 9: Works from Filippo Marinetti's
Les Mots Futuristes en Liberté, 1914.

contradiction. At the same time that it denies the law of contradiction, it
collaterally denies the law of identity. It affirms that A can be A, but also
B at the same time as it remains fully and passionately A. It claims (as
well) that in being A and B at the same time, it can also be non-A. It
affirms contradiction within the essence of society, culture, the word, and
speech; it denies identity and thereby denies that what passes as settled
truth is in fact settled. Its impulse is to undercut the presumption of
ordinary discourse, to make the solemn pretensions of bourgeois speech
contemptible, but as well to elaborate a doctrine which denies the imputation of value to any artifact of culture. Its decline is nomadic, rather
than settled; its teaching is a vagabondage of the word and, in the process, the recovery of a cadence and song which humiliates bow ties,
lorgnettes, clapping hands, pipes, homburgs, as well as those items of

Plate 10: Works from Filippo Marinetti's
Les Mots Futuristes en Liberté, 1914.

culture which the futurists admired—machine guns, speed for its own sake, bombs, warfare. *Le fusil,* of course, the single gun for the single shot, understood; the shout, by all means; but sheer terrorism—the terrorism of which Marinetti was an expert and Breton an adept, no, and with contempt, no.

V

My perception of the Dada spirit is that it sought—whether in the calligrams of Marius de Zayas in Stieglitz's *291* or Picabia's astonishing conflagrations of language and image throughout his *391,* or the Huelsenbeck-Janco-Tzara simultaneous poem which appeared in *Cabaret Voltaire* in June 1916, or yet again the productions announced in *Die Schammade* which included Baargeld's "Bimbamresonanz 1" and wild advertisements for Arp's *Die Wolkenpumpe* or Hausmann's simultaneous poem from *Merz 4* which is eviscerated by a hand pointing to the legend "Von der Zensur gestrichen" ("Struck by the Censor")—to oblige a reconception of the relation of spoken word, written speech, settled meaning, and the pictorial ideogram which was once the alphabet and is now twenty-six beautiful and exotic shapes which can slink or lurk, stand erect or be flattened by bar lines, hemmed within squares, wrinkled by italic or compelled to call forth, tiny letters surrounded by giant capitals, to drown beneath the weight of fat faces or lie down on their sides to rest or to hide. Type came alive, living things squirming on the page, requiring that the words be reread and reconceived, that the writing itself be composed as typography and reapprehended as living voice, speaking volumes, shouting and making love.

The reason why such a view of Dada is perhaps unfamiliar and such an interpretation of artisanal typography is unconventional is that Dada is too often seen in disjunction from moods and inquiries elsewhere making their way through European culture at the same time. Dada was manifest assertion about the hopeless dessication of language, the inability of language and image to speak, the necessity to rebuke, humor, humiliate the salons and ballrooms of culture where literature was still high and art was devotion, where education was still genteel and religions respectable—even then, after the carnage of war and despite the efforts of George Grosz, Baader, Hausmann, Heartfield, and others to awaken the bourgeoisie.

Dada was having no more of such a society. It threw up its language; however, others, it should be recalled, confirming the Dada assertion, were making sterner and more permanent inquiries: Ferdinand Ebner,

Friedrich Gogarten, and Eugen Rosenstock-Huessy had brought to the attention of the German Christian world the inability of the word to speak, the primary voice of God and the gods of civilization no longer able to break through the crust of obduracy and intransigence which surrounded and baffled the living voice; the Patmos Circle, which met from 1915–23, brought together the most gifted young theological minds of postwar Germany, Protestant and Catholic, to meet in contemplation of the sources of European civilization and the forces arrayed against them. And no less Martin Buber in 1923, Dadaist not at all, published his *I and Thou* in which the possibilities of dialogic speech, relational language, was affirmed, and Franz Rosenzweig, the greatest of modern Jewish theologians, published *The Star of Redemption* in 1921 in which the principal doctrine revolves about the reconception of the direct speech of man and God, and among French Catholics, the personalist doctrine of Emmanuel Mounier seeking to reclaim realms of intimacy from the world of use, manipulation, and objectification, and Berdyaev and Soloviev, among Russian Orthodox thinkers, contending for a realm of incarnate speech, *sophia,* wisdom as language.

I bring all this unfamiliar association to bear upon this discussion because I contend that Dada is not isolate, not a phenomenon merely outrageous or witty, but a movement of considerable power and internal coherence which contended passionately for the life of speech, for the power of speech to transcend convention and subvert its boring and dry traditionalism in the interest of a personalism which was ardently humanist and ultimately sane in a world of apparent sanity, but about to go mad.

SELECTED BIBLIOGRAPHY

The following titles are proposed as a selected bibliography for the topic under discussion in this essay: Baudin, Fernand. "Typo-DaDA, DaDA-Typo. Au Royaume des Bilingues." *Cahiers-Dada-Surréalisme.* No. 3, Paris, 1969: 36–49; Billoli, Carlo. "La component visuale-tipografica nella poesia d'avanguardia." *Pagina.* Milan, (No. 3 October 1963): 4–47; Bowler, Berjouhi. *The Word as Image.* Studio Vista. London, 1970; Caradec, François. "Dada sans/avec Parangon." *Cahiers-Dada-Surréalisme.* No. 3. Paris, 1969: 51–62; Cohen, Ronny. "Italian Futurist Typography." *Print Collector's Newsletter.* New York (8, No. 6 January–February 1978): 166–70; Damase, Jacques. *Révolution Typographique.* (Geneva: Editions Motte, 1966); Guégan, Bertrand. "Vers Figures et Calligrammes." *Arts et Metiers Graphiques.* Paris (No. 32 November 1932): 27–34; Harrison, Gail, et al. *Constructivism & Futurism: Russian & Other.* Catalogue. Ex Libris. New York, 1977; Livshits, Benedikt. *The One and A Half-Eyed Archer.* Translated by John E. Bowlt. (Newtonville, MA: Oriental Research Partners, 1977); Markov, Vladimir. *Russian Futurism: A History.* London: MacGibbon & Kee Ltd., 1969); Poppard-Lieussou, Y., & Sanouillet, M. (Geneva: *Documents Dada*. Weber, 1974); Spencer, Herbert. *Pioneers of Modern Typography*. (New York: Hastings House Publishers, 1969); Sullerot, François, "Des Mots sur le Marche." *Cahiers—Dada-Surréalisme*. No. 3, Paris, 1969: 63–69; Themerson, Stefan. *Apollinaire's Lyrical Ideograms*. (London: Gaberbocchus, 1968).

KAFKA'S PRAGUE

Caroline Commanville, Flaubert's niece, records in her memoir the sacrifices which her uncle made for literature—his loneliness, his celibacy, his disdain for the attachments of wife or family, and she concludes that he came ultimately to regret his departure from "*la route commune*." She cites in evidence Flaubert's agitated comment upon their leaving the home of a married friend, who sat in evident content, surrounded by her appealing children. As they returned along the Seine to Flaubert's solitary quarters, Madame Commanville reports, her uncle observed "*ils sont dans le vrai*," referring by this phrase to the example of domestic felicity which they had just seen. And, as though persuading himself further of what he had already announced, Flaubert repeated again, but this time with increased gravity, "*ils sont dans le vrai*."

Franz Kafka often cited this remark of Flaubert's as a paradigm of his own situation, Kafka felt himself particularly identified with the great Flaubert as well as with Heinrich von Kleist, whose autobiography resembled in so many ways his own misery of *misalliance* with family, work, friends, and vocation. Both Flaubert and von Kleist suffered in alienation from "*le vrai*"—the common, pedestrian round of days, where routine is ostensibly salvaged from tedium by the affection and intimacy of life *en famille*.

Partisan Review 48 (April–May 1981): 552–63. Estate of Arthur A. Cohen.

If I construe Kafka's life as arid, I do so with full recognition of the superlative achievement which was recognized least by himself. Kafka also failed to find compensation in his personal life: the number of occasions on which he was able to claim pleasure in his days were a half-dozen—perhaps the exuberant night in which he finished his story *The Judgment,* the few days of happiness he spent at Marienbad with Felice Bauer, the intermittent moments of contentment at the very end with Dora Dymant. The *Diaries* and the *Letters* confirm persistent psychogenic and physical distress—migraines, shooting pains, insomnia, feelings of paralysis—and in the last years consumptive attacks, internal bleeding, and anxiety of the deepest order. All these alarums of psychic unease and physical illness served Kafka with excuses for lateness or cancellation of appointments, and engendered a distinctly queer arrangement of lodgings (maintaining, as he did for many years, one apartment in which he slept, another in which he wrote, and a third—the home of his parents—in which he took his meals and kept score for them while they played cards). In Kafka's view, his despair provoked his body to rebel against the orderly seductions of "*le vrai,*" but in his last years he was increasingly confirmed in the sadness of his condition and the decisions he had made on behalf of literature to cut himself off from the possibility of ordinary life. Kafka had left nothing to chance. He saw both his disease and his achievement as fatal necessities.

Kafka's relatively brief life was passed within a small area of his native city, bounded by the precincts of the Altstädter Ring, whose principal monuments were the rococo Kinsky Palace, the baroque church of St. Nicholas (in one of whose converted clergy houses Kafka was born in 1883) a short walk from the Judenstadt whose synagogues, small shops, and brothels marked the presence of a poor and petit bourgeois Jewish community. The gothic and baroque quarter of old Prague was a small city within a sprawling nineteenth-century metropolis in which Czechs from the countryside settled by the tens of thousands, to which Germans from the Sudeten came briefly to study, to which Jews began to come after restrictions against their internal migrations within Bohemia-Moravia had been lifted.

During the years of his childhood, Kafka rarely left Prague, and in his maturity his brief trips to Paris, Italy, Germany, Switzerland, and the Bohemian countryside were few. Rather it was Prague—the city which had, in his words, "claws" to whom one must surrender or else, as he wrote a friend, "we would have to set it on fire from two sides" (the castle complex of Hradcany and the ancient citadel of Vysehrad)—that was the home of Franz Kafka and his enemy. Yet Kafka was constricted by no single Prague: his prison was everywhere, devised according to his own doctrine of penal constructions and justified punishment.

After years of fantasizing escape and urging others to undertake the surrogacy of flight, Kafka managed to leave Prague for Berlin, also a fantasy city, where he imagined that Jews speaking German could make culture without attracting enmity or notice, where life could be engaged with the greatest intensity and anonymity, where loneliness might be bearable. A secular heaven, Berlin was balanced in Kafka's imagination by the hieratic Palestine. At the very end of his life, the two fantasies came to reality—he studied Hebrew seriously and considered moving to Palestine to become a carpenter (not very dissimilar in this respect to Walter Benjamin's contemplated emigration to Palestine at Gershom Scholem's insistence). At the same time he dreamt of the Berlin that would distance him from the oppressive weight of Prague, which contained his family and his employment. He even imagined that flight would cure his illness.

On September 24, 1923, only nine months before his death, Kafka arrived in Berlin and shortly thereafter began to live with Dora Dymant, a young woman of Orthodox Jewish background, in the suburb of Charlottenburg. The privation of those postwar days broke his health and he returned to Prague in March of 1924, spent his last months at the sanatorium in Kierling near Vienna, and went thence on June 3 to Prague's Strasnice Cemetery, marked now by a sign in five languages pointing out the path to the grave where, on June 11, 1924, Franz Kafka was buried alone and then later beside, perhaps even beneath (since he died first), his parents.

In a letter to Max Brod and Felix Weltsch written from Meran on April 10, 1920, the form and substance of Kafka's personal drama of cities is set forth in his description of an evening meal taken at a countryside hotel in Bohemia:

> After the first words it came out that I was from Prague; both of them, the General (who sat opposite me) and the colonel—were acquainted with Prague. Was I Czech? No. So now you explain to those true German military eyes what you really are. Someone else suggested "German-Bohemian," someone else "Kleinseite" (the so-called Little Quarter in which the German bourgeoisie were settled in Prague). Then the subject was dropped and people went on eating, but the General, with his sharp ears linguistically trained in the Austrian army, was not satisfied. After we had eaten, he once more began to wonder about the sound of my German, perhaps more bothered by what he saw than by what he heard. At this

point I tried to clear up the matter by saying I am a Jew. . . . At the same moment, probably by sheer chance, for all the others could not have heard our conversation, but perhaps there was some connection after all, the whole company rose to leave. . . . The General, too, was very restless, though from politeness he brought our little chat to a sort of end before he hurried out with long strides. That hardly satisfied my human feelings. Why must I be a thorn in their flesh? But otherwise it is a good solution. I shall be alone again without ridiculously sitting off by myself, provided that they don't take any measures. . . .

This extract might well have been a fictional fragment, one among the many which express Kafka's sense of comic estrangement and alienation, for, like those others, it is grounded in a detailed registration of ambiguity. The general was, after all, right in his surmise. Kafka was neither a German-Bohemian nor a Czech, although he spoke Czech extremely well, read its literature, supported its national arts, and wrote it with excellence. Kafka's Prague-German accent bore traces, we are told, of the country German which his father spoke. Linguistically, therefore, as well as culturally, intellectually, and emotionally, Kafka was a mélange; he was above all a Jew of Prague whose language was German, whose earthy affections were Czech, and whose literary language transcended the formalism and stiffness of Prague-German (itself cut off from living German speech).

Is it any wonder then that the general should be curious, the colonel unsettled, the guests unnerved by this thin and severe-looking young man with pale eyes so similar to them in speech and so completely alien? Could it be otherwise? To be a Prague Jew at the beginning of the twentieth century was considerably different and more difficult than being a Jew in virtually any other contemporary city of Western Europe.

Czechoslovakia was part of the Hapsburg Empire until the end of World War I, a vassal nation whose institutions and visible power derived from the splendidly impersonal and correct bureaucracy of Austria. But its peasant class, industrial proletariat, and petit bourgeois were Czech, animated by traditions that opposed the aristocratic Austrian attitudes. It contained also a large German-speaking minority who supplied to the church, the army, and the civil service their educated managers, loyal to the Emperor of Austria and the cultural dominion of Germany. The Czechs despised the Germans but worked their factories and lands; the Germans loathed the Czechs, regarding their patrimony as rude and uncultivated. The Jews formed one of the oldest enclaves in the nation, having come to the Moldau before the tenth century, settled within medieval Prague and the towns of Moravia and Bohemia. They became small shopkeepers, hawkers, and tinkers who preserved their religion and customs. At the same time curious about their surroundings, the Jews supplied the first grammarian of the Czech language and provided the first topographic description of Czech lands.

The Jews first migrated to Prague over the Alps from the south and through the Balkans from the east, a Slavic legacy discernible in Hebrew writings of the twelfth and thirteenth centuries. The second and larger migration of Jews from Bavaria and Franconia (attending the call of the Premyslid dynasty for German colonists) settled into the ghetto of Prague, quickly establishing a lively and enthusiastic connection with Czech language and culture which endured throughout the Middle Ages, as the given names and patronymics of many medieval Jews and the Bohemian folk motifs of synagogue tapestries and Torah vestments demonstrate.

The Czechs were far less inhospitable to the Jews among them than were other sectors of the European dispersion. Jews were infrequently slaughtered (the pogrom of 1389 being a horrendous exception) or expelled from their homes. Although, as elsewhere in Europe, they were considered an asset of the crown and restricted in their freedom of movement, they were invited by Otakar II to settle within his borders and enjoy economic advantages generally denied them elsewhere. Even if only briefly, the Jews were considered the legal equals of their Czech neighbors, a benefaction recollected in their literature, in their use of the Czech language to annotate their texts and to communicate with each other and with the general populace. Their earliest artifacts date from the sixth century, and they built a synagogue within the city boundaries of Prague to mark the way station of the great caravan routes which Jews traversed between east and west. Upon those earliest foundations, the Jewish community built first the *Alt Synagoge,* presumably destroyed by fire in 1316, and latterly the splendid early gothic synagogue, known as the *Alt-Neu Synagoge,* completed before 1350, when Jews were prohibited from further synagogue construction, and enduring to the present day, a unique example of architectural syncretism, wholly reminiscent of German gothic and yet condensed and intimate as the Hasidic *klaus* would be.

If the Jews throughout the Middle Ages were the tertium quid between German and Czech, subject to the shifting moods of political and economic interest, their situation changed dramatically, but not happily, in the aftermath of their liberation under Maria Theresa and Joseph II of Austria. The Hapsburgs, determined to Germanize their Czech majority by bringing it under the tighter rein of German-speaking administrators, rescinded the restrictions which until then had governed Jewish life, abolishing the ghetto, permitting internal migration, and allowing Jews to establish new families at will. The Austrian constitution which was promulgated after the revolution of 1848 concluded a long chapter in the history of official anti-Semitism.

Emperor Joseph II had begun even before 1848. In Johann Bauer's amusing phrase, the emperor had commenced in 1781 "to solve the Jewish question in the light of rationalist principles." The Josephine reforms no longer obliged Jews to wear the yellow star; Jews were permitted to learn crafts and pursue higher education; to own land and to serve in the emperor's army. Jews were permitted freedom of religious practice and of migration within the empire. However, since the motive of these reforms was the more efficient and tightfisted control of his realm, the emperor's reforms were essentially repressive in that they promoted not the flourishing of the Jewish community but its assimilation and ultimate disappearance.

Every Jew was required to adopt a German surname to complement his Hebrew patronymic, and knowledge of the German language became mandatory in order to practice a craft or profession; Jewish businessmen were obliged to keep their account books in German to facilitate regulation and tax inspection; finally a *numerus clausus* was established on the number of Jewish families allowed in the countryside and in Prague, the establishment of new families being restricted to the oldest son, and migration from countryside to city was permitted only when a place fell vacant and property qualifications had been satisfied.

Jewish "emancipation" was completed during the early part of the reign of Franz Joseph. The Prague ghetto was abolished in 1850, being incorporated with the rest of the city under the name of Josefstadt in memory of its liberal benefactor. At that time there were 8,500 Jews in Prague as against a Christian population of 115,000. The Czech majority was linguistically and culturally a persecuted population; the country was being delivered by the emperor to the Germans. The Jews made an unfortunate, but unavoidable, decision to Germanize, which resulted in the enmity of the Czechs and the contempt of the Germans.

It could not be helped. The joining of the Jew to the elitist German had been encouraged and then decreed, and when the Jews left the ghetto, acquired German language, attended German schools, were required by law to matriculate in the German universities of the Czech lands, it could not have been anticipated that the beleaguered Czechs would be reborn. But the Germanizing policies of Joseph II produced a reaction which led to a renaissance of the Czech national movement. Prague gradually became again a Czech city, within which a small minority continued to speak German and rule the institutions of the nation. The Prague German community, cut off by hauteur from the German population of the Sudeten and from the Czech majority, continued as a class of rulers by rank and wealth. It became increasingly narrow-minded, denying to itself not only what was Czech but what was cosmopolitan and international within the German realm, rejecting the whole German tradition from Goethe to Thomas Mann. It became, in Pavel Eisner's phrase, "a Ghetto in matters of language and culture."

Who then was the Prague-Jew, speaking German, educated in German language and culture, distant from the religious institutions that surrounded him with their shards and memories, anxious to join himself to the dominant culture and the ruling elite? The German-Jew in Prague, the Prague-Jew become German, the ancient Jew who had preceded the Czech, become Czech, fallen away from the Czech to become German, was rejected but now was tied inexorably to the German.

The Prague German-speaking Jew was, in the period before World War I, industrialist, bank official, doctor, lawyer, university professor; he was wholesale merchant and import-export trader; he controlled fashion and the dissemination of fabrics and furniture. The Jews of the German ruling class were principals and controllers, but the workers were Czechs, and the real power was in the hands of the German Christians. The Jew raised his children with Czech servants, chauffeurs, cooks, and nurses. The Jew's table was supplied by Czech grocers, provisioners, butches; his clothes were mended and patched by their labor. All that was menial and indispensable was supplied by the Czechs, and from the Czech nurse the child learned the rudiments of his language, speaking it as a foreign tongue, a language suitable for domestics and tradespeople. The young German-Jew was fed by a Czech maid and led to his school by her threatening hand, but he was also seduced by her and later found her charms available for purchase, for she was the streetwalker he followed, and his café haunts always admitted the Czech prostitute as one of its permanent recreations. The universities in the city were rigidly divided between Czech and German, and German-Jews attended the latter, sharing only occasional contact with the facilities of its neighbor. The German-Jew went to the *gymnasium,* read German books and the daily newspapers (predominantly edited, but not owned, by Jews), attended German theaters and art galleries. But the German-Christian enclave— the minority within the minority—merely despised the Jews in the familiar terms all European cultures have known. Although, in Kafka's day,

85 percent of the German population of Prague was Jewish, they lived as a beleaguered minority, albeit in elitist segregated neighborhoods around the Stadtpark, while the German ruler looked down on their arrival in his schools and university, and held in contempt their passion for his cultivation and ease.

It is no wonder that the family name of Franz Kafka should already contain the ambiguity of his birth. An authentic Czech name, Kafka was acquired in the background of generations when the family lived in Bohemian lands and was presumably on easy terms with its Czech surroundings. When Hermann Kafka rushed from the country village of Osek in southwest Bohemia to Prague, he attached himself to the German minority, acquired German speech and identity, and raised his children within the German community. He settled in the old ghetto, married a woman from the Alstädter Ring into which the ghetto thrust its promontory, and lived in a house at its edge. In this house Franz Kafka was born and briefly lived, and in this minuscule ancient quarter of ancient Prague, the Kafka family had (with the exception of five months) numerous dwelling places for the remainder of their lives.

The ghetto was ordered razed and rebuilt in 1893, and this was carried out, slowly and before Kafka's eyes, between 1897 and 1917. The Fifth District of Prague, known colloquially as "*bei den Juden,*" by Kafka's time, had become a ghost world. But Kafka could speak to his friend Janouch about the incubus of old Prague "still alive in us—the dark corners, the mysterious alleys, the sightless windows, dirty courtyards, noisy pothouses, and secretive inns. We walk about the broad streets of the new town, but our steps and looks are uncertain, we tremble inwardly as we used to do in the old miserable alleyways. Our hearts know nothing yet of any clearance: the unsanitary old ghetto is much more real than our new, hygienic surroundings. We walk about as in a dream, and we ourselves are only a ghost of former times."

The ghost is always within; the reality never catches hold, having no substance beyond the shadows which photographs retain for us, obliging us to consider not only the photograph of Kafka which occupied Walter Benjamin's attention, but the photographs of old Prague by Sudek, Plicka, Pollak, Marco, and Urzidil already snapped by Kafka's eye. Kafka, who fell in love with a woman he hardly knew and to whom he engaged himself twice, demanded of her endless photographs, by which we may consider that he charted the obsessive totemization of understanding, for Kafka had told Janouch "that nothing can be so deceiving as a photograph," because truth as an affair of the heart can be secured only through art. The photographs he loved (and his library contained many books of photographs and magazines which specialized in photographic documents) were means of collateralizing dreams and dream language, confirming to him that the reality beyond the old Prague of his dwelling place was as near, as violent, as threatening and decayed as the one at hand. He was a devotee not only of photographs but of film. When told that there was a cinema in a working-class quarter of Prague named Cinema of the Blind (Bio Slepcu) he is said by Janouch to have laughed "louder than I ever heard him before or since." "Every cinema should be called that," he said. "Their flickering images blind people to the real."

That the real constituted the true horror—and that to Kafka his own evocation of horror *was* the reality—is illustrated by the question Kafka is said one morning to have asked his neighbor, Karl Thieberger, the father of his friend and Hebrew teacher: "What have you to say about the dreadful things going on in our house?" Kafka was alluding to his story, The Metamorphosis, which he had just finished, but his question was not asked, as one of us might ask it, to prompt the pleasure of revealing the existence of a new work, but rather (as all testified to the question and its transmission throughout the small circle of Prague Jewish writers) that Kafka might express his certainty that the events of his tale were true, that no fiction had been invented, but a dream had been transcribed without the intermediation of familiar devices of the sanity of the writer. Indeed the goings-on in the Kafka house were so dreadful—unspeakable—that Kafka begged his publisher to leave the cover drawing an open door into darkness. Kafka thus admitted the doom in his own house, about him in the city (which all his metaphors addressed as a city of the night), and about him in the continent and the world.

The old city was transformed before Kafka's eyes from the decayed remnants of the ancient ghetto to a well-accoutered commercial district where his father established offices in an old palace and where Kafka lived virtually all of his life. Every city story of Kafka's details without names, situates without identification, makes precise without historical verification. The city is conjured as in a dream and with that particularity out of which dream language is formed, conspicuously concrete, but with the absence of documentation that only the ferreting of the unconscious allows. It is no wonder that the most precise description of his own Prague is evoked in a Diary rendition of a dream situated in a theater where Kafka is both subject and audience:

> In one act the scenery was so enormous that nothing else was visible—neither the stage, nor the darkened auditorium. In fact, the whole audience was itself on the stage, and the scene was that of the Alstädter Ring,

probably seen from the corner of Niklasstrasse. In real life this would have meant that one could not see the part of the square in front of the Rathaus clock, or the Kleiner Ring; but in my dream the stage shifted from time to time in such a way that, for instance, one could see the view of the Kleiner Ring from the Kinsky Palace. The only purpose of this was to display the scene as a whole—it was in fact there in all its perfection and it would have been a thousand pities to leave out any of it, since, as I well knew, it is the most beautiful setting that has ever been seen on earth. The sky was overcast with dark, autumnal clouds; an occasional flash of sunlight was reflected from a coloured window-pane in the southeast corner of the square. Everything was life-size and in perfect detail: it was curious to see windows being blown open and shut by the breeze, soundlessly because the houses were so tall. The square sloped away at a sharp angle; the pavement was almost black; the Tyn church was in its proper place, but in front of it stood a little Imperial palace with a courtyard in which all the other monuments of the square were tidily arranged: the pillar of the Rathaus and which I have never seen, the other fountain in front of St. Nicholas's and the wooden fence around the site that is being excavated for the Hus monument.

The dream is more precise than any story, as though the story were already an edited condensation of the dream, one step removed to daylight, to wakefulness, but still charged with the mysterious disjunctions of the dream. It is no longer Prague in which the cathedral scene in *The Trial* occurs (although every Praguer recognizes it to have been St. Vitus's Cathedral) and the bridge over which characters walk is any bridge joining estranged regions of the city (the Praguer knows that it is the Charles Bridge over the Moldau). Prague was sunk into Kafka as he said—its talons deep in his throat. As he wrote to his friend and doctor, Robert Klopstock, "I believe in the power of places or rather in the powerlessness of people." This is to say that everything is fatality, where one is born, to whom one is born, how one is constituted. These are all the fatalities which the individual is powerless to resist. It is not incorrect, then, to construe the decisions of Kafka's life as a relentless struggle to sever his intimate relations with the world while struggling to succumb to it—to sink himself, had he been fully able, in the clay substance of *le vrai,* learning carpentry, horseback riding, swimming, gardening, Hebrew. But all the time, in the very midst of the most decisive attempts to share a portion of the real, he found the project at hand insupportable, ludicrous to boat on the Moldau or swim in Bohemian lakes. He adored his own contrariety, although he wrote scathingly of antitheses. What life presented in all its contradiction was ineluctable but on that account deserved no elevation to principle. Life does what it can; the real has no opinion. Everything is bespoken in another realm and set forth matter-of-factly in ours. The sufferers are those who have been rendered unfit by their origins. Kafka was finally one who elected to transform the injustice of his condition and elaborate it into a just order, obscurely merited.

Prague was, in its finality, a baroque *scenum,* the setting before which the procedures of withdrawal and severance transpired: Kafka was thrust out—recalling the childhood calamity in which his father locked him weeping on the small balcony overlooking the night city. Kafka was set apart, the oldest child (third after two previous sons had died) who tried to cooperate but couldn't, who wanted to be affectionate but could not bear the intimacy and nakedness. Kafka longed to master the culture around him, but he could not make contact with its earthy immediacy: his body, he observed, lying next to theirs at Bohemian summer resorts, seemed like their own until it began to speak and its language made it the enemy. Among Germans he was cut off as Jew, among the Yiddish traveling players of the Cafe Savoy assimilated, and among the healthy sick to death, obliged, as he wrote in 1916, to "struggle even in order to die." In all things Kafka was beyond *le vrai,* much farther from its prospect than Flaubert, who at least had suffered the healthy misfortune of venereal disease.

Throughout Kafka's writing, Prague is a deposit of memory, not Proustian as some have suggested, for there is little comfort taken in the remembered, few experiences worked and reworked until they became ribbon and cakes laid out to offer at interior shrines. Rather it is that Prague is made mythic, retraced into a past where, as Kafka remarked, "we Jews are old the moment we come into the world," more familiar with what is long gone than with what is at hand, intimate with stones which have long since been removed, ancient buildings and monuments long ago refaced and renovated. There is, however, one monument which Kafka must have passed a thousand times and to which, nowhere in his writings, can I find direct reference. Upon the Charles Bridge, several blocks from the center of his days, "past statues of saints with their faint glimmer of light," stands a crucifix haloed by golden letters in the Hebrew alphabet proclaiming the *kedushah* (Holy, holy, holy is the Lord of Hosts). Beneath this strange and mysterious conjunction appears the explanation. In 1609, in penance for the desecration of the crucifix by an accused Jew of Prague, the community of Israel was obliged to erect above the slighted divinity its own prayer of sanctification. The explanation appears to this day in three languages, Latin, German, and Czech. This is the triple throng of Kafka's Prague.

THE SUFFERINGS OF HEINRICH VON KLEIST

Writing on March 22, 1801, to his fiancée, Wilhemine von Zenge, Heinrich von Kleist described in painstaking detail the collapse of his vision of the universe. He had believed until then (he was twenty-four at the time) that human beings were capable of building a secure and virtuous life by acquiring knowledge that reflected the coherence of reality and perception, of self and world. The previous three years, following his release from the army, Kleist had occupied himself with the study of mathematics, physics, and philosophy. He had disdained a career of easy preferment in the military for the arduous pursuit of philosophic and moral self-understanding, training himself to think clearly and act virtuously. In this undertaking he was behaving as an exemplary offspring of his class and station.

Born on October 18, 1777, into a noble family that had produced generations of Prussian generals, Kleist was expected either to serve in the army or to work for the Prussian state. He tried the first, but after six years, during which time he rose from corporal to second lieutenant in the cavalry, he determined to abandon the boredom and tyranny of army life. Returning from the military, Kleist formulated the first of his many life plans, describing to an old teacher and then to his sister, Ulrike, his

New Criterion 6, no. 4 (December 1982): 26–34. Estate of Arthur A. Cohen.

optimistic quest for moral excellence and the achievement of happiness. He decided to eschew the family's call to practicality, to earning a livelihood, establishing his presence at the Prussian court, and winning his way by social manipulation and slavish conformity to the requirements of his class. Kleist wanted instead to be free to grow in accordance with his own notions of sovereign reason and moral perfection.

Although rebellious against his provincial family, the young Kleist was in all other respects a predictable child of the Enlightenment, enamored of Rousseau's image of natural harmony and of solidly German paragons of humanistic reason. It is improbable that the Kleist we have come to know should have emerged from this genial environment, protected as he was by modest wealth, property, title, and access to the guardians of Prussia; he might easily have grown to be very much like Tolstoy's Pierre, slightly bumbling, full of goodwill and moral self-scrutiny, belabored by bouts of guilt and ennui, troubled by injustice and inequality, but capable finally—at the end—of making a bearable peace or, at the very least, of negotiating a lasting truce between his own ambition for truth and the wretched deceits that were commonplace around him.

As it happened, Kleist was not able to bring off such a halcyon accommodation. During his travels in 1801, he came upon the writings of Immanuel Kant. It is not certain whether he read *The Critique of Pure Reason* or *The Critique of Judgment,* or whether indeed he read an account of Kant's doctrine in an unidentified secondary source.[1] In any event, misunderstanding Kant had a devastating effect upon him. Kleist had wanted to believe that truth could be quantified, built up as packets of certainty that could be carried to his death and beyond into an afterlife where terrestrial truths would be purified and enlarged. Instead, as he reported to Wilhelmine after reading Kant, "we can never be certain that what we call Truth is really Truth, or whether it does not merely appear so to us. If the latter, then the Truth that we acquire here is *not* Truth after our death, and it is all a vain striving for a possession that may never follow us into the grave."

The conviction that a solid, linked, and impermeable universe had been destroyed by what he took to be Kant's persuasive skepticism produced in Kleist another absolute as treacherously negative as the one he despaired of securing had been treacherously positive: "My one, my highest goal has sunk from sight, and I have no other." The "I have no other"—no reserves, no options—compelled Kleist to conclude "that Truth is nowhere to be known on earth." He scuttered like a rat in a sealed maze: "I have not touched another book. I have paced idly in my room, I have sat by the open window, I have run from the house, an inner unrest at last drove me to taverns and coffee houses, I have gone to plays and concerts for distraction and to find some relief I have even committed a folly." (The folly in this instance has been understood to allude to Kleist's first detailed planning of suicide.)

It had all become "stale, flat, and unprofitable." Kleist had left Frankfurt an der Oder, his birthplace and the home of his family and fiancée, to travel in search of self-understanding, but his pursuit of *Bildung* (formation of character) had brought him to the abyss. Had it turned out otherwise, he might have returned to his conventionally pretty and mindless young fiancée, but instead, as his letters of late spring 1801 make clear, it had become necessary for him to prolong his absence, to try Paris in the midst of Napoleon's consulship following the Terror. Wilhelmine became ever more distant, an almost abstract recipient of letters, her person evoked by increasingly formulaic and static images that betray Kleist's growing indifference to her as the real goal of his longing for "wife, my own house and *freedom.*"

It was on the way to Paris in 1801 that Kleist discovered an alternative to the life he had forsworn. In Dresden, he encountered Catholicism and art. Although possessing a strong Protestant contempt for ritual and dogma, Kleist found himself moved by the visual excess of the Church, its appeal to spectacle as a simulacrum of the holy Trinity. ("Ah, a single drop of forgetfulness and I would embrace Catholicism with passion.") "Nothing could have led me with such total forgetfulness from the melancholy fields of learned abstractions as has the art collected in this city. . . . Such things have no need of the intellect to be enjoyed, and work only on the heart and the senses."

After Dresden, Paris was annoying. The French seemed frivolous, ceaselessly chattering the inconsequential. Although the Louvre was to reinforce his experience of Dresden's art, Paris was on the whole unbearable. Kleist was obviously no cosmopolitan and he was by then even less a young bourgeois than his origins might have dictated. He decided to take himself out of the world of competitive sociality and to make a place in nature where beauty could be contemplated and the interior riot of passions could be repatterned as art. Kleist determined to become a poet (*Dichter*), which meant to him a craftsman in images rather than a laborer in ideas. If he could wangle the funds, he would be a farmer as well. Amid nature's solitude, Kleist dreamed he would install his wife, till the soil, and make himself famous.

In one of the earliest formulations of his life plan, Kleist had affirmed that a "single good deed" should be among the goals of life. A good deed was hardly at the core of his ambition, but a great one surely was. Indeed, the virtuous assumption of his youthful planning was a screen to the more desperate and arrogant project which began to emerge during his Paris days in the summer of 1801. Still believing in the infinite prospects of youth and its insatiable ambition, Kleist formulated the demand for greatness. "Nothing is settled and all things are possible." It is a game of chance, where fate proffers the lots but destiny elects one. Why should not that one "assure greatness"?

In 1802 Kleist was able to leave Germany and settle on a deserted island near Lake Thun in Switzerland. Although he was filled with self-criticism for refusing to accommodate himself to the requirements of a young Prussian aristocrat and therefore thought himself a failure in the world's terms, he nonetheless believed himself capable of producing a stunning success that would render his ordinary failures inconsequential. Writing from his island isolation, Kleist affirmed his willingness to die if he could only produce "a child, a beautiful piece of writing, and a great deed." Wife and home passed from his mind; only acts of making remained. Each in its own way was hazardous for a man who was a virgin (and apparently remained one), who had never written anything but private letters, and who still considered virtue so exalted and remote as to be almost inaccessible to mortals. Nonetheless, Kleist's final letter to Wilhelmine, written on May 20, 1802, is decisive. Wilhelmine had refused to play a part in his pastoral romance, his family had closed off all financial support, and only faithful Ulrike—who would herself finally betray him—was willing to underwrite this first and last year of peace in her brother's life.

Kleist's formulation of his intentions is, as always, ultimate and total. Either fame or death. "Either I return to my Fatherland a famous man, or not at all. This remains as decided once and for all as the very nature of my being. . . . [I]t matters not whether in pleasure or displeasure, I have committed myself to writing." At the conclusion of the letter, having informed Wilhelmine that he has no further wish to hear from her, he writes: "I have no other wish than very soon to die." There is no determination here to prefer exile to humiliation, to prefer the atmosphere where free work is unhampered to the obloquy of an acceptable life. Kleist, desperate premodern though he was, knew no language of exile. Exile was wrought from within, in the "inner immigration" of which his countrymen were to speak more than a century later under very different conditions of tyranny. And of all permanent exiles, the only one that made sense to Kleist was death.

At each of the many moments in Kleist's life when the scuttering rat found no exit among the living, the one exit that remained open for him was voluntary death. Kleist could pursue death, hymning it as the single freedom available to the tormented, because among all the absolutes thrust upon him by the world, death seemed the least terrifying. Death was never represented by him as the annihilating end, emplaced like a disgusting finality to a life of enterprise and striving. It was always a viable and considered alternative—not simply a way out of a deceitful human society but a way into a seraphic existence, where he imagined wings would indeed be worn, the best of one's friends would be reassembled in tranquility, and conservation would be superb, where the fields of Elysium would glitter with sunlight and flowers. No wonder that in his early adolescence Kleist signed a suicide pact with his cousin, Carl Otto von Pannwitz (who in fact did—much later—commit suicide), and that he renewed the offer to join in suicide with virtually every other significant person—male or female—in his life. The sole exception was the girl whom he had betrothed. He evidently regarded her as too simple and commonplace to take part in such a grand alliance against ordinary living and ordinary dying.

It is all too easy to convict Kleist of self-destructive mania, to chart the lines of exaltation and despair that marked his indubitably manic-depressive pathology, to do as did the medical autopsists when they examined his brain following his suicide and described its owner as possessed of "a temperament *sanguino cholericus* in the first degree," who "must certainly have suffered from fits of extreme depression." The autopsists added that "a general excess of religious enthusiasm might reasonably be deduced in the case of the male deceased, von Kleist." Kleist was in fact not conventionally religious, but he had fabricated for himself "a personal religion" in which suicide was a central ritual of expiation meticulously designed to convert failed life into excellence, and its violent means into an object of divine approbation. Kleist craved approval with an innocence that would be laughable were its consequences not so horrendous. It is no wonder that at the end, having conspired against himself and his own ambition with complete success, Kleist should have been left with only an infantile divinity to approve his self-destruction.

The inquest concluded that at four o'clock in the afternoon on November 11, 1811, having ordered coffee and rum, as well as writing implements, to be brought along with a table and chairs to the heather-covered knoll that rises above the Kleiner Wannsee some three miles from Berlin on the road to Potsdam, Heinrich von Kleist murdered Henriette Vogel and then, with another pistol, blew his brains out. As Joachim Maass asserts in his recent biography of Kleist,[2] it is not incorrect to regard this suicide as Kleist's first resounding success. The event was noted in the press throughout Germany, Austria, France, even England. Kleist had achieved fame.

During the scant decade between Kleist's decision to write and his death, he produced the whole body of his work: some seven plays (and the notorious fragment of his tragedy, *Robert Guiscard,* which Christoph Martin Wieland, the German romantic, had hailed, when passages were read to him by Kleist, as demonstrating "that nothing is impossible for the genius of the sacred Muse that inspires you"),[3] eight novellas and tales, a body of stunning philosophic journalism and anecdotes (itself a German romantic genre), a score of ordinary, principally patriotic, poems, and a steady stream of totally candid and painful letters. These were to form the corpus on which Kleist staked his claim for immortality. As the years passed, bringing with them few minor successes and even fewer rewards, Kleist's stake became smaller while the wager remained no less than total. Everything was risked, each time. It was a calculus fated to catastrophe from the very beginning.

An essential ingredient of Kleist's aesthetic enterprise—his determination to remain an exile to death if he failed to produce an acknowledged masterpiece—was his refusal of German classicism, represented preeminently by Goethe (then in his prime, his *Werther* and *Torquato Tasso* already behind him) and by Friedrich Schiller, whose heroic dramas dominated the theatrical literature. The basis of Kleist's decision to write for the stage, as motivated as it assuredly was by the wish to commandeer a large public and a considerable income, lay in his not quite unconscious competition with the established classicists of German literature. Wieland had fired that ambition when he reaffirmed his conviction that Kleist's talent would "fill the wide gap in our dramatic literature which, at least in my opinion, even Goethe and Schiller had failed to fill." But at the time of offering his assessment, only one play of Kleist's had been completed and published, his first play had been scrapped, *The Broken Jug* (a comedy which today stands in German literature alongside Lessing's *Minna von Barnhelm*) was incomplete, and *Robert Guiscard,* which tracks the fortunes of a Norman crusader stalled before Constantinople, resisted completion. Only the virtually unplayable *The Schroffenstein Family* (1802) was finished and published (in Switzerland) at the time Kleist received Wieland's enthusiasm. Creaky and mannered in its intricate devices though it was, *The Schroffenstein Family* already manifested the strength that was to invest all of Kleist's work with its nervous energy—the pressing to the foreground of the deepest and hitherto inscrutable complexities of private psychology. Although Georg Lukacs, in his essay "The Tragedy of Heinrich von Kleist," published in *Internationale Literatur* in Moscow in 1937, attacked Kleist's reckless (and, to his view, reactionary and decadent) privatization of the public conscience that had dominated German classical drama, clearly for Kleist the values that ordered the public weal, shored up consensual morality, and supported the status quo ante were simply untrue and, for all their popularity, immoral. Kleist turned his back on the morally acceptable and made the domain of decision and will private: "locked from the inside," as the old retainer in *Schroffenstein* says when he comments on the fate of the unhappy lovers murdered in a dynastic feud.[4]

The Schroffenstein Family, although hailed by some readers and admired by some viewers at its only performance in Graz, was generally ignored. In a fit of despair, Kleist destroyed the manuscript of *Robert Guiscard,* only a fragment of which was later reconstructed by him. It had resisted too long and although Kleist averred that he had spent five hundred hours trying to write it, his imagination remained stubbornly unyielding. Clearly Wieland had misjudged his young friend. Hoping to cheer and inspirit him by his praise of Kleist's abilities, Wieland had only succeeded in blocking him.

Kleist slowly began to unravel. Between 1803 when he returned to Germany from Switzerland and received the encomia of the old romantic, and 1807, when he settled in Dresden, Kleist's commitment to writing was severely tested. The effort to complete *Robert Guiscard,* "to add one more to our family's laurel wreaths," had failed. And he concluded this letter: "I cannot go on." Fame eluded him; *consolatione mortis* beckoned once more. It was several months later, in Paris, that Kleist tore up the manuscript and burned it. Although he then persistently invited his traveling companion to join him in suicide, the usually passive Ernst von Pfuel, angered by Kleist's importunings, lost his temper and stormed out. When he returned Kleist had disappeared. Kleist then made a determined effort to join Napoleon's army, not out of sympathy with Napoleon, for whom he had otherwise wholehearted contempt, but out of a desire for a hero's death. "Heaven denies me fame, the greatest of this earth's treasures; like a stubborn child I am rejecting all the others it has to offer me . . . hurling myself to my death. . . . I shall die a beautiful death in battle. . . . I rejoice at the prospect of an infinitely glorious grave." Kleist was at last apprehended and with mighty intercessions returned to Potsdam. At a family council in Frankfurt an der Oder, he was promised a steady income if he would enter government service and renounce his literary vocation. Already broken, he capitulated. After nine months of social maneuvering in Berlin, where he consolidated his position in the reigning salons of the day (including that of Rahel Levin, soon to be the wife of Varnhagen von Ense[5]), Kleist enrolled in a training program for the Prussian bureaucracy, taking himself to Königsberg to learn economics and political theory.

It was all, however, buying time. In Königsberg, reading Molière's *Amphitryon* and Montaigne's essay on drunkenness, Kleist conceived of his own *Amphitryon* and his exquisite novella *The Marquise of O.*[6] Exposure to the *Märkische Chronik* of Peter Hafftiz, where the career of Michael Kohlhaas is factually detailed, set Kleist's own tale of implacable warfare against injustice into motion. And his reading in classical mythology defined the ground of his soaring, if barbaric, gigantomachy *Penthesilea*.

It could not be helped. Although literature no longer promised him fame, Kleist spoke of it as though it were a disease that could never be shaken. He had relapsed, literally, into prose. He was tormented by insomnia, digestive difficulties, palpitations, eye strain, headaches—the whole equipment of the confirmed neurasthenic who knows that he suffers, as Kleist said, "from insuperable heart sickness." There was no choice but to abandon again the acceptable for the improbable. Kleist petitioned to leave government service. After five months in a French prison, where he had been sent on suspicion of being a spy, he returned to Dresden, the only society in which he had experienced any health and exuberance.

Amphitryon was completed and published in 1807, while Kleist still languished in prison. That tragicomedy, laden with the mistaken identities in which Kleist delighted, is typical in its excavation from the inside. Muddles of identity abound, but they arise from the necessities that the gods feel to mask their absolute dominion in the guise of human passions and from the impotencies that mortal lovers experience when they are pitted against divine power. Goethe didn't like the play, but he thought the playwright promising and undertook to produce *The Broken Jug* in Weimar, where he served as artistic director of the local theater. Moreover, the Dresden interlude found Kleist manically productive, completing *Penthesilea,* which centered on the love-death combat of the Queen of the Amazons with Achilles, and seeing to the publication of *The Broken Jug, The Marquise of O.,* his terrifying story *The Earthquake in Chile,* as well as his drama of maidenly mystification *Käthchen of Heilbronn.* He could write confidently to his disapproving sister that his life was "so full of promise . . . that I hardly know where to begin and end."

As surely as his life was full of promise, however, its end was already predictable. In his introduction to *An Abyss Deep Enough,* a collection of

Kleist's letters published recently,[7] Philip B. Miller correctly emphasizes the "stain on reputation that Goethe must bear for his disdainful treatment of poor, petitioning Kleist." As much as Kleist wished to surpass Goethe ("I'll tear the wreath from his brow"), he had a desperate need to win his approval. Progress in the literary culture of Germany could only be made by gaining sponsored entrance into its tight and internecine society, and Goethe alone could arbitrate the warfare of snobbism and provinciality. Kleist sent Goethe his *Penthesilea* "on the knees of my heart," believing that if Goethe liked *The Broken Jug* he would endorse his tragedy and even deign to contribute to the literary almanac, *Phoebus,* which Kleist and his Dresden associates (once more, with sister Ulrike subscribing his share) were just launching.

Goethe, whose classicism was rooted in a Christianized rendition of the Greek worldview, could not bear the violence of Kleist's play. Whereas Kleist was pressing toward a more faithful rendering of the hitherto unplumbed depths of human emotion—its capacity for contradiction and revenge, its endless quest for reconciliations that lift up and transform the most base and bloodthirsty capacities of the heart—Goethe was wedded to his own vision of a serene, majestic, transcendent classical harmony. Nothing could be more alienating than Kleist's *Penthesilea.* Kleist was creating a tableau of language that was as unprecedented in its bloody lust as it was extreme in its stylization. Here, as elsewhere, despising romantic effusion and classical order, Kleist nonetheless employed the conventions of both to produce an entirely new reading of the classical mythology upon which much German literature drew.

Goethe was as implacable with Kleist as he was what Hölderlin and Caspar David Friedrich. (Lamentably, Goethe had the weakness of admiring second-raters while passing over anyone who threatened his own view of himself or the world he endorsed.) Not content, however, with rejecting *Penthesilea,* Goethe went on to produce a bowdlerized version of *The Broken Jug,* virtually destroying that excellently witty and moderately ribald exposure of a peculating provincial judge who, caught in his own sexual escapades, undertakes to shift blame onto an innocent and fails. Goethe's production was a disaster; however not Goethe, but Kleist, was held to blame.

Kleist could not deal with Goethe's disdain, much less with what he took to be his betrayal. Resorting to a petty device, Kleist circulated two scurrilous epigrams designed to reveal Goethe's own philistinism and only succeeded, as one might suppose, in alienating the rest of his public, who could bear hypocrisy more readily than the abuse of its cultural god. Moreover, Kleist bruited it about—his Prussian honor offended—that he wanted to challenge Goethe to a duel. It never came about, but the whole incident was to mark the beginning of a virtual litany of condemnation and outrage from Goethe toward the younger man and his literary presumption. Goethe was later to say, after Kleist's suicide, that Kleist had filled him with "horror and revulsion, as if a body which nature had intended to be beautiful were afflicted with an incurable disease." Goethe went on to speak of "something barbaric, misshapen" about Kleist; it was as if Kleist were "a Nordic phantom of acrimony and hypochondria." In fact, the core of Goethe's rage was less Kleist's assault on his amour-propre than the recognition that, as Goethe said of *Michael Kohlhaas,* it took a "great spirit of contradiction to generalize on a single instance with such consistent and radical hypochondria." Goethe had framed a canonic principle that Kleist unswervingly denied: "there are unbeautiful, terrifying things in nature, with which literature, however skillfully it may treat them, ought neither to concern nor to reconcile itself." For Kleist the true and revealing subjects of literature were invariably unbeautiful.

Goethe had read Kleist correctly and disapproved. Precisely the point! All the stories, even those bonded to unembellished themes of Gothic horror, have no intention of merely entertaining. They were about terrains of consciousness that no other writer among his contemporaries (setting aside the indubitable morbidity of Goethe's own *Werther*) could even acknowledge existed. Although Kleist moved the *scenum* to distant continents and earlier times, employing unfamiliar devices of spookdom and necromancy, clanking armor and chivalric codes, swoonings, rapes, and murders abundant, he was always intent upon an inversion of sensibility, on externalizing the riot of passions that he discerned within himself and, by extension, within everyone. He used himself continuously as his test case and what he located in his own manic-depressive hallucinations he found abundant tale and incident to make universal as art.

Unrecognized by his contemporaries, Kleist has come to be hailed as a messenger of modernity, presumably for his uncannily prescient talent for bringing out of his own depths a sense of the disorder and estrangement of consciousness, for recognizing in his own psyche the possibilities of malevolence and perfection, of depraved sensuality and pitiable isolation, shared by everyone. It is hardly remarkable that Nietzsche and later Kafka would find Kleist their spiritual kinsman. Nietzsche admired his willingness to live on the edge of the real, where capitulation to conventional reality is a more severe bankruptcy than striving for another reality and falling to one's death. Kafka discerned the Kleistean similitudes to his own embarrassing impotencies and abysmal social ineptitude, his incapacity for intimacy and psychic isolation. But for both Nietzsche and Kafka (and for many others as well), it is Kleist's work, not his life, that remains preeminent.

It seems to me mistaken to ransack the premoderns for signs of modernism, as though our age requires for confirmation of its excellence or misery the proof that its spirit was in the air nearly two centuries ago. What good does it do either ourselves or the reputation of Kleist to make of him our ancestor? If he was a forebear, it was surely not a service to us or our instruction, since he had not really begun to be read and admired (as a putative hero of modernism) until long after the disarray of the modern world had begun to be annotated. If Friedrich Gundolf in 1922 placed Kleist alongside Stendhal, Flaubert, Baudelaire, Mallarmé, Buechner, Hebbel, and Nietzsche, he was only congratulating the age of which he was a gravific exponent. By the war years and beyond, Kleist would be settled into the battles of modernist assessment, trounced by Lukacs as a "radical nihilist," and admired by Thomas Mann "as one of the greatest, boldest, and most ambitious poets Germany has produced."

The core of Kleist's modernity—the quality singled out by virtually every contemporary writer on Kleist—is his utter aloneness. Surely, however, this indubitable mark of his life is less a signature of modernism than a register of the extremity of his creative achievement. Given the documentation of his pathology, the procedure of self-isolation that Kleist pursued with almost fanatic specialization was a portion of his pathology which would have functioned even if Kleist had been the maker of conventional tearjerkers and farce. The Kleist who paid attention to himself, who took a hard look at his own catastrophe and charted its development, who dared to write in a letter twelve days before his suicide that "my soul is so sore, if I so much as poke my nose out of the window, the light of day, I might almost say, is painful on it," is more than isolated and alone.

Kleist had, above all, made the written word a *factum brutum*. Words were never signs or symbols of a generalized condition or civilizational malaise. He broke familiar molds, as Lessing, Goethe, and Schiller had broken them, as Hölderlin, Novalis, Nietzsche, and Kafka would come to break them. He was doing nothing special other than being a genius of awareness. The fact that the pedestrian writers of his day could confect with ruffs and frills and satisfy the conventional expectations of the literate should not be interpreted as proof that Kleist anticipates our age. At its best, modernism is as much despised and misunderstood in our time and practiced by as few as it was in Kleist's day. Goethe towered over all because he wrought a total universe that was finally easy to take—even in its extreme and encompassing formulation in *Faust*—precisely because the elevation and grandeur of its values were held dear by every cultural aspirant. It could be admirable while still remaining the portion of the middle class. Kleist, however, had no such synthetic genius. Neither did he enjoy the early admiration which, with sponsorship and sinecure, would have freed him to tear down the old world with the wholehearted support and misunderstanding of his contemporaries. Besides, Kleist would have destroyed himself as surely and exquisitely even if he had been as celebrated as Goethe.

One is tempted then to forget the horrific details of Kleist's life—the dubious triumph of his suicide—and concentrate on the work, among which the most emblematic, profound, painfully mortal, and sad is the essay "On the Puppet Theater," which he printed in his ill-fated Berlin newspaper, *Die Abendblätter,* less than a year before his death. It was anticipated by a brief note he had written for his paper shortly before, where he inverted the Enlightenment dream of endless progress and described the course of the world as one of irreversible decline. The decline, he wrote, began with the living heroes of antiquity and devolved through the poetry that celebrates them to the codification of the rules of such poetry and the philosophy that abstracts their principles after the poetry has ceased, ending thereafter in simple badness. Not up from savagery to perfection, but down from spontaneity to frozen evil. Obviously Kleist foreshortened for the sake of brevity, for he could have inserted much between the rise of philosophy and the coming of the evil age, but he took it for granted that those few who got the point would fill in the blanks. Pessimism was the point. Nothing further could be expected of civilization. If there was hope it would be only with those intrepid voyagers of the spirit who would not be afraid, as he asserts in "On the Puppet Theater," to travel the long way around and enter paradise from the back. The devolution from unself-conscious grace into the barren narcissism of civilization, from the innocence of the first paradise to the return of innocence in the second, is a passage through infinity and forgetfulness, a retracing of the whole of human history in order that we forget our disenchantment, guile, self-deception—all conditions born of reflection and consciousness. We must, Kleist concludes, eat of the tree of knowledge a second time in order to fall back once again into the grace of innocence. "On the Puppet Theater" was Kleist's last argument for truth and justice. In his own day, the essay was hardly remarked.

The acts of Kleist's last days were all gestures of summation and leavetaking. He sent the fair copy of his masterpiece *The Prince of Hom-*

burg to his cousin, Marie von Kleist, as a testamentary gift. Like *Michael Kohlhaas, The Prince of Homburg* diagrams the paradoxicality of human justice. Ironically, it explores the crisis of conscience of a victorious cavalry commander condemned to death for disobeying orders although by doing so he won a great victory. At its conclusion, the young prince, in a speech before his execution, speaks much as Kleist would write before his suicide several weeks later: "O immortality, you're mine. / Your light, intenser than a thousand suns, / Pierces the bindings of these earthly eyes." Kleist then destroyed all his manuscripts, tidied his room, prepared a trunk that contained his few keepsakes and letters to be delivered after his death, and departed with Henriette Vogel to keep the rendezvous he had been planning since his youth.

NOTES

1. In his critical essay accompanying the Rowohlt selection of Kleist's prose, Curt Grütz-macher discusses the complexity of what is called Kleist's "Kant crisis." Ernst Cassirer, in his essay on the matter, suggested that Kleist might have read J. G. Fichte's just published study *Die Bestimmung des Menschen* (1800).

2. *Kleist: A Biography*, Joachim Maass, translated from the German by Ralph Manheim; Farrar, Straus & Giroux, 313 pages, $22.50. Maass's biography, although the first to be published in the English language, is by no means the best. It covers the life and works, but without critical perspective and orientation. Moreover, it passes over such significant biographical dilemmas as Kleist's famous Würzburg visit, which is regarded by many scholars as having been the occasion for a precarious operation for a penile disorder, his "Kant crisis," and his self-destruction, which, although documented, is hardly interpreted. Beyond these lapses of exegesis, the writing is either orotund or flat, philistine judgments abound, and the usually superb translator, Ralph Manheim, has failed to smooth out the wrinkles in Maass's popular prose.

3. Four of Kleist's plays have recently been published by the German Library. They are edited by Walter Hinderer and include a foreword by E. L. Doctorow: *Plays;* Continuum Publishing Company, 341 pages, $17.50.

4. I am indebted to the young German writer Gunnar Kaldewey for pointing out this passage to me as a touchstone of Kleist's sensibility.

5. See Hannah Arendt's superb account of the Berlin salons in her biography, *Rahel von Varnhagen.*

6. In 1960, Criterion Books published the complete stories of Kleist in *The Marquise of O. and Other Stories.* Splendidly translated and subtly introduced by Martin Greenberg, this edition also carried a translation of the revised version of Thomas Mann's essay on Kleist of 1954. Although long out of print, it should certainly be reissued.

7. *An Abyss Deep Enough: Letters of Heinrich von Kleist* (including a selection of essays and anecdotes), edited, translated, and introduced by Philip B. Miller; E. P. Dutton, 297 pages, $16.95. Miller's carefully selected and translated anthology of Kleist's correspondence, essays, and anecdotes serves, almost better than Maass's biography, to orient the reader to the psychology and metaphor of Kleist. Although marred by the introduction of modern syntactical conventions and paragraphing (where Kleist is all full-blown and breathless), Miller's translations are graceful and passionate, his annotation of the letters provides a biography in miniature, and his interpretations are judicious and unflinching.

From Eastern Europe to Paris and Beyond

With the exception of Marc Chagall's fanciful memoir of his youth in the small city of Vitebsk, we have little or insufficient information about the childhood, youth, or education of the Jewish artists of Eastern Europe who became the Jewish painters and sculptors of Montparnasse. We have the odd (but extraordinarily revealing) story of deprivation and parental cruelty in the childhood of Chaim Soutine in the Lithuanian village of Smilovitchi;[1] we know that Sonia Delaunay's parents sent her away to be brought up by a wealthy uncle in St. Petersburg, Henri Terk, so that she might escape the poverty of their home in the Ukraine; we know about the religious family of Mane-Katz and the fact that Abraham Mintchine (1898–1931) was an apprentice goldsmith in Kiev. But such information offers us only a series of unconnected details without any clear and defined sense of how this remarkable group of artists arose out of Eastern Europe. Moreover, the state of East European Jewish studies does not help matters since, until recently, there has been virtually no interest in clarifying how it came about that Jews of the East first picked up colored pencils and drew, rather than taking up pen and writing texts.[2] In other words, it is difficult to address the problem of how this remarkable group

From *The Circle of Montparnasse: Jewish Artists in Paris, 1905–1945,* edited by Kenneth Silver. New York: The Jewish Museum/Universe Books, 1985.

of artists came together in Montparnasse, formed an association of Jewish artists, dealt with the charges of being Jewish nihilists or mere eclectics preying on the body of advanced French art, achieved notoriety and success (or alternately continued to be obscure and unknown), and all the while, despite the absence of Jewish subject matter (for the most part and for most of the artists involved), were nonetheless seen by others and by themselves as Jewish artists.

In a famous and frequently cited passage from Chagall's Yiddish essay "What is a Jewish artist?," Chagall reports on a conversation over-heard in Paris, through the thin walls of his studio in La Ruche, in which emigrant voices debate the question of whether Mark Antokolsky, Jozef Israels, and Max Liebermann—well-known Jewish artists of the nine-teenth century—are Jewish artists. Chagall finds the question ludicrous. For him the issue is not debatable. A national art is not possible or mean-ingful in a world now dominated by individual talent. What is distinctive and unique among the anonymous artists of the ancient world—he ar-gues—who made Japanese, Egyptian, Persian, Greek art, has all but dis-appeared. Chagall allows for something mysterious in the Jews out of all relation to their numbers in the world: "When it [Judaism] wished, it brought forth Christ and Christianity. When it wanted, it produced Marx and socialism. Can it be, then, that it would not show the world some sort of art?"[3] Having first denied the prospect of Jewish art, Chagall con-cludes with a weak affirmation of its possibility.

As in all things speculative and ideological, Chagall's reflections are thin and rhetorical, but he nonetheless adumbrates several of the essen-tial issues being debated by East European Jewish writers, intellectuals, and artists during the first decades of the twentieth century, a debate echoed but not seriously recapitulated in the West. The debate, it should be noted at the outset, was principally conducted among the Jews of Eastern Europe since their own situation was in the vanguard of the secular search for political emancipation and cultural independence in the period just prior to World War I. Although in the West the issue of Jewish art had been raised primarily as an aspect of the continuing wish of the Jewish minority to maintain some form of independent identity, the reality of Jewish art—unconnected in the assimilated capitals of Western Europe with an indigenous folk tradition—was vigorously op-posed by those who regarded the possibility of Jewish art only in the context of Zionist fulfillment. It is no surprise that Martin Buber in one of his less than persuasive essays should answer the question, "Is a Jewish art possible today?" with a resounding "No," going on to argue in his address at the Fifth Zionist Congress in Basel (December 1901) that "a national art needs a soil from which to spring and a sky toward which to rise . . . a national style needs a homogeneous society from which it grows and for which it exists."[4]

The argument over Jewish art took a very different course among West European Jewish intellectuals than it took among the Jews of the East. For the former, ethnic and national art no longer seemed possible in the emancipated climate of Germany and France, whereas the question of national art remained of considerable importance not only to the latter but to enthusiasts of Slavic culture as well during the last decades of the nineteenth century. It was easier for Buber to displace the question of Jewish art to the time of Zionist fulfillment, leaving behind the many hundreds of practicing European Jewish artists to do the work of bourgeois evocation in which paintings of artists such as Moritz Oppenheim, Isidore Kaufman, Lesser Ury, Jozef Israels, Max Liebermann, and many others became signs of Jewish self-acceptance in an otherwise wholly assimilated bourgeois environment.[5]

The situation in the East was radically different. It should be recalled that in the period just prior to World War I there was a population of roughly five million Jews, still bonded to traditional values, Yiddish-speaking "to the extent that 97 percent . . . spoke Yiddish at the time of the Russian revolution,"[6] living in hundreds of small towns and villages in a wide swath that stretched north to south from Lithuania to the Black Sea, largely self-administered (although constantly interfered with and dislocated since the interventions of Czar Nicholas I after his accession to the throne in 1825),[7] and forming a significant majority in many Eastern provinces. For all this cohesiveness and raw power, the Jews still lacked an awareness of the strength of their political and cultural forces and remained for the most part passive and ineffectual. The pogroms that afflicted East European Jewry at the end of the nineteenth and the beginning of the twentieth centuries generated an upsurge of energy and creative protest among the advanced sectors of Jewry, providing an impetus to radical and Bundist politics, to Zionism, and to programs of cultural autonomy. Among the issues that came to the fore was that of Jewish art, since it served the Jewish artist to supply a cultural rationale for perservering as Jews; just as poetry and fiction served a broader intelligentsia, so visual artifacts were to serve the needs of the people.

Yet it was no longer possible for Jewish artists—cut off as they were from the piety that produced the holy and abstract images that decorated the great stone synagogues of Gothic Germany or the wooden synagogues of Poland and Russia—to create afresh a new folk art. These artists were neither peasants, open and ready for training in colonies like those of

Mamontov's Abramtsevo and Princess Tenisheva's Talashkino, nor urbane craftsmen influenced by William Morris, the Deutscher Werkbund, or the Darmstadt colony of Matildehöle. For the most part the new Jewish artists were painters from secular and assimilated urban Jewish families or children of *shtetl* backgrounds who shared in common one defect of existence that did not afflict comparably motivated Russian and Polish national artists: They were Jews and hence prohibited from attending certain advanced schools for training, unable to gain admission for even temporary settlement in certain cities of Great Russia, and excluded by harassment and police surveillance from even the modest degree of freedom enjoyed by the non-Jewish citizenry.

This is the context of the migration en masse of the East European Jewish artists toward Paris. Denied freedom of movement and access to higher education in the arts at home, for them Paris—as it had been for so many of the world's oppressed since the French Revolution—became a refuge and eventually a new home. Without attempting a comprehensive description of the environment of Eastern Europe from which the Jewish artists of Montparnasse derive, we can identify certain characteristics of their world. For example, if they emigrated from the large cosmopolitan cities of the East—Warsaw, Cracow, Budapest, Lodz, Odessa—it was more than likely that they came from secure, perhaps even rich, middle-class families, enjoyed formal education in the local school system, had mastered at least one and perhaps several non-Jewish languages, and, even if religiously instructed, were not significantly compelled by traditional religious values and hence were spared a painful degree of guilt and melancholy during their resettlement in Paris.

Even before World War I, the process of acculturation and assimilation documented by Ezra Mendelsohn[8] had begun: Jews of the middle class tended to be urban; open to the political polarization introduced by the nationalist parties of Poland, Lithuania, Hungary, and other countries or territories of Eastern Europe; familiar, if not intimate, with Gentiles; conversant in European tongues; and educated in non-Jewish environments. However, this was not the case with Jews from small, unexceptional towns and villages—the *shtelach* of fact and fantasy—which were endemically poor, implicitly segregated, paranoid before Gentile sensibility, fearful of pogrom, and religiously orthodox and conservative.

For example, consider the odd situation of a community like Vitebsk (which became part of White Russia after Poland's partition) from which came Chagall, Oscar Miestchaninoff, and the Yiddish playwright S. Y. An-Ski. Although regarded by the careless as a *shtetl*, Vitebsk was rather more than that for it was a community numbering 67,719 inhabitants in

1895 of which 34,420 were Jews,[9] and a rail junction of some importance and hence the seat of significant light manufacturing. Although its streets were unpaved, its atmosphere insalubrious, and (near the end of the century) only some 650 of its eight thousand houses were of stone,[10] it was still a thriving provincial metropolis in which, despite its lack of sophistication, it was possible for Marc Chagall (and Benjamin Kopman)[11] to have his first experience of painting instruction in the school run by Yehuda Pen, a Jewish academic draftsman of no particular talent. Moreover (and of some importance) is the fact that in nearly every biography we have of the artists of Montparnasse, at least one parent is noted to have supported their child's wish to study art. Often, the father wanted a more economically promising and bourgeois career for his child—as in the case of Jacques Lipchitz's father, a successful building contractor in Druskieniki, who wished his son to be an architect while his mother was willing to allow him to follow the career he wanted, that of a sculptor.[12]

Chagall's narcissistic delight in his origins and history is unique among the Jewish painters of Montparnasse. Only he composed an autobiography (originally intended to be illustrated by a suite of drypoint etchings, which were in fact published by Paul Cassirer in 1923 independently of any text). Chagall's narrative is characterized by romantic enthusiasm for his childhood in Vitebsk[13] and the laying of groundwork for the distinctively Chagallian mythology of alogical associative elements and connections that dominate his imagination. No one else undertook to make of his own childhood an affair consisting of equal parts of affection and calamity. Many among the Jewish artists exhibit that pathetic temperament that some critics have tried to read into their work as distinctively Jewish, but invariably such a characterization breaks apart since it is virtually indescribable, invariably inconsistent, and nowhere documented by the artist's own confessional admission of his intentionally sorrowful brushstroke. There is, therefore, hardly any linkage between remembered episodes of their East European origins and their mature work, except in the narrative and anecdotal paintings of Chagall, Mané-Katz, and Max Weber.

The artists of Montparnasse who came from Eastern Europe had certain sociological and cultural experiences that can be identified as characteristic. In most cases they had their first training in painting or the decorative arts either in their own city of birth, if it was a large and cosmopolitan center (for example, Hayden in Warsaw, Menkès in Lvov, Krémègne in Vilna), or in a traditionally strict academic environment away from home, whether in the West or in the East (in Munich for a considerable number of artists, including Czobel, Epstein, Halicka, Kars, and Pascin; Cracow in the case of Kisling and Mondzain; Hayden, Warsaw for Zak; Minsk for Soutine and Kikoïne; or St. Petersburg or Moscow for Sonia Delaunay, Chagall, and Marevna, if they were fortunate enough to have residence permits or temporary authorization). Moreover, with few exceptions, none of the artists went straight away to Paris. Paris was an almost mythical place to which artists of the East had been traveling for many decades, but for the most part, after a stay of a number of years, they returned to their homelands. It was a new phenomenon for artists during the early decades of the new century to go to Paris and never to return. At the outset, however, Paris was simply a rumored place. "During my years at Vilna," Lipchitz recalled, "I must have learned about Paris as the center for the study of art, and I developed a passionate desire to go there."[14] In the case of Chagall, it was in the studio of Léon Bakst, an assimilated Russian Jew, where he studied in 1905, that he first heard the names of the new Parisian artists and conceived his passion for Paris, finally assisted in his ambition by the support of Max Moisevich Vinaver, a member of the Duma and editor of Jewish cultural periodicals.[15] Paris was by then seen as the city from which artists would not return. Sonia Delaunay reported that her uncle was reluctant to allow her to study in Paris after she completed her preliminary education in Karlsruhe since he feared—correctly—that she would not return to St. Petersburg to assume her bourgeois responsibilities.[16]

Paris was the city where artistic experimentation was being conducted in an atmosphere free of state bureaucracy and government control of bursaries and examinations that marred the Russian atmosphere. In Paris, if an aspiring artist loathed the Ecole des Beaux-Arts, there were a considerable number of options, with academies of drawing and painting maintained by rigorous academics, minor as well as major artists, including the schools of such innovative masters as Henri Matisse. If one had no wish to continue formal training, the society of artists who were making modern art, critics and enthusiasts, collectors and poets was open and unrestricted, and the variety of museums, galleries, and exhibitions was seemingly unlimited. Paris was clearly the city to which to come if one had made up one's mind to seek a life in art.

The price of this migration, though, was an undeniable loss of Jewish self-consciousness. The debate about the Jewishness of Jewish art as it had been elaborated in Eastern Europe, for instance, was for better or worse nullified in Paris, where the lack of any official anti-Semitism—and even, relatively speaking, the absence of any effectual social prejudice (until the late 1930s)—meant an exhilaratingly open field for Jewish artists and, indeed, for artists of whatever ethnic origins. With the notable exceptions of Chagall and Mané-Katz (and a few lesser-known figures), the Jewish artists in Montparnasse wanted first and foremost to be "Parisian" artists—that is, to be equal to the world standard for artists. Which is not to say that these painters and sculptors lost their Jewish identity. A few did attempt to deny or ignore their origins, but for the most part the Jewish artists of Montparnasse simply lived as artists and as Jews, without a necessary relationship between those two identities (although the rapport between the two identities was by no means immutable). This very freedom to choose when, where, and in what way to combine—or not to combine—origins and art is the measure of how far this first generation of Jewish artists in the West had traveled from Eastern Europe.

NOTES

1. Soutine "was the tenth of eleven children of a miserably poor Jewish tailor who wanted him to become a shoemaker. But he was a born painter. . . . At the age of seven, he so desired a colored pencil that he stole some utensils from his mother's kitchen in order to buy one, and was punished by two days' incarceration in the family cellar. . . . He then had the temerity to ask the rabbi to pose for his portrait. The rabbi's son, feeling that his father had been insulted, met him at the door and beat him so brutally that it took him a week to recover." Soutine's mother's support for him was so significant that the settlement of twenty-five rubles, paid over by the rabbi in settlement of her threatened suit for the beating, was used by her to finance her son's early art education in Minsk. Monroe Wheeler, Soutine (New York: The Museum of Modern Art, 1950), 32–33.

2. The recent remarkable book by Avram Kampf, Jewish Experience in the Art of the Twentieth Century (South Hadley, Mass., 1984), is the first systematic attempt to trace the history of the formation of the Jewish esthetic avant-garde. It is not simply a gathering of Jewish names which renders the earlier work edited by Cecil Roth, Jewish Art: An Illustrated History (New York, 1961) an uncritical hodgepodge. Kampf, building on the researches of many scholars (not least among them Rachel Wischnitzer or the contributions of a Journal of Jewish Art) has focused many of the critical questions about the origins of the Jewish allegiance to esthetic modernism and my own discussion in this essay is profoundly indebted to his pioneering work.

3. Marc Chagall, "Eygns," in Gregory Aronson, ed., Vitebsk amol (New York, 1956), 441–44, translated from the Yiddish by Lucy Dawidowicz and published in her remarkable anthology The Golden Tradition (New York, 1967), 331–32.

4. Kampf, Jewish Experience in the Art of the Twentieth Century, 203, fn. 4. Kampf's discussion here was first published as an essay, "In Quest of the Jewish Style in the Era of the Russian Revolution," Journal of Jewish Art, vol. 5 (Chicago, 1978), 48–75. Although Buber denied the existence of a Jewish art in his essay on Lesser Ury in Ost und West, vol. 2 (Berlin, February 1902)—from which Kampf quotes—he allows for the existence of Jewish artists: "Lesser Ury ist ein Jude. Er ist auch in Wahrheit ein jüdischer Künstler." Lesser Ury: Juedische Kuenstler (Berlin, 1903), 71.

5. Kampf, Jewish Experience, 203, fn. 2, in which Alfred Nossig cites the English Jewish painter Frank L. Emmanuel who compiled a list of more than four hundred Jewish artists working in Europe. "Ausstellung Jüdisdher Künstler," Ost und West, vol. 12 (Berlin, December 1907).

6. Kampf, Jewish Experience, 15.

7. Michael Stanislavski, *Tsar Nicholas I and the Jews: The Transformation of Jewish Society in Russia, 1825–1855* (Philadelphia, 1983), passim.

8. Ezra Mendelsohn, *The Jews of East Central Europe Between the World Wars* (Bloomington, Ind., 1983), 2.

9. This information stems from the generous scholarship of Professor Lucjan Dobroscycki of the YTVO Institute for Jewish Research, who prepared a memorandum for me on the composition of many of the cities and *shtetlach* from which the Jewish artists of Eastern Europe came. Also, Dina Abramowicz, librarian at YTVO, was extremely helpful in organizing for me research sources which I consulted during the preparation of this essay.

10. Franz Meyer, *Marc Chagall* (New York, 1961), 21. Meyer credits his information on Vitebsk to W. P. Simenov, *Russia,* vol. 9 (St. Petersburg, 1905).

11. J. Tofel, *B. Kopman* (Paris, n.d.), biographical note preceding essay, p. 6.

12. Jacques Lipchitz, with H. H. Arnason, *My Life in Sculpture* (New York, 1972), 3.

13. Marc Chagall, *My Life* (New York, 1960), passim.

14. Lipchitz, *My Life in Sculpture.*

15. Meyer, *Chagall,* 57, 93.

16. Arthur A. Cohen, *Sonia Delaunay* (New York, 1975), 40, 44.

Franz Kafka: Artist of the Incomplete

I

Franz Kafka would regard lectures about Franz Kafka, essays devoted to elucidating his works, and seminars devoted to explicating his language and his times with immense amusement. Do not for a moment think that Kafka was without humor. It may well be the case that he is the preeminent comedic writer of modern literature, comedy commanding as it does the same material, subtlety, and sensibility as tragedy. Indeed, it is only those who do not read Kafka but hear of his eminence by report (as though he himself were the Great Wall of China, constructed in fragments and linked together in the wilderness, at great distance from the populated centers of the world where people read and compare their readings) who find Kafka so unsettling to ordinary traditions and commonplace realms. Kafka, in fact, was full of humor and amusement. A particular kind of humor and amusement to be sure, one which could hardly irritate a fly or unmask a fool, if flies and fools are imagined to be real creatures of a real universe. Rather, all Kafka's devastating humor—the humor which edged his laughter to tears when he read aloud for the first time his horrific story of 1912, *The Judgment*—is directed against Kafka himself. All the humor, all the savagery, all the brutality is turned

Orim: A Jewish Journal at Yale, 1987. Reprinted by permission.

against its maker—not in an orgy of masochistic punishment, not because of some well-documented crime, not even because of some psychological aberration, but simply because the only reality Kafka could acknowledge, the only world Kafka could abide, was the hell and salvation of making literature. Speaking, interpreting, being wise in public, Kafka regarded with such fear and anguish as to make such enterprise insupportable. Public events made him ill. When once he went to Munich, toward the end of his romance with Felice Bauer, to read in public a story he did not yet consider accomplished, he read so badly he became ill from the experience. Even his own words could make him ill, could alienate him by their inadequacy and untruth. Kafka made himself unbearable. His strife was never with others; indeed, others found him unfailingly courteous and gentle, incapable of dissemblance and falsehood, frequently unable to speak aloud, predisposed by an almost frozen shyness from expressing himself sufficiently. And for these qualities— knowing even then in the Prague of the early century that he was a genius in literature—Kafka could be regarded with circumspection and solicitude, his foibles honored, his curious personal habits respected, since he was treated not as human being with genius, but as genius who was hardly human.

II

Kafka had affinities with other writers only—with Flaubert, who, like him, was envious of those able to live "*dans le vrai*," in the real world, raising children, establishing their paternity, claiming future generations; and with the Danish religious thinker Søren Kierkegaard, who made of Regina Olsen the same project of hopeless unfulfillment as Kafka did with Felice Bauer; and, of course, with the great story writer, playwright, and essayist Heinrich von Kleist.

Kleist is surely his most obscure affinity. The stories Kleist wrote, the plays he devised are certainly different than those of Kafka, although they enjoy the same wobbling foundation in the real which alludes to a commonality of unnerve and anguish. The clue perhaps to Kafka's unreserved admiration for Kleist is revealed in a line given by Kleist to the minor figure of the old retainer who discovers the bodies of the star-crossed lovers in Kleist's early play, *The Schroffenstein Family*. Speaking the plain wisdom of a pleasant, the retainer affirms their ineluctable destiny to die, for their fate, he avers, was "locked from inside." Not destinarian circumstance, not some fatalistic nomenclature of divine will or chivalric transgression, but their inner nature, tormented from within, shriveled them to doom. There is no evidence that Kafka knew this play of Kleist, but then the fatality of all Kleist's heroes, including Michael Kohlhaas, whose tragic destiny Kafka offered in his own public readings from German literature, were "locked from inside."

As was the destiny of Franz Kafa. Nobody of robust health, happily situated in the world, fulfilled by hearth and home produces a grim theology, a theology in which God, like father, is cast over one's own frail body as a long and weighty shadow. Kafka, it is well known, felt himself smothered into sickness by the absolutely incoherent willfulness of his father, stunted in weakness and insufficiency by the irrational authority of a paternal immensity. Of course, it is well recognized that Kafkan neurasthenia was Kafka's own invention. Hermann Kafka, the jackdaw of his life, is never even made mythical in one of Kafka's animal parables. Kafka made no stories of such ravenous birds as his own name bespoke, except perhaps for the tormenting birds that made off with the innards of Prometheus, until even Prometheus was forgotten, the rock to which he was bound forgotten, the pecking eagles forgotten, the legend and its meaning forgotten. After so much torment, after so much self-tormenting, even Kafka wearies of the exercise of self-scrutiny and gives over, to meaninglessness, to inexplicability, to the unfinished.

III

We remain astonished that such an extraordinary genius as Franz Kafka left us so few instructions as to how to understand his genius. He cooperates so little with our passion for explication, for seizing significances and bearing them off in our mouths as morsels of truth, indigestible surely, but still carried like nourishment, in our mouths. Kafka cooperates not at all. Even where he seems to be cooperating—as with his young friend Gustav Jannouch, his Czech hagiographer—he fails, for every moment that we seem about to be given a revelation of conviction, a Kafkan certitude, Kafka backs off and honest Jannouch, obliged to record the truth (even where he would wish to embellish it by wringing from Kafka some definition, some clarity, some morsel of truth to be borne away in the mouth of culture), leaves us with an ambiguity, a "may be," an item that makes it all unsure:

> Out of a house in the Jakobsgasse, where we has arrived in the course of our discussion, ran a small dog looking like a ball of wool; it crossed our path and disappeared round the corner of the Tempelgasse. "A pretty little dog," (Jannouch said). "A dog?" Kafka asked suspiciously and slowly

moved off again. "A small, young dog. Didn't you see it?" "I saw. But was it a dog?" (Kafka asked). "It was a little poodle." "A poodle! It could be a dog, but it could also be a sign. We Jews sometimes make tragic mistakes." "It was only a dog," I said. "It would be a good thing if it were," Kafka nodded, "but the 'only' is true for him who uses it, and for no one else. What one person takes to be a bundle of rags or a dog may, to another person, be a sign." "Odradek in your story 'The Cares of the Father,' " I remarked. But Kafka did not respond to my words and continued his train of thought with the final sentence: "There is always something left unaccounted for." (Jannouch, p. 110)[1]

Of course, Kafka was quite right. There are unavailable to us single readings of the real, unless of course we are persuaded of an orthodox view of revelation, but even such a view leaves the way open to outrageous fanaticism, stripped of the shadows and colorations that render every reading of the real ambiguous. The heart of Kafka is his conviction that nothing that appears in our way is univocal, that no reading is absolute as the world's view, but every reading is as absolute as the reader. For one poodle in ridicious specificity, for another generic dog, and for Kafka, perhaps a sign.

The notion of events and episodes, objects and persons entering into our lives to disclose not merely their physical whatness—their weight and presence—but their significance as signs is distinctively Kafkan. Everything transmits something other than what it seems, but the new question that Kafka poses is the hermeneutics of the real, the doctrine of interpretation that enables not Kafka, but us, to bear away his meaning. It lies lodged, I think, in the use that he made—along with Georg Wilhelm Friedrich Hegel, Søren Kierkegaard, Franc Rosenzweig, and others—of the ineluctable Archimedean fulcrum, the lever that stands outside the universe, but shifts and positions it. In the meantime, Kafka's exchange with Jannouch helps by identifying the allusive, signifying character of the real as part of what Kafka considers to be the Jewish propensity for making tragic mistakes.

What is this Jewish propensity for mistaking the real, for thinking dogs dogs when they are only signs or construing signs when in fact dogs remain only, always, imperturbably dogs? What is this epistemological self-deception? Kafka does not really help us. He always breaks off after he has established the grounds of mystification, leaving us with the imaginative construction of the real, the three or four alternative explanations of it, and the beginning of a resolution that is never completed.

Every story of Kafka's, even those that we know are finished, seems unfinished. Since most of the body of his work remained uncompleted, we have little to judge the ostensibly finished against. Is "The Judgment" a finished story? Is "The Transformation" (which is incorrectly translated as "The Metamorphosis") finished? In a sense, yes. They are finished in the story, but are they finished in the real? And all Kafka's unfinished stories—which we know to be unfinished only because the manuscript breaks off or Kafka has noted in his *Diaries* or in a letter that he can go no further—are these stories unfinished? We have no epistemological criterion for understanding Kafka's notion of the completed or the incomplete; indeed, we have some works like *The Trial* which are surely finished in the story, but profoundly incomplete, while other works like *The Castle* are unfinished in the story but, given the guylines that sustain and hold the fiction, surely complete. We need nothing further in order to become interpreters and begin to misread the story.

The reason, I suspect, for this confusion between the unreal and the real, the imagined universe that seems unreal and the real universe that seems untrue, the dialectic of finished and complete, is that all these stem from a unique quality of Kafka's intelligence—his taxis for mythologizing, his passion to make new myths out of old, or to relayer the elements of the ancient myth in order to disclose dimensions of it that had been hidden for millennia, and finally to create new myths that have been taken to mean myths that signify modernity.

We now understand myth to be the archaic formulations of origins and beginnings of the race and man. Virtually all the great mythologies—those transmitted by blind singers as well as those redacted as religious scriptures—are marked by the enterprise of establishing the foundations of specific human societies. What enables the myths to endure is that over millennia they yield to us more than an interpretation of our hoary instaurations. Most human beings can barely keep track of their own family histories without taking to themselves the task of transmitting the formulae of the origins of their ancient birthright. What keeps alive and throbbing the energy of old tales—the expulsion from paradise, the Tower of Babel, the giving of the tablets of the Law—is that they are composed in formulae that are carried in our beaks and placed in the mouths of our young as essential nutriment; they serve even in our confused times to propose metaphors of clarification and reconciliation which, despite their ambiguity (because we cannot be certain whether they are real or only signs), enable us to limn an understanding of what takes place fundamentally in the universe. Jews may not like original sin, but they are endlessly perplexed by the differentiation of the Tree of Knowledge and the Tree of Life. Jews may be besotted with the renaissance of the Hebrew language and speak of it as the language of God, but they remain perplexed by the languages of the world in which other visions are created and other gods extolled, and they return to the ancient ziggurat of Babel where languages competed in the enterprise of catching hold of some divine truth. But Kafka has not helped us particularly. He has not told us definitively that he is simply a Jewish mythologist. How much help it would have been if he had written one story in which a Jew appeared as a Jew, or had even used the word Jew to designate something or someone specific in a single of his stories or parables. But he has not been accommodating to us who would wish to rescue him from Christians who delight in stressing his compatibility with Kierkegaard, or Marxists like Georg Lukacs and Bertoldt Brecht who read him as a prognosticator of the collapse of imperial capitalism at the end of the Austro-Hungarian hegemony.

In all matters that would enable us to pin him down, to make of him something that we would find useful to assuage our own anxiety and concern, Kafka eludes us. Or rather, not Kafka, but Kafka's writing eludes us. For finally we hardly know who Kafka is, since even when Kafka is being most forthright he is maintaining ambivalence, and even where he is most specific and concrete—that is, in his prose—his writing is riddled with ambiguity. Of course, not an ambiguity in language, for Kafka's prose is always unambiguous. But like all that is most characteristically modern—Schönberg's opera *Moses and Aaron,* Jean-Luc Godard's films, Samuel Beckett's plays—the ambiguity in a Kafka story is to be found in the interval between written words, that is to say, in the empty spaces or what writers would call transitions. Every transition in prose takes place not on the page, but in the writer's mind. Usually, it is pretty easy to determine from where the writer comes, since the transitions are explicit, the train of associations trackable and lucid. But Kafka doesn't disclose his associations and, hence, his transitions—the silent interval between connections is lost to us. What enables "Blumfeld, an Elderly Bachelor" to move from thinking of dogs (again) to entering his room and finding two irrepressible bouncing balls following him about the room, animate, amusing, but also faintly threatening and dangerous? Not the bouncing balls themselves; they are not threatening, but the *idea* is threatening. And from where does the idea come? *From some arcane source in Kafka's imagination that finds reality always proposing to mind a form to test and challenge that defies the rules of the real.* In "Blumfeld, an Elderly Bachelor," Kafka has proposed a view of literature that turns its conventional appeal on its head. Most people read for no good reason—to amuse, to recreate, to put to sleep, to keep up with peers, to improve oneself; all perfectly legitimate, but fundamentally nerveless notions of ordinary literature. I don't write for you, the reader, although you may read me. Kafka, however, didn't even know you existed. He had no idea that he was making literature *for you*. He could no more explain to you what he was doing than could the ape in his "A Report to an Academy" explain to the academicians what it was like for him to have once been an ape. The interior life of a man is as inscrutable as the past life of an ape. No one can detail it; no one can make it clear. Certainly not if one uses the rules of literature. One can make it clear if one recasts it as a philosophic problem. Then one merely stirs away passion, affections, sorrows, and all the discrete barnacles of the everyday that cling to a human life and tell you about the mind-body relationship, or the confusions of thinking and perceiving, or even talk in much larger terms about being, time, death. Or one can make it clear if it is recast as a religious problem. Then one merely makes of the single man an absurdity in a cosmic whole, ruled (or not ruled) by an ancient being who is God, father, benefactor, sage, tyrant of the race; who has told man what to expect and what to do, and has watched over millenia while man—full and free—disdains obligation, throws off yokes, and is humbled like Job or convicted and slain like Joseph K. But in literature there is no recasting other than by a faculty which is so close to the real that it feels its breath upon its face. The imagination is no simple fantasist. Do not think that because Kafka makes this real world a fabulist's field day, inventing moles, burrows, dogs, apes who talk and cavort, that he is using an imagination none of you possess. He would propose quite differently that he is using an imagination all of you possess, but which you are too timid or too terrified to indulge, lest you retire from the world of enterprise and become, like him, a recluse of the imagination, living better on a schedule that begins at midnight and sleeps until noon, scratching on paper all the while, repudiating girlfriends who wish to sit at your side and imbibe your genius, watching how you do it, making up worlds, all the while throttling solitude with their attentiveness.

Kafka was mad, a little mad, a little paranoid, quite mad, believing that sickness had invaded him as a punishment for writing; he was terribly torn by it all, divided, cut up by prose like a finely carved joint, and yet, with all said and done, incapable of living a healthy life like his father, incapable of screaming at servants and coworkers, incapable of mopping his plate with bread while instructing children to be better mannered. In other words, he was incapable of deceiving with the real (or in the real world), but only of devising in the imagination escape routes that make lucid in dream and fable what is beyond lucidity in the real world.

There is no discontinuity between reality and the imagination; rather, they are delicately composed as compatible radii of the same circle of mystery, the imagination supplying an exegesis of the real that enables the real not merely to be understood but to endure. The imagination makes the real possible, sustains it, bears its burden, interprets its catastrophe. What is made alive in story and in myth sustains the universe. Or, put with slight variation, God exists because reality requires God; but then not because God exists, only because reality requires him. The necessity is not in God, but in the world. The truth is not in the real, but in the fiction it obligates. In this, Kafka is certainly an exceptionally clever and very modern theologian. His Godhead is not different from the profundity of the legends and tales that narrate and imply its nature. Kafka could never be a member in good standing of a religion that had left no mythology or even a poor mythology. His religion was in the first-rate story, since all story is interpretation, and the richer, more complex, and finally more ambiguous its scansion, the more accurate a rendition of the real it becomes. Do not think then that Gregor Samsa was not transformed into "some monstrous kind of insect." He was transformed in the imagination, and (given the potency of the imagination to evoke the horrors of the real) it is only those who cannot see clearly who do not recognize that sitting next to them in any darkened theater, are many who are already transformed into insects and many who are about to be transformed. Indeed many readers of this essay only seem to be ordinary human beings but, believe me, have already become insects, moles, burrows, apes, and dogs, as well as remaining ordinary human beings. I promise you that this statement is true in the imagination and, hence, true in the real.

Let me make this view even more difficult, if I have not been difficult enough already (actually, however, I have been very simple and clear; it is the world that is difficult, while my prose remains simple and clear). I have said that Kafka invests the real with a quality drafted in the imagination and laid over the face of the world with immense care. His predicament, like all those who cover the world with the imagination, is that like sign hangers, they sometimes miss the corners with their large gluing brushes, and the paper that is intended to cover the real begins to flap in the wind, and insects who adore glue begin to feast upon it, until the whole paper shroud of the real comes loose and collapses over the paper hanger. Unlike miserable paper hangers who have no recourse, Kafka has a remedy. He stops the story; he puts it away; he retains the fragment;

and although Kafka destroyed twenty shoe boxes of his manuscripts in Berlin in 1923, burning them in the presence of Dora Dymant, Max Brod, his friend and executor, refused to burn anything and instead translated Kafka into High German (from which he is only now about to be rescued in order to restore him to the Czech German dialect where his living language was to be found). We have many, many Kafkan fragments; indeed, with the exception of perhaps fifteen short works, everything we have of Kafka is fragmentary. May it not be the case that fragmentariness—the reality of the part, the incomplete, the unfinished—is essential to Kafka's literary vision? Instead of the fragment being regarded as something puny and insubstantial, the fragmentary may well be critical to Kafka's epistemology, to his understanding of the universe. I suggest that this is so principally because in Kafka we have a great and profound metaphysician, a great and profound mythologist, a great and profound artist, but nonetheless a person in the world who never mentions an historical event. It is as though Kafka did not live in history, as though the First World War did not break out, as though Eastern European Jews whose theater he loved were not being decimated by the war, as though Communism was not an issue, or Zionism, or any of the other large and small issues of the day. Kafka did not breathe ordinary air. He certainly had no Jewish sense of history—there is little or no evidence that he thought in anyone's terms except his own, that is, he didn't construct the world to be compatible with anyone's tradition except his own, the tradition he carved out and redacted by himself in fragments. Not even the myths that he adored were retained as they were given. Everything was reworked, and not simply once in order to settle a new and correct reading of the Tower of Babel, or the coming of the Messiah, or the Fall from Paradise. No, no. Never a single reading. At least two and contradictory. Or three. Which to choose? Which is right? *We* look for rightness. *We* want instruction. Kafka was content to know that it could be a dog, or a poodle, but more likely a sign. And hence, three versions are always preferable to two.

I have said that it is as though Kafka did not live in history. We know that is untrue. Of course Kafka lived in history. Kafka was a real person. Do we know for certain that Prometheus or Adam and Eve or the Messiah are real persons? No, but we are certain that Franz Kafka was born in 1883 and died in 1924. So he was an historical person, but that does not mean that Kafka lived in history, that history moved through him, that he engaged the historical as episode, gathered it into event, transformed it into continuity, fashioned it as instruction, transmitted it as destiny and tradition. He tells us nothing at all that we should learn from history.

All the Marxist interpreters of Kafka's two great novels do as Marxists always do—they mistake metaphor for lesson: how else could Kafka create the great myth of his childhood and paternity than by using the structure of the late Austro-Hungarian bureaucracy? It is the fact that the novel strains through such a complex webbing a primary and brutal confrontation with the unreasonableness of the real and it is its obstinacy and refusal to be questioned and clarified that gives *The Trial* its particular horror and ferocity. It frightens us precisely because it is nonhistorical, because it hates history, because it refuses to be pinned down to any social-economic-political-historical analysis. It terrifies us because all of us, whoever and however we are, have broken at least one rule and know it, have transgressed once against a premise we hold in our guts to be universal truth (even if terribly trivial and unimportant) and we are able, with passion, to convict ourselves as Kafka convicts himself and convicts all his creations. But this has nothing to do with history. This has nothing to do with war, holocaust, Zionism, Communism, capitalism, decadence, religion, Judaism. Kafka has nothing to do with anything that can be called whole, complete, fully characterizable. He takes part in no historical reality, because historical realities are part of the human code of memory and transmission. Kafka's work is a fragment because Kafka perceives the world in its fragmentariness, in its brokenness, in its incompletion, that requires the other side of the door before the Law, or the other side of the Great Wall of China, or the other side of time where the Messiah curves back to take up the beginning instead of the end, a wholeness that is only in the imagination, never in the real.

IV

Let me conclude this prose poem in honor of Franz Kafka's inability to be of help to us by offering you an interpretation for which I am indebted to Elias Canetti. Canetti proposes (and I agree) that Kafka's real imaginative affinities are not with Christians, Marxists, or Jews, but with Chinese Taoists. "The only writer of the Western world who is essentially Chinese is Kafka. In an observation that might almost come from a Taoist text, he has epitomized what 'smallness' meant for him: 'Two possibilities: making oneself infinitely small or being so. The second is perfection, that is to say, inactivity; the first is beginning, that is to say, action.' "[2] Canetti continues in an elaborate footnote to cite the authority of Arthur Waley, the great connoisseur of Chinese literature, who spoke often and passionately of Kafka's natural Taoism combined with "a special kind of ritualism," borne out most vividly, in Waley's and Canetti's opinion, by

Kafka's stories "The Refusal" and "The Great Wall of China." I should like briefly to embroider this notion. You will see that it ties into everything I have said about Kafka's notion of beginnings, incompletion, the fragment, and indifference to history.

Kafka is generally obsessed with space and distance, and virtually indifferent to time. Only people who expect to live a complete life—a three score ten and more—bargain out their days in temporal terms. My father, for instance, ancient in his eighty-sixth year, used to say, "If I die . . ." He is obsessed with time, but space means very little to him. But Kafka, who died at forty-one, who knew from his early youth that his lungs were weak, his psyche weak, his sex weak, his body weak, his spirit fragile, thought little or nothing about time. Time was like the air, a pressure, a weight, a difficulty in breathing; space, however, was vast and virtually uncharted. Time was never conceived by Kafka in other than mythic terms—endless years waiting before the entrance to the court, years waiting for a message from the castle. Time was never specific, chronological, measuring time. It is vague time and it is precise in its vagueness, mute and mythic, decreed by unknown authorities, set down as the law of the realm by unseen and inaccessible powers, who guard the capitol of the realm (as in Kafka's "The Refusal") in all its inscrutability; it is represented in immediacy by dumb, ritualized authority that deigns to decree and rule. The behavior of the citizens of the realm consists of childlike obedience and innocent conformity as classical Taoism recommends. Indeed, reduction of oneself to the miniscule, self-atomization, the stripping from oneself of all pretension to knowledge and power, total inaction is both Taoist perfection and the Kafkan ideal. If only Joseph K had not tried to fight back, to prove his innocence by trying to find out the charge; if he had behaved like the son in "The Judgment" who willingly accepts the justice of his father's curse and kills himself, obediently, in conformance with his wish, all would have been well with Joseph K. Of course he would have been executed at the end, but the story could have been written and finished in one stroke, since all Taoist fables are very short stories; but because Joseph K protests, tries to find out, to secure counsel to argue his case, to locate supporters, to discuss comparable cases and to develop a sense of the liturgy and traditions of the court, this energy in self-exculpation moves Kafka out of Taoism (in which he could very easily have settled himself, I think, to the ultimate detriment of his imagination since Taoist wisdom intends but one thing—resignation) and back into the nervous Western tradition where the primary myths are about origins and salvation, indeed, about time.

V

I wish I could remember the page in Kafka's prose where I was struck by what I take to be the primary Kafkan befuddlement and confusion. It seems to me that everything that I have been saying about Kafka's imagination and method arises not simply from the fact that Kafka experienced some primal terror that left him scarred, but that he very early elevated that terror into a question that occupies and underlies every single work of his imagination. The question is: why is there something rather than nothing? Why, if there is a God, did God create heaven and earth, rather than nothing? What is the ultimate need in the universe that drives toward concretion, the specific, the charged event, when it is perfectly clear—after the fact of creation—that all sin and corruption, all deceit and lies, all untruth results from concreteness and particularity? If everything in the universe were abstract—numbers, elements, or essences—there would be no sin. Corruption in the human realm, in nature, is part of the order of their realms—their Tao (a Kafkan perception quite opposed to classical Taoism, which sees the essential Tao as one of virtue). Kafka's Western, Czech, Prague, postghetto childhood could not help but revise Lao-Tzu's sixth-century optimistic reading of reality in the direction of something vastly more ambiguous. And the question remains: Why something? Why here and now? Why dog at all, if these do not suggest and signify a possible answer to the ultimate question? And this question, unresolved, ongoing, the question of why is there something? Why is there Franz Kafka? What possible use is Franz Kafka to the demonstration of providence? The question is almost laughable. Of what possible use—Kafka's father early made clear—is this weak, weightless, insubstantial human being? Such a Kafka proves nothing to the universe other than its ambiguity.

VI

Every honest thinker, that is, every thinker who is bonded to telling truth, is trapped between two extremes: to the extent that he cares for others, he fears to tell the truth lest its hardness burden those for whom he cares. To the extent, however, that he values himself and his own enterprise of telling truth, he cannot help but be aware that most human beings thrive on soft truths. Kafka is a man between, always. And, given my sympathy for his predicament, I myself, no less than he—although differently—find myself desperate to make the way straight and generous for others, despite my certainty that the authentic truth of the way is gnarled and ambiguous. Artists and religious thinkers can make the way easy only by lying or by laughing. They can never be serious and unambiguous. Kafka, Kierkegaard, Kleist. These three were hard men. They never gave in. We, who live in the company of others for whom we care and whom we need, do what Kafka, Kierkegaard, and Kleist never did: we arrange, with their approval and connivance, to support the world with lies and deceptions. And in this way, by this accommodation, the world of marriage and friendship, the raising of children, and the foundation of families is accomplished in a moderately orderly and decent way. Not brilliantly, but well. And that should be sufficient. Those poor others—our three Ks—could not marry, could not found homes or raise children. They could not conduct themselves amid the real. For them, everything they did produced and generated a dangerous reality, where the imagination brought into existence every order of hell and alienage. And what we know of their world strengthens us to persevere, for we know—as they did not—that reality is only *sometimes* as they fabled it to be always. Not all the time, only *sometimes*. And this should be sufficient to make life bearable.

NOTES

1. Gustav Jannouch, *Conversations with Kafka by Gustav Jannouch,* trans. G. Rees, 2nd ed. (New York: New Directions, 1971).

2. Elias Canetti, *Kafka's Other Trial: The Letters to Felice,* trans. C. Middleton. (New York: Schocken, 1974), 94.

VIII.

PERSONAL TESTIMONIES

Introduction

David Stern

Everything Arthur Cohen wrote was marked by an indelible, unmistakable style, the syntax, diction, and train of thought that was his literary and intellectual signature. The fact that Cohen wrote few formally autobiographical works is, therefore, both insignificant and revealing. It is insignificant because everything Cohen wrote was intensely personal, but it is surely telling that he never expressed an interest or intention to write memoirs or the story of his life. In an age of narcissistic autobiographers, Cohen's modesty in this respect can only be viewed with great admiration.

The four short essays included in this section are all exceptional works in Cohen's literary corpus inasmuch as they are openly autobiographical. None of them, however, were originally written with that purpose in mind. For example, Cohen wrote his wonderfully affectionate memoir of his relationship with Milton Steinberg as an introduction to his edition of Milton Steinberg's *An Anatomy of Faith;* it is only our good fortune that the portrait of the student shines forth as vividly as the teacher's, which is its manifest content. "Hasidic Encounter," with its sly but appreciative account of Cohen's meeting with the Lubavitcher Rebbe, is excerpted from the introductory essay Cohen wrote to the book of photographs by Philip Garvin entitled *A People Apart: Hasidism in America* (1970). "How to Avoid Disappearing," the final selection, is actually a

525

small homily in praise of Hebrew literacy—that is, the knowledge of Hebrew and of Hebrew literature as a prerequisite for Jewish survival. In making this homily, Cohen briefly sketches his own career as a Hebraist, telling the story of the renewal of his personal commitment to Hebrew literacy for himself. The final selection in this anthology, this short but compelling essay is a perfect example of the kind of personal essay that Cohen excelled in writing.

MY RABBI:
A MEMOIR OF MILTON STEINBERG

If life as a Jew has become for me an ineluctable destiny (avoided in my youth, repudiated in my adolescence, and embraced—with all its joy and disappointment—in my maturity), it may be ascribed, in large measure, to the patience, tenacity, intellectual power, and affectionate warmth of Milton Steinberg, the rabbi of his generation in America and brilliant *defensor fides* of *The Making of the Modern Jew, Partisan Guide to the Jewish Problem, Basic Judaism.*

But of these accomplishments I was less aware during the years that we were friends. We were not colleagues nor was he master and I disciple. It was only years later when his widow asked that I edit for publication his unpublished theological writings and prepare a general biographical introduction to his work (*Anatomy of Faith*, 1960) that I became familiar with the intimate detail of his life before we had met. For I had met him toward the close of his life; indeed, we became close only during his last five years, when the ambit of his activities was already severely restricted by the crippling coronary attack which he had suffered in Brownswood, Texas on December 7, 1942.

Jewish Heritage 8, no. 3 (winter 1965–66): 5–9. Reprinted by permission of the B'nai B'rith Commission of Continuing Jewish Education.

It is as friend that I recall him now—as that most rare of friends who opens to another, honest, unabashed, joyously, what anguishes him in the universe. When we met he was most eminent. To say the least I was obscure. But I was young—just past my sixteenth birthday, an undergraduate in my second year at that then wondrously innovating institution, the University of Chicago. And, I confess readily, I was vastly confused, but confused with what I can only presume was an attractive confusion, one that took all things seriously while managing to maintain an order of amusement and levity which undercut, but never deprecated, seriousness.

The occasion for our meeting was unexceptional. It has happened no doubt a thousand, ten thousand times. Parents in dismay consult the rabbi before the psychoanalyst. A Jewish boy is always meshuga before he's pronounced mad. In all events, my early University of Chicago days had brought forth full-blown a quasi-skeptical neurasthenia, not at all unusual in American Jewish life. Simple: I found Judaism unattractive, Christianity more attractive. I refused to go to synagogue for the High Holy Days in 1945. Synagogue didn't interest me. It was tiresome, uneventful, flat.

Moreover, I had at the time come under the influence of a distinguished Anglican theologian and historian of religion (himself a direct descendant of the converted composer Felix Mendelssohn). I read much Christian theology in those days—a great deal of Kierkegaard, Barth, Brunner, Schweitzer, and great Christian mystics, and many miserably unhappy novelists and poets. It was good reading. I regret none of it; however, it did no good for a Jewish boy who knew nothing about Judaism, but had the intelligence to regard the issues raised as being preeminent.

It was simply that Jewish thinkers were hard to come by; one had to work exceedingly hard to be a Jew, particularly when most institutions of Jewish learning and instruction managed to keep the best of contemporary Jewish thought almost wholly unavailable. There was practically no Buber available in those days, no Rosenzweig, no Hermann Cohen, Heschel had yet to write his suggestive books. And the marvelous Jewish Publication Society had yet to discover the importance of Jewish religious philosophy with the exception of the Schiff Classics and Solomon Schechter.

Needless to say, my parents wrote their rabbi, Milton Steinberg, described their perplexity, and shortly thereafter I made Milton's acquaintance. I don't remember the details. Undoubtedly it was a Sabbath afternoon. Milton and his wife Edith would always have a *Havdalah* in their home late in the day as the Sabbath ebbed. Precarious characters like myself would come early before favored friends and congregants. It was a tense first meeting. I was aware why I had been invited. It depressed me; it delighted Milton. He took my perplexity seriously, but not lugubriously. It became a furious intellectual battle between the jejune and Jewishly illiterate undergraduate and the ferocious, but humane, interpreter of Judaism.

I went back several times thereafter. It was the winter recess of 1945. I was none too happy at our meetings. Clearly Milton had succeeded in touching that residual vein from which both virtue and atavism may be quarried. He fought me quite literally, combatting my metaphysical flights, my mysticism with hard, essentially unpalatable philosophic rationalism, citing Bentham, Mill, James, Pierce, his favorite Bergson, even Santayana, to provide the background for the most fundamental of his didactic convictions, the necessity for giving, not simply reason, but *open* inquiry a chance. I was prepared, at sixteen, to close the debate. Milton fought to keep it open.

Milton won. I remember the winning. I had been visiting Milton almost daily during that vacation. Despite Edith's premonitory rationing of our time together (as he wrote me in early 1946: "We miss the experience of having you ensconced in the chair at the foot of my bed like the fabled immovable object on which beats incessantly the irresistible force of Edith's cry: 'Arthur, go home.' "), I had stayed late one afternoon. Fitful I was and undoubtedly unbearable—defending doggedly my belief that to be a Jew was an open and free option and, if free, free as well to be refused. It was at this juncture that Milton played, to my mind, a triumphant trump. He granted my position, but urged that if such a decision were to be made, it must be made out of knowledge rather than out of ignorance. A simple issue of intellectual conscience. Become a Christian if you choose, he argued, but only from the starting place of Judaism; become a Christian as the early Christians had become Christian, by first having been a Jew. It seemed then, it seems now, to have been a daring risk. "How does one become a Jew?" I had asked. "By study," he had answered and the study began.

We began a course of instruction which Milton once gaily titled: "Orientations: Religious and Jewish, offered at all times to properly qualified students, with no academic credit but, it is hoped, with some spiritual gain. Instructor: Rabbi Milton Steinberg." Given the fact that I was then a wildly precocious undergraduate with endless academic commitments, the reading program he developed was formidable. My Hebrew was then nonexistent; English would have to do. It included *Hebrew Origins* by Theophile Meek; S. R. Driver, *Introduction to the Literature of the Old Testament;* Pfeiffer, *Introduction to the Old Testament;* Fleming James, *Personalities of the Old Testament;* and assorted works by Smith, George Foot Moore, Schechter, Louis Ginzberg, Montefiore, and Loewe's *A Rabbinic Anthology*. And, of course, the Bible, the Bible, and more Bible, with reference to all and sundry general and particular commentaries, Jewish and non-Jewish.

There was nothing parochial about Milton's passion for scholarship. It was capacious, broad, and above all tolerant. He was the first to affirm his knowledge, but equally ready to disclaim it where it was defective. Over those years, what began as a relation of instruction deepened into something more. I cannot claim that I ever influenced Milton's thought. That would be not only presumptuous but patently untrue. I did, however, along with Professor Albert Salomon, to whom Milton later introduced me, and Will Herberg, with whom he had become combative friends, define an ambiance of uncertainty which raised for him as many questions as he had helped resolve for me.

In those days (his first reference to it was in a letter to me of November 2, 1947) he described a private seminar he was taking with Albert Salomon: "I've read Max Scheler for him. I'm going on to Weber and other of the German social philosophers of whom I know very little. He's a great mind and an equally great spirit and it's tremendously stimulating to meet with him." In March 1948 he wrote: "One of my most exciting current experiences is that of reading Kierkegaard with Albert Salomon. We've put the German sociologists aside for the time being, having had enough of Weber and Dilthey, et al., and are concentrating on the continental theologians."

Paragraphs such as these would be inserted between descriptions of his writing of the never-completed novel, *Prophet's Wife,* and an outline study history of the Jews; correcting proofs for *Partisan Guide to the Jewish Problem* and later *Basic Judaism:* the writing of his famous address for the United Jewish Appeal, "When I Remember Seraye"; and descriptions of my parents, synagogue events, and human gossip, and he was always and insistently napping at my heels to get on with the task of Jewish learning.

In early 1949, having just completed my Master's Degree in philosophy, I returned to New York City. It was clear by then that I was hopelessly wedded to Jewish thought and study. Quite inevitably the time of rumination and reflection had passed and a different order of religious life had begun. It was parlously observant. Milton was never more magnificent, for as much as he delighted in my commitment to Jewish study and observance, he was concerned lest I embrace more than I could bear. He would repeatedly caution me with the Talmudic injunction that one never put upon a community more burdens than it is able to sustain. He warned me against zeal, but energized me to study.

He arranged that I study Hebrew—first with a brilliant friend of his who spent two hopeless sessions instructing me in the Kabbalistic significance of the Hebrew alphabet without ever teaching me the alphabet; later he sought Rabbi Gerson Cohen to teach me. That worked better. I knew nothing. I left Gerson knowing at least how to read the siddur and understand what I was reading. At that time (it was spring of 1949) Milton conceived the idea that I should go and spend six months in Israel, simply to study Hebrew.

I left in June. Shortly before my leaving I saw Milton and said that I wanted to lay tefillin in Jerusalem, but that I didn't know how; in fact, I hardly knew what tefillin looked like. It was an unknown mitzvah to me. We discussed tefillin. Milton was doubtful whether I was genuine or whether it was simply part of what he had begun to call, with amusement, my "religious pathology." One afternoon, the week before I was to leave, he called and told me to come see him the following day at about ten in the morning.

I entered and found him seated at his desk in the living room, wearing tallith and tefillin and studying. I had never seen a Jew so casually holy. It seemed to me miraculous—an unhidden Jew in tallith and tefillin, studying. Knowing some halakhah, I asked whether he had already eaten, since if he was waiting to say the morning *Shahrit* in order to eat we could learn to put on tefillin another time. Milton laughed and answered that sometimes his stomach growled more loudly than God, that he wasn't that pious, and that he had already eaten a light breakfast. Reaching into his desk drawer he withdrew a small blue bag from which he took out the black phylacteries protected with little yellow box covers and wound about with long black leather thongs. He instructed me patiently for more than an hour, reassuring my shaking hand as it made the *retsuah,* teaching me the words and their meaning. Those tefillin were a parting gift.

We wrote while I was in Israel, long, complex, demanding letters— letters theological and historical, each letter from me bringing forth from him the fruits of the generosity of a lifetime. When I returned from Israel in January 1950, he had but two months to live. We saw each other many times, the last time only two (or was it three?) days before his final illness. He had decided that we should study Midrash together. He had chosen the Midrash on Ecclesiastes. It was an all too fitting contemplation for the last study of his life: mordantly beautiful, ironic, full with the wisdom of sages making peace out of the suffering of the Preacher.

I have written as much here about myself as I have about Milton Steinberg. But that is unavoidable, for we were friends. He was no datum in my life. He was and will remain for me the paradigm of what a rabbi in this time should be.

Hasidic Encounter

What returns to me as I remember my earliest involvement with Hasidic thought and life is not history and argumentation, but the loneliness of my life in those years.

I had just returned from Israel where I had gone to live for six months to acquire the rudiments of the Hebrew language in order to prepare myself to take up a fellowship in medieval Jewish literature offered me by the Jewish Theological Seminary of America. I returned in the winter of 1950 and a year later left my parents' home to live in a small apartment on West Seventy-third Street in New York City. It was an apartment where one conducted solitude. There was room for nothing else.

I was not to become a medievalist so quickly. First I had to learn a great deal of Bible and an even greater deal of Talmud. I confess now to finding it all rather dreary. At that time, however, I had permitted myself no alternative.

An eminent scholar, given to such disingenuous rhetoric, had told me that I had the intellectual gifts to become the generation's Maimonides. I thought it a fatuous enlargement. A Maimonides for a generation

Jewish Heritage 13, no. 2 (spring–summer 1971): 46–53. Reprinted by permission of the B'nai B'rith Commission of Continuing Jewish Education.

and then another and another. Maimonides was not someone to be reproduced, and my own vanity would not have been satisfied by struggling to become a third Moses and last for only twenty years.

My days were spent in study. I rose early, put on my tallith and tefillin (prayer shawl and phylacteries), and studied Talmud, propping the large folio on my knees (of all things, *Mesechet Sotah,* the tractate which elaborates the judicial procedures for trying a suspected adulteress), and sitting, I recall, not very piously in a high-backed antique chair covered in a chintz of green and brown rosettes. It was uncomfortable. Later I faced the east wall of the apartment where I had hung a small eighteenth-century illuminated vellum, executed by some good lady of Germany, which marked the direction of the Holy Land, and prayed long and loud. I had seen Hasidim pray in Jerusalem.

Around the corner from where I lived in Jerusalem in an old Arab house near Meah Shaarim, there was a Hasidic synagogue where I had gone for Purim in 1949. It was late afternoon. Old Jews dozed amid the disarray of bottles of vodka and brandy, their cheeks pressed lightly against open folios. They snored. The rebbe entered—which rebbe I have no idea—a young boy who preceded him clapped his hands and shouted, "Jews, awaken," and suddenly the thirty or so tired and weary followers, dizzy no doubt from having observed the injunction to drink to the point where they could no longer distinguish between the saintly Mordecai and the hated Haman, awoke. A song began in the back of the room; taken up, it moved to the front. An old man, crippled with arthritis, stepped carefully into the center of the room before the Ark of the Torah and began to dance, moving from side to side, his toes pointing with an almost feminine delicacy. His arms, outstretched, pushed upward in a gesture of strength, his bearded head turned against his hunched shoulder, he danced, singing all the while one of those wordless invocations of God for which the Hasidim are famous, occasionally interrupting his melody with a beseeching "tatenu" (beloved little father) or an equally felt, but apparently apposite, lamentation of "Oi, veh" ("Oh, woe"). Others rose to dance and before long all the old men and boys were dancing together, separately in their address to God, unified as a community dancing before the Lord.

New York offered as many opportunities as Israel to observe—more than observe: to be drawn into the whorl of Hasidic life. On my block up near Central Park West, if I remember correctly, was the home and house of study of the Bobover Rebbe, who later moved his congregation to Brooklyn where the courts of the Lubavitch, the Satmar, Stoliner and other rebbes were located. The Hasidim of the Bobover (the names are always the towns in Poland, Hungary, or Russia where the founding rebbe had had his court) were a small community; how many exactly, I have no idea. At the time, not concerned as I am now with telling something of the life and beliefs of Hasidim in the New World, numbers, occupations, social structure, politics, and polity were of no importance to me. What mattered was that I was alone and they, acknowledging that I was a Jew, took me into their circle, allowed me to rise with their community on Holy Days to be a priest among priests administering the benediction to all Israel, to be called to the reading of the Torah—very occasionally—as a visiting *Kohen* (priest). But more important than these honorifics, I felt at home with them.

I learned to pray with the Hasidim of Bobov; learned to rock back and forth on the balls of my feet and turn rhythmically from side to side, interrupting the Readers' repetition of the Eighteen Benedictions with bursts of personal greeting to God, to intersperse my own prayer (embarrassed as I sometimes was, for I was not, as were most of my fellow congregants, one who had passed through the holocaustal fire and survived, although I never doubted that I had survived without escaping) with Yiddish punctuations, to bow to the Ark, to extend my arms in salutation to the Torah when it was removed from its domicile, to blow a kiss to it when it was returned, to cover my eyes with my prayer shawl during the *Shema Yisrael* (the fundamental confession of Jewish faith), to do those multiple gestures of prayer which are the deepest felt liturgical language of people worshipping God.

I would have put on a *gartel*—the usually black, twined rope belt which Hasidim wear at prayer—to mark the separation of the head and heart from the lower (presumably profane) organs of the body—and their concentrated reunification in prayer—but I could not do this in good faith. My own mysticism, however, was too self-conscious. The *mehitzah* (separation) of the *gartel* was artificial and seemed to me somewhat neurotic, although for those who had been raised in such a style of life it was quite normal.

On Saturday afternoon, particularly in the summertime, I would go to the Bobover or walk uptown to 103rd Street between Broadway and West End Avenue where the Grand Rabbi of Sassov (otherwise the Sassover Rebbe) had his *bet midrash* and take part in that remarkable Hasidic feast, the so-called Third Meal of the Sabbath. The Third Meal is not restricted to Hasidim, but it was transformed by the Hasidim from the concluding Sabbath meal into a means of celebrating the intimacy between the rebbe and his community and the community and the Sabbath.

Normally, at twilight, before the ritual of havdalah that separates the Sabbath from the workweek, the last meal of the Sabbath day is eaten—bread, a piece of fish, cake, perhaps tea or wine. But Hasidim were not anxious to allow the workweek to begin. The Sabbath was the preeminent occasion for drawing out prayer, reflection, study, for attaching oneself wholly to God and if not to God himself then to his surrogate exemplification, the rebbe.

At the Third Meal, the Sassover Rebbe spoke Torah. He would enter the small room—actually two rooms with a sliding door and a long table on which stood bottles of wine and brandy, several loaves of twisted bread, in the anteroom, the women of the rebbe's household distributed pieces of gefilte fish on paper plates to be served when the rebbe was finished with his discourse.

It was an ordinary Sabbath, not a Sabbath intermediate to holy days or a Sabbath before a festival. The rebbe did not speak long, but he spoke without interruption, in a low voice, punctuating his argument with slight motions of his white, almost transparent hands. When he finished his Torah—he spoke in Yiddish and all I could understand was an occasional Hebrew quotation—his community nodded vigorously, broke into song, and one of the women placed before him a plate of fish with which to begin the Third Meal. It was by now dark. It had been dark for an hour already. The Sabbath was over, and still the rebbe had not ended the Sabbath.

The Sabbath continued. The rebbe called out a name and a man to my left shouted a greeting to the rebbe and received, thrown across the table, a piece of bread which the rebbe had broken off from the bread he then used to scrape up a portion of fish, the so-called gift of "leavings." And then the rebbe called another name and lifted a glass to salute him and received in return a shouted l'hayim.

And so the evening progressed, greetings, song, words of instruction; until at nine-thirty or so the rebbe, tired, separated the holy from the profane, ended the Sabbath, and rose with his congregation to recite the evening prayers of the new week.

The Sabbath had not been as prolonged on that occasion as it would be on others, some communities of old extending the Sabbath until the early hours of the next morning.

The Sassover Rebbe was not one of the great contemporary masters of hasidut, although he descended from the great Moshe Leib of Sassov. He was pious, learned, intense. Wonders were ascribed to him, profound thoughts, loving gestures, and stern discipline. What counted to me was that I—a Jew of America, raised in comfort and ease—was among people who had struggled. Survivors of the Holocaust most of them, dressed poorly, with bad complexions and irregular teeth, with hats pushed far back on their heads, without ties many, with cheap silk ties others. These were companion Jews, joined together by the presence of an emissary among them to whom they felt the bond of love and loyalty, whom they expected to think of them, to raise them up in his prayers and by his instruction.

Distant by generations from the great founding leaders of Hasidism, these messengers could still transmit, however pallidly, however incompletely, not only the direct instruction of the Baal Shem Tov or Schneur Zalman or Levi Yitzhak, but, more, could give them the sense that by holding to his coattails they could be closer by a little to the God of their ancient fathers and their dead and murdered fathers who alone gave them comfort.

It would be disrespectful to suggest that I was any different from these fellow Jews in the house of Sassov or Bobov, dancing with them— confessedly self-consciously on Purim or Simhat Torah (the Festival of the Rejoicing of the Law), and self-consciously at the Third Meal, and self-consciously at prayer, but with them, for I was in need of them, and through them of their teacher whose words I could not understand, whose dress of black silk robe with *gartel,* with white knee socks, with black shoes and silver buckles, with fur *straimel* could be mine to purchase, but whose beard I had not age enough to grow and whose knowledge and faith I doubted I could ever have.

It was toward the end of my brief sojourn in the land of the Seminary—a wilderness as my language suggests—that I was privileged to have an audience with Rabbi Menachem Mendel Schneerson, the Lubavitcher Rebbe at the headquarters of the worldwide movement of Lubavitch Hasidim on Eastern Parkway in Brooklyn. A very orthodox student at the conservative Seminary, Dov Slotnik I think it was, knew of my attachment to theology and no doubt thought I would benefit from the purgative, corrective, and authentic witness that a meeting with the rebbe would assure.

He arranged the audience.

A Sunday night in winter. It was 1951, February or March, I think. Cold, wet, blustery, and the hour of eleven o'clock at night when the Lubavitcher Rebbe received petitioners, a fact which seemed to me somewhat mysterious. In my world, people were less than likely to be at their best near midnight. But this was not the case on Eastern Parkway. The vestibule where we sat—Dov Slotnik, two others from the Seminary and myself—was crowded with people going back and forth, some waiting simply to speak with those who came out from the rebbe's study, to hear anything the rebbe might have said that could be of meaning to them.

We waited nearly two hours. It was almost one o'clock when we entered; a desk, books, and a line of simple chairs on which visitors were to sit. We remained standing until the rebbe asked us to be seated. Dov Slotnik spoke for us. The rebbe offered to speak in English, but he said he preferred to talk in Yiddish. He talked in Yiddish and I understood scarcely anything. The few words I spoke to him, in reply to questions, I phrased in hating Hebrew. I don't remember anything that was said. It was a simple theological argument, with simple rhetoric, uncomplicated analogies, benign exemplifications from science and secular learning which the rebbe seemed pleased to have at his command (he had studied engineering some years before at the Sorbonne). None of the rebbe's words impressed me. What was moving was the fact that he consented to see us, that he took two hours out of his life for us—we who were engaged in Torah but were less than meticulously orthodox (other than Dov), were studying at a less than acceptable institution of Jewish learning, and were clearly not Hasidim.

I could not understand enough to be impressed, and what was related to me by my companions after the audience concluded at about three in the morning was not up to my excessively rigid and uncharitable theological standards. In those days God and theology were a revenge.

But what remains? That example of openness and willingness and care is retained. It was foolish to expect more, to anticipate revelations and mysteries, miracles and conversions. The rebbe might well have had the power to plant the seed, but I was not the ground to receive it.

Nearly twenty years later, many theologies later, many books read and written later, many experiences with Hasidim later, I am still moved by the undertaking of their life.

How to Avoid Disappearing

It was exactly thirty years ago that I began to study Hebrew with Gerson Cohen, now chancellor of the Jewish Theological Seminary in New York. The late Rabbi Milton Steinberg persuaded Gerson to take me on, and with considerable patience and affection, he conducted me through the rudiments. Six months later I was living in Jerusalem, where I made a vow not to speak English until sundown. Each day began with Hebrew and concluded with Hebrew. Communication was rather limited for many months, but by the time I was ready to return to New York in January 1949, I had a substantial vocabulary, was quite able to read without vowel pointing and to write with plausible style.

In the thirty years that have passed since that Hebrew sunrise, my vocabulary has thinned, but I have not forgotten. I have an adequate vocabulary, the gift of a turn of phrase here and there, a sprung rhyme or two. Hebrew is part of my psyche. A month ago I renewed a vow. Not a week would go by without spending at least some time reading Hebrew, serious Hebrew—Hebrew of the imagination, novels, poetry, the mystic literature, religious philosophy.

I was moved to renovate and renew my vow by Yehezkel Kaufmann's essay, "The Hebrew Language and Our National Future," which appeared

Present Tense 5, no. 3 (spring 1978): 64.

in Martin Buber's remarkable monthly, *Der Jude* (*The Jew*), in 1917. Kaufmann, then a young man and not yet the author of the magisterial *History of the Faith of Israel* or his *Exile and Alienage,* argues persuasively that language, not religion, is the bond which connects the Jew to the Jewish people. The great Spanish-Arabic Jewries of the Middle Ages were able to sustain authentic national self-awareness because they conducted their cultural life in Hebrew. It did not matter, Kaufmann observes, that their daily life was transacted in Arabic or medieval Spanish. What counted was that Jews created, thought, and prayed in Hebrew. It was Hebrew which defined them as Jews and transcended their professions as lawyers, doctors, or businessmen and because of that Hebrew vitality, their literatures and philosophies survived the destruction of their community.

By contrast, consider the fate of Alexandrian Jewry, the most thriving intellectual and religious settlement of first century Jewry outside Palestine and Babylonia. With the exception of the philosopher and biblical exegete, Philo of Alexandria, who is remembered and who survives? Indeed, until Harry Wolfson called Philo to our attention again in this century, who, but Protestant divines read Philo? Besides Philo no other of reputation is still read, although in its day Alexandria boasted an enormous and cosmopolitan Jewish center.

The reason, Kaufmann adduces, is that the Jews of Alexandria conducted not only their secular life, but their imagination, in Greek. They thought in Greek and Greek thought through them. However they might have wished it, they were assimilated through the pores of language.

I do not believe that all Jews will make aliyah. It is conceivable; it is a normative religious expectation, but it is an improbable hope. Those who remained behind in the Diaspora, presuming they do not will to disappear, will have to make provision against it. Principal among these provisions is the recovery of the Hebrew language. Not the Hebrew of ordinariness—which mimics the Hebrew used daily in Israel by ordering foods or shopping in Hebrew. Such an employment of Hebrew is an exercise in futility.

The real challenge of Hebrew, as the language of the Jewish psyche, is that the millenial conversation between the Jewish people and God is not restricted to the prayerbook or even to the Midrashim, Talmud, and biblical commentators. The conversation has acquired modes and styles throughout the centuries which presently encompass poetry, romances, philosophic texts, travel diaries, mystic tracts, and since the renaissance of modern Hebrew and the founding of the State of Israel, works of history, archaeology, literature of all genres and sensibilities. Hebrew is again a living language and once more the language of revelation.

As surely as there are minimum obligations we must fulfill to maintain our self-consciousness and communal loyalty as Jews, the knowledge of Hebrew must be numbered among them. Hebrew is work, but it is also life. It is not enough that Jews master the techniques of adapting successfully to the free form of American life. Such skills will render the body of the Jew safe and secure, while the spirit withers and dies. The Jews of Diaspora must maintain no less successfully the energies of classic Israel—and those energies are conducted through the Hebrew language.

Afterword:
A Passion for Theology:
Reflections on
Arthur A. Cohen's Legacy

Paul Mendes-Flohr

Arthur Aharon Cohen was a bewitchingly affable and gregarious individual. Yet, paradoxically, his life was shrouded in loneliness. He dwelt in what Kafka called *"das Grenzland zwischen Einsamkeit und Gemeinschaft"*—he was a denizen of an anguished land at the border between loneliness and fellowship. But unlike Kafka, who regarded his residence in this unhappy region as a curse, which he sought to escape, Cohen, I suspect, was—despite the pain—content to dwell in this ambiguous realm at the margins between social respectability and the lonely existence of an outsider. He was, to be sure, a prominent New York intellectual—a highly acclaimed publisher, writer, and collector of art and rare books. He was also a connoisseur of friendship. Blessed with a prodigious capacity for sharing, he took an active interest in others and generously expressed his affection in the fastidious and caring attention he gave to his many, many friends. Yet in the urbane, literate world of Manhattan, which was Cohen's turf, he was an anomaly—an anomaly by disposition and, he would say, by fate. Cohen was a theologian.

Indeed, Cohen's abiding passion was theology. For him theology had an existential urgency born of his need to be a Jew by faith and religious commitment. As a form of knowledge, Cohen contended, theology is sui generis; it begins with what it wishes to know, God and his revealed word. Prima facie, theology is based on a grand tautology, which Cohen regarded to be the source of "its humility and its arrogance." The theologian begins with what he has learned in faith; he does not set forth to find God. But, Cohen argued, it would be mistaken to view the theologian as "locked into a massive *petito principii,* building an edifice to exemplify what is already revealed, to explicate what he already believes as certainty." This common misconception of theology, Cohen held, stems from an erroneous premise shared by believers and nonbelievers alike that theology is preeminently an edifying discourse—thus, in effect little more than sermons—designed to strengthen belief. Sermons, no matter how learned, are not theology, Cohen emphasized. He held that the sermonic conception of theology renders it a species of ideology, a mere rhetorical exercise to shore up civil consensus. His own view of theology was far more modest.

> I would suggest that theological method and language . . . are devised to render privacy accountable: to remove from the welter of private speech—where emotion, history, presupposition, the unconscious, the living passion of the human being has precedence—common terms, generalizable characteristics, transmissable judgments and form for them a language that opens each human being to the other, in time forging for them a community of shared gesture, symbol, expression, and ratiocination in which the struggle to speak truth about God and man is the highest goal.

Theology in this sense is a rational form of thinking, and thus its affinity to philosophical method and language. It requires no surrender of intellect. To the contrary: Reason and its rules of argument are enjoined to release belief from the trammels of solipsism and ideology and thus serve to guard it as the fount of truth.

In order to assure that theology be open to reason, Cohen maintained, it must not be a mere reformulation—a re-outfitting in new garments—of inherited doctrines and catechized positions. To resist this understandable temptation, he urged that the theologian begin by re-thinking the presuppositions of his or her particular faith-community. Such rethinking, he underscored, initially entails a radical deconstruction of those very presuppositions. Guided by a hermeneutics of suspicion, one is to examine anew the very fundaments and teachings of one's tradition:

> The theological imagination is [accordingly] continually engaged in testing the rescription and trasmission of the old sources in order not only that our contemporary faith be tested and secured, but that the interpretations which the classic texts placed upon the primary religious events may be

adjudged to have retained or lost their transmissable significance. It is not that the old must pass the test of the contemporary (for no one could deny the implicit sophistry of such a procedure) but rather that the contemporary can and often does enclose explosive and decisive events that demand that the old be reshaped in their light.

The objective of theological deconstruction, Cohen explained, is to open the tradition to the onrushing flow of experience—to the ever unfolding experience of the intellect and of history. Only such a procedure allows for the possibility of a genuine retrieval of a tradition as a living reality, pulsating with the life force of the thought, imagination, and passion of human beings creatively engaged in an unfettered quest for truth and moral integrity. Conversely, Cohen believed that to treat a tradition as a closed system, impervious to the present experience of intellect and history, is to forfeit the possibility of engaging tradition in a dialogue that is both existentially and intellectually compelling. Modern Jewish education, he contended, thus commits a grave error by neglecting theology, not to say discouraging it. Dogmatics, he cautioned, is not theology; orthodoxy—be it spelt with a capital "O" or with a silent "o" accompanying alternative visions of "correct" Jewish doctrine and practice—is the hobgoblin of an intellectually and spiritually vital Jewish life.

Cohen also warned that one should not construe the history of Jewish religious thought as theology; for a mere rehearsal of positions articulated by thinkers of the past is not theology. Nor is historical consciousness per se, Cohen argued, sufficient ground for a spiritually engaging Judaism. He would surely have endorsed Nietzsche's admonishment that a surfeit of history can deaden thinking. Indeed, Cohen averred, the nurturing of historical consciousness as a means of engendering a firm Jewish identity had come at the expense of hard thinking. Already as a young man in search of theological support for his decision to become a Jew by faith, he was profoundly disappointed to learn that Jewish institutions of learning, even rabbinical seminaries, distrusted theology and were ill-disposed to approach issues of faith with the rigor Cohen had sought. Bereft of institutional support, Cohen would never find a home in organized Jewish religious life.

The modern Jew, Cohen insisted, has no choice but continually to rethink his or her way back to Judaism. In the first instance, theology was for Cohen an act of "self-clarification"—both of one's life before God and of one's life with one's fellow human beings. Jealously affirming the integrity of one's experience, the theologian unabashedly and paradoxically speaks a private language while pursuing a public discourse. "In this," Cohen observed, "theology resembles literature." In both literature and theology, the author speaks in a private language, grounded in his or her experience, and for the sake of the very integrity of that experience seeks to extend it before the review of the public, hoping his or her testimony will sound familiar and credible. Though employing different grammars and rules of discourse, theology and literature both acknowledge, albeit implicitly, the moral and epistemological authority of public discourse. Indeed, Cohen regarded literature and theology as comparable attempts to restore the dignity of language, in an age when it had been debased as a mere instrument of communication, often cynically employed. "Words no longer command us," he bemoaned, "precisely because they no longer reflect concepts and convictions which directly govern and thereby agitate conscience." Language was for Cohen the most delicate and precious tool vouchsafed to human beings.

To have read Cohen—to have known him personally—is to have realized how crucial indeed language was to him. He loved words; he delighted in hearing them chime properly and achieve a dramatic, evocative cadence. Graced with a mellifluous voice of his own, he took great pleasure in uttering words well chosen and euphoniously articulated. His speech and elaborately braided, interlaced language, however, were no mere aesthetic affection of an individual blessed with an unusually rich vocabulary. Words are the matrix of culture, he believed: the life of the spirit is conducted through and within language.

In his reverence for language—in his cultivation of learned, even esoteric inflections of speech—Cohen was also an anomaly, even in the self-consciously sophisticated circles of New York. To Cohen's amusement and sometimes chagrin, more than one reviewer complained about his diction, his predilection, in both his theological essays and novels, for obscure and "hyper" cultured language. Indeed, in rereading Cohen's voluminous writings in preparation for this essay I filled many pages with words I encountered for the first time. But Cohen's language had a subtext: a hidden hermeneutical and theological agenda.

Cohen was alert to the disordering capacity of language—he profoundly appreciated the power of language to cause us, his readers, to pause—and not solely to scuttle to our dictionaries in embarrassed search of the meaning of the obscure polysyllables he used, but to make us think, to break our habit of routine reflection; in his often surprising use of language Cohen obliged us to recognize that our ordinary, doxic-ladden speech shields a thoughtlessness.

At another level, Cohen shared Walter Benjamin's eagerness to restore to language its distinctive cultural, if not theological, role. Benjamin traced the cultural emasculation of language to the ascendency of news-papers. With their demand for crispy, entertaining, readily processed in-formation, newspapers have altered the governing conception of language. No knowledge other than that which is conveyed in the news item or report is to be demanded of the reader. Language, as Benjamin noted, is in effect divorced from tradition. Not only is literacy endangered by the imperious dictates of journalism, but the humanistic ground of Western culture is likewise threatened. In the name of a mass readership, newspapers ban language that appeals to culture, that assumes a learning resonating past wisdom. If secularization means inter alia the severence of the present from the past, then the journalistic conception of linguistic democracy has secularized language, ripping it from its moorings in the past and tradition. Like Benjamin, Arthur lamented the debasement of language, precisely because it was perhaps the one medium left to the modern individual providing access to the truths nurtured by tradition.

Cohen was an aristocrat, or rather *ein Geistesaristokrat*—an aristocrat of the spirit. But he was no snob. To the very marrow of his being he was a democrat. He loved the simple individual, and in particular the simple Jew whose fantasy and passion have yet to be corrupted by the material success bequeathed by the twentieth century. Thus Cohen's active sup-port of the YIVO Institute for Jewish Research in New York City, which despite his distance from its militant secularism and anachronistic Yid-dishism, he saw as representing the simple, disestablished Jew.

With similar affection, Cohen was solicitous of the "natural Jew"—the Jew facing the raw need to survive in the mundane reality of history (what he called the natural order)—and to endure with a maximum of material and political dignity. On the other hand, he was anguished by what he perceived to be the dialectical limits of the Jews' successful ac-commodation to the material and political promise of the modern world. The triumph of the natural Jew had led to the eclipse of the "supernatural Jew"—the Jew beholden to a covenant with God. The overarching thrust of Cohen's novels was to expose the contradictions (to use the Marxist term) between the material and political success of the Jews in the mod-ern world (at least as represented by America), and the insidious and unfortunate effects of their embourgeoisement on their spiritual life. Cohen also recognized that embourgeoisement as historically necessary. The modern era has been the era of the natural Jew—a fact that Cohen beseeched us to celebrate. The alignment of the Jew's hopes and energy with those of the liberal era has unambiguously led to the enhancement of his natural dignity. The challenge now, Cohen contended, was to de-termine how to guard the Jew's firm footing in the natural world while reorienting his energies and hopes to his primordial calling as a servant of the supernatural.

Modern Jewish thought, Cohen observed, has been lamentably divided by strategies devised to promote either the natural or the supernatural Jew. For Cohen the question, however, was to establish a creative balance between the two. Thus despite his great affection for Franz Rosenzweig, whom he otherwise regarded as his theological alter ego, Cohen rejected the German Jewish sage's conception of Israel as a metahistorical community standing apart from the natural world. Certainly after the Holocaust this position was particularly untenable, if not grotesque. The Jews have no choice but to return to history and master its tools in order to assure their sheer survival. Nonetheless, something of the metahistorical posture must also be preserved. The metahistorical, supernatural Jew must maintain a solidarity with the natural Jew. (Cohen tended to identify the supernatural Jew with Rosenzweig's metahistorical Jew.) Yet this solidarity, to Cohen's mind, was not just the tragic imperative of the post-Holocaust situation. At the very moment he "adopted" Jewish faith, he came to realize that Jewish solidarity was theologically necessary. Solidarity with one's fellow Jews was a sine qua non of Israel's covenant.

In the last months of the illness to which he eventually succumbed, Cohen and I corresponded on how he could acquire Israeli citizenship without making the for him then arduous journey to Israel. Although not a Zionist, he regarded Israeli citizenship to be a necessary—for him theologically necessary—expression of solidarity with the Jewish people. But he was also acutely sensitive to the danger that solidarity could readily degenerate into mere nationalism or worse. This danger, he passionately argued, should not deter one from accepting the moral and political imperatives of solidarity. The challenge, he held, was how to assure that Jewish solidarity—as an expression of love, care, and family—will serve to promote Israel's fulfillment of its supernatural vocation to be God's witness.

BIBLIOGRAPHY

Works by and about Arthur A. Cohen

1951

Articles and Essays

"Being and Existence: The Prospect of Israel Philosophy." *Israel: Life and Letters* 7, no. 3 (March 1951): 8–9.

"The Encounter of Judaism and Christendom." *Cross Currents* 3 (March 1951): 91–95.

Book Reviews

Review of *The Jewish People and Jesus Christ,* by Jacob Jocz. *The Journal of Religion* 31, no. 1 (January 1951): 66–67.

1952

Articles and Essays

"Revelation and Law: Reflections on Martin Buber's Views on Halakhah." *Judaism* 1, no. 3 (July 1952): 250–56.

1953

Book Reviews

Review of *The Eclipse of God,* by Martin Buber. *Judaism* 2, no. 3 (July 1953): 280–83.

1954

Book Reviews

Review of *Religion and Humanity,* by Eugene Kohn. *Judaism* 3, no. 3. (summer 1954): 275–82.

1955

Articles and Essays

"Messianism and the Jew." *Commonweal* 62, no. 15 (July 1955): 367–69.
"On Scriptual Exegesis." *Cross Currents* 5, no. 1 (winter 1955): 39–50.

1956

Articles and Essays

"The Possibilities of Belief: Nathanael West's Holy Fool." *Commonweal* 64, no. 11 (June 15, 1956): 276–78. (A shortened version of this essay is reprinted in *Twentieth Century Interpretations of Miss Lonelyhearts,* edited by Thomas H. Jackson, 46–48. New York: Prentice-Hall, 1971).
"Moses, Mystery, and Jesus." *Jewish Frontier* 23, no. 6 (June 1956): 24–28.
"Religion as a Sacred Ideology." *Partisan Review* 23, no. 4 (fall 1956): 495–505.

Book Reviews and Letters

"The Continuing Debate." Letter to the Editor of *Commonweal* 65, no. 3 (October 19, 1956): 74–75. (Refers to an article by Gunner Kumlien of September 28, 1956.)
"Hutchins." Letter to the Editor of *The New Leader* 39, no. 17 (April 23, 1956): 28. (Response to the article "Six Fallacies of Robert Hutchins," by Sidney Hook, March 19, 1956.)
"A One-Sided Discussion." Review of *The Bridge: A Yearbook of Judaeo-Christian Studies,* vol. 1, edited by John M. Oesterreicher. *Jewish Frontier* 23, no. 4 (April 1956): 28–30.
"The Polemicist and the Professor." Review of *The Professor and the Fossil,* by Maurice Samuel. *Jewish Frontier* 23, no. 11 (December 1956): 28–35.
"Pragmatic Religiousity." Review of *Protestant-Catholic-Jew: An Essay in American Religious Sociology,* by Will Herberg. *Partisan Review* 23, no. 1 (winter 1956): 128–30.
Review of *Contemporary Problems in Religion,* by Howard Basilius. *Judaism* 5, no. 4 (fall 1956): 370–72.

Articles, Reviews, and Letters about Arthur Cohen

"Publishers on the Square." *University of Chicago Magazine* 48, no. 4 (January 1956): 17–18.

1957

Books: Nonfiction

Martin Buber. London: Bowes and Bowes, 1957.

Articles and Essays

"For a New Center of Creativity." *The New Leader* 40, no. 12 (March 25, 1957): 21–22.
"The Jewish Press." *Commonweal* 67, no. 3 (October 18, 1957): 65–68. (The article was part of a symposium on religious journalism in America.)
"Martin Buber: The Bible and Hasidim." *Jewish Frontier* 24, no. 9 (November 1957): 33–38; 24, no. 10 (November 1957): 13–16.
"Our Present Situation." *Conservative Judaism* 11, no. 2 (winter 1957): 13–19. (This essay was delivered as a sermon preached at the Jewish Theological Seminary, Yom Kippur 5717.)
"Pacifism and Violence." *Jewish Frontier* 24, no. 5 (May 1957): 5–7.

"Religion behind the Iron Curtain: The Plight of Judaism." *Commonweal* 66, no. 9 (May 1957): 226–28.

"Semite According to the Flesh." *Christian Century* 74, no. 38 (September 1957): 1097–99. (An altered version appears in *The Myth of the Judeo-Christian Tradition and Other Dissenting Essays*. New York: Harper and Row, 1970.)

"Three We Have Lost: The Problem of Conversion." *Conservative Judaism* 11, no. 4 (summer 1957): 7–19.

Book Reviews and Letters

"Imprudent, Muddled?" Letter to the Editor of *Christian Century* 74 (March 20, 1957): 363.

Response to Rabbi Steven S. Schwarzschild's criticism of his article "Pacificism and Violence" (May 5, 1957), *Jewish Frontier* 24, no. 10 (November 1957): 25–27.

Review of *The Bridge,* edited by John M. Oesttereicher. *Judaism* 6, no. 4 (fall 1957): 374–76.

"Revival in Judaism, Too: A Review Article." Review of *American Judaism,* by Nahum Glazer. *The Christian Century* 74, no. 42 (October 16, 1957): 1232–33.

"The Secular and the Divine." Review of *An Historian's Approach to Religion,* by Arnold Toynbee. *World Alliance News Letter* 33, no. 1 (January 1957): 6.

Articles, Reviews, and Letters about Arthur Cohen

Cain, Seymour. "Semite Also." *Christian Century* 74, no. 42 (October 16, 1957): 1236–37.

Schwartschild, Steven S. Response to "Pacifism and Violence." *Jewish Frontier* 24, no. 10 (November 1957): 25–27.

1958

Books: Nonfiction

Martin Buber. New York: Hillary House, 1958. (U.S. publication of book published in U.K., 1957).

Books: Edited

Handbook of Christian Theology: Definition Essays on Concepts and Movements of Thought in Contemporary Protestantism. Edited by Arthur A. Cohen and Marvin Halverson. New York: Meridian Books, 1958.

Articles and Essays

"Atheism." In *Handbook of Christian Theology: Definition Essays on Concepts and Movements of Thought in Contemporary Protestantism.* Edited by Arthur A. Cohen and Marvin Halverson, 17–19. New York: Meridian Books, 1958.

"The Jewish Christian Contradiction: It Means Profound Differences in Approach to World Affairs." *Worldview* 1, no. 2 (February 1958): 3–5.

"Judaism." In *Handbook of Christian Theology: Definition Essays on Concepts and Movements of Thought in Contemporary Protestantism.* Edited by Arthur A. Cohen and Marvin Halverson, 188–91. New York: Meridian Books, 1958.

"The Problem of Pluralism." *Religion and Free Society.* Edited by William Lee Miller, et al., 35–48. New York: The Fund for the Republic, 1958.

Book Reviews and Letters

Comments on Father Gustave Weigel's essay "How Relevant is Morality." Letter to the Editor of *Worldview* 1, no. 5 (May 1958): 10–11.

"Martin Buber." Review of *Martin Buber: The Life of Dialogue,* by Maurice Friedman. *Conservative Judaism* (winter 1958): 29–33.

"The Philosophy." Review of *Hasidism and the Modern Man,* by Martin Buber. *Saturday Review* (June 7, 1958): 18.

Review of *Prayer, Humility and Compassion,* by Samuel H. Dresner. *Conservative Judaism* 12, no. 4 (summer 1958): 42–43.

"Variety. George Santayana on Existentialism: An Unpublished Letter." *Partisan Review* 25, no. 4 (fall 1958): 632, 635, 637.

"The Westernization of Judaism." Review of *The Course of Modern Jewish History,* by Howard M. Sachar. *Saturday Review* (June 1958): 27.

"Who's Offending Whom?" Review of *David,* by D. H. Lawrence, Union Theological Seminary, directed by Tom F. Driver. *Christian Century* 75, no. 17 (April 23, 1958): 11.

Articles, Reviews, and Letters about Arthur Cohen

Altizer, Thomas J. J. "The Paradox of Faith and the World." Review of *Martin Buber,* by Arthur A. Cohen. *Worldview* 1, no. 4 (April 1958): 10.

Salomon, Albert. Review of *Martin Buber,* by Arthur A. Cohen. *Social Research* 25, no. 3 (autumn 1958): 370–72.

Schonfeld, Gabriel. "II. The Philosopher." Review of *Martin Buber,* by Arthur A. Cohen. *Saturday Review* (June 7, 1958): 19.

1959

Articles and Essays

"Book Design." *Art in America* 47, no. 4 (1959): 32–33.

"The Natural and the Supernatural Jew: Two Views of the Church." In *American Catholics: A Protestant-Jewish View,* edited by Phillip Sharper, 127–57. New York: Sheed and Ward, 1959.

"On Judaism and Catholicism." *Reconstructionist* 25, no. 8 (May 29, 1959): 3–8.

"On Judaism and Catholicism, II." *Reconstructionist* 25, no. 9 (June 15, 1959): 19–24.

"The Seminary and the Modern Rabbi." *Conservative Judaism* 14, no. 3 (spring 1959): 1–12.

"Why I Choose to be a Jew." *Harper's Magazine* 218, no. 1307 (April 1959): 63–66.

Book Reviews

"Herman Wouk's Orthodoxy." Review of *This is My God,* by Herman Wouk. *Congress Bi-Weekly* 26, no. 16 (November 2, 1959): 13–14.

"The Judeo-Christian Dialogue." Interview with the staff of *Apostolic Perspectives* 6, no. 1 (December–January 1959): 29–31.

"Precious Little Being Said." Review of *Yale Literary Magazine* (spring 1959). *Yale Daily News* 80, no. 148 (May 13, 1959): 2.

"Selected." Review of *Between God and Man: An Interpretation of Judaism. From the Writings of Abraham J. Heschel,* edited by Fritz A. Rothschild. *The Christian Century* 76, no. 24 (June 24, 1959): 751.

Articles, Reviews, and Letters about Arthur Cohen

"Arthur A. Cohen." *The Supplement to Who's Who.* (March–May 1959): 2377.

Anonymous. "Letter to a Young Man about to Enter Publishing." *Harper's Magazine* 219, no. 1313 (October 1959): 183–90.

Cohen, Jacob. "Third Generation: Choosing or Chosen." *Jewish Frontier* 26 (October 1959): 10–14. (Response to "Why I Choose to be a Jew." *Harper's Magazine* 218, no. 1307 [April 1959]: 63–66.)

1960

Books: Edited

Steinberg, Milton. *Anatomy of Faith.* Edited by Arthur A. Cohen. New York: Harcourt, Brace and Co., 1960.

Handbook of Christian Theology: Definition Essays on Concepts and Movements of Thought in Contemporary Protestantism. Edited by Arthur A. Cohen and Marvin Halverson. London: Fontana Books, 1960. (First published in New York by Meridian Books in 1958.)

Articles and Essays

"An Analysis of Milton Steinberg's *Anatomy of Faith:* A Reply to the Critics." *Conservative Judaism* 14, no. 4 (summer 1960): 14–21.

Cohen, Arthur A., and Rev. Gustave Weigel, S. J., "American Catholics: A Jewish View." *The Catholic Hour* (May 22, 1960): 1–7.

"Atheism." In *Handbook of Christian Theology: Definition Essays on Concepts and Movements of Thought in Contemporary Protestantism,* edited by Arthur A. Cohen and Marvin Halverson, 17–19. London: Fontana Books, 1960.

"Judaism." In *Handbook of Christian Theology: Definition Essays on Concepts and Movements of Thought in Contemporary Protestantism,* edited by Arthur A. Cohen and Marvin Halverson, 188–91. London: Fontana Books, 1960.

"The Problem of Pluralism." In *An Understanding in Our Time: Catholic Responsibility in a Pluralistic Society.* Washington, D.C.: National Federation of Catholic College Students, 1960. (First published in *Religion and the Free Society,* 1958.)

"Religion as Gadfly." In *The Churches and the Public,* edited by Robert Lekachman et al., 41–52. Santa Barbara, Calif.: Center for the Study of Democratic Institutions, 1960.

"Why I Choose to be a Jew." In *Essays of Our Time,* edited by Leo Hamalian and Edmond L. Volpe, 287–96. New York: McGraw-Hill, 1960. (First published in *Harper's Magazine,* 218, no. 1307 [April 1959]: 63–66.)

Book Reviews

"A Religious Confrontation." Review of *An American Dilemma,* by Robert McAfee Brown and Gustave Weigel. *The New Leader* 43, no. 47 (December 5, 1960): 24–25.

Articles, Reviews, and Letters about Arthur Cohen

"Arthur A. Cohen." *Current Biography* 21, no. 8 (September 1960): 92–93.

Anonymous. "Letter to a Young Man about to Enter Publishing." In *Writing in America,* edited by John Fischer and Robert B. Silvers, 150–68. New Jersey: Rutgers University Press, 1960. (First published in *Harper's Magazine,* 219, no. 1313 [October 1959]: 183–90.)

Cohen, Jacob. "Third Generation Choosing or Chosen." *Jewish Frontier* (October 1959): 10–14.

Girson, Rochelle. "Portraits of Publishers—Alfred A. Knopf, Arthur A. Cohen, James Laughlin and Savoie Lotinville." *Amerika, Amerika Illustrated* 25 (1960): 26–27. (Issued by the United States Information Agency for Poland.)

————. *Amerika, Amerika Illustrated* 25 (1960): 50–51. (Issued by the United States Information Agency for the Soviet Union.)

1961

Articles and Essays

"The Church III: The Great Withdrawal." In *The Agreeable Autocracies: A Series of Conversations with American Institutions,* edited by Joseph P. Lyford, 156–71. New York: Oceana, 1961. (Originally broadcast as "The American Republic" on WBAI-FM, New York City.)

"The God of Israel—Pursuer and Pursued." *Judaism* 10, no. 4 (fall 1961): 296–97.

Cohen, Arthur A., et al. "Religion and American Society: A Statement of Principles." Santa Barbara, Calif.: Center for the Study of Democratic Institutions, 1961.

Cohen, Arthur A., Arthur Hertzberg, and Ruth Hyman. "Of Books, Readers and Writers." *Our Age* 3, no. 2 (November 12, 1961): 3–6.

"Why I Choose to be a Jew." In *Fields of Learning: A College Reader,* edited by Hans J. Gottlieb and Edwin B. Knowles, 155–64. New York: Harper and Brothers, 1961. (First published in *Harper's Magazine.* 218, no. 1307 [April 1959]: 63–66.)

"Why I Choose to be a Jew." In *A Nation of Nations: Ethnic Literature in America,* edited by Theodore L. Gross, 263–73. New York: Free Press, 1961. (First Published in *Harper's Magazine,* 218, no. 1307 [April 1959]: 63–66.)

Letters to the Editor

"Letter to the Editor." *The Reconstructionist* 27, no. 1 (February 24, 1961): 28–29.

"Symposium II." Letter to the Editor of *Commentary* 32, no. 1 (July 1961): 69–70.

1962

Books: Nonfiction

The Natural and the Supernatural Jew. New York: Pantheon, 1962.

Articles and Essays

"Foreword." *Triangle* 2, no. 2 (fall 1962): iii.

"Judaism and the Academy: The Philosopher and the Jew." *Judaism* 11, no. 4 (fall 1962): 309–19. (Based on the lecture "Hebrew Studies and Philosophy," delivered at the University of Wisconsin, Milwaukee, March 18, 1962.)

"Notes toward a Jewish Theology of Politics." *Commonweal* 77, no. 1 (September 28, 1962): 10–11.

"Silence in the Aftermath—Jewish Christian Dialogue: The Wish to Transform." *Christianity and Crisis* 22, no. 11 (June 25, 1962): 112–15.

"Talk." *International Design Conference Papers.* Aspen: 1962, 23–27.

Book Reviews and Letters

"Author Meets His Critic." Letter to the Editor of *America* 107 (April 7, 1962). (Letter in response to Christopher Emmet's article "Threat to Unity on Berlin." *America* 106 [February 17, 1962]).

"Faith and Truth." Letter to the Editor of *Commentary* 33, no. 6 (June 1962): 536.

"Honest Thinking." Review of *The Faith of a Heretic,* by Walter Kaufman. *Commentary* 33, no. 1 (January 1962): 88–90.

Articles, Reviews, and Letters about Arthur Cohen

Hargrove, Kathrine, R.S.C.J. "Spiritual Semites." Review of "The Natural and Supernatural Jew: Two Views of the Church," *Religious Education* 57, no. 1 (January–February 1962): 47–52.

1963

Books: Nonfiction

The Hebrew Bible in Christian, Jewish, and Muslim Art. New York: Jewish Museum, 1963.

Articles and Essays

"Books That Have Influenced Me." *The Christian Century* 79 (January 2, 1963): 75–76.

"Discussion: Comments on Paul Weiss's 'The Religious Turn.' " *Judaism* 12, no. 1 (winter 1963): 3–27.

"The Jew, Secularity, and Christian Culture." *Ramparts* 2, no. 2 (autumn 1963): 49–56.

"Jewish Theology for the Interregnum." In *Living Legacy: Essays in Honor of Hugo Hahn,* edited by Bernard N. Cohn, 69–79. New York: Congregation Habonim, 1963.

"Judaism and Culture: Does Judaism Have a Definable Relation to the Realities of Culture?" *Worldview* 6, no. 1 (January 1963): 3–5.

"Paperbacks in the College." *College and Research Libraries* 24, no. 2 (March 1963): 109–12. (Originally given as a lecture at the University of Michigan, Ann Arbor, February 21, 1962.)

"The Past and Future of Eschatological Thinking." In *Religion and Contemporary Society,* edited by Harold Stahmer, 116–41. New York: Macmillan, 1963. (An altered version can be found in *The Myth of the Judeo-Christian Tradition and other Dissenting Essays,* 3–31. New York: Harper and Row, 1970.)

"Reflections on the History of Jewish Thought." In *Religion and Contemporary Society,* edited by Harold Stahmer, 116–41. New York: Macmillan, 1963.

"A Theology of Jewish Existence." *The Christian Century* 80, no. 4 (January 23, 1963): 104–7.

Book Reviews and Letters

"The Absence of Heroism." Review of *German Catholics and Hitler's Wars,* by Gordon Zahn. *Worldview* 6, no. 9 (September 1962): 10–11.

Review of *The Root and the Branch: Judaism and the Free Society,* by Robert Gordis. *Revue des Etudes Juives,* fourth series, 11, no. 3–4 (July–December 1963): 454–55.

"An Uncontentious Responsum to Will Herberg." *Judaism* 12, no. 4 (fall 1963): 487–92.

Articles, Reviews, and Letters about Arthur Cohen

Eckardt, A. Roy. "The Jew." Review of *The Natural and Supernatural Jew,* by Arthur A. Cohen. *The Journal of Bible & Religion* 31, no. 3 (July 1963): 240–42.

1964

Books: Nonfiction

The Negative Way: A Collaboration. Lithographs by Paul Brach. New York: Tamarind Workshop, 1964 (limited edition).

Books: Edited

Humanistic Education and Western Civilization: Essays for Robert M. Hutchins. Edited with an introduction by Arthur A. Cohen. New York: Holt, Rinehart and Winston, 1964.

Articles and Essays

"The Temper of Jewish Anti-Christianity." In *Christianity: Some Non-Christian Appraisals,* edited by David W. McKain, 205–22. New York: McGraw Hill, 1964. (This essay is a revised and expanded version of the lecture "Common Ground and Difference," delivered at Perspectives on the Good Society: A Jewish-Protestant Colloquium, sponsored by the Divinity School, University of Chicago, and the Anti-Defamation League of B'nai B'rith, Chicago, Ill., April 23, 1963.)

"A Theology of Jewish Existence." In *What's Ahead for the Churches: A Report from the Christian Century,* 44–52. New York: Sheed and Ward, 1964.

"Why I Chose to be a Jew." In *Breakthrough: A Treasury of Contemporary American-Jewish Literature,* edited by Irving Malin and Irwin Stark, 367–76. New York: McGraw-Hill, 1964. (First published in *Harper's Magazine,* 218, no. 1307 [April 1959]: 63–66.)

Book Reviews

"Americans Confront the Past: History in the Guise of Drama." Review of the play *The Deputy,* by Rolf Hochhuth. *Christianity and Crisis* 24, no. 5 (March 30, 1964): 51–53.

"Hugo Rahner's Pursuit of Christian Archetypes." Review of *Greek Myths and Christian Mystery,* by Hugo Rahner. *Commonweal* 79, no. 20 (February 14, 1964): 605–6.

"In Search of the Divine." Review of *The Problem of God,* by John Courtney and S. J. Murray. *The Critic* 23, no. 1 (August–September 1964): 62–63.

Articles, Reviews, and Letters about Arthur Cohen

Halpern, Ben. "A Theological Jew." Review of *The Natural and Supernatural Jew. The Jewish Frontier* (February 1964): 11–13.

Heer, Friedrich. "The Future Needs the Past." Review of *The Natural and Supernatural Jew. The Christian Century* 81, no. 20 (May 13, 1964): 635–38.

1965

Articles and Essays

Cohen, Arthur A., Krister Stendahl, and John Yoder. "Colloquy: A Comment on a Paper by Krister Stendahl." *Fellowship* 31, no. 5 (May 1965): 30–31.

"Martin Buber: An Appreciation." *American Judaism* 15, no. 1 (fall 1965): 11.

"My Rabbi: A Memoir of Milton Steinberg." *Jewish Heritage* 8, no. 3 (winter 1965–66): 5–9.

"One: A Jew's Lament." *Ramparts* 4, no. 6 (October 1965): 31.

"Why I Choose to be a Jew." In *The Dynamics of Emancipation: The Jew in the Modern Age,* edited by Nahum N. Glatzer, 240–51. Boston: Beacon Press, 1965. (First published in *Harper's Magazine,* 218, no. 1307 [April 1959]: 63–66.)

Book Reviews

"Freedom How?" Review of *Freedom of the Individual,* by Stuart Hampshire. *Book Week* 3, no. 13 (December 5, 1965): 38, 40.

"Soaring Up, Up, and Away." Review of *Nietzsche: An Introduction to the Understanding of his Philosophical Activity,* by Karl Jaspers. *Book Week* 2, no. 52 (September 5, 1965): 5, 15.

1966

Books: Nonfiction

Der Naturliche und der Übernatürliche Jude. Munich: Verlag Karl Alber, 1966. (Translation of The Natural and Supernatural Jew, New York: Pantheon, 1962.)

Articles and Essays

"Between Two Traditions." Midstream 12, no. 6 (June/July 1966): 26–35.

"Doomsday in Dogpatch: The McLuhan Thesis Examined." Journal of the American Institute of Graphic Arts 3 (1966): 2–5. (Originally delivered as an address at the Fifty Books Show Dinner, Waldorf Astoria, New York, April 18, 1966.)

"Further Reflections on the Natural and Supernatural." In Varieties of Jewish Belief, edited by Ira Eisenstein, 29–42. New York: Reconstructionist Press, 1966.

"Negro-Jewish Relations in America." Midstream 12, no. 10 (December 1966): 8–11.

"The Retrieval of the Human: Some Reflections on Morality." American Judaism 16, no. 1 (fall 1966): 10–11, 24.

"Silence and Laughter." Jewish Heritage 8, no. 4 (spring 1966): 37–39.

Book Reviews

"A Guide to Jewish Journals." Review of The Commentary Reader, edited by Norman Podhoretz. Commonweal 84, no. 23 (September 30, 1966): 639–41.

"Rediscovering Judaism." Review of Rediscovering Judaism, edited by Arnold Jacob Wolf. Commonweal 83, no. 21 (March 4, 1966): 634–35.

Articles, Reviews, and Letters about Arthur Cohen

Kresh, Paul. "Hurt or Puzzled." Letter to the Editor of Commonweal 84 (October 28, 1966): 117–18. (Reaction to the exclusion of American Judaism in Cohen's "Guide to Jewish Journals.")

Levitan, Tina. "The New Generation: A Random Sampling of Young Jewish Achievers." Jewish Heritage 9, no. 1 (summer 1966): 27–38. (Cohen's profile appears on pages 32–33.)

Review of The Carpenter Years. Kirkus Reviews 34 (December 15, 1966): 1298.

1967

Books: Fiction

The Carpenter Years. New York: Signet Press, 1967. (Hardcover edition published in New York by The New American Library, 1967; English edition published in London by Hart Davis, 1967.)

Books: Nonfiction

The Natural and Supernatural Jew. London: Valentine, Mitchell, 1967. (First published in New York by Pantheon, 1962.)

Articles and Essays

"Comments." In Negro and Jew: An Encounter in America, edited by Shlomo Katz, 7–11. New York: Macmillan Paperback, 1967. (First published in Midstream 12, no. 10 [December 1966]: 8–11.)

"English Novels-American Novels." *Owl among the Colophons.* Holt Rinehart and Winston 3, no. 2 (May 1967): 3.

"The Jewish Intellectual in an Open Society." In *Confrontations with Judaism—A Symposium,* edited by Phillip Longworth, 17–34. London: Anthony Blond, Ltd., 1967.

"The Jewish Museum: Victim of Confusion." *Congress Bi-Weekly* 15 (November 20, 1967): 7–8.

"Reflections on Theological Method: The Task of Jewish Theology." Unpublished manuscript, 1967. Estate of Arthur A. Cohen.

Review of *Athens and Jerusalem,* by Lev Shestov. *Commonweal* 85, no. 22 (March 10, 1967): 661–62.

"Truth is Not Good Enough." *American Judaism* 16, no. 3 (spring 1967): 10–11, 37–39.

Articles, Reviews, and Letters about Arthur Cohen

Elman, Richard M. "Edgar Morrison's Choice." Review of *The Carpenter Years. New York Times Book Review* 72, no. 6 (February 7, 1967): 45.

Fremont-Smith, Elliot. "Schlepp's Progress." *New York Times* 116, February 8, 1967, 29.

Review of *The Carpenter Years. Publisher's Weekly* 192 (December 11, 1967): 49.

Review of *The Carpenter Years. Times Literary Supplement* (April 27, 1967): 364.

1968

Book Reviews

"Commentary." Review of "Homeland and the Holocaust: Issue in the Jewish Religious Situation." In *The Religious Situation: 1968,* edited by Donald L. Cutler, 87–91. New York: Beacon Press, 1968.

"The Dirty Little Secret." Review of *Making It,* by Norman Podhoretz. *Congress Bi-Weekly* 35, no. 7 (April 8, 1968): 17–19.

"Identities." Review of *Elder and Younger Brothers,* by Roy Eckhardt. *Commentary* 45, no. 6 (June 1968): 79–84.

"Laying Fuses Under Rome." Review of *Those Incredible Christians,* by Hugh J. Schonfield. *New Republic* 159, no. 12 (September 21, 1968): 29–30.

"The Metaphysics of Survival." Review of *The Chocolate Deal,* by Chaim Gouri. *Midstream* 14, no. 9 (November 1968): 77–79.

"A Relish Tray of Goodies." Review of *Explorations: An Annual on Jewish Themes,* edited by Murray Mindlin and Chaim Bermant. *Hadassah Magazine* 50, no. 1 (September 1968): 27–28.

Review of *Portrait of Yahweh as a Young God,* by Greta Wels-Schon. *Commonweal* 89, no. 12 (December 20, 1969): 418–19.

Review of *The Religious Imagination: A Study in Psychoanalysis and Jewish Theology,* Richard L. Rubenstein. *New York Times Book Review* 73 (1968): 8–9.

1969

Articles and Essays

"Doomsday in Dogpatch: The McLuhan Thesis Examined." In *McLuhan: Pro and Con,* edited by Raymond Rosenthal, 234–41. Baltimore, Md.: Penguin Books, 1969. (Expanded version of "Doomsday in Dogpatch: The McLuhan Thesis Examined." *Journal of the American Institute of Graphic Arts* 3 [1966]: 2–5.)

"Israel, Its Dilemma and Ours." *Commonweal* 89, no. 16 (January 24, 1969): 518–19.

"The Myth of the Judeo-Christian Tradition." *Commentary* 48, no. 5 (November 1969): 73–77.

"The Philosophy." In *Sacramentum Mundi: An Encyclopedia of Philosophy,* 6 vols., edited by Karl Rahner, Cornelius Ernst, and Kevin Smyth, III, 222–26. Basle: Herder and Herder, 1969. (Reprinted in German in *Sacramentum Mundi: Theologisches Lexicon fur die Praxis,* 1000–1009. Basle: Herder and Herder, 1969.)

Book Reviews

"Job and the Modern Imagination." Review of *The Dimensions of Job: A Study and Selected Readings,* by Nahum N. Glatzer. *Congress Bi-Weekly* 36, no. 7 (May 12, 1969): 21–22.

"Judaism and Metaphysics." Review of *Jewish Philosophy in Modern Times,* by Nathan Rotenstreich. *Midstream* 15, no. 4 (April 1969): 73–76.

"Rethinking Judaism." Review of *A New Jewish Theology in the Making,* by Eugene Borowitz; *The Non-Jewish Jew and Other Essays,* by Isaac Deutscher; *The Jews: Story of a People,* by Howard Fast; *Albert H. Leo Baeck: Teacher of Theresienstadt,* by S. Friedlander; *Post Mortem: The Jews in Germany Today,* by Leo Katcher; *Choose Life,* by Bernard Mandelbaum; *Jewish Philosophy in Modern Times: From Mendelssohn to Rosenzweig,* by Nathan Rotenstreich; *The Evolution of the American Jew from 1921 to the Present,* by Judd L. Teller; *The American Jews,* by James Yaffe. *New Republic* 160, no. 11 (March 15, 1969): 28, 30–31.

Review of *Kurt Gerstein,* by Saul Friedlander. *New York Times Book Review* 74 (April 13, 1969): 10.

Review of *The Non-Jewish Jew and Other Essays. The New Republic* 160 (March 15, 1969): 28.

Articles, Reviews, and Letters about Arthur Cohen

Marty, Martin E. "Commentaries on the World Religious Situation: The American Situation in 1969." In *The Religious Situation, 1969,* edited by Donald R. Cutler, 25–43. Boston: Beacon Press, 1969.

Review of *The Myth of the Judeo-Christian Tradition. Publisher's Weekly* 196 (October 27, 1969): 58.

1970
Books: Nonfiction

Arguments and Doctrines: A Reader of Jewish Thinking in the Aftermath of the Holocaust. New York: The Jewish Publication Society and Harper and Row, 1970.

Cohen, Arthur A., and Garvin Phillip. *A People Apart: Hasidism in America.* New York: Dutton, 1970.

The Myth of the Judeo-Christian Tradition and Other Dissenting Essays. New York: Harper and Row, 1970.

Articles and Essays

"El Mito de la Tradicion Judeo-Christiana." *Commentario* 17, no. 70 (January–February 1970): 29–36. (Translation of "The Myth of the Judeo-Christian Tradition." *Commentary* 48, no. 5 [November 1969]: 73–77.)

Book Reviews and Letters

"The Besht." Review of *In Praise of the Baal Shem Tov,* edited and translated by Dan Ben-Amos and Jerome R. Mintz. *Commentary* 50, no. 3 (September 1970): 88–90.

"Dialogue." Review of *Judaism Despite Christianity: "The Letters on Christianity and Judaism"* *Between Eugene Rosenstock-Huessy and Franz Rosenzweig*, edited by Eugene Rosenstock-Huessy. *Commentary* 49, no. 6 (June 1970): 90–92.

"The Holy Spirit Comes to Rest on Holy Discontents." Review of *Divine Disobedience: Profiles in Catholic Radicalism*, by Francine du Pessix Gray. *Commonweal* 92, no. 12 (June 12, 1970): 298–99.

"Letter to the Editor." *Commentary* 49, no. 1 (January 1970): 4, 6, 8.

Articles, Reviews, and Letters about Arthur Cohen

Chinitz, Jacob Rabbi. Letter to the Editor of *Commentary* 49, no. 1 (January 1970): 4–6.

Kaplan, Edward. Letter to the Editor of *Commentary* 49, no. 1 (January 1970): 6.

Meyer, Michael A. Review of *Arguments and Doctrines*. *Commentary* 50 (November 1970): 103.

Neusner, Jacob. "Beyond Accomodation." Review of *The Myth of the Judeo-Christian Tradition*. *Midstream* 16, no. 3 (March 1970): 77–80.

Pepper, George. Review of *Arguments and Doctrines*. *Cross Currents* 20 (summer 1970): 344.

Plotkin, Frederick. "Judaism, Christianity, and the Gate of God." Review of *The Myth of the Judeo-Christian Tradition*. *Congress Bi-Weekly* 37, no. 9 (September 25, 1970): 17–19.

Proskauer, Joseph M. "Letter to the Editor." *Commentary* 49, no. 1 (January 1970): 4.

Review of *Arguments and Doctrines*. *Kirkus Reviews* 38 (April 1, 1970): 399.

Review of *Arguments and Doctrines*. *Publisher's Weekly* 197 (April 27, 1970): 75.

Review of *The Myth of the Judeo-Christian Tradition*. *Choice* 7 (September 1970): 854.

Teeple, Howard M. Review of *Arguments and Doctrines*. *Library Journal* 95 (July 1970): 2483.

1971

Books: Nonfiction

The Myth of the Judeo-Christian Tradition and Other Dissenting Essays. New York: Schocken Press, 1971. (First paperback edition.)

Articles and Essays

"Hasidic Encounter." *Jewish Heritage* 13, no. 2 (spring-summer 1971): 46–53.

"Museum or Mausoleum." *New York Times,* February 7, 1971, 21, 23.

"The Possibility of Belief: Nathanael West's Holy Fool." In *Twentieth Century Interpretations of Miss Lonelyhearts,* edited by Thomas H. Jackson, 46–48. Englewood Cliffs, N.J.: Prentice-Hall, 1971. (Longer version of this article first appeared in *Commonweal* 64, no. 11 [June 15, 1956]: 276–78.)

Cohen, Arthur A., contributor. "Religion and Culture." In *The United States and Canada: A Handbook*. London: Anthony Blond, Ltd., 1971.

"Theology as Creative Art: Franz Rosenzweig's *The Star of Redemption:* An Inquiry into Its Psychological Origins." *Midstream* 18, no. 2 (February 1971): 13–33.

"Three Points in Rosenzweig's Star." *Sh'ma* 2, no. 22 (December 17, 1971): 9–12.

"Why I Choose to be a Jew." In *A Nation of Nations: Ethnic Literature in America,* edited by Theodore L. Gross, 263–73. New York: The Free Press, 1971. (First published in *Harper's Magazine,* 218, no. 1307 [April 1959]: 63–66.)

Book Reviews and Letters

"Criticism among Brothers." Letter to the Editor of *Christianity and Crisis* 31, no. 20 (November 29, 1971): 262.

"Doctrine of Concept." Review of *Jesus and Israel,* by Isaac Jules. *Commentary* 52, no. 3 (September 1971): 92–95.

"Friedrich Heer and the Jews: The Passion of a Mind Possessed." Review of *God's First Love,* by Friedrich Heer. *Commonweal* 94, no. 9 (May 7, 1971): 218–20.

"The Gift of the Human." Review of *Adam Resurrected,* by Yoram Kaniuk. *Congress Bi-Weekly* 38, no. 13 (December 10, 1971): 19.

"New Truths and Revelations." Review of *The Pagan Rabbi and Other Stories,* by Cynthia Ozick. *Congress Bi-Weekly* 38, no. 9 (September 17, 1971): 22–23.

"Our Young." Review of *The New Jews,* edited by James A. Sleeper and Alan L. Mintz. *Midstream* 17, no. 6 (June/July 1971): 71–76.

"Response to Irving Fineman." Letter to the Editor of *Commentary* 52, no. 6 (December 1971): 18, 20.

"Return to Judaism." Review of *Paganism-Christianity-Judaism: A Confession of Faith,* by Max Brod. *Commentary* 51, no. 5 (May 1971): 85–86.

Review of *Amen: The Diary of Martin Siegel,* edited by Mel Ziegler. *Commonweal* 94, no. 15 (July 9, 1971): 364–65.

Review of *The Pagan Rabbi and Other Stories,* by Cynthia Ozick. *Commonweal* 94, no. 19 (September 3, 1971): 461–63.

Articles, Reviews, and Letters about Arthur Cohen

Neusner, Jacob. Review of *Arguments and Doctrines. American Jewish Historical Quarterly* 60 (June 1971): 395.

Review of *A People Apart. Choice* 8 (June 1971): 562.

Unterman, Alan. Review of *The Myth of the Judeo-Christian Tradition. Jerusalem Post,* September 3, 1971: 22.

1972

Books: Nonfiction

The Delaunays, Apollinaire and Cendrars. New York: The Cooper Union School of Art and Architecture, 1972. (This paper was originally delivered as a lecture at Cooper Union, New York City, February 9, 1972.)

Articles and Essays

"Beyond Politics, Vision." *Congress Bi-Weekly* 39, no. 5 (March 10, 1972): 33–47. (First presented to the Ninth Annual American Jewish Congress Dialogue in Israel, Weizmann Institute, Rehovot, Israel, August 1–4, 1971.)

"Discussion, Response to Arthur J. Lelyveld, 'A Minority People becomes a Majority,'" *Congress Bi-Weekly* 39, no. 5 (March 10, 1972): 5–13.

"Fortunato Depero—Depero Futurista." *Art News* (May 1972): 117.

"Franz Rosenzweig's *The Star of Redemption:* An Inquiry into Its Psychological Origins." *Midstream* 18, no. 2 (February 1972): 13–33. (This essay was delivered, in an abbreviated form as the Hugo Hahn Memorial Lecture on November 12, 1971, at Congregation Habonim in New York City.)

"The Last Jew on Earth: A Fable." *Commentary* 54, no. 5 (November 1972): 48–59.

"Willing a Messianic Marginality." *Sh'ma* 3, no. 44 (December 22, 1972): 29–30.

Book Reviews

Review of *The Avenue of the Americas,* by James Scully. *Commonweal* 97, no. 11 (December 15, 1972): 259–60.

Articles, Reviews, and Letters about Arthur Cohen

Neusner, Jacob. *American Judaism: Adventures in Modernity.* New York: Prentice-Hall, 1972. (A discussion of Cohen's work appears on pages 121–27, 155, 156.)

1973

Books: Nonfiction

The Book Stripped Bare: A Survey of Books by 20th Century Artists and Writers: An Exhibition of Books from the Arthur Cohen and Elaine Lustig Cohen Collection. New York: Hofstra University Press, 1973.

Cohen, Arthur A., and Mordecai M. Kaplan. *If Not Now, When? Toward a Reconstitution of the Jewish People: Conversations between Mordecai M. Kaplan and Arthur A. Cohen.* New York: Schocken Books, 1973.

Books: Fiction

In the Days of Simon Stern. New York: Random House, 1973.

Articles and Essays

"The Birth of Simon Stern." *Response* 16, no. 16 (winter 1972–73): 43–52.

"David Shapiro." In *Contemporary Poets of The English Language,* 147–48. London: St. James Press, Ltd., 1973.

Introductory essay. In *Judaism and Tragic Theology,* by Frederick S. Plotkin. New York: Schocken Books, 1973.

"Nahum Glatzer as Friend and Teacher." *Jewish Heritage* 15, no. 1 (summer/fall 1973): 51–53.

"The Last Jew on Earth." *Commentary* 55 (June 1973): 49–59.

"The Play of Job—1945." *Midstream* 19, no. 1 (January 1973): 35–40.

"Revelation and Law—Reflections on Martin Buber's Views on Halakah." In *Faith and Reason: Essays in Judaism,* edited by Robert Gordis and Ruth B. Waxman, 250–56. New York: Ktav Publishing House, 1973. (Reprint of article in *Judaism* 1, no. 3 [July 1952]: 250–56.)

"Selections from *In the Days of Simon Stern.*" In *Works in Progress,* no. 8. New York: Literary Guild, 1973.

Book Reviews and Letters

"Critics Choices." Review of *A Maimonides Reader,* edited by Isadore Twersky; *From Politics to Piety: The Emergence of Pharisaic Judaism,* by Jacob Neusner; *The Messianic Idea in Judaism,* by Gershom Scholem; *The Collected Stories,* by Franz Kafka. *Commonweal* 97, no. 20 (February 23, 1973): 477.

"The First Futurist." Review of *Marinetti: Selected Writings,* edited by R. W. Flint. *Commentary* 55, no. 5 (May 1973): 92–94.

"How to Arouse Americans." *New York Times,* April 13, 1973, C38.

"The Inventor of Splendid Arguments with Death." Review of *Our Lord Don Quixote: The Life of Don Quixote and Sancho with Related Essays, The Tragic Sense of Life in Men and Nations,* and *The Agony of Christianity,* by Miguel de Unamuno. *New York Times Book Review* 78, no. 50 (December 16, 1973): 19–22.

Review of *Firstfruits: A Firstfruits of 25 Years of Israeli Writings,* edited by James Michener. *New York Times Book Review* 78, no. 30 (September 30, 1973): 46–47.

Review of *Selected Poems,* by Joseph Brodsky. *New York Times Book Review* 78, no. 52 (December 30, 1973): 1–2.

Articles, Reviews, and Letters about Arthur Cohen

Aksler, Samuel M. "Work in Judaica, 1970–72: A Sampling." *American Jewish Yearbook* 74 (1973): 244–63.

Bandler, Michael J. Review of *In the Days of Simon Stern. Commonweal* 98 (September 28, 1973): 530–13.

"Briefly Noted—Fiction." *New Yorker* 49 (July 16, 1973): 79.

Haupt, Christopher-Lehman. Review of *In the Days of Simon Stern. New York Times* 122 (June 5, 1973): 39.

Maddocks, Melvin. "Everyman a Jew." Review of *In the Days of Simon Stern. Time* 102 (July 9, 1973): 60.

Prescott, Peter. "The Last Jew." Review of *In the Days of Simon Stern. Newsweek* 81 (June 11, 1973): 108.

Review of *In the Days of Simon Stern. Kirkus Reviews* 41 (April 15, 1973): 472.

Review of *In the Days of Simon Stern. Publisher's Weekly* 203 (May 14, 1973): 42.

1974

Books: Fiction

In the Days of Simon Stern. London: Secker and Warburg, Ltd., 1974. (British edition of 1973 American edition.)

Books: Nonfiction

Osip Emilevich Mandelstam: An Essay in Antiphon. Ann Arbor, Mich.: Ardis, 1974.

Thinking the Tremendum: Some Theological Implications of the Death Camps. Leo Baeck Memorial Lecture #18. New York: Leo Baeck Institute, 1974.

Articles and Essays

"Abstraction as the Story of Feeling: A Note on the Graphics of Robert Motherwell." Foreward to *Robert Motherwell: Selected Prints: 1961–74.* New York: Brooke Alexander, Inc., 1974. (This essay was translated by Francesco Paolini in the Italian edition of *Robert Motherwell.* Rome: De Luca Editore, 1977.)

"Ferreting the Word." *Congress Bi-Weekly* 41, no. 8 (June 21, 1974): 16–17.

Foreword to *Robert Motherwell: Selected Prints, 1961–1974.* New York: Brooke Alexander, 1974.

"Jewish Messianism and Sabbatai Sevi." *Midstream* 20 (October 1974): 30–49. (First delivered as a lecture at Oberlin College, Oberlin, Ohio, 1974.)

"Lost in the Desert of Nations." *Hadassah Magazine* 55, no. 5 (January 1974): 6, 28–29.

Book Reviews

"Critics Choices." Review of *Invitation to the Talmud,* by Jacob Neusner; *Moses Mendelssohn,* by Alexander Altmann; *Sabbatai Sevi,* by Gershom Scholem; *The Foundation Pit,* by Andrei Plantonov; *Selected Poems,* by Joseph Brodsky; *Hope Abandoned,* by Osip Mandelstam; *Selected Poems,* by Osip Mandelstam; *Mozart and Salieri,* by Osip Mandelstam. *Commonweal* 99, no. 20 (February 22, 1974): 513–14.

Articles, Reviews, and Letters about Arthur Cohen

Stern, David. "Theology into Art: An Appreciation of Arthur A. Cohen." *Response* 21 (spring 1974): 63–71.

1975

Books: Nonfiction

Sonia Delaunay. New York: Harry N. Abrams, 1975.

Articles and Essays

"Critics Choices: Selections for Religious Book Week." *Commonweal* (February 28, 1975): 427–28.

"George Wittenborn, 1905- 1974." *Art News* 74, no. 2 (February 1975): 54–55.

"Hans Cassebeer and the Virgin's Rose." *TriQuarterly* 33 (summer 1975): 79–111.

"Mann in His Letters." *Commentary* 60 (November 1975): 62–65.

"What Is a Jewish Book?" *Jewish Heritage Review* 1, no. 1 (January 1975): 13.

Book Reviews

Review of *Power Struggle,* by Richard L. Rubenstein. *Commonweal* 101, no. 1 (January 3, 1975): 305–6.

Articles, Reviews, and Letters about Arthur Cohen

Bespaloff, Alexis. "Eight Great Wine Cellars." *New York Magazine* 9 (November 17, 1975): 71.

Friedlander, Albert. *European Judaism* 10, no. 2 (1975): 44–46.

Review of *A Hero in His Time. Kirkus Reviews* 41 (November 1, 1975): 1250.

Review of *A Hero in His Time. Publisher's Weekly* 208 (October 27, 1975): 46.

1976

Books: Fiction

A Hero in His Time. New York: Random House, 1976.

Articles and Essays

"Aggadah and the Fictional Imagination." *Sh'ma* 6, no. 106 (January 23, 1976): 45–46.

"Arthur Cohen." In *Self Portrait: Book People Picture Themselves,* 136. New York: Random House, 1976.

"Futurism and Constructivism: Russian and Others." *The Print Collector's Newsletter* 7, no. 1 (March–April 1976): 2–4.

"Nothing Succeeds Like Success. Right? Wrong." *New York Times,* March 10, 1976, Op-Ed page.

Book Reviews

Review of *On Jews and Judaism in Crisis: Selected Essays,* by Gershom Scholem. *New York Times Book Review* (September 11, 1977): 40.

Review of *The Abyss,* by Margaret Yourcenar. *New York Times Book Review* (July 11, 1976): 7.

Review of *The Holocaust and the Literary Imagination,* by Lawrence L. Langer. *New York Times Book Review* (January 18, 1976): 19.

Articles, Reviews, and Letters about Arthur Cohen

Broyard, Anatole. "The Politics of Poetry." Review of *A Hero in His Time. New York Times,* January 5, 1976, 27.

Grumbach, Doris. "Arthur Cohen Catches Fires." Review of *A Hero in His Time. The Village Voice* 21 (March 15 1976): 15.

Jefferson, Margo. "Innocent Abroad." Review of *A Hero in His Time. Newsweek* 87 (January 12, 1976): 65–66.

Lehman-Haupt, Christopher. Review of *A Hero in His Time. New York Times,* July 30, 1976, C19.

Morgan, Edwin. "A Russian in New York." Review of *A Hero in His Time. The Times Literary Supplement* (February 27, 1976): 213.

Phillip, Robert. Review of *A Hero in His Time. Commonweal* 103 (March 26, 1976): 215–16.

Review of *A Hero in His Time. Choice* 13 (June 1976): 516.

Skow, John. "A Lyre for the K.G.B." *Time* 107 (January 5, 1976): 45.

Wisse, Ruth R. "The Pen and the Sword." Review of *A Hero in His Time. Commentary* 62 (October 1976): 92–96.

Wolff, Geoffrey. Review of *A Hero in His Time. New York Times Book Review* 81 (January 25, 1976): 6.

1977

Articles and Essays

"Fathers Neither Named Nor Slain." *Confrontation* 14 (spring–summer 1977): 180–82.

"Human Fraternity: The Liturgy of Theological Enmity." In *Modern Jewish Thought: A Source Reader,* edited by Nahum Glatzer, 175–80. New York: Schocken Books, 1977.

"In Motherwell Country." *Vogue* 167 (March 1977): 230–33.

"Paradisical Origins and Disenchantments." In *All Our Sons and Daughters,* edited by John Garvey, 102–13 London: Templegate Publishers, 1977.

Book Reviews

"Passionate Scholar." Review of *Jews and Judaism in Crisis,* by Gershom Scholem. *New York Times Book Review* 82 (September 11, 1977): 40.

Review of *In Pursuit of the Messiah,* by Mark J. Mirsky. *Commonweal* 104, no. 20 (September 30, 1977): 637–38.

Articles, Reviews, and Letters about Arthur Cohen

Lanser, Faye. "Interview." *The Feminist Art Journal* 5, no. 4 (winter 1976–77): 5–11.

1978

Books: Nonfiction

Cohen, Arthur A., ed. *The New Art of Color: The Writings of Robert and Sonia Delaunay.* New York: Viking Press, 1978.

Articles and Essays

"Critic's Choice." *Commonweal* 105, no. 5 (March 3, 1978): 156–57.

Foreword to *Behold a Great Image,* edited by Sharon Strassfeld and Arthur Kurzwil, 7–9. Philadelphia, Penn.: Jewish Publication Society of America Press, 1978.

"The Last Word: How to Avoid Disappearing." *Present Tense* 5, no. 3 (spring 1978): 64.

"Marinetti and Futurism." *Print Collector's Newsletter* 8, no. 6 (January–February 1978): 170.

"The Monumental Sculptor." *TriQuarterly* 41 (winter 1978): 169.

Letters, Reviews, and Letters about Arthur Cohen

"Arthur A. Cohen." *The Author Speaks—Selected PW Interviews: 1967–76,* by Publishers Weekly Editors and Contributors, 27. New York: RR Bowker, 1978.

1979

Books: Nonfiction

The Natural and Supernatural Jew. 2d ed. New York: Behrman House, 1979.

Articles and Essays

"In the Matter of *Mein Kampf.*" *New York Times,* October 4, 1979, A31.

"Ramsch auf dem Weltraum." In *Die Ausserirdischen sind da.* Munich: Matthes and Seitz, 1979.

"The Typographic Revolution: Antecedents and Legacy of Dada Graphic Design." In *Dada Spectrum: The Dialectics of Revolt,* edited by Stephen C. Foster and Rudolf Kuenzli, 71–89. Iowa: University of Iowa and Coda Press, 1979.

Book Reviews

Reviews of *Decadence: The Strange Life of an Epithet,* by Richard Gilman. *Commonweal* 106 (August 31, 1979): 474.

Review of *New York,* by Gunner Kaldeway. *Print Collector's Newsletter* (November–December 1979): 156.

Articles, Reviews, and Letters about Arthur Cohen

Review of *Acts of Theft. Kirkus Reviews* 47 (December 15, 1979): 1443.

1980

Books: Fiction

Acts of Theft. New York: Harcourt Brace Jovanovich, 1980.

Books: Nonfiction

The Jew: Essays from Martin Buber's Journal Der Jude: 1916–1928. Translated by Joachim Neugroschel. Alabama: University of Alabama Press, 1980.

Articles and Essays

"Dada Obsession: Notes on Collecting the Dada Movement." *American Book Collector* 2 (March–April, 1980): 3.

"I Dream with No Ring of Gyges." In *Inseln im Ich. Ein Buch der Wuensche,* edited by Ruth Hagengruber. Munich: Matthes and Seitz, 1980.

"Liberalism and the Jews." *Commentary* 69, no. 1 (January 1980): 27.

"Martin Buber and Der Jude." *Midstream* 20 (June/July 1980): 29.

"Martin Buber and Judaism." *Leo Baeck Institute Yearbook* 25. London: Secker and Warburg, 1980.

"Our Narrative Condition." *Present Tense* (summer 1980): 58–60. (Originally delivered as the first talk at the Smilen Awards for Jewish Literature.)

"Painting Every Surface of the World." *American Craft* 40 (February–March 1980): 36.

"Richard Meier: Creator of a New Harmony." *Mainliner* (March 1980): 66.

"Sonia Delaunay: Memories of an Optimist." *Art News* 79 (March 1980): 127.

"The Tremendum as Caesura: A Phenomological Comment on the Holocaust." *Cross Currents* 30, no. 4 (winter 1980–81): 421–40.

Book Reviews and Letters

"Letter to the Editor." *New York Times Book Review* (1980): 34.

Review of *Passages in Modern Sculpture,* by Rosalind E. Krauss. *Partisan Review* 1 (1980): 146–49.

Review of *Tormented Master: A Life Rabbi Nahman of Bratzlav,* by Arthur Green. *New York Times Book Review* 85 (January 13, 1980): 9.

Articles, Reviews, and Letters about Arthur Cohen

Hochfield, Sylvia. Review of *Acts of Theft. Art News* 79 (September 1980): 28.

Lask, Thomas. "From Art Books to a Novel about Art." Review of *Acts of Theft. Publishing* (February 22, 1980): 34.

Leonard, John. Review of *Acts of Theft. New York Times,* February 12, 1980, C9.

Macoby, Hyam. Review of *The Jew. Commentary* 171, no. 4 (April 1981): 77.

Malin, Irving. "Acts of Faith." Review of *Acts of Theft, The Carpenter Years, In the Days of Simon Stern,* and *A Hero in his Time. Congress Bi-Monthly* 47, no. 4 (May 1980): 15.

McHale, Brian. Review of *Acts of Theft. Jerusalem Post Magazine* (October 17, 1980): 26.

McLellen, Joseph. Review of *Acts of Theft. Washington Post,* February 22, 1980, D6.

Ratcliff, Carter. Review of *Acts of Theft. Art in America* 68 (Summer 1980): 21.

Review of *Acts of Theft. Publisher's Weekly* 217 (January 11, 1980): 77.

Review of *The Jew. Choice* 71 (December 1980): 544.

Review of *The Jew. Library Journal* 105 (August 1980): 1629.

Riemer, Jack. Review of *The Jew. America* 143 (November, 1980): 274.

Schechner, Mark. Review of *Acts of Theft. New York Times Book Review* 85 (March 9, 1980): 9.

Washburn, Martin. Review of *Acts of Theft. The Village Voice* 47 (December 15, 1979): 1443.

1981

Books: Nonfiction

The American Imagination after War. Syracuse N.Y.: Syracuse University Press, 1981. (This paper was first delivered at The B. G. Rudolph Lectures in Judaic Studies, Syracuse University,

New York, March 1981. It was later presented under the title "Judaism and the Imagination: The Situation of the American Novel after the War" at Williams College, Williamstown, Mass., March 5, 1981.)

The Avant-Garde in Print. 5 vols. New York: A.G.P. Matthews, 1981.

Piet Zwart. New York: Ex Libris, 1981.

The Tremendum: A Theological Interpretation of the Holocaust. New York: Crossroad Publishing Co., 1981.

Articles and Essays

"Franz Rosenzweig's The Star of Redemption: Mystic Epistemology without Kabbalah." In Unfinished Essays in Honor of Roy L. Hart, edited by Mark C. Taylor, 65–81. A thematic series of the Journal of the American Academy of Religion 48, no. 1.

"Kafka's Prague." Partisan Review 4 (April–May 1981): 552–63. (Originally delivered as a lecture in the series "The Writer and the City," Columbia University, New York City, February 15, 1979.)

"Points of Origin: Where My Mind Comes From." Fiction 6, no. 3 (1981): 130–36. (Excerpt from the novel An Admirable Woman, 1983.)

Book Reviews

Review of The World Backwards: Russian Futurist Books 1912–16, by Susan P. Compton. American Book Collector 2, no. 3 (May–June 1981): 52–57.

Articles, Reviews, and Letters about Arthur Cohen

Berger, Dr. Alan A. "From Dispersion to Exile: Responding to the Holocaust in Jewish American Fiction." (Paper delivered at The B.G. Rudolph Lectures in Judaic Studies, Syracuse University, March 1981.)

Cole, Diane. "Profession: Renaissance Man, Arthur A. Cohen." Present Tense 9, no. 1 (autumn 1981): 32–35.

Eckhardt, Roy. Review of The Tremendum. Christian Century 98 (October 7, 1981).

McGarry, Michael B. Review of The Tremendum. America 145 (August 15, 1981): 77–78.

McGary, Michael B. Review of The Tremendum. Commonweal 108 (July 31, 1981): 439.

Neusner, Jacob. Review of The Tremendum. Journal of Ecumenical Studies 18, no. 4 (fall 1981): 675.

Review of The Tremendum. Library Journal 106 (May 1, 1981): 982.

Rubenstein, Aryeh. Review of The Jew. Jerusalem Post Magazine (March 27, 1981): 17.

1982

Articles and Essays

"Birth of a Zionist." Commonweal 109, no. 15 (September 10, 1982): 457.

"The 'Bolted Machine Book' of Fortunato Despero." Art News 81 (March 1982): 118–19.

"Collecting Rare Books." Dollar Magazine 1, no. 4 (April 1982): 32–37.

"The Holocaust and Christian Theology: An Interpretation of the Problem." In Papers Presented to the International Symposium on Judaism and Christianity under the Impact of National Socialism (1919–1945), 415. Jerusalem: The Historical Society of Israel, June 1982.

"Living One's Own life." Present Tense 9, no. 2 (winter 1982): 30–31.

"In Memoriam: Great Uncle Salomon." Forthcoming 1, no. 1 (November 1982): f3–f13; insert in Moment 7, no. 10 (November 1982).

"Mysterium Tremendum." In *Judische Theologie des Holocaust,* edited by Michael Brocke and Herbert Jochum. Munich: Kaiser, 1982.

"The Religious Center of the Jews: An Essay in Historical Theology." In *Religion in America,* edited by Mary Douglas and Steven M. Tipton. Boston, Mass.: Beacon Press, 1982–83.

"Russian Avant-Garde Books at Sotheby's." *Print Collector's Newsletter* 13, no. 1 (March–April 1982): 17.

"Sepera Futurista." *Art News* (March 1982): 118–19.

"The Sufferings of Heinrich von Kleist." *New Criterion* 6, no. 4 (December 1982): 26–34.

Book Reviews

Review of *Discovering the Way: A Theology of Jewish-Christian Reality,* by Paul Van Buren. *Journal of Religion* 62 (April 1982): 210–17.

Review of *The Seriousness of Life: An Autobiography,* by Mircea Eliade. *Commonweal* (March 26, 1982): 188–90.

"A Short, Rich, and Tortured Life." Review of *Walter Benjamin: The Story of a Friendship,* by Gershom Scholem. *New York Times Book Review* 87 (May 16, 1982): 12.

1983

Books: Fiction

An Admirable Woman. Boston: David R. Godine, 1983.

Articles and Essays

"Autobiographical Fragment: The Holocaust." *Forthcoming* 1, no. 3/4 (1983): 27.

"The Contemporaneity of Ahad Ha'am." *Jewish Frontier* 50 (May 1983): 6.

"Franz Rosenzweig and the Crucifixion: An Historical Episode in Judeo-Christian Communication." Unpublished manuscript, 1983. Estate of Arthur A. Cohen.

"The Homily of the Roses." In *New City: A Treasury of Modern Jewish Tales,* edited by Howard Schwartz. New York: Avon Books, 1983.

"The Last Word from Berlin." *Present Tense* 10, no. 4 (summery 1983): 43–47.

Preface to *Dada Once and For All.* Introduction by Trevor Winkfield. New York: Ex Libris, 1983.

"Tenth Anniversary Address." *Present Tense* 10 (May 11, 1983): 45–46.

Book Reviews

"A Land of Two Peoples." Review of *Martin Buber on Jews and Arabs,* edited by Paul Mendes-Flohr. *Commonweal* 110, no. 18 (October 21, 1983): 556.

"Man Revealed." Review of *Thomas Mann Diaries, 1918–1939,* translated by Richard and Clara Winston. *New Criterion* 1, no. 6 (February 1983): 65.

"On Emil Fackenheim's *To Mend the World*: A Review Essay." Review of *To Mend the World: Foundations of Future Jewish Thought,* by Emil Fackenheim. *Modern Judaism* 3, no. 2 (May 1983): 225–36.

Articles, Reviews, and Letters about Arthur Cohen

Broyard, Anatole. Review of *An Admirable Woman. New York Times,* November 9, 1983, C31.

Dirlam, Sharon. Review of *An Admirable Woman. Los Angeles Times Book Review* (November 20, 1983): 10.

Filer, Martin. "From Bauhaus to Their House." *House and Garden* 155 (July 1983): 30.

McDowell, Edwin. "Was That Hannah Arendt or Not?" Review of *An Admirable Woman.* *New York Times,* December 9, 1983, C31.

Miller, Jim. Review of *An Admirable Woman. Newsweek* 102 (November 14, 1983): 114.

Ozick, Cynthia. "A Library of Rediscoveries." In *Writers' Choice,* edited by Linda Sternberg and Bill Katz, 26. Reston, Va.: Reston Publishers, 1986.

Review of *An Admirable Woman. Kirkus Reviews* 51 (September 1, 1983): 964.

Review of *An Admirable Woman. Library Journal* 108 (January 1983): 1888.

Review of *An Admirable Woman. Publisher's Weekly* 224 (September 23, 1983): 62.

Shorris, Earl. Review of *An Admirable Woman. New York Times Book Review* 88 (November 23, 1983): 9.

1984

Books: Nonfiction

Herbert Bayer: The Complete Works. Cambridge, Mass.: MIT Press, 1984.

Articles and Essays

"Addressing Letters to Israel." *Jewish Frontier* (November/December 1984): 11.

"In Our Terrible Age: The Tremendum of the Jews." In *Concillium: The Holocaust as Interpretation,* by Elizabeth Schussler and David Tracy, 11. Edinburgh, Scotland: T and T Clark, Ltd., 1984. (Translated into French, German, Italian, and Spanish.)

Book Reviews and Letters

"God The Implausible Kinsman." Review of *Against the Apocalypse: Responses to Catastrophe in Modern Jewish Culture,* by David G. Roskies. *New York Times Book Review* 89 (June 17, 1984): 28–29.

"Letter to the Editor." *New York Times Book Review* 89 (December 23, 1984): 3.

"On Theological Method (A Response on Behalf of *The Tremendum*)." *Journal of Reform Judaism* 31 (spring 1984): 56–65.

Review of *Cinema Calendrier du Coeur Abstrait. Fine Print* 10, no. 3 (July 1984): 126–28.

Articles, Reviews, and Letters about Arthur Cohen

Elkin, Lillian. Review of *An Admirable Woman. Jewish Frontier* 51 (January 1984): 24.

Tracy, David. Review of *An Admirable Woman. Commonweal* 140 no. 4 (February 10, 1984): 92.

1985

Books: Fiction

An Admirable Woman. Manchester, UK: Carcanet Press, Ltd, 1985. (American edition published by David R. Godine, 1983.)

Articles and Essays

"Castilian Odyssey on Horseback." *New York Times,* travel section, January 6, 1985, 20.

"Embarrassed by Principle." *Present Tense* 12, no. 2 (winter 1985): 40.

"From Eastern Europe to Paris and Beyond." In *The Circle of Montparnasse: Jewish Artists in Paris, 1905–1945,* edited by Kenneth Silver. New York: The Jewish Museum/Universe Books, 1985.

Letters

"The Hidden Persuasion." Letter to the Editor of *Commonweal* (November 1, 1985): 596, 623.

Articles, Reviews, and Letters about Arthur Cohen

Berger, Alan L. "Arthur A. Cohen." In *Crisis and Covenant: The Holocaust in American Jewish Fiction,* 42–48. Albany, N.Y.: State University of New York, 1985.

Brookner, Anita. Review of *An Admirable Woman. Times* (London), March 10, 1985, 45.

Fern, Alan. Review of *Herbert Bayer: The Complete Work,* by Arthur A. Cohen. *AIGA Journal of Graphic Design* 3, no. 3 (1985): 7.

McPherson, Michael. Review of *Herbert Bayer: The Complete Work,* by Arthur A. Cohen. *Fine Print* (October 1985): 12.

Steiner, Deborah. Review of *An Admirable Woman. Times Literary Supplement* (March 15, 1985): 283.

1986

Articles and Essays

Afterword to *Erasmus and the Jews,* by Shimon Markish, 144–54. Chicago and London: University of Chicago Press, 1986.

"Life amid the Paradigms or the Absence of a Jewish Critique of Culture." *Journal of the American Academy of Religion* 54, no. 3 (fall 1986): 499–519.

"Zionism and Theology." *Sh'ma* 17, no. 324 (December 1986): 25–27.

Articles, Reviews, and Letters about Arthur Cohen

Review of *Artists and Enemies. Publisher's Weekly* 230 (December 26, 1986): 38.

1987

Books: Fiction

Artists and Enemies: Three Novellas. Boston.: David R. Godine, 1987.

Books: Nonfiction

Cohen, Arthur A., and Paul Mendes-Flohr, eds. *Contemporary Jewish Religious Thought: Original Essays on Critical Concepts, Movements, and Beliefs.* New York: Charles Scribner's Sons, 1987.

The Unknown Steinhardt: Prints by Jakob Steinhardt Produced between 1907 and 1934. New York: The Jewish Museum, 1987.

Articles and Essays

"Franz Kafka: Artist of the Incomplete." *Orim: A Jewish Journal at Yale* (1987).

"The Holocaust and Christian Theology: An Interpretation of the Problem." In *Judaism and Christianity under the Impact of National Socialism, 1940–1945,* edited by Otto Dov Kulka and Paul R. Mendes-Flohr, 473–97. Jerusalem: The Historical Society of Israel and The Zalman Shazar Center for Jewish History, 1987. (This essay was originally delivered as a paper at the Symposium "Judaism and Christianity under the Impact of National Socialism [1919–1945]," sponsored by the Historical Society of Israel, Jerusalem, June 1982.)

"On Judaism and Modernism," *Partisan Review* 3 (1987): 437–42. (This paper was originally delivered at the National Jewish Book Awards, New York Public Library, New York City, May 17, 1984.)

"My Rabbi: A Memoir of Milton Steinberg." Foreword to *Basic Judaism,* by Milton Steinberg. Northvale, N.J.: Jason Aronson, Inc., 1987. (Reprint of an article published in *Jewish Heritage* 8, no. 3 [winter 1965–66]: 5–9.)

"Myths and Riddles: Some Observations about Literature and Theology." *Prooftexts* 7, no. 2 (May 1987): 107–22. (This paper was originally delivered at the conference "Continuity and Transformation: Jewish Writing Since WWII," Bellagio, Italy, 1982.)

"Observations on the Danish Rescue." In *The Rescue of the Danish Jews: Moral Courage Under Stress,* edited by Leo Goldberger, 191–94. New York and London: New York University Press, 1987. (This paper was adapted from one originally given at the Conference on the Rescue of Danish Jewry, Sutton Place Synagogue, New York City, October 23, 1983.)

Articles, Reviews, and Letters about Arthur Cohen

Gold, Ivan. Review of *Artists and Enemies. Partisan Review* 1 (1988): 159.

Gottschalk, Alfred. "The Wisdom of the Moderns." Review of *Contemporary Jewish Religious Thought,* edited by Arthur A. Cohen and Paul Mendes-Flohr. *New York Times Book Review* 92 (March 29, 1987): 6–7.

Phillipson, Morris. Review of *Artists and Enemies. New York Times Book Review* 92 (April 12, 1987): 20.

Plagens, Peter. Review of *Artists and Enemies. Art in America* 75 (July 1987): 27.

Stern, David. "Arthur A. Cohen: In Memoriam." *Orim: A Jewish Journal at Yale* 2, no. 2 (spring 1987): 109–15.

1988

Books

Acts of Theft. Chicago and London: The University of Chicago Press, 1988. (Paperback edition of book originally published by Harcourt Brace Jovanovich, 1980.)

Cohen, Arthur A., and Paul Mendes-Flohr, eds. *Contemporary Jewish Religious Thought: Original Essays on Critical Concepts, Movements and Beliefs.* London: Collier Macmillan, 1988.

A Hero in His Time. Chicago and London: The University of Chicago Press, 1988. (Paperback edition of book originally published by Random House, 1976.)

In the Days of Simon Stern. Chicago and London: The University of Chicago Press, 1988. (Paperback edition of book originally published by Random House, 1973.)

Sonia Delaunay. 2d ed. New York: Harry N. Abrams, Inc., 1988.

The Tremendum: A Theological Interpretation of the Holocaust. 2d ed. New York: Crossroad Press, 1988. (First edition published by Crossroad in 1981.)

Articles, Reviews, and Letters about Arthur Cohen

Gold, Ivan. Review of *Artists and Enemies. Partisan Review* 1 (1988): 159.

1989

Articles, Reviews, and Letters about Arthur Cohen

Kremer, S. Lillian. "Eternal Faith, Eternal People: The Holocaust and Redemption in Arthur A. Cohen's *In the Days of Simon Stern.*" In *Witness through the Imagination: Jewish American Holocaust Literature.* Detroit, Mich.: Wayne State University Press, 1989.

1992

Articles and Essays

"Jepthah's Vow." *Conjunctions* 19 (1992): 313–15.
"Marginality." *Conjunctions* 19 (1992): 316–17.

Articles, Reviews, and Letters about Arthur Cohen

Katz, Steven T. " 'The Tremendum': Arthur Cohen's Understanding of Faith after the Holocaust." *The Journal of Jewish Thought and Philosophy* 1 (1992): 28–303.